HP-UX 11.x
SYSTEM ADMINISTRATION
HANDBOOK AND TOOLKIT

ISBN 0-13-012514-8

90000

9 780130 125149

Hewlett-Packard® Professional Books

Hewlett-Packard Professional Books

MORE BOOKS FROM MARTY PONIATOWSKI

HP-UX 11.x System Administration "How To" Book,
Second Edition

◆

HP NetServer Guide for Windows NT®

◆

HP-UX System Administration Handbook and Toolkit

◆

Windows NT® and HP-UX System Administrator's
"How To" Book

◆

HP-UX 10.x System Administration "How To" Book

◆

Learning the HP-UX Operating System

HP-UX 11.x
SYSTEM ADMINISTRATION
HANDBOOK AND TOOLKIT

Marty Poniatowski

http://www.hp.com/go/retailbooks

Prentice Hall PTR
Upper Saddle River, NJ 07458
www.phptr.com

Library of Congress Cataloging-in-Publication Data

Poniatowski, Marty
    HP-UX 11.x system administration handbook and toolkit / Marty
    Poniatowski.
        p. cm. -- (Hewlett-Packard Press series)
        ISBN 0-13-012514-8 (paper : alk. paper)
        1. HP-UX. 2. Operating systems (Computers) I. Title.
    II. Series.
    QA76.76.O63P647   1999
    005.4'469--dc21   99-24948
                                          CIP

Editorial/production supervision: *Patti Guerrieri*
Acquisitions editor: *Jill Pisoni*
Marketing manager: *Lisa Konzelmann*
Manufacturing manager: *Alexis R. Heydt*
Editorial assistant: *Linda Ramagnano*
Cover design director: *Jerry Votta*
Cover designer: *Talar Agasyan*
Manager, Hewlett-Packard Press: *Patricia Pekary*
Editor, Hewlett-Packard Press: *Susan Wright*

©1999 by Hewlett-Packard Company

Published by Prentice Hall PTR
Prentice-Hall, Inc.
Upper Saddle River, NJ 07458

Prentice Hall books are widely used by corporations and government agencies
for training, marketing, and resale.

The publisher offers discounts on this book when ordered in bulk quantities.
For more information, contact: Corporate Sales Department, Phone: 800-382-3419;
Fax: 201-236-7141; E-mail: corpsales@prenhall.com; or write: Prentice Hall PTR,
Corp. Sales Dept., One Lake Street, Upper Saddle River, NJ 07458.

Hummingbird Communications, Exceed, NFS Maestro, and TCP/IP Maestro are registered trademarks of Hummingbird Communications Ltd. UNIX is a registered trademark licensed through X/Open Company, Ltd. X Window System is a trademark and product of the Massachusetts Institute of Technology. HP-UX, HP OpenView, GlancePlus, PerfView, and Measureware are registered trademarks of Hewlett-Packard Company. Microsoft, Windows NT, and MS/DOS are registered trademarks of Microsoft Corporation. OS/2 is a registered trademark of International Business Machines Corporation. All other products or services mentioned in this book are the trademarks or service marks of their respective companies or organizations.

Printed in the United States of America
10 9 8 7 6 5 4 3

ISBN 0-13-012514-8

Prentice-Hall International (UK) Limited, *London*
Prentice-Hall of Australia Pty. Limited, *Sydney*
Prentice-Hall Canada Inc., *Toronto*
Prentice-Hall Hispanoamericana, S.A., *Mexico*
Prentice-Hall of India Private Limited, *New Delhi*
Prentice-Hall of Japan, Inc., *Tokyo*
Prentice-Hall (Singapore) Pte. Ltd., *Singapore*
Editora Prentice-Hall do Brasil, Ltda., *Rio de Janeiro*

PREFACE

Our job as system administrators is to make the magic of HP-UX work. You know very well as a system administrator that most of what you make work is magic to those around you. When the data warehouse is running slowly the users report this fact to you and expect that you will perform some magic to make it run faster. When a user is short on space they ask you to increase their limit using whatever magic you need to employ. When the boss realizes that you need to have a disaster recovery scheme in place that will allow you to replicate your system in one hour it may as well be magic that makes this work.

Welcome to *HP-UX 11.x System Administration Handbook & Toolkit*. The purpose of this, and all of my other books, is to cover all essential system administration topics that you need to set up and maintain your system(s) that to others are magic.

I could never tell you everything you need to know to be administrator of your HP-UX systems. I can, however, walk you through the commonly performed administration tasks of setting up a system, loading HP-UX, and using System Administration Manager (SAM) to perform common system administration tasks; run through the basics of performance analysis; cover Common Desktop Environment (CDE) administration; introduce shell programming; and so on. I also provide copies of the on-line manual pages for many of the commands used throughout the book so that you can refer to them when reviewing a section of the book.

As with my other books, this book includes a blueprint from which you can work, and many tips and recommendations from my experience working with HP-UX, as well as what I have learned working with many HP-UX system administrators over the years.

No matter how detailed a training course or manual, it always leaves out some of the specific tasks you'll need to perform. Instead of getting mired down in excruciating detail, I'll provide the common denominator of information every HP-UX system administrator needs to know. I'll provide you with all the essential information you need so that you'll be able to take on new and unforeseen system administration challenges with a good knowledge base.

The blueprint I provide consists of many things; among them is a setup flowchart. As I describe the specific steps in the flowchart, I'll also provide pertinent background information. This means that as you learn how to perform a specific system administration function, I'll also provide background that will help you understand why you are performing it and what is taking place on your system.

This approach sometimes means that I'll be describing a procedure and use a command or procedure covered earlier. As a result, you may see the same command and corresponding output more than once in this book. The reason is that this setup saves you the time and confusion of trying to flip back to where you originally saw the command.

You may very well find that you'll need additional resources as your system administration challenges increase. No matter what anyone tells you, no one resource can answer everything you need to know about HP-UX system administration. Just when you think you know everything there is to know about HP-UX system administration you'll be asked to do something you've never dreamed of before. That's why I'm not trying to be all things to all people with this book. I cover what everyone needs to know and leave topics in specific areas to other people. You may need training courses, manuals, other books, or consulting services to complete some projects. In any case, I'll bet that every topic in this book would be worthwhile to know for every HP-UX system administrator. *HP-UX 11.x System Administration Handbook & Toolkit* covers tasks all system administrators need to perform: It shows you how to perform each task, tells why you are doing it, and explains how it is affecting your system. Much of the knowledge I have gained has come from the fine HP-UX manual set and the concise on-line manual pages. Some of the procedures in the book are based on those in the HP-UX manual set and some of the command summaries in the book are based on the on-line manual pages. I am grateful for all of the hard work my HP associates have put into both the manual set and the on-line manual pages.

Speaking of examples, I sometimes use a workstation (Series 700) and sometimes a server (Series 800) in the examples. When it is required, I use both a workstation and server to show the differences. Sometimes I use the term *workstation* instead of *Series 700* and sometimes *server system* instead of *Series 800*. In general, though, I use *Series 700* and *Series 800*.

HP-UX 11.x System Administration Handbook & Toolkit is comprised of the following chapters:

- Chapter 1:   Setting Up Your HP-UX System

- Chapter 2:   HP-UX File System and Related Commands

- Chapter 3:   Networking

- Chapter 4:   System Administration Manager (SAM)

- Chapter 5:   Introduction to HP-UX Performance Tools

- Chapter 6:   Common Desktop Environment (CDE)

- Chapter 7:   Shell Programming for System Administrators

- Chapter 8:   HP-UX System Auditing

- Chapter 9:   System Recovery with Ignite-UX

- Chapter 10:   The vi Editor

- Chapter 11:   Windows® NT and HP-UX Interoperability - The X Window System

- Chapter 12:   Windows NT and HP-UX Interoperability - Networking

- Chapter 13:   The Windows NT Command Line - Advanced Server for UNIX®

- Chapter 14: The Windows NT Command Line - NET Commands, POSIX Utilities, and Others

- Chapter 15: SFU

Covered in these chapters is everything you need to get started and work through advanced topics in HP-UX system administration.

Manual Pages Supplied with This Book

I am most grateful to Hewlett Packard Company for having allowed us to include select HP-UX manual pages in this book. Although specific options for a given command often vary among the UNIX® variants it is useful to have a manual page to turn to when reviewing a command. I included the manual pages for select commands where I thought they would be especially helpful. Our special thanks to John Verrochi, Susanne Sonderhoff, and Susan Wright of Hewlett Packard for having taken a lead role in helping us receive permission for using the manual pages.

Software Supplied with This Book

One CD-ROM accompanies this book. Information on the suppliers of this software, order forms, and other such material are supplied on the CD-ROM. Here is a brief description of the contents of the CD-ROM.

Performance   The CD-ROM contains extensive trial performance software for HP-UX, Sun, AIX, and NCR.

This is a full suite of software including: HP GlancePlus; HP Measureware Agent; and HP PerfView. Most of the software on this CD-ROM will run for a 60-day trial period, after which you can use the information on the CD-ROM to buy a permanent license for the software. Every HP-UX installation should run some of the performance software on this CD-ROM in order to monitor system performance as well as tune the system. There is no better way to determine the software that best suits the needs of your environment than to test the software for 60 days and make your own determinations.

Interoperability   The CD-ROM also contains several pieces of useful interoperability software. The first is a suite of software from Hummingbird Communications, Ltd. This software is covered in the Windows NT and HP-UX interoperability chapter of this book and includes X Windows and NFS products. This software runs on Windows NT.

The software and information included on the CD-ROM is very useful in HP-UX installations. No installation should be without some performance tools. With Windows NT and HP-UX coexisting in more and more installations I think it is important to know what interoperability tools exist, such as those from Hummingbird, and test them to determine which are best suited to enhance the interoperability in your environment.

Please don't hesitate to contact the vendors that have offered to put their software on the CD-ROM. I'm sure they'll be happy to hear from you.

I hope you enjoy reading the book and learning the material as much as I did writing it.

Marty Poniatowski

marty_poniatowski@hp.com

An Overview of My Other Books

This is my eighth book centered around Hewlett Packard products. The primary difference in the books is the audience for whom the book is written. For instance *The HP-UX 11.x System Administration Handbook & Toolki*t covers only the HP-UX operating system and goes into great detail. *Windows NT and HP-UX System Administrator's "How To" Book* covers both the Windows NT and HP-UX operating systems for system administrators at an introductory level. The following brief descriptions provide an overview of each book and the intended audience. All my books have been published by Prentice Hall PTR.

HP-UX 11.x System Administrator's "How To" Book

(0-13-012515-6)

This book covers system administration specifically for the HP-UX 11.x operating system release. It is for new system administrators who need to get up and running quickly. This book starts with the first task of loading the HP-UX operating system on both servers and workstations. It then progresses through all of the topics new system administrators need to know such as networking, the System Administration Manager (SAM), performance analysis, managing the Common Desktop Environment (CDE), and other useful topics.

HP NetServer Guide for Windows NT

(ISBN 0-13-989682-1)

This book covers the HP NetServer family running the Microsoft Windows NT operating system. In this book I cover many topics including: installing an HP NetServer using the *HP Navigator Kit*; Windows NT topics such as file systems and system administration tools; Windows NT and HP-UX interoperability; and the command line. There is a CD-ROM included with this book. The CD-ROM contains Windows NT interoperability tools such the X Window System and Network File System, background material on HP NetServers, and more. With this book and the CD-ROM I have put together a package to get you up and running with Windows NT on your NetServer and some tools to help you have a successful installation.

HP-UX System Administration Handbook & Toolkit

(ISBN 0-13-905571-1)

This is the most detailed of my system administration books. In this book I cover many HP-UX topics in detail which you will not find covered in any other source. I cover HP-UX system auditing, for instance, by discussing aspects of your system that should be regularly audited **and** by providing several audit scripts you can use. There are two CD-ROMs included with this book and a four-panel quick reference card. This book, along with the next book described, *Windows NT and HP-UX System Administrator's "How To" Book*, are meant to be companion books in the sense that the greatest coverage of both HP-UX and Windows NT topics is achieved by having both books. The topics covered in both books combined with the software supplied with this book will put you well on your way to achieving HP-UX, Windows NT, and interoperability expertise.

Windows NT and HP-UX System Administrator's "How To" Book
(ISBN 0-13-861709-0)

This book covers both the Windows NT and HP-UX operating systems. It is intended for system administrators who are new to one or both of these operating systems. There is a chapter devoted to each system administration topic for both Windows NT and HP-UX. In addition, there are five chapters covering Windows NT and HP-UX system interoperability topics such as networking, software development, X windows, and so on.

Learning the HP-UX Operating System

(ISBN 0-13-258534-0)

This book is useful for anyone new to the HP-UX operating system, including users, system administrators, operators, and so on. This book covers all the topics new users need to get started quickly, including the most often used commands, a thorough discussion of the vi editor, shell programming, and so on.

HP-UX 10.x System Administrator's "How To" Book

(ISBN 0-13-125873-7)

This book covers system administration specifically for the HP-UX 10.x operating system release. It is for new system administrators who need to get up and running quickly. This book starts with the first task of loading the HP-UX operating system on both servers and workstations. It then progresses through all the topics new system administrators need to know, such as networking, the System Administration Manager (SAM), performance analysis, managing the Common Desktop Environment (CDE), and other useful topics.

The HP-UX System Administrator's "How To" Book

(ISBN 0-13-099821-4)

This book covers system administration specifically for the HP-UX 9.x operating system release. This book covers all of the same topics as *HP-UX 10.x System Administrator's "How To" Book* for HP-UX 9.x.

All my books are written from the point of view of a system administrator or user of Windows NT or HP-UX, not from the point of view of a super operating system expert. The reason is that I work with users and system administrators every day, so I know what topics are important to you.

I hope that you find this and my other books useful and that they make your installation more successful and smoother running. That is the reason I write these books.

Conventions Used in the Book

I don't use a lot of complex notations in the book. Here are a few simple conventions I've used to make the examples clear and the text easy to follow:

$ and #	The HP-UX command prompt. Every command issued in the book is preceded by one of these prompts.
italics	Italics are used primarily in Chapter 4 when referring to functional areas and menu picks in the System Administration Manager (SAM).
bold and " "	Bold text is the information you would type, such as the command you issue after a prompt or the information you type when running a script. Sometimes information you would type is also referred to in the text explaining it, and the typed information may appear in quotes.
<----	When selections have to be made, this convention indicates the one chosen for the purposes of the example.

One additional convention is that used for command formats. I don't use command formats more than I have to because I could never do as thorough a job describing commands as the HP-UX manual pages. The manual pages go into detail on all HP-UX commands. Here is the format I will use when I cover commands:

```
form 1      command [option(s)] [arg(s)]
form 2      command [option(s)] [arg(s)]
form n      command [option(s)] [arg(s)]
```

I try not to get carried away with detail when covering a command but, there are sometimes many components that must be covered in order to understand a command. Here is a brief description of the components listed above:

form # -There are sometimes many forms of a command. If there is more than one form of a command that requires explanation, then I will show more than one form.

command - The name of the executable.

option(s) - Several options may appear across a command line.

cmd_arg(s) - Command arguments such as path name.

There are man pages at the end of many chapters for some of the commands used in the chapter. The Table of Contents contains a complete list of the man pages appearing at the end of each chapter. The man pages for a command appear in the chapter to which the command is most applicable, even if it is not the first chapter in which the command is used. Commands pertaining to performance, for instance, have their man pages in the performance chapter even if those commands were used in an earlier chapter. The man pages were copied from an HP Washroom for HP-UX release 10.x. The commands used in the book changed minimally, if at all, going from HP-UX 10.x to 11.x.

Acknowledgments

There were too many people involved in helping me with this book to list them all. I have decided to formally thank those who wrote sections of the book and those who took time to review it. I'm still not sure whether it takes more time to write something or review something that has been written to ensure it is correct.

William Russell

Bill Russell is Vice President and General Manager of Enterprise Systems and Software Group for Hewlett Packard. Bill acted as executive champion and sponsor of this book. His support was invaluable in helping get the resources necessary to complete this book.

Donna Kelly

Donna took on the mammoth task of updating much of this book from the 10.x to 11.x release of the HP-UX operating system. Donna and I have collaborated on a number of projects together. Donna has painstakingly reviewed many of my books for both technical accuracy and readability. Donna is both a technical expert in many operating systems and an excellent evaluator of the usefulness of a topic and the way it is covered. She not only ensures that the material is technically accurate she also makes certain each topic is covered in a useful manner and that it is easy to read and comprehend.

Donna has been responsible for a number of computing environments of Hewlett Packard in Roseville, CA. She has experience with several operating systems including HP-UX, Windows NT, MPE, and AS/400.

The Author - Marty Poniatowski

Marty has been a Senior Technical Specialist with Hewlett Packard for twelve years in the New York area. He has worked with hundreds of

Hewlett Packard customers in many industries, including on-line services, financial, and manufacturing.

Marty has been widely published in computer industry trade publications. He has published over 50 articles on various computer-related topics. In addition to this book, he is the author of seven other Prentice Hall books: *HP-UX 11.x System Administrator's "How To" Book* (1998); *HP NetServer Guide for Windows NT* (1998); *HP-UX System Administration Handbook & Toolkit* (1997); *Windows NT and HP-UX System Administrator's "How To" Book* (1997); *Learning the HP-UX Operating System* (1996); *HP-UX 10.x System Administrator's "How To" Book* (1995); and *The HP-UX System Administrator's "How To" Book* (1993).

Marty holds an M.S. in Information Systems from Polytechnic University (Brooklyn, NY), an M.S. in Management Engineering from the University of Bridgeport (Bridgeport, CT), and a B.S. in Electrical Engineering from Roger Williams University (Bristol, RI).

Reviewers

I'm not sure what makes someone agree to review a book. You don't get the glory of a contributing author, but it is just as much work. I would like to thank the many people who devoted a substantial amount of time to reviewing this book to ensure that I included the topics important to new system administrators and covered those topics accurately.

My special thanks to Mark Bichlmeier of Microsoft for both supplying Microsoft software used in the book and reviewing many of the sections related to UNIX and Windows NT interoperability.

CHAPTER 1

Setting Up
Your HP-UX System

You are going to have a great time setting up your HP-UX system(s). I know you are, because I have set up hundreds and hundreds of systems and my customers always enjoy it. Why? Because you think it's going to be one thing - pain and misery, and it turns out to be another - smooth, easy, and a great learning experience.

The systems I have helped set up have come in all shapes and sizes. They range from a network of hundreds of low-end desktop systems to massive data center systems with thousands of users. In the distributed environment, networking is more of an issue; in the data center environment, disk management is more of an issue. In either case, though, HP-UX is HP-UX and what you know about one system applies to the other. What I am hoping you get from this book is **the common denominator of HP-UX system administration knowledge that applies to all systems**.

I am in a good position to help you with this knowledge. I have been setting up HP-UX systems since they were introduced. Before that, I set up other UNIX systems. This means that although I haven't learned much else, I *really* know UNIX systems. In addition, I have a short memory, so I write down most things that work. The result is this book for HP-UX 11.x and its predecessors for HP-UX 9.x and HP-UX 10.x.

To help you understand the tasks you will have to perform, I have included a flowchart for setting up HP-UX systems. One of the most intimidating aspects to setting up a new system is because there are so many tasks to perform, it is easy to get lost in the detail. Figure 1-2 helps put in perspective the tasks to be performed and the sequence of performing them. I hope this helps make your setup more manageable.

The nature of learning HP-UX system administration is that in addition to the specific steps to be performed there is also some background information you need to know. What I have done is include the background in the appropriate setup step. This way, you're not reading background information for the sake of reading background information. Instead, you're reading background information that applies to a specific setup step. Two examples of this are providing background information about the program used to load software and background on the HP-UX 11.x file system under the setup step called "Install HP-UX 11.x." You need to know about the software installation program in order to load software, and you should also know the file system layout when you load software. It, therefore, makes sense to put this background information under this step of the setup flowchart.

Although I can't include every possible step you might need to perform, I have included the steps common to most installations. If a step is irrelevant to your site, you can skip it. Based on the many installations I have performed, I think I have discovered the common denominator of most installations. In any event, you can use this flowchart as an effective step-by-step approach to getting your system(s) up and running.

SAM

Many of the steps you'll see in the flowchart are simple procedures you can perform with the System Administration Manager (SAM). SAM is an HP-UX system administrator's best friend. I have devoted all of Chapter 3 to SAM because, except for initial system setup, you can perform most of your *routine* system administration functions with SAM. As a preview, here are the *major* headings under the SAM main menu:

- Accounts for Users and Groups
- Auditing and Security
- Backup and Recovery
- Disks and File Systems
- Display
- Kernel Configuration
- Networking and Communications
- Performance Monitors
- Peripheral Devices
- Printers and Plotters
- Process Management
- Routine Tasks
- Run SAM on Remote Systems
- Software Management
- Time

Figure 1-1 shows the graphical user interface (GUI) of SAM through which you could select any of the areas. There is also a terminal user interface (TUI) for SAM if you do not have a graphics display.

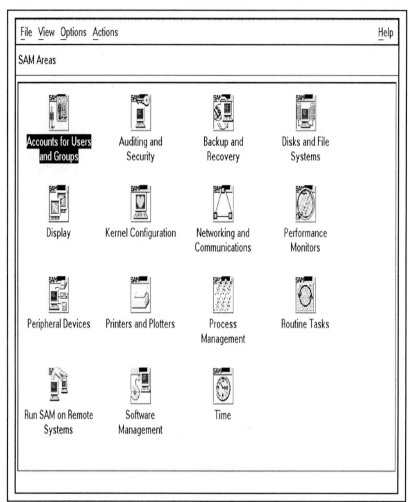

Figure 1-1 SAM Startup Window in Graphics Mode

You select one of these headings, such as *Accounts for Users and Groups*, and SAM walks you through the process of adding users, deleting users, and so on. Because SAM does a great job with the routine system administration functions it helps you perform, I don't spend a lot of time with these tasks in the flowcharts. I cover the tasks you can do with SAM at a cursory level and refer you to Chapter 3 for more detail. I discuss all of the non-SAM topics in detail. Although I recommend that you use SAM because it makes system administration so much easier, I also suggest that you understand what SAM is doing so that you can attack system problems intelligently. If, for instance, you allow SAM to configure your networking and you don't know what has occurred in the background, you won't know where to begin troubleshooting a problem if one should arise.

Server vs. Workstation Implementation

Although one of the most important advancements in HP-UX 11.x is the convergence of workstation (Series 700) and servers (Series 800) functionality, there are still some minor differences between the two. When I come across one of these differences while covering a topic, I point it out. Because the differences are minor, I do not devote a lot of space to covering them. There are, however, a few differences worth mentioning here.

When covering the **ioscan** command, for instance, I will provide the Series 700, Series 800, and V class examples. Because of the differences in hardware, you see somewhat different results when you run this command. This is true even within the Series 700 and Series 800 for different models.

Another area where I spend some time pointing out the differences between the Series 700 and Series 800 is installing the operating system. When installing the operating system, you may see one Boot program on one system and a different sequence on another system, even within the Series 700 and Series 800 families. When I cover installing software, I show two different Boot possibilities depending on how old your Series 700 is. When covering such differences, I have decided to cover them to the extent necessary. That is, I will share with you the more important points and not get dragged down into excruciating detail in differences. You will see a variety of systems used in the examples throughout the book. Keep in mind that although there may, indeed, be differences among models, the procedures are very similar for different models.

Your knowledge of the Series 700 is directly applicable to the Series 800 and vice versa. I have seen many system administrators move from a workstation environment to a data center environment and vice versa with very little difficulty. You will almost certainly need to learn new applications if you choose to make such a switch. You may, for instance, go from scientific and engineering applications to database or other commercial applications if you make a switch from workstations to the data center. For the most part, though, you can take comfort in knowing that your HP-UX knowledge is directly applicable to both environments.

If you are currently using HP-UX 10.x, then you should find moving to HP-UX 11.x easy. You should obtain the Software Transition Tools kit that provides analysis and conversion tools from HP before you make the move. This kit, referred to as STK tools, is available free of charge from Hewlett Packard and can be downloaded from the World Wide Web via **http://www.software.hp.com/STK**. Running this on your 10.x systems will asssist in identifying any potential software compatibility issues. This will help you perform a smooth migration.

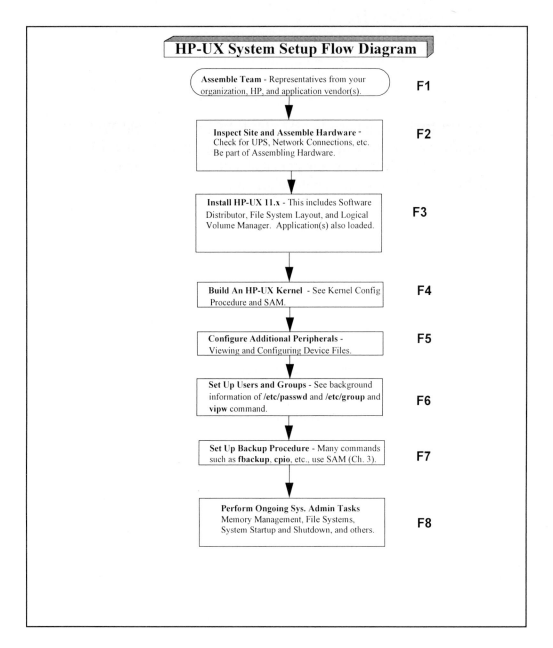

Figure 1-2 System Setup Flow Diagram

Using the Setup Flowchart

The goal is to get the system up and running as soon as possible, doing as little rework as possible after users are on the system. Although you might plan to have the system exclusively for setup-related work for a few weeks after it is delivered, you will probably find that users are eager to get on the system. This situation usually means that the setup gets compromised in the interest of getting users on the system. If possible, don't let this happen to you. Although the setup flowchart looks straightforward and gives you the impression that you can get your system going step by step, there are, invariably, some steps you'll want to revisit. This situation will, of course, affect any users who jump on the system before you have had a chance to complete the setup and do adequate testing.

The simplified setup flow diagram in Figure 1-2 can be of great value to you for three reasons:

1. It gives you an overview of the tasks you'll need to perform.

2. It serves as a checklist as you complete activities.

3. It serves as a basis for your own custom flowchart, which includes your application installation procedures.

Although system administration books and manuals abound with information about how to perform a particular setup step such as adding users or performing backups, I have never seen a setup flowchart like the one in this chapter that encompasses HP-UX systems. I encourage you to copy this flowchart and modify it to reflect the process at your site.

This flowchart is by no means complete. However, it acts as a good common denominator. You may need to perform additional tasks, but virtually every new HP-UX installation involves the tasks shown in the flowchart.

The next sections cover the steps shown in the flowchart.

Assemble Team (F1)

What a fascinating process I have found this to be. When you consider the number of team members that might be required for a large, distributed project, this might seem to be an impossible task. I have found the converse to be true. In general, I have found application vendors, consultants, hardware vendors, customer representatives, and others involved in a project happy to have the opportunity to carefully plan a project and devote resources to ensure its success.

I think that those of us involved in technology know the importance of both planning and working together as a team. I am often pleasantly surprised at how well planning can proceed when the right group of people are brought together. Although you are in the best position to determine who should be part of the team, I offer a few suggestions here.

- Within your organization. you have a variety of people interested in the project, including: application developers; system administrators; managers responsible for the installation; network administrators; data center managers; help desk representatives; users; and others whom you may want to consider making part of your team.

- Hewlett Packard may have a number of representatives involved in making your installation successful, including: a sales representative; consultants in the Professional Services Organization; support people in the System Support Organization; and others.

- You may have several application vendors who will play a part in your project. If these representatives can be made part of your team rather than just software suppliers, you may find that you'll encounter fewer unforeseen problems such as software incompatibility, and when you do encounter problems, you may get a better response.

- You may have other consultants who fill a void within your organization. If they are part of the team, they may have prior experience they can share with the group that may be valuable.

You may have others you wish to be part of the team. As long as you have a team made up of people important to the project, you will know who is responsible for what and may end up with a more smoothly running project.

Inspect Site and Assemble Hardware (F2)

The systems used in the examples throughout this book were delivered with owner's manuals that included illustrated steps for setting up the system. There isn't really much to assembling the hardware. Just unpack the boxes, connect the cables, and power up. The manual for the Series 800 Model K400 used in some of the examples went into some detail about the environment for the system, but in general, there isn't much to setting up one of the smaller systems.

A large T500, on the other hand, may require a lot of work to assemble. For a modest fee, the HP System Support Organization (SSO) will perform the hardware setup for you. I normally recommend that my customers use this service for a number of reasons. First, if you don't have a lot of experience with HP, you will meet your Customer Engineer (CE). Although HP equipment is highly reliable, you may need to see your CE for possible future hardware problems, so it makes sense to become acquainted with him or her. Secondly, it may be comforting to have a CE set up the system, tell you "it's working great," and give you some tips. Finally, the CE will take down all the serial numbers of the equipment and verify that all your hardware support is in order. It's good to take care of this detail when the system is set up to ensure there won't be a delay when you need service.

The really important part of this step is what you do *BEFORE* you set up the equipment. I always recommend that the CE perform a site inspection to verify that your physical environment can accommodate the system(s) you have ordered. In the case of the systems used in the examples in this book, which operate in a standard office environment, you wouldn't think there is a lot to inspect. A trained eye, however, can uncover hidden problems. The most common of these is lack of sufficient power. Even though these systems consume a modest amount of power, some offices aren't wired for more than an adding machine and calculator charger!

There is no greater disappointment than setting up your system only to find that you have insufficient power to run it. Your CE can point out all such potential problems.

Consider all of the material you think you'll need to get your systems up and running. Here is a checklist of items I recommend that my customers review.

Logistical Considerations

Cabling   LAN cable (twisted pair, thin net, etc.) of the length you require. Don't measure distance "as the crow flies." Remember that if your office is not prewired, you'll have to run wires up the wall, across the ceiling, and back down the wall to go from office to office.

Media Attachment Unit   MAU to attach cable to the connector on the back of the computer. An example is attaching twisted pair cable to the AUI connector on the back of the computer. HP workstations come with both a thin net connector and AUI. Order the system with the interface you want so you don't have to mess with this when you connect your systems.

Power   Make sure you have sufficient power and power outlets. Many offices already have PCs in them, so you want to make sure you have enough power and outlets in the office. If your Series 800 system is going in a computer room, you will be pleasantly surprised by how little space it consumes compared to the dinosaurs for which computer rooms were originally designed.

Air Conditioning   Make sure you have sufficient air conditioning. Servers, especially the V class systems, have air conditioning requirements that need to be met in order to keep the systems running at peak performance. Also, since the Series 700s are so small, some people tend to hide them on the floor behind boxes where they can overheat.

Software Configuration

System Names   Think about system names. The most common delay I encounter when installing systems is waiting for users to select the names of their systems. It doesn't matter what theme you choose for system names, just be sure that you, the administrator, are happy with the theme.

Some good themes for system names are colors, planets, and sports teams. Choose a theme that can accommodate additional systems later.

Addresses Have IP addresses ready. If you don't now use IP addresses, HP can provide you with class C addresses. Ask your HP Technical Consultant (TC) how to obtain these addresses from HP. IP addressing and networking will be discussed in detail in Chapter 2.

Network Diagram Since I recommend having your HP TC assist you with the installation on a consulting basis, I also recommend that you ask your TC to give a rundown on what he or she will do to get your systems running. I normally produce a flowchart similar to Figure 1-2, only more customer specific. A formal document isn't necessary, but it will be helpful to you to understand your TC's plan. TCs do this kind of work every day and can help you get your system installed quickly. But you won't know what he or she is doing unless you're involved.

Order Documentation

As part of preparing for your system, you also want to consider your documentation needs when you buy your system. Very little documentation delivered is with either a new Series 800 or a new Series 700 unit; however, there are many manuals you can order with your system. The documentation is well organized into sets of manuals covering related topics. An extensive HP-UX 11.x documentation set is available. Be sure to order the documentation sets you need, such as system administration, programming reference, CDE, etc., when ordering your system. You can also order the manuals set on CD-ROM called Instant Information.

If you are an HP-UX 10.x user, the single most important document to you may be *Release Notes for HP-UX 11.0*. This covers all the important information about HP-UX 11.x, including many topics not covered in my book, such as the new way in which 64-bit applications are implemented. Release notes can also be downloaded from the World Wide Web via **http://www.software.hp.com/STK/partner/relnotes/11.00/relnotes_11.00.** They also can be obtained on CD-ROM by ordering part number 5967-0055.

Install HP-UX 11.x (F3)

Installing HP-UX means building an initial "bare bones" HP-UX 11.x system and later building your complete full-function HP-UX system. The initial system is loaded from the HP-UX Install media for both the Series 700 and Series 800 or from another system on the network, a process not covered in this book. The full-function system is loaded from the HP-UX 11.0 Install and Core OS CD and Applications CD or from another system on the network.

You can have your system delivered with instant ignition, which means that HP-UX has been loaded on your system and you'll only have to add to it the application software you need. I cover the complete installation process for both a Series 700 and Series 800 from CD-ROM so you can see the process start to finish. If you have instant ignition on your system, you may need to install additional software on your system in the future and can, therefore, use some of the techniques described in this section to load that software.

The K4xx server systems I have worked with that were delivered with instant ignition did not have the **/SD_CDROM** directory, which is the default directory used to load software and which I use in the examples in this chapter. Although I don't cover instant ignition in this chapter, you may have your systems delivered with instant ignition and probably will choose to not reinstall the operating system. If you have instant ignition and wish to load software using the **/SD_CDROM** directory, you may have to create **/SD_CDROM**.

The Install media that you use to install HP-UX 11.x on the Series 700 and Series 800 is self-contained; that is, it has on it everything you need for the initial installation. I will use CD-ROM media for the installation process for both the Series 700 and Series 800.

Before you start installing anything, make sure that your hardware configuration is a supported HP-UX 11.x configuration. If your system is not supported for HP-UX 11.x, you are taking a risk by installing it. A number of generic requirements must be met, such as having a minimum of

64 MBytes of RAM and 1 GByte of disk space. However, 128 MB RAM and 2 GB disk space are recommended for the 32-bit version of 11.x (all supported 700s, and D,E,F,G,H,I, and K-class and T600 servers), and 512 MBytes of RAM and 6 GB disk space are recommended for the 64-bit version of 11.x (K-class, T600, and V-class servers). In addition, you want to make sure that your processor is one of the supported devices for HP-UX 11.x. For example, models 715/64, 715/80, and 715/100 are the only 715 class systems supported for 11.x. Models 715/33, 715/50, and 715/75 are not.

One of the features of moving to the 11.x operating system is the option of taking advantage of 64-bit computing. Whereas previous versions of HP-UX supported only the 32-bit processor, with 11.x, you have the option of running either the 32-bit or the 64-bit version. Which version of the operating system you choose is dependent on 2 things: what hardware you are using and what your application requirements are. The 64-bit version is not supported on the Series 700 workstations and many of the low-end Series 800s, but it is required for the V Class servers. With other Series 800s, most notably the K Class and T Class servers, you have the option to install either the 32-bit or the 64-bit version. But don't worry too much if you are unsure whether your hardware supports 64-bit or not. If your hardware doesn't support the 64-bit version, you won't be prompted as to which version to install. The 32-bit version will be installed automatically. If you do have the option to install the 32-bit or 64-bit version, then your hardware supports either.

Your application requirements will also help determine whether you will install the 32-bit or 64-bit operating system. If your applications are 32-bit, then you really have no reason to run the 64-bit version. If, however, you will be running a 64-bit application, then you obviously will need to install the 64-bit operating system. The good news is that if you install the 32-bit operating system and then find that the application you want to install is 64-bit, you can upgrade to the 64-bit operating system, assuming, of course, that your hardware also supports it.

Loading HP-UX 11.x - Installation Options

The HP-UX 11.x installation process gives you two user interface options as to how to set up your system. Guided Installation leads you through a basic system configuration setup. It allows for only a few system-specific options. Advanced Installation is much more flexible and allows for extensive system specific parameters to be set.

In addition to the two user interface options, the HP-UX 11.x installation process gives you three source location options. Of the three options, we will use only the first: Media-only installation. This selection assumes that you will load the software from CD. The other two options are network-based installations. The first, media with network enabled, allows for use with Software Distributor-HP-UX depots. Software Distributor-HP-UX is covered later in this chapter. The second, Ignite-UX server-based installation, makes use of an Ignite-UX server to load the installation options. Ignite-UX, a part of the 11.x operating system, is reviewed in Chapter 7 of this book.

The two installation examples I present both make use of the CD-ROM media.

Also, I want to show you a bit of the differences in beginning an installation on a Series 700 and a Series 800. To this end, the first section, Loading HP-UX 11.x Software Using "Guided Installation," depicts the installation of a Series 700 workstation. A Series 800 server is installed in the second section, Loading HP-UX 11.x Software Using "Advanced Installation."

Loading HP-UX 11.x Software Using "Guided Installation"

In order to install HP-UX software, place the "HP-UX 11.00 Extension Pack Install and Core OS Software CD" into the CD-ROM drive. Be sure to insert the CD-ROM before you begin the installation. When you boot an older Series 700 unit and press the escape key before it autoboots, a screen appears that looks something like Figure 1-3.

```
Selecting a system to boot.
To stop selection process, press and hold the ESCAPE key.

Selection process stopped.

Searching for Potential Boot Devices.
To terminate search, press and hold the ESCAPE key

Device Selection   Device Path   Device Type
-----------------------------------------------------------------

P0                 scsi.6.0      HP       C2235
P1                 scsi.3.0      TOSHIBA CD-ROM XM-3301TA
P2                 scsi.0.0      TEAC     FC-1      HF    07


b)    Boot from specified device
s)    Search for bootable devices
a)    Enter Boot Administration mode
x)    Exit and continue boot sequence

Select from menu: BOOT P1
```

Figure 1-3 Booting a Series 700, Example #1

What are shown in Figure 1-3 (Example #1) are the bootable devices found. Some workstations may show the menu of boot commands instead of the potential boot devices, as shown in Figure 1-4 (Example #2) .

```
--------------------------------------------------------------------
Command                            Description
-------                            -----------
Auto [boot|search] [on|off]        Display or set auto flag

Boot [pri|alt|scsi.addr] [isl]     Boot from primary,alt or SCSI

Boot lan[.lan_addr] [install] [isl] Boot from LAN

Chassis [on|off]                   Enable chassis codes

Diagnostic [on|off]                Enable/disable diag boot mode

Fastboot [on|off]                  Display or set fast boot flag

Help                               Display the command menu

Information                        Display system information

LanAddress                         Display LAN station addresses

Monitor [type]                     Select monitor type

Path [pri|alt] [lan.id|SCSI.addr]  Change boot path

Pim [hpmc|toc|lpmc]                Display PIM info

Search [ipl] [scsi|lan [install]]  Display potential boot devices

Secure [on|off]                    Display or set security mode
--------------------------------------------------------------------
BOOT_ADMIN>
```

Figure 1-4 Booting a Series 700, Example #2

If indeed you have booable devices attached to your system the
SEARCH command will show these as shown in Figure 1-5.

```
BOOT_ADMIN> SEARCH

Searching for potential boot device.
This may take several minutes

To discontinue, press ESCAPE.


    Device Path               Device Type
    -----------               -----------
    scsi.6.0                  HP       C2247
    scsi.3.0                  HP       HP35450A
    scsi.2.0                  Toshiba  CD-ROM
    scsi.1.0                  HP       C2247

BOOT_ADMIN> BOOT SCSI.2.0
```

Figure 1-5   Series 700 Boot **SEARCH** Example

Once the bootable devices have been displayed, you may select an entry from the list. In this case, I have the HP-UX 11.x Install media on CD-ROM, so I can boot from P1 with the command shown in Example #1 (**BOOT P1**). In Example #2, I specify the CD-ROM at SCSI address 2 to boot from (**BOOT SCSI.2.0**) after running **SEARCH** to see what bootable devices exist.

You will then be asked what language you want, such as U.S. English. You will notice that you have two choices for U.S. English: *PS2_DIN_ITF_US_English* and *PS2_DIN_US_English*. If you have an older 700 with an HIL adapter for your keyboard and mouse, you will need to select the ITF version. Otherwise, choose *PS2_DIN_US_English*.

After selecting your language, the "Welcome to HP-UX installation/ recovery process" menu is displayed, as in Figure 1-6.

```
        Welcome to HP-UX installation/recovery process!
   Use the <tab> key to navigate between fields, and the
   arrow keys within fields. Use the <return/enter> key
   to select an item. Use the <return> or <space-bar> to
   pop-up a choices list. If the menus are not clear, select
   the "Help" item for more information.


   Hardware Summary:     System Model:  9000/715/G
   +-----------------+------------+-------------+
   |Disks: 2 (4.0 GB)|Floppies: 0 |LAN cards: 1 |   [Scan Again]
   |CDs:   1         |Tapes:    0 |Memory: 80 Mb|
   |Graphics Ports: 1|IO Buses: 2 |             |   [H/W Details]
   |                 |            |             |
   |                 |            |             |
   |                 |            |             |
   +-----------------+------------+-------------+
               [ Install HP-UX ]
           [ Run a Recovery Shell ]
             [ Advanced Options ]
      [ Reboot ]                              [ Help ]
```

Figure 1-6 Installation Options on Series 700 HP-UX 11.x Install Media

The *Welcome to HP-UX* menu is the first menu displayed. It gives a summary of the hardware on your system. If you want to see more detail, select the H/W Details option. This takes you to a detailed listing of your hardware. It includes such items as hardware paths, disk drive capacities, and LAN addresses. From this menu, I select *Install HP-UX*.

Next comes the *User Interface and Media Options* menu, as in Figure 1-7.

```
  User Interface and Media Options

This screen lets you pick from options that will determine
if an Ignite-UX server is used, and your user interface
preference.

Source Location Options:
[*] Media only installation
[ ] Media with Network enabled (allows use of SD depots)
[ ] Ignite-UX server based installation
User Interface Options:
[*] Guided Installation (recommended for basic installs)
[ ] Advanced Installation (recommended for disk and
    filesystem management)
Hint: If you need to make LVM size changes, or want to set
the final networking parameters during the install,
you will need to use the Advanced mode (or remote
graphical interface).

[OK]                    [Cancel]                    [Help]
```

Figure 1-7   Installation Options on Series 700 HP-UX 11.x Install Media

As explained earlier, the *User Interface and Media Options* menu gives you the option of installing from the Install CD only, the Install CD combined with software depots on your network, or the Ignite-UX product. I have selected the defaults of Media only installation and Guided Installation.

The next set of displays guides you through the basic setup for installing the operating system. The displays, titled *Install HP-UX Wizard*, suggest the default options. You just need to select *Next* at the bottom of each display in order to select the default option.

The default options for the next four setup screens are listed below in the order presented by the *Install HP-UX Wizard*. In each case, I have selected the default option.

- Configuration: HP-UX B.11.00 Default

- Environments: 32-Bit CDE HP-UX Environment

- Root Disk: SEAGATE_ST32151N, 2/0/1.6.0, 2048 MB

- Root Swap (MB)   160 Physical Memory (RAM) = 80 MB

   If you have not reviewed the Logical Volume Manager section of this chapter, you want to do so before you make the next selection (LVM is Logical Volume Manager). I am a strong advocate of using Logical Volume Manager and the journaled file system (VxFS) whenever possible. Many advantages exist to using Logical Volume Manager, and you should be aware of these. In HP-UX 9.x, Logical Volume Manager was not available on Series 700 units, so I expect that some system administrators may select "whole disk (not LVM) with HFS configuration" because this is what they have grown accustomed to for the Series 700. I would recommend using Logical Volume Manager. Among the many advantages of Logical Volume Manager is that it extends the size of a logical volume if it is insufficient for your needs.

   I want to select *Logical Volume Manager (LVM) with VxFS* (which is the journaled file system). In order to change the default, "wholedisk (not LVM) with HFS," the space bar is pressed to get more options. Using the down arrow, I was able to highlight *Logical Volume Manager (LVM) with VxFS*, as in Figure 1-8.

```
      Select a file system type


Now that you have made your root swap selection, you
need to choose which type of file system you would like
to use. The current choice displayed in the selector is
recommended. If you are unsure of what to choose, keep
the default selection. You may then safely proceed
to the next step.

File system:[Whole disk (not LVM) with HFS]
           [Logical Volume Manager (LVM) with HFS]
           [Logical Volume Manager (LVM) with VxFS]


[Back]          [Next]              [Cancel]              [Help]
```

Figure 1-8 Installation Options on Series 700 HP-UX 11.x Install Media

The next display, Select Languages, needs to be carefully reviewed. Initially, only English is marked to be installed. If your setup requires multiple languages, here's the place to install them. Again, use the space bar and arrow keys to view all options and select any others you might want.

The next displays were left with the proposed defaults:

- User Licenses: HP-UX 2-User License

- Additional Software: leave defaults

Under Additional Software, even though I left the defaults marked, you need to be aware of what the defaults are. Specifically, the installation CD includes the latest *Extension Pack*, which is a compilation of the latest general release patches to the HP-UX 11.x operating system. This includes patches to enable newly released hardware to work under the HP-UX 11.x environment as of the date on the Extension Pack. Hewlett Packard recommends that these patches be installed, and this selection is the default.

We now arrive at "Pre-installation Checks." This section of the installation process checks for anything that may cause you problems later on.

Because my disk drive had been previously used, I was warned that it would be overwritten and I was asked whether I wanted to continue or not. Since I already knew that the installation process would overwrite my disk, I selected continue.

Finally, a display is presented saying "Congratulations, you have successfully defined your system." A "show summary" option allows you to review everything you have done up to this point. After viewing this and finding everything to my satisfaction, I select "Finish" to complete the installation process.

The system now loads the operating system from the CD-ROM. This process takes about one and one-half (1 1/2) hours to complete. Once it is done, your system will reboot and then display "Welcome to HP-UX." You are now asked to link the system to your network.

Boot after Installation

When the system comes up after installation, a series of windows appears that allows you to configure your system name, time zone, root password, Internet Protocol (IP) address, subnet mask, and other networking setup (IP address and subnet mask background is provided in Chapter 2). One of the first questions you are asked is whether or not you wish to use DHCP to obtain networking information. This is new with 11.x. DHCP, dynamic host configuration protocol, works with an Ignite-UX server that automatically assigns system name, IP address, etc. Since my installation does not use this, I answered "no."

The system-specific information to be entered next can also be entered, after your system boots, by running **/sbin/set_parms**. This program can be used to set an individual system parameter or all the system parameters that would be set at boot time. **/sbin/set_parms** uses one of the arguments in Table 1-1, depending on what you would like to configure.

TABLE 1-1   /sbin/set_parms ARGUMENTS

set_parms Argument	Comments
hostname	Set hostname.
timezone	Set time zone.
date_time	Set date and time.
root_passwd	Set root password.
ip_address	Set Internet Protocol address (see Chapter 2 for networking background).
addl_network	Configure subnet mask, Domain Name System, and Network Information Service.
initial	Go through the entire question-and-answer session you would experience at boot time.

If you use the **initial** argument, you interact with a variety of dialog boxes asking you for information. The system host name dialog box appears in Figure 1-9.

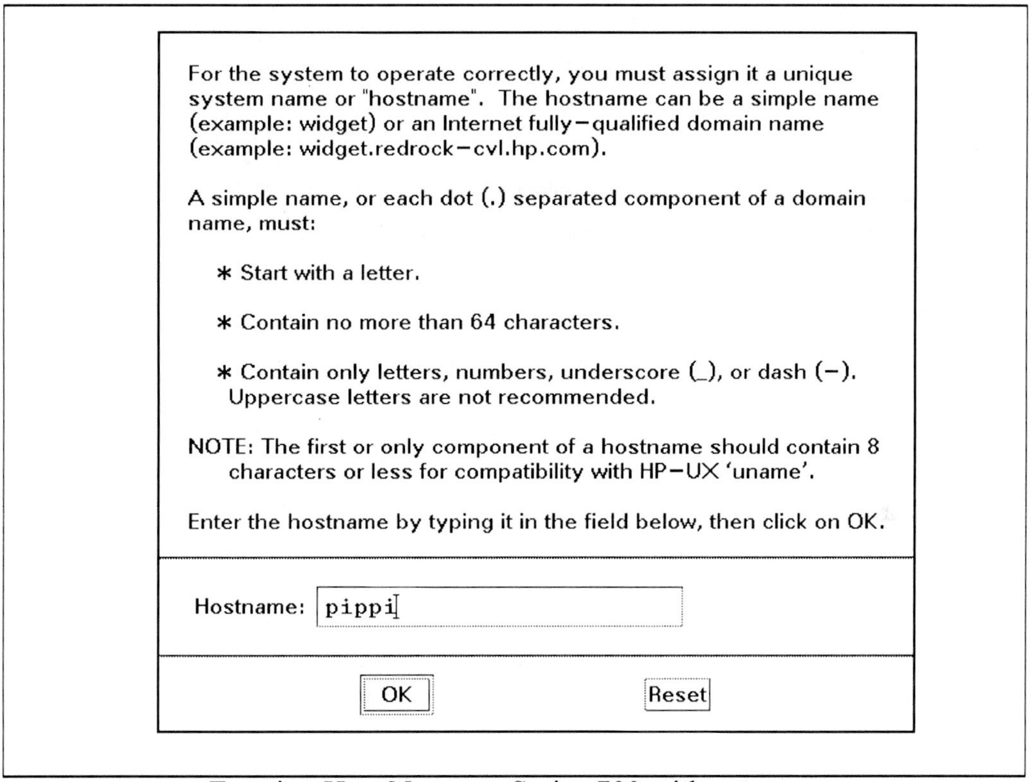

For the system to operate correctly, you must assign it a unique system name or "hostname". The hostname can be a simple name (example: widget) or an Internet fully−qualified domain name (example: widget.redrock−cvl.hp.com).

A simple name, or each dot (.) separated component of a domain name, must:

* Start with a letter.

* Contain no more than 64 characters.

* Contain only letters, numbers, underscore (_), or dash (−). Uppercase letters are not recommended.

NOTE: The first or only component of a hostname should contain 8 characters or less for compatibility with HP−UX 'uname'.

Enter the hostname by typing it in the field below, then click on OK.

Hostname: | pippi |

| OK | | Reset |

Figure 1-9   Entering Host Name on Series 700 with **set_parms**

You are then asked for your time zone and root password. Figure 1-10 shows the dialog box for entering your IP address.

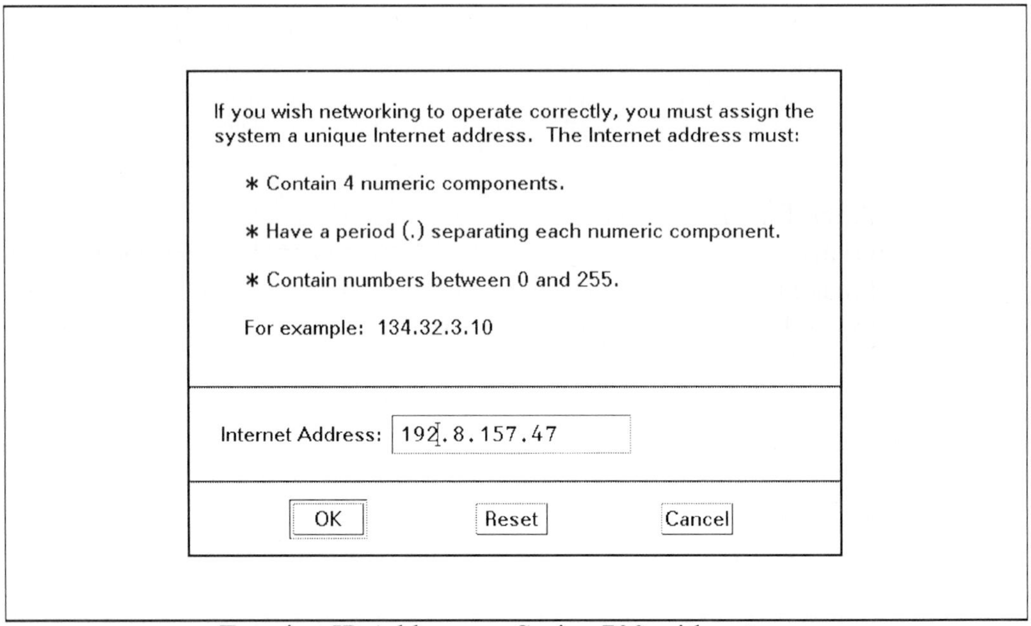

If you wish networking to operate correctly, you must assign the
system a unique Internet address. The Internet address must:

    ∗ Contain 4 numeric components.

    ∗ Have a period (.) separating each numeric component.

    ∗ Contain numbers between 0 and 255.

    For example: 134.32.3.10

Internet Address: | 192.8.157.47 |

| OK | | Reset | | Cancel |

Figure 1-10 Entering IP Address on Series 700 with **set_parms**

You can then configure your subnet mask and other networking configuration.

Please be careful if you configure some of the additional networking parameters (**set_parms addl_netwrk**). Do not configure a system as an NIS client if it hasn't been set up on the NIS server. I have encountered some interesting problems booting if the system is configured as an NIS client *and* I select the option "Wait For NIS Server on Bootup: yes." This means your system will wait forever for the NIS server to respond before the system boot will complete. If you are having problems with your NIS server, you can forget about booting (this is a problem I encountered on a K400 server acting as an NIS client). Your system won't boot and you'll have no way of running **set_parms** to change to "Wait For NIS Server on Bootup: no." I found there are two ways to make this change if your system won't complete the boot process. The first is to shut off the system and boot into single-user state from the ISL prompt with the following command:

```
ISL> hpux -is boot
```

When the system boots, it is in single-user mode with root already logged in. If you run **set_parms** and change to "Wait For NIS Server on Bootup: no," you would think you have changed this variable to "no," but the file where this is changed (**/etc/rc.config.d/namesvrs**) has not been updated, because you are in single-user mode and the commands required to make this change are on a logical volume that has not yet been mounted.

After finding out that the change had not been made by running **set_parms**, I decided to manually edit **/etc/rc.config.d/namesvrs**, where I could make this change. The logical volume **/usr** is not mounted in single-user mode, however, so access to the **/usr/bin/vi** editor I wanted to use to make this change doesn't exist. To mount **/usr**, I issued the following commands (the **fsck** is required because the system was improperly shut down earlier):

```
$ fsck /dev/vg00/rlvol7
$ mount /dev/vg00/lvol7 /usr
```

I then edited **/etc/rc.config.d/namesvrs** and changed the variable in this file to WAIT_FOR_NIS_SERVER="FALSE" and proceeded with the boot process. This fixed the problem but not without a lot of monkeying around. This is an area where you must be careful when setting up your system(s).

Loading HP-UX 11.x Software Using "Advanced Installation"

Loading software using the "Advanced Installation" option is very different from the Guided Installation and has many more options from which to choose. You will find a couple of the initial steps that are the same, and the final setup is the same. But with "Advanced Installation," you will be able to modify the information to suit your particular environment.

In order to install HP-UX software, place the "HP-UX 11.00 Extension Pack Install and Core OS Software CD" into the CD-ROM drive. Be sure to insert the CD-ROM Install media before you begin the installation. As your Series 800 unit boots, you will see a variety of messages fly by, including information about your processors, buses, boot paths, and so on.

You are then given some time to press any key before the system autoboots. If you do this, you'll see the menu shown in Figure 1-11.

```
--------------- Main Menu -----------------------------------

Command                         Descripton
-------                         ----------

BOot [PRI|ALT|<path>]           Boot from specified path

PAth [PRI|ALT| [<path>]         Display or modify a path

SEArch [DIsplay|IPL] [<path>]   Search for boot devices

COnfiguration menu              Displays or sets boot values

INformation menu                Displays hardware information

SERvice menu                    Displays service commands

DIsplay                         Redisplay the current menu

HElp [<menu>|<command>]         Display help for menu or cmd

RESET                           Restart the system

--------

Main Menu: Enter command or menu >
```

Figure 1-11   Booting a Series 800

You can view the bootable devices with the **SEARCH** command, as
shown in Figure 1-12.

```
Main Menu: Enter command or menu > SEARCH

Searching for potential boot device(s)
This may take several minutes.

To discontinue search, press any key
(termination may not be immediate).

Path Number    Device Path (dec)    Device Type
-----------    -----------------    -----------
P0             10/0.6               Random access media
P1             10/0.5               Random access media
P2             10/0.4               Random access media
P3             10/0.3               Random access media
P4             10/12/5.2            Random access media
P5             10/12/5.0            Sequential access media
P6             10/12/6.0            LAN Module

Main Menu: Enter command or menu >
```

Figure 1-12 Series 800 Boot **SEARCH** Example

The information from this screen does not tell us what devices exist at each address. In fact, it can be a guess at this point. I doubt that people with little HP-UX experience know that such things as "Random access media" are disk drives and CD-ROMs, and "Sequential access media" are tape drives. But since I know I ordered a system with four identical internal disk drives and I have what appear to be four indentical entries at P0, P1, P2, and P3, I assume that none of these is a CD-ROM. And since the default address for a CD-ROM is address 2, I'll guess that my CD-ROM is the next entry, which is P4:

```
Main Menu: Enter command or menu > BOOT P4
Interact with IPL (Y or N)?> N
```

This was a lucky guess! Actually, this information can be gleaned by looking at the inside of the front door of the Series 800, which listed the devices and their corresponding addresses. Going back to the Series 700 boot examples shown earlier, they were much clearer what devices were present. With the Series 800, the categories of devices appear to be much more broad.

When your system first begins to boot up, you will be asked what language you want, such as U.S. English. You will notice that you have two choices for U.S. English:

PS2_DIN_ITF_US_English and *PS2_DIN_US_English.*

For a Series 800 server, you want to select *PS2_DIN_US_English.*

After selecting your language, the "Welcome to HP-UX installation/ recovery process!" menu is displayed as in Figure 1-13.

```
        Welcome to HP-UX installation/recovery process!
Use the <tab> key to navigate between fields, and the
arrow keys within fields. Use the <return/enter> key
to select an item. Use the <return> or <space-bar> to
pop-up a choices list. If the menus are not clear, select
the "Help" item for more information.

Hardware Summary:    System Model:   9000/869/K420
+-----------------+-----------+-------------+
|Disks: 4(16.0 GB)|Floppies: 1|LAN cards: 1 |   [Scan Again]
|CDs:    1        |Tapes:    1|Memory:1024Mb|
|Graphics Ports: 1|IO Buses: 2|             |   [H/W Details]
|                 |           |             |
|                 |           |             |
+-----------------+-----------+-------------+
              [ Install HP-UX ]
            [ Run a Recovery Shell ]
            [ Advanced Options ]
   [ Reboot ]                          [ Help ]
```

Figure 1-13 Installation Options on Series 800 HP-UX 11.x Install Media

The Welcome to HP-UX menu is the first menu displayed. It gives a summary of the hardware on your system. If you want to see more detail, select the H/W Details option. This takes you to a detailed listing of your hardware. It includes such items as hardware paths, disk drive capacities, and LAN addresses. From this menu, I select *Install HP-UX.*

Next comes the User Interface and Media Options menu, as in Figure 1-14.

```
┌─────────────────────────────────────────────────────────────────────┐
│           User Interface and Media Options                          │
│                                                                     │
│ This screen lets you pick from options that will determine          │
│ if an Ignite-UX server is used, and your user interface             │
│ preference.                                                         │
│                                                                     │
│ Source Location Options:                                            │
│                                                                     │
│ [*] Media only installation                                         │
│ [ ] Media with Network enabled (allows use of SD depots)            │
│ [ ] Ignite-UX server based installation                             │
│ User Interface Options:                                             │
│ [ ] Guided Installation (recommended for basic installs)            │
│ [*] Advanced Installation (recommended for disk and                 │
│     filesystem management)                                          │
│ Hint: If you need to make LVM size changes, or want to set          │
│ the final networking parameters during the install,                 │
│ you will need to use the Advanced mode (or remote                    │
│ graphical interface).                                               │
│                                                                     │
│ [OK]                    [Cancel]                       [Help]        │
│                                                                     │
└─────────────────────────────────────────────────────────────────────┘
```

Figure 1-14 Installation Options on Series 800 HP-UX 11.x Install Media

As explained earlier, the *User Interface and Media Options* menu gives you the option of installing from the Install CD only, the Install CD combined with software depots on your network, or the Ignite-UX product.

This time, besides Media only installation, we select Advanced Installation.

The display that now appears is similar to that used by Ignite-UX. In fact, it is the same except that Ignite-UX uses a graphical user interface (GUI) and this is the terminal user interface (TUI) . Figure 1-15 shows this display.

```
                    /opt/ignite/bin/itool


/-------\/----------\/--------\/-------------\/----------\
| Basic || Software || System || File System || Advanced |
\        \-----------------------------------------------/

Configurations:[HP-UX B.11.00 Default ->] [Description...]

Envionments: [32-Bit CDE HP-UX Environment ->]  [HP-UX B.11.00]
[Root Disk...] SEAGATE_ST34572WC, 10/0.6,4095 MB
File System: [Logical Volume Manager (LVM) with VxFS ->]
[Root Swap (MB)...] 1024 Physical Memory (RAM)= 1024 MB
[Languages...] English   [Keyboards...] [Additional...]


\----------------------------------------------------------/


[Show Summary]   [Save As...]   [Reset  Configuration]



[Go!]                    [Cancel]                    [Help]
```

Figure 1-15 Advanced Installation Display - Basic Screen on Series 800

This installation set-up works differently from the installation process for prior releases of HP-UX. Rather than going from display to display in a sequential order, this Advanced Installation menu lets you choose among the menu tab areas with the ability of going back and forth among them until you are satisfied with your choices.

Across the top of the main menu display are five tab areas: Basic, Software, System, File System, and Advanced. By pressing the tab key, each tab area can be highlighted. To select the highlighted tab area, press the Enter/Return key. This will cause that tab area's screen to be displayed. Within each of these areas are several parameters that can be modified for your specific system. Listed below are the main features of each tab area:

- Basic - configuration and environment information.

- Software - ability to choose optional software to be installed. Same options as under Guided Installation.

- System - networking parameters. Also configurable via the **set_parms** command.

- File System - disk space allocation.

- Advanced - advanced disk, file system, logical volume, and volume group parameters.

We configure our system beginning with the Basic screen as shown in Figure 1-15.

Items of particular importance are discussed below:

- Configuration - we use "HP-UX B.11.00 Default."

- Environment - the 32-Bit CDE HP-UX Environment is the default for Series 800 servers. If 64-bit were supported, we would have the option of selecting either the 32-bit or 64-bit version of HP-UX 11.x. However, our hardware doesn't support 64-bit, so we aren't given the choice.

- Root Disk - the default selection is the first internal disk drive, which is usually the disk drive at address 6. If you want, you can select a different disk drive on your system.

- File System - as in the Guided Installation, we are given the option of choosing wholedisk (not LVM) with HFS, Logical Volume Manager with HFS, or Logical Volume Manager with VxFS. If you have not reviewed the Logical Volume Manager section of this chapter, you will want to do so before you make this selection (LVM is Logical Volume Manager). I am a strong advocate of using Logical Volume Manager whenever possible with both the Series 800 and Series 700. I find many advantages to using Logical Volume Manager, and you should be aware of them. Among the many advantages of Logical Volume Manager is its ability to extend the size of a logical volume across multiple disk drives if it is insufficient for your needs. On the Series 800 servers, LVM with VxFS is the default.

- Root Swap - the system automatically selects an amount twice the size of your main memory or a maximum of 1024 MB. You want to consider your primary swap space very carefully. A detailed discussion about swap space appears later in this chapter under the "Memory Management" section.

- Languages - initially, English is the only language selected. However, if you want to install other languages, here is where you do so.

- Additional - this is the pick at the bottom right corner of the screen, not the tab area. Here is where you can configure such things as a second swap area, adding a second disk drive to the root volume, and disabling DHCP. New with 11.x, DHCP, dynamic host configuration protocol, works with an Ignite-UX server that automatically assigns system name, IP address, etc. Since my installation does not use this, I changed it to disable.

Moving to the Software tab area, we find software on the installation CD that has been marked for installation. Please note that the installation CD includes the latest Extension Pack. This is a compilation of the latest general release patches to the HP-UX 11.x operating system. This includes patches to enable newly released hardware to work under the HP-UX 11.x environment as of the date on the Extension Pack. Hewlett Packard recommends that these patches be installed, and this is selected for you as the default.

Other software you may want to install can be selected from the installation CD. However, most likely you will be wanting to install application software from the HP-UX Application CD set. This is done using Software Distributor. An overview of the Software Distributor product used for installing all HP-UX 11.x software appears later in this chapter. You may want to take a look at this overview to get a feel for the type of functionality Software Distributor offers. The **swinstall** program is the Software Distributor program used to install software. If you have application software to be installed, you will interact with **swinstall,** and possibly be asked for codeword information for some of the software to be installed. If your software is protected, you will have to enter the codeword information. If you need a codeword, it should be printed on the CD-ROM certificate you received with your software. This codeword is tied to the ID number of a hardware device of your system.

The System tab area is where networking configuration can be found. Since I want to install these parameters after the installation is complete, I have changed only the first item on this screen. The options are:

Final system parameters: [Set parameters now]

[Ask at first boot]

I selected "Ask at first boot."

File System is the area of particular importance. Here is where you can change file system sizes. Figure 1-16 shows the default system layout for a Series 800. It also shows that I am ready to increase the disk space allocated to **/home** from 20 MB to 200 MB.

```
                        /opt/ignite/bin/itool

/--------\/-----------\/--------\/--------------\/----------\
| Basic || Software|| System || File System || Advanced |
\----------------------------\          \----------/

Mount Dir   Usage    Size(MB)    %Used    VG name

/stand      HFS          68       29      vg00
primary     SWAP+D     1024        0      vg00        Add
/           VxFS         84       19      vg00        Modify
/tmp        VxFS         32        0      vg00        Remove
/home       VxFS         20        0      vg00
/opt        VxFS        240       37      vg00
/usr        VxFS        376       81      vg00
/var        VxFS        500       16      vg00


\---------------------------------------------------------/
   Usage: [VxFS]      Vg Name: [vg->]      Mount Dir: /home

   Size: [Fixed]  200         Avail: 1748 MB

   [Add/Remove Disks...]          [--Additional Tasks-- ->]
\---------------------------------------------------------/


[Show Summary]    [Save As...]    [Reset  Configuration]

[Go!]                  [Cancel]                  [Help]
```

Figure 1-16 Advanced Installation Display - File System Screen on Series 800

If indeed you have selected Logical Volume Manager, here is where you can adjust the size of any logical volume including /, swap, and **/home**. You will get different default mount directory sizes depending on the size of the disk you have selected to load HP-UX 11.x onto. The mount directory default sizes are the same as for a Series 700. (Had we done a "show summary" before we completed the installation for the Series 700, we could have seen that fact.) However, since I have a 4.0 GB disk drive, I can make these defaults bigger to accommodate more application software and user disk space.

To make logical volume size changes, you select the mount directory of the logical volume, tab down to "Size" and enter the desired new size. With 11.x, you get some new features with "Size." You'll notice that it shows "Fixed" in Figure 1-16. This means that the default is a fixed size. If you tab to "Fixed" and press the space bar, you will see other options such as all remaining, size range, free percent, and free size. These allow you to be very flexible in allocating your disk space. In Figure 1-16, I left the size as "Fixed" and just increased the default of 20 MB to 200 MB. In order to apply the change, I next tabbed up to Modify and pressed Return.

You will notice that "Avail" shows you how much disk space is left to be allocated on your disk drive. It is perfectly all right to leave some disk space unallocated. This will give you a cushion for when you need to increase disk space down the road.

In addition to making changes to **/home**, I want to look at the size of swap. In this case with a K400 with four processors and a lot of RAM, it would make sense to increase the size of primary swap.

After making all these modifications, I am ready to go ahead and install the system. However, first, I want to choose the "Show Summary" option towards the bottom of the screen. This option will show me a summary of all the changes I have made. This gives me a chance to make sure that I didn't forget something. Since everything is fine, I next choose "Go!". Like "Show Summary," this appears at the bottom of every screen.

Series 800 Boot after Installation

When the system comes up after installation, the boot path will be displayed for you. For the K400 used in the example, the following message appeared:

```
Boot:
: disc3(10/0.6.0;0)/stand/vmunix
```

When the system comes up after installation, a series of windows appears that allows you to configure your system name, time zone, root password, Internet Protocol (IP) address, subnet mask, and other networking setup (IP address and subnet mask background is provided in Chapter 2). One of the first questions you will be asked is whether or not you wish to use DHCP to obtain networking information. This is new with 11.x. DHCP, dynamic host configuration protocol, works with an Ignite-UX server that automatically assigns system name, IP address, etc. Since my installation does not use this, I answered "no."

The system-specific information to be entered next can also be entered, after your system boots, by running **/sbin/set_parms**. This program can be used to set an individual system parameter or all the system parameters that would be set at boot time. **/sbin/set_parms** uses one of the arguments in Table 1-2, depending on what you would like to configure.

TABLE 1-2 /sbin/set_parms ARGUMENTS

set_parms Argument	Comments
hostname	Set hostname.
timezone	Set time zone.
date_time	Set date and time.
root_passwd	Set root password.
ip_address	Set Internet Protocol address (see Chapter 2 for networking background).
addl_network	Configure subnet mask, Domain Name System, and Network Information Service.
initial	Go through the entire question-and-answer session you would experience at boot time.

If you use the **initial** argument, you'll interact with a variety of dialog boxes asking you for information. The system host name dialog box is shown in Figure 1-17.

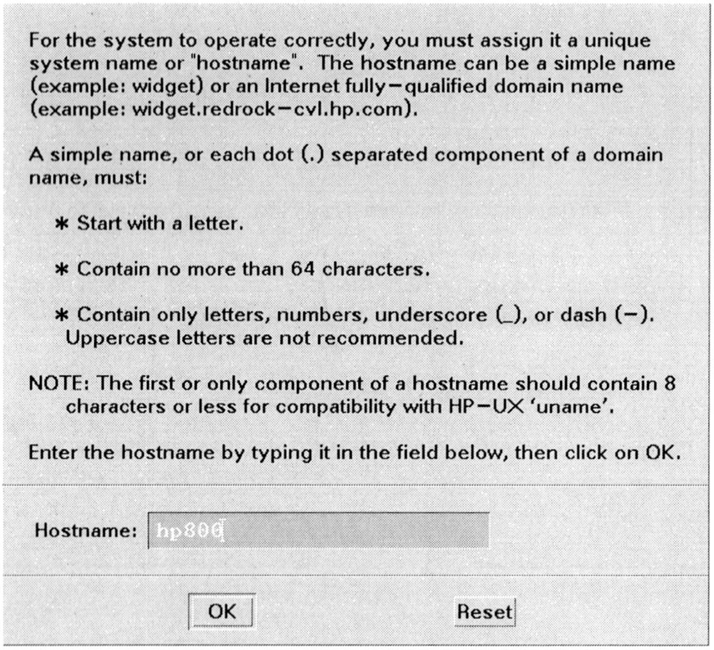

For the system to operate correctly, you must assign it a unique system name or "hostname". The hostname can be a simple name (example: widget) or an Internet fully-qualified domain name (example: widget.redrock-cvl.hp.com).

A simple name, or each dot (.) separated component of a domain name, must:

* Start with a letter.

* Contain no more than 64 characters.

* Contain only letters, numbers, underscore (_), or dash (-). Uppercase letters are not recommended.

NOTE: The first or only component of a hostname should contain 8 characters or less for compatibility with HP-UX 'uname'.

Enter the hostname by typing it in the field below, then click on OK.

Hostname: hp800

[OK]   [Reset]

Figure 1-17 Entering Host Name on Series 800 with **set_parms**

You'll then be asked for your time zone and root password. Figure 1-18 shows the dialog box for entering your IP address.

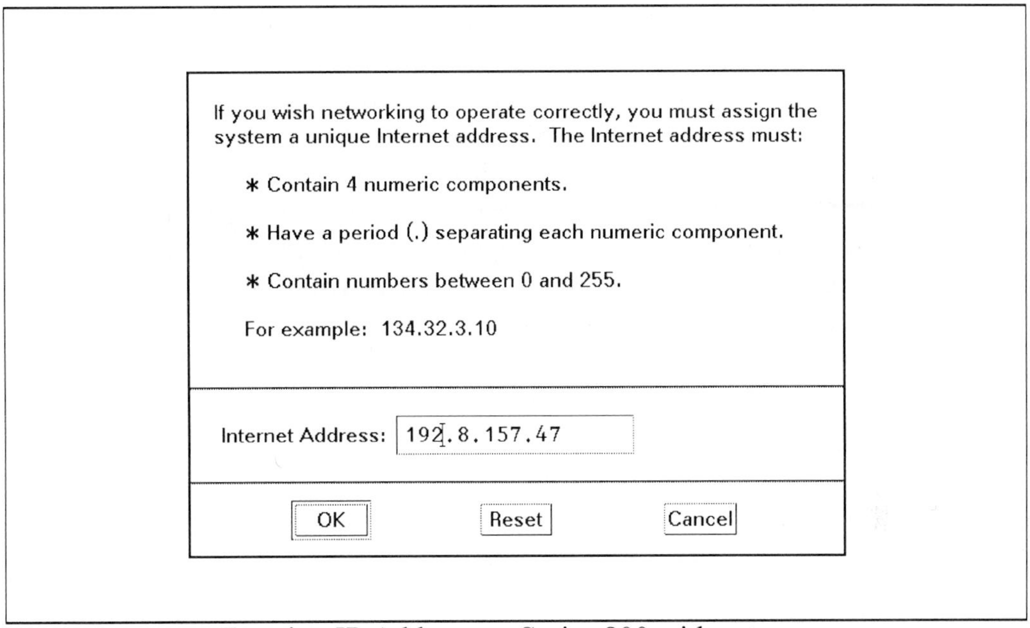

If you wish networking to operate correctly, you must assign the system a unique Internet address. The Internet address must:

* Contain 4 numeric components.

* Have a period (.) separating each numeric component.

* Contain numbers between 0 and 255.

For example: 134.32.3.10

Internet Address: 192.8.157.47

OK   Reset   Cancel

Figure 1-18 Entering IP Address on Series 800 with **set_parms**

You can then configure your subnet mask and other networking configuration.

Please be careful if you configure some of the additional networking parameters (**set_parms addl_netwrk**). Do not configure a system as an NIS client if it hasn't been set up on the NIS server. I have encountered some interesting problems booting if the system is configured as an NIS client *and* I select the option "Wait For NIS Server on Bootup: yes." This means your system will wait forever for the NIS server to respond before the system boot will complete. If you are having problems with your NIS server, you can forget about booting (this is a problem I encountered on a K400 server acting as an NIS client). Your system won't boot and you'll have no way of running **set_parms** to change to "Wait For NIS Server on Bootup: no." I found two ways to make this change if your system won't complete the boot process. The first is to shut off the system and boot into single-user state from the ISL prompt with the following command:

```
ISL> hpux -is boot
```

When the system boots, it is in single user mode with root already logged in. If you run **set_parms** and change to "Wait For NIS Server on Bootup: no," you would think that you have changed this variable to "no," but the file where this is changed (**/etc/rc.config.d/namesvrs**) has not been updated because you are in single-user mode, and the commands required to make this change are on a logical volume, which has not yet been mounted.

After finding out that the change had not been made by running **set_parms,** I decided to manually edit **/etc/rc.config.d/namesvrs** where I could make this change. The logical volume **/usr** is not mounted in single-user mode, however, so I didn't have access to the **/usr/bin/vi** editor I wanted to use to make this change. To mount **/usr**, I issued the following commands (the **fsck** is required because the system was improperly shut-down earlier):

```
$ fsck /dev/vg00/rlvol7
$ mount /dev/vg00/lvol7 /usr
```

I then edited **/etc/rc.config.d/namesvrs** and changed the variable in this file to WAIT_FOR_NIS_SERVER="FALSE" and proceeded with the boot process. This fixed the problem but not without a lot of monkeying around. In this area, you must be careful when setting up your system(s).

Installing Software with Software Distributor-HP-UX

Software Distributor-HP-UX (I'll call this Software Distributor throughout the book; HP documentation typically uses SD-UX) is the program used in HP-UX 11.x to perform all tasks related to software management. Software Distributor will be used in an example to install software on a Series 700 and Series 800 shortly. Software Distributor is a standards-based way to perform software management. It conforms to the Portable Operating System Interface (POSIX) standard for packaging software and utilities related to software managment. The Software Distributor product described in this section comes with your HP-UX system. Additional functionality can be obtained by buying the OpenView Software Distributor (SD-OV) product. SD-OV provides support for additional platforms, allows you to push soft-ware out to target systems, allows for centralized monitoring, and provides a job browser to assist in managing software on target systems. In this section, I won't cover SD-OV, but will make some comments about SD-OV functionality where appropriate.

Software Distributor can be invoked using the commands described in this section, by using SAM (which I cover in Chapter 3) or by installing software for the first time as described earlier in this chapter. Although I don't cover upgrading from HP-UX 10.x to 11.x, you can use Software Distributor to match what is on your HP-UX 10.x system to produce an 11.x system. This process is described in detail in the HP-UX upgrade manual part number B2355-90153.

The following are the four phases of software installation performed with Software Distributor:

- Selection - You can select the source and software you wish to load during this phase. In the upcoming example, the graphical user interface of Software Distributor is used and you'll see how easily you can select these.

- Analysis- All kinds of checks are performed for you, including free disk space; dependencies; compatibility; mounted volumes; and others. Among the very useful outputs of this phase is the amount of space the software you wish to load will consume on each logical volume. This will be shown in the example.

- Load - After you are satisfied with the analysis, you may proceed with loading the software.

- Configuration - The software you load may require kernel rebuilding and a system reboot. Startup and shutdown scripts may also need to be modified.

There is some terminology associated with Software Distributor that I tend to use somewhat loosely. I have nothing but good things to say about Software Distributor, but I don't tend to conform to the official Software Distributor terminology as much as I should. I tend, for instance, to use the word *system* a lot, which could mean many different things in the Software Distributor world. For instance, Software Distributor uses *local host* (a system on which Software Distributor is running or software is to be

installed or managed by Software Distributor), *distribution depot* (a directory that is used as a place for software products), and *development system*
(a place where software is prepared for distribution). I will use the word
system to mean the system on which we are working in the examples,
because software is loaded onto the system from CD-ROM.

Here are some of the common software management-related tasks you
can perform with Software Distributor.

Installing and Updating Software (Command Line or GUI)

The **swinstall** command is used to install and update software. The source
of the software you are loading can come from a variety of places, including, CD-ROM, magnetic tape, or a "depot" directory from which software
can be distributed. Using the depot, you can load software into a directory
and then install and update software on other nodes from this directory.
Software loaded from CD-ROM with Software Distributor must be loaded
onto the local system; this technique is used in the upcoming example. You
have a lot of flexibility with SD-OV only when selecting the target system
onto which you want to load software and the source from which you will
load the software. You can, for instance, load software from a depot that is
on another system on your network. This command can be run at the command line or with the graphical user interface.

Copying Software to a Depot (Command Line or GUI)

The **swcopy** command is used to copy software from one depot to another.
The depot used in the upcoming examples is a CD-ROM. By setting up
depots, you can quickly install or update software to other nodes simultaneously with SD-OV only. This command can be run at the command line
or with the graphical user interface.

Removing Software from a System (Command Line or GUI)

The **swremove** command is used to remove software from a system that has had software loaded with Software Distributor. This includes removing installed and configured software from a system or removing software from a depot. This command can be run at the command line or with the graphical user interface.

List Information about Installation Software

The **swlist** command provides information about the depots that exist on a system, the contents of a depot, or information about installed software. Examples of using this command are provided shortly. This command can be run at the command line or with the graphical user interface.

Configure Installed Software

The **swconfig** command configures or unconfigures installed software. Configuration of software normally takes place as part of **swinstall,** but configuration can be deferred until a later time.

Verify Software

The **swverify** command confirms the integrity of installed software or software stored in a depot.

Package Software That Can Later Be Installed (Local System Only)

You may want to produce "packages" of software that you can later put on tape or in a depot with the **swpackage** command. This packaged software can then be used as a source for **swinstall** and be managed by other Software Distributor commands.

Control Access to Software Distributor Objects

You may want to apply restricted access to Software Distributor objects such as packaged software. Using the **swacl** command, you can view and change the Access Control List (ACL) for objects.

Modify Information about Loaded Software (Local System Only)

The Installed Products Database (IPD) and associated files are used to maintain information about software products you have loaded. **swmodify** can be run at the command line to modify these files.

Register or Unregister a Depot

A software depot can be registered or unregistered with **swreg**. This means you don't have to remove a depot; if you temporarily don't want it used, you can unregister it.

Manage Jobs (Command Line or GUI, this is SD-OV only)

Software Distributor jobs can be viewed and removed with **swjob**. The graphical user interface version of this command can be invoked with **sd** or **swjob -i**.

Software Distributor Example

The example of Software Distributor in this section describes the process of loading software from CD-ROM to the local system. What I show here only begins to scratch the surface of functionality you have with Software Distributor, but since I want to get you up and running quickly, this overview should be helpful. You can load software from a variety of media as well as across the network. The graphical user interface that appears throughout this section makes the process of dealing with software easy. You don't, however, have to use this graphical user interface. You can use the **swinstall** command from the command line specifying source, options, target, etc. I would recommend using the graphical user interface because this is so much easier. If, however, you like to do things the "traditional UNIX" way, you can issue the **swinstall** command with arguments. You can look at the manual page for **swinstall** to understand its arguments and options and use this command from the command line. The graphical user interface of Software Distributor works with the **sd** (this is an SD-OV command and may also be invoked with **swjob -i**), **swcopy**, **swremove**, **swlist**, and **swinstall** commands. There is also an interactive terminal user interface for these commands if you don't have a graphics display.

The first step when loading software from CD-ROM is to insert the media and mount the CD-ROM. The directory **/SD_CDROM** should already exist on your HP-UX 11.x system. If not, you can create this directory or use any name you like. You can use SAM to mount the CD-ROM for you or do this manually. If you forget, the **swinstall** and **swcopy** commands will automount the CD-ROM for you at **/SD_CDROM**. I issued the following commands to mount a CD-ROM at SCSI address two on a workstation and start Software Distributor:

```
$ mount /dev/dsk/c0t2d0 /SD_CDROM
```

```
$ swinstall
```

Software Distributor may look for a software depot on your local system as a default source location for software. If this is not found, you receive a dialog box in which you can change the source depot path. In this case, I changed the source depot path to the default for a CD-ROM, **/SD_CDROM**. This is the Selection process described earlier, whereby you select the source and target for software to be loaded. You can now select the specific software you wish to load.

When the Software Selection Window is opened for you, you can perform many different operations. To identify software bundles you wish to load on your system, you can highlight these and *Mark For Install* from the *Actions* menu, as I have done in Figure 1-19 for The C/ANSI C Developer's Bundle.

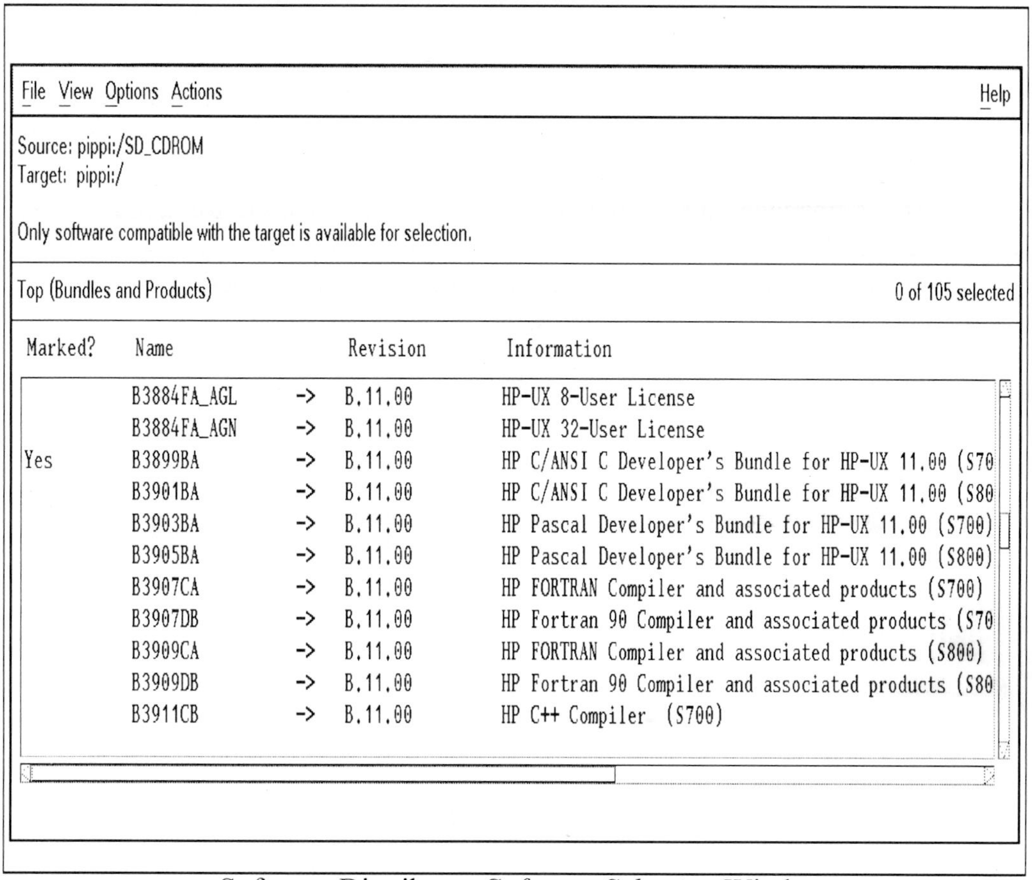

File View Options Actions   Help

Source: pippi:/SD_CDROM
Target: pippi:/

Only software compatible with the target is available for selection.

Top (Bundles and Products)   0 of 105 selected

Marked?	Name		Revision	Information
	B3884FA_AGL	->	B.11.00	HP-UX 8-User License
	B3884FA_AGN	->	B.11.00	HP-UX 32-User License
Yes	B3899BA	->	B.11.00	HP C/ANSI C Developer's Bundle for HP-UX 11.00 (S70
	B3901BA	->	B.11.00	HP C/ANSI C Developer's Bundle for HP-UX 11.00 (S80
	B3903BA	->	B.11.00	HP Pascal Developer's Bundle for HP-UX 11.00 (S700)
	B3905BA	->	B.11.00	HP Pascal Developer's Bundle for HP-UX 11.00 (S800)
	B3907CA	->	B.11.00	HP FORTRAN Compiler and associated products (S700)
	B3907DB	->	B.11.00	HP Fortran 90 Compiler and associated products (S70
	B3909CA	->	B.11.00	HP FORTRAN Compiler and associated products (S800)
	B3909DB	->	B.11.00	HP Fortran 90 Compiler and associated products (S80
	B3911CB	->	B.11.00	HP C++ Compiler (S700)

Figure 1-19   Software Distributor *Software Selection* Window

A bundle, such as the one selected, may be comprised of products, subproducts, and filesets. You can select *Open Item* from the *Actions* menu if you want to drop down one level to see the subproducts or filesets. Figure 1-20 shows *Open Item* for C/ANSI C Developer's Bundle.

```
┌──────────────────────────────────────────────────────────────────────────┐
│ ┌────────────────────────────────────────────────────────────────────────┐ │
│ │ File  View  Options  Actions                                     Help  │ │
│ │ ────  ────  ───────  ───────                                     ────  │ │
│ │ Source: pippi:/SD_CDROM                                                │ │
│ │ Target:  pippi:/                                                       │ │
│ │ Only software contained in the parent bundle is shown.                 │ │
│ │ Only software compatible with the target is available for selection.   │ │
│ │                                                                        │ │
│ │ Products:B3899BA                                       0 of 13 selected │ │
│ │                                                                        │ │
│ │ Marked?     Name             Revision      Information                 │ │
│ │ ..(go up)                                                              │ │
│ │ Yes        AudioDevKit    -> B.11.00.01   HP-UX Audio Developer Kit    │ │
│ │ Yes        Auxiliary-Opt  -> B.11.00      Auxiliary Optimizer for HP Languages. │ │
│ │ Yes        BLINKLINK      -> B.11.00      Blink Link (HP Incremental Linking Facility) │ │
│ │ Yes        C-ANSI-C       -> B.11.00      HP C/ANSI C Compiler         │ │
│ │ Yes        C-Analysis-Tools -> B.11.00    C Language Analysis Tools    │ │
│ │ Yes        C-Dev-Tools    -> B.11.00      C Language Development Tools │ │
│ │ Yes        CDEDevKit      -> B.11.00.01   CDE Developer Kit            │ │
│ │ Yes        DDE            -> B.11.00      Distributed Debugging Environment │ │
│ │ Yes        DebugPrg       -> B.11.00      Debugging Support Tools      │ │
│ │ Yes        HPPAK          -> B.11.00      HP Programmer's Analysis Kit │ │
│ │                                                                        │ │
│ └────────────────────────────────────────────────────────────────────────┘ │
└──────────────────────────────────────────────────────────────────────────┘
```

Figure 1-20   Software Distributor *Open Item*

After you have specified items to *Mark For Install,* you can select *Install (analysis)* from the *Actions* menu. Before starting analysis or before loading software, you should select *Show Description Of Software* from the *Actions* menu to see whether a system reboot is required (you may have to scroll down the window to see the bottom of the description). You want to know this information before you load software so that you don't load software that requires a reboot at a time that is inconvenient. Figure 1-21 is an example *Install Analysis* window for installing C/ANSI C Developer's Bundle.

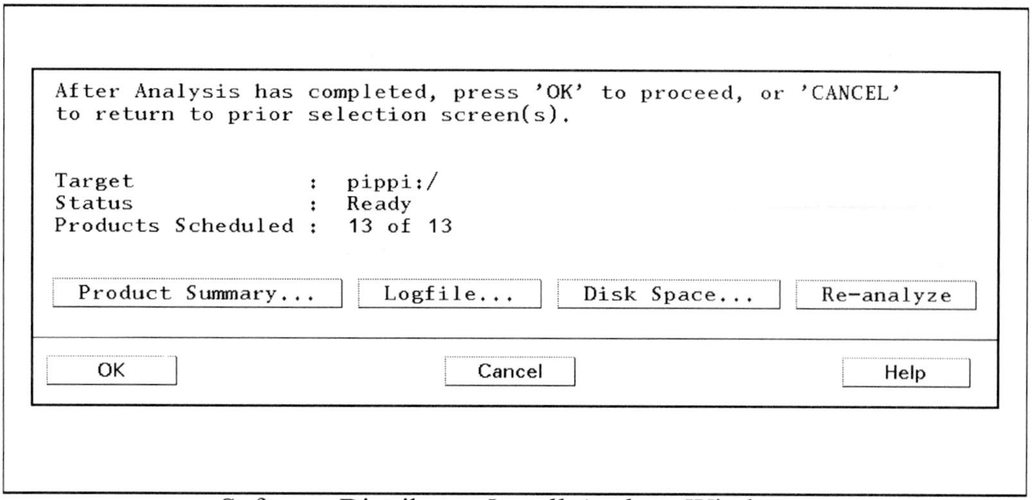

```
After Analysis has completed, press 'OK' to proceed, or 'CANCEL'
to return to prior selection screen(s).


Target           :  pippi:/
Status           :  Ready
Products Scheduled :  13 of 13


   Product Summary...      Logfile...      Disk Space...      Re-analyze


   OK                          Cancel                          Help
```

Figure 1-21 Software Distributor *Install Analysis* Window

You can see that 13 products are to be loaded in this bundle. Among the many useful pieces of information that analysis provides you is a *Logfile* that contains a good review of the analysis and a *Disk Space* window that shows the amount of space that will be consumed by the software you plan to load. Figure 1-22 shows the *Disk Space* window, which includes the amount of disk space available on the affected Logical Volumes both before and after the software load takes place.

File View Options Actions   Help

Target: pippi:/   Sizes shown in Kbytes.
All affected file systems on pippi:/ are listed.
To view software affecting a filesystem, open the filesystem.

File Systems   0 of 4 selected

File System Mount Point		Available Before	Available After	Capacity After	Must Free
/	->	63424	63420	26%	0
/opt	->	147895	74981	69%	0
/usr	->	83580	46536	87%	0
/var	->	146186	145250	11%	0

Figure 1-22   Software Distributor *Disk Space* from Analysis

This window is a dream come true for system administrators who have traditionally not had a lot of good information about either the amount of space consumed by the software they are loading or the destination of the software they are loading. You also have menus here that allow you to further investigate the software you're about to load on your system.

After you are satisfied with the analysis information, you may proceed with loading the software.

Software Distributor Background

You need to have some background on the way software is organized in Software Distributor. Software bundles contain filesets from a variety of different products. Figure 1-23 shows the hierarchy of software bundles.

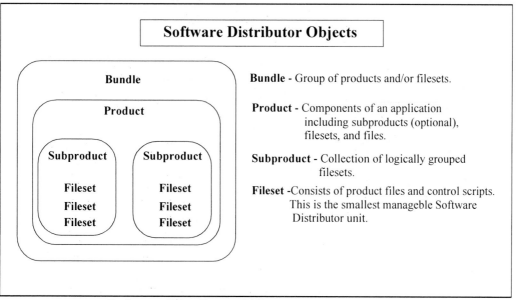

Figure 1-23   Software Distributor Objects

    You can look at the bundle in Figure 1-23 as a group of software. This can be products, subproducts, and filesets, as shown in the diagram. The concept here is to organize software in such a way that it is easy to manage. The diagram is somewhat oversimplified in that a bundle can contain a whole or partial product. This possibility allows a fileset to be in more than one   product.

Listing Software

Although I like the graphical user interface of **swinstall,** you can also issue Software Distributor commands at the command line. One example is the **swlist** command. The **swlist** command is useful for viewing the software you have loaded on your system, viewing the software you have loaded in a depot, or producing a list of depots. A graphical user interface to the **swlist** command can be invoked with the **-i** option and is also available in SAM. With the **swlist** command, you perform many functions, including the following:

- List the software you have at the specified level with the **-l** option. I will show several examples shortly. The levels you can specify are:

  root
  depot
  bundle
  product
  subproduct
  fileset
  file

Levels are delineated by "." so you will see *bundle.[product].[sub-product].[fileset]*. You can get all kinds of useful information out of **swlist** and use this for other purposes. Some of the things you can do with **swlist** are:

- Display the table of contents from a software source.

- Specify which attributes you wish to see for a level of software such as name, size, revision, etc.

- Create a list of products that can be used as input to other Software Distributor commands such as **swinstall** and **swremove**.

When you run **swlist** with no options, you get a list of the software products installed on your system. Let's try a few **swlist** commands with the **-l** option to view software installed on a system (by default, **swlist** will list installed products; you can use the **-s** option to specify a software depot or other source). The following example shows listing software at the *bundle* level.

```
$ swlist -l bundle

# various header information
#             .
#
B2491BA      B.11.00 MirrorDisk/UX
B3701AA_TRY  B 11.00.31 Trial HP GlancePlus/UX Pak for s800
B3929BA      B11.00   HP OnLineJFS (Advanced VxFS)
B3947BA      B.11.00 HP Process Resource Manager
B5725AA      B.1.4    HP-UX Installation Utilities (Ignite-UX)
HPUXEng32RT  B 11.00 English HP-UX 32-bit Runtime Environment
```

This system has the HP-UX runtime environment, GlancePlus/UX trial software, HP OnLineJFS, and MirrorDisk/UX.

If we run **swlist** at the product level, the following is produced for GlancePlus/UX trial software:

```
$ swlist -l product B3701AA_TRY

# various header information
#            .
#            .
#            .
B3701AA_TRY                    B.11.00.31  Trial HP GlancePlus/UX
Pak for s800 11.00
B3701AA_TRY.MeasurementInt B.11.00.31  HP-UX Measurement In-
terface for 11.00
B3701AA_TRY.MeasureWare     B.11.00.31   MeasureWare Software/
UX
B3701AA_TRY.Glance          B.11.00.31   HP GlancePlus/UX

  (bundle)   (product)
```

GlancePlus/UX is comprised of the two products shown in this example. Are there any subproducts of which GlancePlus/UX is comprised? The following example will help us determine the answer.

```
$ swlist -l subproduct B3701AA_TRY

# various header information
#            .
#            .
#            .
B3701AA_TRY                    B.11.00.31  Trial HP GlancePlus/UX
Pak for s800 11.00
B3701AA_TRY.MeasurementInt B.11.00.31  HP-UX Measurement In-
terface for 11.00
B3701AA_TRY.MeasureWare     B.11.00.31 MeasureWare Software/UX
B3701AA_TRY.Glance          B.11.00.31 HP GlancePlus/UX

  (bundle)    (product)
```

The output of the products and subproducts levels is the same; therefore, there are no subproducts in GlancePlus/UX. We can go one step further and take this to the fileset level, as shown in the following example.

```
$ swlist -l fileset B3701AA_TRY

# various header information
#            .
#            .
#            .
B3701AA_TRY                    B.11.00.31   Trial HP GlancePlus/UX
Pak for s800 11.00
B3701AA_TRY.MeasurementInt  B.11.00.31  HP-UX Measurement In-
terface for 11.00
B3701AA_TRY.MeasurementInt.ARM  B.11.00.31  HP-UX Application
Response Measurement for 11.00
B3701AA_TRY.MeasurementInt.MI   B.11.00.31 HP-UX Measurement
Interface for 11.00
B3701AA_TRY.MeasureWare         B.11.00.31  MeasureWare Soft-
ware/UX
B3701AA_TRY.MeasureWare.MWA      B.11.00.31  MeasureWare Soft-
ware files
B3701AA_TRY.MeasureWare.MWANO   B.11.00.31  MeasureWare  NOS
Connectivity Module Software files
B3701AA_TRY.MeasureWare.PERFDSI B.11.00.31 HP PCS Data Source
Integration
B3701AA_TRY.Glance              B.11.00.31 HP GlancePlus/UX
B3701AA_TRY.Glance.GLANC        B.11.00.31 HP GlancePlus files
B3701AA_TRY.Glance.GPM          B.11.00.31    HP GlancePlus Motif
interface files

(bundle)    (product) (fileset)
```

With the **swlist** command and the **-l** option, we have worked our way
down the hierarchy of HP GlancePlus/UX. Going down to the file level
with the **-l file** option produces a long list of files associated with this
product.

The other Software Distributor commands listed earlier can also be
issued at the command line. You may want to look at the manual pages for
these commands as you prepare to do more advanced Software Distributor
work than loading software from CD-ROM or tape.

To system administrators familiar with HP-UX 9.x, this is a different
organization of software, but the graphical user interface of **swinstall** combined with the better organization of Software Distributor makes this an
advantage of HP-UX 11.x.

Build an HP-UX Kernel (F4)

I can think of a variety of reasons to build a new HP-UX kernel on your system, as well as a variety of ways to build the kernel. I would recommend that you use the System Administration Manager (SAM) covered in Chapter 3 to build your kernel. There is, however, no substitute for understanding the process by which you would manually build an HP-UX kernel and, therefore, be more informed when you have SAM do this for you in the future. In this chapter, I discuss various commands related to kernel generation and cover the process by which you would manually create a kernel. As with most other system administration functions in HP-UX 11.x, creating an HP-UX kernel is the same for both a workstation and server system.

You may need to create a new HP-UX kernel in order to add device drivers or subsystems, to tune the kernel to get improved performance, to alter configurable parameters, or to change the dump and swap devices.

Dynamically Loadable Kernel Modules

New with 11.x is the introduction of dynamically loadable kernel modules. In 11.x, the infrastructure for this feature is put into place, providing for a separate system file for each module. With 11.x is provided the ability of specially created modules to be loaded or unloaded into the kernel without having to reboot the system as long as the module is not being used. Future releases of the operating system will support the on-line version. This new mechanism provides great flexibility and improved system uptime. Detailed information about this advanced feature can be reviewed in the HP-UX 11.x Release Notes. Release notes can also be downloaded from the World Wide Web via **http://www.software.hp.com/STK/partner/rel-notes/11.00/relnotes_11.00,** or they can be obtained on CD-ROM by ordering part number 5967-0055.

Building a Kernel

To begin, let's take a look at an existing kernel running on a Series 700. The **sysdef** command is used to analyze and report tunable parameters of a currently running system. You can specify a particular file to analyze if you don't wish to use the currently running system. The following is a *partial* listing of having run **sysdef** on both the Series 700, used in the earlier installation example, showing some of the "max" parameters:

                                                                    (on Series 700)

```
#  /usr/sbin/sysdef

NAME                VALUE   BOOT    MIN-MAX         UNITS   FLAGS

maxdsiz             16384    -      256-655360      Pages     -
maxfiles               60    -       30-2048                  -
maxfiles_lim         1024    -       30-2048                     -
maxssiz              2048    -      256-655360      Pages     -
maxswapchuncks        256    -        1-16384                    -
maxtsize            16384    -      256-655360      Pages     -
maxuprc                50    -        3-                       -
maxvgs                 10    -        -                        -
```

In addition to the tunable parameters, you may want to see a report of all the hardware found on your system. The **ioscan** command does this for you. Using **sysdef** and **ioscan,** you can see what your tunable parameters are set to and what hardware exists on your system. You will then know the way your system is set up and can then make changes to your kernel. The following is an **ioscan** output of the same Series 700 for which **sysdef** was run. (Using **-f** would have created a full listing; you should try this with and without **-f.**)

                                                                    (on Series 700)

```
$ /usr/sbin/ioscan

H/W Path      Class               Description
========================================================================

              bc
1             graphics            Graphics
2             ba
2/0           unknown
2/0/1           ext_bus           Built-in SCSI
2/0/1.1           target
2/0/1.1.0           disk          HP      C2247
2/0/1.2           target
2/0/1.2.0           disk          TOSHIBA CD-ROM XM-3301TA
2/0/1.6           target
2/0/1.6.0           disk          HP      C2247
```

```
2/0/2              lan              Built-in LAN
2/0/4              tty              Built-in RS-232C
2/0/6              ext_bus          Built-in Parallel Interface
2/0/8              audio            Built-in Audio
2/0/10             pc               Built-in Floppy Drive
2/0/10.1             floppy         HP_PC_FDC_FLOPPY
2/0/11             ps2              Built-in Keyboard
8                  processor        Processor
9                  memory           Memory
```

The following is an **ioscan** output of a Series 800 (using **-f** would have created a full listing; you should try this with and without **-f**). Note the four processors shown in this output.

(on Series 800)

$ /usr/sbin/ioscan

```
H/W Path        Class              Description
=================================================================

                bc
8               bc                 I/O Adapter
10              bc                 I/O Adapter
10/0               ext_bus         GSC built-in Fast/Wide SCSI
10/0.3               target
10/0.3.0               disk        HP        C2490WD
10/0.4               target
10/0.4.0               disk        HP        C2490WD
10/0.5               target
10/0.5.0               disk        HP        C2490WD
10/0.6               target
10/0.6.0               disk        HP        C2490WD
10/4            bc                 Bus Converter
10/4/0               tty           MUX
10/12           ba                 Core I/O Adapter
10/12/0            ext_bus         Built-in Parallel Interface
10/12/5            ext_bus         Built-in SCSI
10/12/5.0            target
10/12/5.0.0            tape        HP        HP35480A
10/12/5.2            target
10/12/5.2.0            disk        TOSHIBA CD-ROM XM-4101TA
10/12/6            lan             Built-in LAN
10//12/7           ps2             Built-in Keyboard/Mouse
32              processor          Processor
34              processor          Processor
36              processor          Processor
38              processor          Processor
49              memory             Memory
```

The file **/stand/vmunix** is the currently running kernel. Here is a long listing of the directory **/stand** on the Series 800, which shows the file **/stand/vmunix**:

```
$ ll  /stand

-rw-r--r--  1 root    sys         190 Jul 12 18:09 bootconf
drwxr-xr-x  2 root    root       1024 Jul 12 18:37 build
-rw-r--r--  1 root    root        684 Jul 12 18:05 ioconfig
-rw-r--r--  1 root    sys          82 Jul 12 18:31 kernrel
-rw-r--r--  1 root    sys         609 Jul 12 18:15 system
-rwxr-xr-x  1 root    root    6938348 Jul 12 18:37 vmunix
```

In order to make a change to the kernel, we would change to the **/stand/build** directory, where all work in creating a new kernel is performed, and issue the **system_prep** command as shown below:

```
# cd /stand/build
# /usr/lbin/sysadm/system_prep  -s  system
```

We can now proceed to make the desired changes to the kernel, including adding a driver or subsystem such as cdfs for CD-ROM filesystem. With the dynamically loadable kernel module (DLKM) structure in place with 11.x, we must use **kmsystem** and **kmtune** to make changes to the kernel system and system description files.

With the desired changes having been made, we can create the new kernel, which will be generated as **/stand/build/vmunix_test** using the command shown below:

```
# mk_kernel  -s  system
```

At this point, the new kernel exists in the **/stand/build** directory. The existing kernel is updated with the newly generated kernel with **kmupdate**. **kmupdate** moves the new kernel files into the **/stand** directory. I would first recommend moving the existing **/stand/system** kernel file to a backup file name and then updating the new kernel as shown below:

```
# mv /stand/system /stand/system.prev

# kmupdate /stand/build/vmunix_test
```

kmupdate will automatically create backup copies of **/stand/vmunix** and **/stand/dlkm** for you. These will be created as **/stand/vmunix.prev** and **/stand/dlkm.vmunix.prev,** respectively.

You can now shut down the system and automatically boot from the new kernel.

In HP-UX 11.x, you may want to rebuild the kernel for dynamic buffer cache. You can, for instance, specify a buffer cache boundary using *dbc_min_pct* as a lower boundary and *dbc_max_pct* as an upper boundary.

Figure 1-24 summarizes the process of building a new kernel in HP-UX 11.x.

<u>Step</u>	<u>Comments</u>
1) run **sysdef** and **ioscan -f**	Analyzes and reports tunable parameters of currently running kernel.
2) perform long listing of /**stand** directory	The file **vmunix** is the existing kernel, and **system** is used to build a new kernel.
3) **cd /stand/build**	This is the directory where the new kernel will be built.
4) /**usr/lbin/sysadm/system_prep -s system**	This extracts the **system** file from the currently running kernel.
5) use **kmsystem** and **kmtune** to make changes	Takes place in the /**stand/build** directory.
6) **mk_kernel -s system**	Makes a new kernel in the /**stand/build** directory called **vmunix_test**. DLKM files are produced in **dlkm.vmunix_test/***.
7) **mv /stand/system /stand/system.prev**	Saves the existing **system** file as /**stand/system.prev**.
7) **kmupdate /stand/build/vmunix_test**	Updates the kernel with the newly generated kernel. Automatically saves the old versions in /**stand** as follows: **vmunix** as /**stand/vmunix.prev** **dlkm** as /**dlkm.vmunix.prev**
8) **cd /** **shutdown -r 0**	Changes directory to / and shuts down the sytem sothat it comes up with the new kernel.

Figure 1-24 Creating a Kernel in HP-UX 11.x

Configure Additional Peripherals (F5)

As you progress through the installation flow, you reach a point where it makes sense to add the additional peripherals that are part of your system. A typical installation will have terminals, printers, a tape drive, a CD-ROM drive, etc. Some devices are "standard," meaning that they are HP products or third-party products officially supported by HP. You have to be careful here, though, because what may seem as if it should work may not work after all and may not be supported. Almost always you can find a way to get things working eventually, but beware of devices you may be adding that aren't supported and may cause you trouble.

As you add additional peripherals to your system, you will have to either add device files manually or use SAM to create them for you. Most all devices you add can be added through SAM. I find adding peripherals to be much like setting up networking; that is, I almost always use SAM but I find it important to know what is going on in the background. As an example, you could add a printer to your system using SAM and never know what has been done to support the new printer. In the event that the printer does not work for some reason, you really can't begin troubleshooting the problem without an understanding of device files.

I touched on device files in the file system section but did not want to go into too much detail. Here is the rest of the story on device files.

All About Device Files in HP-UX 11.x

What could be more confusing in the UNIX world than device files? Fortunately, in HP-UX, device files for the Series 700 and Series 800 are nearly identical, so if you learn one, it applies to the other. In this section, I cover:

- The structure of device files.

- Some commands associated with helping you work with device files.

- Some examples of creating device files.

A device file provides the HP-UX kernel with important information about a specific device. The HP-UX kernel needs to know a lot about a device before Input/Output operations can be performed. With HP-UX 11.x, the device file naming convention is the same for workstations and server systems. Device files are in the **/dev** directory. There may also be a subdirectory under **/dev** used to further categorize the device files. An example of a subdirectory would be **/dev/dsk,** where disk device files are usually located, and **/dev/rmt**, where tape drive device files are located. Figure 1-25 shows the HP-UX 11.x device file naming convention.

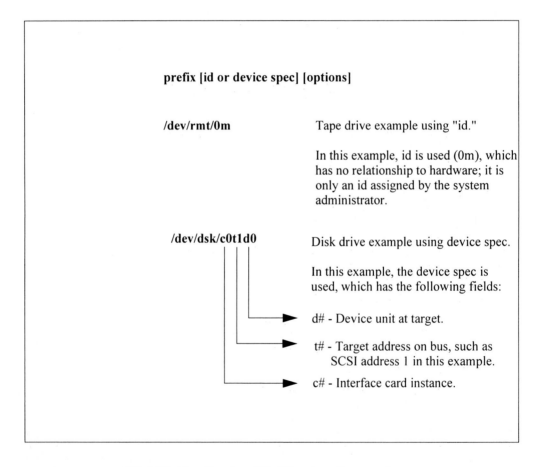

Figure 1-25 HP-UX 11.x Device File Naming Convention

There are a number of commands you use as you go about creating device files. The **ioscan** command is the first of these. This command was covered earlier under "Building a Kernel in HP-UX 11.x," but I go over this again here and provide the same **ioscan** examples for the Series 700 and Series 800 shown earlier, so you don't have to flip back to the earlier section. The following is an **ioscan** output of the same Series 700, for which **sysdef** was run when describing how a kernel is created. (Using **-f** with **ioscan** would have created a full listing; you should try it with and without **-f.**)

(on Series 700)

```
$ /usr/sbin/ioscan

H/W Path        Class                   Description
===============================================================

                bc
1               graphics                Graphics
2               ba
2/0             unknown
2/0/1             ext_bus               Built-in SCSI
2/0/1.1             target
2/0/1.1.0             disk              HP        C2247
2/0/1.2             target
2/0/1.2.0            disk               TOSHIBA  CD-ROM XM-3301TA
2/0/1.6             target
2/0/1.6.0            disk               HP        C2247
2/0/2           lan                     Built-in LAN
2/0/4           tty                     Built-in RS-232C
2/0/6           ext_bus                 Built-in Parallel Interface
2/0/8           audio                   Built-in Audio
2/0/10          pc                      Built-in Floppy Drive
2/0/10.1          floppy                HP_PC_FDC_FLOPPY
2/0/11          ps2                     Built-in Keyboard
8               processor               Processor
9               memory                  Memory
```

The following is an **ioscan** output of the same Series 80, for which **sysdef** was run when describing how a kernel is created. (Using **-f** would have created a full listing; you should try with and without **-f.**) Note the four processors shown in this output.

                                                                    (on Series 800)

```
$ /usr/sbin/ioscan

H/W Path      Class              Description
==============================================================

              bc
8             bc                 I/O Adapter
10            bc                 I/O Adapter
10/0              ext_bus        GSC built-in Fast/Wide SCSI
10/0.3                target
10/0.3.0                disk     HP        C2490WD
10/0.4                target
10/0.4.0                disk     HP        C2490WD
10/0.5                target
10/0.5.0                disk     HP        C2490WD
10/0.6                target
10/0.6.0                disk     HP        C2490WD
10/4          bc                 Bus Converter
10/4/0                tty        MUX
10/12         ba                 Core I/O Adapter
10/12/0           ext_bus        Built-in Parallel Interface
10/12/5           ext_bus        Built-in SCSI
10/12/5.0             target
10/12/5.0.0             tape     HP        HP35480A
10/12/5.2             target
10/12/5.2.0             disk     TOSHIBA CD-ROM XM-4101TA
10/12/6           lan            Built-in LAN
10//12/7          ps2            Built-in Keyboard/Mouse
32            processor          Processor
34            processor          Processor
36            processor          Processor
38            processor          Processor
49            memory             Memory
```

And last is an **ioscan** output from a V class server. (Using **-f** would have created a full listing; you should try this with and without **-f**.) Note the eight processors shown in this output.

                                                                    (on V Class)

```
$ /usr/sbin/ioscan

H/W Path     Class              Description
==========================================
             bc
0            ba                 PCI Bus Bridge - epic
0/0/0             lan           PCI(10110019)
```

```
0/1/0               unknown         PCI(107e0008)
2             ba                    PCI Bus Bridge - epic
2/0/0               ext_bus         Ultra Wide SCSI
2/0/0.5               target
2/0/0.5.0               disk        SEAGATE ST34371W
2/0/0.6               target
2/0/0.6.0               disk        SEAGATE ST34371W
2/0/0.7               target
2/0/0.7.0               ctl         Initiator
2/1/0             lan               PCI(10110019)
4             ba                    PCI Bus Bridge - epic
4/1/0               fc              HP Fibre Channel Mass
                                       Storage Adapter
4/1/0.5           lan               HP Fibre Channel Mass
                                       Storage Cntl
4/1/0.8             fcp             FCP Protocol Adapter
4/2/0               ext_bus         Ultra Wide SCSI
4/2/0.0               target
4/2/0.0.0               disk        TOSHIBA CD-ROM XM-5701TA
4/2/0.1               target
4/2/0.1.0               tape        HP C1537A
4/2/0.7               target
4/2/0.7.0               ctl         Initiator
6             ba                    PCI Bus Bridge - epic
8             memory
15            ba                    Core I/O Adapter
15/1            tty                 Built-in Serial Port DUART
15/2            tty                 Built-in Serial Port DUART
15/3            unknown             Unknown
17            processor             Processor
19            processor             Processor
20            processor             Processor
22            processor             Processor
25            processor             Processor
27            processor             Processor
28            processor             Processor
30            processor             Processor
```

The next command that helps you when creating device files is **lsdev**. **lsdev** lists the drivers configured into your system. When adding a device file, you need to have the driver for the device you use configured into the system. If it is not configured into the system, you can use SAM to configure it or use the manual kernel configuration process covered earlier in this chapter. There is a column for the major number for a character device and block device, the driver name, and class of the driver. Here is an example of running **lsdev** on the same Series 700 in which **ioscan** was run:

(on Series 700)

```
$ /usr/sbin/lsdev
```

Character	Block	Driver	Class
0	-1	cn	pseudo
1	-1	ansio0	tty
3	-1	mm	pseudo
16	-1	ptym	ptym
17	-1	ptys	ptys
24	-1	hil	hil
27	-1	dmem	pseudo
46	-1	netdiag1	unknown
52	-1	lan2	lan
64	64	lv	lvm
66	-1	audio	audio
69	-1	dev_config	pseudo
72	-1	clone	pseudo
73	-1	strlog	pseudo
74	-1	sad	pseudo
75	-1	telm	strtelm
76	-1	tels	strtels
77	-1	tlctls	pseudo
78	-1	tlcots	pseudo
79	-1	tlcotsod	pseudo
114	-1	ip	pseudo
115	-1	arp	pseudo
116	-1	echo	pseudo
119	-1	dlpi	pseudo
130	-1	rawip	pseudo
136	-1	tcp	pseudo
137	-1	udp	pseudo
138	-1	stcpmap	pseudo
139	-1	nuls	pseudo
140	-1	netqa	pseudo
141	-1	tun	pseudo
142	-1	btlan3	unknown
143	-1	fddi3	unknown
144	-1	fddi0	unknown
145	-1	fcT1_cntl	unknown
156	-1	ptm	strptym
157	-1	ptm	strptys
159	-1	ps2	ps2
164	-1	pipedev	unknown
168	-1	beep	graf_pseudo
169	-1	fcgsc_lan	lan
170	-1	lpr0	unknown
174	-1	framebuf	graf_pseudo
183	-1	diag1	diag
188	31	sdisk	disk
189	-1	klog	pseudo

```
        196              -1         eeprom        da
        203              -1         sctl          ctl
        205              -1         stape         tape
        207              -1         sy            pseudo
        216              -1         CentIF        ext_bus
        227              -1         kepd          pseudo
        229              -1         ite           graf_pseudo
        232              -1         diag2         diag
```

Here is an example of running **lsdev** on the same Series 800 on which **ioscan** was run:

(on Series 800)

```
$ /usr/sbin/lsdev

Character        Block        Driver        Class
        0          -1         cn            pseudo
        1          -1         asio0         tty
        3          -1         mm            pseudo
       16          -1         ptym          ptym
       17          -1         ptys          ptys
       28          -1         diag0         diag
       46          -1         netdiag1      unknown
       52          -1         lan2          lan
       64          64         lv            lvm
       69          -1         dev_config    pseudo
       72          -1         clone         pseudo
       73          -1         strlog        pseudo
       74          -1         sad           pseudo
       75          -1         telm          strtelm
       76          -1         tels          strtels
       77          -1         tlctls        pseudo
       78          -1         tlcots        pseudo
       79          -1         tlcotsod      pseudo
      114          -1         ip            pseudo
      116          -1         echo          pseudo
      119          -1         dlpi          pseudo
      130          -1         rawip         pseudo
      136          -1         lpr0          unknown
      137          -1         udp           pseudo
      138          -1         stcpmap       pseudo
      139          -1         nuls          pseudo
      140          -1         netqa         pseudo
      141          -1         tun           pseuod
      142          -1         btlan3        unknown
      143          -1         fddi3         unknown
      144          -1         fddi0         unknown
```

```
156            -1      ptm        strptym
157            -1      ptm        strptys
159            -1      ps2        ps2
164            -1      pipedev    unknown
168            -1      beep       graf_pseudo
174            -1      framebuf   graf_pseudo
188            31      sdisk      disk
189            -1      klog       pseudo
193            -1      mux2       tty
203            -1      sctl       ctl
205            -1      stape      tape
207            -1      sy         pseudo
216            -1      CentIF     ext_bus
227            -1      kepd       pseudo
229            -1      ite        graf_pseudo
```

And last, here is an example of running **lsdev** on the same V class server on which **ioscan** was run:

(on V class)

$ /usr/sbin/lsdev

```
Character     Block      Driver       Class
       0        -1      cn           pseudo
       3        -1      mm           pseudo
      16        -1      ptym         ptym
      17        -1      ptys         ptys
      27        -1      dmem         pseudo
      28        -1      diag0        diag
      46        -1      netdiag1     unknown
      64        64      lv           lvm
      69        -1      dev_config   pseudo
      72        -1      clone        pseudo
      73        -1      strlog       pseudo
      74        -1      sad          pseudo
      75        -1      telm         strtelm
      76        -1      tels         strtels
      77        -1      tlclts       pseudo
      78        -1      tlcots       pseudo
      79        -1      tlcotsod     pseudo
     114        -1      ip           pseudo
     115        -1      arp          pseudo
     116        -1      echo         pseudo
     119        -1      dlpi         pseudo
     130        -1      rawip        pseudo
     136        -1      tcp          pseudo
     137        -1      udp          pseudo
     138        -1      stcpmap      pseudo
     139        -1      nuls         pseudo
     140        -1      netqa        pseudo
     141        -1      tun          pseudo
```

```
     142            -1      fddi4           unknown
     143            -1      fcT1_cntl       lan
     144            -1      fcgsc_lan       lan
     145            -1      lpr0            unknown
     156            -1      ptm             strptym
     157            -1      pts             strptys
     164            -1      pipedev         unknown
     169            -1      consp1          tty
     170            -1      btlan6          lan
     171            -1      fcp             fcp
     188            31      sdisk           disk
     189            -1      klog            pseudo
     203            -1      sctl            ctl
     205            -1      stape           tape
     207            -1      sy              pseudo
     227            -1      kepd            pseudo
     232            -1      diag2           diag
```

From these three **lsdev** outputs, you can observe some minor differences in the devices. The Series 700, for instance, has such classes as audio and floppy, the Series 800 has a multiplexer, and the V class has a BaseTen network card.

You can use **ioscan** to show you the device files for a particular peripheral. Going back to the Series 800 that had four disks and a CD-ROM attached to it, you could issue the following **ioscan** command to see the device files associated with *disk:*

(on Series 800)

```
$ /usr/sbin/ioscan -fn -C disk

Class  I  H/W Path     Driver  S/W State  H/W Type    Description
===============================================================
disk   0 10/0.3.0      sdisk   CLAIMED    DEVICE      HP C2490WD
                       /dev/dsk/c0t3d0  /dev/rdsk/c0t3d0

disk   1 10/0.4.0      sdisk   CLAIMED    DEVICE      HP C2490WD
                       /dev/dsk/c0t4d0  /dev/rdsk/c0t4d0

disk   2 10/0.5.0      sdisk   CLAIMED    DEVICE      HP C2490WD
                       /dev/dsk/c0t5d0  /dev/rdsk/c0t5d0

disk   3 10/0.6.0      sdisk   CLAIMED    DEVICE      HP C2490WD
                       /dev/dsk/c0t6d0  /dev/rdsk/c0t6d0

disk   3 10/12/5/2/0   sdisk   CLAIMED    DEVICE      CD-ROM
                       /dev/dsk/c1t2d0  /dev/rdsk/c1t2d0
```

You can see from this **ioscan** all of the device files associated with *disk,* including the CD-ROM.

You could find out more information about one of these devices with the **diskinfo** command and the character device you want to know more about, as shown below (using the **-v** option for verbose provides more detailed information).

```
$ diskinfo /dev/rdsk/c0t5d0

SCSI describe of /dev/rdsk/c0t5d0
            vendor: HP
        product id: C2490WD
              type: direct access
              size: 2082636 bytes
   bytes per sector: 512
```

An Example of Adding a Peripheral

Before we construct a device file, let's view two existing device files on the Series 700 and see where some of this information appears. The first long listing is that of the tape drive, and the second is the disk, both of which are on the Series 700 in the earlier listing.

(on Series 700)

```
$ ll /dev/rmt/0m

crw-rw-rw- 2 bin bin 205 0x003000 Feb 12 03:00 /dev/rmt/0m
```

(on Series 700)

```
$ ll /dev/dsk/c0t1d0

brw-r----- 1 bin sys 31 0x001000 Feb 12 03:01 /dev/dsk/c0t1d0
```

   The tape drive device file, **/dev/rmt/0m**, shows a major number of 205 corresponding to that shown for the *character* device driver *stape* from **lsdev**. The disk drive device file, **/dev/dsk/c0t6d0**, shows a major number of 31 corresponding to the *block* device driver *sdisk* from **lsdev**. Since the tape drive requires only a character device file and no major number exists for a block *stape* device, as indicated by the **-1** in the block column of **lsdev**, this file is the only device file that exists for the tape drive. The disk, on the other hand, may be used as either a block device or a character device (also referred to as the *raw device*). Therefore, we should see a character device file, **/dev/rdsk/c0t6d0**, with a major number of 188, as shown in **lsdev** for sdisk.

(on Series 700)

```
$ ll /dev/rdsk/c0t0d0


crw-r-----  1  root   sys   188   0x001000   Feb   12   03:01
/dev/rdsk/c0t1d0
```

   We can now create a device file for a second tape drive, this time at SCSI address 2, and a disk device file for a disk drive at SCSI address 5, using the **mksf** command. You can run **mksf** two different ways. The first form of **mksf** requires you to include less specific information such as the minor number. The second form requires you to include more of this specific information. Some of these arguments relate only to the specific form of **mksf** you use.

       -d   Use the device driver specified. A list of device drivers is obtained with the **lsdev** command.

       -C   The device specified belongs to this class. The class is also obtained with the **lsdev** command.

-H   Use the hardware path specified. Hardware paths
                               are obtained with the **ioscan** command.

-m   The minor number of the device is supplied.

-r   Create a character, also known as a raw device
                               file. The default is to create a block file.

-v   Use verbose output, which prints the name of
                               each special file as it is created.

We will now create the device files for a disk drive. Both a block and
a character device file are required. The 0x005000 in the example corresponds to the address of 5 on the disk drive. This number, used in both the
block and character device files, is unique for every disk drive created.

We can now create a *block* device file for a disk at SCSI address 5
using the following **mksf** command:

(on Series 700)

```
$ /sbin/mksf -v -C disk -m 0x005000 /dev/dsk/c0t5d0

     making /dev/dsk/c0t5d0 b 31 0x005000
```


Similarly, we can now create a *character* device file for a disk at SCSI
address 5 using form two of **mksf**:

(on Series 700)

```
$ /sbin/mksf -v -r -C disk -m 0x005000 /dev/dsk/c0t5d0

     making /dev/rdsk/c0t5d0 c 188 0x005000
```

The **-v** option used in these examples prints out each device file as it is created. If you wanted to add a second tape drive at SCSI address 2 to your system in addition to the existing tape drive (**/dev/rmt/0m**), you might use the following **mksf** command:

(on Series 700)

```
$ /sbin/mksf  -v -C tape -m 0x002000 /dev/rmt/1m

     making /dev/rmt/1m c 205 0x002000
```

Character devices are automatically produced for tape drives, since no block device drivers are required. This fact was found in the output from the **lsdev** command, as indicated by a **-1** in the "Block" column.

With this level of device file background, you should have a good understanding of the device files that SAM will build for you when you add peripherals. By the way, printer device files look much different from the device files I covered here, but all the same principles apply.

Set Up Users and Groups (F6)

As you may have guessed by now, performing system administration functions on your HP-UX system is easy; the planning is what takes time and effort. Setting up users and groups is no exception. Thanks to SAM, doing just about anything with users and groups is simple.

One exception exists to this easy setup: HP CDE customization. SAM doesn't really help with HP CDE customization and it can be quite tricky to modify one's HP CDE setup manually. I have Chapter 5 to assist you with HP CDE customization.

You need to make a few basic decisions about users. Where should users' data be located? Who needs to access data from whom, thereby defining "groups" of users? What kind of particular startup is required by users and applications? Is there a shell that your users will prefer? Then, again, the subject of HP CDE customization is covered in Chapter 5.

You will want to put some thought into these important user-related questions. I spend a lot of time working with my customers, rearranging user data, for several reasons. It doesn't fit on a whole disk (for this reason, I strongly recommend using Logical Volume Manager), users can't freely access one another's data, or even worse, users *can* access one another's data too freely.

We will consider these questions, but first, let's look at the basic steps to adding a user, whether you do this manually or rely on SAM. Here is a list of activities:

- Select a user name to add
- Select a user ID number
- Select a group for the user
- Create an **/etc/passwd** entry
- Assign a user password (including expiration options)
- Select and create a home directory for user
- Select the shell the user will run (I strongly recommend the default POSIX shell)
- Place startup files in the user's home directory
- Test the user account

This list may seem like a lot of work, but there is nothing to it if you run SAM and answer the questions. Most of what you do is entered in the **/etc/passwd** file, where information about all users is stored. You can make these entries to the **/etc/passwd** file with the **/usr/sbin/vipw** command. Figure 1-26 is a sample **/etc/passwd** entry.

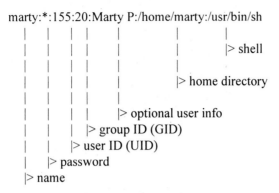

Figure 1-26 Sample **/etc/passwd** Entry

Here is a description of each of these fields:

name.   The user name you assign. This name should be easy for the user and other users on the system to remember. When sending electronic mail or copying files from one user to another, the easier it is to remember the user name the better. If a user has a user name on another system, you may want to assign the same user name on your HP-UX system. Some systems don't permit nice, easy user names, so you may want to break the tie with the old system and start using sensible, easy-to-remember user names on your HP-UX system. Remember, no security is tied to the user name; security is handled through the user's password and the file permissions.

password.   This is the user's password in encrypted form. If an asterisk appears in this field, the account can't be used. If it is empty, the user has no password assigned and can log in by typing only his or her user name. I strongly recommend that each user have a password that he or she changes periodically. Every system has different security needs, but at a minimum, every user on every system should have a password. When setting up a new user, you can force the user to create a password at first login by putting a ,.. in the password field. Password aging can easily be set in SAM.

Some features of a good password are:

- A minimum of six characters that should include special characters such as a slash (/), a dot (.), or an asterisk (*).

- No words should be used for a password.

- Don't make the password personal such as name, address, favorite sports team, etc.

- Don't use something easy to type such as 123456, or qwerty.

- Some people say that misspelled words are acceptable, but I don't recommend using them. Spell check programs that match misspelled words to correctly spelled words can be used to guess at words that might be misspelled for a password.

- A password generator that produces intelligible passwords works the best.

user ID (UID).   The identification number of the user. Every user on your system should have a unique UID. There are no conventions for UIDs. SAM will assign a UID for you when you add users, but you can always change this. I would recommend that you reserve UIDs less than 100 for system-level users.

group ID (GID).   The identification number of the group. The members of the group and their GID are in the **/etc/group** file. You can change the GID assigned if you don't like it, but you may also have to change the GID of many files. As a user creates a file, his or her UID is assigned to the file as well as the GID. This means if you change the GID well after users of the same group have created many files and directories, you may have to change the GID of all these. I usually save GIDs less than 10 for system groups.

optional user info.   In this space, you can make entries, such as the user's phone number or full name. SAM asks you for this information when you create a user. You can leave this blank, but if you manage a system or network with many users, you may want to add the user's full name and extension so that if you need to get in touch with him or her, you'll have the information at your fingertips. (This field is sometimes referred to as the GECOs field.)

home directory. The home directory defines the default location for all the users' files and directories. This is the present working directory at the time of login.

shell. This is the startup program the user will run at the time of login. The shell is really a command interpreter for the commands the user issues from the command line. I recommend using the default POSIX shell (**/usr/bin/sh**), but there are also three traditional popular shells in the HP-UX environment: C shell (**/usr/bin/csh**); Bourne shell (**/usr/old/bin/sh**); and Korn shell (**/usr/bin/ksh**). Shell programming for the system administrator is covered in Chapter 6.

The location of the user's home directory is another important entry in the **/etc/passwd** file. You have to select a location for the user's "home" directory in the file system where the user's files will be stored. With some of the advanced networking technology that exists, such as NFS, the user's home directory does not even have to be on a disk that is physically connected to the computer he or she is using! The traditional place to locate a user's home directory on an HP-UX system is the **/home** directory in HP-UX 11.x.

The **/home** directory is typically the most dynamic in terms of growth. Users create and delete files in their home directory on a regular basis. This means you have to do more planning related to your user area than in more static areas, such as the root file system and application areas. You would typically load HP-UX and your applications and then perform relatively few accesses to these in terms of adding and deleting files and directories. The user area is continuously updated, making it more difficult to maintain.

Assigning Users to Groups

After defining all user-related information, you need to consider groups. Groups are often overlooked in the HP-UX environment until the system administrator finds that all his or her users are in the very same group, even though from an organizational standpoint, they are in different groups. Before I cover the groups in general, let's look at a file belonging to a user and the way access is defined for a file:

```
$ ll
-rwxr-x--x    1 marty        users       120 Jul 26 10:20 sort
```

For every file on the system, HP-UX supports three classes of access:

- User access (u). Access granted to the owner of the file

- Group access (g). Access granted to members of the same group as the owner of the file

- Other access (o). Access granted to everyone else

These access rights are defined by the position of r (read), write (w), and execute (x) when the long listing command is issued. For the long listing (**ll**) above, you see the permissions in Table 1-3.

TABLE 1-3   LONG LISTING PERMISSIONS

Access	User Access	Group Access	Other
Read	r	r	-
Write	w	-	-
Execute	x	x	x

You can see that access rights are arranged in groups of three. Three groups of permissions exist with three access levels each. The owner, in this case, marty, is allowed read, write, and execute permissions on the file. Anyone in the group users is permitted read and execute access to the file. Others are permitted only execute access of the file.

These permissions are important to consider as you arrange your users into groups. If several users require access to the same files, then you will want to put those users in the same group. The trade-off here is that you can give all users within a group rwx access to files, but then you run the risk of several users editing a file without other users knowing it, thereby causing confusion. On the other hand, you can make several copies of a file so that each user has his or her personal copy, but then you have multiple versions of a file. If possible, assign users to groups based on their work.

When you run SAM and specify the groups to which each user belongs, the file **/etc/group** is updated. The **/etc/group** file contains the group name, an encrypted password (which is rarely used), a group ID, and a list of users in the group. Here is an example of an **/etc/group** file:

```
root::0:root
other::1:root, hpdb
bin::2:root,bin
sys::3:root,uucp
adm::4:root,adm
daemon::5:root,daemon
mail::6:root
lp::7:root,lp
tty::10:
nuucp::11:nuucp
military::25:jhunt,tdolan,vdallesandro
commercial::30:ccascone,jperwinc,devers
nogroup:*:-2:
```

This **/etc/group** file shows two different groups of users. Although all users run the same application, a desktop publishing tool, some work on documents of "commercial" products while others work on only "military" documents. It made sense for the system administrator to create two groups, one for commercial document preparation and the other for military document preparation. All members of a group know what documents are current and respect one another's work and its importance. You will have few problems among group members who know what each other is doing and you will find that these members don't delete files that shouldn't be deleted. If you put all users into one group, however, you may find that you spend more time restoring files, because users in this broader group don't find files that are owned by other members of their group to be important. Users can change group with the **newgrp** command.

Set Up Backup Procedure (F7)

The best way to manage backups in HP-UX is through SAM. Backup with SAM is covered in Chapter 3. SAM uses the commands **fbackup** and **frecover** to perform backups and restore data. The reason SAM is the best way to specify backups in HP-UX is that it prompts you for all the relevant information related to backups. SAM helps you manage both *Automated Backups* and *Interactive Backup and Recovery*. There are, however, a variety of commands you can use to back up your system, some of which I'll give a brief overview of. There are also some advanced backup programs you can procure from both HP and third parties. In general, I find the capabilities of **fbackup** and **frecover** are sufficient for new HP-UX installations. If, however, you have a highly distributed environment or need to back up large amounts of data to several devices simultaneously, you may want to consider a more advanced product. Here are some of the more important factors related to backup and recovery that you should know.

To begin, let's consider why you perform backups. A backup is a means of recovering from any system-related problem. System-related problems range from a disk hardware problem that ruins every byte of data on your disk to a user who accidentally deletes a file he or she really needs. The disk hardware problem is a worst-case scenario: You will need an entire (full) backup of your system performed regularly in order to recover from this. The minor problem that your user has created can be recovered from with regular incremental backups. This means you need to perform full system backups regularly and incremental backups as often as possible. Depending on the amount of disk space you have and the backup device you will use, you may be in the comfortable position of performing backups as often as you want. Assuming you have the backup device, what is the full and incremental backup technique you should employ? I am a strong advocate of performing a full backup, and then performing incremental backups of every file that has changed since the **last full backup**. This means that to recover from a completely "hosed" (a technical term meaning *destroyed*) system, you need your full backup tape and only one incremental tape. If, for instance, you performed a full backup on Sunday and an incremental backup on Monday through Friday, you would need to load only Sunday's full backup tape and Friday's incremental backup tape to completely restore your system. **fbackup** supports this scheme.

SAM supports all the options of the **fbackup** command, such as whether this is a full or incremental backup, but it is worthwhile to know what is taking place with **fbackup**. Here is an explanation of the **fbackup** command and *some* of its options:

/usr/sbin/fbackup -f device [-0-9] [-u] [-i path] [-e path] [-g graph]

-f device	The tape drive for the backup, such as **/dev/rmt/ 0m** for your local tape drive.
[-0-9]	This is the level of backup. If you run a full backup on Sunday at level 0, then you would run an incremental backup at level 1 the other days of the week. An incremental backup will back up all information changed since a backup was made at a lower level. You could back up at 0 on Sunday, 1 on Monday, 2 on Tuesday, and so on. However, to recover your system, you would need to load Sunday's tape, then Monday's tape, then Tuesday's tape, and so on, to fully recover.
[-u]	This updates the database of past backups so that it contains such information as the backup level, time of the beginning and end of the backup session, and the graph file (described below) used for the backup session. This is valid only with the **-g** (graph) option.
[-i path]	The specified path is to be included in the backup. This can be issued any number of times.
[-e path]	The specified path is to be excluded from the backup. This can also be specified any number of times.
[-g graph]	The graph file contains the list of files and directories to be included or excluded from the backup.

Although **fbackup** is quite thorough and easy to use, it does not have embedded in it the day and time at which full and incremental backups will be run. You have to make a **cron** entry to run **fbackup** automatically. SAM will make a **cron** entry for you, thereby running **fbackup** whenever you like. (**cron** is covered in detail in Chapter 3.)

Since SAM runs the **fbackup** for you, there really isn't much more you have to know about **fbackup**. However, many other backup programs are widely used in the UNIX world of which you should be aware. Some of these may prove important to you because they are widely used in exchanging information between UNIX systems of different manufacturers. They can also be used for backup purposes, but I recommend using **fbackup** through SAM. Keep in mind that **fbackup** runs under HP-UX only, so you can restore only to an HP-UX system.

Here is a brief overview of some other backup methods:

tar   **tar** is the most popular generic backup utility. You will find that many applications are shipped on tar tapes. This is the most widely used format for exchanging data with other UNIX systems. **tar** is the oldest UNIX backup method and therefore runs on all UNIX systems. You can append files to the end of a **tar** tape, which you can't do with **fbackup**. When sending files to another UNIX user, I would strongly recommend **tar**. **tar** is as slow as molasses, so you won't want to use it for your full or incremental backups. One highly desirable aspect of **tar** is that when you load files onto a tape with **tar** and then restore them onto another system, the original users and groups are retained. For instance, to back up all files belonging to frank and load them onto another system, you would use the following commands:

$ **cd /home/frank**

$ **tar -cvf /dev/rmt/0m 'ls'**   (grav around **ls**)

You could then load frank's files on another system even if the user frank and his group don't yet exist on that system.

cpio   **cpio** is also portable and easy to use, like **tar**. In addition, **cpio** is much faster than **tar** - not as fast as **fbackup**, but much faster than **tar**. **cpio** is good for replicating directory trees.

dd   This is a bit-for-bit copy. It is not smart in the sense that it does not copy files and ownerships; it just copies bits. You could not, therefore, select only a file from a **dd** tape as you could with **fbackup**, **tar**, or **cpio**. **dd** is mainly used for converting data such as EBCDIC to ASCII.

dump   **dump** is similar to **fbackup**. If you use **fbackup** on HP-UX, you will see much similarity when you use **dump**. **dump** provides the same level backup scheme as **fbackup** and creates **/var/adm/dumpdates,** which lists the last time a file system was backed up. **dump**, however, works only with HFS file systems and not VxFS, and it assumes that you are using a reel tape.

Perform Ongoing System Administration Tasks (F8)

A system administrator's job is never done. This fact is good news if you need to keep making a living for a few more years. Enough ongoing tasks and new technologies will be introduced into your environment to keep you busy.

Many of my fastest-paced customers find new technology to implement every month! Some of this technology is unproven, and some of it you would not normally think would work well together. However, business needs are forcing many companies, possibly your company, to continue to press ahead with such technology. A lot of the burden of making this new technology work and maintaining it will be your job. Although you don't need to pay overly close attention to the way your system is being used, I do have some recommendations:

- Monitor overall system resource utilization, including:
  - CPU
  - Disk (file system usage)
  - Networking
  - Swap space

- Devise a thorough backup strategy in which you have 100 percent confidence. This means that you test it out by restoring select files, and then restoring your entire system. The backup commands I covered earlier are only commands, not a strategy. You have to be confident that any or all of your data can be restored whenever necessary.

- Keep printers and plotters running.

- Have a network map that you keep current. Change the network configuration to keep collisions low, and tune the network whenever necessary.

- Update applications with new releases and, if possible, have a test system on which you can test new releases of HP-UX and applications.

- Update HP-UX on the test system if this is available.

- Keep a book of all hardware and software and be sure to update these whenever you change the configuration of a system.

- Keep a record of the kernel configuration of all your systems and be sure to update this whenever you rebuild a kernel.

- Record the patches you apply to each system.

- Make a detailed list of the logical volumes on all your systems.

As the system administrator, you can't rely on HP to handle your system and HP-UX-related issues and on the application vendor to handle your application-related issues. There are just too many system dependencies. Congratulations, this is your job.

The next section, "Memory Management," will cover many basic commands and procedures you'll need to handle.

Memory Management

What is swap? HP-UX system administrators spend a lot of time worrying about swap. It must be very important. Swap is one part of the overall HP-UX memory management scheme, one of three parts to be exact. As any student of computer science will tell you, computers have three types of memory: cache memory, Random Access Memory (RAM), and disk memory. These are listed in order of their speed; that is, cache is much faster than RAM, which is much faster than disk.

Cache Memory

The HP Precision Architecture chip set is configured with both data and instruction cache, which, I might add, is used very efficiently. You must rely on the operating system to use cache efficiently, since you have very little control over this. If you need information from memory and it is loaded in cache (probably because you recently accessed this information or accessed some information that is located close to what you now want), it will take very little time to get the information out of cache memory. This access, called a cache "hit," is instantaneous for all practical purposes. One of the reasons cache memory is so fast is that it typically is physically on the same chip with the processor. If putting large amounts of cache on-chip with the processor were possible, this would obviate the need for RAM and disk. This, however, is not currently possible, so efficient use of memory is a key to good overall system performance.

Checking Available RAM

Your system spells out to you what RAM is available. **/sbin/dmesg** gives you the amount of "physical" memory installed on the system, as shown below for a 64-MByte system:

```
Physical: 65536 Kbytes
```

Don't get too excited when you see this number, because it is not all "available" memory. Available memory is what is leftover after some memory is reserved for kernel code and data structures. You'll also see the available memory, in this case approximately 54 MBytes, with **/sbin/ dmesg**:

```
available: 55336 Kbytes
```

Some of the available memory can also be "lockable." Lockable memory is that which can be devoted to frequently accessed programs and data. The programs and data that lock memory for execution will remain memory-resident and run more quickly. You will also see the amount of lockable memory, in this case approximately 44 MBytes, at the time of system startup:

```
lockable: 45228
```

/sbin/dmesg shows you these values and a summary of system-related messages. You should issue this command on your system to see what it supplies you.

Managing Cache and RAM

If the information you need is not in cache memory but in RAM, then the access will take longer. The speed of all memory is increasing and RAM speed is increasing at a particularly rapid rate. You have a lot of control over the way in which RAM is used. First, you can decide how much RAM is configured into your system. The entire HP product line, both workstations and server systems, supports more RAM than you will need in the system. RAM, at the time of this writing, is inexpensive and getting less expensive all the time. RAM is not a good area in which to cut corners in the configuration of your system. Second, you can use whatever RAM you have configured efficiently. One example is in configuring an HP-UX kernel that is efficient. The HP-UX kernel is always loaded in RAM. This means if it is 1 or 2 MBytes too big for your needs, then this is 1 or 2 MBytes you don't have for other purposes. If you need to access some information in RAM, it will take roughly one order of magnitude longer to access than if it were in cache.

Virtual Memory

If your system had only cache and, say, 64 MBytes of RAM, then you would be able to have user processes that consumed only about 64 MBytes of physical memory. With memory management, you can have user processes that far exceed the size of physical memory by using virtual memory. Virtual memory allows you to load into RAM only parts of a process while keeping the balance on disk. You move blocks of data back and forth between memory and disk in pages.

Swap

Swap is used to extend the size of memory, that is, reserve an area on the disk to act as an extension to RAM. When the load on the system is high, swap space is used for part or all of the processes for which space is not available in physical memory. HP-UX handles all this swapping for you with the **vhand**, **statdaemon**, and **swapper** processes. You want to make sure that you have more than enough swap space reserved on your disk so that memory management can take place without running out of swap space.

Three types of swap space exist: primary swap, secondary swap, and file system swap. These are described next:

Primary swap   Swap that is available at boot. Primary swap is located on the same disk as the root file system. If a problem occurs with this primary swap, you may have a hard time getting the system to boot.

Secondary swap   Swap that is located on a disk other than the root disk.

File system swap This is a file system that supports both files and data structures as well as swapping.

Don't labor too much over the amount of swap to configure. At a minimum, swap should be twice the size of physical memory (this is the installation process default size). Also, our primary applications will define the amount of swap required. Most of the applications I've worked with make clear the maximum amount of swap required for the application. If you are running several applications, add together the swap required for each application if they are going to be running simultaneously.

System Startup and Shutdown Scripts

Startup and shutdown scripts for HP-UX 11.x are based on a mechanism that separates the actual startup and shutdown scripts from configuration information. In order to modify the way your system starts or stops, you don't have to modify scripts, which in general is considered somewhat risky; you can instead modify configuration variables. The startup and shutdown sequence is based on an industry standard that is similar to many other UNIX-based systems, so your knowledge of HP-UX applies to many other systems.

Startup and shutdown are going to become increasingly more important to you as your system administration work becomes more sophisticated. As you load and customize more applications, you will need more startup and shutdown knowledge. What I do in this section is give you an overview of startup and shutdown and the commands you can use to shut down your system.

The following three components are in the startup and shutdown model:

Execution Scripts

> Execution scripts read variables from configuration variable scripts and run through the startup or shutdown sequence. These scripts are located in **/sbin/init.d**.

Configuration Variable Scripts

> These are the files you would modify to set variables that are used to enable or disable a subsystem or perform some other function at the time of system startup or shutdown. These are located in **/etc/rc.config.d**.

Link Files   These files are used to control the order in which scripts execute. These are actually links to execution scripts to be executed when moving from one run level to another. These files are located in the directory for the appropriate run level, such as **/sbin/rc0.d** for run level 0, **/sbin/rc1.d** for run level 1, and so on.

Sequencer Script

> This script invokes execution scripts based on run-level transition. This script is **/sbin/rc**.

Figure 1-27 shows the directory structure for startup and shutdown scripts.

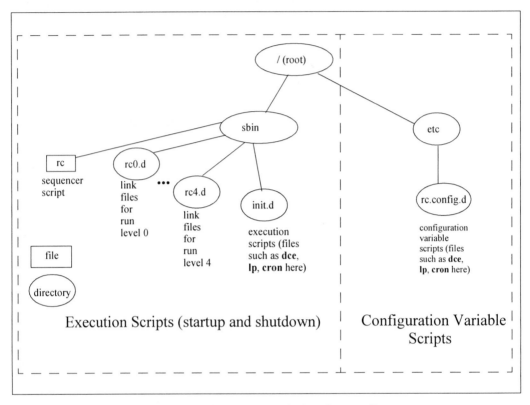

Figure 1-27 Organization of Startup and Shutdown Files

Execution scripts perform startup and shutdown tasks. **/sbin/rc** invokes the execution script, with the appropriate start or stop arguments, and you can view the appropriate start or stop messages on the console. The messages you see will have one of the three following values:

OK	This indicates that the execution script started or shut down properly.
FAIL	A problem occurred at startup or shutdown.
N/A	The script was not configured to start.

In order to start up a subsystem, you would simply edit the appropriate configuration file in **/etc/rc.config.d**. An example showing **/etc/rc.config.d/audio** is shown with the **AUDIO_SERVER** variable set to **1**.

```
#    *********** File:  /etc/rc.config.d/audio **************
# Audio server configuration.  See audio(5)
#
# AUDIO_SER:        Set to 1 to start audio server daemon
#

AUDIO_SERVER=1
```

This results in the following message being shown at the time the system boots:

```
Start audio server daemon .......................[ OK ]
```

and this message at the time the system is shut down:

```
Stopping audio server daemon ......................OK
```

I have mentioned run levels several times in this discussion. Both the startup and shutdown scripts described here, as well as the **/etc/inittab** file, depend on run levels. In HP-UX 11.x, the following run levels exist:

0	Halted run level.
s	Run level s, also known as single-user mode, is used to ensure that no one else is on the system so you can proceed with system administration tasks.
1	Run level 1 starts various basic processes.

2	Run level 2 allows users to access the system. This is also known as multi-user mode.
3	Run level 3 is for exporting NFS file systems.
4	Run level 4 starts the graphical manager including HP Common Desktop Environment (HP CDE).
5 and 6	Not currently used.

/etc/inittab is also used to define a variety of processes that will be run, and is used by **/sbin/init**. The **/sbin/init** process ID is 1. It is the first process started on your system and it has no parent. The **init** process looks at **/etc/inittab** to determine the run level of the system.

Entries in the **/etc/inittab** file have the following format:

id:run state:action:process

id:	The name of the entry. The id is up to four characters long and must be unique in the file. If the line in **/etc/inittab** is preceded by a "#," the entry is treated as a comment.
run state:	Specifies the run level at which the command is executed. More than one run level can be specified. The command is executed for every run level specified.
action:	Defines which of 11 actions will be taken with this process. The 11 choices for action are *initdefault, sysinit, boot, bootwait, wait, respawn, once, powerfail, powerwait, ondemand,* and *off.*
process	The shell command to be executed *if* the run level and/or action field so indicates.

Here is an example of an **/etc/inittab** entry:

cons:123456:respawn:/usr/sbin/getty   console console

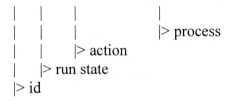

This is in the **/etc/inittab** file, as opposed to being defined as a startup script, because the console may be killed and have to be restarted whenever it dies, even if no change has occurred in run level. **respawn** starts a process if it does not exist and restarts the process after it dies. This entry shows all run states, since you want the console to be activated at all times.

Another example is the first line from **/etc/inittab**:

```
init:3:initdefault:
```

The default run level of the system is defined as 3.

The basics of system startup and shutdown described here are important to understand. You will be starting up and shutting down your system and possibly even modifying some of the files described here. Please take a close look at the startup and shutdown files before you begin to modify these.

Now let's take a look at the commands you can issue to shut down your system.

System Shutdown

What does it mean to shut down the system? Well, in its simplest form, a shutdown of the system simply means issuing the **/sbin/shutdown** command. The **shutdown** command is used to terminate all processing. It has many options, including the following:

-r   Automatically reboots the system, that is, brings it down and brings it up.

-h	Halts the system completely.
-y	Completes the shutdown without asking you any questions it would normally ask.
grace	Specifies the number of seconds you wish to wait before the system is shut down, in order to give your users time to save files, quit applications, and log out.

Here are some of the things your system does when you issue the **shutdown** command:

- Checks to see whether the user who executed shutdown does indeed have permission to execute the command.
- Changes the working directory to root (/).
- Sets *PATH* to **/usr/bin/:/usr/sbin:/sbin**.
- Updates all superblocks.
- Informs the users that a **shutdown** has been issued and asks them to log out.
- Executes **/sbin/rc,** which does such things as shut down subsystems via shutdown scripts such as the spooler and CDE, unmount file systems and other such tasks.
- Runs **/sbin/reboot** if the **-r** options is used.

To shut down and automatically reboot the system, you would type:

```
$ shutdown -r
```

To halt the system, you would type:

```
$ shutdown -h
```

You will be asked whether you want to type a message to users informing them of the impending system shutdown. After you type the message, it is immediately sent to all users. After the specified time elapses (60 seconds is the default), the system begins the shutdown process. Once you receive a message that the system is halted, you can power off all your system components.

To shut down the system in two minutes without being asked any questions, type:

```
$ shutdown -h -y 120
```

At times, you will need to go into single-user mode with **shutdown**, to perform some task such as a backup or to expand a logical volume, and then reboot the system to return it to its original state.

To shut down the system into single-user mode, you would type:

```
$ shutdown
```

The **shutdown** command with no options puts you into single-user mode. On older versions of the operating system, you could go to single-user mode by using the **init** command with the **s** option (**init s**). However, this is highly discouraged because this command does not terminate other system activity nor does it log users off, and, therefore, it does not result in a true single-user state.

If the system is already in single-user mode or you like to live dangerously, you can execute **/usr/sbin/reboot**. I strongly suggest that you issue **shutdown,** which will call **reboot**. The **reboot** command abruptly terminates all processes and then halts or reboots the system. Also, with dynamically loadable kernel modules, **reboot** will not load these modules; only **shutdown** will.

Again, I recommend using the **shutdown** command, not **reboot**.

Manual Pages for Commands Used in Chapter 1

The following section contains copies of the manual pages of commands used in Chapter 1. This makes for a quick reference for you of commands commonly used throughout your system administration day. The manual pages, more commonly referred to as man pages, are listed in detail with the exception of the Software Distributor (SD-UX). Because Software Distributor is commonly used from the GUI interface, only a summary of the command-line version of these commands is given. These commands are listed under "sw command summaries." The summaries are listed last.

cpio

cpio - Save or restore archives.

---

cpio(1)   cpio(1)

NAME
     cpio - copy file archives in and out; duplicate directory trees

SYNOPSIS

     cpio -o [-e extarg] [achvxABC]

     cpio -i[bcdfmrstuvxBPRSU6] [pattern...]

     cpio -p [-e extarg] [adlmruvxU] directory

DESCRIPTION
     The cpio command saves and restores archives of files on magnetic
     tape, other devices, or a regular file, and copies files from one
     directory to another while replicating the directory tree structure.

     cpio -o   (copy out, export) Read standard input to obtain a list
                 of path names, and copy those files to standard output
                 together with path name and status information. The
                 output is padded to a 512-byte boundary.

     cpio -i   (copy in, import) Extract files from standard input,
                 which is assumed to be the result of a previous cpio -o.

                 If pattern..., is specified, only the files with names
                 that match a pattern according to the rules of Pattern
                 Matching Notation (see regexp(5)) are selected. A leading
                 ! on a pattern indicates that only those names that do
                 not match the remainder of the pattern should be selected.
                 Multiple patterns can be specified. The patterns are
                 additive. If no pattern is specified, the default is *
                 (select all files). See the f option, as well.

                 Extracted files are conditionally created and copied into
                 the current directory tree, as determined by the options
                 described below. The permissions of the files match the
                 permissions of the original files when the archive was
                 created by cpio -o unless the U option is used. File
                 owner and group are that of the current user unless the
                 user has appropriate privileges, in which case cpio
                 retains the owner and group of the files of the previous
                 cpio -o.

     cpio -p   (passthrough) Read standard input to obtain a list of
                 path names of files which are then conditionally created
                 and copied into the destination directory tree as
                 determined by the options described below. directory must
                 exist. Destination path names are interpreted relative to
                 directory.

     Options
        cpio recognizes the following options, which can be appended as

appropriate to -i, -o, and -p. Whitespace and hyphens are not permitted between these options and -i, -o, or -p.

a   Reset access times of input files after they are copied.

b   Swap both bytes and half-words. Use only with -i. See the P option for details; see also the s and S options.

c   Write or read header information in ASCII character form for portability.

d   Create directories as needed.

-e extarg
    Specifies the handling of any extent attributes of the file(s) to be archived or copied. extarg takes one of the following values.

        warn   Archive or copy the file and issue a warning message if extent attributes cannot be preserved.
        ignore Do not issue a warning message even if extent attributes cannot be preserved.
        force   Any file(s) with extent attributes will not be archived and a warning message will be issued.

    When using the -o option, extent attributes are not preserved in the archive. Furthermore, the -p option will not preserve extent attributes if the files are being copied to a file system that does not support extent attributes. If -e is not specified, the default value for extarg is warn.

f   Copy in all files except those selected by pattern....

h   Follow symbolic links as though they were normal files or directories. Normally, cpio archives the link.

l   Whenever possible, link files rather than copying them. This option does not destroy existing files. Use only with -p.

m   Retain previous file modification time. This option does not affect directories that are being copied.

r   Rename files interactively. If the user types a null line, the file is skipped.

s   Swap all bytes of the file. Use only with -i. See the P option for details; see also the s and S options.

t   Print only a table of contents of the input. No files are created, read, or copied.

u   Copy unconditionally (normally, an older file does not replace a newer file with the same name).

v   Print a list of file names as they are processed. When used with the t option, the table of contents has the format:

      numeric-mode owner-name blocks date-time filename

where numeric-mode is the file privileges in numeric format, owner-name is the name of the file owner, blocks is the size of the file in 512-byte blocks, date-time is the date and time the file was last modified, and filename is the path name of the file as recorded in the archive.

x   Save or restore device special files. Since mknod() is used to recreate these files on a restore, -ix and -px can be used only by users with appropriate privileges (see mknod(2)). This option is intended for intrasystem (backup) use only. Restoring device files from previous versions of the OS, or from different systems can be very dangerous. cpio may prevent the restoration of certain device files from the archive.

A   Suppress warning messages regarding optional access control list entries. cpio does not back up optional access control list entries in a file's access control list (see acl(5)). Normally, a warning message is printed for each file that has optional access control list entries.

B   Block input/output at 5120 bytes to the record (does not apply to cpio -p). This option is meaningful only with data directed to or from devices that support variable-length records such as magnetic tape.

C   Have cpio checkpoint itself at the start of each volume. If cpio is writing to a streaming tape drive with immediate-report mode enabled and a write error occurs, it normally aborts and exits with return code 2. With this option specified, cpio instead automatically restarts itself from the checkpoint and rewrites the current volume. Alternatively, if cpio is not writing to such a device and a write error occurs, cpio normally continues with the next volume. With this option specified, however, the user can choose to either ignore the error or rewrite the current volume.

P   Read a file written on a PDP-11 or VAX system (with byte-swapping) that did not use the c option. Use only with -i. Files copied in this mode are not changed. Non-ASCII files are likely to need further processing to be readable. This processing often requires knowledge of file contents, and thus cannot always be done by this program. The b, s, and S options can be used when swapping all the bytes on the tape (rather than just in the headers) is appropriate. In general, text is best processed with P and binary data with one of the other options.

           (PDP-11 and VAX are registered trademarks of Digital Equipment Corporation.)

R   Resynchronize automatically when cpio goes "out of phase", (see DIAGNOSTICS).

S   Swap all half-words in the file. Use only with -i. See the P option for details; see also the b and s options.

U   Use the process's file-mode creation mask (see umask(2)) to modify the mode of files created, in the same manner as creat(2).

      6   Process a UNIX Sixth-Edition-format file. Use only with
                -i.

Note that cpio archives created using a raw device file must be read
using a raw device file.

When the end of the tape is reached, cpio prompts the user for a new
special file and continues.

If you want to pass one or more metacharacters to cpio without the
shell expanding them, be sure to precede each of them with a backslash
(\).

Device files written with the -ox option (such as /dev/tty03) do not
transport to other implementations of HP-UX.

EXTERNAL INFLUENCES
   Environment Variables
     LC_COLLATE determines the collating sequence used in evaluating
     pattern matching notation for file name generation.

     LC_CTYPE determines the interpretation of text as single and/or
     multi-byte characters, and the characters matched by character class
     expressions in pattern matching notation.

     LC_TIME determines the format and content of date and time strings
     output when listing the contents of an archive with the v option.

     LANG determines the language in which messages are displayed.

     If LC_COLLATE, LC_CTYPE, or LC_TIME is not specified in the
     environment or is set to the empty string, the value of LANG is used
     as a default for each unspecified or empty variable. If LANG is not
     specified or is set to the empty string, a default of "C" (see
     lang(5)) is used instead of LANG. If any internationalization
     variable contains an invalid setting, cpio behaves as if all
     internationalization variables are set to "C". See environ(5).

   International Code Set Support
     Single- and multi-byte character code sets are supported.

RETURN VALUE
    cpio returns the following exit codes:

      0   Successful completion. Review standard error for files that
           could not be transferred.

      1   Error during resynchronization. Some files may not have
           been recovered.

      2   Out-of-phase error. A file header is corrupt or in the
           wrong format.

DIAGNOSTICS
   Out of phase--get help
   Perhaps the "c" option should[n't] be used

     cpio -i could not read the header of an archived file. The
     header is corrupt or it was written in a different format.
     Without the R option, cpio returns an exit code of 2.

     If no file name has been displayed yet, the problem may be the
     format. Try specifying a different header format option: null
     for standard format; c for ASCII; b, s, P, or S, for one of the

byte-swapping formats; or 6 for UNIX Sixth Edition.

Otherwise, a header may be corrupt. Use the R option to have
cpio attempt to resynchronize the file automatically.
Resynchronizing means that cpio tries to find the next good
header in the archive file and continues processing from there.
If cpio tries to resynchronize from being out of phase, it
returns an exit code of 1.

Other diagnostic messages are self-explanatory.

EXAMPLES
Copy the contents of a directory into a tape archive:

        ls | cpio -o > /dev/rmt/c0t0d0BEST

Duplicate a directory hierarchy:

        cd olddir
        find . -depth -print | cpio -pd newdir

The trivial case

        find . -depth -print | cpio -oB >/dev/rmt/c0t0d0BEST

can be handled more efficiently by:

        find . -cpio /dev/rmt/c0t0d0BEST

WARNINGS
Because of industry standards and interoperability goals, cpio does
not support the archival of files larger than 2GB or files that have
user/group IDs greater than 60K. Files with user/group IDs greater
than 60K are archived and restored under the user/group ID of the
current process.

Do not redirect the output of cpio to a named cpio archive file
residing in the same directory as the original files belonging to that
cpio archive. This can cause loss of data.

cpio strips any leading ./ characters in the list of filenames piped
to it.

Path names are restricted to PATH_MAX characters (see <limits.h> and
limits(5)). If there are too many unique linked files, the program
runs out of memory to keep track of them. Thereafter, linking
information is lost. Only users with appropriate privileges can copy
special files.

cpio tapes written on HP machines with the -ox[c] options can
sometimes mislead (non-HP) versions of cpio that do not support the x
option. If a non-HP (or non-AT&T) version of cpio happens to be
modified so that the (HP) cpio recognizes it as a device special file,
a spurious device file might be created.

If /dev/tty is not accessible, cpio issues a complaint and exits.

The -pd option does not create the directory typed on the command
line.

The -idr option does not make empty directories.

The -plu option does not link files to existing files.

POSIX defines a file named TRAILER!!! as an end-of-archive marker.
Consequently, if a file of that name is contained in a group of files

being written by cpio -o, the file is interpreted as end-of-archive,
and no remaining files are copied. The recommended practice is to
avoid naming files anything that resembles an end-of-archive file
name.

To create a POSIX-conforming cpio archive, the c option must be used.
To read a POSIX-conforming cpio archive, the c option must be used and
the b, s, S, and 6 options should not be used. If the user does not
have appropriate privileges, the U option must also be used to get
POSIX-conforming behavior when reading an archive. Users with
appropriate privileges should not use this option to get POSIX
-conforming behavior.

Using Cartridge Tape Drives
For an explanation of the constraints on cartridge tapes, see ct(7).

Using cpio to write directly to a cartridge tape unit can severely
damage the tape drive in a short amount of time, and is therefore
strongly discouraged. The recommended method of writing to the
cartridge tape unit is to use the tcio command (see tcio(1)) in
conjunction with cpio (note that the B option must not be used by cpio
when tcio is used). tcio buffers data into larger pieces suitable for
cartridge tapes. The B option must be used when writing directly
(that is, without using tcio) to a CS/80 cartridge tape unit.

DEPENDENCIES
If the path given to cpio contains a symbolic link as the last
element, this link is traversed and pathname resolution continues.
cpio uses the symbolic link's target, rather than that of the link.

SEE ALSO
ar(1), find(1), tar(1), tcio(1), cpio(4), acl(5), environ(5), lang(5),
regexp(5).

STANDARDS CONFORMANCE
cpio: SVID2, SVID3, XPG2, XPG3

dd

dd - Copy the specified input file to the specified output.

---

dd(1)   dd(1)

NAME
     dd - convert, reblock, translate, and copy a (tape) file

SYNOPSIS

     dd [option=value] ...

DESCRIPTION
     dd copies the specified input file to the specified output with
     possible conversions. The standard input and output are used by
     default. Input and output block size can be specified to take
     advantage of raw physical I/O.

  Options
     dd recognizes the following option=value pairs:

          if=file   Input file name; default is standard input.

          of=file   Output file name; default is standard output. The
                         output file will be created using the same owner
                         and group used by creat().

          ibs=n   Input block size is n bytes (default 512).

          obs=n   Output block size is n bytes (default 512).

          bs=n   Set both input and output block size to the same
                         size, superseding ibs and obs. This option is
                         particularly efficient if no conversion is
                         specified, because no in-core copy is necessary.

          cbs=n   Conversion buffer size is n bytes.

          skip=n   Skip n input blocks before starting copy.

          seek=n   Seek n blocks from beginning of output file before
                         copying. This option is ignored on a raw magnetic
                         tape device. See mt(1) for information about
                         operations on raw magnetic tape devices.

          count=n   Copy only n input blocks.

          conv=option   Data conversion option. Use one of the following:

                              conv=ascii   Convert EBCDIC to ASCII.

                              conv=ebcdic   Convert ASCII to EBCDIC.

                              conv=ibm   Convert ASCII to EBCDIC
                                              using an alternate
                                              conversion table

conv=lcase	Map US ASCII alphabetics to lowercase
conv=ucase	Map US ASCII alphabetics to uppercase
conv=swab	Swap every pair of bytes
conv=noerror	Do not stop processing on an error
conv=sync	Pad every input block to input block size (ibs)
conv=notrunc	Do not truncate existing file on output
conv=block	Convert input record to a fixed length specified by cbs
conv=unblock	Convert fixed length records to variable length
conv=..., ...	Multiple comma-separated conversions

Where sizes are required, n indicates a numerical value in bytes. Numbers can be specified using the forms:

n	for n bytes
nk	for n Kbytes (n * 1024),
nb	for n blocks (n * 512), or
nw	for n words (n * 2).

To indicate a product, use x to separate number pairs.

The cbs option is used when block , unblock , ascii or ebcdic conversion is specified. In case of ascii , cbs characters are placed into the conversion buffer, converted to ASCII, trailing blanks are trimmed, and a new-line is added before sending the line to the output. In case of ebcdic , ASCII characters are read into the conversion buffer, converted to EBCDIC, and blanks are added to make up an output block of size cbs.

Upon completion, dd reports the number of whole and partial input and output records.

EXTERNAL INFLUENCES
   International Code Set Support
      Single- and multibyte character code sets are supported.

   Environment Variables
      The following environment variables will affect execution of dd :

      LANG determines the locale when LC_ALL and a corresponding variable (beginning with LC_) do not specify a locale.

      LC_ALL determines the locale used to override any values set by LANG or any environment variables beginning with LC_.

      The LC_CTYPE variable determines the locale for the interpretation of sequences of bytes of text data as characters (single/multiple byte characters, upper/lower case characters).

The LC_MESSAGES variable determines the language in which messages should be written.

RETURN VALUE
    Exit values are:

        0   Successful completion.
        >0   Error condition occurred.

DIAGNOSTICS
    f+p records in   Number of full and partial blocks read.
    f+p records out   Number of full and partial blocks written.

EXAMPLES
    Read an EBCDIC tape blocked ten 80-byte EBCDIC card images per block
    into an ASCII file named x:

        dd if=/dev/rmt/c0t0d0BEST of=x ibs=800 cbs=80
        conv=ascii,lcase

    Note the use of the raw magnetic tape device file. dd is especially
    suited to I/O on raw physical devices because it allows reading and
    writing in arbitrary block sizes.

WARNINGS
    You may experience trouble writing directly to or reading directly
    from a cartridge tape. For best results, use tcio(1) as an input or
    output filter. For example, use

        ... |dd ... |tcio -ovVS 256 /dev/rct/c4t1d0

    for output to a cartridge tape, or

        tcio -ivS 256 /dev/rct/c4t1d0 |dd ... | ...

    for input from a cartridge tape.

    Some devices, such as 1/2-inch magnetic tapes, are incapable of
    seeking. Such devices must be positioned prior to running dd by using
    mt(1) or some other appropriate command.

    ASCII and EBCDIC conversion tables are taken from the 256-character
    ACM standard, Nov, 1968. The ibm conversion, while less widely
    accepted as a standard, corresponds better to certain IBM print train
    conventions. There is no universal solution.

    New-line characters are inserted only on conversion to ASCII; padding
    is done only on conversion to EBCDIC. These should be separate
    options.

    If if or of refers to a raw disk, bs should always be a multiple of
    sector size of disk. The default bs size used by dd is 512 bytes. If
    sector size of disk is different from 512 bytes, a bs multiple of
    sector size should be specified. The character special (raw) device
    file should always be used for devices.

    It is entirely up to the user to insure there is enough room in the
    destination file, filesystem and/or device to contain the output since
    dd(1) cannot pre-determine the required space after conversion.

SEE ALSO
    cp(1), mt(1), tr(1), disk(7), mt(7).

STANDARDS CONFORMANCE
    dd: SVID2, SVID3, XPG2, XPG3, XPG4, POSIX.2

diskinfo

diskinfo - Describe a disk device.

---

diskinfo(1M)   diskinfo(1M)

NAME
     diskinfo - describe characteristics of a disk device

SYNOPSIS

     /usr/sbin/diskinfo [-b|-v] character_devicefile

DESCRIPTION
     The diskinfo command determines whether the character special file
     named by character_devicefile is associated with a SCSI, CS/80, or
     Subset/80 disk drive. If so, diskinfo summarizes the disk's
     characteristics.

     The diskinfo command displays information about the following
     characteristics of disk drives:

          Vendor name   Manufacturer of the drive (SCSI only)
          Product ID   Product identification number or ASCII name
          Type   CS/80 or SCSI classification for the device
          Disk   Size of disk specified in bytes
          Sector   Specified as bytes per sector

     Both the size of disk and bytes per sector represent formatted media.

     Options
     The diskinfo command recognizes the following options:

          -b   Return the size of the disk in 1024-byte sectors.

          -v   Display a verbose summary of all of the
                         information available from the device. (Since the
                         information returned by CS/80 drives and SCSI
                         drives differs, the associated descriptions also
                         differ.)

                         - CS/80 devices return the following:
                                Device name
                                Number of bytes/sector
                                Geometry information
                                Interleave
                                Type of device
                                Timing information

                         - SCSI disk devices return the following:
                                Vendor and product ID
                                Device type
                                Size (in bytes and in logical blocks)
                                Bytes per sector
                                Revision level
                                SCSI conformance level data

DEPENDENCIES
   General
      The diskinfo command supports only CS/80, subset/80, and HP SCSI disk
      devices.

   SCSI Devices
      The SCSI specification provides for a wide variety of device-dependent
      formats. For non-HP devices, diskinfo may be unable to interpret all
      of the data returned by the device. Refer to the drive operating
      manual accompanying the unit for more information.

AUTHOR
      diskinfo was developed by HP.

SEE ALSO
      lsdev(1M), disktab(4), disk(7).

dmesg

dmesg - Print system diagnostic information.

```
dmesg(1M)                                                           dmesg(1M)

NAME
     dmesg - collect system diagnostic messages to form error log

SYNOPSIS

     /usr/sbin/dmesg [-] [core] [system]

DESCRIPTION
     dmesg looks in a system buffer for recently printed diagnostic
     messages and prints them on the standard output.  The messages are
     those printed by the system when unusual events occur (such as when
     system tables overflow or the system crashes).  If the - argument is
     specified, dmesg computes (incrementally) the new messages since the
     last time it was run and places these on the standard output.  This is
     typically used with cron (see cron(1)) to produce the error log
     /var/adm/messages by running the command:

          /usr/sbin/dmesg - >> /var/adm/messages

     every 10 minutes.

     The arguments core and system allow substitution for the defaults
     /dev/kmem and /stand/vmunix respectively, where core should be a file
     containing the image of the kernel virtual memory saved by the
     savecore(1M) command and system should be the corresponding kernel.
     If the system is booted with a kernel other than /stand/vmunix say
     /stand/vmunix_new, dmesg must be passed this name, the command must
     be,

          /usr/sbin/dmesg [-] /dev/kmem /stand/vmunix_new

WARNINGS
     The system error message buffer is of small, finite size.  dmesg is
     run only every few minutes, so there is no guarantee that all error
     messages will be logged.

AUTHOR
     dmesg was developed by the University of California, Berkeley.

FILES
     /var/adm/messages          error log (conventional location)
     /var/adm/msgbuf            memory scratch file for - option
     /dev/kmem                  special file containing the image of kernel
                                virtual memory
     /stand/vmunix              the kernel, system name list

SEE ALSO
     savecore(1M).
```

dump

dump - Copy files to tape that have been changed.

---

dump(1M)   dump(1M)

NAME
    dump, rdump - incremental file system dump, local or across network

SYNOPSIS

    /usr/sbin/dump [option [argument ...] filesystem]

    /usr/sbin/rdump [option [argument ...] filesystem]

DESCRIPTION
    The dump and rdump commands copy to magnetic tape all files in the
    filesystem that have been changed after a certain date. This
    information is derived from the files /var/adm/dumpdates and
    /etc/fstab. option specifies the date and other options about the
    dump. option consists of characters from the set 0123456789bdfnsuWw.
    The dump and rdump commands work only on file systems of type hfs. If
    the given file system is not of type hfs, dump and rdump will abort
    after printing an error message.

    Options
            0-9   This number is the "dump level". All files modified
              .   since the last date stored in file /var/adm/dumpdates
                    for the same file system at lesser levels will be
                    dumped. If no date is determined by the level, the
                    beginning of time is assumed. Thus, the option 0
                    causes the entire file system to be dumped.

            b   The blocking factor is taken from the next argument
                    (default is 10 if not specified). Block size is
                    defined as the logical record size times the blocking
                    factor. dump writes logical records of 1024 bytes.
                    When dumping to tapes with densities of 6250 BPI or
                    greater without using the b option, the default
                    blocking factor is 32.

            d   The density of the tape (expressed in BPIs) is taken
                    from the next argument. This is used in calculating
                    the amount of tape used per reel. The default value of
                    1600 assumes a reel tape.

            f   Place the dump on the next argument file instead of the
                    tape. If the name of the file is -, dump writes to the
                    standard output. When using rdump, this option should
                    be specified, and the next argument supplied should be
                    of the form machine:device.

            n   Whenever dump and rdump require operator attention,
                    notify all users in group operator by means similar to
                    that described by wall(1).

            s   The size of the dump tape is specified in feet. The
                    number of feet is taken from the next argument. When

the specified size is reached, dump and rdump wait for
reels to be changed. The default tape size value of
2300 feet assumes a reel tape.

u   If the dump completes successfully, write on file
              /var/adm/dumpdates the date when the dump started.
              This file records a separate date for each file system
              and each dump level. The format of /var/adm/dumpdates
              is user-readable and consists of one free-format record
              per line: file system name, increment level, and dump
              date in ctime(3C) format. The file /var/adm/dumpdates
              can be edited to change any of the fields if necessary.

W   For each file system in /var/adm/dumpdates, print the
              most recent dump date and level, indicating which file
              systems should be dumped. If the W option is set, all
              other options are ignored and dump exits immediately.

w   Operates like W, but prints only file systems that need
              to be dumped.

If no arguments are given, option is assumed to be 9u and a default
file system is dumped to the default tape.

Sizes are based on 1600-BPI blocked tape; the raw magnetic tape device
must be used to approach these densities. Up to 32 read errors on the
file system are ignored. Each reel requires a new process; thus
parent processes for reels already written remain until the entire
tape is written.

The rdump command creates a server, /usr/sbin/rmt or /etc/rmt, on the
remote machine to access the tape device.

dump and rdump require operator intervention for any of the following
conditions:

- end of tape,
- end of dump,
- tape-write error,
- tape-open error, or
- disk-read error (if errors exceed threshold of 32).

In addition to alerting all operators implied by the n option, dump
and rdump interact with the control terminal operator by posing
questions requiring yes or no answers when it can no longer proceed or
if something is grossly wrong.

Since making a full dump involves considerable time and effort, dump
and rdump each establish a checkpoint at the start of each tape
volume. If, for any reason, writing that volume fails, dump and rdump
will, with operator permission, restart from the checkpoint after the
old tape has been rewound and removed and a new tape has been mounted.

dump and rdump periodically report information to the operator,
including typically low estimates of the number of blocks to write,
the number of tapes it will require, the time needed for completion,
and the time remaining until tape change. The output is verbose to
inform other users that the terminal controlling dump and rdump is
busy and will be for some time.

Access Control Lists (ACLs)
    The optional entries of a file's access control list (ACL) are not
    backed up with dump and rdump. Instead, the file's permission bits
    are backed up and any information contained in its optional ACL

entries is lost (see acl(5)).

EXAMPLES
In the following example, assume that the file system /mnt is to be
attached to the file tree at the root directory, (/). This example
causes the entire file system (/mnt) to be dumped on
/dev/rmt/c0t0d0BEST and specifies that the density of the tape is 6250
BPI.

/usr/sbin/dump 0df 6250 /dev/rmt/c0t0d0BEST /mnt

WARNINGS
dump will not backup a file system containing large files.

Tapes created from file systems containing files with UID/GIDs greater
than 60,000 will have a new magic number in the header to prevent
older versions of restore(1M) from incorrectly restoring ownerships
for these files.

AUTHOR
dump and rdump were developed by the University of California,
Berkeley.

FILES
/dev/rdsk/c0d0s0	Default file system to dump from.
/dev/rmt/0m	Default tape unit to dump to.
/var/adm/dumpdates	New format-dump-date record.
/etc/fstab	Dump table: file systems and frequency.
/etc/group	Used to find group operator.

SEE ALSO
restore(1M), rmt(1M), fstab(4), acl(5).

extendfs

extendfs - Increase the capacity of a file system (this is generic man page, there is also a man page for hfs and vxfs.)

```
extendfs(1M)                                                    extendfs(1M)

NAME
     extendfs (generic) - extend a file system size

SYNOPSIS
     /usr/sbin/extendfs [-F FStype] [-q] [-v] [-s size] special

DESCRIPTION
     If the original file system image created on special does not make use
     of all of the available space, extendfs can be used to increase the
     capacity of a file system by updating the file system structure to
     include the extra space.

     The command-line parameter special specifies the device special file
     of either a logical volume or a disk partition. The special must be
     un-mounted before extendfs can be run (see mount(1M)).

   Options
     extendfs recognizes the following options:

          -F FStype Specify the file system type on which to operate (see
                    fstyp(1M) and fs_wrapper(5)). If this option is not
                    included on the command line, then the file system type
                    is determined from the file /etc/default/fs.

          -q        Query the size of special. No file system extension
                    will be done.

          -v        Verbose flag.

          -s size   Specifies the number of DEV_BSIZE blocks to be added to
                    the file system. If size is not specified, the
                    maximum possible size is used.

EXAMPLES
     To increase the capacity of a file system created on a logical volume,
     enter:

          umount /dev/vg00/lvol1

          lvextend -L larger_size /dev/vg00/lvol1

          extendfs -F hfs /dev/vg00/rlvol1

          mount /dev/vg00/lvol1 mount_directory

SEE ALSO
     fstyp(1M), lvextend(1M), mkfs(1M), mount(1M), umount(1M), fs(4),
     fs_wrapper(5).
```

fbackup

fbackup - Perform a high speed selective backup.

---

fbackup(1M)   fbackup(1M)

NAME
     fbackup - selectively back up files

SYNOPSIS
     /usr/sbin/fbackup -f device [-f device] ... [-0-9] [-nsuvyAEl] [-i
     path] [-e path] [-g graph] [-d path] [-I path] [-V path] [-c config]

     /usr/sbin/fbackup -f device [-f device] ... [-R restart] [-nsuvyAEl]
     [-d path] [-I path] [-V path] [-c config]

DESCRIPTION
     fbackup combines features of dump and ftio to provide a flexible,
     high-speed file system backup mechanism (see dump(1M) and ftio(1)).
     fbackup selectively transfers files to an output device. For each
     file transferred, the file's contents and all the relevant information
     necessary to restore it to an equivalent state are copied to the
     output device. The output device can be a raw magnetic tape drive,
     the standard output, a DDS-format tape, a rewritable magneto-optical
     disk or a file.

     The selection of files to backup is done by explicitly specifying
     trees of files to be included or excluded from an fbackup session.
     The user can construct an arbitrary graph of files by using the -i or
     -e options on the command line, or by using the -g option with a graph
     file. For backups being done on a regular basis, the -g option
     provides an easier interface for controlling the backup graph.
     fbackup selects files in this graph, and attempts to transfer them to
     the output device. The selectivity depends on the mode in which
     fbackup is being used; i.e., full or incremental backup.

     When doing full backups, all files in the graph are selected. When
     doing incremental backups, only files in the graph that have been
     modified since a previous backup of that graph are selected. If an
     incremental backup is being done at level 4 and the -g option is used,
     the database file is searched for the most recent previous backup at
     levels 0-3. If a file's modification time is before the time when the
     last appropriate session began and the i-node change time is before
     the time that same session ended, the file is not backed up.
     Beginning at HP-UX Release 8.0, all directories lying on the path to a
     file that qualifies for the incremental backup will also be on the
     backup media, even if the directories do not qualify on their own
     status.

     If fbackup is used for incremental backups, a database of past backups
     must be kept. fbackup maintains this data in the text file
     /var/adm/fbackupfiles/dates, by default. Note that the directory
     /var/adm/fbackupfiles must be created prior to the first time fbackup
     is used for incremental backups. The -d option can be used to specify
     an alternate database file. The user can specify to update this file
     when an fbackup session completes successfully. Entries for each
     session are recorded on separate pairs of lines. The following four

items appear on the first line of each pair: the graph file name,
backup level, starting time, and ending time (both in time(2) format).
The second line of each pair contains the same two times, but in
strftime(3C) format. These lines contain the local equivalent of
STARTED:, the start time, the local equivalent of ENDED:, and the
ending time. These second lines serve only to make the dates file
more readable; fbackup does not use them. All fields are separated by
white space. Graph file names are compared character-by-character
when checking the previous-backup database file to ascertain when a
previous session was run for that graph. Caution must be exercised to
ensure that, for example, graph and ./graph are not used to specify
the same graph file because fbackup treats them as two different graph
files.

The general structure of a fbackup volume is the same, no matter what
type of device is used. There are some small specific differences due
to differing capabilities of devices. The general structure is as
follows:

  - Reserved space for ASCII tape label (1024 bytes)
  - fbackup specific volume label (2048 bytes)
  - session index (size in field of volume label)
  - data

Each file entry in the index contains the volume number and the
pathname of the file. At the beginning of every volume, fbackup
assumes that all files not already backed up will fit on that volume;
an erroneous assumption for all but the last volume. Indices are
accurate only for the previous volumes in the same set. Hence, the
index on the last volume may indicate that a file resides on that
volume, but it may not have actually been backed up (for example, if
it was removed after the index was created, but before fbackup
attempted to back it up). The only index guaranteed to be correct in
all cases is the on-line index (-I option), which is produced after
the last volume has been written. Specific minor differences are
listed below:

  - When using 9-track tape drives or DDS-format tape drives
    several small differences exist. The main blocks of
    information are separated by EOF. fbackup checkpoints the
    media periodically to enhance error recovery. If a write
    error is detected, the user normally has two options: First, a
    new volume can be mounted and that volume rewritten from the
    beginning. Second, if the volume is not too severely damaged,
    the good data before the error can be saved, and the write
    error is treated as a normal end-of-media condition. The
    blocks of data with their checkpoint records are also
    separated by EOF. In addition if the DDS-format drive
    supports Fast Search Marks these will be used to enhance
    recovery speed by placing them between blocks of files.

  - For a magneto-optical device, a disk, a file, or standard
    output, there are no special marks separating the information
    pieces. Using standard output results in only one volume.

fbackup provides the ability to use UCB-mode tape drives. This makes
it possible to overlap the tape rewind times if two or more tape
drives are connected to the system.

Set-up
There are several things the user will want to consider when setting
fbackup up for regular use. These include type of device and media,
full versus incremental frequency, amount of logging information to
keep on-line, structure of the graph file, and on-line versus off-line
backup.

The type of device used for backups can affect such things as media
expenses, ability to do unattended backup and speed of the backup.
Using 9-track tapes will probably result in the highest performance,
but require user intervention for changing tapes. A magneto-optical
autochanger can provide an unattended backup for a large system and
long life media, however the media cost is high. The lowest cost will
probably be achieved through DDS-format devices, but at the lowest
performance.

It is also important to consider how often full backups should be
made, and how many incremental backups to make between full backups.
Time periods can be used, such as a full backup every Friday and
incrementals on all other days. Media capacities can be used if
incremental backups need to run unattended. The availability of
personnel to change media can also be an important factor as well as
the length of time needed for the backup. Other factors may affect
the need for full and incremental backup combinations such as
contractual or legal requirements.

If backup information is kept online; i.e., output from the -V or -I
options, the required storage space must also be considered. Index
file sizes are hard to predict in advance because they depend on
system configuration. Each volume header file takes less than 1536
bytes. Of course the more information that is kept on-line, the
faster locating a backup media for a recovery will be.

There are several ways to structure the graph file or files used in a
system backup. The first decision involves whether to use one or more
than one graph files for the backup. Using one file is simpler, but
less flexible. Using two or more graph files simplifies splitting
backups into logical sets. For example, one graph file can be used
for system disks where changes tend to be less frequent, and another
graph file for the users area. Thus two different policies can be
implemented for full and incremental backups.

fbackup was designed to allow backups while the system is in use by
providing the capability to retry an active file. When absolute
consistency on a full backup is important, the system should probably
be in single-user mode. However, incremental backups can be made
while the system is in normal use, thus improving system up-time.

Options
  -c config   config is the name of the configuration file, and can
                    contain values for the following parameters:

- Number of 1024-byte blocks per record,
- Number of records of shared memory to allocate,
- Number of records between checkpoints,
- Number of file-reader processes,
- Maximum number of times fbackup is to retry an
  active file,
- Maximum number of bytes of media to use while
  retrying the backup of an active file,
- Maximum number of times a magnetic tape volume
  can be used,
- Name of a file to be executed when a volume
  change occurs. This file must exist and be
  executable.
- Name of a file to be executed when a fatal error
  occurs. This file must exist and be executable.

- The number of files between the Fast Search Marks
  on DDS-format tapes. The cost of these marks are
  negligible in terms of space on the DDS-format
  tape. Not all DDS-format devices support fast
  search marks.

Each entry in the configuration file consists of one line of text in the following format: identifier, white space, argument. In the following sample configuration file, the number of blocks per record is set to 16, the number of records is set to 32, the checkpoint frequency is set to 32, the number of file reader processes is set to 2, the maximum number of retries is set to 5, the maximum retry space for active files is set to 5,000,000 bytes, the maximum number of times a magnetic tape volume can be used is set to 100, the file to be executed at volume change time is /var/adm/fbackupfiles/chgvol, the file to be executed when a fatal error occurs is /var/adm/fbackupfiles/error, and the number of files between fast search marks is set to 200.

```
blocksperrecord        16
records                32
checkpointfreq         32
readerprocesses        2 (maximum of 6)
maxretries             5
retrylimit             5000000
maxvoluses             100
chgvol                 /var/adm/fbackupfiles/chgvol

error                  /var/adm/fbackupfiles/error

filesperfsm            200
```

Each value listed is also the default value, except chgvol and error, which default to null values.

-d path This specifies a path to a database for use with incremental backups. It overrides the default database file /var/adm/fbackupfiles/dates.

-e path path specifies a tree to be excluded from the backup graph. This tree must be a subtree of part of the backup graph. Otherwise, specifying it will not exclude any files from the graph. There is no limit on how many times the -e option can be specified.

-f device device specifies the name of an output file. If the name of the file is -, fbackup writes to the standard output. There is no default output file; at least one must be specified. If more than one output file is specified, fbackup uses each one successively and then repeats in a cyclical pattern. Patterns can be used in the device name in a manner resembling file name expansion as done by the shell (see sh-bourne(1) and other shell manual entries. The patterns must be protected from expansion by the shell by quoting them. The expansion of the pattern results in all matching names being in the list of devices used.

There is slightly different behavior if remote devices are used. A device on the remote machine can be specified in the form machine:device. fbackup creates a server process from /usr/sbin/rmt on the remote machine to access the tape device. If /usr/sbin/rmt does not exist on the remote system, fbackup creates a server process from /etc/rmt on the remote machine to access the tape device. Only half-inch 9-track magnetic tapes or DDS-format tapes can be remote devices. The fast search and save set marks capabilities are not used when remote DDS-format devices are used.

-g graph   graph defines the graph file. The graph file is a text file containing the list of file names of trees to be included or excluded from the backup graph. These trees are interpreted in the same manner as when they are specified with the -i and -e options. Graph file entries consist of a line beginning with either i or e, followed by white space, and then the path name of a tree. Lines not beginning with i or e are treated as an error. There is no default graph file. For example, to backup all of /usr except for the subtree /usr/lib, a file could be created with the following two records:

```
i /usr
e /usr/lib
```

-i path   path specifies a tree to be included in the backup graph. There is no limit on how many times the -i option can be specified.

-n   Cross NFS mount points. By default fbackup does not cross NFS mount points, regardless of paths specified by the -i or -g options.

-l   Includes LOFS files specified by the backup graph. By default, fbackup does not cross LOFS mount points. If -l is specified, and the backup graph includes files which are also in a LOFS that is in the backup graph, then those files will backed up twice.

-s   Backup the object that a symbolic link refers to. The default behavior is to backup the symbolic link.

-u   Update the database of past backups so that it contains the backup level, the time of the beginning and end of the session, and the graph file used for this fbackup session. For this update to take place, the following conditions must exist: Neither the -i nor the -e option can be used; the -g option must be specified exactly once (see below); the fbackup must complete successfully.

-v   Run in verbose mode. Generates status messages that are otherwise not seen.

-y   Automatically answer yes to any inquiries.

-A   Do not back up optional entries of access control lists (ACLs) for files. Normally, all mode information is backed up including the optional ACL entries. With the -A option, the summary mode information (as returned by stat()) is backed up. Use this option when backing up files from a system that contains ACL to be recovered on a system that does not understand ACL (see acl(5)).

-E   Do not back up extent attributes. Normally, all extent attributes that have been set are included with the file. This option only applies to file systems which support extent attributes.

-I path   path specifies the name of the on-line index file to be generated. It consists of one line for each file backed up during the session. Each line contains the volume number on which that file resides and the file name. If the -I option is omitted, no index file is generated.

-V path   The volume header information is written to path at the end of a successful fbackup session. The following fields from the header are written in the format label:value with one pair per line.

Magic Field	On a valid fbackup media it contains the value FBACKUP_LABEL (HP-UX release 10.20 and beyond). Before HP-UX release 10.20, it contained the value FBACKUP LABEL.
Machine Identification	This field contains the result of uname -m.
System Identification	This field contains the result of uname -s.
Release Identification	This field contains the result of uname -r.
Node Identification	This field contains the result of uname -n.
User Identification	This field contains the result of cuserid() (see cuserid(3S)).
Record Size	This field contains the maximum length in bytes of a data record.
Time	This field contains the clock time when fbackup was started.
Media Use	This field contains the number of times the media has been used for backup. Since the information is actually on the media, this field will always contain the value 0.
Volume Number	This field contains a # character followed by 3 digits, and identifies the number of volumes in the backup.
Checkpoint Frequency	This field contains the frequency of backup-data-record checkpointing.
Index Size	This field contains the size of the index.
Backup Identification Tag	This field is composed of two items: the process ID (pid) and the start time of that process.
Language	This field contains the language used to make the backup.

-R restart   Restart an fbackup session from where it was previously interrupted. The restart file contains all the information necessary to restart the interrupted session. None of the -[ieg0-9] options can be used together with the restart option.

-0-9   This single-digit number is the backup level. Level 0
                    indicates a full backup. Higher levels are generally
                    used to perform incremental backups. When doing an
                    incremental backup of a particular graph at a
                    particular level, the database of past backups is
                    searched to find the date of the most recent backup of
                    the same graph that was done at a lower level. If no
                    such entry is found, the beginning of time is assumed.
                    All files in the graph that have been modified since
                    this date are backed up.

    Access Control Lists (ACLs)
        If a file has optional ACL entries, the -A option is required to
        enable its recovery on a system whose access control lists capability
        is not present.

EXTERNAL INFLUENCES
    Environment Variables
        LC_COLLATE determines the order in which files are stored in the
        backup device and the order output by the -I option.

        LC_TIME determines the format and contents of date and time strings.

        LC_MESSAGES determines the language in which messages are displayed.

        If LC_COLLATE and LC_TIME and LC_MESSAGES are not all specified in the
        environment or if either is set to the empty string, the value of LANG
        is used as a default for each unspecified or empty variable. If LANG
        is not specified or is set to the empty string, a default of "C" (see
        lang(5)) is used instead of LANG. If any internationalization
        variable contains an invalid setting, fbackup behaves as if all
        internationalization variables are set to "C". See environ(5).

    International Code Set Support
        Single- and multi-byte character code sets are supported.

RETURN VALUE
        fbackup returns 0 upon normal completion, 1 if it is interrupted but
        allowed to save its state for possible restart, and 2 if any error
        conditions prevent the session from completing.

EXAMPLES
        In the following two examples, assume the graph of interest specifies
        all of /usr except /usr/lib (as described in the g key section above).

        The first example is a simple case where a full backup is done but the
        database file is not updated. This can be invoked as follows:

            /usr/sbin/fbackup -0i /usr -e /usr/lib -f /dev/rmt/c0t0d0BEST

        The second example is more complicated, and assumes the user wants to
        maintain a database of past fbackup sessions so that incremental
        backups are possible.

        If sufficient on-line storage is available, it may be desirable to
        keep several of the most recent index files on disk. This eliminates
        the need to recover the index from the backup media to determine if
        the files to be recovered are on that set. One method of maintaining
        on-line index files is outlined below. The system administrator must
        do the following once before fbackup is run for the first time
        (creating intermediate level directories where necessary):

            -   Create a suitable configuration file called config in the
                directory /var/adm/fbackupfiles

- Create a graph file called usr-usrlib in the directory
  /var/adm/fbackupfiles/graphs

- Create a directory called usr-usrlib in the directory
  /var/adm/fbackupfiles/indices

A shell script that performs the following tasks could be run for each
fbackup session:

- Build an index file path name based on both the graph file
  used (passed as a parameter to the script) and the start time
  of the session (obtained from the system). For example:

      /var/adm/fbackupfiles/indices/usr-usrlib/871128.15:17
      (for Nov 28, 1987 at 3:17 PM)

- Invoke fbackup with this path name as its index file name.
  For example:

      cd /var/adm/fbackupfiles
      /usr/sbin/fbackup -Ouc config -g graphs/usr-usrlib\
          -I indices/usr-usrlib/871128.15:17\
              -f /dev/rmt/c0t0d0BEST

When the session completes successfully, the index is automatically
placed in the proper location.

Note that fbackup should be piped to tcio when backing up to a CS/80
cartridge tape device see tcio(1)). The following example copies the
entire contents of directory /usr to a cartridge tape:

      /usr/sbin/fbackup i /usr -f - | tcio -oe /dev/rct/c0d1s2

WARNINGS
    With release 10.20, HP-UX supports large files (greater than 2GB) and
    increased UID/GIDs (greater than 60,000). Archives containing files
    with these attributes would cause severe problems on systems that do
    not support the increased sizes. For this reason, fbackup creates
    tapes with a new magic number ("FBACKUP_LABEL"). This prevents
    fbackup tape archives from being restored on pre-10.20 HP-UX systems.
    frecover still reads both tape formats so that fbackup tape archives
    created on pre-10.20 HP-UX systems can be restored.

    Starting with HP-UX Release 8.0, fbackup does not back up network
    special files because RFA networking is obsolete. A warning message
    is issued if a network special file is encountered in the backup graph
    and the file is skipped.

    The use of fbackup for backing up NFS mounted file systems is not
    guaranteed to work as expected if the backup is done as a privileged
    user. This is due to the manner in which NFS handles privileged-user
    access by mapping user root and uid 0 to user nobody, usually uid -2,
    thus disallowing root privileges on the remote system to a root user
    on the local system.

    The utility set comprised of fbackup and frecover was originally
    designed for use on systems equipped with not more than one gigabyte
    of total file system storage. Although the utilities have no
    programming limitations that restrict users to this size, complete
    backups and recoveries of substantially larger systems can cause a
    large amount system activity due to the amount of virtual memory (swap
    space) used to store the indices. Users who want to use these
    utilities, but are noticing poor system-wide performance due to the
    size of the backup, are encouraged to backup their systems in multiple

smaller sessions, rather than attempting to backup the entire system at one time.

Due to present file-system limitations, files whose inode data, but not their contents, are modified while a backup is in progress might be omitted from the next incremental backup of the same graph. Also, fbackup does not reset the inode change times of files to their original value.

fbackup allocates resources that are not returned to the system if it is killed in an ungraceful manner. If it is necessary to kill fbackup, send it a SIGTERM; not a SIGKILL.

For security reasons, configuration files and the chgvol and error executable files should only be writable by their owners.

If sparse files are backed up without using data compression, a very large amount of media can be consumed.

fbackup does not require special privileges. However, if the user does not have access to a given file, the file is not backed up.

fbackup consists of multiple executable objects, all of which are expected to reside in directory /usr/sbin.

fbackup creates volumes with a format that makes duplication of volumes by dd impossible (see dd(1)). Copying an fbackup volume created on one media type to another media type does not produce a valid fbackup volume on the new media because the formats of volumes on 9-track tape, backup to a file, rewritable optical disks and DDS-format tapes are not identical.

When configuring the parameter blocksperrecord (see -c option), the record size is limited by the maximum allowed for the tape drive. Common maximum record sizes include 16 1-Kbyte blocks for tape drive models HP7974 and HP7978A, 32 blocks for the HP7978B, 60 blocks for the HP7980, and 64 blocks for DDS tape drives. Note also that the blocksize used in earlier releases (7.0 and before) was 512 bytes, whereas it is now 1024 bytes. This means that the same value specified in blocksperrecord in an earlier release creates blocks twice their earlier size in the current release (i.e., a blocksperrecord parameter of 32 would create 16-Kbyte blocks at Release 7.0, but now creates 32-Kbyte blocks). If blocksperrecord exceeds the byte count allowed by the tape drive, the tape drive rejects the write, causing an error to be communicated to fbackup which fbackup interprets as a bad tape. The resulting write error message resembles the following:

> fbackup (3013): Write error while writing backup at tape block 0.
> Diagnostic error from tape 11...... SW_PROBLEM (printed by
> driver on console)
> fbackup (3102): Attempting to make this volume salvageable.
> etc.

DEPENDENCIES
  NFS
    Access control lists of networked files are summarized (as returned in st_mode by stat()), but not copied to the new file (see stat(2)).

  Series 800
    On NIO-bus machines there can be problems when a CS/80 cartridge tape device is on the same interface card as hard disk devices. If writes longer than 16K bytes are made to the tape device, it is possible to have disk access time-out errors. This happens because the tape device has exclusive access to the bus during write operations. Depending on the system activity, this problem may not be seen. The

```
           default write size of fbackup is 16 Kbytes.

    Series 700/800
         fbackup does not support QIC-120, and QIC-150 formats on QIC devices.
         If fbackup is attempted for these formats, fbackup fails and the
         following message is displayed :

              mt lu X: Write must be a multiple of 512 bytes in QIC 120 or QIC
              150

AUTHOR
      fbackup was developed by HP.

FILES
      /var/adm/fbackupfiles/dates                    database of past backups

SEE ALSO
      cpio(1), ftio(1), tcio(1), dump(1M), frecover(1M), ftio(1M),
      restore(1M), rmt(1M), stat(2), acl(5), mt(7).
```

ioscan

ioscan - Scan system and list the results.

---

ioscan(1M)   ioscan(1M)

NAME
     ioscan - scan I/O system

SYNOPSIS

     /usr/sbin/ioscan [-k|-u] [-d driver|-C class] [-I instance] [-H
     hw_path] [-f[-n]|-F[-n]] [devfile]

     /usr/sbin/ioscan -M driver -H hw_path [-I instance]

DESCRIPTION
     ioscan scans system hardware, usable I/O system devices, or kernel I/O
     system data structures as appropriate, and lists the results. For
     each hardware module on the system, ioscan displays by default the
     hardware path to the hardware module, the class of the hardware
     module, and a brief description.

     By default, ioscan scans the system and lists all reportable hardware
     found. The types of hardware reported include processors, memory,
     interface cards and I/O devices. Scanning the hardware may cause
     drivers to be unbound and others bound in their place in order to
     match actual system hardware. Entities that cannot be scanned are not
     listed.

     In the second form shown, ioscan forces the specified software driver
     into the kernel I/O system at the given hardware path and forces
     software driver to be bound. This can be used to make the system
     recognize a device that cannot be recognized automatically; for
     example, because it has not yet been connected to the system, does not
     support autoconfiguration, or because diagnostics need to be run on a
     faulty device.

   Options
     ioscan recognizes the following options:

          -C class   Restrict the output listing to those devices
                             belonging to the specified class. Cannot be
                             used with -d.

          -d driver   Restrict the output listing to those devices
                             controlled by the specified driver. Cannot be
                             used with -C.

          -f   Generate a full listing, displaying the
                             module's class, instance number, hardware path,
                             driver, software state, hardware type, and a
                             brief description.

          -F   Produce a compact listing of fields (described
                             below), separated by colons. This option
                             overrides the -f option.

-H hw_path	Restrict the scan and output listing to those devices connected at the specified hardware path. When used with -M, this option specifies the full hardware path at which to bind the software modules.
-I instance	Restrict the scan and output listing to the specified instance, when used with either -d or -C. When used with -M, specifies the desired instance number for binding.
-k	Scan kernel I/O system data structures instead of the actual hardware and list the results. No binding or unbinding of drivers is performed. The -d, -C, -I, and -H options can be used to restrict listings. Cannot be used with -u.
-M driver	Specifies the software driver to bind at the hardware path given by the -H option. Must be used with the -H option.
-n	List device file names in the output. Only special files in the /dev directory and its subdirectories are listed.
-u	Scan and list usable I/O system devices instead of the actual hardware. Usable I/O devices are those having a driver in the kernel and an assigned instance number. The -d, -C, -I, and -H options can be used to restrict listings. The -u option cannot be used with -k.

The -d and -C options can be used to obtain listings of subsets of the I/O system, although the entire system is still scanned. Specifying -d or -C along with -I, or specifying -H or a devfile causes ioscan to restrict both the scan and the listing to the hardware subset indicated.

Fields
The -F option can be used to generate a compact listing of fields separated by colons (:), useful for producing custom listings with awk. Fields include the module's bus type, cdio, is_block, is_char, is_pseudo, block major number, character major number, minor number, class, driver, hardware path, identify bytes, instance number, module path, module name, software state, hardware type, a brief description, and card instance. If a field does not exist, consecutive colons hold the field's position. Fields are defined as follows:

class	A device category, defined in the files located in the directory /usr/conf/master.d and consistent with the listings output by lsdev (see lsdev(1M)). Examples are disk, printer, and tape.
instance	The instance number associated with the device or card. It is a unique number assigned to a card or device within a class. If no driver is available for the hardware component or an error occurs binding the driver, the kernel will not assign an instance number and a (-1), is listed.
hw path	A numerical string of hardware components, notated sequentially from the bus address to the device address. Typically, the initial number is appended by slash (/), to represent a bus converter (if required by your machine), and

subsequent numbers are separated by periods (.).
Each number represents the location of a hardware
component on the path to the device.

driver   The name of the driver that controls the hardware
             component. If no driver is available to control
             the hardware component, a question mark (?) is
             displayed in the output.

software state The result of software binding.

CLAIMED	software bound successfully
UNCLAIMED	no associated software found
DIFF_HW	software found does not match the associated software
NO_HW	the hardware at this address is no longer responding
ERROR	the hardware at this address is responding but is in an error state
SCAN	node locked, try again later

hardware type Entity identifier for the hardware component. It
             is one of the following strings:

UNKNOWN	There is no hardware associated or the type of hardware is unknown
PROCESSOR	Hardware component is a processor
MEMORY	Hardware component is memory
BUS_NEXUS	Hardware component is bus converter or bus adapter
INTERFACE	Hardware component is an interface card
DEVICE	Hardware component is a device

bus type   Bus type associated with the node.

cdio   The name associated with the Context-Dependent I/O
             module.

is_block   A boolean value indicating whether a device block
             major number exists. A T or F is generated in this
             field.

is_char   A boolean value indicating whether a device
             character major number exists. A T or F is
             generated in this field.

is_pseudo   A boolean value indicating a pseudo driver. A T or
             F is generated in this field.

block major The device block major number. A -1 indicates that
             a device block major number does not exist.

character major

The device character major number. A -1 indicates
that a device character major number does not
exist.

minor   The device minor number.

identify bytes The identify bytes returned from a module or
                 device.

module path   The software components separated by periods (.).

module name   The module name of the software component
                 controlling the node.

description   A description of the device.

card instance   The instance number of the hardware interface
                 card.

RETURN VALUE
      ioscan returns 0 upon normal completion and 1 if an error occurred.

EXAMPLES
      Scan the system hardware and list all the devices belonging to the
      disk device class.

            ioscan -C disk

      Forcibly bind driver tape1 at the hardware path 8.4.1.

            ioscan -M tape1 -H 8.4.1

AUTHOR
      ioscan was developed by HP.

FILES
      /dev/config
      /dev/*

SEE ALSO
      config(1M), lsdev(1M), ioconfig(4).

lsdev

lsdev - List devices configured into the system.

NAME
     lsdev - list device drivers in the system

SYNOPSIS

     /usr/sbin/lsdev [-h] [-d driver | -C class] [-b block_major]
          [-c char_major] [-e major] [major ...]

DESCRIPTION
     The lsdev command lists, one pair per line, the major device numbers
     and driver names of device drivers configured into the system and
     available for invocation via special files. A -1 in either the block
     or character column means that a major number does not exist for that
     type.

     If no arguments are specified, lsdev lists all drivers configured into
     the system.

     If the -h option is specified, lsdev will not print a heading. This
     option may be useful when the output of lsdev will be used by another
     program.

     The -d, -C, -b, -c, and -e options are used to select specific device
     drivers for output. If more than one option is specified, all drivers
     that match the criteria specified by those options will be listed.
     These search options are divided into two types: name search keys (the
     -d and -C options) and major number search keys (the -b, -c, and -e
     options). If both types of options are present, only entries that
     match both types are printed. The same type of option may appear more
     than once on the command line with each occurrence providing an ORing
     effect of that search type. The -d and -C options may not be
     specified at the same time.

     The ability to process major arguments is provided for compatibility
     and functions like the -e option.

     Options
          -C class   List device drivers that match class.

          -d driver   List device drivers with the name driver.

          -b block_major   List device drivers with a block major number
                              of block_major.

          -c char_major   List device drivers with a character major
                              number of char_major.

          -e major   List device drivers with either a character
                              major number or block major equal to major.

DIAGNOSTICS

    Invalid combination of options
         The -d and -C options may not be specified at the same time.

    Invalid major number
         A major number is malformed or out of range.

EXAMPLES
    To output entries for all drivers in the pseudo class:

         lsdev -C pseudo

    To output entries that are in the class disk that have either a block
    or character major number of 0:

         lsdev -C disk -e 0

    To get the character major number of my_driver into a shell
    environment variable:

         C_MAJOR=$(lsdev -h -d my_driver | awk '{print $1}')

WARNINGS
    Some device drivers available from the system may be intended for use
    by other drivers. Attempting to use them directly from a special file
    may produce unexpected results.

    A driver may be listed even when the hardware requiring the driver is
    not present. Attempts to access a driver without the corresponding
    hardware will fail.

    lsdev only lists drivers that are configured into the currently
    executing kernel. For a complete list of available drivers, please
    run sam (see sam(1M).

DEPENDENCIES
    Since lsdev relies on the device driver information provided in a
    driver_install routine, lsdev may not list drivers installed by other
    means.

AUTHOR
    lsdev was developed by HP.

SEE ALSO
    sam(1M).

    Section 7 entries related to specific device drivers.

    HP-UX System Administration Tasks

mksf

mksf - Make a special device file in the devices directory.

---

mksf(1M)   mksf(1M)

NAME
     mksf - make a special (device) file

SYNOPSIS

     /sbin/mksf [-C class | -d driver] [-D directory] [-H hw-path]
          [-I instance] [-q|-v] [driver-options] [special-file]

     /sbin/mksf [-C class | -d driver] [-D directory] [-H hw-path]
          -m minor [-q|-v] [-r] special-file

DESCRIPTION
     The mksf command makes a special file in the devices directory,
     normally /dev, for an existing device, a device that has already been
     assigned an instance number by the system. The device is specified by
     supplying some combination of the -C, -d, -H, and -I options. If the
     options specified match a unique device in the system, mksf creates a
     special file for that device; otherwise, mksf prints an error message
     and exits. If required, mksf creates any subdirectories relative to
     the device installation directory that are defined for the resulting
     special file.

     For most drivers, mksf has a set of built-in driver options,
     driver-options, and special-file naming conventions. By supplying
     some subset of the driver options, as in the first form above, the
     user can create a special file with a particular set of
     characteristics. If a special-file name is specified, mksf creates
     the special file with that special file name; otherwise, the default
     naming convention for the driver is used.

     In the second form, the minor number and special-file name are
     explicitly specified. This form is used to make a special file for a
     driver without using the built-in driver options in mksf. The -r
     option specifies that mksf should make a character (raw) device file
     instead of the default block device file for drivers that support
     both.

     Options
     mksf recognizes the following options:

          -C class   Match a device that belongs to a given device
                        class, class. Device classes can be listed with
                        the lsdev command (see lsdev(1M)). They are
                        defined in the files in the directory
                        /usr/conf/master.d. This option is not valid for
                        pseudo devices. This option cannot be used with
                        -d.

          -d driver   Match a device that is controlled by the specified
                        device driver, driver. Device drivers can be
                        listed with the lsdev command (see lsdev(1M)).
                        They are defined in the files in the directory

/usr/conf/master.d. This option cannot be used
with -C.

-D directory   Override the default device installation directory
                /dev and install the special files in directory
                instead. directory must exist; otherwise, mksf
                displays an error message and exits. See
                WARNINGS.

-H hw-path   Match a device at a given hardware path, hw-path.
                Hardware paths can be listed with the ioscan
                command (see ioscan(1M)). A hardware path
                specifies the addresses of the hardware components
                leading to a device. It consists of a string of
                numbers separated by periods (.), such as 52 (a
                card), 52.3 (a target address), and 52.3.0 (a
                device). If a hardware component is a bus
                converter, the following period, if any, is
                replaced by a slash (/) as in 2, 2/3, and 2/3.0.
                This option is not valid for pseudo devices.

-I instance   Match a device with the specified instance number.
                Instances can be listed with the -f option of the
                ioscan command (see ioscan(1M)). This option is
                not valid for pseudo devices.

-m minor   Create the special file with the specified minor
                number minor. The format of minor is the same as
                that given in mknod(1M) and mknod(5).

-q   Quiet option. Normally, mksf displays a message
                as each driver is processed. This option
                suppresses the driver message, but not error
                messages. See the -v option.

-r   Create a character (raw) special file instead of a
                block special file.

-v   Verbose option. In addition to the normal
                processing message, display the name of each
                special file as it is created. See the -q option.

Naming Conventions
  Many special files are named using the ccardttargetddevice naming
  convention. These variables have the following meaning wherever they
  are used.

      card   The unique interface card identification number from
                ioscan (see ioscan(1M)). It is represented as a
                decimal number with a typical range of 0 to 255.

      target   The device target number, for example the address on a
                HP-FL or SCSI bus. It is represented as a decimal
                number with a typical range of 0 to 15.

      device   A address unit within a device, for example, the unit
                in a HP-FL device or the LUN in a SCSI device. It is
                represented as a decimal number with a typical range of
                0 to 15.

Special Files
  The driver-specific options (driver-options) and default special file
  names (special-file) are listed below.

    asio0

-a access-mode   Port access mode (0-2). The default access mode
is 0 (Direct connect). The access-mode meanings
are:

access-mode	Port Operation
0	Direct connect
1	Dial out modem
2	Dial in modem

-c   CCITT.

-f   Hardware flow control (RTS/CTS).

-i   Modem dialer. Cannot be used with -l.

-l   Line printer. Cannot be used with -i.

-r fifo-trigger

fifo-trigger should have a value between 0 and 3.
The following table shows the corresponding FIFO
trigger level for a given fifo-trigger value.

fifo-trigger	Receive FIFO Trigger Level
0	1
1	4
2	8
3	14

-t   Transparent mode (normally used by diagnostics).

-x xmit-limit   xmit-limit should have a value between 0 and 3.
The following table shows the corresponding
transmit limit for a given xmit-limit value.

xmit-limit	Transmit Limit
0	1
1	4
2	8
3	12

special-file   The default special file name depends on the
access-mode and whether the -i and -l options are
used.

access-mode	-i	-l	Special File Name
-	no	yes	ccardp0_lp
2	no	no	ttydcardp0
1	no	no	culcardp0

```
            |     0       | yes | no  | cuacardp0           |
            |     0       | no  | no  | ttycardp0           |
            |_____|_____|_____|_____|
```

audio

    -f format   Audio format (0-3). The format meanings are:

| | | File Name Modifier |
format	Audio Format	format-mod
0	No change in audio format	
1	8-bit Mu-law	U
2	8-bit A-law	A
3	16-bit linear	L

    -o output-dest Output destination (0-4). The output-dest should
                  have a value between 0 and 4. The following table
                  shows the corresponding output destinations for a
                  given output-dest value.

| | | File Name Modifier |
output-dest	Output Destinations	output-mod
0	All outputs	B
1	Headphone	E
2	Internal Speaker	I
3	No output	N
4	Line output	L

    -r   Raw, control access. This option cannot be used
                     with either the -f or -o options.

    special-file   The default special file name depends on the
                     options specified.

Options	Special File Name
-r	audioCtl_card
-f 0	audio_card
all others	audiooutput-modformat-mod_card

                     The optional output-mod and format-mod values are
                     given in the tables above. Note the underscore
                     (_) before card in each special file name. Also
                     note that for card 0, each file will be linked to
                     a simpler name without the trailing _card.

autox0 schgr

    Note that -i cannot be used with either -r or -p.

    -i   Ioctl; create picker control special file.

    -p optical-disk[:last-optical-disk]
                     The optical disk number (starts with 1). If the

optional :last-optical-disk is given then special
files for the range of disks specified will be
created.

-r   Raw; create character, not block, special file.

special-file   A special file cannot be given if a range of
                       optical disks is given with the -p option. If one
                       is given for the single disk case, the name will
                       have an a appended to the end for the A-side
                       device and a b appended to the end for the B-side
                       device. The default special file name depends on
                       whether the -r option is used.

-r	Special File Name
yes	rac/ccardttargetddevice_optical-diska
	rac/ccardttargetddevice_optical-diskb
no	ac/ccardttargetddevice_optical-diska
	ac/ccardttargetddevice_optical-diskb

Note the underscore (_) between device and
optical-disk.

CentIf

   -h handshake-mode

Handshake mode. Valid values range from 1 to 6:

handshake-mode	Handshake operation
1	Automatic NACK/BUSY handshaking
2	Automatic BUSY only handshaking
3	Bidirectional read/write
4	Stream mode (NSTROBE only, no handshaking)
5	Automatic NACK/BUSY with pulsed NSTROBE
6	Automatic BUSY with pulsed NSTROBE

special-file   The default special file name is ccardt0d0_lp for
                       handshake-mode 2 and ccardt0d0hhandshake-mode_lp
                       for all others.

disc1

-c   This option must be present if the unit is a
                       cartridge tape.

-r   Raw; create character, not block, special file.

-s section   The section number.

-t   Transparent mode (normally used by diagnostics).

-u unit   The CS/80 unit number (for example, unit 0 for
                       disk, unit 1 for tape).

special-file   The default special file name depends on whether
                       the -c, -r, and -s options are used:

-c	-r	-s	Special File Name
yes	yes	invalid	rct/ccardttargetddevice
no	yes	no	rdsk/ccardttargetddevice
no	yes	yes	rdsk/ccardttargetddevicessection
yes	no	invalid	ct/ccardttargetddevice
no	no	no	dsk/ccardttargetddevice
no	no	yes	dsk/ccardttargetddevicessection

disc2

    -r   Raw; create character, not block, special file.

    -s section   The section number.

    -t   Transparent mode (normally used by diagnostics).

    -u unit   The cs80 unit number (typically 0).

    special-file   The default special file name depends on whether
                     the -r and -s options are used:

-r	-s	Special File Name
yes	no	rdsk/ccardttargetddevice
yes	yes	rdsk/ccardttargetddevicessection
no	no	dsk/ccardttargetddevice
no	yes	dsk/ccardttargetddevicessection

disc3

    -f   Floppy.

    -r   Raw; create character, not block, special file.

    -s section   The section number.

    special-file   The default special file name depends on whether
                     the -r and -s options are used:

-r	-s	Special File Name
yes	no	rdsk/ccardttargetddevice and
		rfloppy/ccardttargetddevice
yes	yes	rdsk/ccardttargetddevicessection
no	no	dsk/ccardttargetddevice and
		floppy/ccardttargetddevice
no	yes	dsk/ccardttargetddevicessection

disc4 sdisc

    -r   Raw; create character, not block, special file.

    -s section   The section number.

    special-file   The default special file name depends on whether the -r and -s options are used:

-r	-s	Special File Name
yes	no	rdsk/ccardttargetddevice
yes	yes	rdsk/ccardttargetddevicessection
no	no	dsk/ccardttargetddevice
no	yes	dsk/ccardttargetddevicessection

instr0

-a address   The HP-IB instrument address (0-30). Cannot be used with the -t option.

-t   Transparent mode (normally used by diagnostics). Cannot be used with the -a option.

special-file   The default special file name depends on the arguments -a and -t:

-a	-t	Special File Name
no	no	hpib/ccard
no	yes	diag/hpib/ccard
yes	no	hpib/ccardttargetdaddress

hil

Note that only one of -a, -k, or -r is allowed.

-a address   The link address (1-7).

-k   Cooked keyboard.

-n   The hil controller device.

special-file   The default special file name depends on the -a, -k, and -r options:

Option	Special File Name
-a	hil_card.address
-k	hilkbd_card
-r	rhil_card

Note the underscore (_) before card. Also note that for card 0, each file will be linked to a simpler name without _card, either hiladdress, hilkbd, or rhil.

lan0 lan1 lan2 lan3

Note that only one of -e or -i is allowed.

-e   Ethernet protocol.

-i   IEEE 802.3 protocol.

-t   Transparent mode (normally used by diagnostics).

special-file   The default special file name depends on the -e,
                      -i, and -t options:

Option	-t	Special File Name
-e	no	ethercard
-e	yes	diag/ethercard
-i	no	lancard
-i	yes	diag/lancard

lantty0

-e   Exclusive access.

special-file   The default special file name depends on whether
                      the -e option is used:

-e	Special File Name
no	lanttycard
yes	diag/lanttycard

lpr0 lpr1 lpr2 lpr3

-c   Capital letters. Convert all output to uppercase.

-e   Eject page after paper-out recovery.

-n   No form-feed.

-o   Old paper-out behavior (abort job).

-r   Raw.

-t   Transparent mode (normally used by diagnostics).

-w   No wait. Don't retry errors on open.

special-file   The default special file name depends on whether
                      the -r option is used:

-r	Special File Name
no	ccardttargetddevice_lp
yes	ccardttargetddevice_rlp

mux0 mux2 mux4 eisa_mux0

-a access-mode   Port access mode (0-2). The default access mode
                      is 0 (Direct connect). The access-mode meanings
                      are:

```
                          |access-mode | Port Operation |
                          |_____|_____|
                          |     0      | Direct connect |
                          |     1      | Dial out modem |
                          |     2      | Dial in modem  |
                          |_____|_____|
```

-c   CCITT.

-f   Hardware flow control (RTS/CTS).

-i   Modem dialer. Cannot be used with -l.

-l   Line printer. Cannot be used with -i.

-p port   Multiplexer port number (0-15 for mux0 and mux2;
                0-1 for mux4; 0-256 for eisa_mux0). Some MUX
                cards controlled by a particular driver have fewer
                than the maximum supported ports.

-t   Transparent mode (normally used by diagnostics).

special-file   The default special file name depends on the
                access-mode and whether the -i and -l options are
                used.

```
          _____
          |access-mode |  -i  |  -l  | Special File Name |
          |_____|_____|_____|_____|
          |     -      |  no  | yes  | ccardpport_lp     |
          |     2      |  no  | no   | ttydcardpport     |
          |     1      |  no  | no   | culcardpport      |
          |     0      | yes  | no   | cuacardpport      |
          |     0      |  no  | no   | ttycardpport      |
          |_____|_____|_____|_____|
```

pflop sflop

-r   Raw; create character, not block, special file.

special-file   The default special file name depends on whether
                the -r option is used:

```
          _____
          |-r  |          Special File Name               |
          |____|_____|
          |no  | floppy/ccardttargetddevice               |
          |yes | rfloppy/ccardttargetddevice              |
          |____|_____|
```

ps2

Note that only one of -a, or -p is allowed.

-a auto_device Autosearch device. An auto_device value of 0
                means first mouse; a value of 1 means first
                keyboard.

-p port   PS2 port number.

special-file   The default special file name depends on the -a,
                and -p options:

```
 _____
|Option | Special File Name |
|_____|_____|
| -a 0  | ps2mouse         |
| -a 1  | ps2kbd           |
|  -p   | ps2_port         |
|_____|_____|
```

Note the underscore (_) before port.

scc1

    -a access-mode Port access mode (0-2). The default access mode
                    is 0. The access-mode meanings are:

```
 _____
|access-mode | Port Operation |
|_____|_____|
|     0      | Direct connect |
|     1      | Dial out modem |
|     2      | Dial in modem  |
|_____|_____|
```

    -b   Port B.

    -c   CCITT.

    -i   Modem dialer. Cannot be used with -l.

    -l   Line printer. Cannot be used with -i.

    special-file   The default special file name depends on the
               access-mode and whether the -i and -l options are
               used.

```
 _____
|access-mode | -i  | -l  | Special File Name |
|_____|_____|_____|_____|
|     -      | no  | yes | ccardpport_lp     |
|     2      | no  | no  | ttydcardpport     |
|     1      | no  | no  | culcardpport      |
|     0      | yes | no  | cuacardpport      |
|     0      | no  | no  | ttycardpport      |
|_____|_____|_____|_____|
```

schgr   See autox0.

sdisk   See disc4.

sflop   See pflop.

stape

    -a   AT&T-style rewind/close.

    -b bpi   Bits per inch or tape density. The recognized
               values for bpi are:
               BEST, D1600, D3480, D3480C, D6250, D6250C, D800,
               D8MM_8200, D8MM_8200C, D8MM_8500, D8MM_8500C,
               DDS1, DDS1C, DDS2, DDS2C, NOMOD, QIC_1000, QIC_11,
               QIC_120, QIC_1350, QIC_150, QIC_2100, QIC_24,
               QIC_2GB, QIC_525, QIC_5GB,
               or a decimal number density code.

-c [code]   Compression with optional compression code. The optional decimal code is used to select a particular compression algorithm on drives that support more than one compression algorithm. This option must be specified at the end of an option string. See mt(7) for more details.

-e   Exhaustive mode. This option allows the driver to experiment with multiple configuration values in an attempt to access the media. The default behavior is to use only the configuration specified.

-n   No rewind on close.

-p   Partition one.

-s [block-size]
           Fixed block size mode. If a numeric block-size is given, it is used for a fixed block size. If the -s option is used alone, a device-specific default fixed block size is used. This option must be specified at the end of an option string.

-u   UC Berkeley-style rewind/close.

-w   Wait (disable immediate reporting).

-x index   Use the index value to access the tape device driver property table entry. Recognized values for index are decimal values in the range 0 to 30.

special-file   Put all tape special files in the /dev/rmt directory. This is required for proper maintenance of the Tape Property Table (see mt(7)). Device files located outside the /dev/rmt directory may not provide consistent behavior across system reboots. The default special file names are dependent on the tape drive being accessed and the options specified. All default special files begin with rmt/ccardttargetddevice. See mt(7) for a complete description of the default special file naming scheme for tapes.

tape1 tape2

-a   AT&T-style rewind/close.

-b bpi   Bits per inch or tape density. The recognized values for bpi are:
BEST, D1600, D3480, D3480C, D6250, D6250C, D800, D8MM_8200, D8MM_8200C, D8MM_8500, D8MM_8500C, DDS1, DDS1C, DDS2, DDS2C, NOMOD, QIC_1000, QIC_11, QIC_120, QIC_1350, QIC_150, QIC_2100, QIC_24, QIC_2GB, QIC_525, QIC_5GB, DLT_42500_24, DLT_42500_56, DLT_62500_64, DLT_81633_64, DLT_62500_64C, DLT_81633_64C, or a decimal number density code.

-c [code]   Compression with optional compression code. The optional decimal code is used to select a particular compression algorithm on drives that support more than one compression algorithm. This option must be specified at the end of an option string. See mt(7) for more details.

-n   No rewind on close.

-o   Console messages disabled.

-t   Transparent mode, normally used by diagnostics.

-u   UC Berkeley-style rewind/close.

-w   Wait (disable immediate reporting).

-x index   Use the index value to access the tape device
                driver property table entry. The recognized
                values for index are decimal values in the range 0
                to 30.

-z   RTE compatible close.

special-file   Put all tape special files in the /dev/rmt
                directory. This is required for proper
                maintenance of the Tape Property Table (see
                mt(7)). Device files located outside the /dev/rmt
                directory may not provide consistent behavior
                across system reboots. The default special file
                names are dependent on the tape drive being
                accessed and the options specified. All default
                special files begin with rmt/ccardttargetddevice.
                See mt(7) for a complete description of the
                default special file naming scheme for tapes.

RETURN VALUE
     mksf exits with one of the following values:

     0   Successful completion.
     1   Failure. An error occurred.

DIAGNOSTICS
     Most of the diagnostic messages from mksf are self-explanatory.
     Listed below are some messages deserving further clarification.
     Errors cause mksf to abort immediately.

   Errors
     Ambiguous device specification

          Matched more than one device in the system. Use some combination
          of the -d, -C, -H, and -I options to specify a unique device.

     No such device in the system

          No device in the system matched the options specified. Use
          ioscan to list the devices in the system (see ioscan(1M)).

     Device driver name is not in the kernel
     Device class name is not in the kernel

          The indicated device driver or device class is not present in the
          kernel. Add the appropriate device driver and/or device class to
          the config input file and generate a new kernel (see config(1M)).

     Device has no instance number

          The specified device has not been assigned an instance number.
          Use ioscan to assign an instance to the device.

Directory *directory* doesn't exist

The directory argument of the -D option doesn't exist. Use mkdir
to create the directory (see mkdir(1)).

EXAMPLES
Make a special file named /dev/printer for the line printer device
associated with instance number 2.

mksf -C printer -I 2 /dev/printer

Make a special file, using the default naming convention, for the tape
device at hardware path 8.4.1. The driver-specific options specify
1600 bits per inch and no rewind on close.

mksf -C tape -H 8.4.1 -b D1600 -n

WARNINGS
Many commands and subsystems assume their device files are in /dev;
therefore, the use of the -D option is discouraged.

AUTHOR
mksf was developed by HP.

FILES
/dev/config   I/O system special file

/etc/mtconfig   Tape driver property table database

SEE ALSO
mkdir(1), config(1M), insf(1M), ioscan(1M), lsdev(1M), mknod(1M),
rmsf(1M), mknod(2), ioconfig(4), mknod(5), mt(7).

shutdown

shutdown - Terminate all running processes in an orderly fashion.

---

shutdown(1M)   shutdown(1M)

NAME
     shutdown - terminate all processing

SYNOPSIS

     /sbin/shutdown [-h|-r] [-y] [-o] [grace]

DESCRIPTION
     The shutdown command is part of the HP-UX system operation procedures.
     Its primary function is to terminate all currently running processes
     in an orderly and cautious manner. shutdown can be used to put the
     system in single-user mode for administrative purposes such as backup
     or file system consistency checks (see fsck(1M)), and to halt or
     reboot the system. By default, shutdown is an interactive program.

     Options and Arguments
     shutdown recognizes the following options and arguments.

          -h   Shut down the system and halt.

          -r   Shut down the system and reboot automatically.

          -y   Do not require any interactive responses from the user.
                    (Respond yes or no as appropriate to all questions,
                    such that the user does not interact with the shutdown
                    process.)

          -o   When executed on the cluster server in a diskless
                    cluster environment, shutdown the server only and do
                    not reboot clients. If this argument is not entered the
                    default behavior is to reboot all clients when the
                    server is shutdown.

          grace   Either a decimal integer that specifies the duration in
                    seconds of a grace period for users to log off before
                    the system shuts down, or the word now. The default is
                    60. If grace is either 0 or now, shutdown runs more
                    quickly, giving users very little time to log out.

     If neither -r (reboot) nor -h (halt) is specified, standalone and
     server systems are placed in single-user state. Either -r
     (reboot) or -h (halt) must be specified for a client; shutdown to
     single-user state is not allowed for a client. See dcnodes(1M),
     init(1M).

     Shutdown Procedure
     shutdown goes through the following steps:

          - The PATH environment variable is reset to
             /usr/bin:/usr/sbin:/sbin.

          - The IFS environment variable is reset to space, tab, newline.

- The user is checked for authorization to execute the shutdown command. Only authorized users can execute the shutdown command. See FILES for more information on the /etc/shutdown.allow authorization file.

- The current working directory is changed to the root directory (/).

- All file systems' super blocks are updated; see sync(1M). This must be done before rebooting the system to ensure file system integrity.

- The real user ID is set to that of the superuser.

- A broadcast message is sent to all users currently logged in on the system telling them to log out. The administrator can specify a message at this time; otherwise, a standard warning message is displayed.

- The next step depends on whether a system is standalone, a server, or a client.

  - If the system is standalone, /sbin/rc is executed to shut down subsystems, unmount file systems, and perform other tasks to bring the system to run level 0.

  - If the system is a server, the optional -o argument is used to determine if all clients in the cluster should also be rebooted. The default behavior (command line parameter -o is not entered) is to reboot all clients using /sbin/reboot; entering -o results in the server only being rebooted and the clients being left alone. Then /sbin/rc is executed to shut down subsystems, unmount file systems, and perform other tasks to bring the system to run level 0.

  - If the system is a client, /sbin/rc is executed to bring the system down to run-level 2, and then /sbin/reboot is executed. Shutdown to the single-user state is not an allowed option for clients.

- The system is rebooted or halted by executing /sbin/reboot if the -h or -r option was chosen. If the system was not a cluster client and the system was being brought down to single-user state, a signal is sent to the init process to change states (see init(1M)).

DIAGNOSTICS

device busy

This is the most commonly encountered error diagnostic, and happens when a particular file system could not be unmounted; see mount(1M).

user not allowed to shut down this system

User is not authorized to shut down the system. User and system must both be included in the authorization file /etc/shutdown.allow.

EXAMPLES
Immediately reboot the system and run HP-UX again:

```
        shutdown -r 0
```

Halt the system in 5 minutes (300 seconds) with no interactive
questions and answers:

```
        shutdown -h -y 300
```

Go to run-level s in 10 minutes:

```
        shutdown 600
```

FILES
    /etc/shutdown.allow

            Authorization file.

            The file contains lines that consist of a system host name
            and the login name of a user who is authorized to reboot or
            halt the system. A superuser's login name must be included
            in this file in order to execute shutdown. However, if the
            file is missing or of zero length, the root user can run the
            shutdown program to bring the system down.

            This file does not affect authorization to bring the system
            down to single-user state for maintenance purposes; that
            operation is permitted only when invoked by a superuser.

            A comment character, #, at the beginning of a line causes
            the rest of the line to be ignored (comments cannot span
            multiple lines without additional comment characters).
            Blank lines are also ignored.

            The wildcard character + can be used in place of a host name
            or a user name to specify all hosts or all users,
            respectively (see hosts.equiv(4)).

            For example:

                # user1 can shut down systemA and systemB
                systemA user1
                systemB user1
                # root can shut down any system
                + root
                # Any user can shut down systemC
                systemC +

WARNINGS
    The user name compared with the entry in the shutdown.allow file is
    obtained using getlogin() or, if that fails, using getpwuid() (see
    getlogin(3) and getpwuid(3)).

    The hostname in /etc/shutdown.allow is compared with the hostname
    obtained using gethostbyname() (see gethostbyname(3)).

    shutdown must be executed from a directory on the root volume, such as
    the / directory.

    The maximum broadcast message that can be sent is approximately 970
    characters.

    When executing shutdown on an NFS diskless cluster server and the -o
    option is not entered, clients of the server will be rebooted. No
    clients should be individually rebooted or shutdown while the cluster
    is being shutdown.
```
```

SEE ALSO
      dcnodes(1M), fsck(1M), init(1M), killall(1M), mount(1M), reboot(1M),
      sync(1M), dcnodes(3), gethostbyname(3), getpwuid(3), hosts.equiv(4).

sysdef

sysdef - Analyze the currently running system and report on its tunable configuration parameters.

```
sysdef(1M)                                                        sysdef(1M)

NAME
     sysdef - display system definition

SYNOPSIS

     /usr/sbin/sysdef [kernel [master]]

DESCRIPTION
     The command sysdef analyzes the currently running system and reports
     on its tunable configuration parameters.  kernel is the file used to
     retrieve the kernel namelist; if not specified, /stand/vmunix is used.
     master is not used, but can be specified for standards compliance.

     For each configuration parameter, the following information is
     printed:

          NAME          The name and description of the parameter.

          VALUE         The current value of the parameter.

          BOOT          The value of the parameter at boot time, if
                        different from the current value.

          MIN           The minimum allowed value of the parameter, if
                        any.

          MAX           The maximum allowed value of the parameter, if
                        any.

          UNITS         Where appropriate, the units by which the
                        parameter is measured.

          FLAGS         Flags that further describe the parameter.  The
                        following flag is defined:

                        M  Parameter can be modified without rebooting.

EXAMPLES
     Analyze the system using the /stand/vmunix kernel file:

          sysdef

     Analyze the system using the kernel file /os_file:

          sysdef /os_file

WARNINGS
     Users of sysdef must not rely on the exact field widths and spacing of
     its output, as these will vary depending on the system, the release of
     HP-UX, and the data to be displayed.
```

FILES
    /stand/vmunix   Default kernel file

    /usr/conf/master.d   Directory containing master files

tar

tar - Save and restore archives of files.

```
tar(1)                                                              tar(1)

NAME
     tar - tape file archiver

SYNOPSIS

     tar [-]key [arg ...] [file | -C directory] ...

DESCRIPTION
     The tar command saves and restores archives of files on a magnetic
     tape, a flexible disk, or a regular file.  The default archive file is
     /dev/rmt/0m.  See the -f option below.  Its actions are controlled by
     the key argument.

     Arguments
     key                is a string of characters containing an optional version
                        letter, exactly one function letter, and possibly one or
                        more function modifiers, specified in any order.
                        Whitespace is not permitted in key.  The key string can
                        be preceded by a hyphen (-), as when specifying options
                        in other HP-UX commands, but it is not necessary.

     arg ...            The b and f function modifiers each require an arg
                        argument (see below).  If both b and f are specified,
                        the order of the arg arguments must match the order of
                        the modifiers.  If specified, the arg arguments must be
                        separated from the key and each other by whitespace.

     file               specifies a file being saved or restored.  If file is a
                        directory name, it refers to the files and (recursively)
                        the subdirectories contained in that directory.

     -C directory       causes tar to perform a chdir() to directory (see
                        chdir(2)).  Subsequent file and -C directory arguments
                        must be relative to directory.  This allows multiple
                        directories not related by a close or common parent to
                        be archived using short relative path names.

     The value of file is stored in the archive.  The value of directory is
     not stored.

     Version Keys
     The version portion of the key determines the format in which tar
     writes the archive.  tar can read either format regardless of the
     version.  The version is specified by one of the following letters:


             N    Write a POSIX format archive.  This format allows file names
                  of up to 256 characters in length, and correctly archives
                  and restores the following file types: regular files,
                  character and block special devices, links, symbolic links,
                  directories, and FIFO special files.  It also stores the
                  user and group name of each file and attempts to use these
```

names to determine the user-ID and group-ID of a file when restoring it with the p function modifier. This is the default format.

O   Write a pre-POSIX format archive.

Function Keys

The function portion of the key is specified by exactly one of the following letters:

c   Create a new archive. Write from the beginning of the archive instead of appending after the last file. Any previous information in the archive is overwritten.

r   Add the named file to the end of the archive. The same blocking factor used to create the archive must be used to append to it.

t   List the names of all the files in the archive. Adding the v function modifier expands this listing to include the file modes and owner numbers. The names of all files are listed each time they occur on the tape.

u   Add any named file to the archive if it is not already present or has been modified since it was last written in the archive. The same blocking factor used to create the archive must be used to update it.

x   Extract the named file from the archive and restore it to the system. If a named file matches a directory whose contents were written to the archive, this directory is (recursively) extracted. If a named file on tape does not exist on the system, the file is created as follows:

- The user, group, and other protections are restored from the tape.

- The modification time is restored from the tape unless the m function modifier is specified.

- The file user ID and group ID are normally those of the restoring process.

- The set-user-ID, set-group-ID, and sticky bits are not set automatically. The o and p function modifiers control the restoration of protection; see below for more details.

If the files exist, their modes are not changed, but the set-user-id, set-group-id and sticky bits are cleared. If no file argument is given, the entire content of the archive is extracted. Note that if several files with the same name are on the archive, the last one overwrites all earlier ones.

Function Modifier Keys

The following function modifiers can be used in addition to the function letters listed above (note that some modifiers are incompatible with some functions):

A   Suppress warning messages that tar did not archive a file's access control list. By default, tar writes a warning message for each file with optional ACL entries.

b   Use the next arg argument as the blocking factor for archive
        records. The default is 20; the maximum is at least 20.
        However, if the f - modifier is used to specify standard
        input, the default blocking factor is 1.

        The blocking factor is determined automatically when reading
        nine-track tapes (key letters x and t). On nine-track
        tapes, the physical tape record length is the same as the
        block size. The block size is defined as the logical record
        size times the blocking factor (number of logical records
        per block).

        The blocking factor must be specified when reading flexible
        disks and cartridge tapes if they were written with a
        blocking factor other than the default.

        If a tar file is read using a blocking factor not equal to
        the one used when the file was written, an error may occur
        at the end of the file but there may or may not be an actual
        error in the read. To prevent this problem, a blocking
        factor of 1 can be used, although performance may be reduced
        somewhat.

        tar writes logical records of 512 bytes, independent of how
        logical records may be defined elsewhere by other programs
        (such as variable-length records (lines) within an ASCII
        text file).

e   Fail if the extent attributes are present in the files to be
        archived. If tar fails for this reason, the partially
        created destination file is not be removed.

f   Use the next arg argument as the name of the archive instead
        of the default, /dev/rmt/0m. If the name of the file is -,
        tar writes to standard output or reads from standard input,
        whichever is appropriate, and the default blocking factor
        becomes 1. Thus, tar can be used as the head or tail of a
        pipeline (see EXAMPLES).

h   Force tar to follow symbolic links as if they were normal
        files or directories. Normally, tar does not follow
        symbolic links.

l   Tell tar to complain if it cannot resolve all of the links
        to the files being saved. If l is not specified, no error
        messages are printed.

m   Tell tar not to restore the modification time written on the
        archive. The modification time of the file will be the time
        of extraction.

o   Suppress writing certain directory information that older
        versions of tar cannot handle on input. tar normally writes
        information specifying owners and modes of directories in
        the archive. Earlier versions of tar, when encountering
        this information, give error messages of the form:

            name - cannot create

        When o is used for reading, it causes the extracted file to
        take on the user and group IDs of the user running the
        program rather than those on the tape. This is the default
        for the ordinary user and can be overridden, to the extent
        that system protections allow, by using the p function
        modifier.

      p   Cause file to be restored to the original modes and
ownerships written on the archive, if possible. This is the
default for the superuser, and can be overridden by the o
function modifier. If system protections prevent the
ordinary user from executing chown(), the error is ignored,
and the ownership is set to that of the restoring process
(see chown(2)). The set-user-id, set-group-id, and sticky
bit information are restored as allowed by the protections
defined by chmod() if the chown() operation above succeeds.

      nd   Specify a particular nine-track tape drive and density,
where n is a tape drive number: 0-7, and d is the density: l
= low (800 bpi); m = medium (1600 bpi); h = high (6250 bpi).
This modifier selects the drive on which the nine-track tape
is mounted. The default is 0m.

      v   Normally, tar does its work silently. The v (verbose)
function modifier causes tar to type the name of each file
it treats, preceded by the function letter. With the t
function, v gives more information about the archive entries
than just the name.

      V   Same as the v function modifier except that, when using the
t option, tar also prints out a letter indicating the type
of the archived file.

      w   Cause tar to print the action being taken, followed by the
name of the file, then wait for the user's confirmation. If
the user answers y, the action is performed. Any other
input means "no".

When end-of-tape is reached, tar prompts the user for a new special
file and continues.

If a nine-track tape drive is used as the output device, it must be
configured in Berkeley-compatibility mode (see mt(7)).

EXTERNAL INFLUENCES
    Environment Variables
      LC_TIME determines the format and contents of date and time strings
      output when listing the contents of an archive with the -v option.

      LANG determines the language equivalent of y (for yes/no queries).

      If LC_TIME is not specified in the environment or is set to the empty
      string, the value of LANG is used as the default.

      If LANG is not specified or is set to the empty string, it defaults to
      "C" (see lang(5)).

      If any internationalization variable contains an invalid setting, tar
      behaves as if all internationalization variables are set to "C". See
      environ(5).

    International Code Set Support
      Single- and multibyte character code sets are supported.

ERRORS
    tar issues self-explanatory messages about bad key characters, tape
    read/write errors, and if not enough memory is available to hold the
    link tables.

EXAMPLES
    Create a new archive on /dev/rfd.0 and copy file1 and file2 onto it,
    using the default blocking factor of 20. The key is made up of one

function letter (c) and two function modifiers (v and f):

        tar cvf /dev/rfd.0 file1 file2

Archive files from /usr/include and /etc:

        tar cv -C /usr/include -C /etc

Use tar in a pipeline to copy the entire file system hierarchy under
fromdir to todir:

        cd fromdir ; tar cf - . | (cd todir ; tar xf -i)

Archive all files and directories in directory my_project in the
current directory to a file called my_project.TAR, also in the current
directory:

        tar -cvf my_project.TAR my_project

WARNINGS
        Because of industry standards and interoperability goals, tar does not
        support the archival of files larger than 2GB or files that have
        user/group IDs greater than 60K. Files with user/group IDs greater
        than 60K are archived and restored under the user/group ID of the
        current process.

        The default version has changed from O to N, beginning with HP-UX
        Release 8.0.

        Due to internal limitations in the header structure, not all file
        names of fewer than 256 characters fit when using the N version key.
        If a file name does not fit, tar prints a message and does not archive
        the file.

        Link names are still limited to 100 characters when using the N
        version key.

        There is no way to ask for the n-th occurrence of a file.

        Tape errors are handled ungracefully.

        The u function key can be slow.

        If the archive is a file on disk, flexible disk, or cartridge tape,
        and if the blocking factor specified on output is not the default, the
        same blocking factor must be specified on input, because the blocking
        factor is not explicitly stored in the archive. Updating or appending
        to the archive without following this rule can destroy it.

        Some previous versions of tar have claimed to support the selective
        listing of file names using the t function key with a list. This
        appears to be an error in the documentation because the capability
        does not appear in the original source code.

        There is no way to restore an absolute path name to a relative
        position.

        tar always pads information written to an archive up to the next
        multiple of the block size. Therefore, if you are creating a small
        archive and write out one block of information, tar reports that one
        block was written, but the actual size of the archive might be larger
        if the b function modifier is used.

        Note that tar cOm is not the same as tar cmO.

        Do not create archives on block special devices. Attempting to do so

can causes excessive wear, leading to premature drive hardware
failure.

DEPENDENCIES
   Series 700/800
      The r and u function keys are not supported on QIC or 8mm devices. If
      these options are used with QIC or 8mm devices, tar fails and displays
      the message:

            tar: option not supported for this device

AUTHOR
      tar was developed by AT&T, the University of California, Berkeley, HP,
      and POSIX.

FILES
      /dev/rmt/*
      /dev/rfd.*
      /tmp/tar*

SEE ALSO
      ar(1), cpio(1), acl(5), mt(7).

STANDARDS CONFORMANCE
      tar: SVID2, SVID3, XPG2, XPG3

"sw" command summaries

"sw" commands - Command summaries related to software distribution.

```
swacl(1M)                   Hewlett-Packard Company              swacl(1M)

NAME
     swacl - View or modify the Access Control Lists (ACLs) which protect
     software products

SYNOPSIS
     swacl -l level [-M acl_entry| -D acl_entry| -F acl_file] [-x
     option=value]
     [-X option_file] [-f software_file] [-t target_file]
     [software_selections] [@ target_selections]




swagentd(1M)                Hewlett-Packard Company            swagentd(1M)
swagent(1M)                                                     swagent(1M)

NAME
     swagentd - Serve local or remote SD software management tasks,
     including invoking a swagent command.

     swagent - Perform SD software management tasks as the agent of an SD
     command.

     SWAGENTD.EXE - Perform HP OpenView Software Distributor PC software
     management tasks, or serve local PC software for distribution. See
     "Remarks:" below.

SYNOPSIS
     swagentd [-k] [-n] [-r] [-x option=value] [-X option_file]

     SWAGENTD.EXE (HP OpenView Software Distributor only)




swcluster(1M)                                                 swcluster(1M)

NAME
     swcluster - install or remove software from diskless server

SYNOPSIS
     swcluster [XToolkit Options] [-v][v] [-i] [-p] [-f] [-r] [-b] [-l
     list_class] [-n] [-s source]
     [-C session_file] [-S session_file] [-x option=value] [-X option_file]
     [software_selections] [@ target_selections]
```

swconfig(1M)   Hewlett-Packard Company   swconfig(1M)

NAME
     swconfig - Configure, unconfigure, or reconfigure installed software

SYNOPSIS

     swconfig [-p] [-v] [-u] [-x option=value] [-X option_file] [-f
     software_file] [-t target_file]
     [-C session_file] [-S session_file] [-Q date] [-J jobid]
     [software_selections] [@ target_selections]

swgettools(1M)   Hewlett-Packard Company   swgettools(1M)

NAME
     swgettools - Utility for retrieving the SD product from new SD media

SYNOPSIS

     swgettools -s <source_media_location> [-t <temp_dir_location>]

swinstall(1M)   Hewlett-Packard Company   swinstall(1M)
swcopy(1M)   swcopy(1M)

NAME
     swinstall - Install and configure software products

     swcopy - Copy software products for subsequent installation or
     distribution

SYNOPSIS

     swinstall [XToolkit Options] [-i] [-p] [-v] [-r] [-s source] [-x
     option=value] [-X option_file]
     [-f software_file] [-t target_file] [-C session_file] [-S session_file]
     [-Q date] [-J jobid]
     [software_selections] [@ target_selections]

     swcopy [XToolkit Options] [-i] [-p] [-v] [-s source] [-x option=value]
     [-X option_file]
     [-f software_file] [-t target_file] [-C session_file] [-S session_file]
     [-Q date] [-J jobid]
     [software_selections] [@ target_selections]

swjob(1M)   Hewlett-Packard Company   swjob(1M)
sd(1M)   sd(1M)

NAME
     swjob - Display job information and remove jobs.

     sd - Interactive interface for creating and monitoring jobs.

     For a description of the HP OpenView Software Distributor objects,

attributes and data formats, see the sd(4) manual page by typing:
        man 4 sd

For an overview of all HP OpenView Software Distributor commands, see
the sd(5) manual page by typing:
        man 5 sd

SYNOPSIS

        swjob [-i] [-u] [-v] [-R] [-a attribute] [-x option=value] [-X
        option_file] [-f jobid_file]
        [-t target_file] [-C session_file] [-S session_file] [jobid(s)] [
        @ target_selections]

        sd [-x option=value] [-X option_file]

swlist(1M)   Hewlett-Packard Company   swlist(1M)

NAME
        swlist - Display information about software products

SYNOPSIS

        swlist [-d|-r] [-l level] [-v] [-a attribute] [-R] [-s source] [-x
        option=value] [-X option_file]
        [-f software_file] [-t target_file] [-C session_file] [-S session_file]
        [software_selections] [@ target_selections]

swmodify(1M)   Hewlett-Packard Company   swmodify(1M)

NAME
        swmodify - Modify software products in a target root or depot

SYNOPSIS

        swmodify [-d|-r] [-p] [-P pathname_file] [-v[v]] [-V] [-u]
        [-s product_specification_file| -a attribute=[value]] [-x option=value]
        [-X option_file]
        [-f software_file] [-C session_file] [-S session_file]
        [software_selections] [@ target_selection]

swpackage(1M)   Hewlett-Packard Company   swpackage(1M)

NAME
        swpackage - Package software products into a target depot or tape

For a description of the Product Specification File used as input to
the swpackage command, see the swpackage(4) manual page by typing:
        man 4 swpackage

SYNOPSIS

        swpackage [-p] [-v[v]] [-V] [-s product_specification_file|directory]

```
[-d directory|device]
[-x option=value] [-X option_file] [-f software_file] [-C session_file]
[-S session_file]
[software_selections] [@ target_selection]
```

swreg(1M)   Hewlett-Packard Company   swreg(1M)

NAME
     swreg - Register or unregister depots and roots

SYNOPSIS

```
swreg -l level [-u] [-v] [-x option=value] [-X option_file] [-f
object_file] [-t target_file]
[-C session_file] [-S session_file] [objects_to_(un)register] [
@ target_selections]
```

swremove(1M)   Hewlett-Packard Company   swremove(1M)

NAME
     swremove - Unconfigure and remove software products

SYNOPSIS

```
swremove [XToolkit Options] [-i] [-p] [-v] [-d|-r] [-x option=value]
[-X option_file] [-f software_file] [-t target_file] [-C session_file]
[-S session_file] [-Q date] [-J jobid] [software_selections] [
@ target_selections]
```

swverify(1M)   Hewlett-Packard Company   swverify(1M)

NAME
     swverify - Verify software products

SYNOPSIS

```
swverify [-v] [-d|-r] [-x option=value] [-X option_file] [-f
software_file] [-t target_file]
[-C session_file] [-S session_file] [-Q date] [-J jobid]
[software_selections] [@ target_selections]
```

CHAPTER 2

The HP-UX File System and Related Commands

Introduction

A thorough understanding of the HP-UX file system is essential to performing system administation. In this chapter, I cover the following topics:

- HP-UX File Types - This section describes the different types of files in HP-UX and using the **file** command to determine the file type.

- File System Layout - You need to know the layout of the file system including important directories and their contents.

- Logical Volume Manager (LVM) - You will probably be using LVM to mananage the data on your system. I provide LVM background in this section.

- Example of Using LVM to Reconfigure Disks - I included an example of a complex disk reconfiguration performed on a real system to show how many LVM commands are used. Although this disk reconfiguration does not apply to your system(s), it is a good example of using LVM commands.

• Some Additional File System Commands.

HP-UX File Types

There are a variety of different file types on an HP-UX system. A file is a means by which information is stored on an HP-UX system. The commands you issue, the applications you use, the data you store, and the devices you access such as printers and keyboard are all contained in files. This is one of the aspects of HP-UX that makes it both simple and complex, simple because you know everything out there is a file, complex because the contents of a file could be anything, ranging from simple data you can read to a device file that is created by your system administrator with a unique set of commands.

Every file on the system has a file name. The operating system takes care of all file system-related tasks; you just need to know the name of the file and how to use it. The file types we will look at are:

• Text Files

• Data Files

• Source Code Files

• Executable Files

• Shell Programs

• Links

• Device Files

Text Files

What could be simpler than a file that contains characters, just like the ones you're now reading in this chapter? These ASCII characters are letters and numerals that represent the work you perform. If, for instance, you use an HP-UX editor to create an electronic mail message or a letter, you are creating a text file in most cases. Here is an example of part of a text file:

```
*                                                          *
  *                                                      *
    *                    HP LaserROM/UX                 *
      *                   README File                  *
        * * * * * * * * * * * * * * * * * * * * * * * * * * * * * * * * * * * * * * * * * * * *


This version of HP LaserROM/UX can only be installed and run
on HP-UX Operating System Release 10.x or better.

The graphical user interface of HP LaserROM/UX requires the X
Window System version 11, Release 5 or later.
```

This text file is easy to read, has no data or other information in it, and can easily be modified.

Data Files

A file that contains data used by one of your applications is a data file. If you use a sophisticated desktop publishing tool such as FrameMaker®

to write a book, you create data files that FrameMaker uses. These data files contain data, which you can usually read, and formatting information, which you can sometimes read but is usually hidden from you. If your HP-UX installation uses a database program, then you may have data files that you can partially read.

Source Code File

A source code file is a text file that contains information related to a programming language such as C, C++, Pascal, Fortran, and so on. When a programmer develops a source code file, they create a file that conforms to the naming convention of the program language being used, such as adding a ".c" to the end of the file if creating a C program.

The following is an example of a C source code file:

```
/* this is K & R sort program */

# include <stdio.h>
# include <stdlib.h>

        int N;
        int v[1000000];        /* v is array to be sorted */
        int left = 0;          /* left pointer */
        int right;
        int swapcount, comparecount = 0;
                               /* count swaps and compares*/

         int i, j, t;
        char print;
        char pr_incr_sorts;



main()


{
    printf("Enter number of numbers to sort : ");
    scanf("%10d", &N);                      /* 10d used for a BIG input */
    printf ("\n");                          /* select type of input to sort */

    printf("Enter rand(1), in-order(2), or reverse order (3)   sort : ");
    scanf("%2d", &type);
    printf ("\n");                          /* select type of input to sort */

    if (type == 3)
            for (i=0; i<N; ++i)     /* random         */
                v[i] = (N - i);

    else if (type == 2)
            for (i=0; i<N; ++i)
                v[i]= (i + 1);              /* in order       */
```

```
else if (type == 1)
        for (i=0; i<N; ++i)
            v[i]=rand();            /* reverse order */
fflush(stdin);
printf("Do you want to see the numbers before sorting (y or n)? : ");
scanf("%c", &print);
printf ("\n");                      /* View unsorted numbers?  */
if (print == 'y')
   {
        printf ("\n");
      for (i=0; i<N; ++i)
        printf("a[%2d]= %2d\n", i, v[i]);
        printf ("\n");
   }


    fflush(stdin);
    printf("Do you want to see the array at each step as it sorts? (y or n)? : ");
    scanf("%c", &pr_incr_sorts);
    printf ("\n");                  /* View incremental sorts?  */


     right = N-1;                    /* right pointer         */

            qsort(v, left, right);




    {

    fflush(stdin);
    printf ("Here is the sorted list of %2d items\n", N);
        printf ("\n");
    for (i=0; i<N; ++i)
        printf ("%2d\n ", v[i]);
        printf ("\n");
        printf ("\n");              /* print sorted list       */
            }
                printf ("number of swaps = %2d\n ", swapcount);
                printf ("number of compares = %2d\n ", comparecount);
   }

/* qsort function */

        void qsort( v, left, right)
                int v[], left, right;
   {
            int i, last;
            if (left > right)
             return;

            swap(v, left, (left + right)/2);
            last = left;
            for (i=left+1; i <= right; i++)
            {
                comparecount = ++comparecount;
                  if (v[i] < v[left])
            swap(v, ++last, i);
            }
            swap(v, left, last);
            qsort(v, left, last-1);
            qsort(v, last+1, right);
            }

            /* swap function  */

            swap(v, i, j)
               int v[], i, j;

               {int temp;
```

```
                    swapcount = swapcount++;
                    temp = v[i];
                    v[i] = v[j];
                    v[j] = temp;


    if (pr_incr_sorts == 'y')
        {
                    printf("Incremental sort of array = ");
            printf ("\n");
            for (i=0;  i<N;  ++i)
                printf("a[%2d]= %2d\n", i, v[i]);
                printf ("\n");
        }
    }
```

Executable Files

Executable files are compiled programs that can be run. You can't read executable files, and you'll typically get a bunch of errors, unreadable characters, and beeps from your HP-UX system when you try to look at one of these. It is also possible you will lose your screen settings and cause other problems.

You don't have to go far in HP-UX to find executable files; they are everywhere. Many of the HP-UX commands you issue are executable files that you can't read. In addition, if you are developing programs on your system, you are creating your own executables.

Here is an example of what you see if you attempt to send an executable to the screen:

```
unknown/etc/ttytyperunknown<@=>|<@=>|:unknown<@=>
callocLINESCOLUMNSunknownPackaged for
argbad aftger%3
parmnumber missing <@=>|<@=>|:
@ @ 3### @@@A:2TTO|>@#<|2X00R
EraseKillOOPS<@=>|<@=>|:
<@=>|<@=>|:
<@=>|<@=>|:<@=>|ATOO<@=>|:<@=>|<@=>|:<@=>|<@=>|:<@=>|<@=>|:
```

Shell Programs

A shell program is both a file you can run to perform a task and a file that you can read. So yes, even though you can run this file because it is executable, you can also read it. I'm going to describe shell programming in more detail in an upcoming chapter.

I consider shell programming to be an important skill for every user to have. I'll spend some time going over the basics of shell programming. Some of the background I'm about to cover relating to file types and permissions is important when it comes to shell programming, so this is important information for you to understand.

Here is an example of part of a shell program from an old startup file:

```
# Check if login script contains non-comment to "VUE"
# If it does, assume it's VUE safe, and set VUESOURCEPROFILE
# to true.

if [ "${SHELL:-}" -a -d "${HOME:-}; then
 case ${SHELL##*/} in
  sh | ksh ) shellprofile="$HOME/.profile" ;;
       csh ) shellprofile="$HOME/.login" ;;
         * ) shellprofile="" ;;

 esac
 if [[ -r "$shellprofile"]] ; then
   [ 'grep -c '^[^#:].*VUE' $shellprofile' !=0 ] &&
     VUERESOURCEPROFILE="true"
 fi
fi

# Place customization code beyond this point.

PATH="$PATH:/usr/local/bin:/usr/sbin:$HOME:."
export PATH

mesg y

umask 022
```

The shell program is text you can read and modify if indeed you have permissions to do so. In addition to programming information, shell programs contain comments indicated by lines beginning with a #.

Links

A link is a pointer to a file stored elsewhere on the system. Instead of having two or more copies of a file on your system, you can link to a file that already exists on your system.

One particularly useful way that links have been used in HP-UX is related to new releases of the operating system. The locations of files sometimes change going from one release to another, and rather than learn all the new locations, there are links produced from the old location to the new one. When you run a command using the old location, the link points to the new location.

Links are also useful for centralizing files. If a set of identical files has to be updated often, it is easier to link to a central file and update it rather than have to update several copies of the file in several different locations.

Device Files

Device files, sometimes called device special files, contain information about the hardware connected to your system. Devices on your system can often be accessed with different device files. A disk, for instance, can be accessed with either a block device file or a character device file. I include extensive coverage of device files in this book.

There are other types of files on your system as well, but for the purposes of getting started with HP-UX, the file types I describe supply sufficient background to get you started.

The file Command

The **file** command is used to determine the file type. This command is useful because the name of a file does not always indicate its file type. The following examples perform a long listing of a file to provide some background information on the file, and then the **file** command is run to show the file type.

Text File

(Described by the **file** command as ascii text.)

```
# ll  .mosaic-global-history
-rw-r--r--  1 201      users      587 Dec 22  1996 .mosaic-global-history
# file  .mosaic-global-history
.mosaic-global-history: ascii text
#
```

Data File

(Described by the file command as data.)

```
# ll Static.dat
-rw-r--r--  1 201      users      235874 Aug 26  1997 Static.dat
# file Static.dat
Static.dat:     data
#
```

Source Code File

(Described by the file command as c program text.)

```
# ll krsort.c
-rwxrwxrwx   1 201        users        3234 Nov 16  1996 krsort.c
# file krsort.c
krsort.c:       c program text
#
```

Executable File

(Described by the file command as shared executable.)

```
# ll krsort
-rwxr-xr-x   1 201        users       34592 Nov 16  1996 krsort
# file krsort
krsort:         PA-RISC1.1 shared executable dynamically linked -not stripped
#
```

Shell Program

(Described by the file command as commands text.)

```
# ll llsum
-rwxrwxrwx   1 root       sys          1267 Feb 23  1997 llsum
# file llsum
llsum:          commands text
#
```

Link

(The link is not referenced by the file command, this is shown as a shared executable dynamically linked. The reference to dynamically linked does not mean that this is a link.)

```
# ll /usr/bin/ar
lr-xr-xr-t   1 root      sys           15 Mar 23  1997 ar -> /usr/ccs/bin/ar
# file /usr/bin/ar
/usr/bin/ar:           s800 shared executable dynamically linked
#
```

Block Device File

(Described by the file command as block special.)

```
# ll /dev/dsk/c0t1d0
brw-r--r--   1 bin      sys          31 0x001000 Apr 17  1997 /dev/dsk/c0t1d0
# file /dev/dsk/c0t1d0
/dev/dsk/c0t1d0:       block special (31/4096)
#
```

Character Device File

(Described by the file command as character special.)

```
# ll /dev/rdsk/c0t1d0
crw-r-----   1 root     sys         188 0x001000 Mar 23  1997 /dev/rdsk/c0t1d0
# file /dev/rdsk/c0t1d0
/dev/rdsk/c0t1d0:      character special (188/4096)
#
```

The HP-UX 11.x File System Layout

The 11.x file system layout is derived from the OSF/1 layout, which is based on the AT&T SVR4 layout. The layout of the file system is directly related to loading software, so I have placed this under installing HP-UX 11.x.

Before I get into the layout of the file system, you should know that there are different types of file systems. This is important to know for several reasons, including the fact that many HP-UX commands allow you to specify the option **-F** followed by the file system type. Some of the commands that support this option are **dcopy**, **fsck**, **mksf**, **mount**, **newfs**, and others. Here is a brief description of five file system types supported by HP-UX:

- Journal File System (JFS) is the HP-UX implementation of the Veritas journaled file system (VxFS), which supports fast file system recovery. With the 10.30 release of HP-UX, JFS has become the default HP-UX file system.

- High Performance File System (HFS) is HP's version of the UNIX File System. This was the most common file system under earlier versions of HP-UX.

- CD-ROM File System (CDFS) is used when you mount a CD-ROM. A CD-ROM is read-only, so you can't write to it.

- Network File System (NFS) is a way of accessing files on other systems on the network from your local system. An NFS mounted file system looks as though it is local to your system, even though it is located on another system. NFS is covered in Chapter 3.

- Loopback File System (LOFS) allows you to have the same file system in multiple places.

You'll be very happy to read that all the file-system-related information in this section applies to both HP 9000 Series 800 and Series 700 systems. This means that you can take the information in this section and apply it to all HP 9000 systems.

HP-UX 11.x File System Layout

Figure 2-1 is a high-level depiction of the HP-UX 11.x file system.

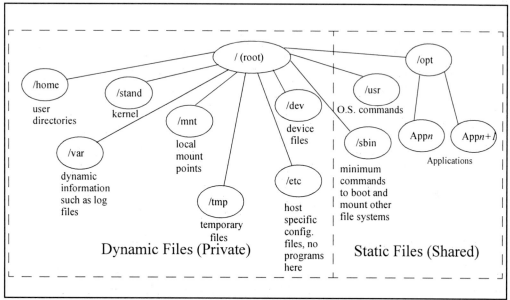

Figure 2-1 HP-UX 11.x File System Layout

Here are some of the more important features of the 11.x file system layout:

- Files and directories are organized by category. The two most obvious categories that appear in Figure 2-1 are static versus dynamic files. Also, other categories exist, such as executable, configuration, and data files. From a system administration perspective, this file system layout is easy to manage. The static files are also labeled "shared" because other hosts on the network may share these. The directories **/usr**, **/sbin**, and **/opt** are shared directories. When **/opt** is shared, the subdirectories of **/opt** should be mounted and not **/opt**. Dynamic files are those that are either host-specific such as configuration files, device files, or kernel files, or those whose contents are dynamic such as logfiles, temporary files, or files in users' home directories. The directories for **/stand**, **/home**, **/tmp**, **/dev**, **/etc**, and   **/var** are dynamic.

- The operating system and applications are kept separate from one another. For those of us who have loaded many applications over the years, we have been practicing this technique because of its benefits. Application vendors don't care where their applications are loaded; that is up to you. But as a system administrator it is highly desirable to keep applications separate from the operating system so you don't inadvertently have application files overwriting operating system files. In addition, if your applications are loaded in a separate area, they are "modular," meaning you can add, remove, and modify them without affecting the operating system or other applications. Applications are kept in the **/opt** directory.

- Intra-system files are kept in a separate area from inter-system, or network accessible, files. As a system administrator, you can now be selective when specifying to what files and directories other systems will have access. **/usr** and **/sbin** are shared operating system directories. No host-specific information is in these two directories. **/etc** is used to hold the host-specific configuration files.

- Executable files are kept separate from system configuration files so that the executables may be shared among hosts. Having the configuration files separate from the programs that use them also means that updates to the operating system won't affect the configuration files.

Here are descriptions of some important 11.x directories:

/	This is the root directory, which is the base of the file system's hierarchical tree structure. A directory is logically viewed as being part of /. Regardless of the disk on which a directory or logical volume is stored, it is logically viewed as a part of the root hierarchy.
/dev	Contains host-specific device files.

/etc   Contains host-specific system and application configuration files. The information in this directory is important to the operation of the system and is of a permanent nature. There are also additional configuration directories below **/etc**. Two **/etc** subdirectories are of particular interest:

/etc/rc.config.d contains configuration *data* files for startup and shutdown programs.

/etc/opt contains host-specific application configuration data.

/export   This is used for diskless file sharing only. Servers export root directories for networked clients.

/home   Users' home directories are located here. Since the data stored in users' home directories will be modified often, you can expect this directory to grow in size, so plan accordingly.

/lost+found   This is the lost files directory. Here you will find files that are in use but are not associated with a directory. These files typically become "lost" as a result of a system crash that caused the link between the physical information on the disk and the logical directory to be severed. The program **fsck**, which is run at the time of boot and interactively by you if you wish, finds these files and places them in the **lost+found** directory. Note: do not remove this directory. Administration functions such as expanding file systems use this directory and can fail if it doesn't exist. If it is accidentally removed, it can be rebuilt using the special **mklost+found** command.

/mnt   This directory is reserved as a mount point for
                        local file systems. You can either mount directly
                        to **/mnt** or have **/mnt** subdirectories as mount
                        points, such as **/mnt1**, **/mnt2**, **/mnt3**, etc.

/net   The name reserved as mount points for remote
                        file systems.

/opt   The directory under which applications are
                        installed. As system administrators, we have
                        always used our best judgment to install applica-
                        tions in a sensible directory. As a rule, application
                        vendors never specified a particular location for
                        their applications to be installed. Now, with **/opt**,
                        we have a standard directory under which appli-
                        cations should be installed. This is an organiza-
                        tional improvement for system administrators,
                        because we can now expect applications to be
                        loaded under **/opt** and the application name.

/sbin   This contains commands and scripts used to boot,
                        shut down, and fix file system mounting prob-
                        lems. **/sbin** is available when a system boots,
                        because it contains commands required to bring
                        up a system.

/stand   This contains kernel configuration and binary
                        files that are required to bring up a system. Three
                        significant files contained in this directory are the
                        system, **vmunix**, and **dlkm** files.

/tmp   This is a free-for-all directory where any user can *temporarily* store files. Because of the loose nature of this directory, it should not be used to store anything important, and users should know that whatever they have stored in **/tmp** can be deleted without notice. In 11.x, application working files should go in **/var/tmp** or **/var/opt/app-name**, not in **/tmp**.

/usr   Most of the HP-UX operating system is contained in **/usr**. Included in this directory are commands, libraries, and documentation. A limited number of subdirectories can appear in **/usr**. Here is a list of some of **/usr** subdirectories:

/usr/bin - Common utilities and applications are stored here.

/usr/ccs - Tools and libraries used to generate C programs are stored here.

/usr/conf - A static directory containing the sharable kernel build environment.

/usr/contrib - The contributed software directory.

/usr/include - This contains header files.

/usr/lib - This contains libraries and machine-dependent databases.

/usr/local - Another contributed software directory.

/usr/newconfig - This contains default operating system data files.

/usr/old - Old files from an operating system update will be stored here.

/usr/sbin - System administration commands are in this directory.

/usr/share - This contains files that are architecture-independent and can be shared.

/usr/share/man - The directory for manual pages.

/var   Holds files that are primarily temporary. Files such as log files, which are frequently deleted and modified, are stored here. Think of this as a directory of "variable" size. Files that an application or command creates at runtime should be placed in this directory including log and spool files. There may, however, be some applications which store static information in **/var**. Be careful if you delete files from this directory in order to free up disk space.

/var/adm - Directory for administrative files, log files, and databases such as kernel crash dumps will be stored here.

/var/adm/crash - Kernel crash dumps will be placed here.

/var/adm/sw - Software Distributor log files, etc.

/usr/var/cron - Log files for **cron**.

/var/mail - Incoming mail messages are kept here.

/var/opt - Application runtime files, such as log files, for applications mounted in **/opt** will be stored in **/var/opt** under the application name.

/var/spool -Spool files are stored here.

Figure 2-2 is an HP CDE file manager window showing the top-level file system with the **/sbin** directory selected.

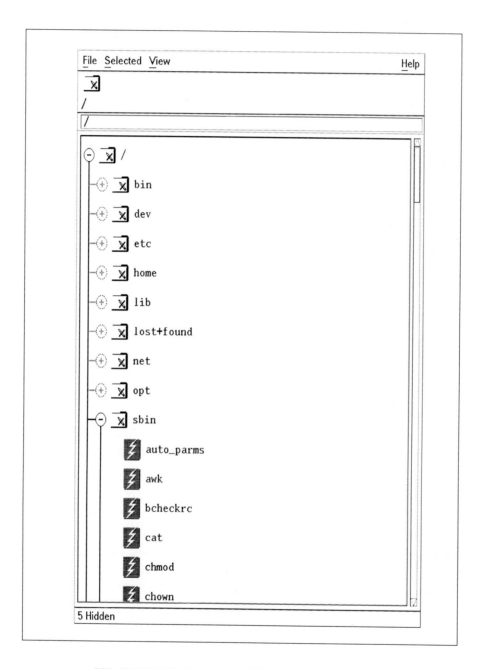

Figure 2-2 HP CDE File Manager Window Showing the HP-UX 11.x File System

Logical Volume Manager Background

Logical Volume Manager is a disk management subsystem that allows you to manage physical disks as logical volumes. This means that a file system can span multiple physical disks. You can view Logical Volume Manager as a flexible way of defining boundaries of disk space that are independent of one another. Not only can you specify the size of a logical volume, but you can also change its size if the need arises. This possibility is a great advancement over dedicating a disk to a file system or having fixed-size partitions on a disk. Logical volumes can hold file systems, raw data, or swap space. You can now specify a logical volume to be any size you wish, have logical volumes that span multiple physical disks, and then change the size of the logical volume if you need!

So what do you need to know in order to set up Logical Volume Manager and realize all these great benefits? First, you need to know the terminology, and second, you need to know Logical Volume Manager commands. As with many other system administration tasks, you can use SAM to set up Logical Volume Manager for you. I recommend that you use SAM to set up Logical Volume Manager on your system(s). But, as usual, I recommend that you read this overview and at least understand the basics of Logical Volume Manager before you use SAM to set up Logical Volume Manager on your system. The SAM chapter (Chapter 3) has an example of using SAM to create logical volumes. After reading this section, you may want to take a quick look at that example.

For use with the journaled file system (JFS), Hewlett-Packard has an add-on product called HP OnLineJFS. This handy product allows you to perform many of the LVM functions without going into single-user mode. For example, when a file system needs to be expanded, the logical volume on which it resides needs to be unmounted before the expansion takes place. Normally, that unmounting would mean shutting the system down into single-user mode so that no user or process could access the volume and it could then be unmounted. With OnLineJFS, the logical volumes and file systems are simply expanded with the system up and running and no interruption to users or processes.

Logical Volume Manager Terms

The following terms are used when working with Logical Volume Manager. They are only some of the terminology associated with Logical Volume Manager, but they are enough for you to get started with Logical Volume Manager. You can work with Logical Volume Manager without knowing all these terms if you use SAM. It is a good idea, however, to read the following brief overview of these terms if you plan to use Logical Volume Manager, so you have some idea of what SAM is doing for you.

Volume
A volume is a device used for file system, swap, or raw data. Without Logical Volume Manager, a volume would be either a disk partition or an entire disk drive.

Physical Volume

A disk that has been not been initialized for use by Logical Volume Manager. An entire disk must be initialized if it is to be used by Logical Volume Manager; that is, you can't initialize only part of a disk for Logical Volume Manager use and the rest for fixed partitioning.

Volume Group
A volume group is a collection of logical volumes that are managed by Logical Volume Manager. You would typically define which disks on your system are going to be used by Logical Volume Manager and then define how you wish to group these into volume groups. Each individual disk may be a volume group, or more than one disk may form a volume group. At this point, you have created a pool of disk space called a *volume group*. A disk can belong to only one volume

group. A volume group may span multiple physical disks.

Logical Volume This is space that is defined within a volume group. A volume group is divided up into logical volumes. This is like a disk partition, which is of a fixed size, but you have the flexibility to change its size. A logical volume is contained within a volume group, but the volume group may span multiple physical disks. You can have a logical volume that is bigger than a single disk.

Physical Extent A set of contiguous disk blocks on a physical volume. If you define a disk to be a physical volume, then the contiguous blocks within that disk form a physical extent. Logical Volume Manager uses the physical extent as the unit for allocating disk space to logical volumes. If you use a small physical extent size such as 1 MByte, then you have a fine granularity for defining logical volumes. If you use a large physical extent size such as 256 MBytes, then you have a coarse granularity for defining logical volumes. The default size is 4 MBytes.

Logical Extents A logical volume is a set of logical extents. Logical extents and physical extents are the same size within a volume group. Although logical and physical extents are the same size, this doesn't mean that two logical extents will map to two contiguous physical extents. It may be that you have two logical extents that end up being mapped to physical extents on different disks!

Figure 2-3 graphically depicts some of the logical volume terms I just covered. In this diagram, you can see clearly that logical extents are not mapped to contiguous physical extents, because some of the physical extents are not used.

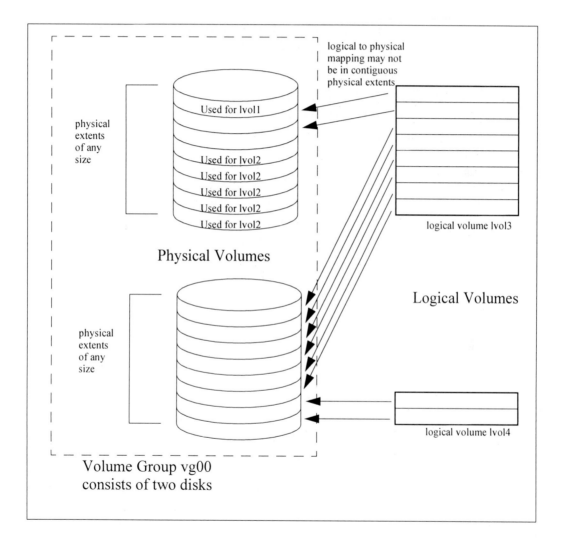

Figure 2-3 Logical Volume Manager Partial Logical to Physical Mapping

Disk Mirroring

Logical volumes can be mirrored one or more times creating an identical image of the logical volume. This means a logical extend can map to more than one physical extent if mirrored.

You may have an environment where you wish to mirror some or all of the logical volumes. SAM can be used to set up disk mirroring for you. You must first, however, decide the characteristics of your mirroring. There is a mirroring policy called "strict." You define one of the following three strict policies when you create the logical volume using the following options:

n   No, this is not a strict allocation policy, meaning that mirrored copies of a logical extent can share the same physical volume. This means that your original data and mirrored data may indeed be on the same physical disk. If you encounter a disk mechanism problem of some type, you may lose both your original and mirrored data.

y   Yes, this is a strict allocation policy, meaning that mirrored copies of a logical extent may not share the same physical volume. This is safer than allowing mirrored copies of data to share the same physical volume. If you have a problem with a disk in this scenario, you are guaranteed that your original data is on a different physical disk from your mirrored data. Original data and mirrored data are always part of the same volume group even if you want them on different physical volumes.

g   Mirrored data will not be on the same physical volume group (PVG) as the original data. This policy is called a PVG-strict allocation policy.

The strict allocation policy depends on your environment. Most installations that employ mirroring buy sufficient disk drives to mirror all data. In an environment such as this, I would create two volume groups, one for the original data and one for the mirrored data, and use the "strict -g" option when creating logical volumes, so that the original data is on one volume group and the mirrored data on the other.

Logical Volume Manager Commands

The following are definitions of some of the more common Logical Volume Commands. Many of these commands are found in the log file that SAM creates when setting up logical volumes for you. I am giving a description of these commands here so that when you see them, you'll have an idea of each command's use. Although these are not all of the Logical Volume Manager commands, these are the ones I use most often and are the commands you should have knowledge of when using Logical Volume Manager. The commands are grouped by physical volume (pv) commands, volume group (vg) commands, and logical volume (lv) commands. These commands are found in the manual pages. Some of the commands such as **vgdisplay**, **pvdisplay**, and **lvdisplay** were issued so that you could see examples of these. The following output of **bdf** will be helpful to you when you view the output of Logical Volume Manager commands that are issued. The output of **bdf** shows several logical volumes mounted (**lvol1**, **lvol3**, **lvol4**, **lvol5**, **lvol6**, **lvol7**, **lvol8**), all of which are in volume group **vg00** (see the **bdf** command overview later in this chapter).

$ bdf

Filesystem	kbytes	used	avail	%used	Mounted on
/dev/vg00/lvol3	47829	18428	24618	43%	/
/dev/vg00/lvol1	67733	24736	36223	41	/stand
/dev/vg00/lvol8	34541	8673	22413	28%	/var
/dev/vg00/lvol7	299157	149449	119792	56%	/usr
/dev/vg00/lvol4	23013	48	20663	0%	/tmp
/dev/vg00/lvol6	99669	32514	57188	36%	/opt
/dev/vg00/lvol5	19861	9	17865	0%	/home
/dev/dsk/c0t6d0	802212	552120	169870	76%	/mnt/9.x

Physical Volume Commands

pvchange   This command is used to change the physical volume in some way. For example, you may wish to allow additional physical extents to be added to the physical volume if they are not permitted, or prohibit additional physical extents from being added to the physical volume if, indeed, they are allowed.

pvcreate   This command is used to create a physical volume that will be part of a volume group. Remember that a volume group may consist of several physical volumes. The physical volumes are the disks on your system.

pvdisplay   This command shows information about the physical volumes you specify. You can get a lot of information about the logical to physical mapping with this command if you use the verbose (**-v**) option. With **-v pvdisplay** will show you the mapping of logical to physical extents for the physical volumes specified.

You get a lot of other useful data from this command, such as the name of the physical volume; the name of the volume group to which the physical volume belongs; the status of the physical volume; the size of physical extents on the physical volume; the total number of physical extents; and the number of free physical extents.

The following is a partial example of running **pvdisplay**:

```
$  pvdisplay -v /dev/dsk/c0t6d0

--- Physical volumes ---
PV Name                 /dev/dsk/c0t1d0
VG Name                 /dev/vg00
PV Status               available
Allocatable             yes
VGDA                    2
Cur LV                  7
PE Size (Mbytes)        4
Total PE                157
Free PE                 8
Allocated PE            149
Stale PE                0

    --- Distribution of physical volume ---
    LV Name             LE of LV      PE for LV
    /dev/vg00/lvol1     12            12
    /dev/vg00/lvol2     17            17
    /dev/vg00/lvol6     75            75
    /dev/vg00/lvol7     9             9
    /dev/vg00/lvol4     25            25
    /dev/vg00/lvol5     6             6
    /dev/vg00/lvol3     5             5
```

```
--- Physical extents ---
PE     Status  LV                      LE
0000 current  /dev/vg00/lvol1         0000
0001 current  /dev/vg00/lvol1         0001
0002 current  /dev/vg00/lvol1         0002
0003 current  /dev/vg00/lvol1         0003
0004 current  /dev/vg00/lvol1         0004
0005 current  /dev/vg00/lvol1         0005
0006 current  /dev/vg00/lvol1         0006
0007 current  /dev/vg00/lvol1         0007
0008 current  /dev/vg00/lvol1         0008
0009 current  /dev/vg00/lvol1         0009
0010 current  /dev/vg00/lvol1         0010
0011 current  /dev/vg00/lvol1         0011
0012 current  /dev/vg00/lvol2         0000
0013 current  /dev/vg00/lvol2         0001
0014 current  /dev/vg00/lvol2         0002
0015 current  /dev/vg00/lvol2         0003
0016 current  /dev/vg00/lvol2         0004
0017 current  /dev/vg00/lvol2         0005
0018 current  /dev/vg00/lvol2         0006
0019 current  /dev/vg00/lvol2         0007
0020 current  /dev/vg00/lvol2         0008
0021 current  /dev/vg00/lvol2         0009
0022 current  /dev/vg00/lvol2         0010
0023 current  /dev/vg00/lvol2         0011
0024 current  /dev/vg00/lvol3         0000
0025 current  /dev/vg00/lvol3         0001
0026 current  /dev/vg00/lvol3         0002
0027 current  /dev/vg00/lvol3         0003
0028 current  /dev/vg00/lvol3         0004
0029 current  /dev/vg00/lvol4         0000
0030 current  /dev/vg00/lvol4         0001
0031 current  /dev/vg00/lvol4         0002
0032 current  /dev/vg00/lvol4         0003
0033 current  /dev/vg00/lvol4         0004
0034 current  /dev/vg00/lvol4         0005
0035 current  /dev/vg00/lvol4         0006



           .
           .
           .
0156 free                             0000
```

From this listing you can see that lvol1, which is roughly 48 MBytes, has many more physical extents assigned to it than lvol3, which is roughly 20 MBytes.

pvmove   You can move physical extents from one physical volume to other physical volumes with this command. By specifying the source physical volume and one or more destination physical volumes, you can spread data around to the physical volumes you wish with this command.

Volume Group Commands

vgcfgbackup   This command is used to save the configuration information for a volume group. Remember that a volume group is made up of one or more physical volumes. SAM automatically runs this command after you make an LVM change.

vgcfgrestore   This command is used to restore the configuration information for a volume group.

vgchange   This command makes a volume group active or inactive. With the **-a** option, you can deactivate (**-a n**) a volume group or activate (**-a y**) a volume group.

vgcreate   You can create a volume group and specify all of its parameters with this command. You specify a volume group name and all of the associated parameters for the volume group when creating it.

vgdisplay   This displays all information related to the vol-
                       ume group if you use the verbose (**-v**) option,
                       including volume group name; the status of the
                       volume group; the maximum, current, and open
                       logical volumes in the volume group; the maxi-
                       mum, current, and active physical volumes in the
                       volume group; and physical extent-related infor-
                       mation.

                       The following is an example of using **vgdisplay**
                       for the volume group vg00:

```
$ vgdisplay /dev/vg00

--- Volume groups ---
VG Name                   /dev/vg00
VG Write Access           read/write
VG Status                 available
Max LV                    255
Cur LV                    7
Open LV                   7
Max PV                    16
Cur PV                    1
Act PV                    1
Max PE per PV             2000
VGDA                      2
PE Size (Mbytes)          4
Total PE                  157
Alloc PE                  149
Free PE                   8
Total PVG                 0
```

vgexport   This command removes a logical volume group
                       from the system but does not modify the logical
                       volume information on the physical volumes.
                       These physical volumes can then be imported to
                       another system using **vgimport.**

vgextend   Physical volumes can be added to a volume group
                       with this command by specifying the physical
                       volume to be added to the volume group.

vgimport   This command can be used to import a physical volume to another system.

vgreduce   The size of a volume group can be reduced with this command by specifying which physical volume(s) to remove from a volume group. Make sure that the physical volume to be removed has no data on it before doing this.

vgremove   A volume group definition can be completely removed from the system with this command.

vgscan   In the event of a catastrophe of some type, you can use this command to scan your system in an effort to rebuild the **/etc/lvmtab** file.

vgsync   There are times when mirrored data in a volume group becomes "stale" or out of date. **vgsync** is used synchronize the physical extents in each mirrored logical volume in the volume group.

Logical Volume Commands

lvcreate   This command is used to create a new logical volume. A logical volume is created within a volume group. A logical volume may span multiple disks but must exist within a volume group. SAM will execute this command for you when you create a logical volume using SAM. Many options exist for this command, and two that you would often use are **-L** to define the size of the logical volume and **-n** to define the name of the logical volume.

lvchange   This command is used to change the logical volume in
                            some way. For example, you may wish to change
                            the permission on a logical volume to read-write
                            (w) or to read (r) with the **-p** option. Or you may
                            want to change the strict policy (described under
                            Disk Mirroring) to strict (y), to not strict (n), or to
                            PVG strict (g).

lvdisplay   This command shows the status and characteris-
                            tics of every logical volume that you specify. If
                            you use the verbose (**-v**) option of this command,
                            you get a lot of useful data in many categories,
                            including:

                            1) Information about the way in which the logical
                            volumes are set up, such as the physical volume
                            on which the logical extents appear; the number
                            of local extents on a physical volume; and the
                            number of physical extents on the physical vol-
                            ume.

                            2) Detailed information for logical extents,
                            including the logical extent number and some
                            information about the physical volume and physi-
                            cal extent for the logical extent.

                            The following is an example of **lvdisplay** for the
                            first of the logical volumes (lvol1) shown in the
                            earlier **bdf** example:

```
$  lvdisplay -v /dev/vg00/lvol1

--- Logical volumes ---
LV Name               /dev/vg00/lvol1
VG Name               /dev/vg00
```

```
LV Permission                read/write
LV Status                    available/syncd
Mirror copies                0
Consistency Recovery         MWC
Schedule                     parallel
LV Size (Mbytes)             48
Current LE                   12
Allocated PE                 12
Stripes                      0
Stripe Size (Kbytes)         0
Bad block                    off
Allocation                   strict/contiguous

   --- Distribution of logical volume ---
   PV Name                LE on PV   PE on PV
   /dev/dsk/c0t1d0        12         12

   --- Logical extents ---
   LE    PV1                  PE1     Status 1
   0000 /dev/dsk/c0t1d0       0000    current
   0001 /dev/dsk/c0t1d0       0001    current
   0002 /dev/dsk/c0t1d0       0002    current
   0003 /dev/dsk/c0t1d0       0003    current
   0004 /dev/dsk/c0t1d0       0004    current
   0005 /dev/dsk/c0t1d0       0005    current
   0006 /dev/dsk/c0t1d0       0006    current
   0007 /dev/dsk/c0t1d0       0007    current
   0008 /dev/dsk/c0t1d0       0008    current
   0009 /dev/dsk/c0t1d0       0009    current
   0010 /dev/dsk/c0t1d0       0010    current
   0011 /dev/dsk/c0t1d0       0011    current
```

Although most of what is shown in this example is self-explanatory, some entries require explanation. The size of the logical volume is 48 MBytes, which consists of 12 Logical Extents (LE) and 12 physical extents (PE). This means that each physical extent is 4 MBytes in size (4 MBytes x 12 extents = 48 MBytes), which we can verify when we display the characteristics of the physical volume in an upcoming example. At the bottom of this listing, you can see the mapping of logical extents onto physical extents. In this case there is a direct mapping takes place between logical extents 0000 - 0011 and physical extents 0000 - 0011.

lvextend   This command is used to increase the number of
                      physical extents allocated to a logical volume. We
                      sometimes underestimate the size required for a
                      logical volume, and with this command you can
                      easily correct this problem. You may want to
                      extend a logical volume to increase the number of
                      mirrored copies (using the **-m** option), to increase
                      the size of the logical volume (using the **-L**
                      option), or to increase the number of logical
                      extents (using the **-l** option).

extendfs   Use this command after **lvextend**. Whereas the
                      lvextend command expands the logical volume,
                      extendfs expands the file system within the logi-
                      cal volume. If you forget to issue the **extendfs**
                      command, the logical volume inside SAM will
                      look expanded, but issuing the **bdf** command will
                      not show the expansion.

lvlnboot   Use this to set up a logical volume to be a root,
                      boot, primary swap, or dump volume (this can be
                      undone with **lvrmboot**). Issuing the **lvlnboot**
                      command with the **-v** option gives the current set-
                      tings.

lvsplit & **lvmerge**

                      These commands are used to split and merge mir-
                      rored logical volumes, respectively. If you have a
                      mirrored logical volume, **lvsplit** will split this into
                      two logical volumes. **lvmerge** merges two logical
                      volumes of the same size, increasing the number
                      of mirrored copies.

lvmmigrate   This command prepares a root file system in a disk partition for migration to a logical volume. You would use this if you had a partition to convert into a logical volume.

lvreduce   Use this to decrease the number of physical extents allocated to a logical volume. When creating logical volumes, we sometimes overestimate the size of the logical volume. This command can be used to set the number of mirrored copies (with the **-m** option), decrease the number of logical extents (with the **-l** option), or decrease the size of the logical volume (with the **-L** option). Be careful when decreasing the size of a logical volume. You may make it smaller than the data in it. If you choose to do this, make sure that you have a good backup of your data.

lvremove   After emptying a logical volume, you can use this command to remove logical volumes from a volume group.

lvrmboot   Use this if you don't want a logical volume to be root, boot, primary swap, or a dump device (this is the converse of the **lvlnboot** command). However, unless you have a disk partition to boot from, don't leave the system without a root or boot device designated with the **lvlnboot** command or else the system won't know where to boot from.

lvsync   There are times when mirrored data in a logical volume becomes "stale" or out of date. **lvsync** is used to synchronize the physical extents in a logical volume.

Reconfiguring Some Disks - An Example of Using Some Logical Volume Commands

I have always advised in my books and articles to take great care when you first set up disks on your HP-UX systems to make sure the disk layout you select is one you can live with for a long time. No matter how careful you are, however, you often need to perform some logical volume reconfiguration. It is much more difficult to make changes to an existing logical volume layout than it is to set up your system right when it is first installed. This section describes the steps performed to make some changes to the dump and mirror on an existing system.

This is not a procedure you should follow. It is an example of some advanced Logical Volume Manager (LVM) commands used to reconfigure some disks on a specific system. It is a good procedure for illustrating how several LVM commands can be used.

Why Change?

Figure 2-4 shows the original configuration of disks on a system and the updated configuration we wish to implement.

The overall objective here is to move the 4 GByte disk used as the mirror of the root disk to a different SCSI channel and to install a 2 GByte dump device on the same SCSI channel as the root disk.

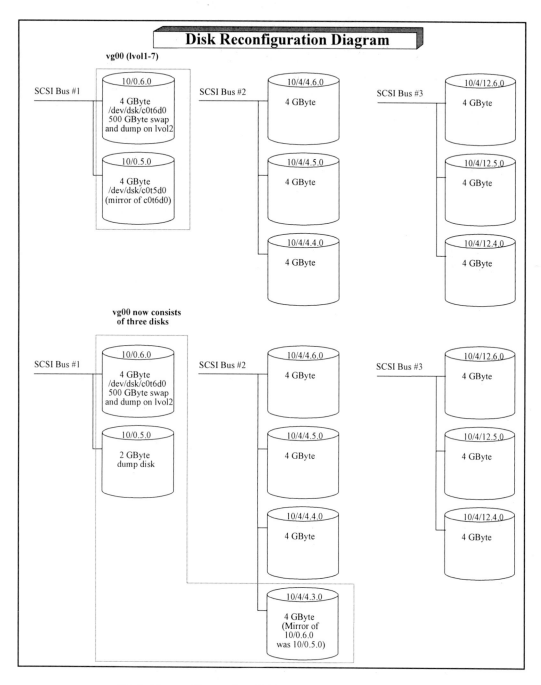

Figure 2-4   Disk Reconfiguration Diagram

The procedure consists of several parts. The first is to obtain a snapshot of the system before any reconfigurations. This serves two purposes. The first is to have documentation of the original system configuration that can be included in the system administration notebook. Should any questions arise in the future as to the original configuration and changes made to it, the original configuration will be in the system administration notebook. The second purpose of having this information is to have all of the relevant information about the configuration available as you proceed with the reconfiguration process.

The second part of the procedure is to shut down the system and install the new 2 GByte disk and move the 4 GByte disk.

The next part of the procedure is to perform the system administration reconfiguration of the dump and mirror.

Figures 2-5, 2-6, and 2-7 show a flowchart showing the procedure we'll follow throughout this section. The step numbers in the upcoming procedure correspond to the step numbers shown in these figures. Let's now proceed beginning with the snapshot of the system.

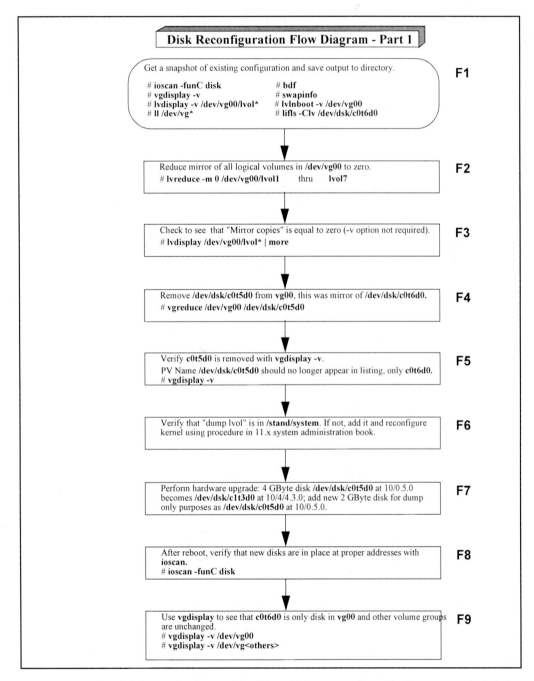

Disk Reconfiguration Flow Diagram - Part 1

Get a snapshot of existing configuration and save output to directory. **F1**

ioscan -funC disk   # bdf
vgdisplay -v   # swapinfo
lvdisplay -v /dev/vg00/lvol*   # lvlnboot -v /dev/vg00
ll /dev/vg*   # lifls -Clv /dev/dsk/c0t6d0

Reduce mirror of all logical volumes in **/dev/vg00** to zero. **F2**
lvreduce -m 0 /dev/vg00/lvol1   thru   lvol7

Check to see that "Mirror copies" is equal to zero (-v option not required). **F3**
lvdisplay /dev/vg00/lvol* | more

Remove **/dev/dsk/c0t5d0** from **vg00**, this was mirror of **/dev/dsk/c0t6d0**. **F4**
vgreduce /dev/vg00 /dev/dsk/c0t5d0

Verify **c0t5d0** is removed with **vgdisplay -v**. **F5**
PV Name **/dev/dsk/c0t5d0** should no longer appear in listing, only **c0t6d0**.
vgdisplay -v

Verify that "dump lvol" is in **/stand/system**. If not, add it and reconfigure **F6**
kernel using procedure in 11.x system administration book.

Perform hardware upgrade: 4 GByte disk **/dev/dsk/c0t5d0** at 10/0.5.0 **F7**
becomes **/dev/dsk/c1t3d0** at 10/4/4.3.0; add new 2 GByte disk for dump
only purposes as **/dev/dsk/c0t5d0** at 10/0.5.0.

After reboot, verify that new disks are in place at proper addresses with **F8**
ioscan.
ioscan -funC disk

Use **vgdisplay** to see that **c0t6d0** is only disk in **vg00** and other volume groups **F9**
are unchanged.
vgdisplay -v /dev/vg00
vgdisplay -v /dev/vg<others>

Figure 2-5 Disk Reconfiguration Flow Diagram - Part 1 (Rearrange Disks)

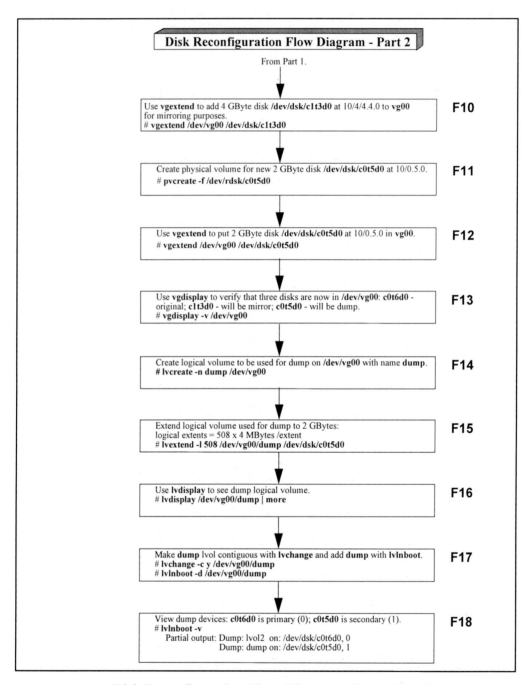

Disk Reconfiguration Flow Diagram - Part 2

From Part 1.

Use **vgextend** to add 4 GByte disk **/dev/dsk/c1t3d0** at 10/4/4.4.0 to **vg00** for mirroring purposes.
vgextend /dev/vg00 /dev/dsk/c1t3d0

F10

Create physical volume for new 2 GByte disk **/dev/dsk/c0t5d0** at 10/0.5.0.
pvcreate -f /dev/rdsk/c0t5d0

F11

Use **vgextend** to put 2 GByte disk **/dev/dsk/c0t5d0** at 10/0.5.0 in **vg00**.
vgextend /dev/vg00 /dev/dsk/c0t5d0

F12

Use **vgdisplay** to verify that three disks are now in **/dev/vg00**: **c0t6d0** - original; **c1t3d0** - will be mirror; **c0t5d0** - will be dump.
vgdisplay -v /dev/vg00

F13

Create logical volume to be used for dump on **/dev/vg00** with name **dump**.
lvcreate -n dump /dev/vg00

F14

Extend logical volume used for dump to 2 GBytes:
logical extents = 508 x 4 MBytes /extent
lvextend -l 508 /dev/vg00/dump /dev/dsk/c0t5d0

F15

Use **lvdisplay** to see dump logical volume.
lvdisplay /dev/vg00/dump | more

F16

Make **dump** lvol contiguous with **lvchange** and add **dump** with **lvlnboot**.
lvchange -c y /dev/vg00/dump
lvlnboot -d /dev/vg00/dump

F17

View dump devices: **c0t6d0** is primary (0); **c0t5d0** is secondary (1).
lvlnboot -v
   Partial output: Dump: lvol2 on: /dev/dsk/c0t6d0, 0
                   Dump: dump on: /dev/dsk/c0t5d0, 1

F18

Figure 2-6   Disk Reconfiguration Flow Diagram - Part 2 (Set Up Dump)

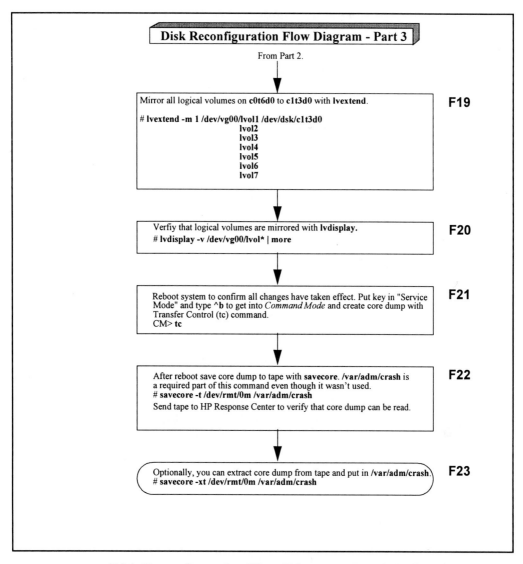

Disk Reconfiguration Flow Diagram - Part 3

From Part 2.

Mirror all logical volumes on **c0t6d0** to **c1t3d0** with **lvextend**.

\# **lvextend -m 1 /dev/vg00/lvol1 /dev/dsk/c1t3d0**
             lvol2
             lvol3
             lvol4
             lvol5
             lvol6
             lvol7

F19

Verfiy that logical volumes are mirrored with **lvdisplay**.
\# **lvdisplay -v /dev/vg00/lvol* | more**

F20

Reboot system to confirm all changes have taken effect. Put key in "Service Mode" and type ^**b** to get into *Command Mode* and create core dump with Transfer Control (tc) command.
CM> **tc**

F21

After reboot save core dump to tape with **savecore**. **/var/adm/crash** is a required part of this command even though it wasn't used.
\# **savecore -t /dev/rmt/0m /var/adm/crash**
Send tape to HP Response Center to verify that core dump can be read.

F22

Optionally, you can extract core dump from tape and put in **/var/adm/crash**.
\# **savecore -xt /dev/rmt/0m /var/adm/crash**

F23

Figure 2-7   Disk Reconfiguration Flow Diagram - Part 3 (Reinstate Mirrors)

F1

First let's run **ioscan** to see the disks on the system.

```
$ /usr/sbin/ioscan -funC disk
```

```
Class      I  H/W Path    Driver      S/W State H/W Type   Description
============================================================================
disk       2  10/0.5.0     sdisk       CLAIMED   DEVICE     SEAGATE ST15150W
                           /dev/dsk/c0t5d0   /dev/rdsk/c0t5d0
disk       3  10/0.6.0     sdisk       CLAIMED   DEVICE     SEAGATE ST15150W
                           /dev/dsk/c0t6d0   /dev/rdsk/c0t6d0
disk       6  10/4/4.4.0   sdisk       CLAIMED   DEVICE     SEAGATE ST15150W
                           /dev/dsk/c1t4d0   /dev/rdsk/c1t4d0
disk       7  10/4/4.5.0   sdisk       CLAIMED   DEVICE     SEAGATE ST15150W
                           /dev/dsk/c1t5d0   /dev/rdsk/c1t5d0
disk       8  10/4/4.6.0   sdisk       CLAIMED   DEVICE     SEAGATE ST15150W
                           /dev/dsk/c1t6d0   /dev/rdsk/c1t6d0
disk       9  10/4/12.4.0  sdisk       CLAIMED   DEVICE     SEAGATE ST15150W
                           /dev/dsk/c2t4d0   /dev/rdsk/c2t4d0
disk      10  10/4/12.5.0  sdisk       CLAIMED   DEVICE     SEAGATE ST15150W
                           /dev/dsk/c2t5d0   /dev/rdsk/c2t5d0
disk      11  10/4/12.6.0  sdisk       CLAIMED   DEVICE     SEAGATE ST15150W
                           /dev/dsk/c2t6d0   /dev/rdsk/c2t6d0
disk       5  10/12/5.2.0  sdisk       CLAIMED   DEVICE     TOSHIBA CD-ROM XM-5401TA
                           /dev/dsk/c3t2d0   /dev/rdsk/c3t2d0
```

Note that the disks in this configuration correspond to those on the top of Figure 2-4. We haven't yet looked at the logical volume information related to these disks, only their physical addresses.

F1

Next run **vgdisplay** to see the volume groups. **lvol2** on **vg00** is the dump logical volume we are going to move to a separate 2 GByte disk. We don't yet know if **lvol1-7** on **vg00** are all mirrored.

```
# vgdisplay -v
 --- Volume groups ---
VG Name                 /dev/vg00
VG Write Access         read/write
VG Status               available
Max LV                  255
Cur LV                  7
Open LV                 7
Max PV                  16
Cur PV                  2
```

```
Act PV                  2
Max PE per PV           1023
VGDA                    4
PE Size (Mbytes)        4
Total PE                2046
Alloc PE                688
Free PE                 1358
Total PVG               0

     --- Logical volumes ---
LV Name                 /dev/vg00/lvol1
LV Status               available/syncd
LV Size (Mbytes)        92
Current LE              23
Allocated PE            46
Used PV                 2

LV Name                 /dev/vg00/lvol2
LV Status               available/syncd
LV Size (Mbytes)        500
Current LE              125
Allocated PE            250
Used PV                 2

LV Name                 /dev/vg00/lvol3
LV Status               available/syncd
LV Size (Mbytes)        20
Current LE              5
Allocated PE            10
Used PV                 2

LV Name                 /dev/vg00/lvol4
LV Status               available/syncd
LV Size (Mbytes)        252
Current LE              63
Allocated PE            126
Used PV                 2

LV Name                 /dev/vg00/lvol5
LV Status               available/syncd
LV Size (Mbytes)        32
Current LE              8
Allocated PE            16
Used PV                 2

LV Name                 /dev/vg00/lvol6
LV Status               available/syncd
LV Size (Mbytes)        320
Current LE              80
Allocated PE            160
Used PV                 2
LV Name                 /dev/vg00/lvol7
LV Status               available/syncd
LV Size (Mbytes)        160
Current LE              40
Allocated PE            80
Used PV                 2

     --- Physical volumes ---
PV Name                 /dev/dsk/c0t6d0
PV Status               available
Total PE                1023
Free PE                 679

PV Name                 /dev/dsk/c0t5d0
PV Status               available
Total PE                1023
Free PE                 679
```

F1

View detailed logical volume information with **lvdisplay**. Note that all of these logical volumes are mirrored and that each has "current" status. Only **lvol1** and **lvol2** are shown in the listing. **lvol3** through **lvol7** are not shown.

```
# lvdisplay -v /dev/vg00/lvol*
 --- Logical volumes ---
LV Name                  /dev/vg00/lvol1
VG Name                  /dev/vg00
LV Permission            read/write
LV Status                available/syncd
Mirror copies            1
Consistency Recovery     MWC
Schedule                 parallel
LV Size (Mbytes)         92
Current LE               23
Allocated PE             46
Stripes                  0
Stripe Size (Kbytes)     0
Bad block                off
Allocation               strict/contiguous

--- Distribution of logical volume ---
PV Name             LE on PV  PE on PV
/dev/dsk/c0t6d0     23          23
/dev/dsk/c0t5d0     23          23


--- Logical extents ---
LE    PV1             PE1    Status 1 PV2             PE2    Status 2
0000 /dev/dsk/c0t6d0  0000  current  /dev/dsk/c0t5d0  0000  current
0001 /dev/dsk/c0t6d0  0001  current  /dev/dsk/c0t5d0  0001  current
0002 /dev/dsk/c0t6d0  0002  current  /dev/dsk/c0t5d0  0002  current
0003 /dev/dsk/c0t6d0  0003  current  /dev/dsk/c0t5d0  0003  current
0004 /dev/dsk/c0t6d0  0004  current  /dev/dsk/c0t5d0  0004  current
0005 /dev/dsk/c0t6d0  0005  current  /dev/dsk/c0t5d0  0005  current
0006 /dev/dsk/c0t6d0  0006  current  /dev/dsk/c0t5d0  0006  current
0007 /dev/dsk/c0t6d0  0007  current  /dev/dsk/c0t5d0  0007  current
0008 /dev/dsk/c0t6d0  0008  current  /dev/dsk/c0t5d0  0008  current
0009 /dev/dsk/c0t6d0  0009  current  /dev/dsk/c0t5d0  0009  current
0010 /dev/dsk/c0t6d0  0010  current  /dev/dsk/c0t5d0  0010  current
0011 /dev/dsk/c0t6d0  0011  current  /dev/dsk/c0t5d0  0011  current
0012 /dev/dsk/c0t6d0  0012  current  /dev/dsk/c0t5d0  0012  current
0013 /dev/dsk/c0t6d0  0013  current  /dev/dsk/c0t5d0  0013  current
0014 /dev/dsk/c0t6d0  0014  current  /dev/dsk/c0t5d0  0014  current
0015 /dev/dsk/c0t6d0  0015  current  /dev/dsk/c0t5d0  0015  current
0016 /dev/dsk/c0t6d0  0016  current  /dev/dsk/c0t5d0  0016  current
0017 /dev/dsk/c0t6d0  0017  current  /dev/dsk/c0t5d0  0017  current
0018 /dev/dsk/c0t6d0  0018  current  /dev/dsk/c0t5d0  0018  current
0019 /dev/dsk/c0t6d0  0019  current  /dev/dsk/c0t5d0  0019  current
0020 /dev/dsk/c0t6d0  0020  current  /dev/dsk/c0t5d0  0020  current
0021 /dev/dsk/c0t6d0  0021  current  /dev/dsk/c0t5d0  0021  current
0022 /dev/dsk/c0t6d0  0022  current  /dev/dsk/c0t5d0  0022  current

LV Name                  /dev/vg00/lvol2
VG Name                  /dev/vg00
LV Permission            read/write
LV Status                available/syncd
Mirror copies            1
Consistency Recovery     MWC
Schedule                 parallel
LV Size (Mbytes)         500
```

```
Current LE              125
Allocated PE            250
Stripes                 0
Stripe Size (Kbytes)    0
Bad block               off
Allocation              strict/contiguous

--- Distribution of logical volume ---

PV Name            LE on PV  PE on PV
/dev/dsk/c0t6d0    125       125
/dev/dsk/c0t5d0    125       125

--- Logical extents ---

LE    PV1                 PE1   Status 1  PV2                 PE2   Status 2

0000  /dev/dsk/c0t6d0     0023  current   /dev/dsk/c0t5d0     0023  current
0001  /dev/dsk/c0t6d0     0024  current   /dev/dsk/c0t5d0     0024  current
0002  /dev/dsk/c0t6d0     0025  current   /dev/dsk/c0t5d0     0025  current
0003  /dev/dsk/c0t6d0     0026  current   /dev/dsk/c0t5d0     0026  current
0004  /dev/dsk/c0t6d0     0027  current   /dev/dsk/c0t5d0     0027  current
0005  /dev/dsk/c0t6d0     0028  current   /dev/dsk/c0t5d0     0028  current
0006  /dev/dsk/c0t6d0     0029  current   /dev/dsk/c0t5d0     0029  current
0007  /dev/dsk/c0t6d0     0030  current   /dev/dsk/c0t5d0     0030  current
0008  /dev/dsk/c0t6d0     0031  current   /dev/dsk/c0t5d0     0031  current
0009  /dev/dsk/c0t6d0     0032  current   /dev/dsk/c0t5d0     0032  current
0010  /dev/dsk/c0t6d0     0033  current   /dev/dsk/c0t5d0     0033  current
0011  /dev/dsk/c0t6d0     0034  current   /dev/dsk/c0t5d0     0034  current
0012  /dev/dsk/c0t6d0     0035  current   /dev/dsk/c0t5d0     0035  current
0013  /dev/dsk/c0t6d0     0036  current   /dev/dsk/c0t5d0     0036  current
                            .
                            .
                            .
0111  /dev/dsk/c0t6d0     0134  current   /dev/dsk/c0t5d0     0134  current
0112  /dev/dsk/c0t6d0     0135  current   /dev/dsk/c0t5d0     0135  current
0113  /dev/dsk/c0t6d0     0136  current   /dev/dsk/c0t5d0     0136  current
0114  /dev/dsk/c0t6d0     0137  current   /dev/dsk/c0t5d0     0137  current
0115  /dev/dsk/c0t6d0     0138  current   /dev/dsk/c0t5d0     0138  current
0116  /dev/dsk/c0t6d0     0139  current   /dev/dsk/c0t5d0     0139  current
0117  /dev/dsk/c0t6d0     0140  current   /dev/dsk/c0t5d0     0140  current
0118  /dev/dsk/c0t6d0     0141  current   /dev/dsk/c0t5d0     0141  current
0119  /dev/dsk/c0t6d0     0142  current   /dev/dsk/c0t5d0     0142  current
0120  /dev/dsk/c0t6d0     0143  current   /dev/dsk/c0t5d0     0143  current
0121  /dev/dsk/c0t6d0     0144  current   /dev/dsk/c0t5d0     0144  current
0122  /dev/dsk/c0t6d0     0145  current   /dev/dsk/c0t5d0     0145  current
0123  /dev/dsk/c0t6d0     0146  current   /dev/dsk/c0t5d0     0146  current
0124  /dev/dsk/c0t6d0     0147  current   /dev/dsk/c0t5d0     0147  current
```

F1

Next, view **/dev/vg00** to have a record of the logical volumes.

```
# ll /dev/vg00

/dev/vg00:
total 0
crw-r--r--  1 root    sys        64 0x000000 May 29 04:44 group
brw-r-----  1 root    sys        64 0x000001 May 29 04:44 lvol1
brw-r-----  1 root    sys        64 0x000002 Jul  9 17:10 lvol2
brw-r-----  1 root    sys        64 0x000003 May 29 04:44 lvol3
brw-r-----  1 root    sys        64 0x000004 May 29 04:44 lvol4
brw-r-----  1 root    sys        64 0x000005 May 29 04:44 lvol5
brw-r-----  1 root    sys        64 0x000006 May 29 04:44 lvol6
brw-r-----  1 root    sys        64 0x000007 May 29 04:44 lvol7
crw-r-----  1 root    sys        64 0x000001 May 29 04:44 rlvol1
```

```
crw-r-----  1 root      sys     64 0x000002 Jul  9 17:10 rlvol2
crw-r-----  1 root      sys     64 0x000003 May 29 04:44 rlvol3
crw-r-----  1 root      sys     64 0x000004 May 29 04:44 rlvol4
crw-r-----  1 root      sys     64 0x000005 May 29 04:44 rlvol5
crw-r-----  1 root      sys     64 0x000006 May 29 04:44 rlvol6
crw-r-----  1 root      sys     64 0x000007 May 29 04:44 rlvol7
```

F1

Next, view **/dev/vg_nw** and any other volume groups.

```
# ll /dev/vg_nw

/dev/vg_nw:
total 0
crw-rw-rw-  1 root      sys     64 0x010000 Jul  9 12:03 group
brw-r-----  1 root      sys     64 0x010003 Jul  9 13:01 lv_nwbackup
brw-r-----  1 root      sys     64 0x010004 Jul  9 13:01 lv_nwlog
brw-r-----  1 root      sys     64 0x010002 Jul  9 12:54 lv_nwsys
brw-r-----  1 root      sys     64 0x010001 Jul  9 12:53 lv_nwtext
crw-r-----  1 root      sys     64 0x010003 Jul  9 13:01 rlv_nwbackup
crw-r-----  1 root      sys     64 0x010004 Jul  9 13:01 rlv_nwlog
crw-r-----  1 root      sys     64 0x010002 Jul  9 12:55 rlv_nwsys
crw-r-----  1 root      sys     64 0x010001 Jul  9 12:54 rlv_nwtext
```

F1

Next, view the file systems with **bdf**. Notice that **lvol2** is not shown because this is a swap and dump device.

```
# bdf
Filesystem                  kbytes     used    avail %used Mounted on
/dev/vg00/lvol1              91669    31889    50613   39% /
/dev/vg00/lvol7             159509    83630    59928   58% /var
/dev/vg00/lvol6             319125   197912    89300   69%
/usr /dev/vg00/lvol5         31829    11323    17323   40% /tmp
/dev/vg00/lvol4             251285    67854   158302   30% /opt
/dev/vg_nw/lv_nwtext       4099465  2070905  1618613   56% /nwtext
/dev/vg_nw/lv_nwsys        4099465  1063909  2625609   29% /nwsys
/dev/vg_nw/lv_nwlog          99669    17313    72389   19% /nwlog
/dev/vg_nw/lv_nwbackup     2552537   377388  1919895   16% /nwbackup
/dev/vg00/lvol3             19861     2191    15683   12% /home
```

F1

Next, run **swapinfo** to see that **lvol2** is the only swap device.

```
# swapinfo
               Kb       Kb       Kb   PCT  START/      Kb
TYPE        AVAIL     USED     FREE  USED  LIMIT RESERVE  PRI  NAME
dev        512000        0   512000   0%      0       -    1  /dev/vg00/lvol2
reserve         -   512000  -512000
memory    1670828  1474704   196124  88%
```

F1

Next, look at the boot information with **lvlnboot**. **lvol2** on **vg00** is the dump device.

```
# lvlnboot -v /dev/vg00
Boot Definitions for Volume Group /dev/vg00:
Physical Volumes belonging in Root Volume Group:
        /dev/dsk/c0t6d0 (10/0.6.0) -- Boot Disk
        /dev/dsk/c0t5d0 (10/0.5.0) -- Boot Disk
Root: lvol1        on: /dev/dsk/c0t6d0
                       /dev/dsk/c0t5d0
Swap: lvol2        on: /dev/dsk/c0t6d0
                       /dev/dsk/c0t5d0
Dump: lvol2        on: /dev/dsk/c0t6d0, 0
```

F1

Look at the boot area with **lifls**.

```
#lifls -Clv /dev/dsk/c0t6d0

volume ISL10 data size 7984 directory size 8 94/11/04 15:46:53
filename   type   start   size   implement  created
===================================================================
ODE       -12960  584    496      0         95/05/19 13:36:50
MAPFILE   -12277 1080     32      0         95/05/19 13:36:50
SYSLIB    -12280 1112    224      0         95/05/19 13:36:50
CONFIGDATA -12278 1336    62      0         95/05/19 13:36:50
SLMOD     -12276 1400     70      0         95/05/19 13:36:50
SLDEV     -12276 1472     68      0         95/05/19 13:36:50
SLDRIVERS -12276 1544    244      0         95/05/19 13:36:50
MAPPER    -12279 1792     93      0         95/05/19 13:36:51
IOTEST    -12279 1888    150      0         95/05/19 13:36:51
PERFVER   -12279 2040     80      0         95/05/19 13:36:51
PVCU      -12801 2120     64      0         95/05/19 13:36:51
SSINFO    -12286 2184      1      0         96/09/16 09:04:01
ISL       -12800 2192    240      0         94/11/04 15:46:53
AUTO      -12289 2432      1      0         94/11/04 15:46:53
HPUX      -12928 2440    800      0         94/11/04 15:46:54
LABEL      BIN   3240      8      0         96/05/29 01:49:55
```

F2

After all the appropriate information has been saved for the existing configuration, we can begin the reconfiguration. First, we break the mirror with **lvreduce** and the **-m** option.

```
# lvreduce -m 0 /dev/vg00/lvol1
Logical volume "/dev/vg00/lvol1" has been successfully reduced.
Volume Group configuration for /dev/vg00 has been saved in /etc/lvmconf/vg00.conf
# lvreduce -m 0 /dev/vg00/lvol2
Logical volume "/dev/vg00/lvol2" has been successfully reduced.
Volume Group configuration for /dev/vg00 has been saved in /etc/lvmconf/vg00.conf
# lvreduce -m 0 /dev/vg00/lvol3
Logical volume "/dev/vg00/lvol3" has been successfully reduced.
Volume Group configuration for /dev/vg00 has been saved in /etc/lvmconf/vg00.conf
# lvreduce -m 0 /dev/vg00/lvol4
Logical volume "/dev/vg00/lvol4" has been successfully reduced.
Volume Group configuration for /dev/vg00 has been saved in /etc/lvmconf/vg00.conf
# lvreduce -m 0 /dev/vg00/lvol5
Logical volume "/dev/vg00/lvol5" has been successfully reduced.
Volume Group configuration for /dev/vg00 has been saved in /etc/lvmconf/vg00.conf
# lvreduce -m 0 /dev/vg00/lvol6
Logical volume "/dev/vg00/lvol6" has been successfully reduced.
Volume Group configuration for /dev/vg00 has been saved in /etc/lvmconf/vg00.conf
# lvreduce -m 0 /dev/vg00/lvol7
Logical volume "/dev/vg00/lvol7" has been successfully reduced.
Volume Group configuration for /dev/vg00 has been saved in /etc/lvmconf/vg00.conf
```

You can type each command or make a file with the **lvreduce** commands in it and run the file. You can call the file **/tmp/reduce** with the following entries:

```
lvreduce -m 0 /dev/vg00/lvol1
lvreduce -m 0 /dev/vg00/lvol2
lvreduce -m 0 /dev/vg00/lvol3
lvreduce -m 0 /dev/vg00/lvol4
lvreduce -m 0 /dev/vg00/lvol5
lvreduce -m 0 /dev/vg00/lvol6
lvreduce -m 0 /dev/vg00/lvol7
```

After you create this file, change it to executable and then run with the following two commands.

```
# chmod 555 /tmp/reduce
# /tmp/reduce
```

You will then see all the output of having run the **lvreduce** commands.

F3

Check to see that mirroring of **lvol1-7** has been reduced with **lvdisplay**. Look to see that mirrored copies are equal to 0. Only **lvol1** through **lvol3** are shown in this listing.

```
# lvdisplay -v /dev/vg00/lvol* | more

--- Logical volumes ---
LV Name                 /dev/vg00/lvol1
VG Name                 /dev/vg00
LV Permission           read/write
LV Status               available/syncd
Mirror copies           0
Consistency Recovery    MWC
Schedule                parallel
LV Size (Mbytes)        92
Current LE              23
Allocated PE            23
Stripes                 0
Stripe Size (Kbytes)    0
Bad block               off
Allocation              strict/contiguous

LV Name                 /dev/vg00/lvol2
VG Name                 /dev/vg00
LV Permission           read/write
LV Status               available/syncd
Mirror copies           0
Consistency Recovery    MWC
Schedule                parallel
LV Size (Mbytes)        500
Current LE              125
Allocated PE            125
Stripes                 0
Stripe Size (Kbytes)    0
Bad block               off
Allocation              strict/contiguous

LV Name                 /dev/vg00/lvol3
VG Name                 /dev/vg00
LV Permission           read/write
LV Status               available/syncd
Mirror copies           0
Consistency Recovery    MWC
Schedule                parallel
LV Size (Mbytes)        20
Current LE              5
Allocated PE            5
Stripes                 0
Stripe Size (Kbytes)    0
Bad block               on
Allocation              strict
```

F4

Now remove **c0t5d0** from **vg00** with **vgreduce**. Since there is no mirroring in place, this approach will work. This disk will be put on a different SCSI controller and again used for mirroring later in the procedure.

```
# vgreduce /dev/vg00 /dev/dsk/c0t5d0
Volume group "/dev/vg00" has been successfully reduced.
Volume Group configuration for /dev/vg00 has been saved in /etc/lvmconf/vg00.conf
```

F5

At this point **c0t5d0** is no longer in **vg00**. Verify that "PV Name" **c0t5d0** is no longer in **vg00** with **vgdisplay**.

```
# vgdisplay -v
```

There should be no **c0t5d0** in **vg00**.

F6

Verify that "dump lvol" is in **/stand/system**. If not, add "dump vol" and reconfigure the kernel. See kernel the rebuild procedure in Chapter 1.

F7

Now the hardware upgrade takes place. The system is shut down, disk drives are added and moved, and the system is rebooted. The 4 GByte disk **/dev/dsk/c0t5d0** becomes **/dev/dsk/c1t3d0** at address 10/4/4.3.0, and a new 2 GByte disk is introduced as 10/0.5.0 with the device name **/dev/dsk/c0t5d0**. The second half of Figure 2-4 depicts this change.

F8

The first activity to perform after the hardware upgrade is to view the new disks with **ioscan**. There is now a 2 GByte disk at 10/0.5.0 and a 4 GByte disk at 10/4/4.3.0.

```
# ioscan -funC disk
Class     I  H/W Path     Driver    S/W State H/W Type  Description
===================================================================
disk      2  10/0.5.0     sdisk       CLAIMED   DEVICE SEAGATE        ST32550W
                          /dev/dsk/c0t5d0    /dev/rdsk/c0t5d0
disk      3  10/0.6.0     sdisk       CLAIMED   DEVICE    SEAGATE ST15150W
                          /dev/dsk/c0t6d0    /dev/rdsk/c0t6d0
disk     12  10/4/4.3.0   disc3       CLAIMED   DEVICE    SEAGATE ST15150W
                          /dev/dsk/c1t3d0       /dev/rdsk/c1t3d0
                          /dev/floppy/c1t3d0    /dev/rfloppy/c1t3d0
disk      6  10/4/4.4.0   disc3       CLAIMED   DEVICE    SEAGATE ST15150W
                          /dev/dsk/c1t4d0       /dev/rdsk/c1t4d0
                          /dev/floppy/c1t4d0    /dev/rfloppy/c1t4d0
disk      7  10/4/4.5.0   disc3       CLAIMED   DEVICE    SEAGATE ST15150W
                          /dev/dsk/c1t5d0       /dev/rdsk/c1t5d0
                          /dev/floppy/c1t5d0    /dev/rfloppy/c1t5d0
disk      8  10/4/4.6.0   disc3       CLAIMED   DEVICE    SEAGATE ST15150W
                          /dev/dsk/c1t6d0       /dev/rdsk/c1t6d0
                          /dev/floppy/c1t6d0    /dev/rfloppy/c1t6d0
disk      9  10/4/12.4.0  disc3       CLAIMED   DEVICE    SEAGATE ST15150W
                          /dev/dsk/c2t4d0       /dev/rdsk/c2t4d0
                          /dev/floppy/c2t4d0    /dev/rfloppy/c2t4d0
disk     10  10/4/12.5.0  disc3       CLAIMED   DEVICE    SEAGATE ST15150W
                          /dev/dsk/c2t5d0       /dev/rdsk/c2t5d0
                          /dev/floppy/c2t5d0    /dev/rfloppy/c2t5d0
disk     11  10/4/12.6.0  disc3       CLAIMED   DEVICE    SEAGATE ST15150W
                          /dev/dsk/c2t6d0       /dev/rdsk/c2t6d0
                          /dev/floppy/c2t6d0    /dev/rfloppy/c2t6d0
disk      5  10/12/5.2.0  sdisk       CLAIMED   DEVICE    TOSHIBA CD-ROM XM-5401TA
                          /dev/dsk/c3t2d0    /dev/rdsk/c3t2d0
```

F9

Now we run **vgdisplay** to see new volume group information. Only **c0t6d0** is in **vg00** and no mirroring is yet configured. The other volume groups have remained the same. Only **lvol1** through **lvol3** are shown.

```
# vgdisplay -v /dev/vg00

--- Volume groups ---
VG Name               /dev/vg00
VG Write Access       read/write
VG Status             available
Max LV                255
```

```
Cur LV                  7
Open LV                 7
Max PV                  16
Cur PV                  1
Act PV                  1
Max PE per PV           1023
VGDA                    2
PE Size (Mbytes)        4
Total PE                1023
Alloc PE                344
Free PE                 679
Total PVG               0

--- Logical volumes ---
LV Name                 /dev/vg00/lvol1
LV Status               available/syncd
LV Size (Mbytes)        92
Current LE              23
Allocated PE            23
Used PV                 1

LV Name                 /dev/vg00/lvol2
LV Status               available/syncd
LV Size (Mbytes)        500
Current LE              125
Allocated PE            125
Used PV                 1

LV Name                 /dev/vg00/lvol3
LV Status               available/syncd
LV Size (Mbytes)        20
Current LE              5
Allocated PE            5
Used PV                 1
```

(F9 continued)

Only the first three logical volumes in **/dev/vg_nw** are shown.

```
# vgdisplay -v /dev/vg_nw
VG Name                 /dev/vg_nw
VG Write Access         read/write
VG Status               available
Max LV                  255
Cur LV                  4
Open LV                 4
Max PV                  16
Cur PV                  6
Act PV                  6
Max PE per PV           1023
VGDA                    12
PE Size (Mbytes)        4
Total PE                6138
Alloc PE                5416
Free PE                 722
Total PVG               2
   --- Logical volumes ---
LV Name                 /dev/vg_nw/lv_nwtext
LV Status               available/syncd
LV Size (Mbytes)        4092
Current LE              1023
Allocated PE            2046
Used PV                 2

LV Name                 /dev/vg_nw/lv_nwsys
```

```
LV Status                available/syncd
LV Size (Mbytes)         4092
Current LE               1023
Allocated PE             2046
Used PV                  2

LV Name                  /dev/vg_nw/lv_nwbackup
LV Status                available/syncd
LV Size (Mbytes)         2548
Current LE               637
Allocated PE             1274
Used PV                  2
```

F10

Use **vgextend** to add the 4 GByte disk to **vg00** for mirroring (you may also have to run **pvcreate** here, too).

```
# vgextend /dev/vg00 /dev/dsk/c1t3d0
Volume group "/dev/vg00" has been successfully extended. Volume Group configuration for
/dev/vg00 has been saved in /etc/lvmconf/vg00.conf
```

F11

Now we can create the new 2 GByte disk and add it to **vg00** using the two following commands: **pvcreate** (F11) to create the physical volume and **vgextend** (F12) to extend the volume group.

```
# pvcreate -f /dev/rdsk/c0t5d0
Physical volume "/dev/rdsk/c0t5d0" has been successfully created.
```

F12

```
# vgextend /dev/vg00 /dev/dsk/c0t5d0
Volume group "/dev/vg00" has been successfully extended.
Volume Group configuration for /dev/vg00 has been saved in /etc/lvmconf/vg00.conf
```

F13

We can check to see that these two disks have indeed been added to **vg00** with **vgdisplay**. Only **lvol1** through **lvol3** are shown. The end of the display is the significant part of the listing showing three physical volumes.

```
# vgdisplay -v /dev/vg00

 --- Volume groups ---
VG Name                  /dev/vg00
VG Write Access          read/write
VG Status                available
Max LV                   255
Cur LV                   7
Open LV                  7
Max PV                   16
Cur PV                   3
Act PV                   3
Max PE per PV            1023
VGDA                     6
PE Size (Mbytes)         4
Total PE                 2554
Alloc PE                 344
Free PE                  2210
Total PVG                0

--- Logical volumes ---

LV Name                  /dev/vg00/lvol1
LV Status                available/syncd
LV Size (Mbytes)         92
Current LE               23
Allocated PE             23
Used PV                  1

LV Name                  /dev/vg00/lvol2
LV Status                available/syncd
LV Size (Mbytes)         500
Current LE               125
Allocated PE             125
Used PV                  1

LV Name                  /dev/vg00/lvol3
LV Status                available/syncd
LV Size (Mbytes)         20
Current LE               5
Allocated PE             5
Used PV                  1

                    .
                    .
                    .

--- Physical volumes ---

PV Name                  /dev/dsk/c0t6d0
PV Status                available
Total PE                 1023
Free PE                  679

PV Name                  /dev/dsk/c1t3d0
```

```
PV Status              available
Total PE               1023
Free PE                1023

PV Name                /dev/dsk/c0t5d0
PV Status              available
Total PE               508
Free PE                508
```

F14

We can now create the dump logical volume in **vg00** with **lvcreate** (F14), extend it to 2 GBytes with **lvextend** (F15), and view it with **lvdisplay** (F16).

```
# lvcreate -n dump  /dev/vg00
Logical volume "/dev/vg00/dump" has been successfully created with character device
"/dev/vg00/rdump".
Volume Group configuration for /dev/vg00 has been saved in /etc/lvmconf/vg00.conf
```

F15

```
# lvextend -l 508 /dev/vg00/dump /dev/dsk/c0t5d0
Logical volume "/dev/vg00/dump" has been successfully extended.
Volume Group configuration for /dev/vg00 has been saved in /etc/lvmconf/vg00.conf
```

F16

```
# lvdisplay /dev/vg00/dump | more

--- Logical volumes ---
LV Name                /dev/vg00/dump
VG Name                /dev/vg00
LV Permission          read/write
LV Status              available/syncd
Mirror copies          0
Consistency Recovery   MWC
Schedule               parallel
LV Size (Mbytes)       2032
Current LE             508
Allocated PE           508
Stripes                0
Stripe Size (Kbytes)   0
Bad block              on
Allocation             strict


--- Distribution of logical volume ---
PV Name              LE on PV   PE on PV
```

```
/dev/dsk/c0t5d0     508        508
                     .
                     .
                     .
```

F17

In order to make **/dev/vg00/dump** the dump device, we must first make it contiguous with **lvchange** and then make it a dump device with **lvl-nboot**.

```
# lvchange -C y /dev/vg00/dump
```

```
# lvlnboot -d /dev/vg00/dump
```

F18

View dump devices.

```
# lvlnboot -v | more
Boot Definitions for Volume Group /dev/vg00:
Physical Volumes belonging in Root Volume Group:
            /dev/dsk/c0t6d0 (10/0.6.0) -- Boot Disk
            /dev/dsk/c1t3d0 (10/4/4.3.0) -- Boot Disk
            /dev/dsk/c0t5d0 (10/0.5.0)
Root: lvol1      on:      /dev/dsk/c0t6d0
Swap: lvol2      on:      /dev/dsk/c0t6d0
Dump: lvol2      on:      /dev/dsk/c0t6d0, 0
Dump: dump       on:      /dev/dsk/c0t5d0, 1
```

This may not be what we want. The primary dump device, as indicated by the "0" is **/dev/dsk/c0t6d0** and the secondary dump device, indicated by the "1," is **/dev/dsk/c0t5d0**. We can optionally redo this. Let's proceed with mirroring the lvols on **/dev/vg00** and come back to dump devices.

F19

Let's now extend all the volumes in **vg00** for one mirror using **lvextend**.

```
# lvextend -m 1 /dev/vg00/lvol1 /dev/dsk/c1t3d0
The newly allocated mirrors are now being synchronized.
This operation will take some time. Please wait ....
Logical volume "/dev/vg00/lvol1" has been successfully extended.
Volume Group configuration for /dev/vg00 has been saved in /etc/lvmconf/vg00.conf
```

Put the following in **/tmp/mirror** and run. **lvol1** was extended earlier; **lvol2** is swap and doesn't need to be extended:

```
lvextend -m 1 /dev/vg00/lvol3 /dev/dsk/c1t3d0
lvextend -m 1 /dev/vg00/lvol4 /dev/dsk/c1t3d0
lvextend -m 1 /dev/vg00/lvol5 /dev/dsk/c1t3d0
lvextend -m 1 /dev/vg00/lvol6 /dev/dsk/c1t3d0
lvextend -m 1 /dev/vg00/lvol7 /dev/dsk/c1t3d0

The newly allocated mirrors are now being synchronized.
This operation will take some time.
Please wait .... Logical volume "/dev/vg00/lvol2" has been successfully extended.
Volume Group configuration for /dev/vg00 has been saved in /etc/lvmconf/vg00.conf
                    .
                    .
                    .
```

F20

Let's now verify that the mirroring is in place with **lvdisplay** (only **lvol1** and **lvol2** are shown).

```
# lvdsisplay -v /dev/vg00/lvol* | more

--- Logical volumes ---
LV Name                 /dev/vg00/lvol1
VG Name                 /dev/vg00
LV Permission           read/write
LV Status               available/syncd
Mirror copies           1
Consistency Recovery    MWC
Schedule                parallel
LV Size (Mbytes)        92
Current LE              23
Allocated PE            46
Stripes                 0
Stripe Size (Kbytes)    0
Bad block               off
Allocation              strict/contiguous

--- Distribution of logical volume ---
PV Name             LE on PV   PE on PV
/dev/dsk/c0t6d0     23         23
/dev/dsk/c1t3d0     23         23
```

```
--- Logical extents ---
LE    PV1                    PE1  Status 1 PV2              PE2   Status 2
0000 /dev/dsk/c0t6d0         0000 current  /dev/dsk/c1t3d0  0000 current
0001 /dev/dsk/c0t6d0         0001 current  /dev/dsk/c1t3d0  0001 current
0002 /dev/dsk/c0t6d0         0002 current  /dev/dsk/c1t3d0  0002 current
0003 /dev/dsk/c0t6d0         0003 current  /dev/dsk/c1t3d0  0003 current
                               .
                               .
                               .
```

You can see from this listing that **c0t6d0** is mirrored on **c1t3d0**.

F21

Reboot the system to confirm that all changes have taken effect.

After reboot, do the following to create a dump. The key must be in the "Service" position for **^b** to work (you must be on a server for this to work).

Use **^b** to get the **CM>** prompt.

Use the **tc** command at the **CM>** prompt to create core dump

---

F22

The system will automatically reboot after a core dump. Use the following command to save the core dump to tape. The **/var/adm/crash** file name is required even though the core dump is in the dump logical volume and not in the **/var/adm/crash** directory.

```
# savecore -t /dev/rmt/0m /var/adm/crash
```

F23

Then use **savecore -xt** and the directory name to the extract core dump. If you do not have room for the core dump, or you want a more thorough check, you can place a call and ask the HP Response Center to verify the **savecore** to tape has worked.

```
# savecore -xt /dev/rmt/0m /var/adm/crash
```

The core dump space requirement is calculated from the end of dump back toward the front. For this reason about roughly 1.5 GBytes is written to the **dump** logical volume and then roughly 600 MBytes are written to **lvol2**.

Optional Procedure to Exchange Dump Priorities

This procedure removes all boot definitions, including swap and dump, from **/dev/vg00** with **lvrmboot** and replaces them with **lvlnboot**. This needs to be done because **lvol2** is the primary dump logical volume (0) and dump is the secondary dump logical volume (1).

You must reboot in order for these changes to take effect. Figure 2-8 shows the steps required to complete this optional procedure.

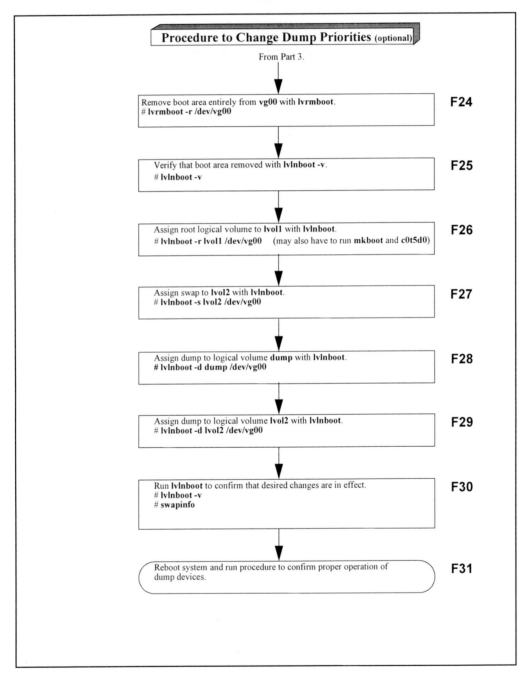

Procedure to Change Dump Priorities (optional)

From Part 3.

Remove boot area entirely from **vg00** with **lvrmboot**.
\# **lvrmboot -r /dev/vg00**   **F24**

Verify that boot area removed with **lvlnboot -v**.
\# **lvlnboot -v**   **F25**

Assign root logical volume to **lvol1** with **lvlnboot**.
\# **lvlnboot -r lvol1 /dev/vg00**   (may also have to run **mkboot** and **c0t5d0**)   **F26**

Assign swap to **lvol2** with **lvlnboot**.
\# **lvlnboot -s lvol2 /dev/vg00**   **F27**

Assign dump to logical volume **dump** with **lvlnboot**.
\# **lvlnboot -d dump /dev/vg00**   **F28**

Assign dump to logical volume **lvol2** with **lvlnboot**.
\# **lvlnboot -d lvol2 /dev/vg00**   **F29**

Run **lvlnboot** to confirm that desired changes are in effect.
\# **lvlnboot -v**
\# **swapinfo**   **F30**

Reboot system and run procedure to confirm proper operation of
dump devices.   **F31**

Figure 2-8 Procedure to Change Dump Priorities (Optional)

F24

Remove the boot area entirely from **vg00** with **lvrmboot**.

```
# lvrmboot -r /dev/vg00
```

F25

Verify that the boot area was removed with **lvlnboot.**

```
# lvlnboot -v
Boot Definitions for Volume Group /dev/vg00: The Boot Data Area is empty.
```

F26

Assign the root logical volume to **lvol1** on **/dev/vg00** with **lvlnboot**.

```
# lvlnboot -r lvol1 /dev/vg00
```

F27

Assign the swap to **lvol2** on **/dev/vg00**.

```
# lvlnboot -s lvol2 /dev/vg00

# swapinfo
           Kb       Kb       Kb    PCT   START/      Kb
TYPE     AVAIL    USED     FREE   USED   LIMIT RESERVE  PRI  NAME
dev     512000       0   512000    0%       0       -    1  /dev/vg00/lvol2
reserve      -   23144   -23144
memory 1671008   27324  1643684    2%
```

F28

Assign the dump to the logical volume **dump** on **/dev/vg00**.

```
# lvlnboot -d dump /dev/vg00
```

F29

Assign the secondary dump device as **lvol2** (primary swap) on **lvol2**.

```
# lvlnboot -d lvol2 /dev/vg00
```

F30

Run **lvlnboot** to confirm that the dump and swap are properly configured with priority "0" on 2 GByte disk **c0t5d0** and "1" on **c0t6d0**.

```
# lvlnboot -v       # after adding lvol2 as secondary dump

Boot Definitions for Volume Group /dev/vg00:
Physical Volumes belonging in Root Volume Group:
                  /dev/dsk/c0t6d0 (10/0.6.0) -- Boot Disk
                  /dev/dsk/c1t3d0 (10/4/4.3.0) -- Boot Disk
                  /dev/dsk/c0t5d0 (10/0.5.0)
Root: lvol1       on:    /dev/dsk/c0t6d0
                         /dev/dsk/c1t3d0
Swap: lvol2       on:    /dev/dsk/c0t6d0
                         /dev/dsk/c1t3d0
Dump: dump        on:    /dev/dsk/c0t5d0, 0
Dump: dump        on:    /dev/dsk/c0t6d0, 1
```

F31

Reboot the system and run steps 21-23 to confirm proper operation of
dump devices.

Although this procedure to reconfigure disks is for a specific system,
it is useful for illustrating the many LVM commands required to perform
such tasks. LVM, and disk management in general, are the areas I find consumes the most system administration time in mature HP-UX installations.
There are many commands used in this procedure for which there is no
way to "back out," so use caution whenever using LVM commands.

Some Additional File System-Related Commands

Viewing File Systems with bdf

You can manually view the file systems you have mounted with the **bdf** command. **bdf** provides the following output:

File system	Block device file system name. In the following example, several logical volumes are shown.
KBytes	Number of KBytes of total disk space on the file system.
used	The number of used KBytes on the file system.
avail	The number of available KBytes on the file system.
%used	The percentage of total available disk space that is used on the file system.
Mounted on	The directory name on which the file system is mounted.
iused	Number of inodes in use (only if you use the **-i** option with **bdf**).
ifree	Number of free inodes (only if you use the **-i** option with **bdf**).
%iuse	Percent of inodes in use (only if you use the **-i** option with **bdf**).

Here is an example of **bdf** that is also in "Logical Volume Manager Background," covered earlier in this chapter:

$ /usr/bin/bdf

File system	kbytes	used	avail	%used	Mounted on
/dev/vg00/lvol3	47829	18428	24618	43%	/
/dev/vg00/lvol1	67733	24736	36223	41%	/stand
/dev/vg00/lvol8	34541	8673	22413	28%	/var
/dev/vg00/lvol7	299157	149449	119792	56%	/usr
/dev/vg00/lvol4	23013	48	20663	0%	/tmp
/dev/vg00/lvol6	99669	32514	57188	36%	/opt
/dev/vg00/lvol5	19861	9	17865	0%	/home
/dev/dsk/c0t6d0	802212	552120	169870	76%	/mnt/9.x

File System Maintenance with fsck

fsck is a program used for file system maintenance on HP-UX systems. **fsck** checks file system consistency and can make many "life-saving" repairs to a corrupt file system. **fsck** can be run with several options, including the following:

-F   This option allows you to specify the file system type (see the explanation of file system types earlier in this chapter). If you do not specify a file system type, then the **/etc/fstab** file will be used to determine the file system type. See the **fstab** description later in this section.

-m   This is a sanity check of the file system. If you run this, you'll be told whether your file system is okay or not. I did the following to check lvol5, which is mounted as **/home**:

```
$ umount /home
$ fsck -m /dev/vg00/lvol5
```

```
vxfs fsck: sanity check: /dev/vg00/lvol5 OK
```

-y   **fsck** will ask questions if run in interactive mode, which is the default. Using the **-y** option causes a "yes" response to all questions asked by **fsck**. Don't use this! If you have a serious problem with your file system, data will probably have to be removed, and the **-y** indicates that the response to every question, including removing data, will be yes.

-n   The response to all questions asked by **fsck** will be "no." Don't use this, either. If your file system is in bad shape, you may have to respond "yes" to some questions in order to repair the file system. All "no" responses will not do the job.

Since your system runs **fsck** on any file systems that were not marked as clean at the time you shut down the system, you can rest assured that when your system boots, any disks that were not properly shut down will be checked. It is a good idea to run **fsck** interactively on a periodic basis just so you can see firsthand that all of your file systems are in good working order.

Should **fsck** find a problem with a directory or file, it would place these in the **lost+found** directory, which is at the top level of each file system. If a file or directory appears in **lost+found,** you may be able to identify the file or directory by examining it and move it back to its original location. You can use the **file**, **what**, and **strings** commands on a file to obtain more information about a file to help identify its origin.

How are file system problems created? The most common cause for a file system problem is improper shutdown of the system. The information written to file systems is first written to a buffer cache in memory. It is later written to the disk with the **sync** command by unmounting the disk, or through the normal use of filling the buffer and writing it to the disk. If you walk up to a system and shut off the power, you will surely end up with a file system problem. Data in the buffer that was not synced to the disk will be lost. The file system will not be marked as properly shut down, and **fsck** will be run when the system boots. A sudden loss of power can also cause an improper system shutdown.

Proper shutdown of the system is described in this chapter. Although **fsck** is a useful utility that has been known to work miracles on occasion, you don't want to take any unnecessary risks with your file systems. So be sure to properly shut down your system.

The **/etc/fstab** file mentioned earlier is used by **fsck** to determine the sequence of the file system check if it is required at the time of boot. The sequence of entries in **/etc/fstab** is important if a "pass number" for any of the entries does not exist. Here is an example of the **/etc/fstab** file:

```
# System /etc/fstab file. Static information about the file
# systems. See fstab(4) and sam(1m) for further details.

/dev/vg00/lvol3     /             vxfs    delaylog    0    1
/dev/vg00/lvol1     /stand        hfs     defaults    0    1
/dev/vg00/lvol4     /tmp          vxfs    delaylog    0    2
/dev/vg00/lvol6     /opt          vxfs    delaylog    0    2
/dev/vg00/lvol5     /home         vxfs    delaylog    0    2
/dev/vg00/lvol7     /usr          vxfs    delaylog    0    2
/dev/vg00/lvol8     /var          vxfs    delaylog    0    2
/dev/dsk/c0tt6d0    /tmp/mnt9.x   hfs     rw, suid    0    2

       |             |            |          |        |    |

       v             v            v          v        v    v
```

device special file	directory	type	options	backup frequency	pass #

device special file

    This is the device block file, such as **/dev/vg00/lvol1** in the example.

directory

    The name of the directory under which the device special file is mounted.

type

    Can be one of several types including:
cdfs (local CD-ROM file system)

hfs (high performance local file system)
nfs (network file system)
vxfs (journaled file system)
swap
swapfs

options   Several options are available, including those
                       shown in the example. rw is read and write; ro is
                       read only.

backup frequency

                       To be used by backup utilities in the future.

pass #   Used by **fsck** to determine the order in which file
                       system checks (**fsck**) will take place.

comment   Anything you want, as long as it's preceded by a
                       #.

Initialize with mediainit

A command you probably won't use, but should be aware of, is **mediainit**.
When you use SAM to set up disks for you, the **mediainit** command may
be run.

Here are some of the options of **mediainit**:

-v   This is the verbose option. **mediainit** normally
                       just prints error messages to the screen. You can
                       get continuous feedback on what **mediainit** is
                       doing with the **-v** option.

-i interleave   This allows you to specify the interleave factor,
                       which is the relationship between sequential logi-
                       cal and physical records. **mediainit** will provide
                       this if one is not specified.

-f format   The format option allows you to specify format
                       options for devices, such as floppy disks, that sup-
                       port different format options. This is not required
                       for hard disks.

pathname   This is the character device file to be used for
                       mediainit.

newfs is used to create a new file system. **newfs** calls the **mksf** command earlier covered. **newfs** builds a file system of the type you specify
(this is one of the commands that uses the **-F** option, so you can specify the
file system type).

Manual Pages for Commands Used in Chapter 2

The following section contains copies of the manual pages of commands used in Chapter 2. This makes for a quick reference for you of commands commonly used throughout your system administration day. The manual pages, more commonly referred to as man pages, are listed in detail with the exception of the LVM commands. Since I strongly encourage you to use SAM to make any LVM alterations, I am giving a synopsis of these commands only. They are listed under "vg command summaries," "lv command summaries," and "pv command summaries."

bdf

bdf - Produce a report of free disk blocks.

---

bdf(1M)   bdf(1M)

NAME
     bdf - report number of free disk blocks (Berkeley version)

SYNOPSIS

     /usr/bin/bdf [-b] [-i] [-l] [-t type | [filesystem|file] ...]

DESCRIPTION
     The bdf command displays the amount of free disk space available
     either on the specified filesystem (/dev/dsk/c0d0s0, for example) or
     on the file system in which the specified file (such as $HOME), is
     contained. If no file system is specified, the free space on all of
     the normally mounted file systems is printed. The reported numbers
     are in kilobytes.

     Options
     The bdf command recognizes the following options:

          -b   Display information regarding file system
                          swapping.

          -i   Report the number of used and free inodes.

          -l   Display information for local file systems only
                          (for example, HFS and CDFS file systems).

          -t type   Report on the file systems of a given type (for
                          example, nfs or hfs).

RETURN VALUE
     The bdf command returns 0 on success (able to get status on all file
     systems), or returns 1 on failure (unable to get status on one or more
     file systems).

WARNINGS
     If file system names are too long, the output for a given entry is
     displayed on two lines.

     The bdf command does not account for any disk space reserved for swap
     space, or used for the HFS boot block (8 KB, 1 per file system), HFS
     superblocks (8 KB each, 1 per disk cylinder), HFS cylinder group
     blocks (1 KB - 8 KB each, 1 per cylinder group), and inodes (currently
     128 bytes reserved for each inode). Non-HFS file systems may have
     other items not accounted for by this command.

AUTHOR
     bdf was developed by the University of California, Berkeley.

FILES
     /etc/fstab   Static information about the file systems.
     /etc/mnttab   Mounted file system table.

```
        /dev/dsk/*          File system devices.
```

SEE ALSO
        df(1M), fstab(4), mnttab(4).

fsck

fsck - File system check and repair (this is generic man page, there is also a man page for hfs and vxfs.)

---

fsck(1M)   fsck(1M)

NAME
     fsck (generic) - file system consistency check and interactive repair

SYNOPSIS

     /usr/sbin/fsck [-F FSType] [-m] [-V] [special]

     /usr/sbin/fsck [-F FSType] [-o FSspecific-options] [-V] [special ...]

DESCRIPTION
     The fsck command audits and interactively repairs inconsistent
     conditions for HP-UX file systems on mass storage device files
     identified by special. If the file system is consistent, the number
     of files on that file system and the number of used and free blocks
     are reported. If the file system is inconsistent, fsck provides a
     mechanism to fix these inconsistencies, depending on which form of the
     fsck command is used.

     special represents a special device (e.g., /dev/rdsk/c1d0s8).

   Options
     fsck recognizes the following options:

        -F FStype   Specify the file system type on which to operate
                         (see fstyp(1M) and fs_wrapper(5)). If this option
                         is not included on the command line, then the file
                         system type is determined from the file /etc/fstab
                         by matching special with an entry in that file.
                         If there is no entry in /etc/fstab, then the file
                         system type is determined from the file
                         /etc/default/fs.

        -m   Perform a sanity check only. fsck will return 0 if
                         the file system is suitable for mounting. If the
                         file system needs additional checking, the return
                         code is 32. If the file system is mounted, the
                         return code is 33. Error codes larger than 33
                         indicate that the file system is badly damaged.

        -o FSspecific-options
                         Specify options specific to each file system type.
                         FSspecific-options is a list of suboptions and/or
                         keyword/attribute pairs intended for a file-
                         system-specific version of the command. See the
                         file-system-specific manual entries for a
                         description of the specific_options supported, if
                         any.

        -V   Echo the completed command line, but perform no
                         other action. The command line is generated by
                         incorporating the user-specified options and other
                         information derived from /etc/fstab. This option

allows the user to verify the command line.

RETURN VALUES
     The following values are returned by the -m option to fsck:

          0   Either no errors were detected or all errors were corrected.

          32   The file system needs additional checking.

          33   The file system is mounted.

     Return values greater that 33 indicate that file system is badly
     corrupted. File system specific versions of fsck will have their own
     additional return values (see fsck_FSType(1M)).

WARNINGS
     This command may not be supported for all file system types.

FILES
     /etc/default/fs   Specifies the default file system type
     /etc/fstab   Default list of file systems to check

STANDARDS CONFORMANCE
     fsck: SVID3

SEE ALSO
     fsck_FSType(1M), mkfs(1M), newfs(1M), fstab(4), fs_wrapper(5).

"lv" command summaries

"lv" commands - Command summaries related to logical volumes.

```
lvchange(1M)                                                    lvchange(1M)

NAME
      lvchange - change LVM logical volume characteristics

SYNOPSIS

      /sbin/lvchange [-a availability] [-A autobackup]
            [-c mirror_consistency] [-C contiguous] [-d schedule]
            [-M mirror_write_cache] [-p permission] [-r relocate] [-s strict]
            lv_path
```

```
lvcreate(1M)                                                    lvcreate(1M)

NAME
      lvcreate - create logical volume in LVM volume group

SYNOPSIS

      /sbin/lvcreate [-A autobackup] [-c mirror_consistency] [-C contiguous]
            [-d schedule] [-i stripes -I stripe_size]
            [-l le_number | -L lv_size] [-m mirror_copies]
            [-M mirror_write_cache] [-n lv_name] [-p permission]
            [-r relocate] [-s strict] vg_name
```

```
lvdisplay(1M)                                                   lvdisplay(1M)

NAME
      lvdisplay - display information about LVM logical volumes

SYNOPSIS

      /sbin/lvdisplay [-k] [-v] lv_path  ...
```

```
lvextend(1M)                                                    lvextend(1M)

NAME
```

```
              lvextend - increase space, increase mirrors for LVM logical volume

SYNOPSIS

        /sbin/lvextend [-A autobackup]
              {-l le_number | -L lv_size | -m mirror_copies}
              lv_path [pv_path ... | pvg_name ...]
```

```
lvlnboot(1M)                                                                  lvlnboot(1M)

NAME
        lvlnboot - prepare LVM logical volume to be root, boot, primary swap,
        or dump volume

SYNOPSIS

        /sbin/lvlnboot [[-A autobackup]
              { -b boot_lv | -d dump_lv | -r root_lv | -R | -s swap_lv }] [-v]
              [vg_name]
```

```
lvmerge(1M)                                                                    lvmerge(1M)
                      Requires Optional HP MirrorDisk/UX Software

NAME
        lvmerge - merge two LVM logical volumes into one logical volume

SYNOPSIS

        /sbin/lvmerge [-A autobackup] dest_lv_path src_lv_path
```

```
lvmmigrate(1M)                                                              lvmmigrate(1M)

NAME
        lvmmigrate - prepare root file system for migration from partitions to
        LVM logical volumes

SYNOPSIS

        /usr/sbin/lvmmigrate [-d disk_special_file] [-e file_system ...] [-f]
              [-i file_system ...] [-n] [-v]
```

```
lvreduce(1M)                                                                  lvreduce(1M)

NAME
```

lvreduce - decrease number of physical extents allocated to LVM
logical volume

SYNOPSIS

/sbin/lvreduce [-A autobackup] [-f] -l le_number lv_path

/sbin/lvreduce [-A autobackup] [-f] -L lv_size lv_path

/sbin/lvreduce [-A autobackup] -m mirror_copies lv_path [pv_path ...]

/sbin/lvreduce [-A autobackup] -k pvkey -m mirror_copies lv_path
[pv_path ...]

lvremove(1M)   lvremove(1M)

NAME
lvremove - remove one or more logical volumes from LVM volume group

SYNOPSIS

/sbin/lvremove [-A autobackup] [-f] lv_path ...

lvrmboot(1M)   lvrmboot(1M)

NAME
lvrmboot - remove LVM logical volume link to root, primary swap, or
dump volume

SYNOPSIS

/sbin/lvrmboot [-A autobackup] [-d dump_lv] [-r] [-s] [-v] vg_name

lvsplit(1M)   lvsplit(1M)
                    Requires Optional HP MirrorDisk/UX Software

NAME
lvsplit - split mirrored LVM logical volume into two logical volumes

SYNOPSIS

/sbin/lvsplit [-A autobackup] [-s suffix] lv_path ...

lvsync(1M)   lvsync(1M)
                    Requires Optional HP MirrorDisk/UX Software

NAME
     lvsync - synchronize stale mirrors in LVM logical volumes

SYNOPSIS

     /sbin/lvsync lv_path ...

mediainit

mediainit - Initialize mass storage media.

---

mediainit(1)   mediainit(1)

NAME
     mediainit - initialize disk or cartridge tape media, partition DDS
     tape

SYNOPSIS

     mediainit [-vr] [-f fmt_optn] [-i interleave] [-p size] pathname

DESCRIPTION
     mediainit initializes mass storage media by formatting the media,
     writing and reading test patterns to verify media integrity, then
     sparing any defective blocks found. This process prepares the disk or
     tape for error-free operation. Initialization destroys all existing
     user data in the area being initialized.

     mediainit can also used for partitioning DDS tape media. See the -p
     option below for further details.

   Options
     The following command options are recognized. They can be specified
     in any order, but all must precede the pathname. Options without
     parameters can be listed individually or grouped together. Options
     with parameters must be listed individually, but white space between
     the option and its parameter is discretionary.

          -v   Normally, mediainit provides only fatal error
                         messages which are directed to standard error.
                         The -v (verbose) option sends device-specific
                         information related to low-level operation of
                         mediainit to standard output (stdout). This
                         option is most useful to trained service personnel
                         because it usually requires detailed knowledge of
                         device operation before the information can be
                         interpreted correctly.

          -r   (re-certify) This option forces a complete tape
                         certification whether or not the tape has been
                         certified previously. All record of any
                         previously spared blocks is discarded, so any bad
                         blocks will have to be rediscovered. This option
                         should be used only if:

                              - It is suspected that numerous blocks on
                                 the tape have been spared which should not
                                 have been, or

                              - It is necessary to destroy (overwrite) all
                                 previous data on the tape.

          -f fmt_optn   The format option is a device-specific number in
                         the range 0 through 239. It is intended solely

for use with certain SS/80 devices that support multiple media formats (independent from interleave factor). For example, certain microfloppy drives support 256-, 512-, and 1024-byte sectors. mediainit passes any supplied format option directly through to the device. The device then either accepts the format option if it is supported, or rejects it if it is not supported. Refer to device operating manuals for additional information. The default format option is 0.

-i interleave   The interleave factor, interleave, refers to the relationship between sequential logical records and sequential physical records. It defines the number of physical records on the media that lie between the beginning points of two consecutively numbered logical records. The choice of interleave factor can have a substantial impact on disk performance. For CS/80 and SS/80 drives, consult the appropriate device operating manual for details. For Amigo drives, see WARNINGS.

-p size   Partition DDS cartridge media into two logical separate volumes: partition 0 and partition 1:

- size specifies the minimum size of partition 1 (in Mbytes).

- Partition 0 is the remainder of the tape (partition 0 physically follows partition 1 on the tape).

The actual size of partition 1 is somewhat larger than the requested size to allow for tape media errors during writing. Thus, a size of 400 formats the DDS tape into two partitions where partition 1 holds at least 400 Megabytes of data, and the remainder of the tape is used for partition 0 (for a 1300 Mbyte DDS cartridge, this means that partition 0 has a size somewhat less than 900 Mbytes).

Note that it is unnecessary to format a DDS tape before use unless the tape is being partitioned. Unformatted DDS media does not require initialization when used as a single partition tape. Accessing partition 1 on a single-partition tape produces an error. To change a two-partition tape to single-partition, use mediainit with 0 specified as the size.

pathname   pathname is the path name to the character (raw) device special file associated with the device unit or volume that is to be initialized. mediainit aborts if you lack either read or write permission to the device special file, or if the device is currently open for any other process. This prevents accidental initialization of the root device or any mounted volume. mediainit locks the unit or volume being initialized so that no other processes can access it.

Except for SCSI devices, pathname must be a device special file whose minor number of the device being initialized has the diagnostic bit set. For

device special files with the diagnostic bit set,
the section number is meaningless. The entire
device is accessed.

When a given CS/80 or SS/80 device contains multiple units, or a given
unit contains multiple volumes as defined by the drive controller, any
available unit or volume associated with that controller can be
initialized, independent of other units and volumes that share the
same controller. Thus, you can initialize one unit or volume to any
format or interleave factor without affecting formats or data on
companion units or volumes. However, be aware that the entire unit or
volume (as defined by the drive controller) is initialized without
considering the possibility that it may be subdivided into smaller
structures by the the operating software. When such structures exist,
unexpected loss of data is possible.

mediainit dominates controller resources and limits access by
competing processes to other units or volumes sharing the same
controller. If other simultaneous processes need access to the same
controller, some access degradation can be expected until
initialization is complete; especially if you are initializing a tape
cartridge in a drive that shares the root disk controller.

In general, mediainit attempts to carefully check any -f (format
option) or -i (interleave options) supplied, and aborts if an option
is out of range or inappropriate for the media being initialized.
Specifying an interleave factor or format option value of 0 has the
same effect as not specifying the option at all.

For disks that support interleave factors, the acceptable range is
usually 1 (no interleave) through n-1, where n is the number of
sectors per track. With SS/80 hard disks, the optimum interleave
factor is usually determined by the speed (normal or high) of the HP-
IB interface card used and whether DMA is present in the system. The
optimum interleave factor for SS/80 flexible disk drives is usually a
constant (often 2), and is independent of the type of HP-IB interface
used. The optimum interleave factor for CS/80 disks is usually 1 and
is also usually not related to the type of HP-IB interface being used.
In any case, refer to the appropriate device operating manual for
recommended values.

If a disk being initialized requires an interleave factor but none is
specified, mediainit provides an appropriate, though not necessarily
optimum default. For CS/80 and SS/80 disks, mediainit uses whatever
the device reports as its current interleave factor. SS/80 floppy
drives report their minimum (usually best) interleave factor, if the
currently installed media is unformatted.

When a given device supports format options, the allowable range of
interleave factors may be related to the specified format option. In
such instances, mediainit cannot check the interleave factor if one is
specified.

Notes
Most types of mass storage media must be initialized before they can
be used. HP hard disks, flexible disks, and cartridge tapes require
some form of initialization, but 9-track tapes do not. Initialization
usually involves formatting the media, writing and reading test
patterns, then sparing any defective blocks. Depending upon the media
and device type, none, some, or all of the initialization process may
have been performed at the factory. mediainit completes whatever
steps are appropriate to prepare the media for error-free operation.

Most HP hard disks are formatted and exhaustively tested at the
factory by use of a process more thorough but also more time-consuming
than appropriate for mediainit. However, mediainit is still valuable

for ensuring the integrity of the media after factory shipment, formatting with the correct interleave factor, and sparing any blocks which may have become defective since original factory testing was performed.

HP flexible disks are not usually formatted prior to shipment, so they must undergo the entire initialization process before they can be used.

All HP CS/80 cartridge tapes are certified and formatted prior to shipment from the factory. When a tape is certified, it is thoroughly tested and defective blocks are spared. mediainit usually certifies a tape only if it has not been certified previously. If the tape has been previously certified and spared, mediainit usually reorganizes the tape's spare block table, retaining any previous spares, and optimizing their assignment for maximum performance under sequential access. Reorganizing the spare block table takes only a few seconds, whereas complete certification takes about a half-hour for 150-foot tapes, and over an hour for 600-foot tapes.

HP CS/80 cartridge tape drives have a feature called "auto-sparing". If under normal usage the drive has trouble reading a block, the drive logs the fact and automatically spares out that block the next time data is written to it. Thus, as a tape is used, any marginal blocks that were not spared during certification are spared automatically if they cause problems. This sparing is automatic within the device, and is totally independent of mediainit.

Reorganization of a tape's spare block table technically renders any existing data undefined, but the data is not usually destroyed by overwriting. To ensure that old tape data is destroyed, which is useful for security, complete tape re-certification can be forced with the -r option.

Some applications may require that a file system be placed on the media before use. mediainit does not create a file system; it only prepares media for writing and reading. If such a file system is required, other utilities such as newfs, lifinit, or mkfs must be invoked after running mediainit (see newfs(1M), lifinit(1), and mkfs(1M)).

RETURN VALUE
       mediainit returns one of the following values:

       0   Successful completion.
       1   A device-related error occurred.
       2   A syntax-related error was encountered.

ERRORS
       Appropriate error messages are printed on standard error during execution of mediainit.

EXAMPLES
       Format an HP 9122 SS/80 3-1/2-inch flexible disk with an interleave factor of 2, 1024-byte sectors, and double-sided HP format:

              mediainit -i 2 -f 3 /dev/rdsk/9122

WARNINGS
       For a device that contains multiple units on a single controller, each unit can be initialized independently from any other unit. It should be noted, however, that mediainit requires that there be no other processes accessing the device before initialization begins, regardless of which unit is being initialized. If there are accesses currently in progress, mediainit aborts.

Aborting mediainit is likely to leave the medium in a corrupt state,
even if it was previously initialized. To recover, the initialization
must be restarted.

During the initialization process, open() rejects all other accesses
to the device being initialized, producing the error EACCES (see
open(2)).

DEPENDENCIES
     Series 800
          Partitioning of DDS tape media (-p option) is not supported.

AUTHOR
     mediainit was developed by HP.

SEE ALSO
     lifinit(1), mkfs(1M), newfs(1M).

newfs

newfs - Build a new file system by invoking **mkfs** command. (this is generic man page, there is also a man page for hfs and vxfs.)

```
newfs(1M)                                                    newfs(1M)

NAME
     newfs (generic) - construct a new file system

SYNOPSIS

     /usr/sbin/newfs [-F FStype] [-o specific_options] [-V] special

DESCRIPTION
     The newfs command is a "friendly" front-end to the mkfs command (see
     mkfs(1M)).  The newfs command calculates the appropriate parameters
     and then builds the file system by invoking the mkfs command.

     special represents a character (raw) special device.

  Options
     newfs recognizes the following options:

         -F FStype        Specify the file system type on which to operate
                          (see fstyp(1M) and fs_wrapper(5)).  If this option
                          is not included on the command line, then the file
                          system type is determined from the file /etc/fstab
                          by matching special with an entry in that file.
                          If there is no entry in /etc/fstab, then the file
                          system type is determined from the file
                          /etc/default/fs.

         -o specific_options
                          Specify options specific to the file system type.
                          specific_options is a list of suboptions and/or
                          keyword/attribute pairs intended for an FStype-
                          specific module of the command.  See the file
                          system specific manual entries for a description
                          of the specific_options that are supported, if
                          any.

         -V               Echo the completed command line, but perform no
                          other actions.  The command line is generated by
                          incorporating the specified options and arguments
                          and other information derived from /etc/fstab.
                          This option allows the user to verify the command
                          line.

EXAMPLES
     Execute the newfs command to create an HFS file system on
     /dev/rdsk/c1d0s2

         newfs -F hfs /dev/rdsk/c1d0s2
```

AUTHOR
      newfs was developed by HP and the University of California, Berkeley.

FILES
      /etc/default/fs   File that specifies the default file system
                                type.
      /etc/fstab   Static information about the file systems.

SEE ALSO
      fsck(1M), fstyp(1M), mkfs(1M), newfs_FStype(1M), fstab(4),
      fs_wrapper(5).

"pv" command summaries

"pv" commands - Command summaries related to physical volumes.

```
pvchange(1M)                                                  pvchange(1M)

NAME
     pvchange - change characteristics and access path of physical volume
     in LVM volume group

SYNOPSIS

     /sbin/pvchange [-A autobackup] -s pv_path

     /sbin/pvchange [-A autobackup] -S autoswitch pv_path

     /sbin/pvchange [-A autobackup] -x extensibility pv_path

     /sbin/pvchange [-A autobackup] -t IO_timeout pv_path




pvcreate(1M)                                                  pvcreate(1M)

NAME
     pvcreate - create physical volume for use in LVM volume group

SYNOPSIS

     /sbin/pvcreate [-b] [-B] [-d soft_defects] [-s disk_size] [-f]
         [-t disk_type] pv_path




pvdisplay(1M)                                                pvdisplay(1M)

NAME
     pvdisplay - display information about physical volumes within LVM
     volume group

SYNOPSIS

     /sbin/pvdisplay [-v] [-b BlockList] pv_path ...




pvmove(1M)                                                      pvmove(1M)

NAME
     pvmove - move allocated physical extents from one LVM physical volume
     to other physical volumes

SYNOPSIS
```

```
/sbin/pvmove [-A autobackup] [-n lv_path] source_pv_path
     [dest_pv_path ... | dest_pvg_name ...]
```

"vg" command summaries

"vg" commands - Command summaries related to volume groups.

---

vgcfgbackup(1M)   vgcfgbackup(1M)

NAME
    vgcfgbackup - create or update LVM volume group configuration backup
    file

SYNOPSIS

    /sbin/vgcfgbackup [-f vg_conf_path] [-u] vg_name

vgcfgrestore(1M)   vgcfgrestore(1M)

NAME
    vgcfgrestore - display or restore LVM volume group configuration from
    backup file

SYNOPSIS

    /sbin/vgcfgrestore -n vg_name -l

    /sbin/vgcfgrestore -n vg_name [-o old_pv_path] pv_path

    /sbin/vgcfgrestore -f vg_conf_path -l

    /sbin/vgcfgrestore -f vg_conf_path [-o old_pv_path] pv_path

vgchange(1M)   vgchange(1M)

NAME
    vgchange - set LVM volume group availability

SYNOPSIS

  Activate volume group
    /sbin/vgchange -a availability [-l] [-p] [-q quorum] [-s] [-P
    resync_daemon_count] [vg_name ...]

  Assign to high availability cluster and mark volume group sharable
    /sbin/vgchange -c cluster -S cluster vg_name

vgcreate(1M)   vgcreate(1M)

NAME
    vgcreate - create LVM volume group

SYNOPSIS

     /sbin/vgcreate [-A autobackup] [-x extensibility] [-e max_pe]
       [-l max_lv] [-p max_pv] [-s pe_size] [-g pvg_name]
       vg_name pv_path ...

vgdisplay(1M)   vgdisplay(1M)

NAME
    vgdisplay - display information about LVM volume groups

SYNOPSIS

    /sbin/vgdisplay [-v] [vg_name ...]

vgexport(1M)   vgexport(1M)

NAME
    vgexport - export an LVM volume group and its associated logical
    volumes

SYNOPSIS

    /sbin/vgexport [-m mapfile] [-p] [-v] vg_name

    /sbin/vgexport -m mapfile -s -p -v vg_name

vgextend(1M)   vgextend(1M)

NAME
    vgextend - extend an LVM volume group by adding physical volumes

SYNOPSIS

    /sbin/vgextend [-A autobackup] [-g pvg_name] [-x extensibility]
       vg_name pv_path ...

vgimport(1M)   vgimport(1M)

NAME
    vgimport - import an LVM volume group onto the system

SYNOPSIS

    /sbin/vgimport [-m mapfile] [-p] [-v] vg_name pv_path ...

    /sbin/vgimport -m mapfile -s -v vg_name

vgreduce(1M)   vgreduce(1M)

NAME
     vgreduce - remove physical volumes from an LVM volume group

SYNOPSIS

     /sbin/vgreduce vg_name pv_path ...

     /sbin/vgreduce -f vg_name

vgremove(1M)   vgremove(1M)

NAME
     vgremove - remove LVM volume group definition from the system

SYNOPSIS

     /sbin/vgremove vg_name ...

vgscan(1M)   vgscan(1M)

NAME
     vgscan - scan physical volumes for LVM volume groups

SYNOPSIS

     /sbin/vgscan [-a] [-p] [-v]

vgsync(1M)   vgsync(1M)
                         Requires Optional HP MirrorDisk/UX Software

NAME
     vgsync - synchronize stale logical volume mirrors in LVM volume groups

SYNOPSIS

     /sbin/vgsync vg_name ...

CHAPTER 3

Networking

Networking is the aspect of system administration that varies the most from installation to installation. Some installations, such as highly centralized and isolated systems that have only ASCII terminals connected to the system, require the system administrator to pay very little attention to networking. Other installations, such as highly distributed environments in which thousands of systems are connected to a network that may span many geographic sites, may require the system administrator to pay a great deal of attention to networking. In this scenario, the amount of time a system administrator devotes to networking may exceed the amount of time spent on all other system administration functions combined! Rather than ignore networking altogether, as the first system administrator might, or cover all aspects of network administration, as the second system administrator may require, I cover in this chapter the aspects of network administration that most new system administrators care about. This content is based on my experience working in a variety of new HP-UX installations. In the event that you require more networking background than I cover in this chapter, I recommend the following book as an excellent source of networking information - *UNIX Networks* by Bruce H. Hunter and Karen Bradford Hunter (Prentice Hall, ISBN 0-13-08987-1).

In this chapter, I provide both background and setup information on many networking topics. Most of what I cover falls under the "Internet Services" umbrella in HP terminology. This includes ARPA and Berkeley Services. Here is a list of topics I cover:

- Some general UNIX networking background
- Internet Protocol (IP) addressing (classes A, B, and C)
- Subnet mask
- ARPA Services
- Berkeley commands
- Host name mapping
- Network File System (NFS) background
- HP-UX networking commands
- Some examples

I provide summaries and examples of many HP-UX commands in this chapter. A great deal more detail can be found in the manual pages for these commands. I provide the full manual pages at the end of this chapter for many of the commands covered.

UNIX Networking

Connecting to other machines is an important part of every HP-UX network. This means connecting both to other UNIX machines as well as to non-UNIX machines. The machines must be physically connected to one another as well as functionally connected to one another so that you can perform such tasks as transferring files and logging in to other systems. Many commands exist on your HP-UX system that provide you with the functionality to log in and transfer files between systems. These are known as the ARPA commands **telnet** and **ftp**.

The **telnet** command allows remote logins in a heterogenous environment. From your HP-UX system, for instance, you can **telnet** to non-HP-UX systems and log in. After login on the remote system, you need to have an understanding of the operating system running on that system. If you need to connect to a different computer for only the purpose of transferring files to and from the system, then you can use **ftp**. This command allows you to transfer files between any two systems without having an understanding of the operating system running on the remote system.

These commands are somewhat primitive compared to the commands that can be issued between UNIX systems. To UNIX systems, networking is not an afterthought that needs to be added on to the system. The **ftp** and **telnet** commands come with your HP-UX system, as well as more advanced commands and functionality you can use to communicate between your HP-UX system and other UNIX systems. These more advanced commands, known as Berkeley commands, allow you to perform many commands remotely, such as copying files and directories and logging in. This functionality continues to increase to a point where you are working with files that can be stored on any system on the network, and your access to these files is transparent to you with the Network File System (NFS).

Before I cover the setup required on your HP-UX system to achieve the level of network functionality you require, we'll take a look at some of the basics of UNIX networking.

What Is All This Ethernet, IEEE802.3, TCP/IP Stuff, Anyway?

In order to understand how the networking on your HP-UX system works, you first need to understand the components of your network that exist on your HP-UX system. Seven layers of network functionality exist on your HP-UX system, as shown in Figure 3-1. I'll cover the bottom four layers at a cursory level so you can see how each plays a part in the operation of your network and, therefore, be more informed when you configure and troubleshoot networking on your HP-UX system. The top layers are the ones that most HP-UX system administrators spend time working with because they are closest to the functionality you can relate to. The bottom layers are, however, also important to understand at some level so that you can perform any configuration necessary to improve the network performance of your system, which will have a major impact on the overall performance of your system.

Layer Number	Layer Name	Data Form	Comments
7	Application		User applications here.
6	Presentation		Applications prepared.
5	Session		Applications prepared.
4	Transport	Packet	Port-to-port transportation handled by TCP.
3	Network	Datagram	Internet Protocol (IP) handles routing by going directly to either the destination or default router.
2	Link	Frame	Data encapsulated in Ethernet or IEEE 802.3 with source and destination addresses.
1	Physical		Physical connection between systems. Usually thinnet or twisted pair.

Figure 3-1 ISO/OSI Network Layer Functions

I'll start reviewing Figure 3-1 at the bottom with layer 1 and then describe each of the four bottom layers. This is the International Standards Organization Open Systems Interconnection (ISO/OSI) model. It is helpful to visualizing the way in which networking layers interact.

Physical Layer

The beginning is the physical interconnect between the systems on your network. Without the **physical layer,** you can't communicate between systems, and all the great functionality you would like to implement will not be possible. The physical layer converts the data you would like to transmit to the analog signals that travel along the wire (I'll assume for now that whatever physical layer you have in place uses wires). The information traveling into a network interface is taken off the wire and prepared for use by the next layer.

Link Layer

In order to connect to other systems local to your system, you use the link layer that is able to establish a connection to all the other systems on your local segment. This is the layer where you have either IEEE 802.3 or Ethernet. Your HP-UX system supports both of these "encapsulation" methods. This is called encapsulation because your data is put in one of these two forms (either IEEE 802.3 or Ethernet). Data is transferred at the link layer in frames (just another name for data), with the source and destination addresses and some other information attached. You might think that because two different encapsulation methods exist, that they must be much different. This assumption, however, is not the case. IEEE 802.3 and Ethernet are nearly identical. This is the reason your HP-UX system can handle both types of encapsulation. So with the bottom two layers, you have a physical connection between your systems and data that is encapsulated into one of two formats with a source and destination address attached. Figure 3-2 lists the components of an **Ethernet** encapsulation and makes comments about IEEE802.3 encapsulation where appropriate.

destination address	6 bytes	address data is sent to
source address	6 bytes	address data is sent from
type	2 bytes	this is the "length count" in 802.3
data	46-1500 bytes	38-1492 bytes for 802.3; the difference in these two data sizes (MTU) can be seen with the **ifconfig** command
crc	4 bytes	checksum to detect errors

Figure 3-2 Ethernet Encapsulation

One interesting item to note is the difference in the maximum data size between IEEE 802.3 and Ethernet of 1492 and 1500 bytes, respectively. This is the Maximum Transfer Unit (MTU). The **ifconfig** command covered shortly displays the MTU for your interface. The data in Ethernet is called a *frame* (the re-encapsulation of data at the next layer up is called a *datagram* in IP, and encapsulation at two levels up is called a *packet* for TCP).

Keep in mind that Ethernet and IEEE 802.3 will run on the same physical connection, but there are indeed differences between the two encapsulation methods. With your HP-UX systems, you won't have to spend much, if any, time setting up your network interface for encapsulation.

Network Layer

Next we work up to the third layer, which is the network layer. This layer on UNIX systems is synonymous with Internet Protocol (IP). Data at this layer is called *datagrams*. This is the layer that handles the routing of data around the network. Data that gets routed with IP sometimes encounters an error of some type, which is reported back to the source system with an Internet Control Message Protocol (ICMP) message. We will see some ICMP messages shortly. **ifconfig** and **netstat** are two HP-UX commands that are used to configure this routing that I'll cover shortly.

Unfortunately, the information that IP uses does not conveniently fit inside an Ethernet frame, so you end up with fragmented data. This is really re-encapsulation of the data, so you end up with a lot of inefficiency as you work your way up the layers.

IP handles routing in a simple fashion. If data is sent to a destination connected directly to your system, then the data is sent directly to that system. If, on the other hand, the destination is not connected directly to your system, the data is sent to the default router. The default router then has the responsibility of getting the data to its destination. This routing can be a little tricky to understand, so I'll cover it in detail shortly.

Transport Layer

This layer can be viewed as one level up from the network layer, because it communicates with *ports*. TCP is the most common protocol found at this level, and it forms packets that are sent from port to port. The port used by a program is defined in **/etc/services** along with the protocol (such as TCP). These ports are used by network programs such as **telnet**, **rlogin**, **ftp**, and so on. You can see that these programs, associated with ports, are the highest level we have covered while analyzing the layer diagram. **/etc/ services** will be covered in more detail shortly.

Internet Protocol (IP) Addressing

The Internet Protocol address (IP address) is either a class "A," "B," or "C" address (there are also class "D" and "E" addresses I will not cover). A class "A" network supports many more nodes per network than either a class "B" or "C" network. IP addresses consist of four fields. The purpose of breaking down the IP address into four fields is to define a node (or host) address and a network address. Figure 3-3 summarizes the relationships between the classes and addresses.

Address Class	Networks	Nodes per Network	Bits Defining Network	Bits Defining Nodes per Network
A	a few	the most	8 bits	24 bits
B	many	many	16 bits	16 bits
C	the most	a few	24 bits	8 bits
Reserved	-	-	-	-

Figure 3-3 Comparison of Internet Protocol (IP) Addresses

These bit patterns are significant in that the number of bits defines the ranges of networks and nodes in each class. For instance, a class A address uses 8 bits to define networks, and a class C address uses 24 bits to define networks. A class A address therefore supports fewer networks than a class C address. A class A address, however, supports many more nodes per network than a class C address. Taking these relationships one step further, we can now view the specific parameters associated with these address classes in Figure 3-4.

Figure 3-4 Address Classes

Address Class	Networks Supported	Nodes per Network	Address Range		
A	127	16777215	0.0.0.1	-	127.255.255.254
B	16383	65535	128.0.0.1	-	191.255.255.254
C	2097157	255	192.0.0.1	-	223.255.254.254
Reserved	-	-	224.0.0.0	-	255.255.255.255

Looking at the 32-bit address in binary form, you can see how to determine the class of an address:

Class "A"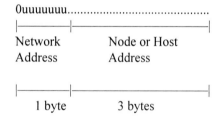

net.host.host.host

A class "A" address has the first bit set to 0. You can see how so many nodes per network can be supported with all of the bits devoted to the node or host address. The first bit of a class A address is 0, and the remaining 7 bits of the network portion are used to define the network. Then a total of 3 bytes are devoted to defining the nodes with a network.

Figure 3-4   Address Classes (Continued)

Class "B"

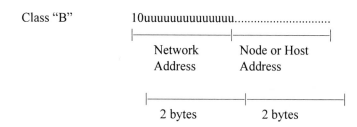

net.net.host.host

A class "B" address has the first bit set to a 1 and the second bit to a 0. More networks are supported here than with a class A address, but fewer nodes per network. With a class B address, 2 bytes are devoted to the network portion of the address and 2 bytes devoted to the node portion of the address.

Class "C"

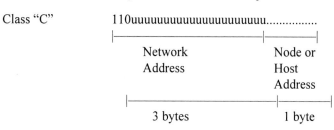

net.net.net.host

A class "C" address has the first bit and second bit set to 1 and the third bit is 0. The greatest number of networks and fewest number of nodes per network are associated with a class C address. With a class C address, 3 bytes are devoted to the network and 1 byte is devoted to the nodes within a network.

These addresses are used in various setup files that are covered later when the **/etc/hosts** file is described. Every interface on your network must have a unique IP address. Systems that have two network interfaces must have two unique IP addresses. If you are about to set up your network for the first time, your HP Technical Consultant can help you obtain your IP addresses. You will need these addresses before you can perform any of the setup steps covered later.

Subnet Mask

Your HP-UX system uses the subnet mask to determine whether an IP datagram is for a host on its own subnet, a host on a different subnet but the same network, or a host on a different network. Using subnets, you can have some hosts on one subnet and other hosts on a different subnet. The subnets can be separated by routers or other networking electronics that connect the subnets.

To perform routing, the only aspects of an address that your router uses are the net and subnet. The subnet mask is used to mask the host part of the address. Because you can set up network addresses in such a way that you are the only one who knows which part of the address is the host, subnet, and network, you use the subnet mask to make your system aware of the bits of your IP address that are for the host and which are for the subnet.

In its simplest form, what you are really doing with subnet masking is defining which portion of your IP address defines the host, and which part defines the network. One of the most confusing aspects of working with subnet masks is that most books show the subnet masks in Figure 3-5 as the most common.

Address Class	Decimal	Hex
A	255.0.0.0	0xff000000
B	255.255.0.0	0xffff0000
C	255.255.255.0	0xffffff00

Figure 3-5   Subnet Masks

This way of thinking, however, assumes that you are devoting as many bits as possible to the network and as many bits as possible to the host and that no subnets are used. Figure 3-6 shows an example of using subnetting with a class B address.

Address Class	Class B		
host IP address	152.128.	12.	1
breakdown	network	subnet	hostid
number of bits	16 bits	8 bits	8 bits
subnet mask in decimal	255.255.	255.	0
subnet mask in hexadecimal	0xffffff00		
Example of different host on same subnet	152.128.	12.	2
Example of host on different subnet	152.128.	13.	1

Figure 3-6 Class B IP Address and Subnet Mask Example

In Figure 3-6 the first two bytes of the subnet mask (255.255) define the network, the third byte (255) defines the subnet, and the fourth byte (0) is devoted to the host ID. Although this subnet mask for a class B address did not appear in the earlier default subnet mask figure, the subnet mask of 255.255.255.0 is widely used in class B networks to support subnetting.

How does your HP-UX system perform the comparison using the subnet mask of 255.255.255.0 to determine that 152.128.12.1 and 152.128.13.1 are on different subnets? Figure 3-7 shows this comparison.

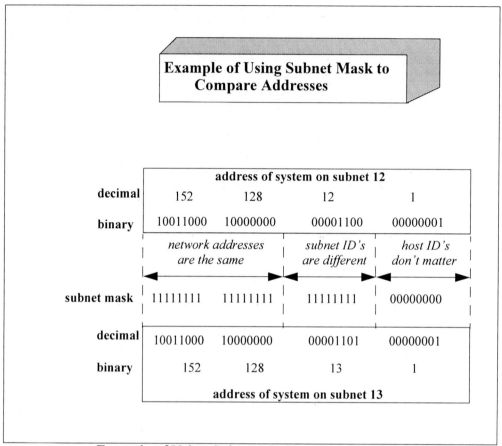

Figure 3-7 Example of Using Subnet Mask to Compare Addresses

Figure 3-8 shows these two systems on the different subnets.

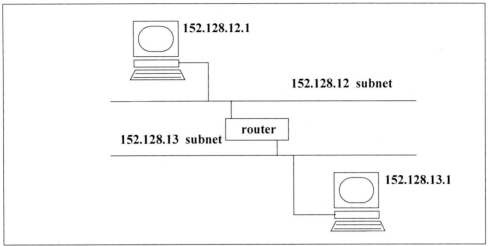

Figure 3-8 Class B Systems on Different Subnets

You don't have to use the 8-bit boundaries to delineate the network, subnet, and host ID fields. If, for instance, you wanted to use part of the subnet field for the host ID, you could do so. A good reason for this approach would be to accommodate future expandability. You might want subnets 12, 13, 14, and 15 to be part of the same subnet today and make these into separate subnets in the future. Figure 3-9 shows this setup.

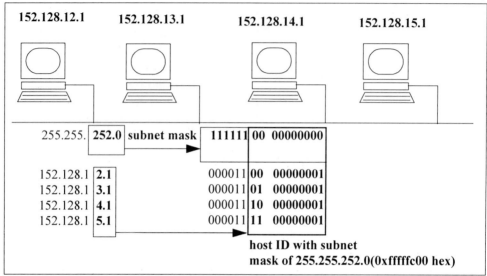

Figure 3-9 Future Expandability Using Subnet Mask

These systems are connected to the same subnet even though part of the third byte, normally associated with the subnet, is used for the host ID. In the future, the subnet mask could be changed to 255.255.252.0 and have four separate subnets of 12, 13, 14, and 15. This would require putting routers in place to route to these separate subnets.

Let's now switch to the high level and look at some networking functionality and then come back to some of the details of configuring networking on HP-UX.

Using Networking

The ISO/OSI model is helpful for visualizing the way in which the networking layers interact. The model does not, however, tell you how to use the networking. This is really your goal. Before you perform any configuration, you need to know how networking is used and then you can perform the appropriate configuration. Two widely used networking services that are worth taking a look at as you set up your system are ARPA and NFS.

The first networking product to configure on your system is HP 9000 ARPA Services - what I have been calling ARPA. ARPA is a combination of "ARPA Services" and "Berkeley Services." ARPA Services supports communications among systems running different operating systems, and Berkeley Services supports UNIX systems. The following is a list of the most common commands. Although many programs can be run under each of these services, the following are the most commonly used ones in the HP-UX world. In some cases, there are examples that show how these commands are used. For all of the examples, the local host is **system1** and the remote host is **system2**.

ARPA Services (Communication among Systems with Different OS)

File Transfer Protocol (ftp) Transfer a file, or multiple files, from one system to another. This is often used when transferring files between an HP-UX workstation and a personal computer or VAX, etc. The following example shows copying the file **/tmp/krsort.c** from system2 (remote host) to the local directory on system1 (local host).

	comments
$ ftp system2	Issue ftp command
Connected to system2.	
system2 FTP server (Version 1.7.212.1) ready.	
Name (system2:root): root	Log in to system2
Password required for root.	
Password:	Enter password
User root logged in.	
Remote system type is UNIX.	
Using binary mode to transfer files.	
ftp> **cd /tmp**	**cd** to **/tmp** on system2
CWD command successful	
ftp> **get krsort.c**	Get krsort.c file
PORT command successful	
Opening BINARY mode data connection for **krsort.c**	
Transfer complete.	
2896 bytes received in 0.08 seconds	

	comments
ftp> **bye**	Exit ftp
Goodbye.	
$	

In this example, both systems are running HP-UX; however, the commands you issue through **ftp** are operating-system-independent. The **cd** for change directory and **get** commands used above work for any operating system on which **ftp** is running. If you become familiar with just a few **ftp** commands, you may find that transferring information in a heterogeneous networking environment is not difficult.

Chances are that you will be using your HP-UX system(s) in a heterogenous environment and may therefore use **ftp** to copy files and directories from one system to another. Since **ftp** is so widely used, I'll describe some of the more commonly used **ftp** commands.

ascii   Set the type of file transferred to ASCII. This means you will be transferring an ASCII file from one system to another. This is the default, so you don't have to set it.

Example: **ascii**

binary   Set the type of file transferred to binary. This means you'll be transferring a binary file from one system to another. If, for instance, you want to have a directory on your HP-UX system that will hold applications that you will copy to non-HP-UX systems, then you will want to use binary transfer.

Example: **binary**

cd	Change to the specified directory on the remote host.
	Example: **cd /tmp**
dir	List the contents of a directory on the remote system to the screen or to a file on the local system, if you specify a local file name.
get	Copy the specified remote file to the specified local file. If you don't specify a local file name, then the remote file name will be used.
lcd	Change to the specified directory on the local host.
	Example: **lcd /tmp**
ls	List the contents of a directory on the remote system to the screen or to a file on the local system, if you specify a local file name.
mget	Copy multiple files from the remote host to the local host.
	Example: **mget *.c**
put	Copy the specified local file to the specified remote file. If you don't specify a remote file name, then the local file name will be used.
	Example: **put test.c**

mput	Copy multiple files from the local host to the remote host.
	Example: **mput *.c**

system	Show the type of operating system running on the remote host.
	Example: **system**

bye/quit	Close the connection to the remote host.
	Example: **bye**

Other **ftp** commands are available in addition to those I have covered here. If you need more information on these commands or wish to review additional **ftp** commands, the HP-UX manual pages for **ftp** will be helpful.

telnet	Used for communication with another host using the telnet protocol. Telnet is an alternative to using **rlogin** described later. The following example shows how to establish a telnet connection with the remote host system2.

	comments
$ telnet system2	
Connected to system2.	Telnet to system2
HP-UX system2	
login: **root**	Log in as root on system2
password:	Enter password
Welcome to system2.	
$	HP-UX prompt on system2

Domain Name System

> This is commonly used to support communication among systems on a large network such as the Internet. I am not going to cover this, but the *Installing and Administering Internet Services* manual thoroughly covers this topic.

Berkeley Commands (Communication between UNIX Systems)

Remote Copy (rcp)

> This program is used to copy files and directories from one UNIX system to another. To copy **/tmp/krsort.c** from system1 to system2, you could do the following:

$ rcp   system2:/tmp/krsort.c /tmp/krsort.c

You need to configure some networking files to get this level of functionality. In this example, the user who issues the command is considered "equivalent" on both systems and has permission to copy files from one system to the other with **rcp**. (These terms will be described shortly.)

Remote login (rlogin)

> Supports login to a remote UNIX system. To remotely log in to system2 from system1, you would do the following:

$ rlogin system2

password:

Welcome to system2

$

If a password is requested when the user issues the **rlogin** command, the users are not equivalent on the two systems. If no password is requested, then the users are indeed equivalent.

Remote shell (remsh)

With the **remsh** command, you can sit on one HP-UX system and issue a command to be run remotely on a different HP-UX system and have the results displayed locally. In this case, a **remsh** is issued to show a long listing of **/tmp/krsort.c**. The command is run on system2, but the result is displayed on system1, where the command was typed:

$ remsh system2 ll /tmp/krsort.c

-rwxrwxrwx 1 root sys 2896 Sept 1 10:54 /tmp/krsort.c

$

In this case, the users on system1 and system2 must be equivalent, or else permission will be denied to issue this command.

Remote who (rwho)

Find out who is logged in on a remote UNIX system. Here is the output of issuing **rwho**:

$ **rwho**

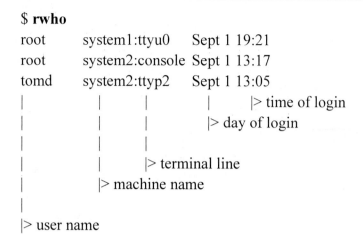

For **rwho** to work, the **rwho** daemon (**rwhod**) must be running.

Host Name Mapping

Your most important decision related to networking is how you will implement host name mapping in ARPA. There are three techniques for host name mapping:

- Berkeley Internet Named Domain (BIND)

- Network Information Service (NIS)

- HP-UX file **/etc/hosts**

The most common and simplest way to implement host name mapping is with **/etc/hosts**, so I'll cover that technique here. Keep in mind that there are networking manuals devoted to many networking topics including NFS, ARPA, and others. These manuals serve as good reference material if you need to know more about networking than is covered here.

/etc/hosts

This file contains information about the other systems to which you are connected. It contains the Internet address of each system, the system name, and any aliases for the system name. If you modify your **/etc/hosts** file to contain the names of the systems on your network, you have provided the basis for **rlogin** to another system. There is an important distinction here that confuses many new HP-UX administrators. Although you can now **rlogin** to other UNIX systems, you cannot yet **rcp** or **remsh** to another system. Don't worry, though; adding **remsh** and **rcp** functionality is easy and I'll show you this next. Here is an example **/etc/hosts** file:

```
127.0.0.1            localhost        loopback
15.32.199.42         a4410827
15.32.199.28         a4410tu8
15.32.199.7          a4410922
15.32.199.21         a4410tu1
15.32.199.22         a4410tu2
15.32.199.62         a4410730
15.32.199.63         hpxterm1
15.32.199.64         a4410rd1
15.32.199.62         a4410750         hp1
```

This file is in the following format:

<internet_address>   <official_hostname>   <alias>

The Internet Protocol address (IP address) is either a class "A," "B," or "C" address. A class "A" network supports many more nodes per network than either a class "B" or "C" network. The purpose of breaking down the IP address into four fields is to define a node (or host) address and a network address. Figures 2-3 through 2-6 described these classes in detail.

Assuming that the above **/etc/hosts** file contains class "C" addresses, the rightmost field is the host or node address, and the other three fields comprise the network address.

You could use either the official_hostname or alias from the **/etc/ hosts** file when issuing one of the ARPA or Berkeley commands described earlier. For instance, either of the following ARPA commands will work:

> **$ telnet a4410750**

> or

> **$ telnet hp1**

Similarly, either of the following Berkeley commands will work:

> **$ rlogin a4410750**

> or

> **$ rlogin hp1**

/etc/hosts.equiv

If you don't want users to have to issue a password when they **rlogin** to a remote system, you can set up equivalent hosts by editing this file. If you have many hosts on your network that you wish to be accessed by the same users, then you will want to create this file. The login names must be the same on both the local and remote systems for **/etc/ hosts.equiv** to allow the user to bypass entering a password. You can either list all the equivalent hosts in **/etc/hosts.equiv** or list the host and user name you wish to be equivalent. Users can now use **rcp** and **remsh** because they are equivalent users on these systems. I usually just enter all the host names on the network. Here is an example of   **/etc/ hosts.equiv**:

> a4410730
> a4410tu1
> a4410tu2
> hpxterm1
> a4410827
> a4410750

Keep in mind the potential security risks of using **/etc/ hosts.equiv**. If a user can log in to a remote system without a password, you have reduced the overall level of security on your network. Even though your users may find it convenient to not have to enter a password when logging into a remote system, you have given every user in **/etc/hosts.equiv** access to the entire network. If you could ensure that all the permissions on all the files and directories on all systems were properly set up, then you wouldn't care who had access to what system. In the real HP-UX world, however, permissions are sometimes not what they are supposed to be. Users have a strong tendency to "browse around," invariably stumbling upon a file they want to copy which they really shouldn't have access to.

/.rhosts

This file is the **/etc/hosts.equiv** for superuser. If you log in as root, you will want to have this file configured with exactly the same information as **/etc/ hosts.equiv**. If you do, however, you have compounded your network security risk by allowing superuser on any system to log in to a remote system without a root password. If you are the undisputed ruler of your network and you're 100 percent certain that no security holes exist, then you may want to set up **/.rhosts** so that you don't have to issue a password when you log in remotely to a system as superuser. From a security standpoint, however, you should know this setup is frowned upon.

Now that you have made the appropriate entries in **/etc/hosts**, **/etc/ hosts.equiv**, and **/.rhosts**, you can use the ARPA Services commands **ftp** and **telnet** as well as the Berkeley commands **rcp**, **rlogin**, **remsh**, and **rwho**.

I have described the process of setting up the appropriate files to get the most commonly used ARPA Services up and running. Virtually every HP-UX system administrator will use the functionality I have described here. It may be that you require additional ARPA functionality such as BIND. You will want to refer to the *HP-UX Networking Manuals* if you need to configure your networking beyond what I have covered here.

Network File System (NFS)

NFS allows you to mount disks on remote systems so that they appear as though they are local to your system. Similarly, NFS allows remote systems to mount your local disk so that it looks as though it is local to the remote system. Configuring NFS to achieve this functionality is simple. You have to perform four activities to get NFS going on your system:

1. Start NFS.

2. Specify whether your system will be an NFS Client, NFS Server, or both.

3. Specify which of your local file systems can be mounted by remote systems.

4. Specify the remote disks you want to mount and view as if they were local to your system.

As with ARPA, you could enable other aspects to NFS, but again, I will again cover what I know to be the NFS functionality that nearly every HP-UX installation uses.

So far, I have been using NFS terminology loosely. Here are definitions of some of the more important NFS terms.

Node	A computer system that is attached to or is part of a computer network.
Client	A node that requests data or services from other nodes (servers).
Server	A node that provides data or services to other nodes (clients) on the network.
File System	A disk partition or logical volume.

Export   Makes a file system available for mounting on remote nodes using NFS.

Mount   Accesses a remote file system using NFS.

Mount Point   The name of a directory on which the NFS file system is mounted.

Import   Mounts a remote file system.

SAM is the best way to enable NFS. Among other things, SAM updates the **/etc/rc.config.d/nfsconf** file. This configuration file contains NFS information such as whether or not your system is an NFS client or an NFS server, and starts the daemon called **/usr/sbin/rpc.mountd**. **mountd** is a remote procedure call server that handles file system mount requests. Here are some of the variables SAM may change for you:

```
NFS_CLIENT=1
NFS_SERVER=1
AUTOMOUNT=1
START_MOUNTD=1
```

You may want to take a look at this file for a good explanation of these and the other variables in this file. The automount variable, for instance, mounts remote file systems only when you make a request to them.

If your system is going to be an NFS server and you will be exporting file systems, SAM will create the **/etc/exports** and **/etc/xtab** files, which specify the file systems to be exported. These files have in them the directory exported and options such as "ro" for read only, and "anon," which handles requests from anonymous users. If "anon" is equal to 65535, then anonymous users are denied access.

The following is an example **/etc/exports** file in which **/opt/app1** is exported to everyone but anonymous users, and **/opt/app2** is exported only to the system named system2:

```
/opt/app1    -anon=65534
/opt/app2    -access=system2
```

You will need to run **/usr/sbin/exportfs -a** if you add a file system to export.

Remote file systems to be mounted locally are put in **/etc/fstab** by SAM. Here is an example of an entry in **/etc/fstab** of a remote file system that is mounted locally. The remote directory **/opt/app3** on system2 is mounted locally under **/opt/app3**:

```
system2:/opt/app3   /opt/app3   nfs   rw,suid   0   0
```

You can use the **showmount** command to show all remote systems (clients) that have mounted a local file system. **showmount** is useful for determining the file systems that are most often mounted by clients with NFS. The output of **showmount** is particularly easy to read because it lists the host name and the directory that was mounted by the client. You have the three following options to the **showmount** command:

-a prints output in the format "name:directory".

-d lists all the local directories that have been remotely mounted by clients.

-e prints a list of exported file systems.

Other Networking Commands and Setup

Setting up networking is usually straightforward. Should you encounter a problem, however, it is helpful to have an understanding of some networking commands that can be lifesavers. In addition, there can be some tricky aspects to networking setup if you have some networking hardware that your HP-UX systems must interface to, such as routers, gateways, bridges, etc. I'll give an example of one such case: connecting an HP-UX system to a router. At the same time, I'll cover some of the most handy networking commands as part of this description.

Consider Figure 3-10, in which an HP-UX system is connected directly to a router.

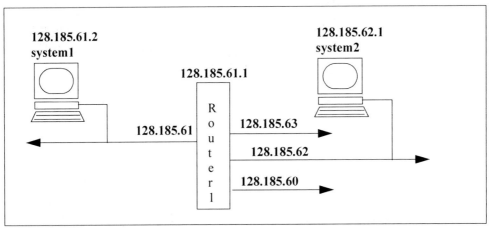

Figure 3-10 HP-UX System and Router Example

Here we have an HP-UX system connected to segment 128.185.61. This is a class "B" Internet address with subnetting enabled.

The **/etc/hosts** file needs to have in it the HP-UX system with node ID 2, the router, and any other systems on this segment or segments on the other side of the router.

If the router is properly configured, we should be able to seamlessly connect to systems on segments 60, 62, and 63 from 61. The router should be configured to allow our system to connect to systems on other segments (60, 62, and 63) by going through the router. Some unforeseen configuration was required to make this simple network operate seamlessly. In this case, a problem occurred getting system1 to connect to systems on the other side of the router on 60, 62, and 63. Before discussing the additional configuration that needed to be done, I'll first show the **/etc/hosts** file and then use some very useful HP-UX commands that show the state of the network. Here is the **/etc/hosts** file showing just the HP-UX system and router:

$ cat /etc/hosts

127.0.0.1   localhosts loopback
128.185.61.1   router1   # router
128.185.61.2   system1   # HP-UX system on 61
128.185.62.1   system2   # HP-UX system on 62

This host file is simple and allows system1 to connect to router1 and system2. The connection from system1 to system2 takes place by going through the router.

ping

How do I know that I have a connection between system1 and the router and the other systems on the other side of the router? I use the **ping** command. **ping** is a simple command that sends an ICMP echo packet to the host you specify once per second. You may recall that ICMP was covered earlier under the network, or third layer. **ping** stands for Packet InterNet Groper. Here is how I know that system1 is connected to router1:

$ ping router1

PING router1: 64 byte packets
64 bytes from 128.185.61.2: icmp_seq=0. time=0. ms
64 bytes from 128.185.61.2: icmp_seq=1. time=0. ms
64 bytes from 128.185.61.2: icmp_seq=2. time=0. ms

Each line of output here represents a response that was returned from the device that was pinged. This means that the device responded. You will continue to get this response indefinitely and have to type **^c** (control c) to terminate the **ping**. If no output is produced, as shown below, then there is no response and you may have a problem between your system and the device you are checking the connection to.

$ ping system2

PING router1: 64 byte packets

You would see this message and that is as far as you would get. A ^**c** will kill the **ping** and you'll see that some number of packets were sent and none were received. I did indeed get this response when issuing the **ping** command, so I know that a problem exists with the connection between system1 and router1.

ping should be used only for testing purposes such as manual fault isolation, because it generates a substantial amount of network traffic. You would not want to use **ping** on an ongoing basis such as in a script that is running continuously.

A nice variation of **ping** that I use is to specify a packet size of 4096 bytes, rather than the default of 64 bytes shown in the previous examples, and count the number of times **ping** will transmit before terminating, rather than having to type ^**c** to terminate **ping**. The following example shows this:

$ ping router1 4096 5

PING router1: 64 byte packets
4096 bytes from 128.185.51.2: icmp_seq=0. time=8. ms
4096 bytes from 128.185.51.2: icmp_seq=1. time=8. ms
4096 bytes from 128.185.51.2: icmp_seq=2. time=9. ms
4096 bytes from 128.185.51.2: icmp_seq=3. time=8. ms
4096 bytes from 128.185.51.2: icmp_seq=4. time=8. ms

Notice that the time required to transmit and receive a response, the round-trip time, is substantially longer than with only 64 bytes transmitted. I usually find that the round-trip time for 64 bytes is 0 ms, although this depends on a number of factors, including network topology and network traffic.

lanscan

lanscan is used to get Local Area Network (LAN) device configuration status. An example is shown below.

```
#   lanscan
Hardware Station          Crd  Hardware  Net-Interface  NM  MAC       HP DLPI Mjr
Path     Address          In#  State     NameUnit State  ID  Type      Support Num
10/16/8  0x080009D91067   1    UP        lan1     DOWN   4   ETHER     Yes     77
10/12/6  0x0060B0834A20   0    UP        lan0     UP     5   ETHER     Yes     52
```

lanscan provides a good summary of the state and configuration of your network interfaces. In this case, two LAN cards are configured in the system. You would receive a line for each LAN card that is configured into your system (many systems have two identical LAN cards or one IEEE 802.3 card and one IEEE 802.5, or token ring, card). Here is a brief description of the **lanscan** headings in the order they appear in the example:

- Series 700 or 800 hardware path.
- The station address, which is sometimes known as the LAN or Ethernet address.
- Card interface number.
- The hardware state of the device, which should be "UP."
- The name of the network interface.
- The network management ID.
- MAC type.
- Whether or not DLPI is supported.
- Major number of driver for LAN interface.

Using the **-v** option produces additional information.

netstat

From the earlier description of the subnet mask, you can see that routing from one host to another can be configured in a variety of ways. The path that information takes in getting from one host to another depends on routing.

You can obtain information related to routing with the **netstat** command. The **-r** option to **netstat** shows the routing tables, which you usually want to know, and the **-n** option can be used to print network addresses as numbers rather than as names. With the **-v** option, you get additional information related to routing, such as subnet mask. In the following examples, **netstat** is issued with the **-r** option (this will be used when describing the **netstat** output), the **-rn** options, and the **-rnv** options, so you can compare the two outputs.

```
# netstat -r

Routing tables
Destination     Gateway      Flags  Refs      Use  Interface  Pmtu  PmtuTime
localhost       localhost    UH        0      465  lo0        4608
system1         localhost    UH        2   837711  lo0        4608
default         wellfleet    UG       12  1051826  lan0       1500
169.200.112     system1      U           751821954 lan0       1500
```

```
# netstat -rn

Routing tables
Destination     Gateway        Flags  Refs      Use  Interface  Pmtu  PmtuTime
127.0.0.1       127.0.0.1      UH        0      465  lo0        4608
169.200.112.1   127.0.0.1      UH        2   837735  lo0        4608
default         169.200.112.250 UG      12  1051827  lan0       1500
169.200.112.0   169.200.112.1  U           751821991 lan0       1500
```

```
# netstat -rnv

Routing tables
Dest/Netmask        Gateway      Flags  Refs      Use  Interface  Pmtu  PmtuTime
127.0.0.1/255.255.255.255
                    127.0.0.1    UH        0      465  lo0        4608
169.200.112.1/255.255.255.255
                    127.0.0.1    UH        1   837756  lo0        4608
default/0.0.0.0 169.200.112.250 UG       14  1051834  lan0       1500
169.200.112.0/255.255.255.0
                    169.200.112.1  U         751822050 lan0       1500
```

With **netstat** some information is provided about the router, which is the middle entry. The **-r** option shows information about routing, but there are many other useful options to this command. Of particular interest in this output is "Flags," which defines the type of routing that takes place. Here are descriptions of the most common flags from the HP-UX manual pages:

1=U   Route to a *network* via a gateway that is the local host itself.

3=UG   Route to a *network* via a gateway that is the remote host.

5=UH   Route to a *host* via a gateway that is the local host itself.

7=UGH   Route to a *host* via a remote gateway that is a host.

The first line is for the local host or loopback interface, called **lo0,** at address 127.0.0.1 (you can see this address in the **netstat -rn** example). The UH flags indicate that the destination address is the local host itself. This class A address allows a client and server on the same host to communicate with one another with TCP/IP. A datagram sent to the loopback interface won't go out onto the network; it will simply go through the loopback.

The second line is for the default route. This entry says to send packets to router1 if a more specific route can't be found. In this case, the router has a UG under Flags. Some routers are configured with a U; others, such as the one in this example, with a UG. I've found that I usually end up determining through trial and error whether a U or UG is required. If a U is in Flags and I am unable to ping a system on the other side of a router, a UG usually fixes the problem.

The third line is for the system's network interface **lan0**. This means to use this network interface for packets to be sent to 169.200.112.

Also, I use two forms of **netstat** to obtain network statistics as opposed to routing information. The first is **netstat -i**, which shows the state of interfaces that are autoconfigured. Since I am most often interested in getting a summary of **lan0**, I issue this command. **netstat -i** gives a good rundown of **lan0**, such as the network it is on, its name, and so on.

The following diagram shows the output of **netstat -i**:

```
# netstat -i

Name  Mtu   Network    Address          Ipkts  Ierrs   Opkts  Oerrs  Coll
ni0*  0     none       none                 0      0       0      0     0
ni1*  0     none       none                 0      0       0      0     0
lo0   4608  loopback   127.0.0.1          232      0     232      0     0
lan0  1500  169.200.112 169.200.112.2 3589746      2   45630      0   104
```

Here is a description of the nine fields in the **netstat** example:

Name	The name of your network interface (Name), in this case, **lan0**.
MTU	The "maximum transmission unit," which is the maximum packet size sent by the interface card.
Network	The network address of the LAN to which the interface card is connected (169.200).
Address	The host name of your system. This is the symbolic name of your system as it appears in the file **/etc/hosts**.

Start of statistical information:

Ipkts	The number of packets received by the interface card, in this case **lan0**.
Ierrs	The number of errors detected on incoming packets by the interface card.
Opkts	The number of packets transmitted by the interface card.
Oerrs	The number of errors detected during the transmission of packets by the interface card.
Collis	The number of collisions that resulted from packet traffic.

netstat provides cumulative data since the node was last powered up; you might have a long elapsed time over which data was accumulated. If you are interested in seeing useful statistical information, you can use **net-stat** with different options. You can also specify an interval to report statistics. I usually ignore the first entry, since it shows all data since the system was last powered up. This means that the data includes non-prime hours when the system was idle. I prefer to view data at the time the system is working its hardest. This following **netstat** example provides network interface information every 5 seconds.

```
# netstat -I lan0 5
```

```
(lan0)-> input            output       (Total)-> input            output
   packets  errs  packets  errs colls      packets  errs  packets  errs colls
   3590505     2    45714     0   104      3590737     2    45946     0   104
       134     0        5     0     0          134     0        5     0     0
       174     0        0     0     0          174     0        0     0     0
       210     0       13     0     0          210     0       13     0     0
       165     0        0     0     0          165     0        0     0     0
       169     0        0     0     0          169     0        0     0     0
       193     0        0     0     0          193     0        0     0     0
       261     0        7     0     0          261     0        7     0     0
       142     0        8     0     0          142     0        8     0     0
       118     0        0     0     0          118     0        0     0     0
       143     0        0     0     0          143     0        0     0     0
       149     0        0     0     0          149     0        0     0     0
```

With this example, you get multiple outputs of what is taking place on the LAN interface. As I mentioned earlier, you may want to ignore the first output, since it includes information over a long time period. This may include a time when your network was idle and therefore the data is not important to you.

You can specifiy the network interface on which you want statistics reported by using **-I interface**; in the case of the example, it was **-I lan0**. An interval of five seconds was also used in this example.

lanadmin

/usr/sbin/lanadmin provides additional information related to network statistics. When you run **lanadmin,** a menu appears that gives you the option to perform various functions, one of which is to display information related to the LAN interface. The following shows the output of **lanadmin** when this option is selected.

```
# lanadmin

              LOCAL AREA NETWORK ONLINE ADMINISTRATION, Version 1.0
                          Wed, May 6  16:03:53

                  Copyright 1994 Hewlett Packard Company.
                        All rights are reserved.

Test Selection mode.

        lan      = LAN Interface Administration
        menu     = Display this menu
        quit     = Terminate the Administration
        terse    = Do not display command menu
        verbose  = Display command menu

Enter command: lan

LAN Interface test mode. LAN Interface Net Mgmt ID = 4

        clear    = Clear statistics registers
        display  = Display LAN Interface status and statistics registers
        end      = End LAN Interface Administration, return to Test Selection
        menu     = Display this menu
        nmid     = Network Management ID of the LAN Interface
        quit     = Terminate the Administration, return to shell
        reset    = Reset LAN Interface to execute its selftest

Enter command: display
                        LAN INTERFACE STATUS DISPLAY
                          Wed, May 6  16:03:57

Network Management ID             = 4
Description                       = lan1 Hewlett-Packard 10/100Base-TX Half-Duplex
 Hw Rev 0
Type (value)                      = ethernet-csmacd(6)
MTU Size                          = 1500
Speed                             = 10000000
Station Address                   = 0x80009d91067
Administration Status (value)     = up(1)
Operation Status (value)          = down(2)
Last Change                       = 0
Inbound Octets                    = 0
Inbound Unicast Packets           = 0
Inbound Non-Unicast Packets       = 0
Inbound Discards                  = 0
Inbound Errors                    = 0
Inbound Unknown Protocols         = 0
Outbound Octets                   = 0
Outbound Unicast Packets          = 0
Outbound Non-Unicast Packets      = 0
Outbound Discards                 = 0
Outbound Errors                   = 0
Outbound Queue Length             = 0
Specific                          = 655367

Press <Return> to continue


Ethernet-like Statistics Group

Index                             = 4
Alignment Errors                  = 0
FCS Errors                        = 0
Single Collision Frames           = 0
Multiple Collision Frames         = 0
Deferred Transmissions            = 0
```

```
Late Collisions                   = 0
Excessive Collisions              = 0
Internal MAC Transmit Errors      = 0
Carrier Sense Errors              = 0
Frames Too Long                   = 0
Internal MAC Receive Errors       = 0


LAN Interface test mode. LAN Interface Net Mgmt ID = 4

        clear    = Clear statistics registers
        display  = Display LAN Interface status and statistics registers
        end      = End LAN Interface Administration, return to Test Selection
        menu     = Display this menu
        nmid     = Network Management ID of the LAN Interface
        quit     = Terminate the Administration, return to shell
        reset    = Reset LAN Interface to execute its selftest

Enter command: quit
#
```

lanadmin gives more detailed information about the LAN interface than **netstat**. The type of interface, Maximum Transfer Unit (MTU), speed, administration and operation status (a quick way to see whether your interface is up), and the LAN interface address in hex. The hex address is often used when access codes are generated for application software or for generating client kernels.

lanadmin also gives much more detailed error information. Although any error slows down your network, having more detailed information on the type of errors and collisions may be helpful in troubleshooting a problem.

With **lanadmin,** you can also "reset" the network interface which is sometimes helpful when the network interface doesn't seem to be working, such as when the LAN interface does not **ping** itself.

route

The information displayed with **netstat** is the routing tables for your system. Some are automatically created with the **ifconfig** command when your system is booted or when the network interface is initialized. Routes to networks and hosts that are not directly connected to your system are entered with the **route** command.

You can make routing changes on the fly, as I did to change the Flags from U to UG:

$ /usr/sbin/route add default 128.185.61.1 3

First is the **route** command. Second, we specify that we wish to add a route; the other option is to delete a route. Third, we specify the destination, in this case, the default. This could be a specific host name, a network name, an IP address, or default that signifies the wildcard gateway route that is shown in our example. Fourth is the gateway through which the destination is reached. In the above example, the IP address was used, but this could also be a host name. The 3 corresponds to the count that is used to specify whether the gateway is the local host or a remote gateway. If the gateway is the local host, then a count of 0 is used. If the gateway is a remote host, which is the case in the example, a count of >0 is used. This will correspond to UG for Flags. This manually changed the network routing table by adding a default route with the appropriate Flags. Issuing this command fixed the problem I encountered trying to get system1 to talk to the systems on the other side of the router (Remember Figure 3-10?).

Before issuing **/usr/sbin/route** with the **add** option, you can first use the **delete** option to remove the existing default route, which is not working.

ifconfig

The **ifconfig** command provides additional information on a LAN interface. The following example provides the configuration of a network interface:

$ /etc/ifconfig lan0
lan0:   flags=863<UP,BROADCAST,NOTRAILERS,RUNNING>
        inet 128.185.61.2 netmask ffff0000 broadcast 128.185.61.255

From this example, we can quickly see that the interface is up, it has an address of 128.185.61.2, and it has a netmask of ffff0000.

You can use **ifconfig** to get the status of a network interface as I have done here to assign an address to a network interface, or to configure network interface parameters. The network address you have will fall into classes such as "A," "B," or "C," as mentioned earlier. You want to be sure that you know the class of your network before you start configuring your LAN interface. This example is a class "B" network, so the netmask is defined as ffff0000 (typical for a class "B" address), as opposed to ffffff00, which is typical for a class "C" network. The netmask is used to determine how much of the address to reserve for subdividing the network into smaller networks. The netmask can be represented in hex, as shown above, or in decimal format, as in the **/etc/hosts** file. Here is the **ifconfig** command I issued to configure the interface:

$ /etc/ifconfig lan0 inet 128.185.61.2 netmask 255.255.0.0

- The 255.255.0.0 corresponds to the hex ffff000 shown earlier for the class "B" subnet mask.

- **lan0** is the interface being configured.

- **inet** is the address family, which is currently the only one supported.

- **128.185.61.2** is the address of the LAN interface for system1.

- **netmask** shows how to subdivide the network

- **255.255.0.0** is the same as ffff0000, which is the netmask for a class "B" address.

I have made good use of **netstat**, **lanscan**, **ping**, and **ifconfig** to help get the status of the network. **ifconfig**, **route**, and **/etc/hosts** are used to configure the network, should you identify changes you need to make. The subnet examples show how flexible you can be when configuring your network for both your current and future needs. In simple networks, you may not need to use many of these commands or complex subnetting. In complex networks, or at times when you encounter configuration difficulties, you may have to make extensive use of these commands. In either case, network planning is an important part of setting up HP-UX systems.

Manual Pages for Commands Used in Chapter 3

The following section contains copies of the manual pages of many of the network commands used in Chapter 3. This makes for a quick reference for you of commands commonly used to configure, monitor, and trouble-shoot your network.

ftp

ftp - Interface for file transfer program.

```
ftp(1)                                                                ftp(1)

NAME
     ftp - file transfer program

SYNOPSIS

     ftp [-g] [-i] [-n] [-v] [-B size] [server-host]

DESCRIPTION
     ftp is a user interface to the File Transfer Protocol.  ftp copies
     files over a network connection between the local ``client'' host and
     a remote ``server'' host.  ftp runs on the client host.

  Options
     The ftp command supports the following options:


          -g   Disable file name ``globbing''; see the glob command, below.
               By default, when this option is not specified, globbing is
               enabled.

          -i   Disable interactive prompting by multiple-file commands; see
               the prompt command, below.  By default, when this option is
               not specified, prompting is enabled.

          -n   Disable ``auto-login''; see the open command, below.  By
               default, when this option is not specified, auto-login is
               enabled.

          -v   Enable verbose output; see the verbose command, below.  If
               this option is not specified, ftp displays verbose output
               only if the standard input is associated with a terminal.

          -B   Set the buffer size of the data socket to size blocks of
               1024 bytes. The valid range for size is an integer from 1 to
               64 (default is 56).
               Note: A large buffer size will improve the performance of
               ftp on fast links (e.g., FDDI), but may cause long
               connection times on slow links (e.g., X.25).

     The name of the server host that ftp communicates with can be
     specified on the command line.  If the server host is specified, ftp
     immediately opens a connection to the server host; see the open
     command, below.  Otherwise, ftp waits for commands from the user.

     File Transfer Protocol specifies file transfer parameters for type,
     mode, form, and struct.  ftp supports the ASCII, binary, and tenex
     File Transfer Protocol types.  ASCII is the default FTP type. (It
     should be noted though that, whenever ftp establishes a connection
     between two similar systems, it switches automatically to the more
     efficient binary type.) ftp supports only the default values for the
     file transfer parameters mode which defaults to stream, form which
     defaults to non-print, and struct which defaults to file.
```

COMMANDS
ftp supports the following commands. Command arguments with embedded
spaces must be enclosed in quotes (for example, "argument with
embedded spaces").

![command [args]]
Invoke a shell on the local host. The SHELL environment variable
specifies which shell program to invoke. ftp invokes /usr/bin/sh
if SHELL is undefined. If command is specified, the shell
executes it and returns to ftp. Otherwise, an interactive shell
is invoked. When the shell terminates, it returns to ftp.

$ macro-name [args]
Execute the macro macro-name that was defined with the macdef
command. Arguments are passed to the macro unglobbed.

account [passwd]
Supply a supplemental password required by a remote system for
access to resources once a login has been successfully completed.
If no argument is included, the user is prompted for an account
password in a non-echoing input mode.

append local-file [remote-file]
Copy local-file to the end of remote-file. If remote-file is
left unspecified, the local file name is used in naming the
remote file after being altered by any ntrans or nmap setting.

ascii
Set the file transfer type to network ASCII. This is the default
type.

bell Sound a bell after each file transfer completes.

binary
Set the file transfer type to binary.

bye Close the connection to the server host if a connection was open,
and exit. Typing an end-of-file (EOF) character also terminates
and exits the session.

case Toggle remote computer file name case mapping during mget
commands. When case is on (the default is off), remote computer
file names with all letters in uppercase are written in the local
directory with the letters mapped to lowercase.

cd remote-directory
Set the working directory on the server host to remote-directory.

cdup Set the working directory on the server host to the parent of the
current remote working directory.

chmod mode file-name
Change the permission modes of the file file-name on the remote
system to mode.

close
Terminate the connection to the server host. The close command
does not exit ftp. Any defined macros are erased.

cr   Toggle carriage return stripping during ascii type file
retrieval. Records are denoted by a carriage-return/line-feed
sequence during ascii type file transfer. When cr is on (the
default), carriage returns are stripped from this sequence to
conform with the UNIX single line-feed record delimiter. Records
on non-UNIX remote systems may contain single line-feeds; when an

ascii type transfer is made, these line-feeds can be
distinguished from a record delimiter only when cr is off.

delete remote-file
    Delete remote-file. The remote-file can be an empty directory.
    No globbing is done.

dir [remote-directory] [local-file]
    Write a remote-directory listing to standard output or optionally
    to local-file. If neither remote-directory nor local-file is
    specified, list the remote working directory to standard output.
    If interactive prompting is on, ftp prompts the user to verify
    that the last argument is indeed the target file for dir output.
    Globbing characters are always expanded.

disconnect
    A synonym for close.

form format
    Set the file transfer form to format. The only supported format
    is non-print

get remote-file [local-file]
    Copy remote-file to local-file. If local-file is unspecified,
    ftp uses the specified remote-file name as the local-file name,
    subject to alteration by the current case, ntrans, and nmap
    settings.

glob Toggle file name globbing. When file name globbing is enabled,
    ftp expands csh(1) metacharacters in file and directory names.
    These characters are *, ?, [,], ~, {, and }. The server host
    expands remote file and directory names. Globbing metacharacters
    are always expanded for the ls and dir commands. If globbing is
    enabled, metacharacters are also expanded for the multiple-file
    commands mdelete, mdir, mget, mls, and mput.

hash Toggle printing of a hash-sign (#) for each 1024 bytes
    transferred.

help [command]
    Print an informative message about the ftp command called ftp-
    command. If ftp-command is unspecified, print a list of all ftp
    commands.

idle [seconds]
    Set the inactivity timer on the remote server to seconds seconds.
    If seconds is omitted, ftp prints the current inactivity timer.

lcd [local-directory]
    Set the local working directory to local-directory. If local-
    directory is unspecified, set the local working directory to the
    user's local home directory.

ls [remote-directory] [local-file]
    Write a listing of remote-directory to local-file. The listing
    includes any system-dependent information that the server chooses
    to include; for example, most UNIX systems produce output from
    the command ls -l (see also nlist). If neither remote-directory
    nor local-file is specified, list the remote working directory.
    If globbing is enabled, globbing metacharacters are expanded.

macdef macro-name
    Define a macro. Subsequent lines are stored as the macro macro-
    name; an empty input line terminates macro input mode. There is
    a limit of 16 macros and 4096 total characters in all defined

macros. Macros remain defined until a close command is executed. The macro processor interprets $ and \ as special characters. A $ followed by a number (or numbers) is replaced by the corresponding argument on the macro invocation command line. A $ followed by an i signals to the macro processor that the executing macro is to be looped. On the first pass $i is replaced by the first argument on the macro invocation command line, on the second pass it is replaced by the second argument, and so on. A \ followed by any character is replaced by that character. Use the \ to prevent special treatment of the $.

mdelete [remote-files]
> Delete remote-files. If globbing is enabled, globbing metacharacters are expanded.

mdir remote-files local-file
> Write a listing of remote-files to local-file. If globbing is enabled, globbing metacharacters are expanded. If interactive prompting is on, ftp prompts the user to verify that the last argument is indeed the target local file for mdir output.

mget remote-files
> Copy remote-files to the local system. If globbing is enabled, globbing metacharacters are expanded. The resulting local file names are processed according to case, ntrans, and nmap settings.

mkdir directory-name
> Create remote directory-name.

mls remote-files local-file
> Write an abbreviated listing of remote-files to local-file. If globbing is enabled, globbing metacharacters are expanded. If interactive prompting is on, ftp prompts the user to verify that the last argument is indeed the target local file for mls output.

mode [mode-name]
> Set the FTP file transfer mode to mode-name. The only supported mode is stream.

modtime remote-file
> Show the last modification time of remote-file.

mput local-files
> Copy local-files from the local system to the remote system. The remote files have the same name as the local files processed according to ntrans and nmap settings. If globbing is enabled, globbing characters are expanded.

newer file-name
> Get the file only if the modification time of the remote file is more recent that the file on the current system. If the file does not exist on the current system, the remote file is considered newer. Otherwise, this command is identical to get.

nlist [remote-directory] [local-file]
> Write an abbreviated listing of remote-directory to local-file. If remote-directory is left unspecified, the current working directory is used. If interactive prompting is on, ftp prompts the user to verify that the last argument is indeed the target local file for nlist output.

nmap [inpattern outpattern]
> Set or unset the filename mapping mechanism. If no arguments are

specified, the filename mapping mechanism is unset. If arguments
are specified, remote filenames are mapped during mput commands
and put commands issued without a specified remote target
filename. If arguments are specified, local filenames are mapped
during mget commands and get commands issued without a specified
local target filename. This command is useful when connecting to
a non-UNIX remote computer with different file naming conventions
or practices. The mapping follows the pattern set by inpattern
and outpattern. inpattern is a template for incoming filenames
(which may have already been processed according to the ntrans
and case settings). Variable templating is accomplished by
including the sequences $1, $2, ..., $9 in inpattern. Use \ to
prevent this special treatment of the $ character. All other
characters are treated literally, and are used to determine the
nmap inpattern variable values. For example, given inpattern
$1.$2 and the remote file name mydata.data, $1 would have the
value mydata, and $2 would have the value data. The outpattern
determines the resulting mapped filename. The sequences $1,
$2, ..., $9 are replaced by any value resulting from the
inpattern template. The sequence $0 is replaced by the original
filename. Additionally, the sequence [seq1,seq2] is replaced by
seq1 if seq1 is not a null string; otherwise it is replaced by
seq2. For example, the command nmap $1.$2.$3 [$1,$2].[$2,file]
would yield the output filename myfile.data for input filenames
myfile.data and myfile.data.old, myfile.file for the input
filename myfile, and myfile.myfile for the input filename
.myfile. Spaces can be included in outpattern, as in the
example: nmap $1 | sed "s/ *$//" > $1 . Use the \ character to
prevent special treatment of the $, [,], and , characters.

ntrans [inchars [outchars]]
> Set or unset the filename character translation mechanism. If no
> arguments are specified, the filename character translation
> mechanism is unset. If arguments are specified, characters in
> remote filenames are translated during mput commands and put
> commands issued without a specified remote target filename. If
> arguments are specified, characters in local filenames are
> translated during mget commands and get commands issued without a
> specified local target filename. This command is useful when
> connecting to a non-UNIX remote computer with different file
> naming conventions or practices. Characters in a filename
> matching a character in inchars are replaced with the
> corresponding character in outchars. If the character's position
> in inchars is longer than the length of outchars, the character
> is deleted from the file name.

open server-host [port-number]
> Establish a connection to server-host, using port-number (if
> specified). If auto-login is enabled, ftp attempts to log into
> the server host.

prompt
> Toggle interactive prompting. By default, ftp prompts the user
> for a yes or no response for each output file during multiple-
> file commands. If interactive prompting is disabled, ftp
> performs the command for all specified files.

proxy ftp-command
> Execute an ftp command on a secondary control connection. This
> command allows simultaneous connection to two remote FTP servers
> for transferring files between the two servers. The first proxy
> command should be an open, to establish the secondary control
> connection. Enter the command proxy ? to see other FTP commands
> executable on the secondary connection. The following commands
> behave differently when prefaced by proxy: open does not define
> new macros during the auto-login process, close does not erase

existing macro definitions, get and mget transfer files from the
host on the primary control connection to the host on the
secondary control connection, and put, mput, and append transfer
files from the host on the secondary control connection to the
host on the primary control connection. Third party file
transfers depend upon support of the FTP protocol PASV command by
the server on the secondary control connection.

put local-file [remote-file]
    Copy local-file to remote-file. If remote-file is unspecified,
    ftp assigns the local-file name, processed according to any
    ntrans or nmap settings, to the remote-file name.

pwd Write the name of the remote working directory to stdout.

quit A synonym for bye.

quote arguments
    Send arguments, verbatim, to the server host. See ftpd(1M).

recv remote-file [local-file]
    A synonym for get.

reget remote-file [local-file]
    reget acts like get, except that if local-file exists and is
    smaller than remote-file, local-file is presumed to be a
    partially transferred copy of remote-file and the transfer is
    continued from the apparent point of failure. This command is
    useful when transferring very large files over networks that tend
    to drop connections.

rhelp [command-name]
    Request help from the server host. If command-name is specified,
    supply it to the server. See ftpd(1M).

rstatus [file-name]
    With no arguments, show status of remote machine. If file-name
    is specified, show status of file-name on remote machine.

rename remote-from remote-to
    Rename remote-from, which can be either a file or a directory, to
    remote-to.

reset
    Clear reply queue. This command re-synchronizes command/reply
    sequencing with the remote FTP server. Resynchronization may be
    necessary following a violation of the FTP protocol by the remote
    server.

restart marker
    Restart the immediately following get or put at the indicated
    marker. On UNIX systems, marker is usually a byte offset into
    the file.

rmdir remote-directory
    Delete remote-directory. remote-directory must be an empty
    directory.

runique
    Toggle storing of files on the local system with unique
    filenames. If a file already exists with a name equal to the
    target local filename for a get or mget command, a .1 is appended
    to the name. If the resulting name matches another existing
    file, a .2 is appended to the original name. If this process
    continues up to .99, an error message is printed, and the
    transfer does not take place. ftp reports the unique filename.

Note that runique does not affect local files generated from a
shell command (see below). The default value is off.

send local-file [remote-file]
    A synonym for put.

sendport
    Toggle the use of PORT commands. By default, ftp attempts to use
    a PORT command when establishing a connection for each data
    transfer. If the PORT command fails, ftp uses the default data
    port. When the use of PORT commands is disabled, ftp makes no
    attempt to use PORT commands for each data transfer. This is
    useful for certain FTP implementations that ignore PORT commands
    but (incorrectly) indicate that they've been accepted. See
    ftpd(1M). Turning sendport off may cause delays in the execution
    of commands.

site arguments
    Send arguments, verbatim, to the server host as a SITE command.
    See ftpd(1M).

size remote-file
    Show the size of remote-file.

status
    Show the current status of ftp.

struct [struct-name]
    Set the FTP file transfer struct to struct-name. The only
    supported struct is file.

sunique
    Toggle storing of files on remote machine under unique file
    names. The remote server reports the unique name. By default,
    sunique is off.

system
    Show the type of operating system running on the remote machine.

tenex
    Set the FTP file transfer type to tenex.

type [type-name]
    Set the FTP file transfer type to type-name. If type-name is
    unspecified, write the current type to stdout. Ascii, binary,
    and tenex are the types currently supported.

umask [newmask]
    Set the default umask on the remote server to newmask. If
    newmask is omitted, the current umask is printed.

user user-name [password] [account]
    Log into the server host on the current connection, which must
    already be open. A .netrc file in the user's local home
    directory can provide the user-name, password, and optionally the
    account; see netrc(4). Otherwise ftp prompts the user for this
    information. The HP-UX FTP server does not require an account.
    For security reasons, ftp always requires a password. It does
    not log into remote accounts that do not have a password.

verbose
    Toggle verbose output. If verbose output is enabled, ftp
    displays responses from the server host, and when a file transfer
    completes it reports statistics regarding the efficiency of the
    transfer.

? [command]
        A synonym for the help command. Prints the help information for
        the specified command.

Aborting A File Transfer
    To abort a file transfer, use the terminal interrupt key (usually
    Ctrl-C). Sending transfers are halted immediately. ftp halts
    incoming (receive) transfers by first sending a FTP protocol ABOR
    command to the remote server, then discarding any further received
    data. The speed at which this is accomplished depends upon the remote
    server's support for ABOR processing. If the remote server does not
    support the ABOR command, an ftp> prompt does not appear until the
    remote server completes sending the requested file.

    The terminal interrupt key sequence is ignored while ftp awaits a
    reply from the remote server. A long delay in this mode may result
    from the ABOR processing described above, or from unexpected behavior
    by the remote server, including violations of the FTP protocol. If
    the delay results from unexpected remote server behavior, the local
    ftp program must be killed manually.

File Naming Conventions
    Files specified as arguments to ftp commands are processed according
    to the following rules.

    -   If the file name - is specified, ftp uses the standard input (for
        reading) or standard output (for writing).

    -   If the first character of the file name is |, ftp interprets the
        remainder of the argument as a shell command. ftp forks a shell,
        using popen() (see popen(3S)) with the supplied argument, and reads
        (writes) from standard output (standard input). If the shell
        command includes spaces, the argument must be quoted, as in:

            "| ls -lt".

    A particularly useful example of this mechanism is:

            "| dir . | more".

    -   Otherwise, if globbing is enabled, ftp expands local file names
        according to the rules used by the C shell (see csh(1)); see the
        glob command, below. If the ftp command expects a single local
        file (e.g. put), only the first filename generated by the globbing
        operation is used.

    -   For mget commands and get commands with unspecified local file
        names, the local filename is named the same as the remote filename,
        which may be altered by a case, ntrans, or nmap setting. The
        resulting filename may then be altered if runique is on.

    -   For mput commands and put commands with unspecified remote file
        names, the remote filename is named the same as the local filename,
        which may be altered by a ntrans or nmap setting. The resulting
        filename may then be altered by the remote server if sunique is on.

WARNINGS
    Correct execution of many commands depends upon proper behavior by the
    remote server.

AUTHOR
    ftp was developed by the University of California, Berkeley.

SEE ALSO

csh(1), rcp(1), ftpd(1M), netrc(4), ftpusers(4), hosts(4).

ftp(1)   Secure Internet Services with Kerberos Authentication   ftp(1)

NAME
     ftp - file transfer program

SYNOPSIS

     ftp [-g] [-i] [-n] [-P] [-v] [-B size] [server-host]

DESCRIPTION
     ftp is a user interface to the File Transfer Protocol. ftp copies
     files over a network connection between the local ``client'' host and
     a remote ``server'' host. ftp runs on the client host.

  Options
     The ftp command supports the following options:

          -g   Disable file name ``globbing''; see the glob command, below.
                By default, when this option is not specified, globbing is
                enabled.

          -i   Disable interactive prompting by multiple-file commands; see
                the prompt command, below. By default, when this option is
                not specified, prompting is enabled.

          -P   Disables Kerberos authentication and authorization. Only
                applicable in a secure environment based on Kerberos V5.
                When this option is specified, a password is required and
                the password is sent across the network in a readable form.
                By default, if this option is not specified, a password is
                not required and Kerberos authentication and authorization
                takes place instead. See sis(5).

          -n   Disable ``auto-login''; see the open command, below. By
                default, when this option is not specified, auto-login is
                enabled.

          -v   Enable verbose output; see the verbose command, below. If
                this option is not specified, ftp displays verbose output
                only if the standard input is associated with a terminal.

          -B   Set the buffer size of the data socket to size blocks of
                1024 bytes. The valid range for size is an integer from 1 to
                64 (default is 56).
                Note: A large buffer size will improve the performance of
                ftp on fast links (e.g., FDDI), but may cause long
                connection times on slow links (e.g., X.25).

     The name of the server host that ftp communicates with can be
     specified on the command line. If the server host is specified, ftp
     immediately opens a connection to the server host; see the open
     command, below. Otherwise, ftp waits for commands from the user.

     File Transfer Protocol specifies file transfer parameters for type,
     mode, form, and struct. ftp supports the ASCII, binary, and tenex
     File Transfer Protocol types. ASCII is the default FTP type. (It
     should be noted though that, whenever ftp establishes a connection
     between two similar systems, it switches automatically to the more
     efficient binary type.) ftp supports only the default values for the
     file transfer parameters mode which defaults to stream, form which
     defaults to non-print, and struct which defaults to file.

COMMANDS

ftp supports the following commands. Command arguments with embedded
spaces must be enclosed in quotes (for example, "argument with
embedded spaces").

![command [args]]
    Invoke a shell on the local host. The SHELL environment variable
    specifies which shell program to invoke. ftp invokes /usr/bin/sh
    if SHELL is undefined. If command is specified, the shell
    executes it and returns to ftp. Otherwise, an interactive shell
    is invoked. When the shell terminates, it returns to ftp.

$ macro-name [args]
    Execute the macro macro-name that was defined with the macdef
    command. Arguments are passed to the macro unglobbed.

account [passwd]
    Supply a supplemental password required by a remote system for
    access to resources once a login has been successfully completed.
    If no argument is included, the user is prompted for an account
    password in a non-echoing input mode.

append local-file [remote-file]
    Copy local-file to the end of remote-file. If remote-file is
    left unspecified, the local file name is used in naming the
    remote file after being altered by any ntrans or nmap setting.

ascii
    Set the file transfer type to network ASCII. This is the default
    type.

bell Sound a bell after each file transfer completes.

binary
    Set the file transfer type to binary.

bye Close the connection to the server host if a connection was open,
    and exit. Typing an end-of-file (EOF) character also terminates
    and exits the session.

case Toggle remote computer file name case mapping during mget
    commands. When case is on (the default is off), remote computer
    file names with all letters in uppercase are written in the local
    directory with the letters mapped to lowercase.

cd remote-directory
    Set the working directory on the server host to remote-directory.

cdup Set the working directory on the server host to the parent of the
    current remote working directory.

chmod mode file-name
    Change the permission modes of the file file-name on the remote
    system to mode.

close
    Terminate the connection to the server host. The close command
    does not exit ftp. Any defined macros are erased.

cr   Toggle carriage return stripping during ascii type file
    retrieval. Records are denoted by a carriage-return/line-feed
    sequence during ascii type file transfer. When cr is on (the
    default), carriage returns are stripped from this sequence to
    conform with the UNIX single line-feed record delimiter. Records
    on non-UNIX remote systems may contain single line-feeds; when an
    ascii type transfer is made, these line-feeds can be

distinguished from a record delimiter only when cr is off.

delete remote-file
> Delete remote-file. The remote-file can be an empty directory.
> No globbing is done.

dir [remote-directory] [local-file]
> Write a remote-directory listing to standard output or optionally
> to local-file. If neither remote-directory nor local-file is
> specified, list the remote working directory to standard output.
> If interactive prompting is on, ftp prompts the user to verify
> that the last argument is indeed the target file for dir output.
> Globbing characters are always expanded.

disconnect
> A synonym for close.

form format
> Set the file transfer form to format. The only supported format
> is non-print

get remote-file [local-file]
> Copy remote-file to local-file. If local-file is unspecified,
> ftp uses the specified remote-file name as the local-file name,
> subject to alteration by the current case, ntrans, and nmap
> settings.

glob Toggle file name globbing. When file name globbing is enabled,
> ftp expands csh(1) metacharacters in file and directory names.
> These characters are *, ?, [,], ~, {, and }. The server host
> expands remote file and directory names. Globbing metacharacters
> are always expanded for the ls and dir commands. If globbing is
> enabled, metacharacters are also expanded for the multiple-file
> commands mdelete, mdir, mget, mls, and mput.

hash Toggle printing of a hash-sign (#) for each 1024 bytes
> transferred.

help [command]
> Print an informative message about the ftp command called ftp-
> command. If ftp-command is unspecified, print a list of all ftp
> commands.

idle [seconds]
> Set the inactivity timer on the remote server to seconds seconds.
> If seconds is omitted, ftp prints the current inactivity timer.

lcd [local-directory]
> Set the local working directory to local-directory. If local-
> directory is unspecified, set the local working directory to the
> user's local home directory.

ls [remote-directory] [local-file]
> Write a listing of remote-directory to local-file. The listing
> includes any system-dependent information that the server chooses
> to include; for example, most UNIX systems produce output from
> the command ls -l (see also nlist). If neither remote-directory
> nor local-file is specified, list the remote working directory.
> If globbing is enabled, globbing metacharacters are expanded.

macdef macro-name
> Define a macro. Subsequent lines are stored as the macro macro-
> name; an empty input line terminates macro input mode. There is
> a limit of 16 macros and 4096 total characters in all defined
> macros. Macros remain defined until a close command is executed.

The macro processor interprets $ and \ as special characters. A
$ followed by a number (or numbers) is replaced by the
corresponding argument on the macro invocation command line. A $
followed by an i signals to the macro processor that the
executing macro is to be looped. On the first pass $i is
replaced by the first argument on the macro invocation command
line, on the second pass it is replaced by the second argument,
and so on. A \ followed by any character is replaced by that
character. Use the \ to prevent special treatment of the $.

mdelete [remote-files]
    Delete remote-files. If globbing is enabled, globbing
    metacharacters are expanded.

mdir remote-files local-file
    Write a listing of remote-files to local-file. If globbing is
    enabled, globbing metacharacters are expanded. If interactive
    prompting is on, ftp prompts the user to verify that the last
    argument is indeed the target local file for mdir output.

mget remote-files
    Copy remote-files to the local system. If globbing is enabled,
    globbing metacharacters are expanded. The resulting local file
    names are processed according to case, ntrans, and nmap settings.

mkdir directory-name
    Create remote directory-name.

mls remote-files local-file
    Write an abbreviated listing of remote-files to local-file. If
    globbing is enabled, globbing metacharacters are expanded. If
    interactive prompting is on, ftp prompts the user to verify that
    the last argument is indeed the target local file for mls output.

mode [mode-name]
    Set the FTP file transfer mode to mode-name. The only supported
    mode is stream.

modtime remote-file
    Show the last modification time of remote-file.

mput local-files
    Copy local-files from the local system to the remote system. The
    remote files have the same name as the local files processed
    according to ntrans and nmap settings. If globbing is enabled,
    globbing characters are expanded.

newer file-name
    Get the file only if the modification time of the remote file is
    more recent that the file on the current system. If the file
    does not exist on the current system, the remote file is
    considered newer. Otherwise, this command is identical to get.

nlist [remote-directory] [local-file]
    Write an abbreviated listing of remote-directory to local-file.
    If remote-directory is left unspecified, the current working
    directory is used. If interactive prompting is on, ftp prompts
    the user to verify that the last argument is indeed the target
    local file for nlist output.

nmap [inpattern outpattern]
    Set or unset the filename mapping mechanism. If no arguments are
    specified, the filename mapping mechanism is unset. If arguments

are specified, remote filenames are mapped during mput commands
and put commands issued without a specified remote target
filename. If arguments are specified, local filenames are mapped
during mget commands and get commands issued without a specified
local target filename. This command is useful when connecting to
a non-UNIX remote computer with different file naming conventions
or practices. The mapping follows the pattern set by inpattern
and outpattern. inpattern is a template for incoming filenames
(which may have already been processed according to the ntrans
and case settings). Variable templating is accomplished by
including the sequences $1, $2, ..., $9 in inpattern. Use \ to
prevent this special treatment of the $ character. All other
characters are treated literally, and are used to determine the
nmap inpattern variable values. For example, given inpattern
$1.$2 and the remote file name mydata.data, $1 would have the
value mydata, and $2 would have the value data. The outpattern
determines the resulting mapped filename. The sequences $1,
$2, ..., $9 are replaced by any value resulting from the
inpattern template. The sequence $0 is replaced by the original
filename. Additionally, the sequence [seq1,seq2] is replaced by
seq1 if seq1 is not a null string; otherwise it is replaced by
seq2. For example, the command nmap $1.$2.$3 [$1,$2].[$2,file]
would yield the output filename myfile.data for input filenames
myfile.data and myfile.data.old, myfile.file for the input
filename myfile, and myfile.myfile for the input filename
.myfile. Spaces can be included in outpattern, as in the
example: nmap $1 | sed "s/ *$//" > $1 . Use the \ character to
prevent special treatment of the $, [,], and , characters.

ntrans [inchars [outchars]]
     Set or unset the filename character translation mechanism. If no
     arguments are specified, the filename character translation
     mechanism is unset. If arguments are specified, characters in
     remote filenames are translated during mput commands and put
     commands issued without a specified remote target filename. If
     arguments are specified, characters in local filenames are
     translated during mget commands and get commands issued without a
     specified local target filename. This command is useful when
     connecting to a non-UNIX remote computer with different file
     naming conventions or practices. Characters in a filename
     matching a character in inchars are replaced with the
     corresponding character in outchars. If the character's position
     in inchars is longer than the length of outchars, the character
     is deleted from the file name.

open server-host [port-number]
     Establish a connection to server-host, using port-number (if
     specified). If auto-login is enabled, ftp attempts to log into
     the server host.

prompt
     Toggle interactive prompting. By default, ftp prompts the user
     for a yes or no response for each output file during multiple-
     file commands. If interactive prompting is disabled, ftp
     performs the command for all specified files.

put local-file [remote-file]
     Copy local-file to remote-file. If remote-file is unspecified,
     ftp assigns the local-file name, processed according to any
     ntrans or nmap settings, to the remote-file name.

pwd Write the name of the remote working directory to stdout.

quit A synonym for bye.

quote arguments

Send arguments, verbatim, to the server host. See ftpd(1M).

recv remote-file [local-file]
    A synonym for get.

reget remote-file [local-file]
    reget acts like get, except that if local-file exists and is
    smaller than remote-file, local-file is presumed to be a
    partially transferred copy of remote-file and the transfer is
    continued from the apparent point of failure. This command is
    useful when transferring very large files over networks that tend
    to drop connections.

rhelp [command-name]
    Request help from the server host. If command-name is specified,
    supply it to the server. See ftpd(1M).

rstatus [file-name]
    With no arguments, show status of remote machine. If file-name
    is specified, show status of file-name on remote machine.

rename remote-from remote-to
    Rename remote-from, which can be either a file or a directory, to
    remote-to.

reset
    Clear reply queue. This command re-synchronizes command/reply
    sequencing with the remote FTP server. Resynchronization may be
    necessary following a violation of the FTP protocol by the remote
    server.

restart marker
    Restart the immediately following get or put at the indicated
    marker. On UNIX systems, marker is usually a byte offset into
    the file.

rmdir remote-directory
    Delete remote-directory. remote-directory must be an empty
    directory.

runique
    Toggle storing of files on the local system with unique
    filenames. If a file already exists with a name equal to the
    target local filename for a get or mget command, a .1 is appended
    to the name. If the resulting name matches another existing
    file, a .2 is appended to the original name. If this process
    continues up to .99, an error message is printed, and the
    transfer does not take place. ftp reports the unique filename.
    Note that runique does not affect local files generated from a
    shell command (see below). The default value is off.

send local-file [remote-file]
    A synonym for put.

sendport
    Toggle the use of PORT commands. By default, ftp attempts to use
    a PORT command when establishing a connection for each data
    transfer. If the PORT command fails, ftp uses the default data
    port. When the use of PORT commands is disabled, ftp makes no
    attempt to use PORT commands for each data transfer. This is
    useful for certain FTP implementations that ignore PORT commands
    but (incorrectly) indicate that they've been accepted. See
    ftpd(1M). Turning sendport off may cause delays in the execution
    of commands.

site arguments

Send arguments, verbatim, to the server host as a SITE command.
See ftpd(1M).

size remote-file
Show the size of remote-file.

status
Show the current status of ftp.

struct [struct-name]
Set the FTP file transfer struct to struct-name. The only
supported struct is file.

sunique
Toggle storing of files on remote machine under unique file
names. The remote server reports the unique name. By default,
sunique is off.

system
Show the type of operating system running on the remote machine.

tenex
Set the FTP file transfer type to tenex.

type [type-name]
Set the FTP file transfer type to type-name. If type-name is
unspecified, write the current type to stdout. Ascii, binary,
and tenex are the types currently supported.

umask [newmask]
Set the default umask on the remote server to newmask. If
newmask is omitted, the current umask is printed.

user user-name [password] [account]
Log into the server host on the current connection, which must
already be open. A .netrc file in the user's local home
directory can provide the user-name, password, and optionally the
account; see netrc(4). Otherwise ftp prompts the user for this
information. In a secure environment based on Kerberos V5, ftp
will not require a password. Instead, Kerberos authentication
and authorization will be performed as described in sis(5). In
all other environments, users are considered authenticated if
they have a password and that password is correct, and authorized
if an account exists for them on the remote system.

verbose
Toggle verbose output. If verbose output is enabled, ftp
displays responses from the server host, and when a file transfer
completes it reports statistics regarding the efficiency of the
transfer.

? [command]
A synonym for the help command. Prints the help information for
the specified command.

Aborting A File Transfer
To abort a file transfer, use the terminal interrupt key (usually
Ctrl-C). Sending transfers are halted immediately. ftp halts
incoming (receive) transfers by first sending a FTP protocol ABOR
command to the remote server, then discarding any further received
data. The speed at which this is accomplished depends upon the remote
server's support for ABOR processing. If the remote server does not
support the ABOR command, an ftp> prompt does not appear until the
remote server completes sending the requested file.

The terminal interrupt key sequence is ignored while ftp awaits a
reply from the remote server. A long delay in this mode may result
from the ABOR processing described above, or from unexpected behavior
by the remote server, including violations of the FTP protocol. If
the delay results from unexpected remote server behavior, the local
ftp program must be killed manually.

File Naming Conventions
  Files specified as arguments to ftp commands are processed according
  to the following rules.

  - If the file name - is specified, ftp uses the standard input (for
    reading) or standard output (for writing).

  - If the first character of the file name is |, ftp interprets the
    remainder of the argument as a shell command. ftp forks a shell,
    using popen() (see popen(3S)) with the supplied argument, and reads
    (writes) from standard output (standard input). If the shell
    command includes spaces, the argument must be quoted, as in:

        "| ls -lt".

    A particularly useful example of this mechanism is:

        "| dir . | more".

  - Otherwise, if globbing is enabled, ftp expands local file names
    according to the rules used by the C shell (see csh(1)); see the
    glob command, below. If the ftp command expects a single local
    file (e.g. put), only the first filename generated by the globbing
    operation is used.

  - For mget commands and get commands with unspecified local file
    names, the local filename is named the same as the remote filename,
    which may be altered by a case, ntrans, or nmap setting. The
    resulting filename may then be altered if runique is on.

  - For mput commands and put commands with unspecified remote file
    names, the remote filename is named the same as the local filename,
    which may be altered by a ntrans or nmap setting. The resulting
    filename may then be altered by the remote server if sunique is on.

WARNINGS
    Correct execution of many commands depends upon proper behavior by the
    remote server.

AUTHOR
    ftp was developed by the University of California, Berkeley.

SEE ALSO
    csh(1), rcp(1), ftpd(1M), netrc(4), ftpusers(4), hosts(4), sis(5).

ifconfig

ifconfig - Display or configure network interface parameters.

```
ifconfig(1M)                                                       ifconfig(1M)

NAME
     ifconfig - configure network interface parameters

SYNOPSIS

     ifconfig interface address_family [address [dest_address]] [parameters]

     ifconfig interface [address_family]

DESCRIPTION
     The first form of the ifconfig command assigns an address to a network
     interface and/or configures network interface parameters.  ifconfig
     must be used at boot time to define the network address of each
     interface present on a machine.  It can also be used at other times to
     redefine an interface's address or other operating parameters.

     The second form of the command, without address_family, displays the
     current configuration for interface.  If address_family is also
     specified, ifconfig reports only the details specific to that address
     family.

     Only a user with appropriate privileges can modify the configuration
     of a network interface.  All users can run the second form of the
     command.

     Arguments
        ifconfig recognizes the following arguments:

              address           Either a host name present in the host name
                                database (see hosts(4)), or a DARPA Internet
                                address expressed in Internet standard dot
                                notation (see inet(3N)).  The host number can be
                                omitted on 10MB/second Ethernet interfaces (which
                                use the hardware physical address), and on
                                interfaces other than the first.

              address_family    Name of protocol on which naming scheme is based.
                                An interface can receive transmissions in
                                differing protocols, each of which may require
                                separate naming schemes.  Therefore, it is
                                necessary to specify the address_family, which
                                may affect interpretation of the remaining
                                parameters on the command line.  The only address
                                family currently supported is inet (DARPA-
                                Internet family).

              dest_address      Address of destination system.  Consists of
                                either a host name present in the host name
                                database (see hosts(4)), or a DARPA Internet
                                address expressed in Internet standard dot
                                notation (see inet(3N)).

              interface         A string of the form nameunit, such as lan0.
```

(See the LAN Card Numbering subsection.)

parameters   One or more of the following operating
                    parameters:

          up   Mark an interface "up". Enables
                              interface after an ifconfig down.
                              Occurs automatically when setting
                              the address on an interface.
                              Setting this flag has no effect if
                              the hardware is "down".

          down   Mark an interface "down". When an
                              interface is marked "down", the
                              system will not attempt to
                              transmit messages through that
                              interface. If possible, the
                              interface will be reset to disable
                              reception as well. This action
                              does not automatically disable
                              routes using the interface.

          broadcast   (Inet only) Specify the address
                              that represents broadcasts to the
                              network. The default broadcast
                              address is the address with a host
                              part of all 1's.

          debug   Enable driver-dependent debugging
                              code. This usually turns on extra
                              console error logging.

          -debug   Disable driver-dependent debugging
                              code.

          ipdst   (NS only) This is used to specify
                              an Internet host that is willing
                              to receive IP packets
                              encapsulating NS packets bound for
                              a remote network. In this case,
                              an apparent point-to-point link is
                              constructed, and the address
                              specified is taken as the NS
                              address and network of the
                              destination.

          metric n   Set the routing metric of the
                              interface to n. The default is 0.
                              The routing metric is used by the
                              routing protocol (see gated(1m)).
                              Higher metrics have the effect of
                              making a route less favorable;
                              metrics are counted as additional
                              hops to the destination network or
                              host.

          netmask mask   (Inet only) Specify how much of
                              the address to reserve for
                              subdividing networks into sub-
                              networks or aggregating networks
                              into supernets. mask can be
                              specified as a single hexadecimal
                              number with a leading 0x, with a
                              dot-notation Internet address, or
                              with a pseudo-network name listed
                              in the network table (see

networks(4)). For subdividing
networks into sub-networks, mask
must include the network part of
the local address, and the subnet
part which is taken from the host
field of the address. mask must
contain 1's in the bit positions
in the 32-bit address that are to
be used for the network and subnet
parts, and 0's in the host part.
The 1's in the mask must be
contiguous starting from the
leftmost bit position in the 32-
bit field. mask must contain at
least the standard network
portion, and the subnet field must
be contiguous with the network
portion. The subnet field must
contain at least 2 bits. The
subnet part after performing a
bit-wise AND operation between the
address and the mask must not
contain all 0's or all 1's. For
aggregating networks into
supernets, mask must only include
a portion of the network part.
mask must contain contiguous 1's
in the bit positions starting from
the leftmost bit of the 32-bit
field.

trailers   Request the use of a "trailer"
                link-level encapsulation when
                sending. If a network interface
                supports trailers, the system
                will, when possible, encapsulate
                outgoing messages in a manner that
                minimizes the number of memory-
                to-memory copy operations
                performed by the receiver. On
                networks that support the Address
                Resolution Protocol, this flag
                indicates that the system should
                request that other systems use
                trailers when sending to this
                host. Similarly, trailer
                encapsulations will be sent to
                other hosts that have made such
                requests. Currently used by
                Internet protocols only. See
                WARNINGS section.

-trailers   Disable the use of a "trailer"
                link-level encapsulation
                (default).

LAN Card Numbering
   The name of an interface associated with a LAN card is lan, and its
   unitnumber is determined as follows. The LAN card installed first in
   the system is given interface unit number 0; the next LAN card
   installed is given interface unit number 1; and so on. When there are
   two or more LAN cards installed at the same time, interface unit
   numbers are assigned according to card positions in the backplane:
   the LAN card that appears "first" in the backplane is given the
   interface unit number N; the next LAN card in the backplane is given
   the number N+1.

The lanscan command can be used to display the name and unit number of each interface that is associated with a LAN card (see lanscan(1M)).

Supernets

A supernet is a collection of smaller networks. Supernetting is a technique of using the netmask to aggregate a collection of smaller networks into a supernet. This technique is particularly useful for class C networks. A Class C network can only have 254 hosts. This can be too restrictive for some companies. For these companies, a netmask that only contains a portion of the network part can be applied to the hosts in these class C networks to form a supernet. This supernet netmask should be applied to those interfaces that connect to the supernet using the ifconfig command. For example, a host can configure its interface to connect to a class C supernet, 192.6, by configuring an IP address of 192.6.1.1 and a netmask of 255.255.0.0 to its interface.

DIAGNOSTICS

Messages indicate if the specified interface does not exist, the requested address is unknown, or the user is not privileged and tried to alter an interface's configuration.

WARNINGS

Currently, all HP 9000 systems can receive trailer packets but do not send them. Setting the trailers flag has no effect.

SEE ALSO

netstat(1), lanconfig(1m), lanscan(1m) hosts(4), routing(7).

lanadmin

lanadmin - Administrative program for Local Area Network (LAN).

```
lanadmin(1M)                                                    lanadmin(1M)

NAME
     lanadmin - local area network administration program

SYNOPSIS

     /usr/sbin/lanadmin [-e] [-t]

     /usr/sbin/lanadmin [-a] [-A station_addr] [-m] [-M mtu_size] [-R]
          [-s] [-S speed] NetMgmtID

DESCRIPTION
     The lanadmin program administers and tests the Local Area Network
     (LAN).  For each interface card, it allows you to:

        -  Display and change the station address.
        -  Display and change the maximum transmission unit (MTU).
        -  Display and change the speed setting.
        -  Clear the network statistics registers to zero.
        -  Display the interface statistics.
        -  Reset the interface card, thus executing its self-test.

     For operations other than display, you must have superuser privileges.

     lanadmin reads commands from standard input, writes prompts and error
     messages to standard error, and writes status information to standard
     output.  When the program is run from a terminal, the interrupt key
     (usually ^C) interrupts a currently executing command; the eof key
     (usually ^D) terminates the program.

     lanadmin operates in two modes: Menu Mode (see the first SYNOPSIS
     line) and Immediate Mode (see the second SYNOPSIS line).  If at least
     one -aAmMRsS option is supplied, lanadmin executes in Immediate Mode.
     Otherwise, it executes in Menu Mode.

  Options and Arguments
     lanadmin recognizes the following Immediate Mode options and
     arguments.  At least one -aAmMRsS option and the NetMgmtID argument
     must be supplied.

          NetMgmtID               The Network Management ID number of the LAN
                                  interface.  This argument is ignored if none
                                  of the -aAmMRsS options is used (Menu Mode).
                                  Any options specified after NetMgmtID are
                                  ignored.  Appropriate values can be displayed
                                  with the lanscan command (see lanscan(1M)).

          -a                      Display the current station address of the
                                  interface corresponding to NetMgmtID.

          -A station_addr         Set the new station address of the interface
                                  corresponding to NetMgmtID.  The station_addr
```

must be entered in hex format with a '0x'
prefix. You must have superuser privileges.

-m   Display the current MTU size of the interface
                             corresponding to NetMgmtID.

-M mtu_size   Set the new MTU size of the interface
                             corresponding to NetMgmtID. The mtu_size
                             value must be within the link specific range.
                             You must have superuser privileges.

-R   Reset the MTU size of the interface
                             corresponding to NetMgmtID to the default for
                             that link type. You must have superuser
                             privileges.

-s   Display the current speed setting of the
                             interface corresponding to NetMgmtID.

-S speed   Set the new speed setting of the interface
                             corresponding to NetMgmtID. You must have
                             superuser privileges.

lanadmin recognizes the following Menu Mode options. They are ignored
if they are given with an Immediate Mode option.

-e   Echo the input commands on the output device.

-t   Suppress the display of the command menu
                             before each command prompt. This is
                             equivalent to the Test Selection Mode terse
                             command. The default is verbose.

Immediate Mode
   In Immediate Mode, you can display the station address, MTU size, and
   link speed of LAN interface NetMgmtID. For certain interfaces, if you
   have superuser privileges you can also modify the station address, MTU
   size, and link speed. See "Options and Arguments" above.

Menu Mode
   In Menu Mode, you can select an interface card, display statistics for
   the selected card, reset the card, and clear the statistics registers.

   Menu Mode accepts either complete command words or unique
   abbreviations, and no distinction is made between uppercase and
   lowercase letters in commands. Multiple commands can be entered on
   one line if they are separated by spaces, tabs, or commas.

Test Selection Mode Menu

   This menu is entered when Menu Mode is first selected. The available
   Test Selection Mode commands are:

lan   Select the LAN Interface Test Mode menu.

menu   Display the Test Selection Mode command menu.

quit   Terminate the lanadmin program.

terse   Suppress the display of command menus.

verbose   Restore the display of command menus.

LAN Interface Test Mode Menu

The following commands are available:

clear   Clear the LAN interface network statistics
                   registers to zero. You must have superuser
                   privileges.

display   Display the RFC 1213 MIB II statistics.
                   Depending on the link, the type-specific MIB
                   statistics may also be displayed. For instance,
                   for Ethernet links, the RFC 1398 Ethernet-like
                   statistics are displayed.

end   Return lanadmin to Test Selection Mode.

menu   Display the LAN Interface Test Mode command menu.

nmid   Prompt for a Network Management ID that
                   corresponds to a LAN interface card. It defaults
                   to the first LAN interface encountered in an
                   internal list. Appropriate values can be
                   displayed with the lanscan command (see
                   lanscan(1M)).

quit   Terminate the lanadmin program.

reset   Reset the local LAN interface card, causing it to
                   execute its self-test. Local access to the
                   network is interrupted during execution of reset.
                   You must have superuser privileges.

AUTHOR
    lanadmin was developed by HP.

SEE ALSO
    netstat(1), lanscan(1M), linkloop(1M), ping(1M), lan(7).

    DARPA Requests for Comments: RFC 1213, RFC 1398.

lanscan

lanscan - Display status of Local Area Network (LAN) device(s).

```
lanscan(1M)                                                    lanscan(1M)

NAME
     lanscan - display LAN device configuration and status

SYNOPSIS

     lanscan [-ainv] [system [core]]

DESCRIPTION
     lanscan displays the following information about each LAN device that
     has software support on the system:

          -   Hardware Path.

          -   Active Station Address (also known as Physical Address).

          -   Card Instance Number

          -   Hardware State.

          -   Network Interface ``Name Unit'' and State.

          -   Network Management ID.

          -   MAC Type.

          -   HP DLPI Supported.  Indicates whether or not the lan device
              driver will work with HP's Data Link Provider Interface.

          -   Major Number associated with the driver for the lan interface.
              A -- implies that a major number does not apply to this LAN
              device.

          -   Extended Station Address for those interfaces which require
              more than 48 bits.  This is displayed only when the -v option
              is selected.

          -   Encapsulation Methods that the Network Interface supports.
              This is displayed only when the -v option is selected.

     The arguments system and core allow substitution for the default
     values /stand/vmunix and /dev/kmem.

   Options
     lanscan recognizes the following command-line options:

          -a      Display station addresses only.  No headings.

          -i      Display interface names only.  No headings.

          -n      Display Network Management IDs only.  No headings.

          -v      Verbose output.  Two lines per interface.  Includes
```

displaying of extended station address and supported encapsulation methods.

WARNINGS

lanscan does not display information about LAN devices that do not have software support such as LAN interface cards that fail to

AUTHOR

lanscan was developed by HP.

SEE ALSO

ifconfig(1M), lanconfig(1M), ioscan(1M), lanadmin(1M).

netstat

netstat - Display statistics related to networking.

NAME
     netstat - show network status

SYNOPSIS

     netstat [-aAn] [-f address-family] [system [core]]
     netstat [-mMnrsv] [-f address-family] [-p protocol] [system [core]]
     netstat [-gin] [-I interface] [interval] [system [core]]

DESCRIPTION
     netstat displays statistics for network interfaces and protocols, as
     well as the contents of various network-related data structures. The
     output format varies according to the options selected. Some options
     are ignored when used in combination with other options.

     Generally, the netstat command takes one of the three forms shown
     above:

          -    The first form of the command displays a list of active
               sockets for each protocol.

          -    The second form displays the contents of one of the other
               network data structures according to the option selected.

          -    The third form displays configuration information for each
               network interface. It also displays network traffic data on
               configured network interfaces, optionally updated at each
               interval, measured in seconds.

     Options are interpreted as follows:

          -a   Show the state of all sockets, including
                             passive sockets used by server processes. When
                             netstat is used without any options (except -A
                             and -n), only active sockets are shown. This
                             option does not show the state of X.25
                             programmatic access sockets. The option is
                             ignored if the -g, -i, -I, -m, -M, -p, -r, -s
                             or interval option is specified.

          -A   Show the address of the protocol control block
                             associated with sockets. This option is used
                             for debugging. It does not show the X.25
                             programmatic access control blocks. This
                             option is ignored if the -g, -i, -I, -m, -M,
                             -p, -r, -s or interval option is specified.

          -f address-family Show statistics or address control block for
                             only the specified address-family. The
                             following address families are recognized: inet
                             for AF_INET, and unix for AF_UNIX. This option

applies to the -a, -A and -s options.

-g Show multicast information for network interfaces. Only the address family AF_INET is recognized by this option. This option may be combined with the -i option to display both kinds of information. The option is ignored if the -m, -M or -p option is specified.

-i Show the state of network interfaces. Interfaces that are statically configured into a system, but not located at boot time, are not shown. This option is ignored if the -m, -M or -p option is specified.

-I interface Show information about the specified interface only. This option applies to the -g and -i options.

-m Show statistics recorded by network memory management routines. If this option is specified, all other options are ignored.

-M Show the multicast routing tables. When -s is used with the -M option, netstat displays multicast routing statistics instead. This option is ignored if the -m or -p option is specified.

-n Show network addresses as numbers. Normally, netstat interprets addresses and attempts to display them symbolically. This option applies to the -a, -A, -i, -r and -v options.

-p protocol Show statistics for the specified protocol. The following protocols are recognized: tcp, udp, ip, icmp, igmp, arp, and probe. This option is ignored if the -m option is specified.

-r Show the routing tables. When -v is used with the -r option, netstat also displays the network masks in the route entries. When -s is used with the -r option, netstat displays routing statistics instead. This option is ignored if the -g, -m, -M, -i, -I, -p or interval option is specified.

-s Show statistics for all protocols. When this option is used with the -r option, netstat displays routing statistics instead. When this option is used with the -M option, netstat displays multicast routing statistics instead. This option is ignored if the -g, -i, -I, -m, -p or interval option is specified.

-v Show additional routing information. When -v is used with the -r option, netstat also displays the network masks in the route entries. This option only applies to the -r option.

The arguments system and core allow substitutes for the defaults, /stand/vmunix and /dev/kmem.

If no options or only the -A or -n option is specified, netstat

displays the status of only active sockets. The display of active and
passive sockets status shows the local and remote addresses, send and
receive queue sizes (in bytes), protocol, and the internal state of
the protocol. Address formats are of the form host.port, or
network.port if the host portion of a socket address is zero. When
known, the host and network addresses are displayed symbolically by
using gethostbyname() and getnetbyname(), respectively (see
gethostbyname(3N) and getnetbyname(3N)). If a symbolic name for an
address is unknown, or if the -n option is specified, the address is
displayed numerically according to the address family. For more
information regarding the Internet ``dot format'', refer to inet(3N).
Unspecified or ``wildcard'' addresses and ports appear as an asterisk
(*).

The interface display provides a table of cumulative statistics
regarding packets transferred, errors, and collisions. The network
addresses of the interface and the maximum transmission unit (MTU) are
also displayed. When the interval argument is specified, netstat
displays a running count of statistics related to network interfaces.
This display consists of a column for the primary interface (the first
interface found during auto-configuration) and a column summarizing
information for all interfaces. To replace the primary interface with
another interface, use the -I option. The first line of each screen
of information contains a summary since the system was last rebooted.
Subsequent lines of output show values accumulated over the preceding
interval.

The routing table display indicates the available routes and their
status. Each route consists of a destination host or network, a
netmask and a gateway to use in forwarding packets. The Flags field
shows whether the route is up (U), whether the route is to a gateway
(G), whether the route is a host or network route (with or without H),
whether the route was created dynamically (D) by a redirect or by Path
MTU Discovery, and whether a gateway route has been modified (M), or
it has been marked doubtful (?) due to the lack of a timely ARP
response.

The Netmask field shows the mask to be applied to the destination IP
address of an IP packet to be forwarded. The result will be compared
with the destination address in the route entry. If they are the same,
then the route is one of the candidates for routing this IP packet.
If there are several candidate routes, then the route with the longest
Netmask field (contiguous 1's starting from the leftmost bit position)
will be chosen. (see routing (7).)

The Gateway field shows the address of the immediate gateway for
reaching the destination. It can be the address of the outgoing
interface if the destination is on a directly connected network.

The Refs field shows the current number of active uses of the route.
Connection-oriented protocols normally hold on to a single route for
the duration of a connection, while connectionless protocols normally
obtain a route just while sending a particular message. The Use field
shows a count of the number of packets sent using the route. The
Interface field identifies which network interface is used for the
route.

The Pmtu and PmtuTime fields apply only to host routes. The Pmtu
field for network and default routes is the same as the MTU of the
network interface used for the route. If the route is created with a
static PMTU value (see route(1M)), the corresponding PmtuTime field
contains the word perm, and the PMTU value permanently overrides the
interface MTU. If the route is created dynamically (D in the Flags
field), the value in the corresponding PmtuTime field is the number of
minutes remaining before the PMTU expires. When the PMTU expires, the
system rediscovers the current PMTU for the route, in case it has

changed. The PmtuTime field is left blank when the PMTU is identical
to the MTU of the interface. An asterisk (*) in the Pmtu field
indicates that user has disabled the PMTU Discovery for the route.

DEPENDENCIES
    X.25:
        -A and -a options do not list X.25 programmatic access information.

AUTHOR
    netstat was developed by the University of California, Berkeley.

SEE ALSO
    hosts(4), networks(4), gethostbyname(3N), getnetbyname(3N),
    protocols(4), route(1M), services(4).

ping

ping - Send information over network and get response.

NAME
     ping - send ICMP Echo Request packets to network host

SYNOPSIS

     ping [-oprv] [-i address] [-t ttl] host [-n count]
     ping [-oprv] [-i address] [-t ttl] host packet-size [[-n] count]

DESCRIPTION
     The ping command sends ICMP Echo Request (ECHO_REQUEST) packets to
     host once per second. Each packet that is echoed back via an ICMP
     Echo Response packet is written to the standard output, including
     round-trip time.

     ICMP Echo Request datagrams ("pings") have an IP and ICMP header,
     followed by a struct timeval (see gettimeofday(2)) and an arbitrary
     number of "pad" bytes used to fill out the packet. The default
     datagram length is 64 bytes, but this can be changed by using the
     packet-size option.

   Options
     The following options and parameters are recognizaed by ping:

             -i address If host is a multicast address, send multicast
                         datagrams from the interface with the local IP
                         address specified by address in ``dot'' notation (see
                         inet_addr(3N)). If the -i option is not specified,
                         multicast datagrams are sent from the default
                         interface, which is determined by the route
                         configuration.

             -o   Insert an IP Record Route option in outgoing packets,
                         summarizing routes taken when the command terminates.

                         It may not be possible to get the round-trip path if
                         some hosts on the route taken do not implement the IP
                         Record Route option. A maximum of 9 Internet
                         addresses can be recorded due to the maximum length
                         of the IP option area.

             -p   The new Path MTU information is displayed when a ICMP
                         "Datagram Too Big" message is received from a
                         gateway. The -p option must be used in conjunction
                         with a large packetsize and with the -v option.

             -r   Bypass the normal routing tables and send directly to
                         a host on an attached network. If the host is not on
                         a directly-connected network, an error is returned.
                         This option can be used to ping the local system
                         through an interface that has no route through it,
                         such as after the interface was dropped by gated (see

gated(1M)).

-t ttl   If host is a multicast address, set the time-to-live
field in the multicast datagram to ttl. This
controls the scope of the multicast datagrams by
specifying the maximum number of external systems
through which the datagram can be forwarded.

If ttl is zero, the datagram is restricted to the
local system. If ttl is one, the datagram is
restricted to systems that have an interface on the
network directly connected to the interface specified
by the -i option. If ttl is two, the datagram can
forwarded through at most one multicast router; and
so forth. Range: zero to 255. The default value is
1.

-v   Verbose output. Show ICMP packets other than Echo
Responses that are received.

host   Destination to which the ICMP Echo Requests are sent.
host can be a hostname or an Internet address. All
symbolic names specified for host are looked up by
using gethostbyname() (see gethostbyname(3N)). If
host is an Internet address, it must be in "dot"
notation (see inet_addr(3N)).

If a system does not respond as expected, the route
might be configured incorrectly on the local or
remote system or on an intermediate gateway, or there
might be some other network failure. Normally, host
is the address assigned to a local or remote network
interface.

If host is a broadcast address, all systems that
receive the broadcast should respond. Normally,
these are only systems that have a network interface
on the same network as the local interface sending
the ICMP Echo Request.

If host is a multicast address, only systems that
have joined the multicast group should respond.
These may be distant systems if the -t option is
specified, and there is a multicast router on the
network directly connected to the interface specified
by the -i option.

packet-size The size of the transmitted packet, in bytes. By
default (when packet-size is not specified), the size
of transmitted packets is 64 bytes. The minimum
value allowed for packet-size is 8 bytes, and the
maximum is 4095 bytes. If packet-size is smaller
than 16 bytes, there is not enough room for timing
information. In that case, the round-trip times are
not displayed.

count   The number of packets ping will transmit before
terminating. Range: zero to 2147483647. The default
is zero, in which case ping sends packets until
interrupted.

When using ping for fault isolation, first specify a local address for
host to verify that the local network interface is working correctly.
Then specify host and gateway addresses further and further away to
determine the point of failure. ping sends one datagram per second,
and it normally writes one line of output for every ICMP Echo Response

that is received. No output is produced if there are no responses.
If an optional count is given, only the specified number of requests
is sent. Round-trip times and packet loss statistics are computed.
When all responses have been received or the command times out (if the
count option is specified), or if the command is terminated with a
SIGINT, a brief summary is displayed.

This command is intended for use in testing, managing and measuring
network performance. It should be used primarily to isolate network
failures. Because of the load it could impose on the network, it is
considered discourteous to use ping unnecessarily during normal
operations or from automated scripts.

AUTHOR
        ping was developed in the Public Domain.

FILES
        /etc/hosts

SEE ALSO
        gethostbyname(3N), inet(3N).

rcp

rcp - Copy files and directories from one system to another.

```
rcp(1)                                                                    rcp(1)

NAME
     rcp - remote file copy

SYNOPSIS

   Copy Single File
     rcp [-p] source_file1 dest_file

   Copy Multiple Files
     rcp [-p] source_file1 [source_file2]... dest_dir

   Copy One or More Directory Subtrees
     rcp [-p] -r source_dir1 [source_dir2]... dest_dir

   Copy Files and Directory Subtrees
     rcp [-p] -r file_or_dir1 [file_or_dir2]... dest_dir

DESCRIPTION
     The rcp command copies files, directory subtrees, or a combination of
     files and directory subtrees from one or more systems to another.  In
     many respects, it is similar to the cp command (see cp(1)).

     To use rcp, you must have read access to files being copied, and read
     and search (execute) permission on all directories in the directory
     path.

   Options and Arguments
     rcp recognizes the following options and arguments:

            source_file    The name of an existing file or directory on a
            source_dir     local or remote machine that you want copied to
                           the specified destination.  Source file and
                           directory names are constructed as follows:

                                  user_name@hostname:pathname/filename

                           or

                                  user_name@hostname:pathname/dirname

                           Component parts of file and directory names are
                           described below.  If multiple existing files
                           and/or directory subtrees are specified
                           (source_file1, source_file2, ..., etc.), the
                           destination must be a directory.  Shell file name
                           expansion is allowed on both local and remote
                           systems.  Multiple files and directory subtrees
                           can be copied from one or more systems to a single
                           destination directory with a single command.

            dest_file      The name of the destination file.  If host name
                           and path name are not specified, the existing file
```

is copied into a file named dest_file in the current directory on the local system. If dest_file already exists and is writable, the existing file is overwritten. Destination file names are constructed the same way as source files except that file name expansion characters cannot be used.

dest_dir   The name of the destination directory. If host name and path name are not specified, the existing file is copied into a directory named dest_dir in the current directory on the local system. If dest_dir already exists in the specified directory path (or current directory if not specified), a new directory named dest_dir is created underneath the existing directory named dest_dir. Destination directory names are constructed the same way as source directory tree names except that file name expansion characters cannot be used.

file_or_dir   If a combination of files and directories are specified for copying (either explicitly or by file name expansion), only files are copied unless the -r option is specified. If the -r option is present, all files and directory subtrees whose names match the specified file_or_dir name are copied.

-p   Preserve (duplicate) modification times and modes (permissions) of source files, ignoring the current setting of the umask file creation mode mask. If this option is specified, rcp preserves the sticky bit only if the target user is superuser.

If the -p option is not specified, rcp preserves the mode and owner of dest_file if it already exists; otherwise rcp uses the mode of the source file modified by the umask on the destination host. Modification and access times of the destination file are set to the time when the copy was made.

-r   Recursively copy directory subtrees rooted at the source directory name. If any directory subtrees are to be copied, rcp recursively copies each subtree rooted at the specified source directory name to directory dest_dir. If source_dir is being copied to an existing directory of the same name, rcp creates a new directory source_dir within dest_dir and copies the subtree rooted at source_dir to dest_dir/source_dir. If dest_dir does not exist, rcp creates it and copies the subtree rooted at source_dir to dest_dir.

Constructing File and Directory Names
  As indicated above, file and directory names contain one, two, or four component parts:

user_name   Login name to be used for accessing directories and files on remote system.

hostname   Hostname of remote system where directories and files are located.

pathname   Absolute directory path name or directory path name
                relative to the login directory of user user_name.

filename   Actual name of source or destination file. File
                name expansion is allowed on source file names.

dirname   Actual name of source or destination directory
                subtree. File name expansion is allowed on source
                directory names.

Each file or directory argument is either a remote file name of the
form hostname:path, or a local file name (with a slash (/) before any
colon (:)). hostname can be either an official host name or an alias
(see hosts(4)). If hostname is of the form ruser@rhost, ruser is used
on the remote host instead of the current user name. An unspecified
path (that is, hostname:) refers to the remote user's login directory.
If path does not begin with /, it is interpreted relative to the
remote user's login directory on hostname. Shell metacharacters in
remote paths can be quoted with backslash (\), single quotes (''), or
double quotes (""), so that they will be interpreted remotely.

The rcp routine does not prompt for passwords. The current local user
name or any user name specified via ruser must exist on rhost and
allow remote command execution via remsh(1) and rcmd(3). remshd(1M)
must be executable on the remote host.

Third-party transfers in the form:

        rcp ruser1@rhost1:path1 ruser2@rhost2:path2

are performed as:

        remsh rhost1 -l ruser1 rcp path1 ruser2@rhost2:path2

Therefore, for a such a transfer to succeed, ruser2 on rhost2 must
allow access by ruser1 from rhost1 (see hosts.equiv(4)).

WARNINGS
    The rcp routine is confused by any output generated by commands in a
    .cshrc file on the remote host (see csh(1)).

    Copying a file onto itself, for example:

        rcp path `hostname`:path

    may produce inconsistent results. The current HP-UX version of rcp
    simply copies the file over itself. However, some implementations of
    rcp, including some earlier HP-UX implementations, corrupt the file.
    In addition, the same file may be referred to in multiple ways, for
    example, via hard links, symbolic links, or NFS. It is not guaranteed
    that rcp will correctly copy a file over itself in all cases.

    Implementations of rcp based on the 4.2BSD version (including the
    implementations of rcp prior to HP-UX 7.0) require that remote users
    be specified as rhost.ruser. If the first remote host specified in a
    third party transfer (rhost1 in the example below) uses this older
    syntax, the command must have the form:

        rcp ruser1@rhost1:path1 rhost2.ruser2:path2

    since the target is interpreted by rhost1. A common problem that is
    encountered is when two remote files are to be copied to a remote
    target that specifies a remote user. If the two remote source
    systems, rhost1 and rhost2, each expect a different form for the
    remote target, the command:

```
rcp rhost1:path1 rhost2:path2 rhost3.ruser3:path3
```

will certainly fail on one of the source systems. Perform such a
transfer using two separate commands.

AUTHOR
      rcp was developed by the University of California, Berkeley.

SEE ALSO
      cp(1), ftp(1), remsh(1), remshd(1M), rcmd(3), hosts(4),
      hosts.equiv(4).

      ftp chapter in Using Internet Services.

rcp(1)   Secure Internet Services with Kerberos Authentication   rcp(1)

NAME
      rcp - remote file copy

SYNOPSIS

   Copy Single File
      rcp [-k realm] [-P] [-p] source_file1 dest_file

   Copy Multiple Files
      rcp [-k realm] [-P] [-p] source_file1 [source_file2]... dest_dir

   Copy One or More Directory Subtrees
      rcp [-k realm] [-P] [-p] -r source_dir1 [source_dir2]... dest_dir

   Copy Files and Directory Subtrees
      rcp [-k realm] [-P] [-p] -r file_or_dir1 [file_or_dir2]... dest_dir

DESCRIPTION
      The rcp command copies files, directory subtrees, or a combination of
      files and directory subtrees from one or more systems to another. In
      many respects, it is similar to the cp command (see cp(1)).

      To use rcp, you must have read access to files being copied, and read
      and search (execute) permission on all directories in the directory
      path.

      In a Kerberos V5 Network Authentication environment, rcp uses the
      Kerberos V5 protocol while initiating the connection to a remote host.
      The authorization mechanism is dependent on the command line options
      used to invoke remshd on the remote host (i.e., -K, -R, -r, or -k).
      Kerberos authentication and authorization rules are described in the
      Secure Internet Services man page, sis(5).

      Although Kerberos authentication and authorization may apply, the
      Kerberos mechanism is not applied when copying files. The files are
      still transferred in cleartext over the network.

   Options and Arguments
      rcp recognizes the following options and arguments:

            source_file   The name of an existing file or directory on a
            source_dir   local or remote machine that you want copied to
                           the specified destination. Source file and
                           directory names are constructed as follows:

                                 user_name@hostname:pathname/filename

            or
```
```

user_name@hostname:pathname/dirname

Component parts of file and directory names are
described below. If multiple existing files
and/or directory subtrees are specified
(source_file1, source_file2, ..., etc.), the
destination must be a directory. Shell file name
expansion is allowed on both local and remote
systems. Multiple files and directory subtrees
can be copied from one or more systems to a single
destination directory with a single command.

dest_file   The name of the destination file. If host name
               and path name are not specified, the existing file
               is copied into a file named dest_file in the
               current directory on the local system. If
               dest_file already exists and is writable, the
               existing file is overwritten. Destination file
               names are constructed the same way as source files
               except that file name expansion characters cannot
               be used.

dest_dir   The name of the destination directory. If host
               name and path name are not specified, the existing
               file is copied into a directory named dest_dir in
               the current directory on the local system. If
               dest_dir already exists in the specified directory
               path (or current directory if not specified), a
               new directory named dest_dir is created underneath
               the existing directory named dest_dir.
               Destination directory names are constructed the
               same way as source directory tree names except
               that file name expansion characters cannot be
               used.

file_or_dir   If a combination of files and directories are
               specified for copying (either explicitly or by
               file name expansion), only files are copied unless
               the -r option is specified. If the -r option is
               present, all files and directory subtrees whose
               names match the specified file_or_dir name are
               copied.

-k realm   Obtain tickets from the remote host in the
               specified realm instead of the remote host's
               default realm as specified in the configuration
               file krb.realms.

-P   Disable Kerberos authentication. Only applicable
               in a secure environment based on Kerberos V5. If
               the remote host has been configured to prevent
               non-secure access, using this option would result
               in the generic error,

                   rcmd: connect: <hostname>: Connection refused

               See DIAGNOSTICS in remshd(1M) for more details.

-p   Preserve (duplicate) modification times and modes
               (permissions) of source files, ignoring the
               current setting of the umask file creation mode
               mask. If this option is specified, rcp preserves
               the sticky bit only if the target user is
               superuser.

               If the -p option is not specified, rcp preserves

the mode and owner of dest_file if it already
exists; otherwise rcp uses the mode of the source
file modified by the umask on the destination
host. Modification and access times of the
destination file are set to the time when the copy
was made.

-r   Recursively copy directory subtrees rooted at the
                source directory name. If any directory subtrees
                are to be copied, rcp recursively copies each
                subtree rooted at the specified source directory
                name to directory dest_dir. If source_dir is
                being copied to an existing directory of the same
                name, rcp creates a new directory source_dir
                within dest_dir and copies the subtree rooted at
                source_dir to dest_dir/source_dir. If dest_dir
                does not exist, rcp creates it and copies the
                subtree rooted at source_dir to dest_dir.

Constructing File and Directory Names
  As indicated above, file and directory names contain one, two, or four
  component parts:

        user_name   Login name to be used for accessing directories and
                        files on remote system.

        hostname   Hostname of remote system where directories and
                        files are located.

        pathname   Absolute directory path name or directory path name
                        relative to the login directory of user user_name.

        filename   Actual name of source or destination file. File
                        name expansion is allowed on source file names.

        dirname   Actual name of source or destination directory
                        subtree. File name expansion is allowed on source
                        directory names.

Each file or directory argument is either a remote file name of the
form hostname:path, or a local file name (with a slash (/) before any
colon (:)). hostname can be either an official host name or an alias
(see hosts(4)). If hostname is of the form ruser@rhost, ruser is used
on the remote host instead of the current user name. An unspecified
path (that is, hostname:) refers to the remote user's login directory.
If path does not begin with /, it is interpreted relative to the
remote user's login directory on hostname. Shell metacharacters in
remote paths can be quoted with backslash (\), single quotes (''), or
double quotes (""), so that they will be interpreted remotely.

rcp does not prompt for passwords. In a non-secure or traditional
environment, user authorization is checked by determining if the
current local user name or any user name specified via ruser exists on
rhost. In a Kerberos V5 Network Authentication or secure environment,
the authorization method is dependent upon the command line options
for remshd (see remshd(1M) for details). In either case, remote
command execution via remsh(1) and rcmd(3) must be allowed and
remshd(1M) must be executable on the remote host.

Third-party transfers in the form:

    rcp ruser1@rhost1:path1 ruser2@rhost2:path2

are performed as:

```
      remsh rhost1 -l ruser1 rcp path1 ruser2@rhost2:path2
```

Therefore, for a such a transfer to succeed, ruser2 on rhost2 must
allow access by ruser1 from rhost1 (see hosts.equiv(4)).

WARNINGS

The rcp routine is confused by any output generated by commands in a
.cshrc file on the remote host (see csh(1)).

Copying a file onto itself, for example:

```
      rcp path `hostname`:path
```

may produce inconsistent results. The current HP-UX version of rcp
simply copies the file over itself. However, some implementations of
rcp, including some earlier HP-UX implementations, corrupt the file.
In addition, the same file may be referred to in multiple ways, for
example, via hard links, symbolic links, or NFS. It is not guaranteed
that rcp will correctly copy a file over itself in all cases.

Implementations of rcp based on the 4.2BSD version (including the
implementations of rcp prior to HP-UX 7.0) require that remote users
be specified as rhost.ruser. If the first remote host specified in a
third party transfer (rhost1 in the example below) uses this older
syntax, the command must have the form:

```
      rcp ruser1@rhost1:path1 rhost2.ruser2:path2
```

since the target is interpreted by rhost1. A common problem that is
encountered is when two remote files are to be copied to a remote
target that specifies a remote user. If the two remote source
systems, rhost1 and rhost2, each expect a different form for the
remote target, the command:

```
      rcp rhost1:path1 rhost2:path2 rhost3.ruser3:path3
```

will certainly fail on one of the source systems. Perform such a
transfer using two separate commands.

AUTHOR

rcp was developed by the University of California, Berkeley.

SEE ALSO

cp(1), ftp(1), remsh(1), remshd(1M), rcmd(3), hosts(4),
hosts.equiv(4), sis(5).

ftp chapter in Using Internet Services.

remsh

remsh - Connect to a remote host and execute a command.

---

remsh(1)   remsh(1)

NAME
     remsh - execute from a remote shell

SYNOPSIS

     remsh host [-l username] [-n] command
     host [-l username] [-n] command

     rexec host [-l username] [-n] command

DESCRIPTION
     remsh connects to the specified host and executes the specified
     command. The host name can be either the official name or an alias as
     understood by gethostbyname() (see gethostent(3N) and hosts(4)).
     remsh copies its standard input (stdin) to the remote command, and the
     standard output of the remote command to its standard output (stdout),
     and the standard error of the remote command to its standard error
     (stderr). Hangup, interrupt, quit, terminate, and broken pipe signals
     are propagated to the remote command. remsh exits when the sockets
     associated with stdout and stderr of the remote command are closed.
     This means that remsh normally terminates when the remote command does
     (see remshd(1M)).

     By default, remsh uses the following path when executing the specified
     command:

          /usr/bin:/usr/ccs/bin:/usr/bin/X11:

     remsh uses the default remote login shell with the -c option to
     execute the remote command. If the default remote shell is csh, csh
     sources the remote .cshrc file before the command. remsh cannot be
     used to run commands that require a terminal interface (such as vi) or
     commands that read their standard error (such as more). In such
     cases, use rlogin or telnet instead (see rlogin(1) and telnet(1)).

     The remote account name used is the same as your local account name,
     unless you specify a different remote name with the -l option. This
     remote account name must be equivalent to the originating account; no
     provision is made for specifying a password with a command. For more
     details about equivalent hosts and how to specify them, see
     hosts.equiv(4). The files inspected by remshd on the remote host are
     /etc/hosts.equiv and $HOME/.rhosts (see remshd(1M)).

     If command, is not specified, instead of executing a single command,
     you will be logged in on the remote host using rlogin (see rlogin(1)).
     Any rlogin options typed in on the command line are transmitted to
     rlogin. If command is specified, options specific to rlogin are
     ignored by remsh.

     By default, remsh reads its standard input and sends it to the remote
     command because remsh has no way to determine whether the remote
     command requires input. The -n option redirects standard input to

remsh from /dev/null. This is useful when running a shell script
containing a remsh command, since otherwise remsh may use input not
intended for it. The -n option is also useful when running remsh in
the background from a job control shell, /usr/bin/csh or /usr/bin/ksh.
Otherwise, remsh stops and waits for input from the terminal keyboard
for the remote command. /usr/bin/sh automatically redirects its input
from /dev/null when jobs are run in the background.

Host names for remote hosts can also be commands (linked to remsh) in
the directory /usr/hosts. If this directory is specified in the $PATH
environment variable, you can omit remsh. For example, if remotehost
is the name of a remote host, /usr/hosts/remotehost is linked to
remsh, and if /usr/hosts is in your search path, the command

    remotehost command

executes command on remotehost, and the command

    remotehost

is equivalent to

    rlogin remotehost

The rexec command, a link to remsh, works the same as remsh except
that it uses the rexec() library routine and rexecd for command
execution (see rexec(3N) and rexecd(1M)). rexec prompts for a
password before executing the command instead of using hosts.equiv for
authentication. It should be used in instances where a password to a
remote account is known but there are insufficient permissions for
remsh.

EXAMPLES
    Shell metacharacters that are not quoted are interpreted on the local
    host; quoted metacharacters are interpreted on the remote host. Thus
    the command line:

        remsh otherhost cat remotefile >> localfile

    appends the remote file remotefile to the local file localfile, while
    the command line

        remsh otherhost cat remotefile ">>" otherremotefile

    appends remotefile to the remote file otherremotefile.

    If the remote shell is /usr/bin/sh, the following command line sets up
    the environment for the remote command before executing the remote
    command:

        remsh otherhost . .profile 2>&- \; command

    The 2>&- throws away error messages generated by executing .profile
    when stdin and stdout are not a terminal.

    The following command line runs remsh in the background on the local
    system, and the output of the remote command comes to your terminal
    asynchronously:

        remsh otherhost -n command &

    The background remsh completes when the remote command does.

    The following command line causes remsh to return immediately without
    waiting for the remote command to complete:

```
remsh otherhost -n "command 1>&- 2>&- &"
```

(See remshd(1M) and sh(1)). If your login shell on the remote system
is csh, use the following form instead:

```
remsh otherhost -n "sh -c \"command 1>&- 2>&- &\""
```

RETURN VALUE
    If remsh fails to set up the secondary socket connection, it returns
    2. If it fails in some other way, it returns 1. If it fully succeeds
    in setting up a connection with remshd, it returns 0 once the remote
    command has completed. Note that the return value of remsh bears no
    relation to the return value of the remote command.

DIAGNOSTICS
    Besides the errors listed below, errors can also be generated by the
    library functions rcmd() and rresvport() which are used by remsh (see
    rcmd(3N)). Those errors are preceded by the name of the library
    function that generated them. remsh can produce the following
    diagnostic messages:

        rlogin: ...
            Error in executing rlogin (rlogin is executed when the user
            does not specify any commands to be executed). This is
            followed by the error message specifying why the execution
            failed.

        shell/tcp: Unknown service
            The ``shell'' service specification is not present in the
            /etc/services file.

        Can't establish stderr
            remsh cannot establish secondary socket connection for
            stderr.

        <system call>: ...
            Error in executing system call. Appended to this error is a
            message specifying the cause of the failure.

        There is no entry for you (user ID uid) in /etc/passwd
            Check with the system administrator to see if your entry in
            the password file has been deleted by mistake.

WARNINGS
    For security reasons, the /etc/hosts.equiv and .rhosts files should
    exist, even if empty, and should be readable and writable only by the
    owner. Note also that all information, including any passwords asked
    for, is passed unencrypted between the two hosts.

    If remsh is run with an interactive command it hangs.

DEPENDENCIES
    remsh is the same service as rsh on BSD systems. The name was changed
    due to a conflict with the existing System V command rsh (restricted
    shell).

AUTHOR
    remsh was developed by the University of California, Berkeley.

FILES
    /usr/hosts/*   for version of the command invoked only with
                          hostname

SEE ALSO
    rlogin(1), remshd(1M), rexecd(1M), gethostent(3N), rcmd(3N),

rexec(3N), hosts.equiv(4), hosts(4).

remsh(1)   Secure Internet Services with Kerberos Authentication   remsh(1)

NAME
     remsh - execute from a remote shell

SYNOPSIS

     remsh host [-l username] [-f/F] [-k realm] [-P] [-n] command
     host [-l username] [-f/F] [-k realm] [-P] [-n] command

     rexec host [-l username] [-n] command

DESCRIPTION
     remsh connects to the specified host and executes the specified
     command. The host name can be either the official name or an alias as
     understood by gethostbyname() (see gethostent(3N) and hosts(4)).
     remsh copies its standard input (stdin) to the remote command, and the
     standard output of the remote command to its standard output (stdout),
     and the standard error of the remote command to its standard error
     (stderr). Hangup, interrupt, quit, terminate, and broken pipe signals
     are propagated to the remote command. remsh exits when the sockets
     associated with stdout and stderr of the remote command are closed.
     This means that remsh normally terminates when the remote command does
     (see remshd(1M)).

     By default, remsh uses the following path when executing the specified
     command:

          /usr/bin:/usr/ccs/bin:/usr/bin/X11:

     remsh uses the default remote login shell with the -c option to
     execute the remote command. If the default remote shell is csh, csh
     sources the remote .cshrc file before the command. remsh cannot be
     used to run commands that require a terminal interface (such as vi) or
     commands that read their standard error (such as more). In such
     cases, use rlogin or telnet instead (see rlogin(1) and telnet(1)).

     The remote account name used is the same as your local account name,
     unless you specify a different remote name with the -l option. In
     addition, the remote host account name must also conform to other
     rules which differ depending upon whether the remote host is operating
     in a Kerberos V5 Network Authentication, i.e., secure environment or
     not. In a non-secure, or traditional environment, the remote account
     name must be equivalent to the originating account; no provision is
     made for specifying a password with a command. For more details about
     equivalent hosts and how to specify them, see hosts.equiv(4). The
     files inspected by remshd on the remote host are /etc/hosts.equiv and
     $HOME/.rhosts (see remshd(1M)).

     In a Kerberos V5 Network Authentication environment, the local host
     must be successfully authenticated before the remote account name is
     checked for proper authorization. The authorization mechanism is
     dependent on the command line options used to invoke remshd on the
     remote host (i.e., -K, -R, -r, or -k). For further information on
     Kerberos authentication and authorization see the Secure Internet
     Services man page, sis(5) and remshd(1M).

     Although Kerberos authentication and authorization may apply, the
     Kerberos mechanism is not applied to the command or to its response.
     All information transferred between the local and remote host is still
     sent in cleartext over the network.

     In a secure or Kerberos V5-based environment, the following command
     line options are available:

-f   Forward the ticket granting ticket (TGT) to the remote
            system. The TGT is not forwardable from there.

-F   Forward the TGT to the remote system and have it
            forwardable from there to another remote system. -f and
            -F are mutually exclusive.

-k realm   Obtain tickets from the remote host in the specified
            realm instead of the remote host's default realm as
            specified in the configuration file krb.realms.

-P   Disable Kerberos authentication.

If a command is not specified, instead of executing a single command,
you will be logged in on the remote host using rlogin (see rlogin(1)).
Any rlogin options typed in on the command line are transmitted to
rlogin. If no command and the option -P is specified, rlogin will be
invoked with -P to indicate that Kerberos authentication (or secure
access) is not required. This will mean that if a password is
requested, the password will be sent in cleartext. If a command is
specified, options specific to rlogin are ignored by remsh.

If a command and the option -n are specified, then standard input is
redirected to remsh by /dev/null. If -n is not specified (the default
case), remsh reads its standard input and sends the input to the
remote command. This is because remsh has no way to determine whether
the remote command requires input. This option is useful when running
a shell script containing a remsh command, since otherwise remsh may
use input not intended for it. The -n option is also useful when
running remsh in the background from a job control shell, /usr/bin/csh
or /usr/bin/ksh. Otherwise, remsh stops and waits for input from the
terminal keyboard for the remote command. /usr/bin/sh automatically
redirects its input from /dev/null when jobs are run in the
background.

Host names for remote hosts can also be commands (linked to remsh) in
the directory /usr/hosts. If this directory is specified in the $PATH
environment variable, you can omit remsh. For example, if remotehost
is the name of a remote host, /usr/hosts/remotehost is linked to
remsh, and if /usr/hosts is in your search path, the command

        remotehost command

executes command on remotehost, and the command

        remotehost

is equivalent to

        rlogin remotehost

The rexec command, a link to remsh, works the same as remsh except
that it uses the rexec() library routine and rexecd for command
execution (see rexec(3N) and rexecd(1M)) and does not support Kerberos
authentication. rexec prompts for a password before executing the
command instead of using hosts.equiv for authentication. It should be
used in instances where a password to a remote account is known but
there are insufficient permissions for remsh.

EXAMPLES
    Shell metacharacters that are not quoted are interpreted on the local
    host; quoted metacharacters are interpreted on the remote host. Thus
    the command line:

        remsh otherhost cat remotefile >> localfile

appends the remote file remotefile to the local file localfile, while
the command line

    remsh otherhost cat remotefile ">>" otherremotefile

appends remotefile to the remote file otherremotefile.

If the remote shell is /usr/bin/sh, the following command line sets up
the environment for the remote command before executing the remote
command:

    remsh otherhost . .profile 2>&- \; command

The 2>&- throws away error messages generated by executing .profile
when stdin and stdout are not a terminal.

The following command line runs remsh in the background on the local
system, and the output of the remote command comes to your terminal
asynchronously:

    remsh otherhost -n command &

The background remsh completes when the remote command does.

The following command line causes remsh to return immediately without
waiting for the remote command to complete:

    remsh otherhost -n "command 1>&- 2>&- &"

(See remshd(1M) and sh(1)). If your login shell on the remote system
is csh, use the following form instead:

    remsh otherhost -n "sh -c \"command 1>&- 2>&- &\""

RETURN VALUE
    If remsh fails to set up the secondary socket connection, it returns
    2. If it fails in some other way, it returns 1. If it fully succeeds
    in setting up a connection with remshd, it returns 0 once the remote
    command has completed. Note that the return value of remsh bears no
    relation to the return value of the remote command.

DIAGNOSTICS
    Besides the errors listed below, errors can also be generated by the
    library functions rcmd() and rresvport() which are used by remsh (see
    rcmd(3N)). Those errors are preceded by the name of the library
    function that generated them. remsh can produce the following
    diagnostic messages:

        rlogin: ...
            Error in executing rlogin (rlogin is executed when the user
            does not specify any commands to be executed). This is
            followed by the error message specifying why the execution
            failed.

        shell/tcp: Unknown service
            The ``shell'' service specification is not present in the
            /etc/services file.

        Can't establish stderr
            remsh cannot establish secondary socket connection for
            stderr.

        <system call>: ...
            Error in executing system call. Appended to this error is a

message specifying the cause of the failure.

There is no entry for you (user ID uid) in /etc/passwd
Check with the system administrator to see if your entry in
the password file has been deleted by mistake.

rcmd: connect: <hostname>: Connection refused
One cause for display of this generic error message could be
due to the absence of an entry for shell in /etc/inetd.conf
on the remote system. This entry may have been removed or
commented out to prevent non-secure access.

Kerberos-specific errors are listed in sis(5).

WARNINGS
For security reasons, the /etc/hosts.equiv and .rhosts files should
exist, even if empty, and should be readable and writable only by the
owner.

If remsh is run with an interactive command it hangs.

DEPENDENCIES
remsh is the same service as rsh on BSD systems. The name was changed
due to a conflict with the existing System V command rsh (restricted
shell).

AUTHOR
remsh was developed by the University of California, Berkeley.

FILES
/usr/hosts/*   for version of the command invoked only with
                      hostname

SEE ALSO
rlogin(1), remshd(1M), rexecd(1M), gethostent(3N), rcmd(3N),
rexec(3N), hosts.equiv(4), hosts(4), sis(5).

rlogin

rlogin - Login to a remote host.

NAME
      rlogin - remote login

SYNOPSIS

      rlogin rhost [-7] [-8] [-ee] [-l username]

      rhost [-7] [-8] [-ee] [-l username]

DESCRIPTION
      The rlogin command connects your terminal on the local host to the
      remote host (rhost). rlogin acts as a virtual terminal to the remote
      system. The host name rhost can be either the official name or an
      alias as listed in the file /etc/hosts (see hosts(4)).

      In a manner similar to the remsh command (see remsh(1)), rlogin allows
      a user to log in on an equivalent remote host, rhost, bypassing the
      normal login/password sequence. For more information about equivalent
      hosts and how to specify them in the files /etc/hosts.equiv and
      .rhosts, see hosts.equiv(4). The searching of the files
      /etc/hosts.equiv and .rhosts occurs on the remote host, and the
      .rhosts file must be owned by the remote user account or by a remote
      superuser.

      If the originating user account is not equivalent to the remote user
      account, the originating user is prompted for the password of the
      remote account. If this fails, a login name and password are prompted
      for, as when login is used (see login(1)).

      The terminal type specified by the current TERM environment variable
      is propagated across the network and used to set the initial value of
      your TERM environment variable on the remote host. Your terminal baud
      rate is also propagated to the remote host, and is required by some
      systems to set up the pseudo-terminal used by rlogind (see
      rlogind(1M)).

      All echoing takes place at the remote site, so that (except for
      delays) the remote login is transparent.

      If at any time rlogin is unable to read from or write to the socket
      connection on the remote host, the message Connection closed is
      printed on standard error and rlogin exits.

   Options
      rlogin recognizes the following options. Note that the options follow
      the rhost argument.

              -7   Set the character size to seven bits. The eighth
                              bit of each byte sent is set to zero (space
                              parity).

              -8   Use an eight-bit data path. This is the default
                              HP-UX behavior.

To use eight-bit characters, the terminal must be configured to generate either eight-bit characters with no parity, or seven bit characters with space parity. The HP-UX implementation of rlogind (see rlogind(1M)) interprets seven bit characters with even, odd, or mark parity as eight-bit non-USASCII characters. You may also need to reconfigure the remote host appropriately (see stty(1) and tty(7)). Some remote hosts may not provide the necessary support for eight-bit characters. In this case, or if it is not possible to disable parity generation by the local terminal, use the -7 option.

-ee   Set the escape character to e. There is no space separating the option letter and the argument character. To start a line with the escape character, two of the escape characters must be entered. The default escape character is tilde (~). Some characters may conflict with your terminal configuration, such as ^S, ^Q, or backspace. Using one of these as the escape character may not be possible or may cause problems communicating with the remote host (see stty(1) and tty(7)).

-l username Set the user login name on the remote host to username. The default name is the current account name of the user invoking rlogin.

Escape Sequences
 rlogin can be controlled with two-character escape sequences, in the form ex, where e is the escape character and x is a code character described below. Escape sequences are recognized only at the beginning of a line of input. The default escape character is tilde (~). It can be changed with the -e option.

The following escape sequences are recognized:

ey If y is NOT a code character described below, pass the escape character and y as characters to the remote host.

ee Pass the escape character as a character to the remote host.

e. Disconnect from the remote host.

e! Escape to a subshell on the local host. Use exit to return to the remote host.

If rlogin is run from a shell that supports job control (see csh(1), ksh(1), and sh-posix(1)), escape sequences can be used to suspend rlogin. The following escape sequences assume that ^Z and ^Y are set as the user's susp and dsusp characters, respectively (see stty(1) and termio(7)).

e^Z Suspend the rlogin session and return the user to the shell that invoked rlogin. The rlogin job can be resumed with the fg command (see csh(1), ksh(1), and sh-posix(1)). e^Z suspends both rlogin processes: the one transmitting user input to the remote login, and the one displaying output from the remote login.

e^Y Suspend the rlogin session and return the user to the shell

that invoked rlogin. The rlogin job can be resumed with the
fg command (see csh(1), ksh(1), and sh-posix(1)). e^Y
suspends only the input process; output from the remote
login continues to be displayed.

If you "daisy-chain" remote logins (for example, you rlogin from host
A to host B and then rlogin from host B to host C) without setting
unique escape characters, you can repeat the escape character until it
reaches your chosen destination. For example, the first escape
character, e, is seen as an escape character on host A; the second e
is passed as a normal character by host A and seen as an escape
character on host B; a third e is passed as a normal character by
hosts A and B and accepted as a normal character by host C.

Remote Host Name As Command
The system administrator can arrange for more convenient access to a
remote host (rhost) by linking remsh to /usr/hosts/rhost, allowing use
of the remote host name (rhost) as a command (see remsh(1)). For
example, if remotehost is the name of a remote host and
/usr/hosts/remotehost is linked to remsh, and if /usr/hosts is in your
search path, the command:

    remotehost

is equivalent to:

    rlogin remotehost

RETURN VALUES
rlogin sends an error message to standard error and returns a nonzero
value if an error occurs before the connection to the remote host is
completed. Otherwise, it returns a zero.

DIAGNOSTICS
Diagnostics can occur from both the local and remote hosts. Those
that occur on the local host before the connection is completely
established are written to standard error. Once the connection is
established, any error messages from the remote host are written to
standard output, like any other data.

login/tcp: Unknown service

    rlogin was unable to find the login service listed in the
    /etc/services database file.

There is no entry for you (user ID username) in /etc/passwd

    rlogin was unable to find your user ID in the password file.

    Next Step: Contact your system administrator.

system call:...
An error occurred when rlogin attempted the indicated system
call. See the appropriate manual entry for information about the
error.

EXAMPLES
Log in as the same user on the remote host remote:

    rlogin remote

Set the escape character to a !, use a seven-bit data connection, and
attempt a login as user guest on host remhost:

    rlogin remhost -e! -7 -l guest

Assuming that your system administrator has set up the links in /usr/hosts, the following is equivalent to the previous command:

    remhost -e! -7 -l guest

WARNINGS
  For security purposes, the /etc/hosts.equiv and .rhosts files should exist, even if they are empty. These files should be readable and writable only by the owner. See host.equiv(4) for more information.

  Note also that all information, including any passwords asked for, is passed unencrypted between the two hosts.

  rlogin is unable to transmit the Break key as an interrupt signal to the remote system, regardless of whether the user has set stty brkint on the local system. The key assigned to SIGINT with the command stty intr c should be used instead (see stty(1)).

AUTHOR
  rlogin was developed by the University of California, Berkeley.

FILES
  $HOME/.rhosts   User's private equivalence list
  /etc/hosts.equiv   List of equivalent hosts
  /usr/hosts/*   For rhost version of the command

SEE ALSO
  csh(1), ksh(1), login(1), remsh(1), sh(1), sh-bourne(1), sh-posix(1), stty(1), telnet(1), rlogind(1M), hosts(4), hosts.equiv(4), inetd.conf(4), services(4), termio(7), tty(7).

rlogin(1)   Secure Internet Services with Kerberos Authentication   rlogin(1)

NAME
  rlogin - remote login

SYNOPSIS

  rlogin rhost [-7] [-8] [-ee] [-f/F] [-k realm] [-l username] [-P]

  rhost [-7] [-8] [-ee] [-f/F] [-k realm] [-l username] [-P]

DESCRIPTION
  The rlogin command connects your terminal on the local host to the remote host (rhost). rlogin acts as a virtual terminal to the remote system. The host name rhost can be either the official name or an alias as listed in the file /etc/hosts (see hosts(4)).

  The terminal type specified by the current TERM environment variable is propagated across the network and used to set the initial value of your TERM environment variable on the remote host. Your terminal baud rate is also propagated to the remote host, and is required by some systems to set up the pseudo-terminal used by rlogind (see rlogind(1M)).

  All echoing takes place at the remote site, so that (except for delays) the remote login is transparent.

  If at any time rlogin is unable to read from or write to the socket connection on the remote host, the message Connection closed is printed on standard error and rlogin exits.

  In a Kerberos V5 Network Authentication environment, rlogin uses the Kerberos V5 protocol to authenticate the connection to a remote host. If the authentication is successful, user authorization will be performed according to the command line options selected for rlogind

(i.e., -K, -R, -r, or -k). A password will not be required, so a
password prompt will not be seen and a password will not be sent over
the network where it can be observed. For further information on
Kerberos authentication and authorization see the Secure Internet
Services man page, sis(5) and rlogind(1M).

Although Kerberos authentication and authorization may apply, the
Kerberos mechanism is not applied to the login session. All
information transferred between your host and the remote host is sent
in cleartext over the network.

Options
    rlogin recognizes the following options. Note that the options follow
    the rhost argument.

-7	Set the character size to seven bits. The eighth bit of each byte sent is set to zero (space parity).
-8	Use an eight-bit data path. This is the default HP-UX behavior.
	To use eight-bit characters, the terminal must be configured to generate either eight-bit characters with no parity, or seven bit characters with space parity. The HP-UX implementation of rlogind (see rlogind(1M)) interprets seven bit characters with even, odd, or mark parity as eight-bit non-USASCII characters. You may also need to reconfigure the remote host appropriately (see stty(1) and tty(7)). Some remote hosts may not provide the necessary support for eight-bit characters. In this case, or if it is not possible to disable parity generation by the local terminal, use the -7 option.
-ee	Set the escape character to e. There is no space separating the option letter and the argument character. To start a line with the escape character, two of the escape characters must be entered. The default escape character is tilde (~). Some characters may conflict with your terminal configuration, such as ^S, ^Q, or backspace. Using one of these as the escape character may not be possible or may cause problems communicating with the remote host (see stty(1) and tty(7)).
-f	Forward the ticket granting ticket (TGT) to the remote system. The TGT is not forwardable from there.
-F	Forward the TGT to the remote system and have it forwardable from there to another remote system. -f and -F are mutually exclusive.
-k realm	Obtain tickets from the remote host in the specified realm instead of the remote host's default realm as specified in the configuration file krb.realms.
-l username	Set the user login name on the remote host to username. The default name is the current account name of the user invoking rlogin.
-P	Disable Kerberos authentication. Only applicable

in a secure environment based on Kerberos V5.
When this option is specified, a password is
required and the password is sent across the
network in cleartext. To bypass the normal
login/password sequence, you can login to a remote
host using an equivalent account in a manner
similar to remsh. See hosts.equiv(4) for details.

rlogin can be controlled with two-character escape sequences, in the
form ex, where e is the escape character and x is a code character
described below. Escape sequences are recognized only at the
beginning of a line of input. The default escape character is tilde
(~). It can be changed with the -e option.

The following escape sequences are recognized:

    ey   If y is NOT a code character described below, pass the
         escape character and y as characters to the remote host.

    ee   Pass the escape character as a character to the remote host.

    e.   Disconnect from the remote host.

    e!   Escape to a subshell on the local host. Use exit to return
         to the remote host.

If rlogin is run from a shell that supports job control (see
csh(1), ksh(1), and sh-posix(1)), escape sequences can be used to
suspend rlogin. The following escape sequences assume that ^Z
and ^Y are set as the user's susp and dsusp characters,
respectively (see stty(1) and termio(7)).

    e^Z Suspend the rlogin session and return the user to the shell
         that invoked rlogin. The rlogin job can be resumed with the
         fg command (see csh(1), ksh(1), and sh-posix(1)). e^Z
         suspends both rlogin processes: the one transmitting user
         input to the remote login, and the one displaying output
         from the remote login.

    e^Y Suspend the rlogin session and return the user to the shell
         that invoked rlogin. The rlogin job can be resumed with the
         fg command (see csh(1), ksh(1), and sh-posix(1)). e^Y
         suspends only the input process; output from the remote
         login continues to be displayed.

If you "daisy-chain" remote logins (for example, you rlogin from host
A to host B and then rlogin from host B to host C) without setting
unique escape characters, you can repeat the escape character until it
reaches your chosen destination. For example, the first escape
character, e, is seen as an escape character on host A; the second e
is passed as a normal character by host A and seen as an escape
character on host B; a third e is passed as a normal character by
hosts A and B and accepted as a normal character by host C.

Remote Host Name As Command
   The system administrator can arrange for more convenient access to a
   remote host (rhost) by linking remsh to /usr/hosts/rhost, allowing use
   of the remote host name (rhost) as a command (see remsh(1)). For
   example, if remotehost is the name of a remote host and
   /usr/hosts/remotehost is linked to remsh, and if /usr/hosts is in your
   search path, the command:

       remotehost

is equivalent to:

        rlogin remotehost

RETURN VALUES
        rlogin sends an error message to standard error and returns a nonzero
        value if an error occurs before the connection to the remote host is
        completed. Otherwise, it returns a zero.

DIAGNOSTICS
        Diagnostics can occur from both the local and remote hosts. Those
        that occur on the local host before the connection is completely
        established are written to standard error. Once the connection is
        established, any error messages from the remote host are written to
        standard output, like any other data.

        login/tcp: Unknown service

            rlogin was unable to find the login service listed in the
            /etc/services database file.

        There is no entry for you (user ID username) in /etc/passwd

            rlogin was unable to find your user ID in the password file.

            Next Step: Contact your system administrator.

        system call:...
            An error occurred when rlogin attempted the indicated system
            call. See the appropriate manual entry for information about the
            error.

        rcmd: connect <hostname>: Connection refused.
            One cause for display of this generic error message could be due
            to the absence of an entry for login in /etc/inetd.conf on the
            remote system. This entry may have been removed or commented out
            to prevent non-secure access.

        Kerberos-specific errors are listed in sis(5).

EXAMPLES
        Log in as the same user on the remote host remote:

            rlogin remote

        Set the escape character to a !, use a seven-bit data connection, and
        attempt a login as user guest on host remhost:

            rlogin remhost -e! -7 -l guest

        Assuming that your system administrator has set up the links in
        /usr/hosts, the following is equivalent to the previous command:

            remhost -e! -7 -l guest

WARNINGS
        For security purposes, the /etc/hosts.equiv and .rhosts files should
        exist, even if they are empty. These files should be readable and
        writable only by the owner. See host.equiv(4) for more information.

        Note also that all information, including passwords, is passed
        unencrypted between the two hosts. In a Kerberos V5 Network
        Authentication environment, a password is not transmitted across the
        network, so it will be protected.

rlogin is unable to transmit the Break key as an interrupt signal to
the remote system, regardless of whether the user has set stty brkint
on the local system. The key assigned to SIGINT with the command stty
intr c should be used instead (see stty(1)).

AUTHOR
      rlogin was developed by the University of California, Berkeley.

FILES
        $HOME/.rhosts   User's private equivalence list
        /etc/hosts.equiv   List of equivalent hosts
        /usr/hosts/*   For rhost version of the command

SEE ALSO
        csh(1), ksh(1), login(1), remsh(1), sh(1), sh-bourne(1), sh-posix(1),
        stty(1), telnet(1), rlogind(1M), hosts(4), hosts.equiv(4),
        inetd.conf(4), services(4), termio(7), tty(7), sis(5).

route

route - Manipulate network routing tables.

```
route(1M)                                                          route(1M)

NAME
     route - manually manipulate the routing tables

SYNOPSIS

     /usr/sbin/route [-f] [-n] [-p pmtu] add [net|host] destination
         [netmask mask] gateway [count]

     /usr/sbin/route [-f] [-n] delete [net|host] destination
         [netmask mask] gateway [count]

     /usr/sbin/route -f [-n]

DESCRIPTION
     The route command manipulates the network routing tables manually.
     You must have appropriate privileges.

     Subcommands
     The following subcommands are supported.

         add               Add the specified host or network route to the
                           network routing table.  If the route already
                           exists, a message is printed and nothing changes.


         delete            Delete the specified host or network route from
                           the network routing table.

     Options and Arguments
     route recognizes the following options and arguments.

         -f                Delete all route table entries that specify a
                           remote host for a gateway.  If this is used with
                           one of the subcommands, the entries are deleted
                           before the subcommand is processed.

         -n                Print any host and network addresses in Internet
                           dot notation, except for the default network
                           address, which is printed as default.

         -p pmtu           Specifies a path maximum transmission unit (MTU)
                           value for a static host route.  The minimum value
                           allowed is 68 bytes; the maximum is the MTU of the
                           outgoing interface for this route.  This option
                           only applies to adding a host route.  In all other
                           cases, this option is ignored and has no effect on
                           a system.

                           You can also disable the Path MTU Discovery for a
                           host route by specifying pmtu as zero.
```

net
or
host

The type of destination address. If this argument
is omitted, routes to a particular host are
distinguished from those to a network by
interpreting the Internet address associated with
destination. If the destination has a local
address part of INADDR_ANY(0), the route is
assumed to be to a network; otherwise, it is
treated as a route to a host.

destination

The destination host system where the packets will
be routed. destination can be one of the
following:

- A host name (the official name or an alias,
  see gethostbyname(3N)).
- A network name (the official name or an
  alias, see getnetbyname(3N)).
- An Internet address in dot notation (see
  inet(3N)).
- The keyword default, which signifies the
  wildcard gateway route (see routing(7)).

netmask
mask

The mask that will be bit-wise ANDed with
destination to yield a net address where the
packets will be routed. mask can be specified as
a single hexadecimal number with a leading 0x,
with a dot-notation Internet address, or with a
pseudo-network name listed in the network table
(see networks(4)). The length of the mask, which
is the number of contiguous 1's starting from the
leftmost bit position of the 32-bit field, can be
shorter than the default network mask for the
destination address. (see routing (7)). If the
netmask option is not given, mask for the route
will be derived from the netmasks associated with
the local interfaces. (see ifconfig (1)). mask
will be defaulted to the longest netmask of those
local interfaces that have the same network
address. If there is not any local interface that
has the same network address, then mask will be
defaulted to the default network mask of
destination.

gateway

The gateway through which the destination is
reached. gateway can be one of the following:

- A host name (the official name or an alias,
  see gethostbyname(3N)).
- An Internet address in dot notation (see
  inet(3N)).

count

An integer that indicates whether the gateway is a
remote host or the local host. If the route leads
to a destination through a remote gateway, count
should be a number greater than 0. If the route
leads to destination and the gateway is the local
host, count should be 0. The default for count is
zero. The result is not defined if count is
negative.

Operation
   All symbolic names specified for a destination or gateway are looked
up first as a host name using gethostbyname(); if the host name is not

found, the destination is searched for as a network name using getnetbyname(). destination and gateway can be in dot notation (see inet(3N)).

If the -n option is not specified, any host and network addresses are displayed symbolically according to the name returned by gethostbyaddr() and getnetbyaddr(), respectively, except for the default network address (printed as default) and addresses that have unknown names. Addresses with unknown names are printed in Internet dot notation (see inet(3N)).

If the -n option is specified, any host and network addresses are printed in Internet dot notation except for the default network address which is printed as default.

If the -f option is specified, route deletes all route table entries that specify a remote host for a gateway. If it is used with one of the subcommands described above, the entries are deleted before the subcommand is processed.

Path MTU Discovery is a technique for discovering the maximum size of an IP datagram that can be sent on an internet path without causing datagram fragmentation in the intermediate routers. In essence, a source host that utilizes this technique initially sends out datagrams up to the the size of the outgoing interface. The Don't Fragment (DF) bit in the IP datagram header is set. As an intermediate router that supports Path MTU Discovery receives a datagram that is too large to be forwarded in one piece to the next-hop router and the DF bit is set, the router will discard the datagram and send an ICMP Destination Unreachable message with a code meaning "fragmentation needed and DF set". The ICMP message will also contain the MTU of the next-hop router. When the source host receives the ICMP message, it reduces the path MTU of the route to the MTU in the ICMP message. With this technique, the host route in the source host for this path will contain the proper MTU.

By default, Path MTU Discovery is enabled for TCP sockets and disabled for UDP sockets.

If the -p pmtu option is specified for a host route, the pmtu value is considered permanent for the host route. Even if the Path MTU Discovery process discovers a smaller pmtu for this route at a later time, the pmtu field in the host route will not be updated. A warning message will be logged with the new pmtu value.

The -p pmtu option is useful only if you knows the network environment well enough to enter an appropriate pmtu for a host route. IP will fragment a datagram to the pmtu specified for the route on the local host before sending the datagram out to the remote. It will avoid fragmentation by routers along the path, if the pmtu specified in the route command is correct.

ping can be used to find the pmtu information for the route to a remote host. The pmtu information in the routing table can be displayed with the netstat -r command (see netstat(1)).

Output
  add destination: gateway gateway

      The specified route is being added to the tables.

  delete destination: gateway gateway

      The specified route is being deleted from the tables.

Flags

The values of the count and destination type fields in the route command determine the presence of the G and H flags in the netstat -r display and thus the route type, as shown in the following table.

Count	Destination Type	Flags	Route Type
=0	network	U	Route to a network directly from the local host
>0	network	UG	Route to a network through a remote host gateway
=0	host	UH	Route to a remote host directly from the local host
>0	host	UGH	Route to a remote host through a remote host gateway
=0	default	U	Wildcard route directly from the local host
>0	default	UG	Wildcard route through a remote host gateway

DIAGNOSTICS
The following error diagnostics can be displayed.

add a route that already exists

The specified entry is already in the routing table.

add too many routes

The routing table is full.

delete a route that does not exist

The specified route was not in the routing table.

WARNINGS
Reciprocal route commands must be executed on the local host, the destination host, and all intermediate hosts if routing is to succeed in the cases of virtual circuit connections or bidirectional datagram transfers.

The HP-UX implementation of route does not presently support a change subcommand.

AUTHOR
route was developed by the University of California, Berkeley.

FILES
/etc/networks
/etc/hosts

SEE ALSO
netstat(1), ifconfig(1M), ping(1M), getsockopt(2), recv(2), send(2), gethostbyaddr(3N), gethostbyname(3N), getnetbyaddr(3N), getnetbyname(3N), inet(3N), routing(7).

rwho

rwho - Produce a list of users on a remote system.

---

rwho(1)   rwho(1)

NAME
     rwho - show who is logged in on local machines

SYNOPSIS

     rwho [-a]

DESCRIPTION
     rwho produces output similar to the output of the HP-UX who command
     for all machines on the local network that are running the rwho daemon
     (see who(1) and rwhod(1M)). If rwhod has not received a report from a
     machine for 11 minutes, rwho assumes the machine is down and rwho does
     not report users last known to be logged into that machine.

     rwho's output line has fields for the name of the user, the name of
     the machine, the user's terminal line, the time the user logged in,
     and the amount of time the user has been idle. Idle time is shown as:

          hours:minutes

     If a user has not typed to the system for a minute or more, rwho
     reports this as idle time. If a user has not typed to the system for
     an hour or more, the user is omitted from rwho's output unless the -a
     flag is given.

     An example output line from rwho would look similar to:

          joe_user   machine1:tty0p1 Sep 12 13:28   :11

     This output line could be interpreted as joe_user is logged into
     machine1 and his terminal line is tty0p1. joe_user has been logged on
     since September 12 at 13:28 (1:28 p.m.). joe_user has not typed
     anything into machine1 for 11 minutes.

WARNINGS
     rwho's output becomes unwieldy when the number of users for each
     machine on the local network running rwhod becomes large. One line of
     output occurs for each user on each machine on the local network that
     is running rwhod.

AUTHOR
     rwho was developed by the University of California, Berkeley.

FILES
     /var/spool/rwho/whod.*   Information about other machines.

SEE ALSO
     ruptime(1), rusers(1), rwhod(1M).

telnet

telnet - Produce a list of users on a remote system.

---

telnet(1)   telnet(1)

NAME
     telnet - user interface to the TELNET protocol

SYNOPSIS

     telnet [[options]host [port]]

DESCRIPTION
     telnet is used to communicate with another host using the TELNET
     protocol. If telnet is invoked without arguments, it enters command
     mode, indicated by its prompt (telnet>). In this mode, it accepts and
     executes the commands listed below. If telnet is invoked with
     arguments, it performs an open command (see below) with those
     arguments.

     Once a connection has been opened, telnet enters an input mode. The
     input mode will be either ``character at a time'' or ``line by line'',
     depending on what the remote system supports.

     In ``character at a time'' mode, most text typed is immediately sent
     to the remote host for processing.

     In ``line by line'' mode, all text is echoed locally, and (normally)
     only completed lines are sent to the remote host. The ``local echo
     character'' (initially ^E) can be used to turn off and on the local
     echo (this would mostly be used to enter passwords without the
     password being echoed).

     In either mode, if the localchars toggle is TRUE (the default in line
     mode; see below), the user's quit and intr characters are trapped
     locally, and sent as TELNET protocol sequences to the remote side.
     There are options (see toggle autoflush and toggle autosynch below)
     which cause this action to flush subsequent output to the terminal
     (until the remote host acknowledges the TELNET sequence) and flush
     previous terminal input (in the case of quit and intr).

     While connected to a remote host, telnet command mode can be entered
     by typing the telnet ``escape character'' (initially ^]). When in
     command mode, the normal terminal editing conventions are available.

     telnet supports eight-bit characters when communicating with the
     server on the remote host. To use eight-bit characters you may need
     to reconfigure your terminal or the remote host appropriately (see
     stty(1)). Furthermore, you may have to use the binary toggle to
     enable an 8-bit data stream between telnet and the remote host. Note
     that some remote hosts may not provide the necessary support for
     eight-bit characters.

     If, at any time, telnet is unable to read from or write to the server
     over the connection, the message Connection closed by foreign host. is
     printed on standard error. telnet then exits with a value of 1.

telnet supports the TAC User ID (also known as the TAC Access Control
System, or TACACS User ID) option. Enabling the option on a host
server allows the user to telnet into that host without being prompted
for a second login sequence. The TAC User ID option uses the same
security mechanism as rlogin for authorizing acces by remote hosts and
users. The system administrator must enable the (telnetd) option only
on systems which are designated as participating hosts. The system
administrator must also assign to each user of TAC User ID the very
same UID on every system for which he is allowed to use the feature.
(See telnetd(1M) and the System Administration Tasks manual, PN 2355-
90051.)

The following telnet options are available:

-8   Enable cs8 (8 bit transfer) on local tty.

-ec   Set the telnet command mode escape character to be ^c
            instead of its default value of ^].

-l   Disable the TAC User ID option if enabled on the client, to
            cause the user to be prompted for login username and
            password. Omitting the -l option executes the default
            setting.

Commands
   The following commands are available in command mode. You need only
   type enough of each command to uniquely identify it (this is also true
   for arguments to the mode, set, toggle, and display commands).

open host [port]
                       Open a connection to the named host at the indicated
                       port. If no port is specified, telnet attempts to
                       contact a TELNET server at the standard TELNET port.
                       The hostname can be either the official name or an
                       alias as understood by gethostbyname() (see
                       gethostent(3N)), or an Internet address specified in
                       the dot notation as described in hosts(4). If no
                       hostname is given, telnet prompts for one.

close   Close a TELNET session. If the session was started
                   from command mode, telnet returns to command mode;
                   otherwise telnet exits.

quit   Close any open TELNET session and exit telnet. An end
                   of file (in command mode) will also close a session and
                   exit.

z   Suspend telnet. If telnet is run from a shell that
                   supports job control, (such as csh(1) or ksh(1)), the z
                   command suspends the TELNET session and returns the
                   user to the shell that invoked telnet. The job can
                   then be resumed with the fg command (see csh(1) or
                   ksh(1)).

mode mode   Change telnet's user input mode to mode, which can be
                   character (for ``character at a time'' mode) or line
                   (for ``line by line'' mode). The remote host is asked
                   for permission to go into the requested mode. If the
                   remote host is capable of entering that mode, the
                   requested mode is entered. In character mode, telnet
                   sends each character to the remote host as it is typed.
                   In line mode, telnet gathers user input into lines and
                   transmits each line to the remote host when the user
                   types carriage return, linefeed, or EOF (normally ^D;
                   see stty(1)). Note that setting line-mode also sets

local echo. Applications that expect to interpret user input character by character (such as more, csh, ksh, and vi) do not work correctly in line mode.

status   Show current status of telnet. telnet reports the current escape character. If telnet is connected, it reports the host to which it is connected and the current mode. If telnet is not connected to a remote host, it reports No connection. Once telnet has been connected, it reports the local flow control toggle value.

display [argument ...]
          Displays all or some of the set and toggle values (see below).

? [command]   Get help. With no arguments, telnet prints a help summary. If a command is specified, telnet prints the help information available about that command only. Help information is limited to a one-line description of the command.

! [shell_command]
          Shell escape. The SHELL environment variable is checked for the name of a shell to use to execute the command. If no shell_command is specified, a shell is started and connected to the user's terminal. If SHELL is undefined, /usr/bin/sh is used.

send arguments Sends one or more special character sequences to the remote host. Each argument can have any of the following values (multiple arguments can be specified with each send command):

                  escape   Sends the current telnet escape character (initially ^]).

                  synch   Sends the TELNET SYNCH sequence. This sequence causes the remote system to discard all previously typed (but not yet read) input. This sequence is sent as TCP urgent data (and may not work to some systems -- if it doesn't work, a lower case ``r'' may be echoed on the terminal).

                  brk   Sends the TELNET BRK (Break) sequence, which may have significance to the remote system.

                  ip   Sends the TELNET IP (Interrupt Process) sequence, which should cause the remote system to abort the currently running process.

                  ao   Sends the TELNET AO (Abort Output) sequence, which should cause the remote system to flush all output from the remote system to the user's terminal.

                  ayt   Sends the TELNET AYT (Are You There) sequence, to which the remote system may or may not choose to respond.

                  ec   Sends the TELNET EC (Erase Character) sequence, which should cause the remote

system to erase the last character
entered.

el   Sends the TELNET EL (Erase Line)
sequence, which should cause the remote
system to erase the line currently being
entered.

ga   Sends the TELNET GA (Go Ahead) sequence,
which likely has no significance to the
remote system.

nop   Sends the TELNET NOP (No OPeration)
sequence.

?   Prints out help information for the send
command.

set variable_name value
Set any one of a number of telnet variables to a
specific value. The special value off turns off the
function associated with the variable. The values of
variables can be shown by using the display command.
The following variable_names can be specified:

echo This is the value (initially ^E) which, when in
line-by-line mode, toggles between doing local
echoing of entered characters (for normal
processing), and suppressing echoing of entered
characters (for entering, for example, a
password).

escape
This is the telnet escape character (initially ^])
which causes entry into telnet command mode (when
connected to a remote system).

interrupt
If telnet is in localchars mode (see toggle
localchars below) and the interrupt character is
typed, a TELNET IP sequence (see send ip above) is
sent to the remote host. The initial value for
the interrupt character is taken to be the
terminal's intr character.

quit If telnet is in localchars mode (see toggle
localchars below) and the quit character is typed,
a TELNET BRK sequence (see send brk above) is sent
to the remote host. The initial value for the
quit character is taken to be the terminal's quit
character.

flushoutput
If telnet is in localchars mode (see toggle
localchars below) and the flushoutput character is
typed, a TELNET AO sequence (see send ao above) is
sent to the remote host. The initial value for
the flush character is ^O.

erase
If telnet is in localchars mode (see toggle
localchars below), and if telnet is operating in
character-at-a-time mode, then when this character
is typed, a TELNET EC sequence (see send ec above)

is sent to the remote system. The initial value
for the erase character is taken to be the
terminal's erase character.

kill If telnet is in localchars mode (see toggle
localchars below), and if telnet is operating in
character-at-a-time mode, then when this character
is typed, a TELNET EL sequence (see send el above)
is sent to the remote system. The initial value
for the kill character is taken to be the
terminal's kill character.

eof If telnet is operating in line-by-line mode,
entering this character as the first character on
a line causes this character to be sent to the
remote system. The initial value of the eof
character is taken to be the terminal's eof
character.

toggle arguments ...
Toggle (between TRUE and FALSE) various flags that
control how telnet responds to events. More than one
argument can be specified. The state of these flags
can be shown by using the display command. Valid
arguments are:

localchars
If TRUE, the flush, interrupt, quit, erase,
and kill characters (see set above) are
recognized locally, and transformed into
appropriate TELNET control sequences
(respectively ao, ip, brk, ec, and el; see
send above). The initial value for this
toggle is TRUE in line-by-line mode, and
FALSE in character-at-a-time mode.

autoflush
If autoflush and localchars are both TRUE,
whenever the ao, intr, or quit characters are
recognized (and transformed into TELNET
sequences - see set above for details),
telnet refuses to display any data on the
user's terminal until the remote system
acknowledges (via a TELNET Timing Mark
option) that it has processed those TELNET
sequences. The initial value for this toggle
is TRUE.

autosynch
If autosynch and localchars are both TRUE,
when either the intr or quit character is
typed (see set above for descriptions of the
intr and quit characters), the resulting
TELNET sequence sent is followed by the
TELNET SYNCH sequence. This procedure should
cause the remote system to begin discarding
all previously typed input until both of the
TELNET sequences have been read and acted
upon. The initial value of this toggle is
FALSE.

binary
Enable or disable the TELNET BINARY option on
both input and output. This option should be

enabled in order to send and receive 8-bit characters to and from the TELNET server.

crlf If TRUE, end-of-line sequences are sent as an ASCII carriage-return and line-feed pair. If FALSE, end-of-line sequences are sent as an ASCII carriage-return and NUL character pair. The initial value for this toggle is FALSE.

crmod
Toggle carriage return mode. When this mode is enabled, any carriage return characters received from the remote host are mapped into a carriage return and a line feed. This mode does not affect those characters typed by the user; only those received. This mode is only required for some hosts that require the client to do local echoing, but output ``naked'' carriage returns. The initial value for this toggle is FALSE.

echo Toggle local echo mode or remote echo mode. In local echo mode, user input is echoed to the terminal by the local telnet before being transmitted to the remote host. In remote echo, any echoing of user input is done by the remote host. Applications that handle echoing of user input themselves, such as C shell, Korn shell, and vi (see csh(1), ksh(1), and vi(1)), do not work correctly with local echo.

options
Toggle viewing of TELNET options processing. When options viewing is enabled, all TELNET option negotiations are displayed. Options sent by telnet are displayed as ``SENT'', while options received from the TELNET server are displayed as ``RCVD''. The initial value for this toggle is FALSE.

netdata
Toggles the display of all network data (in hexadecimal format). The initial value for this toggle is FALSE.

? Displays the legal toggle commands.

RETURN VALUE
In the event of an error, or if the TELNET connection is closed by the remote host, telnet returns a value of 1. Otherwise it returns zero (0).

DIAGNOSTICS
The following diagnostic messages are displayed by telnet:

telnet/tcp: Unknown service
telnet was unable to find the TELNET service entry in the services(4) database.

hostname: Unknown host
telnet was unable to map the host name to an Internet address. Your next step should be to contact the system administrator to check whether there is an entry for the

remote host in the hosts database (see hosts(4)).

?Invalid command
     An invalid command was typed in telnet command mode.

system call>: ...
     An error occurred in the specified system call. See the
     appropriate manual entry for a description of the error.

AUTHOR
     telnet was developed by the University of California, Berkeley.

SEE ALSO
     csh(1), ksh(1), login(1), rlogin(1), stty(1), telnetd(1M), hosts(4),
     services(4), termio(7).

telnet(1)   Secure Internet Services with Kerberos Authentication   telnet(1)

NAME
     telnet - user interface to the TELNET protocol

SYNOPSIS

     telnet [[options]host [port]]

DESCRIPTION
     telnet is used to communicate with another host using the TELNET
     protocol. If telnet is invoked without arguments, it enters command
     mode, indicated by its prompt (telnet>). In this mode, it accepts and
     executes the commands listed below. If telnet is invoked with
     arguments, it performs an open command (see below) with those
     arguments.

     Once a connection has been opened, telnet enters an input mode. The
     input mode will be either ``character at a time'' or ``line by line'',
     depending on what the remote system supports.

     In ``character at a time'' mode, most text typed is immediately sent
     to the remote host for processing.

     In ``line by line'' mode, all text is echoed locally, and (normally)
     only completed lines are sent to the remote host. The ``local echo
     character'' (initially ^E) can be used to turn off and on the local
     echo (this would mostly be used to enter passwords without the
     password being echoed).

     In either mode, if the localchars toggle is TRUE (the default in line
     mode; see below), the user's quit and intr characters are trapped
     locally, and sent as TELNET protocol sequences to the remote side.
     There are options (see toggle autoflush and toggle autosynch below)
     which cause this action to flush subsequent output to the terminal
     (until the remote host acknowledges the TELNET sequence) and flush
     previous terminal input (in the case of quit and intr).

     While connected to a remote host, telnet command mode can be entered
     by typing the telnet ``escape character'' (initially ^]). When in
     command mode, the normal terminal editing conventions are available.

     telnet supports eight-bit characters when communicating with the
     server on the remote host. To use eight-bit characters you may need
     to reconfigure your terminal or the remote host appropriately (see
     stty(1)). Furthermore, you may have to use the binary toggle to
     enable an 8-bit data stream between telnet and the remote host. Note
     that some remote hosts may not provide the necessary support for
     eight-bit characters.

If, at any time, telnet is unable to read from or write to the server over the connection, the message Connection closed by foreign host. is printed on standard error. telnet then exits with a value of 1.

By default (or by use of the -a option or the -l option), this Kerberos version of telnet behaves as a client which supports authentication based on Kerberos V5. As a Kerberos client, telnet will authenticate and authorize the user to access the remote system. (See sis(5) for details on Kerberos authentication and authorization.) However, it will not support integrity-checked or encrypted sessions. telnet supports the TAC User ID (also known as the TAC Access Control System, or TACACS User ID) option. Enabling the option on a host server allows the user to telnet into that host without being prompted for a second login sequence. The TAC User ID option uses the same security mechanism as rlogin for authorizing access by remote hosts and users. The system administrator must enable the (telnetd) option only on systems which are designated as participating hosts. The system administrator must also assign to each user of TAC User ID the very same UID on every system for which he is allowed to use the feature. (See telnetd(1M) and the System Administration Tasks manual)

The following telnet options are available:

-8   Enable cs8 (8 bit transfer) on local tty.

-a   Attempt automatic login into the Kerberos realm and disable
          the TAC User ID option. (Note: this is the default login
          mode.)

          Sends the user name via the NAME subnegotiation of the
          Authentication option. The name used is that of the current
          user as returned by the USER environment variable. If this
          variable is not defined, the name used is that returned by
          getpwnam(3) if it agrees with the current user ID.
          Otherwise, it is the name associated with the user ID.

-e c   Set the telnet command mode escape character to be ^c
          instead of its default value of ^].

-l user   Attempt automatic login into the Kerberos realm as the
          specified user and disable the TAC User ID option. The user
          name specified is sent via the NAME subnegotiation of the
          Authentication option. Omitting the -l option executes the
          default setting. Only one -l option is allowed.

-P   Disable use of Kerberos authentication and authorization.
          When this option is specified, a password is required which
          is sent across the network in a readable form. (See sis(5).)

-f   Allows local credentials to be forwarded to the remote
          system. Only one of -f or -F is allowed.

-F   Allows local credentials to be forwarded to the remote
          system including any credentials that have already been
          forwarded into the local environment. Only one of -f or -F
          is allowed.

Commands
  The following commands are available in command mode. You need only
  type enough of each command to uniquely identify it (this is also true
  for arguments to the mode, set, toggle, and display commands).

  open [-l user] host [port]
                  Open a connection to the named host at the indicated
                  port. If no port is specified, telnet attempts to

contact a TELNET server at the standard TELNET port.
The hostname can be either the official name or an
alias as understood by gethostbyname() (see
gethostent(3N)), or an Internet address specified in
the dot notation as described in hosts(4). If no
hostname is given, telnet prompts for one. The -l
option can be used to specify the user name to use when
automatically logging in to the remote system. Using
this option disables the TAC User ID option.

close   Close a TELNET session. If the session was started
                 from command mode, telnet returns to command mode;
                 otherwise telnet exits.

quit   Close any open TELNET session and exit telnet. An end
                 of file (in command mode) will also close a session and
                 exit.

z   Suspend telnet. If telnet is run from a shell that
                 supports job control, (such as csh(1) or ksh(1)), the z
                 command suspends the TELNET session and returns the
                 user to the shell that invoked telnet. The job can
                 then be resumed with the fg command (see csh(1) or
                 ksh(1)).

mode mode   Change telnet's user input mode to mode, which can be
                 character (for ``character at a time'' mode) or line
                 (for ``line by line'' mode). The remote host is asked
                 for permission to go into the requested mode. If the
                 remote host is capable of entering that mode, the
                 requested mode is entered. In character mode, telnet
                 sends each character to the remote host as it is typed.
                 In line mode, telnet gathers user input into lines and
                 transmits each line to the remote host when the user
                 types carriage return, linefeed, or EOF (normally ^D;
                 see stty(1)). Note that setting line-mode also sets
                 local echo. Applications that expect to interpret user
                 input character by character (such as more, csh, ksh,
                 and vi) do not work correctly in line mode.

status   Show current status of telnet. telnet reports the
                 current escape character. If telnet is connected, it
                 reports the host to which it is connected and the
                 current mode. If telnet is not connected to a remote
                 host, it reports No connection. Once telnet has been
                 connected, it reports the local flow control toggle
                 value.

display [argument ...]
                 Displays all or some of the set and toggle values (see
                 below).

? [command]   Get help. With no arguments, telnet prints a help
                 summary. If a command is specified, telnet prints the
                 help information available about that command only.
                 Help information is limited to a one-line description
                 of the command.

! [shell_command]
                 Shell escape. The SHELL environment variable is
                 checked for the name of a shell to use to execute the
                 command. If no shell_command is specified, a shell is
                 started and connected to the user's terminal. If SHELL
                 is undefined, /usr/bin/sh is used.

send arguments   Sends one or more special character sequences to the

remote host. Each argument can have any of the
following values (multiple arguments can be specified
with each send command):

    escape   Sends the current telnet escape
                character (initially ^]).

    synch   Sends the TELNET SYNCH sequence. This
                sequence causes the remote system to
                discard all previously typed (but not
                yet read) input. This sequence is sent
                as TCP urgent data (and may not work to
                some systems -- if it doesn't work, a
                lower case ``r'' may be echoed on the
                terminal).

    brk   Sends the TELNET BRK (Break) sequence,
                which may have significance to the
                remote system.

    ip   Sends the TELNET IP (Interrupt Process)
                sequence, which should cause the remote
                system to abort the currently running
                process.

    ao   Sends the TELNET AO (Abort Output)
                sequence, which should cause the remote
                system to flush all output from the
                remote system to the user's terminal.

    ayt   Sends the TELNET AYT (Are You There)
                sequence, to which the remote system may
                or may not choose to respond.

    ec   Sends the TELNET EC (Erase Character)
                sequence, which should cause the remote
                system to erase the last character
                entered.

    el   Sends the TELNET EL (Erase Line)
                sequence, which should cause the remote
                system to erase the line currently being
                entered.

    ga   Sends the TELNET GA (Go Ahead) sequence,
                which likely has no significance to the
                remote system.

    nop   Sends the TELNET NOP (No OPeration)
                sequence.

    ?   Prints out help information for the send
                command.

set variable_name value
        Set any one of a number of telnet variables to a
        specific value. The special value off turns off the
        function associated with the variable. The values of
        variables can be shown by using the display command.
        The following variable_names can be specified:

    echo This is the value (initially ^E) which, when in
        line-by-line mode, toggles between doing local
        echoing of entered characters (for normal

processing), and suppressing echoing of entered
characters (for entering, for example, a
password).

escape
This is the telnet escape character (initially ^])
which causes entry into telnet command mode (when
connected to a remote system).

interrupt
If telnet is in localchars mode (see toggle
localchars below) and the interrupt character is
typed, a TELNET IP sequence (see send ip above) is
sent to the remote host. The initial value for
the interrupt character is taken to be the
terminal's intr character.

quit If telnet is in localchars mode (see toggle
localchars below) and the quit character is typed,
a TELNET BRK sequence (see send brk above) is sent
to the remote host. The initial value for the
quit character is taken to be the terminal's quit
character.

flushoutput
If telnet is in localchars mode (see toggle
localchars below) and the flushoutput character is
typed, a TELNET AO sequence (see send ao above) is
sent to the remote host. The initial value for
the flush character is ^O.

erase
If telnet is in localchars mode (see toggle
localchars below), and if telnet is operating in
character-at-a-time mode, then when this character
is typed, a TELNET EC sequence (see send ec above)
is sent to the remote system. The initial value
for the erase character is taken to be the
terminal's erase character.

kill If telnet is in localchars mode (see toggle
localchars below), and if telnet is operating in
character-at-a-time mode, then when this character
is typed, a TELNET EL sequence (see send el above)
is sent to the remote system. The initial value
for the kill character is taken to be the
terminal's kill character.

eof   If telnet is operating in line-by-line mode,
entering this character as the first character on
a line causes this character to be sent to the
remote system. The initial value of the eof
character is taken to be the terminal's eof
character.

toggle arguments ...
Toggle (between TRUE and FALSE) various flags that
control how telnet responds to events. More than one
argument can be specified. The state of these flags
can be shown by using the display command. Valid
arguments are:

localchars
If TRUE, the flush, interrupt, quit, erase,

and kill characters (see set above) are
recognized locally, and transformed into
appropriate TELNET control sequences
(respectively ao, ip, brk, ec, and el; see
send above). The initial value for this
toggle is TRUE in line-by-line mode, and
FALSE in character-at-a-time mode.

autoflush
If autoflush and localchars are both TRUE,
whenever the ao, intr, or quit characters are
recognized (and transformed into TELNET
sequences - see set above for details),
telnet refuses to display any data on the
user's terminal until the remote system
acknowledges (via a TELNET Timing Mark
option) that it has processed those TELNET
sequences. The initial value for this toggle
is TRUE.

autologin
Enable or disable automatic login into the
Kerberos realm. Using this option yields the
same results as using the -a option. The
initial value for this toggle is TRUE.

autosynch
If autosynch and localchars are both TRUE,
when either the intr or quit character is
typed (see set above for descriptions of the
intr and quit characters), the resulting
TELNET sequence sent is followed by the
TELNET SYNCH sequence. This procedure should
cause the remote system to begin discarding
all previously typed input until both of the
TELNET sequences have been read and acted
upon. The initial value of this toggle is
FALSE.

binary
Enable or disable the TELNET BINARY option on
both input and output. This option should be
enabled in order to send and receive 8-bit
characters to and from the TELNET server.

crlf If TRUE, end-of-line sequences are sent as an
ASCII carriage-return and line-feed pair. If
FALSE, end-of-line sequences are sent as an
ASCII carriage-return and NUL character pair.
The initial value for this toggle is FALSE.

crmod
Toggle carriage return mode. When this mode
is enabled, any carriage return characters
received from the remote host are mapped into
a carriage return and a line feed. This mode
does not affect those characters typed by the
user; only those received. This mode is only
required for some hosts that require the
client to do local echoing, but output
``naked'' carriage returns. The initial
value for this toggle is FALSE.

echo Toggle local echo mode or remote echo mode.
In local echo mode, user input is echoed to

the terminal by the local telnet before being
transmitted to the remote host. In remote
echo, any echoing of user input is done by
the remote host. Applications that handle
echoing of user input themselves, such as C
shell, Korn shell, and vi (see csh(1),
ksh(1), and vi(1)), do not work correctly
with local echo.

options
Toggle viewing of TELNET options processing.
When options viewing is enabled, all TELNET
option negotiations are displayed. Options
sent by telnet are displayed as ``SENT'',
while options received from the TELNET server
are displayed as ``RCVD''. The initial value
for this toggle is FALSE.

netdata
Toggles the display of all network data (in
hexadecimal format). The initial value for
this toggle is FALSE.

?   Displays the legal toggle commands.

RETURN VALUE
In the event of an error, or if the TELNET connection is closed by the
remote host, telnet returns a value of 1. Otherwise it returns zero
(0).

DIAGNOSTICS
Diagnostic messages displayed by telnet are displayed below. Kerberos
specific errors are listed in sis(5).

telnet/tcp: Unknown service
telnet was unable to find the TELNET service entry in the
services(4) database.

hostname: Unknown host
telnet was unable to map the host name to an Internet
address. Your next step should be to contact the system
administrator to check whether there is an entry for the
remote host in the hosts database (see hosts(4)).

?Invalid command
An invalid command was typed in telnet command mode.

system call>: ...
An error occurred in the specified system call. See the
appropriate manual entry for a description of the error.

AUTHOR
telnet was developed by the University of California, Berkeley.

SEE ALSO
csh(1), ksh(1), login(1), rlogin(1), stty(1), telnetd(1M), hosts(4),
services(4), termio(7), sis(5).

Keep in mind that you may need to start the telnet daemon, telnetd, in order to run telnet.

See the manual page for telnetd for startup instructions if you do not have telnetd running.

telnetd sends options to the client of a telnet session in order to set up a proper communication exchange during a telnet session.

CHAPTER 4

System Administration Manager (SAM)

SAM Overview

SAM is a program you can use that automates performing various system administration tasks. I would like to go on record right now and suggest that you use System Administration Manager (SAM) for performing routine system administration tasks. You'll talk to UNIX experts who say that any tool that automates system administration tasks is doing things behind your back and is therefore "evil." Don't believe them. SAM is a tool developed by HP-UX gurus who know as much about UNIX as anyone. I have met and worked with some of these people, and they have labored long and hard to give you and me a tool that *helps* us do our job and doesn't hinder us from doing it. Does this mean that you blindly use SAM? Of course not. If you have no idea how TCP/IP works, then you shouldn't have SAM perform networking configuration for you. This is the reason I wrote Chapter 2, to give you an overview of networking so that when you have SAM add Internet Protocol (IP) addresses to your system, you know how these address are constructed and how you use them. Similarly, you wouldn't want SAM to add users to your system without knowing what files will be updated. On the other hand, there is no reason to do this configuration manually if SAM can do this for you. Let SAM help you perform your job better and don't feel guilty about it.

Four features of SAM that make it particularly useful:

1. It provides a central point from which system administration tasks can be performed. This includes both the built-in tasks that come with SAM as well as those you can add into the SAM menu hierarchy. You can run SAM on a remote system and display it locally so that you do truly have a central point of control.

2. It provides an easy way to perform tasks that are difficult, in that you would have to perform many steps. SAM performs these steps for you.

3. It provides a summary of what your system currently looks like for any of the categories of administration tasks you wish to perform. If you want to do something with the disks on your system, SAM first lists the disks you currently have connected. If you want to play with a printer, SAM first lists all your printers and plotters for you. This capability cuts down on mistakes by putting your current configuration right in front of you.

4. You can assign non-root users to perform some of the system administration functions in SAM. If, for instance, you feel comfortable assigning one of your associates to manage users, you can give them permission to perform user-related tasks and give another user permission to perform backups, and so on.

There are some tasks SAM can't perform for you. SAM does most routine tasks for you, but troubleshooting a problem is not considered routine. Troubleshooting a problem gives you a chance to show off and to hone your system administration skills.

When SAM is performing routine tasks for you, it isn't doing anything you couldn't do yourself by issuing a series of HP-UX commands. SAM provides a simple user interface that allows you to perform tasks by selecting menu items and entering pertinent information essential to performing the task.

Running and Using SAM as Superuser

To run SAM, log in as root and type:

```
# sam
```

This will invoke SAM. If you have a graphics display, SAM will run with the Motif interface. If you have a character-based display, SAM will run in character mode. You have nearly all the same functionality in both modes, but the Motif environment is much more pleasant to use.

If you have a graphics display and SAM does not come up in a Motif window, you probably don't have your DISPLAY variable set for root.

Type the following to set the DISPLAY variable for default POSIX, Korn, and Bourne shells:

```
# DISPLAY=system_name:0.0
# export DISPLAY
```

Just substitute the name of your computer for *system_name*. This can be set in your local **.profile** file. If you're running HP CDE, you may want to put these lines in your **.dtprofile** file.

Type the following to set the DISPLAY variable for C shell:

```
# setenv DISPLAY system_name:0.0
```

Again, you would substitute the name of your computer for system_name. This would typically be done in your **.login** file, but if you're running HP CDE, you may want to put this in your **.dtprofile** file.

Figure 4-1 shows the System Administration Manager running in graphics mode. This is the top-level window of the hierarchical SAM environment called the Functional Area Launcher (FAL). The 15 categories or areas of management shown are the default functional areas managed by SAM. You can select one of these functional areas and be placed in a sub-area. Because SAM is hierarchical, you may find yourself working your way down through several levels of the hierarchy before you reach the desired level. I'll cover each of these categories or areas in this chapter.

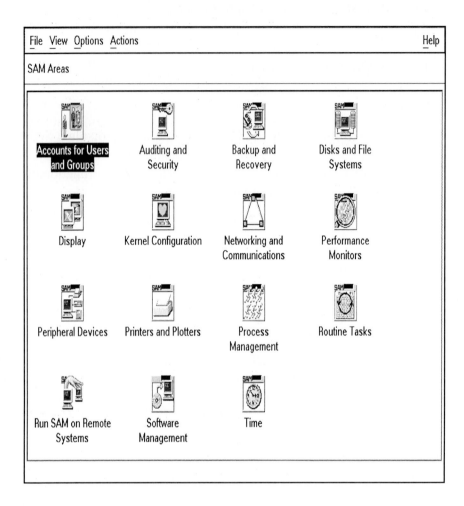

Figure 4-1   SAM Startup Window in Graphics Mode

In addition to selecting a functional area, you can select from the pull-down menu bar across the top of the SAM window. I will indicate selections made in SAM and keyboard keys in this chapter with italics. The five selections are *File, View, Options, Actions,* and *Help.* The title line shown in Figure 4-1 reads *SAM Areas.* If you're running Restricted SAM Builder you will also see a status line with the message "Privileges for user: <username>." As you progress down the hierarchy, the title line will change to reflect your level in the SAM hierarchy. You can move into one of the areas shown, such as *Backup and Recovery*, by double-clicking the left mouse button on this functional area. You move back up the hierarchy by double-clicking the *..(go up)* icon if available or by selecting the *Actions-Close Level* menu pick.

You don't need a graphics display to run SAM. You have access to nearly all the same functionality on a text terminal as you do on a graphics terminal. Figure 4-2 is SAM running in character mode with the same 15 functional areas you have in graphics mode.

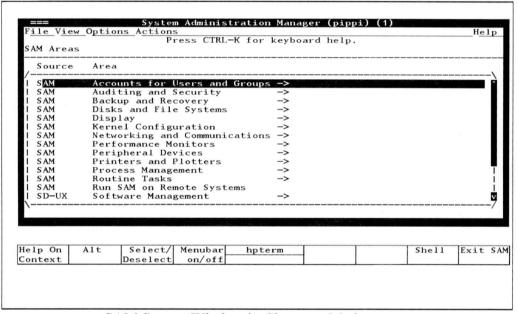

Figure 4-2 SAM Startup Window in Character Mode

The *View* menu can be used in character mode to tailor the information desired, filter out some entries, or search for particular entries.

Because you don't have a mouse on a text terminal, you use the keyboard to make selections. The point-and-click method of using SAM when in graphics mode is highly preferable to using the keyboard; however, the same structure to the functional areas exists in both environments. When you see an item in reverse video on the text terminal (such as *Accounts for Users and Groups* in Figure 4-2), you know that you have that item selected. After having selected *Accounts for Users and Groups* as shown in Figure 4-2, you would then use the *tab* key (or *F4*) to get to the menu bar, use the <- -> keys to select the desired menu, and use the *space bar* to display the menu. This situation is where having a mouse to make your selections is highly desirable. Figure 4-3 shows a menu bar selection for both a text and graphic display. In both cases, the *Actions* menu of *Disks and File Systems* has been selected.

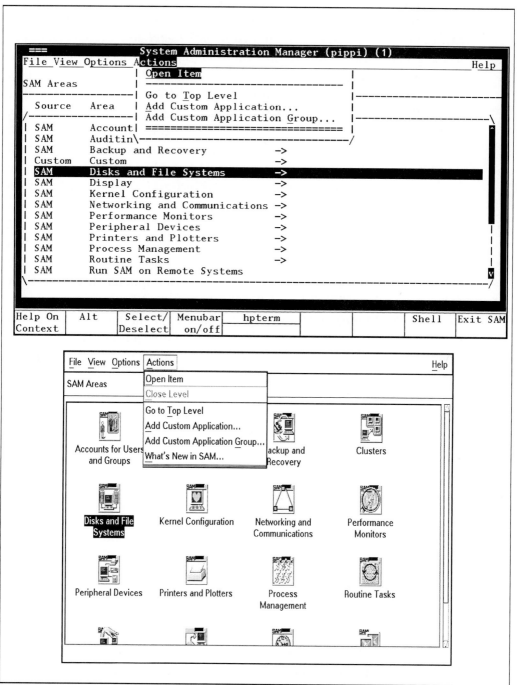

Figure 4-3 SAM Menu Selection for Text and Graphics Displays

Of particular interest on the pull-down menu are *Add Custom Application* and *Add Custom Application Group.* When you use *Add Custom Application Group,* you are prompted for the *Label* and optional *Help File* for the group. After you enter this information, a new icon appears, if you have a graphics display, with the name of your application group. You can then go into this application group and *Add Custom Applications.* This means that you can customize SAM to meet your specific administration needs by adding functionality to SAM. After you familiarize yourself with the aspects of system administration SAM can help you with, you'll want to test adding your own application to SAM. Adding a simple application like opening a log file or issuing the **/usr/bin/find** command will take you only seconds to create.

You can also create users who have restricted access to SAM. You can specify areas within SAM to which specific users can have access. You may have users to whom you would like to give access to backup and restore, or managing users, or handling the print spooler. Invoking SAM with the **-r** option will allow you to select a user to whom you want to give access to a SAM area and then select the specific area(s) to which you want to enable that user to have access. You can also give a user partial access to some areas, such as providing access to backup and recovery but not providing access to handling automated backups. As you progress through the detailed descriptions of SAM areas in this chapter, you'll want to think about which of these areas may be appropriate for some of your users to access.

Running Restricted SAM Builder

SAM can be configured to provide a subset of its overall functionality to specified users such as operators. You may, for instance, wish to give a user the ability to start a backup but not the ability to manage disks and file systems. With the Restricted SAM Builder, you have control of the functional areas to which specified users have access.

When specifying the functionality you wish to give a user, you invoke SAM with the **-r** option, initiating a Restricted SAM Builder session. After you have set up a user with specific functionality, you can then invoke

SAM with both the **-r** and **-f** options with the login name of a user you wish to test. The functionality of the user can be tested using these two options along with the login name.

Initially Setting User Privileges

When you invoke SAM with the **-r** option, you are first asked to select the user to whom you want to assign privileges. You will then be shown a list of default privileges for a new restricted SAM user. Figure 4-4 shows the default privileges SAM recommends for a new restricted user; note that custom SAM functional areas are disabled by default.

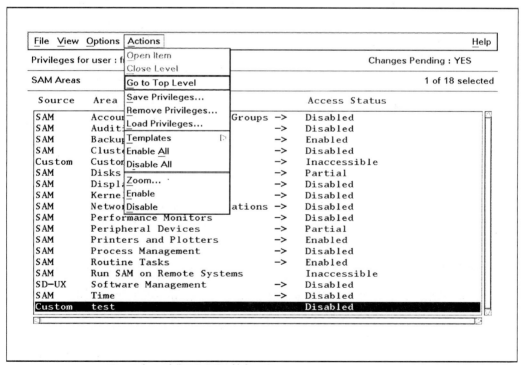

Figure 4-4 Restricted SAM Builder Screen

You can select from the *Actions* shown in Figure 4-4 to control access to functional areas. Of particular interest is the ability to save the privileges which you may later use as a template for other users with *Load User Privileges* from the *Actions* menu.

Verify Restricted Access

After having selected the appropriate privileges for a user by invoking SAM with the **-r** option, you can then use the **-f** option and login name to test the privileges for a user. The command shown below can be used to test user frank's privileges:

```
$ sam -r -f frank
```

When the user invokes SAM, she/he sees only the functional areas to which they have been given access. She/he can then proceed to perform tasks under one of these functional areas.

Accounts for Users and Groups

In Chapter 1, I explained the information that is associated with each user and group. There is an entry in the **/etc/passwd** file for each user and an entry in **/etc/group** for each group. To save you the trouble of flipping back to Chapter 1, Figure 4-5 is an example of a user entry from **/etc/passwd,** and Figure 4-6 is an example of a group entry from **/etc/ group**.

User Example:

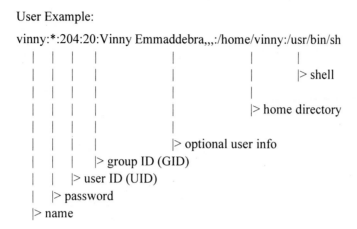

Figure 4-5 Sample **/etc/passwd** Entry

Group Example:

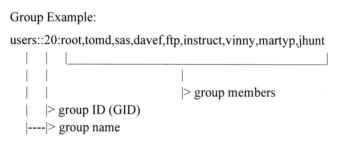

Figure 4-6 Sample **/etc/group** Entry

The *Accounts for Users and Groups* top-level SAM category or area has beneath it only two picks: *Groups* and *Users*. The menu hierarchy for "Users and Groups" is shown in the Figure 4-7.

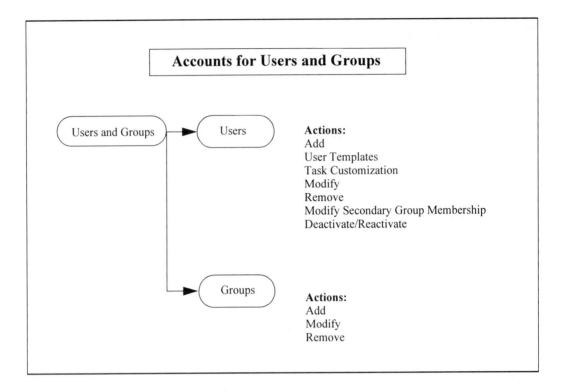

Figure 4-7   Accounts for Users and Groups

When you select *Accounts for Users and Groups* and then *Users* from the
SAM menu, you are provided a list of all the users on your system. Table
4-1 is a partial list of users provided by SAM for the system I am working
on.

TABLE 4-1 LIST OF USERS

Login Name	User ID (UID)	Real Name	Primary Group	Office Phone	Office Location
root	0		sys		
daemon	1		daemon		
bin	2		bin		
adm	4		adm		
uucp	5		sys		
lp	9		lp		
vinny	204	Vinny D.	users	Internal 5611	Stmfd
marty	219	Marty P.	users	Internal 5613	Stmfd
tftp	510	Trivial FTP user	other		
sas	205		users		

Adding a User

SAM is ideal for performing administration tasks related to users and groups. These are routine tasks that are not complex but require you to edit the **/etc/passwd** and **/etc/group** files, make directories, and copy default files, all of which SAM performs for you. Finally, take a minute to check what SAM has done for you, especially if you modify an existing user or group.

To add an additional user, you would select *Add* from the *Actions* menu under *Users* and then fill in the information as shown in Figure 4-8.

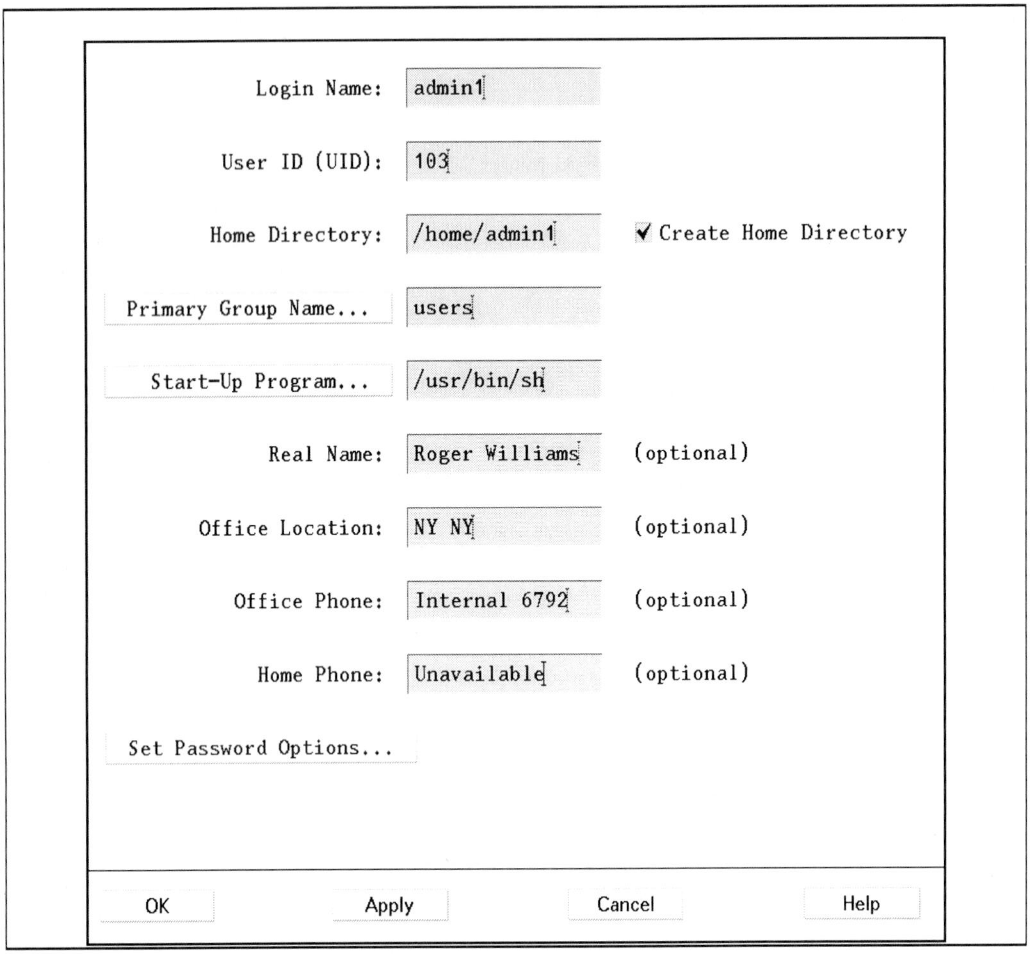

```
              Login Name:    admin1

          User ID (UID):     103

         Home Directory:     /home/admin1        ✔ Create Home Directory

    Primary Group Name...    users

      Start-Up Program...    /usr/bin/sh

               Real Name:    Roger Williams      (optional)

         Office Location:    NY NY               (optional)

            Office Phone:    Internal 6792       (optional)

              Home Phone:    Unavailable         (optional)

    Set Password Options...



        OK              Apply            Cancel              Help
```

Figure 4-8 Example of Adding a New User

There are some restrictions when entering this information. For instance, a comma and colon are not permitted in the Office Location field. When I tried to enter a comma, SAM informed me this was not permitted.

As a result of adding user admin1, the following **/etc/passwd** entry was made. (Notice that no entry exists for password; please make sure that you always enter a password on your system.)

admin1::103:20:Roger Williams,NY NY,Internal 6792,Unavailable:/ home/admin1:/usr/bin/sh

Adding this user gives us an opportunity to look at one of the best features of SAM - the ability to review what took place when this user was added with the "SAM Log Viewer," as shown in Figure 4-9.

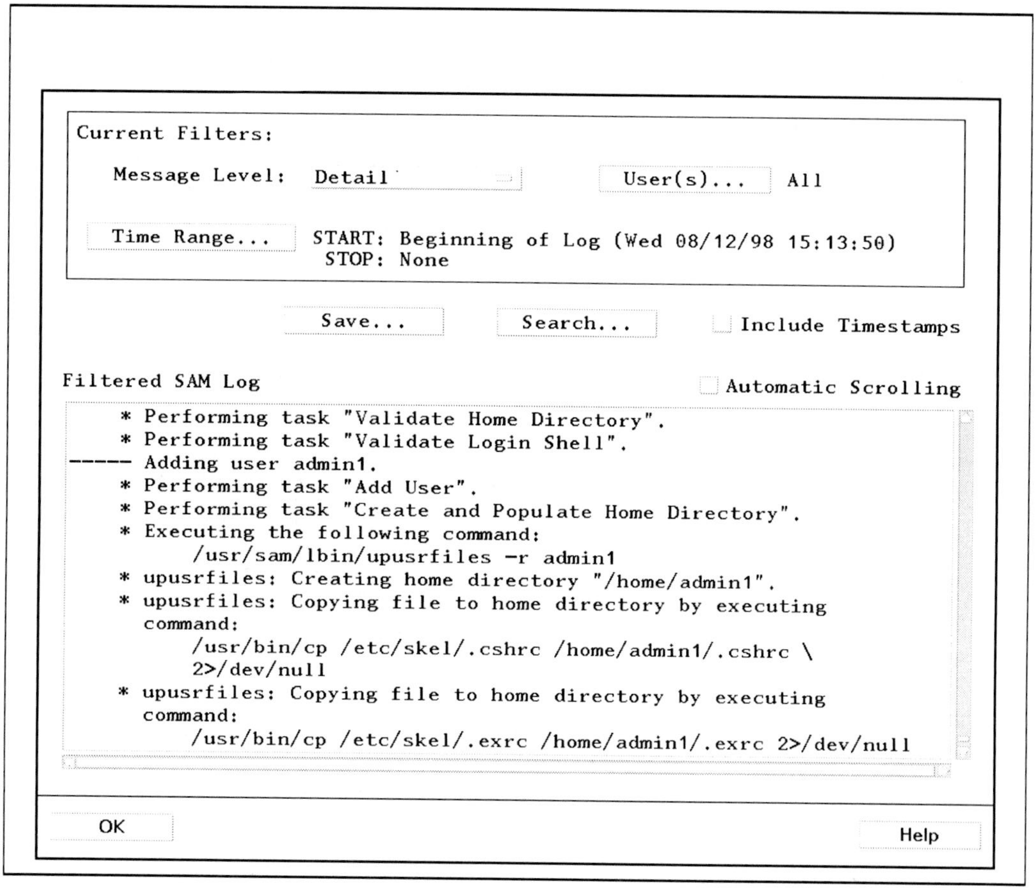

```
Current Filters:

   Message Level:  Detail                 User(s)...  All

   Time Range...    START: Beginning of Log (Wed 08/12/98 15:13:50)
                    STOP: None

            Save...        Search...     ☐ Include Timestamps

Filtered SAM Log                          ☐ Automatic Scrolling

    * Performing task "Validate Home Directory".
    * Performing task "Validate Login Shell".
------ Adding user admin1.
    * Performing task "Add User".
    * Performing task "Create and Populate Home Directory".
    * Executing the following command:
          /usr/sam/lbin/upusrfiles -r admin1
    * upusrfiles: Creating home directory "/home/admin1".
    * upusrfiles: Copying file to home directory by executing
      command:
          /usr/bin/cp /etc/skel/.cshrc /home/admin1/.cshrc \
          2>/dev/null
    * upusrfiles: Copying file to home directory by executing
      command:
          /usr/bin/cp /etc/skel/.exrc /home/admin1/.exrc 2>/dev/null


    OK                                              Help
```

Figure 4-9   SAM Log Viewer for Adding a User

The log file is viewed by selecting *View SAM Log* from the *Actions* menu bar.

The scroll bar on the right-hand side of the SAM Log Viewer allows you to scroll to any point in the log file. We are viewing only the part of the log file that pertains to adding the user Roger Williams. You can select the level of detail you wish to view with the log file. The four levels are *Summary, Detail, Verbose,* and *Commands Only*. The level shown in Figure 4-9 is *Detail*. I like this level because you can see what has taken place without getting mired down in too much detail.

Adding a Group

Adding an additional group is similar to adding a new user. To add an additional group, you would select *Add* from the *Actions* menu under *Groups*. Figure 4-10 shows the Add a New Group window.

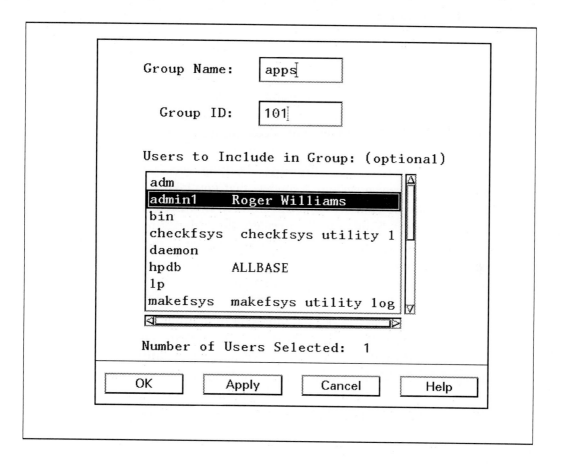

Figure 4-10   Example of Adding a New Group

In Figure 4-10, I added a new group called "apps" with a group ID of 101, and into that group I added the user admin1.

Auditing and Security

Under *Auditing and Security,* you manage the security of your system. This is becoming an increasingly important aspect of system management. Some installations care very little about security, because of well-known, limited groups of users who will access a system. Other installations, such as those connected to the Internet, may go to great pains to make their systems into fortresses with firewalls checking each and every user who attempts to access a system. I suggest that you take a close look at all the ramifications of security, and specifically a trusted system, before you enable security. You'll want to review the "Managing System Security" section of the "Administering A System" chapter of the *Managing Systems and Workgroups* manual, which replaces the 10.x manual *HP-UX System Administration Tasks Manual.* Although SAM makes creating and maintaining a trusted system easy, a lot of files are created for security management that takes place under the umbrella of auditing and security. Among the modifications that will be made to your system, should you choose to convert to a trusted system, is the **/etc/rc.config.d/auditing** file that will be updated by SAM. In addition, passwords in the **/etc/passwd** file will be replaced with "*" and the encrypted passwords are moved to a password database. All users are also given audit ID numbers. Figure 4-11 shows the hierarchy of Auditing and Security.

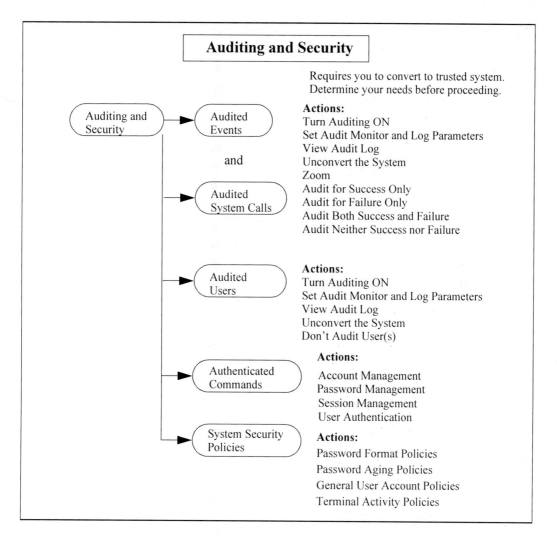

Figure 4-11 Auditing and Security

One choice to observe in Figure 4-11 is an *Actions* menu choice to *Unconvert the System*. This means to reverse the trusted system environment. I have tried this on various systems and it seems to work fine, but you should have a good idea of what a trusted system can do for and to you before you make the conversion.

I hope that I have given you a reasonably good overview of auditing and security, because in order to investigate it yourself, you must first convert to a trusted system. Before you do, please read this section to get an idea of the functionality this will provide and then convert to a trusted system if you think there is adequate benefit.

Audited Events and Audited System Calls

Under *Audited Events,* you can select the particular events you wish to analyze and detect which may cause security breaches. Under *Audited System Calls,* you can monitor system calls. This option is a function of the trusted system to which you must convert in order to perform auditing. You may have in mind particular events and system calls that are most vital to your system's security that you wish to audit, and not bother with the balance. There are a number of events and system calls that you may wish to keep track of for security reasons. Figure 4-12 shows the *Audited Events* window with the *Actions* menu shown as well.

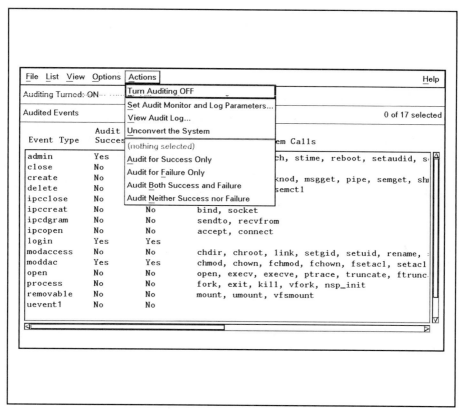

Auditing these events gives you a detailed report of the event. The same is true of system calls. Notice from the *Actions* menu that you have many options for the conditions you do and don't want to monitor. SAM uses the auditing commands of HP-UX such as **audsys**, **audusr**, **audevent**, **audomon**, and **audisp** to perform auditing.

Audited Users

Under *Audited Users,* you can use the *Actions* menu to turn auditing on and off for specific users. Since the audit log files, which you can also control and view through the *Actions* menu, grow large very quickly, you may want to select specific users to monitor to better understand the type of user audit information that is created.

Authenticated Commands

This security feature is the ability to perform authentication based on user, password, session, or account. This industry standard authentication framework is known as Pluggable Authentication Module, or PAM. The PAM framework allows for authentication modules to be implemented without modifying any applications. Authentication is currently provided for CDE components, HP-UX standard commands, trusted systems, and DCE (the Distributed Computing Environment), as well as third party modules.

This advanced feature is discussed in detail in the "Managing System Security" section of the "Administering a System" chapter of the *Managing Systems and Workgroups* manual.

System Security Policies

The most important part of HP-UX security is the policies you put in place. If, for instance, you choose to audit each and every system call but don't impose any restrictions on user passwords, then you are potentially opening up your system to any user. You would be much better off restricting users and not worrying so much about what they're doing. Being proactive is more important in security than being reactive.

You have several options for passwords under *Password Format Policies,* shown in Figure 4-13.

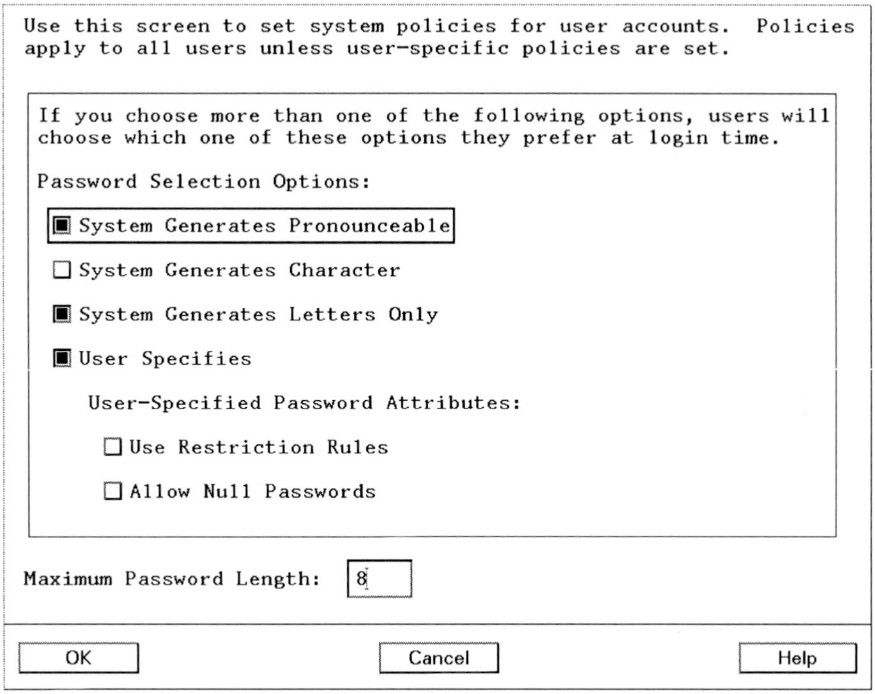

```
Use this screen to set system policies for user accounts.  Policies
apply to all users unless user-specific policies are set.

If you choose more than one of the following options, users will
choose which one of these options they prefer at login time.

Password Selection Options:

■ System Generates Pronounceable

□ System Generates Character

■ System Generates Letters Only

■ User Specifies

   User-Specified Password Attributes:

     □ Use Restriction Rules

     □ Allow Null Passwords


Maximum Password Length:    8
```

OK	Cancel	Help

Figure 4-13 *Password Format Policies* Window

Password Aging Policies, when enabled, allows you to select:

• Time between Password Changes

• Password Expiration Time

• Password Expiration Warning Time

• Password Life Time

• Expire All User Passwords Immediately

General User Account Policies, when enabled, allows you to specify the time in which an account will become inactive and lock it. In addition, you can specify the number of unsuccessful login tries that are permitted.

Terminal Security Policies allows you to set:

• Unsuccessful Login Tries Allowed

• Delay between Login Tries

• Login Timeout Value in Seconds

• Required Login upon Boot to Single-User State

Backup and Recovery

The most important activities you'll perform as a system administrator are system backup and recovery. The SAM team put a lot of thought into giving you all the options you need to ensure the integrity of your system through backup and recovery. Figure 4-14 shows the hierarchy of the *Backup and Recovery* SAM menu.

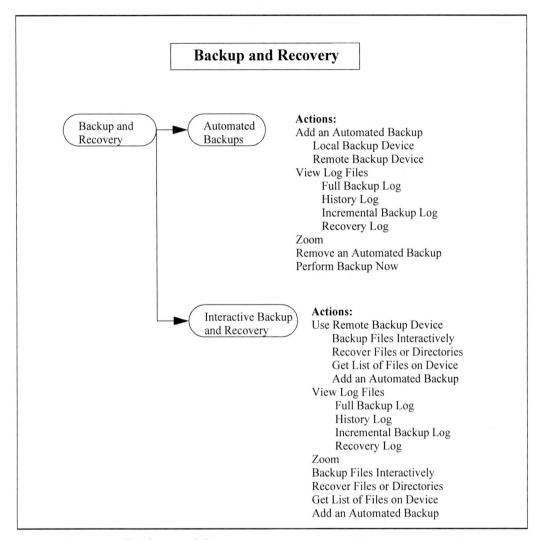

Figure 4-14 Backup and Recovery

Scheduling a Backup

The first step is to enter the *Automated Backups* subarea. You won't see any automated backups appear in the list until you have specified one. Using the *Actions* menu and selecting *Add an Automated Backup,* you can specify all the information about your automated backup. When you select *Add an Automated Backup,* you have to specify whether your backup will be to a local or a remote backup device. You will have to enter information pertaining to the backup scope, backup device, backup time, and additional parameters.

Select Backup Scope

You can view the backup scope as the files that will be included and excluded from the backup. This can include Network File System (NFS) mounted file systems as well. Figure 4-15 shows the window used to specify files to be included and excluded from the backup.

```
    Backup Scope:    Specified Files                          ▭

Cross NFS Mounts:   No  ▭

Type in the files or directories to be included and excluded.

  ┌─────────────────────────────────────┐  ┌─────────────────────────────────────┐
  │ Included Files                       │  │ Excluded Files (optional)           │
  │  Name      Type  Location            │  │  Name           Type  Location      │
  │ ┌───────────────────────────────┐   │  │ ┌───────────────────────────────┐   │
  │ │/var      VxFS  /dev/vg00/lvol17│   │  │ │/home/admin1  VxFS  /dev/vg00/lvol18│ │
  │ │/home     VxFS  /dev/vg00/lvol18│   │  │ │                               │   │
  │ │/mnt/9.x  VxFS  /dev/vg00/lvol3 │   │  │ │                               │   │
  │ └───────────────────────────────┘   │  │ └───────────────────────────────┘   │
  │                                      │  │                                     │
  │ File Name: _____       │  │ File Name: _____       │
  │                                      │  │                                     │
  │  [ Add ]   [ Modify ]  [ Remove ]    │  │  [ Add ]   [ Modify ]  [ Remove ]    │
  └─────────────────────────────────────┘  └─────────────────────────────────────┘

  [    OK    ]              [ Cancel ]                    [  Help  ]
```

Figure 4-15 Selecting the Backup Scope

In the selections shown in Figure 4-15 are three directories specified under included files. You can specify entire directories or individual files to be included or excluded from the backup. Although I want **/home** to be included in the backup, I don't want the home directory of **admin1**, the user we earlier created, to be included in the backup.

Instead of *Specified Files* as shown above, I could have selected *Local File Systems Only,* in which case all local file systems would have appeared in the *Included Files* list. If I had specified *All File Systems,* then all local file systems and NFS file systems (including **/net** by default) would have appeared in the list.

Select Backup Device

If you plan to back up to a local backup device, then those attached to your system will be listed and you select the desired device from the list.

If you plan to use a remote backup device, then you will be asked to specify the remote system name and device file.

Select Backup Time

As with the backup scope, you are provided with a window in which you can enter all the information about backup time for both full and incremental backups, as shown in Figure 4-16. If *Incremental Backup* is *Enabled,* then you must provide all pertinent information about both the full and incremental backup, as shown in the figure.

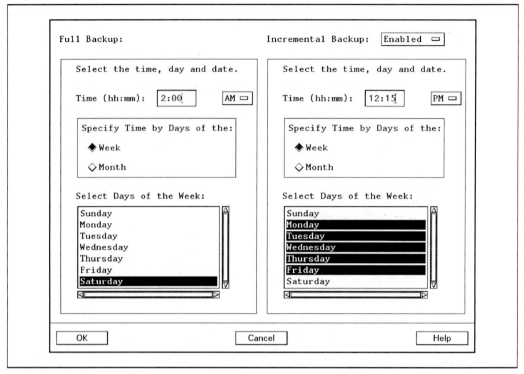

Figure 4-16   Selecting the Backup Time

A key point to keep in mind here is that the incremental backup that SAM creates for you includes files that have been changed *since the last full backup*. This means that you need only the full backup and last incremental backup to recover your system; that is, you do not need to restore the full backup and each incremental backup.

Set Additional Parameters

You can also specify additional parameters such as whether or not to create an index log, which I strongly suggest you do, and to whom to mail the results of the backup. We can now view the **crontab** entry SAM has made for root for these backups. The **crontab** file is used to schedule jobs that are automatically executed by **cron**. **crontab** files are in the **/var/spool/**

cron/crontabs directory. **cron** is a program that runs other programs at the specified time. **cron** reads files that specify the operation to be performed and the date and time it is to be performed. Since we want to perform back-ups on a regular basis, SAM will activate **cron**.

The format of entries in the **crontab** file are as follows:

minute hour monthday   month   weekday   user name command

minute - the minute of the hour, from 0-59
hour - the hour of the day, from 0-23
monthday - the day of the month, from 1-31
month - the month of the year, from 1-12
weekday - the day of the week, from 0 (Sunday) - 6 (Saturday)
user name - the user who will run the command if necessary
             (not used in the example)
command - specifies the command line or script file to run

You have many options in the **crontab** for specifying the *minute, hour, monthday, month,* and *weekday* to perform a task. You could list one entry in a field and then a space, several entries in any field separated by a comma, two entries separated by a dash indicating a range, or an asterisk, which corresponds to all possible entries for the field.

To list the contents of the **crontab** fil, you would issue the following command. The output of this command is the **crontab** file created for the user root in the SAM backup example.

```
$ crontab -l
00 2 * * 6 /usr/sam/lbin/br_backup DAT FULL Y /dev/rmt/0m /etc/
sam/br/graphDCAa02410 root Y 1 N > /tmp/SAM_br_msgs 2>&1 #sam-
backup

15 12 * * 1-5 /usr/sam/lbin/br_backup DAT PART Y /dev/rmt/0m /
etc/sam/br/graphDCAa02410 root Y 1 N > /tmp/SAM_br_msgs 2>&1
#sambackup
```

Although these seem to be excruciatingly long lines, they do indeed conform to the format of the **crontab** file. The first entry is the full backup; the second entry is the incremental backup. In the first entry, the *minute* is 00; in the second entry, the *minute* is 15. In the first entry, the *hour* is 2; in the second entry, the *hour* is 12. In both entries, the *monthday* and *month* are all legal values (*), meaning every *monthday* and *month*. In the first entry, the *weekday* is 6 for Saturday (0 is Sunday); in the second entry, the *weekdays* are 1-5 for Monday through Friday. The optional *user name* is not specified in either example. And finally, the SAM backup command (**/usr/sam/lbin/br_backup**) and its long list of associated information is provided.

minute	hour	monthday	month	weekday	user name	command
00	12	all	all	6	n/a	br_backup
15	12	all	all	1-5	n/a	br_backup

The *graph* file that is used by **/usr/sam/lbin/br_backup** is a list of files to be included and excluded from the backup. The following is the contents of the graph file **/etc/sam/br/graphDCAa02410** that was created for the full and incremental backups:

```
i /mnt/9.x
i /var
i /home
e /home/admin1
```

Lines that start with an "i" are files and directories to be included in the backup, and those starting with an "e" will be excluded from the backup.

You will see various crontab **commands** when you use the *SAM Log Viewer* to see what SAM has done for you to create the **crontab** files. For instance, if you change your backup plan, SAM will remove the old **crontab** file with the command:

```
$ crontab -r
```

This will remove the **crontab** file for the user from the **/var/spool/cron/crontabs** directory.

To place a file in the **crontab** directory, you would simply issue the **crontab** command and the name of the **crontab** file:

```
$ crontab crontabfile
```

You can schedule cron jobs using SAM. The section in this chapter covering *Process Management* has a section called "Scheduling Cron Jobs."

Interactive Backup and Recovery

The *Interactive Backup and Recovery* subarea is used to perform a backup interactively or restore information that was part of an earlier backup. When you enter this area, you are asked to select a backup device from a list that is produced, in the same way that you are asked to select a backup device when you first enter the **Automated Backups** subarea.

After selecting a device from the list, you may select an item from the *Actions* menu shown earlier. If you decide to use *Backup Files Interactively,* you are again provided a window in which you can specify files to be included and excluded from the backup. You are asked to *Select Backup Scope, Specify Tape Device Options*, and *Set Additional Parameters*. You are not, however, asked to *Select Backup Time,* since the backup is taking place interactively.

The steps in this area will vary, depending on the tape devices you have selected.

The log file **/var/sam/log/br_log** reports on the backup. The index files can be reviewed from the *Actions* menu. These are stored in the **/var/sam/log** directory. The following shows the very top and bottom of an index file that is 800 KBytes in size:

```
#   1  /
#   1  /.profile
#   1  /.rhosts
#   1  /.sh_history
#   1  /.sw
#   1  /.sw/sessions
#   1  /.sw/sessions/swinstall.last
#   1  /.sw/sessions/swlist.last
#   1  /.sw/sessions/swmodify.last
#   1  /.sw/sessions/swreg.last
#   1  /.dt
#   1  /.dt/Desktop
#   1  /.dt/Desktop/Two                           TOP
#   1  /.dt/Desktop/Four
#   1  /.dt/Desktop/One
#   1  /.dt/Desktop/Three

                        .
                        .
                        .


#   1  /var/uucp/.Log/uucico
#   1  /var/uucp/.Log/uucp
#   1  /var/uucp/.Log/uux
#   1  /var/uucp/.Log/uuxqt
#   1  /var/uucp/.Old
#   1  /var/uucp/.Status
#   1  /var/varspool/sw
#   1  /var/varspool/sw/catalog/dfiles
#   1  /var/varspool/sw/catalog/swlock
#   1  /var/varspool/sw/swagent.log
#   1  /var/yp
#   1  /var/yp/Makefile                    BOTTOM
#   1  /var/yp/binding
#   1  /var/yp/securenets
#   1  /var/yp/secureservers
#   1  /var/yp/updaters
#   1  /var/yp/ypmake
#   1  /var/yp/ypxfr_1perday
#   1  /var/yp/ypxfr_1perhour
#   1  /var/yp/ypxfr_2perday
```

Performing a Restore

A full or incremental backup, however, is only as good as the files it restores. To retrieve a file from the backup tape, you supply information in three areas: *Select Recovery Scope; Specify Tape Device Options*; and *Set Additional Parameters*. The device options you specify will depend on the tape device you are using.

Select *Recovery Scope* allows you to either enter a file name that contains the files to be recovered or manually list the files to be included in the recovery. You can optionally list files to be excluded from the recovery as well.

A list of tape device files is provided in *Specify Tape Device Options* from which you can select the tape device. In this step, you may select the tape device file; in other cases, you might make selections such as a magneto-optical surface or have nothing to select at all.

Under *Set Additional Parameters,* you can select any of the following options:

Overwrite Newer Files

Preserve Original File Ownership

Recover Files Using Full Path Name

Place Files in Non-Root Directory

After you make all the desired selections, the recovery operation begins. If a file has been inadvertently deleted and you wish to restore it from the recovery tape, you would select the *Preserve Original File Ownership* and *Recover Files Using Full Path Name* options. You will receive status of the recovery as it takes place and may also *View Recovery Log* from the *Actions* menu after the recovery has completed. If you *View Recovery Log,* you will receive a window that provides the name of the index log and the name of the files recovered:

```
Recovery Log (/var/sam/log/br_index.rec)

-rw-r--r--    admin1    users    /home/admin1/for-
tran/makefile
```

Disks and File Systems

Disks and File Systems helps you manage disk devices, file systems, logical volumes, swap, and volume groups (you may also manage HP disk
arrays through SAM if you have these installed on your system). There is
no reason to manually work with these, since SAM does such a good job of
managing these for you. Figures 4-17 and 4-18 show the hierarchy of *Disks
and File Systems*.

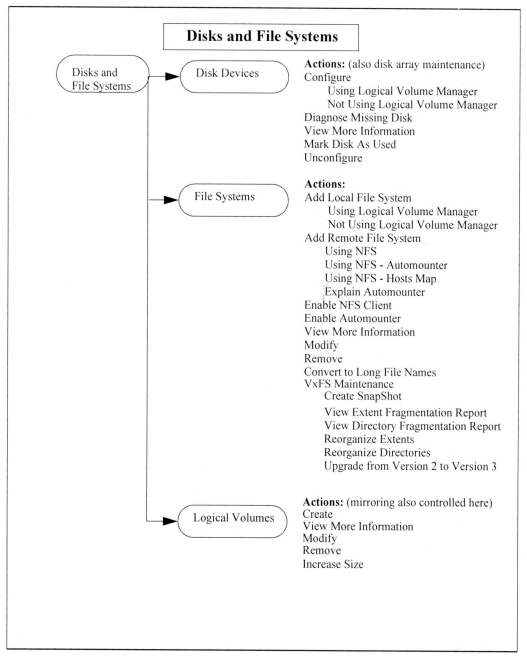

Figure 4-17 Disks and File Systems

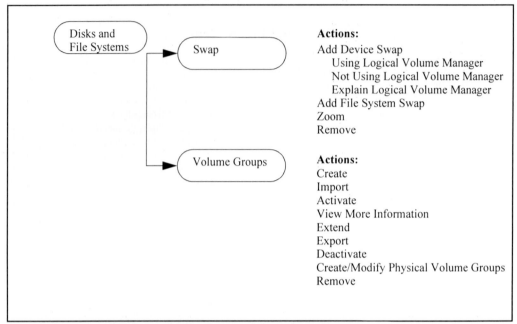

Figure 4-18 Disks and File Systems (continued)

Disk Devices

When you enter this subarea, SAM shows you the disk devices connected to your system. Figure 4-19 shows a listing of the disks for a Series 800 unit.

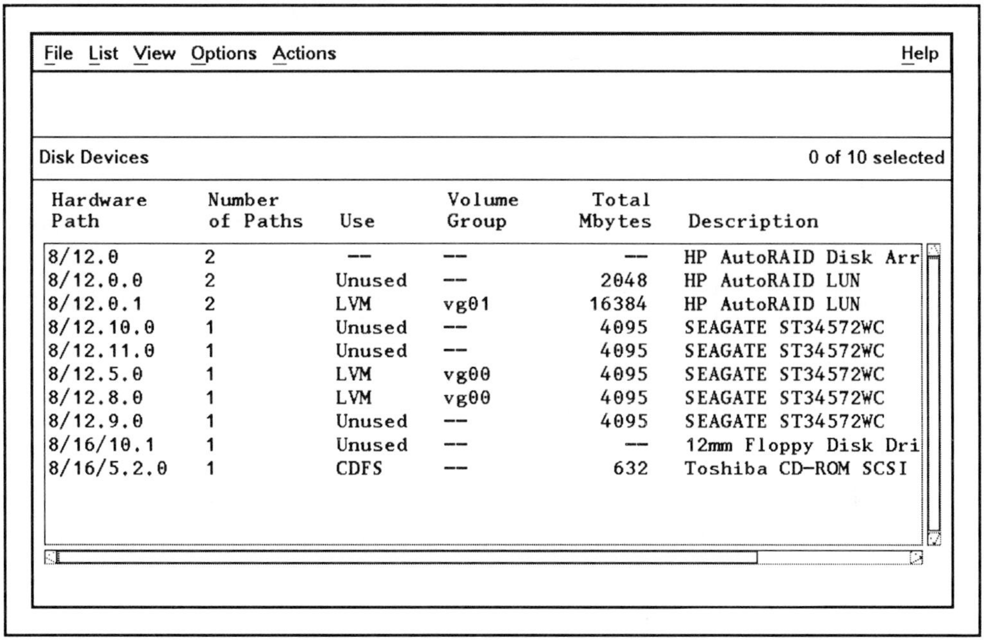

```
┌─────────────────────────────────────────────────────────────────────┐
│ ┌───────────────────────────────────────────────────────────────┐   │
│ │  File  List  View  Options  Actions                    Help   │   │
│ │                                                               │   │
│ ├───────────────────────────────────────────────────────────────┤   │
│ │  Disk Devices                              0 of 10 selected   │   │
│ │                                                               │   │
│ │  Hardware      Number            Volume     Total            │   │
│ │  Path          of Paths   Use    Group      Mbytes  Description│  │
│ │  8/12.0        2          --      --         --     HP AutoRAID Disk Arr│
│ │  8/12.0.0      2          Unused  --         2048   HP AutoRAID LUN │   │
│ │  8/12.0.1      2          LVM     vg01       16384  HP AutoRAID LUN │   │
│ │  8/12.10.0     1          Unused  --         4095   SEAGATE ST34572WC│  │
│ │  8/12.11.0     1          Unused  --         4095   SEAGATE ST34572WC│  │
│ │  8/12.5.0      1          LVM     vg00       4095   SEAGATE ST34572WC│  │
│ │  8/12.8.0      1          LVM     vg00       4095   SEAGATE ST34572WC│  │
│ │  8/12.9.0      1          Unused  --         4095   SEAGATE ST34572WC│  │
│ │  8/16/10.1     1          Unused  --         --     12mm Floppy Disk Dri│
│ │  8/16/5.2.0    1          CDFS    --         632    Toshiba CD-ROM SCSI│ │
│ │                                                               │   │
│ └───────────────────────────────────────────────────────────────┘   │
└─────────────────────────────────────────────────────────────────────┘
```

Figure 4-19 *Disk Devices* Window

The first three entries refer to an AutoRAID disk array. The next five entries are the Fast/Wide 4 GByte SCSI disk drives. Second-to-last is a floppy disk drive. The last entry is the CD-ROM. The following **ioscan** command shows the disk and CD-ROM devices:

(on Series 800)

```
$ /usr/sbin/ioscan -fn -C disk

Class I H/W Path Driver S/W State H/W Type Description
===================================================================
disk  6 8/12.0.0 sdisk   CLAIMED   DEVICE   HP C5447A
                         /dev/dsk/c0t0d0   /dev/rdsk/c0t0d0

disk  7 8/12.0.1 sdisk   CLAIMED   DEVICE   HP C5447A
                         /dev/dsk/c0t0d1   /dev/rdsk/c0t0d1

disk  8 8/12.1.0 sdisk   CLAIMED   DEVICE   HP C5447A
                         /dev/dsk/c0t1d0   /dev/rdsk/c0t1d0

disk  9 8/12.1.1 sdisk   CLAIMED   DEVICE   HP C5447A
                         /dev/dsk/c0t1d1   /dev/rdsk/c0t1d1
```

```
disk  0 8/12.5.0 sdisk    CLAIMED   DEVICE   SEAGATE ST34572WC
                          /dev/dsk/c0t5d0    /dev/rdsk/c0t5d0

disk  1 8/12.8.0  sdisk    CLAIMED   DEVICE   SEAGATE ST34572WC
                          /dev/dsk/c0t8d0    /dev/rdsk/c0t8d0

disk  2 8/12.9.0  sdisk    CLAIMED   DEVICE   SEAGATE ST34572WC
                          /dev/dsk/c0t9d0    /dev/rdsk/c0t9d0

disk 3  8/12.10.0  sdisk    CLAIMED   DEVICE   SEAGATE ST34572WC
                          /dev/dsk/c0t10d0    /dev/rdsk/c0t10d0

disk 4  8/12.11.0  sdisk    CLAIMED   DEVICE   SEAGATE ST34572WC
                          /dev/dsk/c0t11d0    /dev/rdsk/c0t11d0

disk 5 8/16/5.2.0 sdisk    CLAIMED  DEVICE   CD-ROM
                          /dev/dsk/c1t2d0    /dev/rdsk/c1t2d0
```

You can see from this **ioscan** the device files associated with disk, including the CD-ROM. Using SAM to view and manipulate these devices is easier and clearer than typing such commands as **ioscan**. This doesn't mean that you don't have to know the **ioscan** command or that it is not useful, but SAM certainly makes viewing your system a lot easier. We can now add one of the unused disks in SAM by selecting *Add* from the *Actions* menu. Using Logical Volume Manager, we can create a new volume group or select the volume group to which we wish to add the new disk. We would then select the new logical volumes we wanted on the volume group or extend the size of existing logical volumes. Other information such as the mount directory and size of the logical volume would be entered.

Another common disk device that you may configure through SAM is Redundant Arrays of Inexpensive Disks (RAID). The latest RAID from HP can be configured directly through SAM, under Disk Devices. These devices have a Storage Control Processor (SP) and disk that can be configured in a variety of ways. Using SAM you can specify the RAID level, and which disks will bind to which SPs. The manual for the disk arrays (A3232-90001) describes all the nuances related to configuring these arrays.

After the RAID has been configured, you can access it as you would any other disks by specifying logical volumes, and so on.

File Systems

File Systems shows the *Mount Directory*, *Type* of file system, and *Source Device or Remote Directory*. Figure 4-20 shows the information you see when you enter *File Systems* for the Series 800 used in earlier examples.

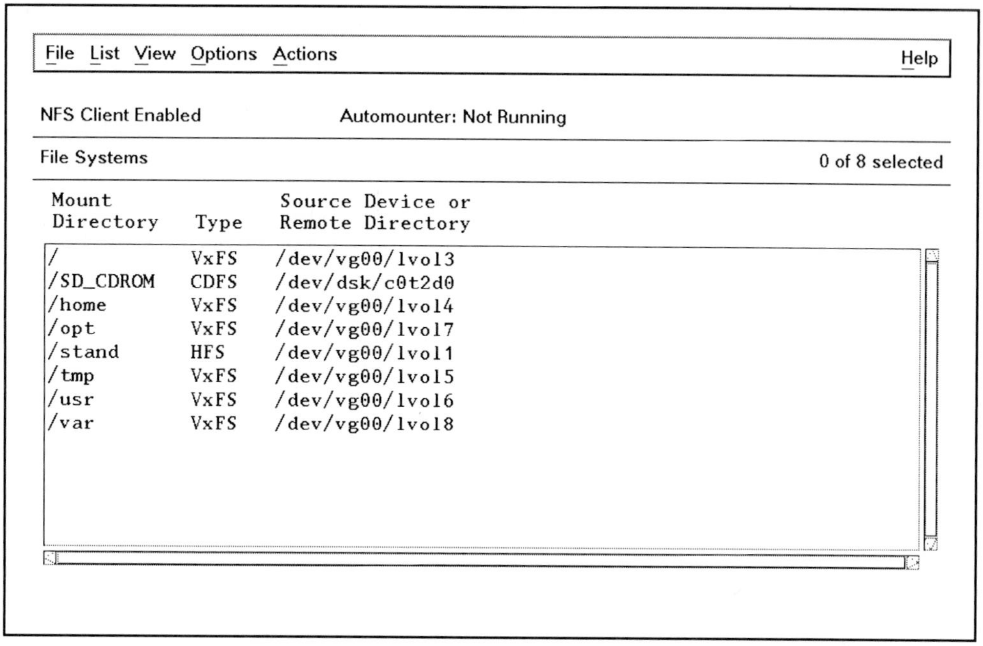

```
File  List  View  Options  Actions                                  Help

NFS Client Enabled                  Automounter: Not Running

File Systems                                              0 of 8 selected

Mount                    Source Device or
Directory      Type      Remote Directory
/              VxFS      /dev/vg00/lvol3
/SD_CDROM      CDFS      /dev/dsk/c0t2d0
/home          VxFS      /dev/vg00/lvol4
/opt           VxFS      /dev/vg00/lvol7
/stand         HFS       /dev/vg00/lvol1
/tmp           VxFS      /dev/vg00/lvol5
/usr           VxFS      /dev/vg00/lvol6
/var           VxFS      /dev/vg00/lvol8
```

Figure 4-20 *File Systems* Window

At this level, you can perform such tasks as *Add Local File System* and *Add Remote File System,* and perform *VxFS Maintenance* from the *Actions* menu.

Several types of file systems may be listed under the Type column. The most common are:

Auto-Indirect Directory containing auto-mountable remote NFS file systems. You may see the **/net** directory here if you have auto-mounter running.

Auto-Mount   Auto-mountable remote NFS file system.

CDFS   CD-ROM file system if it is currently mounted. If, for instance, you have a CD-ROM mounted as /SD_CDROM, you will see this as type CDFS in the list.

HFS   Local HFS file system. These are local HFS file systems that are part of your system. HP's version of the UNIX File System. This was the most common file system under earlier versions of HP-UX.

NFS   Remote NFS file system that is currently mounted.

LOFS   Loopback file system that allows you to have the same file system in multiple places.

VxFS   Local Journal File System (JFS). This is the HP-UX implementation of the Veritas journaled file system (VxFS), which supports fast file system recovery. JFS is the default HP-UX file system.

Add Local File System allows you to mount an unmounted local file system. *Add Remote File System* gives you the ability to mount a file system from another host. The *VxFS Maintenance* subarea is where you can perform some file system maintenance tasks on your JFS file system. Here you can create reports on extent and directory fragmentation. Once these are reviewed and you find that you do indeed need to perform maintenance, you can choose the option to reorganize either the extents or the directory.

Logical Volumes

You can perform several functions related to logical volume manipulation in SAM. Such tasks as *Create, Modify, Remove,* and *Increase Size* can be performed in SAM. Figure 4-21 shows increasing the size of lvol4 (**/home**) from 200 MBytes to 500 MBytes.

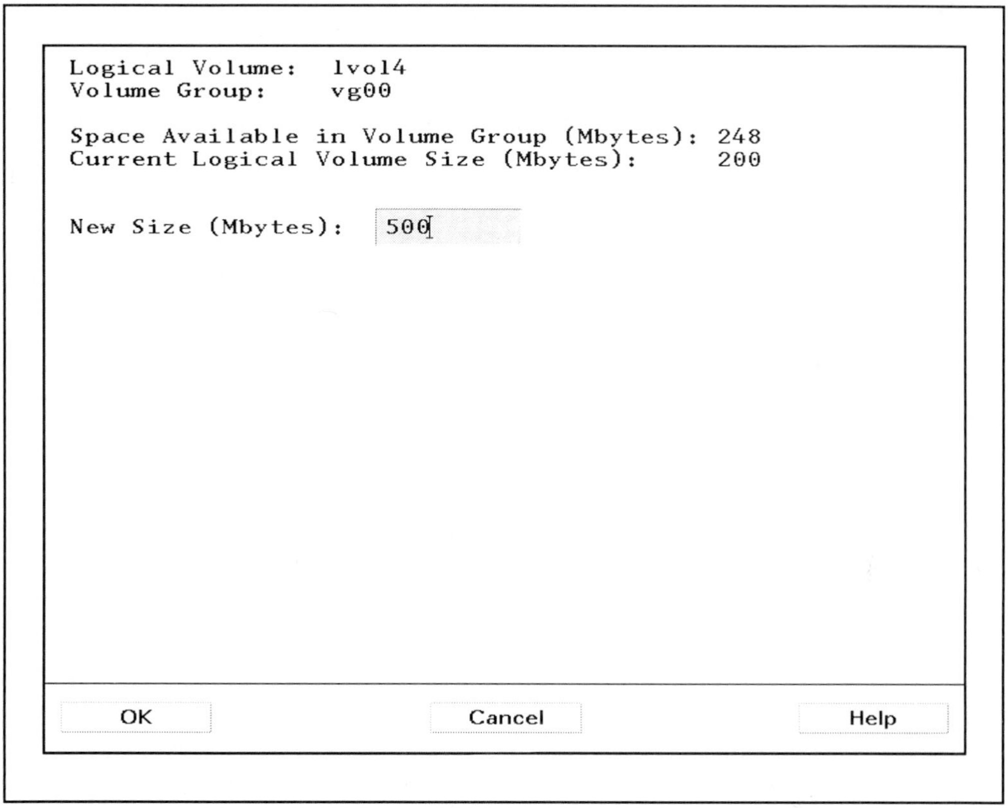

```
Logical Volume:     lvol4
Volume Group:       vg00

Space Available in Volume Group (Mbytes):  248
Current Logical Volume Size (Mbytes):      200

New Size (Mbytes):    500




              OK                        Cancel                        Help
```

Figure 4-21 *Increase Size* Window

SAM will increase the size of the logical volume only if it can be unmounted. Viewing the log file after this task has been completed shows that SAM ran such commands as **/sbin/lvextend** and **/sbin/extendfs** to extend the size of the logical volume and file system, and **/usr/sbin/umount** and **/usr/sbin/mount** to unmount and mount the file system.

See the Logical Volume Manager detail in Chapter 1 for definitions of Logical Volume Manager terms. There is also a description of some Logical Volume Manager commands.

Increasing the Size of a Logical Volume in SAM

SAM may create a unique set of problems when you attempt to increase the size of a logical volume. Problems may be encountered when increasing the size of a logical volume if it can't be unmounted. If, for instance, you wanted to increase the size of the **/opt** logical volume, it would first have to be unmounted by SAM. If SAM can't umount **/opt**, you will receive a message from SAM indicating that the device is busy. You can go into single-user state, but you will have to have some logical volumes mounted, such as **/usr** and **/var,** in order to get SAM to run. You would then need to reboot your system with **shutdown -r** after you have completed your work. This works for directories such as **/opt**, which SAM does not need in order to run.

Alternatively, you could exit SAM and kill any processes accessing the logical volume you wish to extend the size of, and then manually unmount that logical volume. You could then use SAM to increase the size of the logical volume.

The HP OnLineJFS add-on product allows you to perform many of these LVM functions without going into single-user mode. For example, with OnLineJFS, logical volumes and file systems are simply expanded with the system up and running and no interruption to users or processes.

Swap

Both device swap and file system swap are listed when you enter *Swap*. Listed for you are the *Device File/Mount Directory, Type, Mbytes Available*, and *Enabled*. You can get more information about an item by highlighting it and selecting *Zoom* from the *Actions* menu.

Volume Groups

Listed for you when you enter volume groups are *Name, Mbytes Available, Physical Volumes*, and *Logical Volumes*. If you have an unused disk on your system, you can extend an existing volume group or create a new volume group. This window is useful to see how much disk space within a volume group has not been allocated yet. Another function here is the ability to import volume groups from other systems or ready a volume group for export to a remote system. You would use this when moving a volume group contained on an entire disk drive or set of disk drives from one system to another.

Kernel Configuration

Your HP-UX kernel is a vitally important part of your HP-UX system that is often overlooked by HP-UX administrators. Perhaps this is because administrators are reluctant to tinker with such a critical and sensitive part of their system. Your HP-UX kernel, however, can have a big impact on system performance, so you want to be sure that you know how it is configured. This doesn't mean that you have to make a lot of experimental changes, but you should know how your kernel is currently configured so that you can assess the possible impact that changes to the kernel may have on your system.

SAM allows you to view and modify the four basic elements of your HP-UX kernel. There is a great deal of confusion among new HP-UX system administrators regarding these four elements. Before I get into the details of each of these four areas, I'll first give you a brief description of each.

- *Configurable Parameters* - These are parameters that have a value associated with them. When you change the value, there is a strong possibility you will affect the performance of your system. An example of a *Configurable Parameter* is **nfile**, which is the maximum number of open files on the system.

- *Drivers* - Drivers are used to control the hardware on your system. You have a driver called **CentIF** for the parallel interface on your system, one called **sdisk** for your SCSI disks, and so on.

- *Dump Devices* - A dump device is used to store the contents of main memory in the event that a serious kernel problem is encountered. If no dump device is configured, then the contents of main memory are saved on the primary swap device, and this information is copied into one of the directories (usually **/var/adm/crash**) when the system is booted. It is not essential that you have a dump device, but the system will boot faster after a crash if you have a dump device because the contents of main memory don't need to be copied to a file after a crash. A dump device is different from a swap device.

- *Subsystems* - A subsystem is different from a driver. A subsystem is an area of functionality or support on your system such as **CD-ROM/9000**, which is CD-ROM file system support; **LVM,** which is Logical Volume Manager support; and so on.

When you go into one of the four subareas described above, the configuration of your system for the respective subarea is listed for you. The first thing you should do when entering *Kernel Configuration* is to go into each of the subareas and review the list of information about your system in each.

In *Kernel Configuration* is a *current* kernel and *pending* kernel. The *current* kernel is the one you are now running, and the *pending* kernel is the one for which you are making changes.

Figure 4-22 shows the SAM menu hierarchy for *Kernel Configuration.*

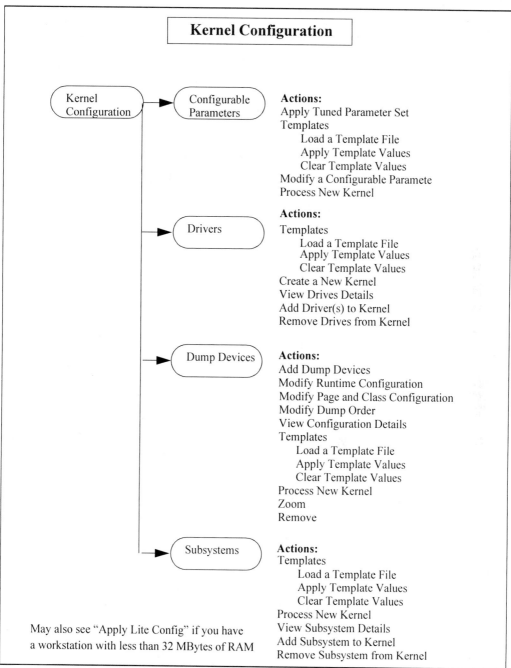

Kernel Configuration

Kernel Configuration → **Configurable Parameters**

Actions:
Apply Tuned Parameter Set
Templates
     Load a Template File
     Apply Template Values
     Clear Template Values
Modify a Configurable Paramete
Process New Kernel

Drivers

Actions:
Templates
     Load a Template File
     Apply Template Values
     Clear Template Values
Create a New Kernel
View Drives Details
Add Driver(s) to Kernel
Remove Drives from Kernel

Dump Devices

Actions:
Add Dump Devices
Modify Runtime Configuration
Modify Page and Class Configuration
Modify Dump Order
View Configuration Details
Templates
     Load a Template File
     Apply Template Values
     Clear Template Values
Process New Kernel
Zoom
Remove

Subsystems

Actions:
Templates
     Load a Template File
     Apply Template Values
     Clear Template Values
Process New Kernel
View Subsystem Details
Add Subsystem to Kernel
Remove Subsystem from Kernel

May also see "Apply Lite Config" if you have
a workstation with less than 32 MBytes of RAM

Figure 4-22   Kernel Configuration

Configurable Parameters

Selecting *Configurable Parameters* lists all your configurable kernel parameters. For each configurable parameter, the following information is listed:

- Name - Name of the parameter.

- Current Value - Value of the parameter in **/stand/vmunix**.

- Pending Value - Value of the parameter in the kernel to be built.

- Type - Shows whether parameters are part of the static kernel or a loadable module.

- Associated Module - Lists module parameter is part of if type is loadable.

- Description - A few words describing the parameter.

You can then take a number of *Actions,* including the following:

Apply Tuned Parameter Set

Several sets of configurable parameters have been tuned for various environments. When you select this from the *Actions* menu, the tuned parameter sets on your system, such as a database server system, are listed for you and you can select from among these.

Templates   You can select a kernel template to load that is basically a different kernel configuration from the one you are currently running.

Process New Kernel

After making whatever changes you like to the *Pending Value* of a configurable parameter, you can have SAM create a new kernel for you.

Modify Configurable Parameter

You can change the value of the parameter in the *pending* kernel. You simply highlight a parameter and select this from the *Actions* menu.

Modifying a configurable parameter is made much easier by SAM. But although the logistics of changing the parameter are easier, determining the value of the parameter is still the most important part of this process.

Many applications recommend modifying one or more of these parameters for optimal performance of the application. Keep in mind, though, that many of these parameters are related; modifying one may adversely affect another parameter. Many applications will request that you change the *maxuprc* to support more processes. Keep in mind that if you have more processes running, you may end up with more open files and also have to change the *maxfiles* per process. If you have a system primarily used for a single application, you can feel more comfortable in modifying these. But if you run many applications, make sure that you don't improve the performance of one application at the expense of another.

When you do decide to modify the value of a configurable parameter, be careful. The range on some of these values is broad. The *maxuprc* (maximum number of user processes) can be reduced as low as three processes. I can't imagine what a system could be used for with this low a value, but SAM ensures that the parameter is set within supported HP-UX ranges for the parameter. "Let the administrator beware" when changing these values. You may find that you'll want to undo some of your changes. Here are some tips: Keep careful notes of the values you change, in case you have to undo a change. In addition, change as few values at a time as possible. That way, if you're not happy with the results, you know which configurable parameter caused the problem.

Drivers

When you select *Drivers*, the drivers for your current kernel, the template file on which your current kernel is based, and the pending kernel are listed. You'll know that the drivers displayed are for more than your current kernel, because you'll see that some of the drivers listed are *Out* of both your current and pending kernels. The following information is listed for you when you enter the *Drivers* subarea:

- Name - Name of the driver.
- Current State - Lists whether the driver is *In* or *Out* of **/stand/vmunix**.
- Pending State - Lists whether the driver is *In* or *Out* of the pending kernel to be built.
- Class - Identifies as a driver or module.
- Type - Identifies as part of the static kernel or a loadable module.
- Load Module at Boot? - Lists whether it is automatically loaded at boot time if it is a loadable module.
- Description - A few words describing the driver.

The Current State indicates whether or not the driver selected is in **/stand/vmunix.**

The Pending State indicates whether or not you have selected this driver to be added to or removed from the kernel. *In* means that the driver is part of the kernel or is pending to be part of the kernel. *Out* means that the driver is not part of the kernel or is pending to be removed from the kernel.

Typically, drivers are added statically. In other words, they are added to the kernel and left there. However, if the driver is a specially created module for a particular purpose, then it may be configured as loadable. This means that it can be loaded and unloaded from the kernel without rebooting the system. This advanced feature is discussed in detail in the "Managing Dynamically Loadable Kernel Modules" chapter of the *Managing Systems and Workgroups* book from Hewlett-Packard.

Using the *Actions* menu, you can select one of the drivers and add or remove it. You can also pick *View Driver Details* from the *Actions* menu after you select one of the drivers. You can select *Process New Kernel* from the *Actions* menu. If you have indeed modified this screen by adding or removing drivers, you want to recreate the kernel. SAM asks whether you're sure that you want to rebuild the kernel before it does this for you. The only recommendation I can make here is to be sure that you have made your selections carefully before you rebuild the kernel.

Dump Devices

When you enter this subarea, both the *Current Dump Devices* and *Pending Dump Devices* are listed for you. A dump device is used when a serious kernel problem occurs with your system, and main memory is written to disk. This information is a core dump that can later be read from disk and used to help diagnose the kernel problem.

Prior to HP-UX 11.x, memory dumps contained the entire image of physical memory. As a result, in order to get a full memory dump, you needed to create a dump area at least as large as main memory. With systems with memory size into the gigabits, a large amount of disk space was wasted just waiting around for a system panic to occur. With HP-UX 11.x comes a new fast dump feature. This allows you to pick and choose what to dump. The fast dump feature not only prevents such things as unused memory pages and user text pages from being dumped, but it also allows you to configure what memory page classes to dump.

The sizes of the dump areas can be configured somewhat smaller than main memory in your system. You can specify a disk or logical volume as a dump device (you can also specify a disk section, but I don't recommend that you use disk sections at all). The entire disk or logical volume is then reserved as a dump device.

If no dump device is specified or if the size of the dump area is less than what is configured to be dumped, then the core dump is written to primary swap. At the time of system boot, the core dump is written out to a core file, usually in **/var/adm/crash**. This is the way most systems I have worked on operate; that is, there is no specific dump device specified and core dumps are written to primary swap and then to **/var/adm/crash**. This approach has sometimes been a point of confusion; that is, primary swap may indeed be used as a dump device, but a dump device is used specifically for core dump purposes whereas primary swap fills this role in the event there is no dump device specified. As long as you don't mind the additional time it takes at boot to write the core dump in primary swap to a file, you may want to forego adding a specific dump device to your system.

Since you probably won't be allocating an entire disk as a dump device, you may be using a logical volume. You must select a logical volume in the root volume group that is unused or is used for non-file-system swap. This is done by selecting *Add* from the *Actions* menu to add a disk or logical volume to the list of dump devices.

You will want to get acquainted with the *View Dump Configuration Details* subarea of *Dump Devices*. It is here where you can see what the current dump configuration is, what the current and pending kernel dump configurations are, and what the current runtime dump configuration is.

Subsystems

Selecting *Subsystems* lists all of your subsystems. For each subsystem, the following information is listed:

- Name - Name of the subsystem.

- Current Value - Lists whether the subsystem is *In* or *Out* of **/stand/vmunix**.

- Pending Value - Lists whether the subsystem is *In* or *Out* of the pending kernel.

- Description - A few words describing the parameter.

You can then take a number of *Actions,* including the following:

Templates	You can select a kernel template to load that is basically a different kernel configuration from the one you are currently running.

Process New Kernel

> After making whatever changes you like to the *Pending State* of a subsystem, you can have SAM create a new kernel for you.

View Subsystem Details

> You get a little more information about the sub-system when you select this.

Add Subsystem to Kernel

> When you highlight one of the subsystems and select this from the menu, the *Pending State* is changed to *In* and the subsystem will be added to the kernel when you rebuild the kernel.

Remove Subsystem from Kernel

> When you highlight one of the subsystems and select this from the menu, the *Pending State* is changed to *Out* and the subsystem will be removed from the kernel when you re-build the kernel.

After making selections, you can rebuild the kernel to include your pending changes or back out of them without making the changes.

Networking and Communications

The menu hierarchy for *Networking and Communications* is shown in Figures 4-23 through 4-25. This area contains many advanced net-working features. Because of their complexity, some of these I will only briefly describe and refer you to the appropriate HP-UX manual for installation and administration of these products.

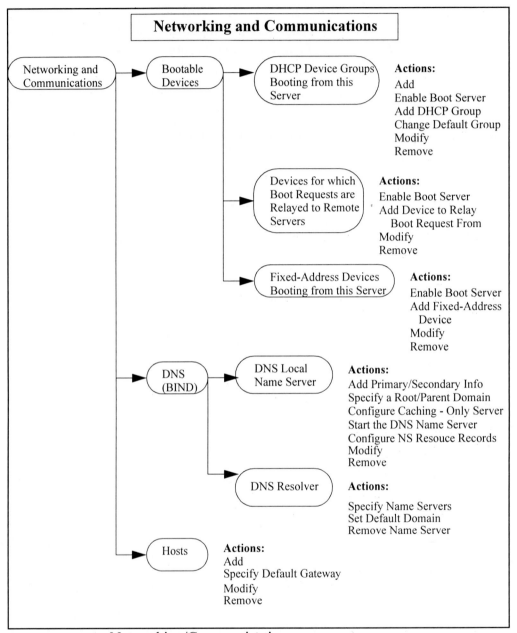

Figure 4-23   Networking/Communications

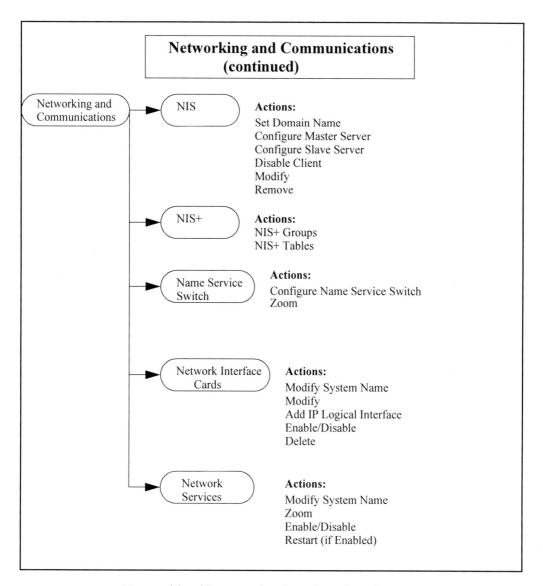

Figure 4-24 Networking/Communications (continued)

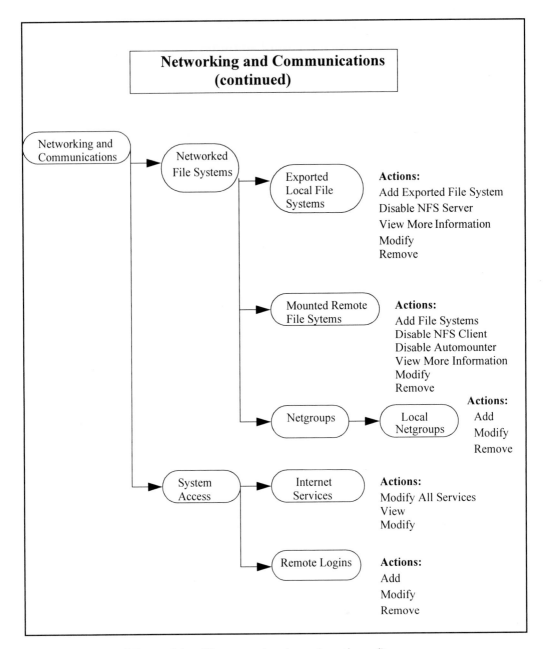

Figure 4-25 Networking/Communications (continued)

Bootable Devices

The *Bootable Devices* area is further subdivided into three subareas: *DHCP Device Groups Booting from this Server*, *Devices for which Boot Requests are Relayed to Remove Servers*, and *Fixed-Address Devices Booting from this Server*. I will briefly describe each subarea and its use. DHCP, dynamic host configuration protocol, is now available on HP-UX and is used by many services. A discussion of DHCP and instructions for setting up a DHCP server is detailed in "Appendix A: Configuring for a DHCP Server" in the HP-UX manual *Installing HP-UX 11.0 and Updating HP-UX 10.x to 11.0*.

The *DHCP Device Groups Booting from this Server* subarea is where the device groups can be configured. Each group would contain a set of IP addresses for use by that device group. Devices could be such things as specific types of printers or specific types of terminals.

In the *Devices for which Boot Requests are Relayed to Remove Servers* subarea, you can view information about Bootp client devices that get their booting information from remote Bootp or DHCP servers. Information is displayed on the client or client groups, including the IP addresses of the remove servers and the maximum number of hops a boot request from a client or client group can be relayed.

In the *Fixed-Address Devices Booting from this Server* subarea you can specify systems that will boot from your system using Bootstrap Protocol (Bootp) or DHCP. Bootp is a means by which a system can discover network information and boot automatically. The Bootp software must be loaded on your system in order for other devices to use it as a boot source (see the **swlist** command in Chapter 1 regarding how to list software installed on your system). Among the many devices that use Bootp are HP X Stations. In this subarea, you can add, modify, or remove a Bootp device. In addition, you can enable or disable the Boot Protocol Server. Similarly, DHCP allows the client to use one of a pool of IP addresses in order to boot automatically. Applications such as Ignite-UX can be configured to use this protocol.

When you enter the *Fixed-Address Devices Booting from this Server* subarea, you immediately receive a list of devices that can boot off your system. You can choose *Add* from the *Actions* menu and you'll be asked to enter the following information about the device you are adding:

- Host Name

- Internet Address

- Subnet Mask (this is optional)

- Station Address in hex or client ID (this is optional)

- Boot File Name

- Whether you'll be using Ethernet or IEEE 802.3 for booting

- Whether to send Hostname to the client or device

You can select *Enable Protocol Server* or *Disable Protocol Server* from the *Actions* menu, depending on whether your system is currently disabled or enabled to support this functionality. When you *Enable Protocol Server,* you also enable Trivial File Transfer Protocol (TFTP), which boot devices use to get boot files. When you enable or disable this, the **/etc/inetd.conf** is edited. This file contains configuration information about the networking services running on your system. If a line in **/etc/inetd.conf** is preceded by a "#", then it is viewed as a comment. The daemon that reads the entries in this file is **/usr/sbin/inetd**. Before enabling or disabling Bootp, you may want to view the **/etc/inetd.conf** file and see what services are enabled. After you make your change through SAM, you can again view **/etc/inetd.conf** to see what has been modified. See *System Access* for security related to **/etc/inetd.conf.** The following is the beginning of the /**etc/inetd.conf** file from a system showing Bootp and TFTP enabled. There is also a brief explanation of the fields in this file appear at the beginning of the file:

```
## Configured using SAM by root on Sat Aug 25 10:12:51 1995
##
#
# Inetd  reads its configuration information from this file
upon ex-
```

```
# ecution and at some later time if it is reconfigured.
#
# A line in the configuration file has the following fields
separated
# by tabs and/or spaces:
#
#    service name          as in /etc/services
#    socket type           either "stream" or "dgram"
#    protocol              as in /etc/protocols
#    wait/nowait            only applies to datagram sockets,
stream
#                          sockets should specify nowait
#    user                      name of user as whom the
server should run
#   server program        absolute pathname for the server inetd
#                          will execute
#  server program args.   arguments server program uses as they
#                          normally are starting with
argv[0] which
#                          is the name of the server.
#
# See the inetd.conf(4) manual page for more information.
##


##
#
#               ARPA/Berkeley services
#
##
ftp        stream tcp nowait root /usr/lbin/ftpd      ftpd -l
telnet     stream tcp nowait root /usr/lbin/telnetd   telnetd

# Before uncommenting the "tftp" entry below, please make sure
# that you have a "tftp" user in /etc/passwd. If you don't
# have one, please consult the tftpd(1M) manual entry for
# information about setting up this service.

tftp       dgram  udp wait   root  /usr/lbin/tftpd    tftpd
bootps     dgram  udp wait   root  /usr/lbin/bootpd   bootpd
#finger    stream tcp nowait bin   /usr/lbing/fingerd fingerd
login      stream tcp nowait bin   /usr/lbin/rlogind  rlogind
shell      stream tcp nowait bin   /usr/lbin/remshd   remshd
exec       stream tcp nowait root  /usr/lbin/rexecd   rexecd
#uucp      stream tcp nowait bin   /usr/sbin/uucpd    uucpd

                         .
                         .
                         .
```

If you select *Fixed-Address Device Client Names*, you can then select *Modify* or *Remove* from the *Actions* menu and either change one of the parameters related to the client, such as its address or subnet mask, or completely remove the client.

DNS (BIND)

Domain Name Service (DNS) is a name server used to resolve host name to IP addressing. HP-UX uses BIND, Berkeley InterNetworking Domain, one of the name services that can be used to implement DNS. A DNS server is responsible for the resolution of all hostnames on a network or subnet. Each DNS client would rely on the server to resolve all IP address-to-hostname issues on the client's behalf. A boot file is used by the server to locate database files. The database files map hostnames to IP addresses and IP addresses to hostnames. Through SAM, a DNS server can be easily set up.

Information about DNS and its setup and administration is described in the HP-UX manual *Installing and Administering Internet Services*.

Hosts

This subarea is for maintaining the default gateway and remote hosts on your system. When you enter this subarea, you receive a list of hosts specified on your system, as shown in Figure 4-26. This information is retrieved from the **/etc/hosts** file on your system.

```
 File  List  View  Options  Actions                                   Help

 Default Gateway: None Specified

 Internet Addresses                                          0 of 9 selected

   Internet          Remote
   Address           System Name          Comments
  ┌──────────────────────────────────────────────────────────────────┐ ▲
  │ 127.0.0.1        localhost                                        │ │
  │ 18.62.199.22     a4410tu2                                         │
  │ 18.62.199.49     yankees                                         │
  │ 18.62.199.51     f4457mfp                                        │
  │ 18.62.199.61     a4410hawk                                       │
  │ 18.62.199.42     a4410827                                        │
  │ 18.62.199.98     xtermpsd                                        │
  │ 18.62.199.33     c4410psd                                        │
  │ 18.62.192.66     f4457mfp                                        │ ▽
  └──────────────────────────────────────────────────────────────────┘
  ◁                                                                  ▷
```

Figure 4-26 Hosts

You can then *Add* a new host, *Specify Default Gateway*, *Modify* one of
the hosts, or *Remove* one of the hosts, all from the *Actions* menu. When
adding a host, you'll be asked for information pertaining to the host,
including Internet Address, system name, aliases for the system, and comments.

NIS

Network Information Service (NIS) is a database system used to propagate
common configuration files across a network of systems. Managed on a
master server are such files as **/etc/passwd**, **/etc/hosts**, and **/etc/auto*** files
used by automounter. Formerly called "yellow pages," NIS converts these
files to its own database files, called maps, for use by clients in the NIS
domain. When a client requests information, such as when a user logs in
and enters their password, the information is retrieved from the server

rather than from the client's system. Thus, this information need be maintained only on the server.

Through SAM, the NIS master server, slave servers, and clients can be configured, enabled, disabled, and removed. Once the master, slaves, and clients are established, you can easily build, modify, and push the various maps to the slaves.

NIS is not available on trusted systems.

NIS+

New with HP-UX 11.x is a new version of NIS called NIS+. This is not an enhancement of NIS, but rather a new service that includes standard and trusted systems and non-HP-UX systems. If you already use NIS, a compatibility mode version of NIS+ allows servers to answer requests from both NIS and NIS+ clients. When NIS+ is configured on a trusted system, in the *Auditing and Security* area of SAM, a new subarea, *Audited NIS+ Users*, is displayed.

More information about NIS+ and its setup is described in the HP-UX manual *Installing and Administering NFS Services*.

Name Service Switch

The Name Service Switch file, **/etc/nsswitch.conf**, can now be configured through SAM. This service allows you to prioritize which name service (FILES, NIS, NIS+, DNS, or COMPAT) to use to look up information. Unless you specifically use one of these services, the default of FILES should be used. The FILES designation supports the use of the **/etc** directory for such administrative files as **/etc/passwd**, **/etc/hosts**, and **/etc/services**. (COMPAT is used with the compatibility mode of NIS+.)

More information about Name Service Switch and its setup is described in the HP-UX manual *Installing and Administering NFS Services*.

Network Interface Cards

This subarea is used for configuring any networking cards in your system. You can *Enable, Disable*, and *Modify* networking cards as well as *Modify System Name,* all from the *Actions* menu. Under *Add IP Logical Interface,* you can add additional logical IP addresses to an existing network card.

The Network Interface Cards screen lists the network cards installed on your system, including the information listed below. You may have to expand the window or scroll over to see all this information.

- Card Type such as Ethernet, IEEE 802.3, Token Ring, FDDI, etc.

- Card Name

- Hardware Path

- Status, such as whether or not the card is enabled

- Internet Address

- Subnet Mask

- Station Address in hex

Included under *Configure* for Ethernet cards is *Advanced Options,* which will modify the Maximum Transfer Unit for this card. Other cards included in your system can also be configured here, such as ISDN, X.25, ATM, and so on.

Network Services

This subarea is used to enable or disable *some* of the network services on your system. You will recognize some of the network services in Figure 4-27 from the **/etc/inetd.conf** file shown earlier. This screen has three columns, which are the name, status, and description of the network services. Figure 4-27 from the *Network Services* subarea shows some of the network services that can be managed.

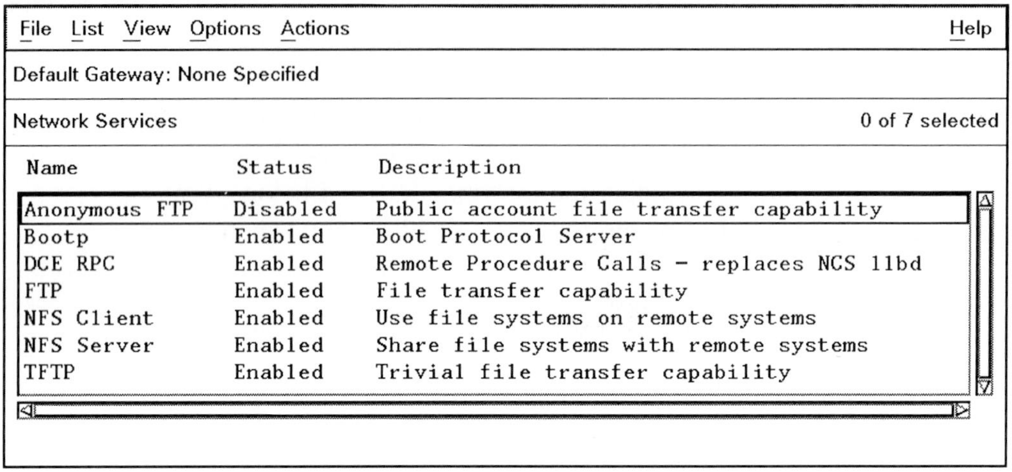

```
 File  List  View  Options  Actions                                      Help

 Default Gateway: None Specified

 Network Services                                              0 of 7 selected

  Name              Status      Description

 Anonymous FTP     Disabled    Public account file transfer capability
 Bootp             Enabled     Boot Protocol Server
 DCE RPC           Enabled     Remote Procedure Calls - replaces NCS 11bd
 FTP               Enabled     File transfer capability
 NFS Client        Enabled     Use file systems on remote systems
 NFS Server        Enabled     Share file systems with remote systems
 TFTP              Enabled     Trivial file transfer capability
```

Figure 4-27 Network Services

After selecting one of the network services shown, you can *Enable* or *Disable* the service, depending on its current status, *Restart* the service if it is currently enabled, get more information about the service with *Zoom*, or *Modify System Name,* all from the *Actions* menu.

Network File Systems

This subarea is broken down into *Exported Local File Systems, Mounted Remote File Systems,* and *Netgroups.* NFS is broken down into these first two areas because you can export a local file system without mounting a remote file system and vice versa. This means you can manage these independently of one another. You may have an NFS server in your environment that won't mount remote file systems, and you may have an NFS client that will mount only remote file systems and never export its local file system. *Entropies*, a part of NIS, allows you to group a set of systems or users to be used together. Among other things, netgroup designations can be used to export file systems to.

Under *Exported Local File Systems,* you can select the file systems you want exported. The first time you enter this screen you have no exported file systems listed. When you select *Add Exported File System* from the *Actions* menu, you enter such information as:

- local directory name

- user ID

- whether or not to allow asynchronous writes

- permissions

After this exported file system has been added, you can select it and choose from a number of *Actions,* including *Modify* and *Remove.*

Under *Mounted Remote File Systems* you have listed for you all of the directories and files that are mounted using NFS. These can be either mounted or mounted on demand with automounter. After selecting one of the mounted file systems, you can perform various *Actions.* For every remote file system mounted, you have the following columns:

- Mount Directory, which displays the name of the local directory name used to mount the remote directory.

- Type, which is either *NFS* for standard NFS or *Auto* for automounter (see the paragraph below).

- Remote Server, which displays the name of the remote system where the file or directory is mounted.

- Remote Directory, which is the name of the directory under which the directory is remotely mounted.

You should think about whether or not you want to use the NFS automounter. With automounter, you mount a remote file or directory on demand, that is, when you need it. Using a master map, you can specify which files and directories will be mounted when needed. The files and

directories are not continuously mounted with automounter, resulting in
more efficiency as far as how system resources are being used. There is,
however, some overhead time is associated with mounting a file or directory on demand, as opposed to having it continuously mounted. From a
user standpoint, this may be slightly more undesirable, but from an administration standpoint, using the automounter offers advantages. Since the
automounter is managed through SAM, there is very little additional work
you need to perform to enable it.

System Access

This subarea is broken down into *Internet Services* and *Remote Logins.*

When you select *Internet Services,* the screen lists the networking services that are started by the internet daemon **/usr/sbin/inetd**. I earlier covered **/etc/inetd.conf**, which is a configuration file that lists all of the
network services supported by a system that is read by **inetd**. There is also
a security file **/var/adm/inetd.sec** that serves as a security check for **inetd**.
Although many other components are involved, you can view **inetd**,
/etc/inetd.conf, and **/var/adm/inetd.sec** as working together to determine
what network services are supported and the security level of each.

Listed for you in the *System Access* subarea are *Service Name,*
Description, Type, and *System Permission*. In Figure 4-28 the *System Per-
mission* for **shell** is "Denied"; for **ftp** is *Selected-Denied*; for **login** is
Selected-Allowed; and for all others is *Allowed.*

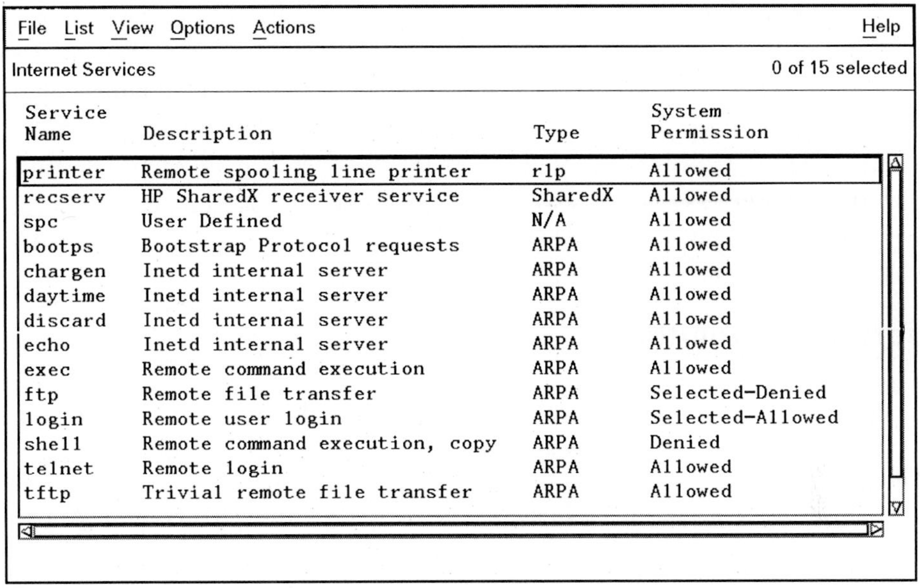

```
 File   List   View   Options   Actions                                    Help

Internet Services                                              0 of 15 selected

    Service                                         System
    Name         Description                 Type   Permission

   printer     Remote spooling line printer   rlp    Allowed
   recserv     HP SharedX receiver service   SharedX  Allowed
   spc         User Defined                   N/A    Allowed
   bootps      Bootstrap Protocol requests    ARPA   Allowed
   chargen     Inetd internal server          ARPA   Allowed
   daytime     Inetd internal server          ARPA   Allowed
   discard     Inetd internal server          ARPA   Allowed
   echo        Inetd internal server          ARPA   Allowed
   exec        Remote command execution       ARPA   Allowed
   ftp         Remote file transfer           ARPA   Selected-Denied
   login       Remote user login              ARPA   Selected-Allowed
   shell       Remote command execution, copy ARPA   Denied
   telnet      Remote login                   ARPA   Allowed
   tftp        Trivial remote file transfer   ARPA   Allowed
```

Figure 4-28 System Access - Internet Services

I changed the permission for **shell** by selecting it and using the *Modify* pick from the *Actions* menu and selecting "Denied." The following are three entries from **/var/adm/inetd.sec**. Note that no entry exists for all the network services that are *Allowed.*

```
ftp          deny         system1
login        allow        system2
shell        deny
```

The four permissions are:

- Denied - All systems are denied access to this service.

- Allowed - All systems are allowed access to the service.

- Selected Denied - Only the selected systems are denied access to this service (**system1** under **ftp**).

- Selected Allowed - Only the selected systems are allowed access to this service (**system2** under **login**).

Remote Logins is used to manage security restrictions for remote users who will access the local system. Two HP-UX files are used to manage users. The file **/etc/hosts.equiv** handles users, and **/.rhosts** handles superusers (root). When you enter this subarea, you get a list of users and the restrictions on each. You can then *Add, Remove*, or *Modify* login security.

Performance Monitors

Under *Performance Monitors,* you can view the performance of your system in several different areas such as disk and virtual memory. Figure 4-29 shows the menu hierarchy of *Performance Monitors.*

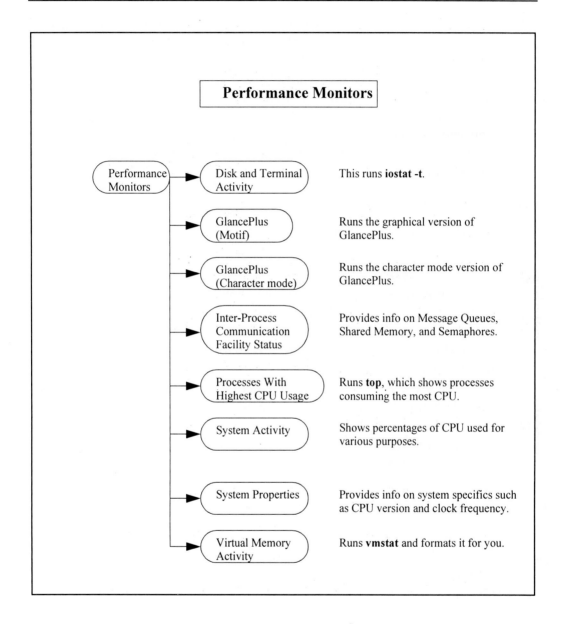

Figure 4-29 Performance Monitors

Performance Monitors provides you a window into several areas of your system. If you are serious about becoming familiar with the tools available on your system to help you understand how your system resources are being used, you should take a close look at Chapter 5. Chapter 5 is devoted to getting a handle on how your system resources are being used, including many built-in HP-UX commands. Some of the performance monitors you can select in this subarea are HP-UX commands, which you'll need some background in before you can use them. I'll cover these areas only briefly because this material will be covered in more detail in Chapter 5.

Disk and Terminal Activity

Selecting *Disk and Terminal Activity* opens a window that shows the output of **iostat -t**. I have included the description of **iostat** from Chapter 4 to save you the trouble of flipping ahead. When the *Disks and Terminal Activity* window with the output of **iostat** is opened for you, it shows a single **iostat** output. When you press *return,* the window is automatically closed for you.

The **iostat** command gives you an indication of the level of effort the CPU is putting into I/O and the amount of I/O taking place among your disks and terminals. The following example shows the **iostat -t** command, which will be executed every three seconds, and associated output from an HP-UX 11.x system.

iostat -t 3

tty			cpu			
tin	tout	us	ni	sy	id	
78	42	2	0	28	70	

/dev/dsk/c0t1d0			/dev/dsk/c0t4d0			/dev/dsk/c0t6d0		
bps	sps	msps	bps	sps	msps	bps	sps	msps
0	0	0	33	8.3	25.2	7	1	19.5

tty			cpu			
tin	tout	us	ni	sy	id	
66	24	0	0	30	70	

/dev/dsk/c0t1d0			/dev/dsk/c0t4d0			/dev/dsk/c0t6d0		
bps	sps	msps	bps	sps	msps	bps	sps	msps
5	12	15.9	36	9.7	21	7	1.2	13.8

tty		cpu			
tin	tout	us	ni	sy	id
90	29	1	0	25	73

/dev/dsk/c0t1d0			/dev/dsk/c0t4d0			/dev/dsk/c0t6d0		
bps	sps	msps	bps	sps	msps	bps	sps	msps
12	1.7	15.5	24	3	19.1	14	2.1	14.6

tty		cpu			
tin	tout	us	ni	sy	id
48	16	1	0	16	83

/dev/dsk/c0t1d0			/dev/dsk/c0t4d0			/dev/dsk/c0t6d0		
bps	sps	msps	bps	sps	msps	bps	sps	msps
0	0	0	62	9.3	18	12	2	17.2

tty		cpu			
tin	tout	us	ni	sy	id
32	48	7	0	14	79

/dev/dsk/c0t1d0			/dev/dsk/c0t4d0			/dev/dsk/c0t6d0		
bps	sps	msps	bps	sps	msps	bps	sps	msps
1	0.3	14.4	5	.9	16.2	171	29.4	18.2

tty		cpu			
tin	tout	us	ni	sy	id
2	40	20	1	42	27

/dev/dsk/c0t1d0			/dev/dsk/c0t4d0			/dev/dsk/c0t6d0		
bps	sps	msps	bps	sps	msps	bps	sps	msps
248	30.9	20.8	203	29.2	18.8	165	30.6	22.1

Descriptions of the reports you receive with **iostat** for terminals, the CPU, and mounted file systems follow.

For every terminal you have connected (tty), you see a "tin" and "tout," which represent the number of characters read from your terminal and the number of characters written to your terminal, respectively. The **-t** option produces this terminal report.

For your CPU, you see the percentage of time spent in user mode ("us"), the percentage of time spent running user processes at a low priority called nice ("ni"), the percentage of time spent in system mode ("sy"), and the percentage of time the CPU is idle ("id").

For every locally mounted file system, you receive information on the kilobytes transferred per second ("bps"), number of seeks per second ("sps"), and number of milliseconds per average seek ("msps"). For disks that are NFS-mounted or disks on client nodes of your server, you will not receive a report: **iostat** reports only on locally mounted file systems.

GlancePlus

GlancePlus is available here if it is installed on your system. You are given the choice of using either the motif (graphical) version or the character mode version of GlancePlus. GlancePlus is covered in detail in Chapter 5.

Inter-Process Communication Facility Status

Inter-Process Communication Facility Status shows categories of information related to communication between processes. You receive status on Message Queues, Shared Memory, and Semaphores. This is a status window only, so again, you press *return* and the window closes.

Processes with Highest CPU Usage

Processes with Highest CPU Usage is a useful window that lists the processes consuming the most CPU on your system. Such useful information as the Process ID, its Resident Set Size, and the Percentage of CPU it is consuming are listed.

System Activity

System Activity provides a report of CPU utilization. You receive the following list:

%usr   Percent of CPU spent in user mode.

%sys   Percent of CPU spent in system mode.

%wio   Percent of CPU idle with some processes waiting
                     for I/O, such as virtual memory pages moving in
                     or moving out.

%idle   Percent of CPU completely idle.

System Properties

System Properties gives you a great overview of system specifics. Included here are those hard-to-find items such as processor information, CPU version, clock frequency, kernel support (32-bit or 64-bit), memory information, operating system version, and network IP and MAC addresses.

Virtual Memory Activity

Virtual Memory Activity runs the **vmstat** command. This too is covered in Chapter 5, but I have included the **vmstat** description here so that you don't have to flip ahead. Some of the columns of **vmstat** are moved around a little when the *Virtual Memory Activity* window is opened for you.

vmstat provides virtual memory statistics. It provides information on the status of processes, virtual memory, paging activity, faults, and the breakdown of the percentage of CPU time. In the following example, the output was produced ten times at five-second intervals. The first argument to the **vmstat** command is the interval; the second is the number of times you would like output produced.

vmstat 5 10:

procs			memory		page							faults			cpu		
r	b	w	avm	free	re	at	pi	po	fr	de	sr	in	sy	cs	us	sy	id
4	0	0	1161	2282	6	22	48	0	0	0	0	429	289	65	44	18	38
9	0	0	1161	1422	4	30	59	0	0	0	0	654	264	181	18	20	62
6	0	0	1409	1247	2	19	37	0	0	0	0	505	316	130	47	10	43
1	0	0	1409	1119	1	10	19	0	0	0	0	508	254	180	69	15	16
2	0	0	1878	786	0	1	6	0	0	0	0	729	294	217	75	17	8
2	0	0	1878	725	0	0	3	0	0	0	0	561	688	435	67	32	1
2	0	0	2166	98	0	0	20	0	0	0	66	728	952	145	8	14	78
1	0	0	2310	90	0	0	20	0	0	0	171	809	571	159	16	21	63
1	0	0	2310	190	0	0	8	1	3	0	335	704	499	176	66	14	20
1	0	0	2316	311	0	0	3	1	5	0	376	607	945	222	4	11	85

You will get more out of the **vmstat** command than you want. Here is a brief description of the categories of information produced by **vmstat**.

Processes are classified into one of three categories: runnable ("r"), blocked on I/O or short-term resources ("b"), or swapped ("w").

Next you will see information about memory. "avm" is the number of virtual memory pages owned by processes that have run within the last 20 seconds. If this number is roughly the size of physical memory minus your kernel, then you are near paging. The "free" column indicates the number of pages on the system's free list. It doesn't mean that the process has finished running and these pages won't be accessed again; it just means that they have not been accessed recently. I suggest that you ignore this column.

Next is paging activity. Only the first field (re) is useful. It shows the pages that were reclaimed. These pages made it to the free list but were later referenced and had to be salvaged. Check to see that "re" is a low number. If you are reclaiming pages that were thought to be free by the system, then you are wasting valuable time salvaging these. Reclaiming pages is also a symptom that you are short on memory.

Next you see the number of faults in three categories: interrupts per second, which usually come from hardware ("in"); system calls per second ("sy"); and context switches per second ("cs").

The final output is CPU usage percentage for user ("us"), system ("sy"), and idle ("id"). This is not as complete as the **iostat** output, which also shows **nice** entries.

Peripheral Devices

With *Peripheral Devices* you can view any I/O cards installed in your system and peripherals connected to your system. These include both used and unused. You can also quickly configure any peripheral, including printers, plotters, tape drives, terminals, modems, and disks. This is a particularly useful area in SAM, because configuring peripherals in HP-UX is tricky. You perform one procedure to connect a printer, a different procedure to connect a disk, and so on, when you use the command line. In SAM these procedures are menu-driven and therefore much easier.

Two of the six subareas, *Disks and File Systems* and *Printers and Plotters,* have their own dedicated hierarchy within SAM and are covered in this chapter. I don't cover these again in this section. The other four subareas, *Cards, Device List, Tape Drives*, and *Terminals and Modems,* are covered in this section.

It's impossible for me to cover every possible device that can be viewed and configured in SAM. What I'll do is give you examples of what you would see on a couple of workstations (models 712 and 715) and a couple of servers (K300 and K400) so that you get a feel for what you can do under **Peripheral Devices** with SAM. From what I show here, you should be comfortable that SAM can help you configure peripherals.

Figure 4-30 shows the hierarchy of *Peripheral Devices*.

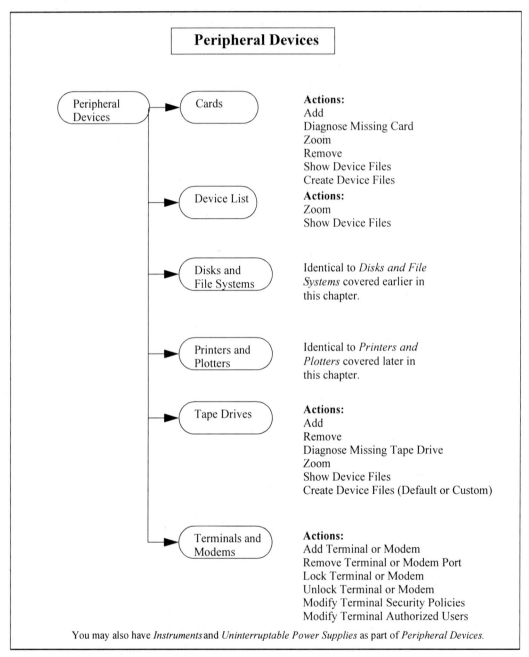

Figure 4-30 Peripheral Devices

Cards

When you select *Cards,* you are provided with a list of I/O cards in your system. You can also perform such tasks as adding and removing cards. Having this list of I/O cards is useful. Figures 4-31 and 4-32 show a listing of I/O cards for a workstation and server, respectively.

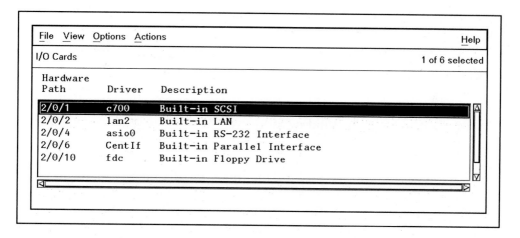

Figure 4-31 *I/O Cards* Window for Workstation

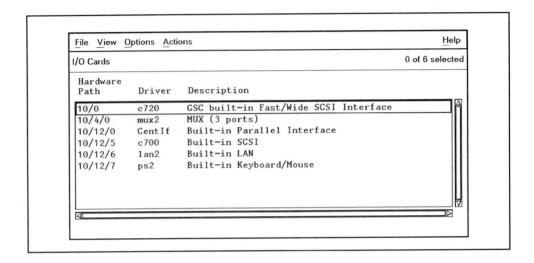

Figure 4-32 *I/O Cards* Window for Server

In *Cards,* you can perform the following *Actions*:

Add
: You can add a new I/O card in the window that is opened for you.

Diagnose Missing Card
: If a card you have installed is not included in the list, you can select this to determine the reason.

Zoom
: If you highlight a card and select *Zoom,* you will be provided such information as the hardware path, driver, and description of the card.

Remove
: If you highlight a card and select *Remove,* a window will appear that walks you through removing the card from the system.

Show Device Files

> If you select this, a window will be opened in which the device files associated with the card will be listed.

Create Device Files

> Creates device files for the selected card. This takes place without any user interaction.

Device List

Device List shows all the peripherals configured into the system. Figures 4-33 and 4-34 show a device list for a workstation and server, respectively.

```
File  View  Options  Actions                                    Help

Peripheral Devices                              0 of 16 selected

Hardware
Path         Driver       Description                  Status

1            graph3       Graphics                     CLAIMED
2            bus_adapter  Core I/O Adapter             CLAIMED
2/0/1        c700         Built-in SCSI                CLAIMED
2/0/1.1.0    sdisk        HP 2213A SCSI Disk Drive     CLAIMED
2/0/1.2.0    sdisk        Toshiba CD-ROM SCSI drive    CLAIMED
2/0/1.3.0    stape        HP35450A 1.3 GB DDS Tape Drive (DAT)  CLAIMED
2/0/1.6.0    sdisk        HP C2247 SCSI Disk Drive     CLAIMED
2/0/2        lan2         Built-in LAN                 CLAIMED
2/0/4        asio0        Built-in RS-232 Interface    CLAIMED
2/0/6        CentIf       Built-in Parallel Interface  CLAIMED
2/0/8        audio        Audio Interface              CLAIMED
2/0/10       fdc          Built-in Floppy Drive        CLAIMED
2/0/10.1     pflop        3.5" PC Floppy Drive         CLAIMED
2/0/11       ps2          Built-in Keyboard            CLAIMED
8            processor    Processor                    CLAIMED
9            memory       Memory                       CLAIMED
```

Figure 4-33 *Peripheral Devices* Window for Workstation

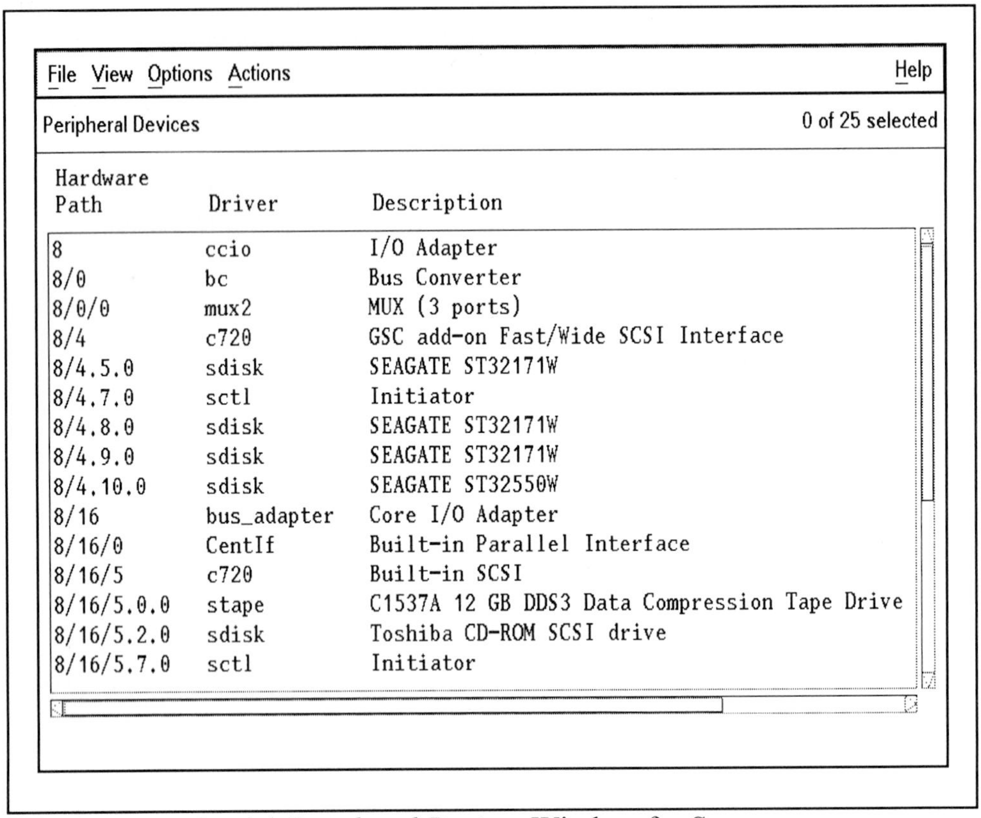

```
  File  View  Options  Actions                                    Help

  Peripheral Devices                                    0 of 25 selected

   Hardware
   Path              Driver          Description
   8                 ccio            I/O Adapter
   8/0               bc              Bus Converter
   8/0/0             mux2            MUX (3 ports)
   8/4               c720            GSC add-on Fast/Wide SCSI Interface
   8/4.5.0           sdisk           SEAGATE ST32171W
   8/4.7.0           sctl            Initiator
   8/4.8.0           sdisk           SEAGATE ST32171W
   8/4.9.0           sdisk           SEAGATE ST32171W
   8/4.10.0          sdisk           SEAGATE ST32550W
   8/16              bus_adapter     Core I/O Adapter
   8/16/0            CentIf          Built-in Parallel Interface
   8/16/5            c720            Built-in SCSI
   8/16/5.0.0        stape           C1537A 12 GB DDS3 Data Compression Tape Drive
   8/16/5.2.0        sdisk           Toshiba CD-ROM SCSI drive
   8/16/5.7.0        sctl            Initiator
```

Figure 4-34 Partial *Peripheral Devices* Window for Server

The two *Action* menu picks here are *Zoom* and *Show Device Files*. Selecting *Zoom* produces a window with such information as hardware path, driver, description, and status. The devices files associated with the item you have highlighted will be shown if you select *Show Device Files*.

Disks and File Systems was covered earlier in this chapter.

Instruments may appear if your system supports HP-IB cards.

Printers and Plotters is covered later in this chapter.

Tape Drives

Tape Drives lists the tape drives connected to your system. You are shown the Hardware Path, Driver, and Description for each tape drive. You can add, remove, diagnose tape drives, list tape drive device files, and add new tape drive device files.

Terminals and Modems

Your system's terminals and modems are listed for you when you enter this subarea. You can perform a variety of tasks from the *Actions* menu, including the following:

- Add Terminal
- Add Modem
- Remove Terminal or Modem Port
- Lock Terminal or Modem Port
- Unlock Terminal or Modem Port
- Modify Terminal Security Policies
- Modify Terminal Security Policies
- Modify Terminal Authorized Users
- Additional Information

Uninterruptable Power Supplies

Your system's uninterruptable power supplies are listed for you when you enter this area, including the UPS type, device file of the UPS, hardware path, port number, and whether or not shutdown is enabled. The *Actions* you can select are: *Modify Global Configuration; Add; Zoom; Remove;* and *Modify.*

Figure 4-35 shows the *Modify Global Configuration* window.

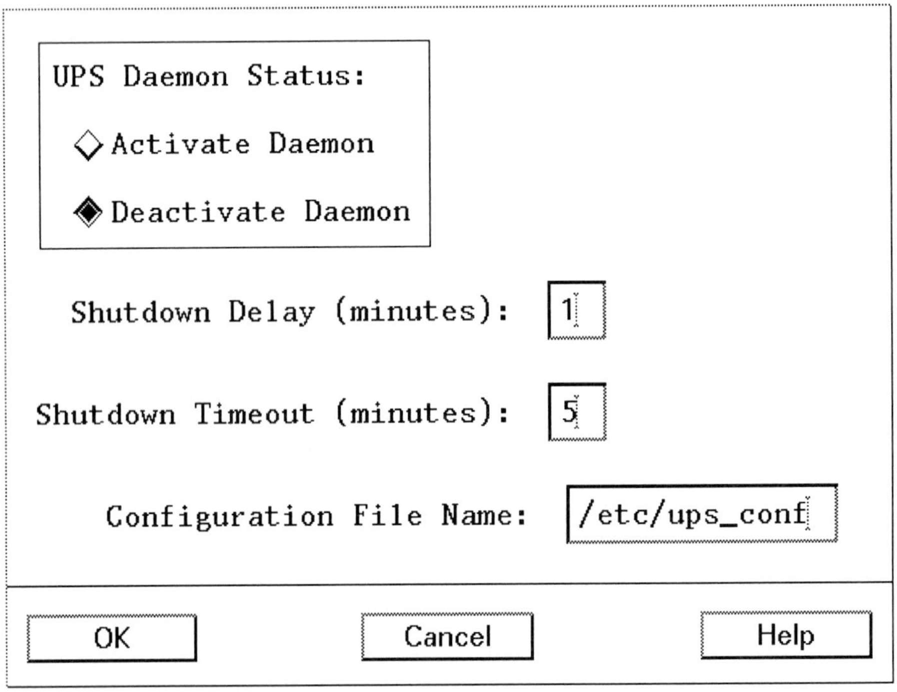

Figure 4-35   *Modify Global Configuration* Window for UPS

Printers and Plotters

Printers and Plotters is divided into two subareas: *HP Distributed Print Service* and *LP Spooler*. *HP Distributed Print Service* (HPDPS) is part of the Distributed Computing Environment (DCE). It is not covered in this book. *LP Spooler* is covered in this section; Figure 4-36 shows the hierarchy of *Printers and Plotters*.

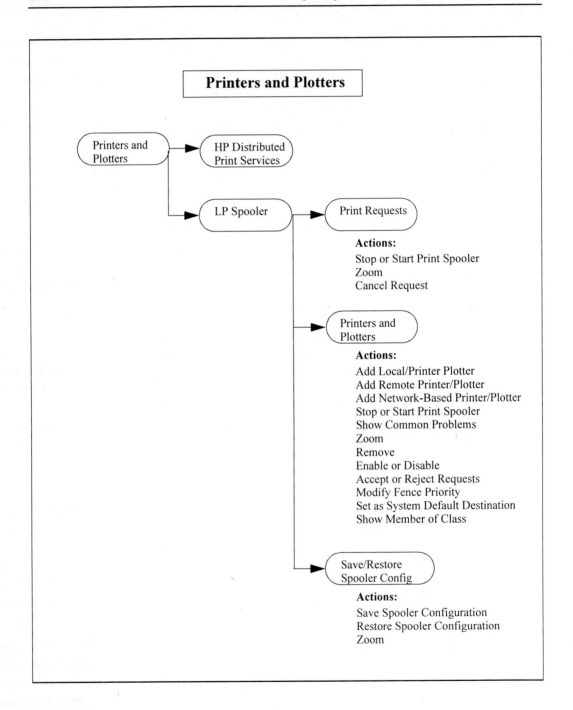

Figure 4-36 Printers and Plotters

Print Requests

Under *Print Requests,* you can manage the print spooler and specific print jobs. You can start or stop the print spooler and cancel print jobs. The following information on print requests is listed for you:

Request ID
: An ID is associated with each print job. This is the Printer Name followed by a number.

Owner
: The name of the user who requested the print job.

Priority
: The priority of a print job is assigned when the job is submitted. The **-p** option of **lp** can be used to assign a priority to a job. Each print destination has a default priority that is assigned to jobs when **-p** is not used on the **lp** command.

File
: The name of the file sent to the print queue.

Size
: The size of the print job in bytes.

The *Actions* menu allows you to act on print jobs by canceling them. In addition, the print spooler can be stopped and started.

Printers and Plotters

You can configure both local and remote printers in *Printers and Plotters.* When you select *Add Local Printer/Plotter* from the *Actions* menu and then the appropriate type of printer, a window is opened for you in which you can supply the specifics about the printer. Before this window is opened, however, you must specify whether the *type* of printer to be added is: parallel serial; HP-IB; non-standard device file; or a printer connected to a TSM terminal, as well as to which I/O card to add the printer. One huge advantage to adding the printer using SAM is that this process is entirely menu-driven, so you only have to select from among the information that is supplied you.

    The window that appears asks you for the following information:

Printer Name   You can pick any name for the printer. I usually like to use a name that is somewhat descriptive, such as ljet4 for a LaserJet 4. The name is limited to 14 alphanumeric characters and underscores.

Printer Model/Interface

               SAM supplies a list of all interface models for you when this window is opened. These models are located in the **/usr/lib/lp/model** directory. Each printer has an interface program that is used by the spooler to send a print job to the printer. When an interface model is selected, the model is copied to **/etc/lp/interface/**<printername>, where it becomes the printer's interface program. Models can be used without modification, or you can create customized interface programs.

Printer Class   You can define a group of printers to be in a class, which means that print requests won't go to a specific printer but instead they will go to the first available printer within the class. This is optional.

Default Request Priority

This defines the default priority level of all requests sent to this printer.

Default Destination

Users who do not specify a printer when requesting a print job will have the print request sent to the default printer.

Figure 4-37 is an example *Add Local Printer/Plotter* window.

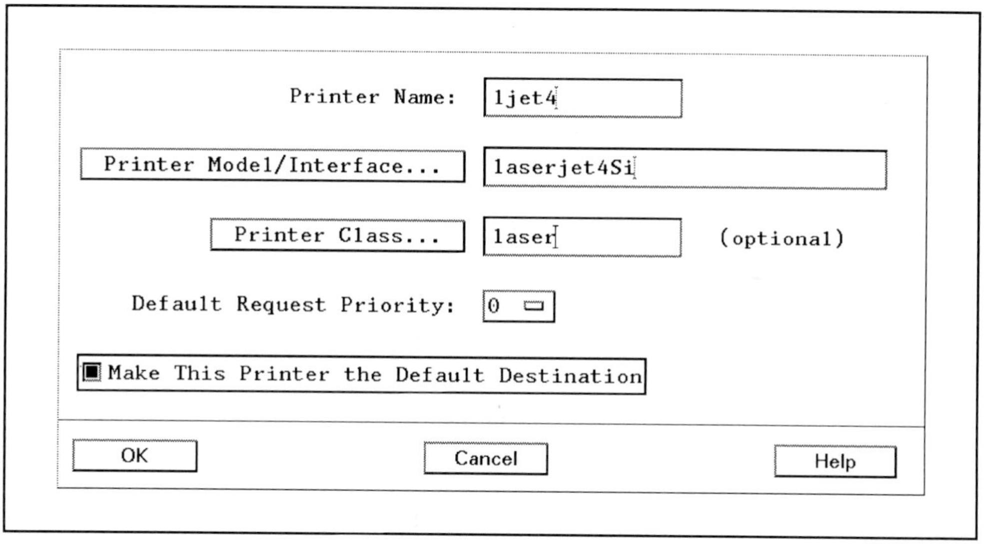

Figure 4-37 *Add Local Printer/Plotter* Window

After this printer has been added, I could use SAM to show me its status or use the **lpstat** command. Here is an example of the **lpstat** command showing ljet4, which was added in the last example.

```
$ /usr/bin/lpstat -t
scheduler is running
system default destination: ljet4
members of class laser:
        ljet4
device for ljet4: /dev/c1t0d0_lp
ljet4 accepting requests since Nov 21 22:45
printer ljet4 is idle. enabled since Nov 21 22:45
        fence priority : 0
no entries
```

As with all the other tasks SAM helps you with, you can manage printers and plotters manually. Doing so manually, however, is a real pain in the neck, and I would strongly recommend that you use SAM for managing printers and plotters. Not only does SAM make this easier for you, but I have also had nothing but good results having SAM do this for me. As you go through the SAM Log file, you will see a variety of **lp** commands issued. Some of the more common commands, including the **lpstat** command issued earlier, are listed in Table 4-2.

TABLE 4-2   lp COMMANDS

COMMAND	DESCRIPTION
/usr/sbin/accept	Start accepting jobs to be queued
/usr/bin/cancel	Cancel a print job that is queued
/usr/bin/disable	Disable a device for printing
/usr/bin/enable	Enable a device for printing
/usr/sbin/lpfence	Set minimum priority for spooled file to be printed
/usr/bin/lp	Queue a job or jobs for printing
/usr/sbin/lpadmin	Configure the printing system with the options provided
/usr/sbin/lpmove	Move printing jobs from one device to another
/usr/sbin/lpsched	Start the **lp** scheduling daemon
/usr/sbin/lpshut	Stop the **lp** scheduling daemon
/usr/bin/lpstat	Show the status of printing based on the options provided
/usr/sbin/reject	Stop accepting jobs to be queued

Save/Restore Spooler Configuration

Occasionally, the spooler can get into an inconsistent state (usually something else has to go wrong with your system that ends up somehow changing or renaming some of the spooler configuration files). SAM keeps a saved version of the spooler's configuration each time SAM is used to make a change (only the most recent one is saved). This saved configuration can be restored by SAM to recover from the spooler having gotten into an inconsistent state. Your latest configuration is automatically saved by SAM, provided that you used SAM to create the configuration, as opposed to issuing **lp** commands at the command line, and it can be restored with *Restore Spooler Configuration* from *Save/Restore Spooler Config*. This screen allows you to save your current spooler configuration or restore previously saved spooler configuration information.

Process Management

Process Management is broken down into two areas that allow you to control and schedule processes. *Process Control* allows you to control an individual process by performing such tasks as viewing it, changing its nice priority, killing it, stopping it, or continuing it. You can also view and schedule **cron** jobs under *Scheduled Cron Jobs*. Figure 4-38 shows the menu hierarchy of *Process Management*.

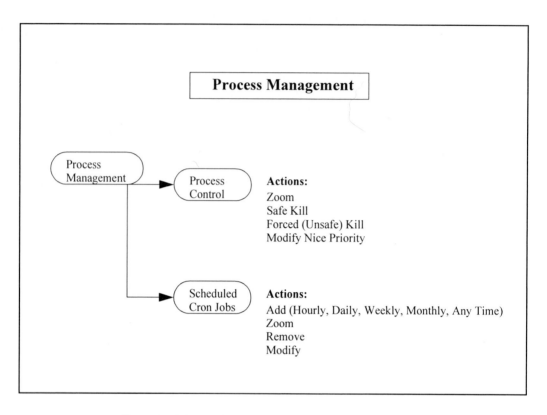

Figure 4-38 Process Management

Process Control

When you pick *Process Control,* SAM lists the processes on your system and allows you to perform various actions. Using *Process Control* is a much easier way of controlling the processes on your system than executing commands such as **ps, nice**, etc. Figure 4-39 shows a partial listing of processes.

File List View Options Actions	Help

Process Control   1 of 88 selected

```
                         Nice
  User       Priority   Priority   Command
 root          154        20       sendmail: accepting connections on po
 root          154        20       /usr/sbin/snmpdm
 root          154        20       /usr/sbin/hp_unixagt
 root          154        20       /usr/sbin/mib2agt
 root          154        20       /usr/sbin/trapdestagt
 root          154        20       /opt/dce/sbin/rpcd
 root           64        20       /usr/sbin/rbootd
 root          154        20       /usr/sbin/pwgrd
 lp            154        20       /usr/sbin/lpsched
 root          154        20       /usr/sbin/cron
 root          154        20       /opt/audio/bin/Aserver
 root          154        20         /opt/audio/bin/Aserver
 root          154        20       /usr/sbin/swagentd -r
 root          154        20       /usr/local/ws/qr/.etc.hppa/qrserviced
 root          154        20       /usr/sbin/rpc.mountd
 root          154        20       /usr/sbin/nfsd 4
 root          154        20         /usr/sbin/nfsd 4
 root          154        20         /usr/sbin/nfsd 4
 root          154        20         /usr/sbin/nfsd 4
 root          154        20       /usr/sbin/rpc.pcnfsd
 root          158        20       /usr/dt/bin/dtrc /usr/dt/bin/dtrc
```

Figure 4-39 Partial *Process Control* Listing.

There are the four columns of information listed for you.

• *User* - The name of the user who owns the process.

• *Priority* - The priority of the process determines its scheduling by the CPU. The lower the number, the higher the priority. Unless you have modified these priorities, they will be default priorities. Changing the priority is done with the **nice** command, which will be covered shortly.

• *Nice Priority* - If you have a process that you wish to run at a lower or higher priority, you could change this value. The lower the value, the higher the CPU scheduling priority.

• *Command* - Lists the names of all the commands on the system.

In addition to these four columns, there are several others you can specify to be included in the list by selecting *Columns* from the *View* menu. You could include such information as the *Process ID, Parent Process ID, Processor Utilization, Core Image Size*, and so on. Adding *Processor Utilization* as a column, for instance, shows me how much of the processor all processes are consuming including SAM.

You can now go select one of the processes and an *Actions* to perform.

When you select a process to kill and pick *Safe Kill* from the *Actions* menu, you see a message that indicates the process number killed and that it may take a few minutes to kill it in order to terminate cleanly. If you select a process to kill and pick *Forced Kill* from the *Actions* menu, you don't get any feedback; SAM just kills the process and you move on.

Chapter 5 covers the **kill** command. To save you the trouble of flipping ahead, I have included some of the information related to **kill** here. The **kill** command can be either **/usr/bin/kill** or **kill** that is part of the POSIX shell. The POSIX shell is the default shell for HP-UX 11.x. The other shells provide their own **kill** commands as well. We use the phrase "kill a process" in the UNIX world all the time, I think, because it has a powerful connotation associated with it. What we are really saying is we want to terminate a process. This termination is done with a signal. The most common signal to send is "SIGKILL," which terminates the process. There are other signals you can send to the process, but SIGKILL is the most common. As an alternative to sending the signal, you could send the corresponding signal number. A list of signal numbers and corresponding signals is shown below:

Signal Number	Signal
0	SIGNULL
1	SIGHUP
2	SIGINT
3	SIGQUIT
9	SIGKILL
15	SIGTERM
24	SIGSTOP
25	SIGTSTP
26	SIGCONT

I obtained this list of processes from the **kill** manual page.

To **kill** a process with a process ID of 234, you would issue the following command:

```
$ kill -9 234
        |    |   |
        |    |   |> process id (PID)
        |    |> signal number
        |> kill command to terminate the process
```

The final selection from the *Actions* menu is to *Modify Nice Priority* of the process you have selected. If you were to read the manual page on **nice,** you will be very happy to see that you can modify this with SAM. Modifying the **nice** value in SAM simply requires you to select a process and specify its new **nice** value within the acceptable range.

Scheduling Cron Jobs

The *Scheduled Cron Jobs* menu selection lists all the **cron** jobs you have scheduled and allows you to *Add, Zoom, Remove*, and *Modify* **cron** jobs through the *Actions* menu. **cron** was described earlier in this chapter in "Backup and Recovery." I have included some of the **cron** background covered earlier to save you the trouble of flipping back.

The **crontab** file is used to schedule jobs that are automatically executed by **cron**. **crontab** files are in the **/var/spool/cron/crontabs** directory. **cron** is a program that runs other programs at the specified time. **cron** reads files that specify the operation to be performed and the date and time it is to be performed. Going back to the backup example earlier in this chapter, we want to perform backups on a regular basis. SAM was used to activate **cron** in the backup example using the following format.

The format of entries in the **crontab** file are as follows:

minute   hour monthday   month   weekday   user name command

minute - the minute of the hour, from 0-59

hour - the hour of the day, from 0-23

monthday - the day of the month, from 1-31

month - the month of the year, from 1-12

weekday - the day of the week, from 0 (Sunday) - 6 (Saturday)

user name - the user who will run the command if necessary (not used in example)

command - specifies the command line or script file to run

You have many options in the **crontab** file for specifying the *minute, hour, monthday, month,* and *weekday* to perform a task. You could list one entry in a field and then a space, several entries in any field separated by a comma, two entries separated by a dash indicating a range, or an asterisk, which corresponds to all possible entries for the field.

To list the contents of the **crontab** file, you would issue the following command. The output of this command is the **crontab** file created for the user root in the SAM backup example earlier in the chapter:


```
$ crontab -l

00 2 * * 6 /usr/sam/lbin/br_backup DAT FULL Y /dev/rmt/0m /etc/
sam/br/graphDCAa02410 root Y 1 N > /tmp/SAM_br_msgs 2>&1 #sam-
backup

15 12 * * 1-5 /usr/sam/lbin/br_backup DAT PART Y /dev/rmt/0m /
etc/sam/br/graphDCAa02410 root Y 1 N > /tmp/SAM_br_msgs 2>&1
#sambackup
```


Although these seem to be excruciatingly long lines, they do indeed conform to the format of the **crontab** file. The first entry is the full backup, and the second entry is the incremental backup. In the first entry, the *minute* is 00; in the second entry, the *minute* is 15. In the first entry, the *hour* is 2; in the second entry, the *hour* is 12. In both entries, the *monthday* and *month* are all legal values (*), meaning every *monthday* and *month*. In the first entry, the *weekday* is 6 for Saturday (0 is Sunday); in the second entry, the *weekdays* are 1-5, or Monday through Friday. The optional *username* is not specified in either example. And finally, the SAM backup command (**/usr/sam/lbin/br_backup**) and its long list of associated information is provided.

minute	hour	monthday	month	weekday	user name	command
00	12	all	all	6	n/a	br_backup
15	12	all	all	1-5	n/a	br_backup

This was done as part of the full and incremental backups that were covered earlier in the chapter. You can, however, schedule **cron** to run any kind of job for you. Using *Add* from the *Actions* menu, you can add *Hourly, Daily, Weekly, Monthly*, or jobs to run *Any Time*. You can also *Remove, Modify*, or *Zoom* in on one of the existing **cron** entries from the *Actions* menu.

Routine Tasks

The following subareas exist under *Routine Tasks* in SAM:

- Backup and Recovery

- Find and Remove Unused Filesets

- Selective File Removal

- System Log Files

- System Shutdown

The hierarchy of *Routine Tasks* is shown in Figure 4-40. Please note that *Backup and Recovery* is identical to the SAM top-level *Backup and Recovery* area discussed earlier in this chapter.

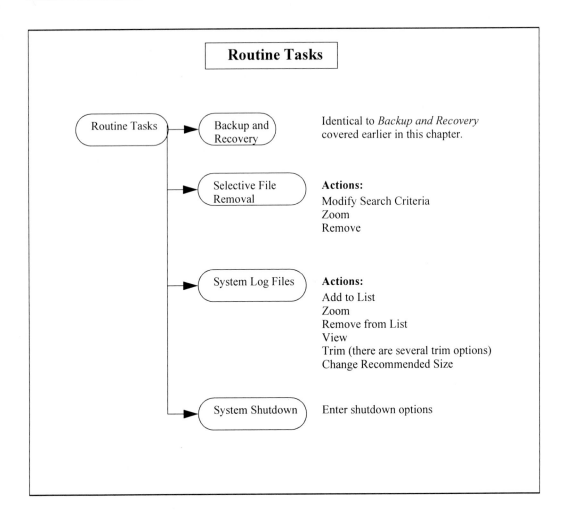

Figure 4-40   Routine Tasks

Backup and Recovery

This is identical to the *Backup and Recovery* area covered earlier in this chapter.

Selective File Removal

Selective File Removal allows you to search for files to remove. You can specify a variety of criteria for selecting files to remove including the following:

Type of file
There are three different file types you can search for: *Large Files, Unowned Files*, and *Core Files*. A pop-up menu allows you to select which of these to search for. Figure 4-41 shows *Large Files* selected. With *Large Files,* you are searching for files of a minimum size that haven't been modified in the specified time. *Unowned Files* are those files owned by someone other than a valid system user. *Core Files* contain a core image of a terminated process when the process was terminated under certain conditions. Core files are usually related to a problem with a process and contain such information as data, stack, etc.

Mount Points
Specify whether or not you want to search across non-NFS mount points. If you select *Yes,* this means that the search will include mount points on your system but not extend to NFS mount points. I chose not to include other mount points in the example.

Beginning Path
Your search can begin at any point in the system hierarchy. You can specify the start point of the search in this field. If you want to search only the **/home** directory for files, then change this entry to **/home** and you will search only that directory, as I did in the example.

Minimum Size   Specify the smallest size file in bytes that you want searched for. Files smaller than this size will not be reported as part of the search. The minimum size in the example is 500,000 bytes.

Last Modification

If you select *Large Files*, you can make an entry in this field. You enter the minimum number of days since the file was last modified, and files that have been modified within that time period will be excluded from the search. This is 30 days in the example.

Figure 4-41 shows an example of specifying which files to search for.

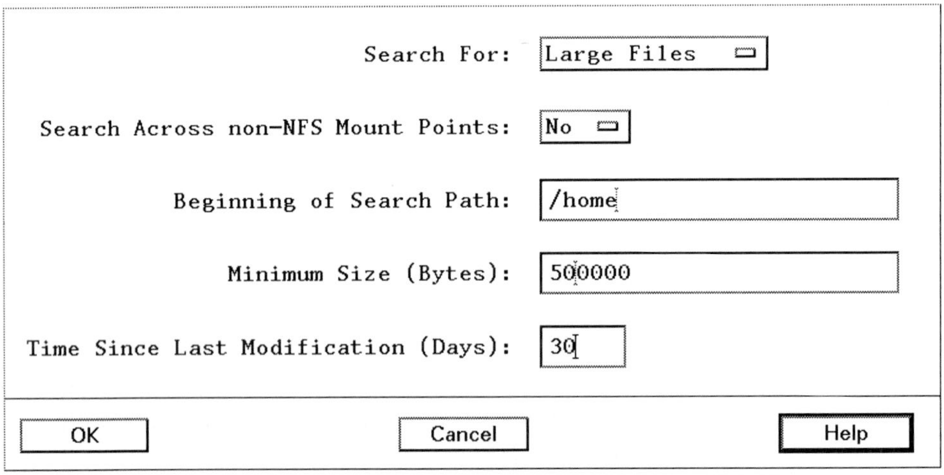

```
              Search For:  | Large Files   ▭ |

Search Across non-NFS Mount Points:  | No  ▭ |

       Beginning of Search Path:  | /home |

          Minimum Size (Bytes):  | 500000 |

Time Since Last Modification (Days):  | 30 |


 | OK |              | Cancel |              | Help |
```

Figure 4-41   Searching for Files to Remove

The list of files reported for removal was too long with a minimum size of only 500 KBytes. I increased the minimum size to 5 MBytes and received the list of files in table 4-3 after my search.

TABLE 4-3 Files Reported for Removal

File Name	Size (Bytes)	Last Modified
/home/denise/demo.mpg	5215336	Jun 19 1995
/home/denise/rock.mpg	17698880	Aug 12 1995
/users/tomd/tst.sasdata2	15666920	Sep 11 1995
/home/joe/testdatabase	23496520	Sep 13 1995

The way to approach removing files is to start with an exceptionally large file size and work your way down in size. It may be that you have a few "unexpected" large files on your system that you can remove and ignore the smaller files.

System Log Files

System Log Files is used to manage the size of your system log files. Log files are generated by HP-UX for a variety of reasons, including backup, shutdown, cron, etc. Your applications may very well be generating log files as well. Some of these log files can grow in size indefinitely, creating a potential catastrophe on your system by growing and crashing your system. You can be operative and manage these log files in this subarea.

SAM is aware of many of the log files generated by HP-UX. When you enter the *System Log Files* subarea, information related to log files is listed. You can add to the list of log files SAM knows about and have a complete list of log files presented to you each time you enter this subarea. SAM lists the following information related to log files each time you enter this subarea. (You may have to increase the size of the window to see all this information.)

File Name   The full path name of the log file.

Percent Full   SAM has what it thinks should be the maximum
                   size of a log file. You can change this size by
                   selecting *Change Recommended Size* from the
                   Actions menu. The percent full is the percentage
                   of the recommended size the log file consumes.

Current Size   The size of the file in bytes is listed for you. You
                   may want to take a look at this. The current size of
                   a log file may be much bigger than you would
                   like. You could then change the recommended
                   size and quickly see which files are greater than
                   100 percent. The converse may also be true. You
                   may think the recommended size for a log file is
                   far too small and change the recommended size to
                   a larger value. In either case, you would like to
                   quickly see which files are much bigger than rec-
                   ommended.

Recommended Size

                   This is what you define as the recommended size
                   of the file. Check these to make sure that you
                   agree with this value.

Present on System

                   Yes if this file is indeed present on your system;
                   No if it is not present on your system. If a file is
                   not present on your system and it simply does not
                   apply to you, then you can select *Remove from
                   List* from the *Actions* menu. For example, you
                   may not be running UUCP and therefore want to
                   remove all the UUCP related log files.

File Type   The only file types listed are *ASCII* and *Non-ASCII*. I found it interesting that **/var/sam/log/samlog** was not one of the log files listed. This is not an ASCII file and must be viewed through *View SAM Log* from the *Actions* menu, but it is indeed a log file that I thought would appear in the list.

You can trim a log file using the *Trim* pick from the *Actions* menu. You then have several options for trimming the file.

System Shutdown

SAM offers you the following three ways to shut down your system:

- *Halt the System*

- *Reboot (Restart) the System*

- *Go to Single-User State*

In addition, you can specify the number of minutes before shutdown occurs.

Run SAM on Remote Systems

I think SAM is great. If it works well on one system, then you, as the system administrator, may as well use it on other systems from a central point of control. *Run SAM on Remote Systems* allows you to set up the system on which you will run SAM remotely from a central point of control.

You can specify any number of remote systems to be controlled by a central system. With the *Actions* menu, you can:

Add System   A window opens up in which you can specify the name of the remote system you wish to administer locally.

Run SAM   You can select the remote system on which you want to run SAM.

Remove System(s)

                    Remote systems can be removed from the list of systems on which you will run SAM remotely.

Software Management

Software Management under SAM uses Software Distributor-HP-UX (I'll call this Software Distributor), which was covered in detail in Chapter 1. I will go over the basics of *Software Management* in SAM so that you can see how some of these tasks are performed in SAM. If you read Chapter 1, you will recognize a lot of the information presented here. The following subareas exist under *Software Management* in SAM:

- Copy Software to Depot
- Install Software to Local Host
- List Software
- Remove Software

The hierarchy of *Software Management* is shown in Figure 4-42.

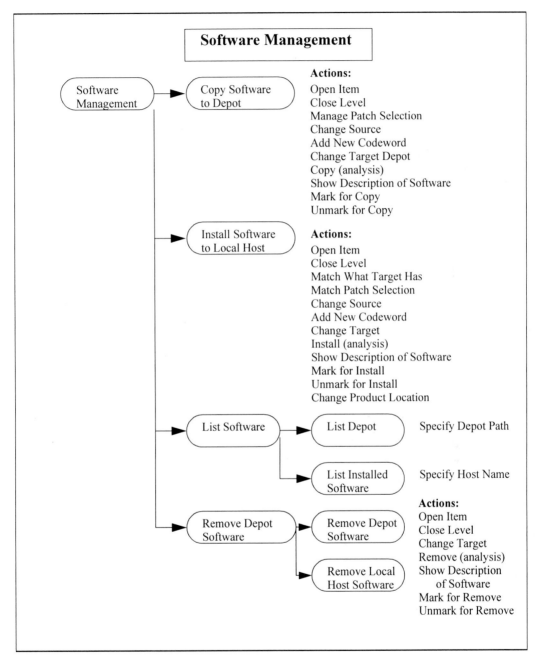

Software Management

Software Management → **Copy Software to Depot**

Actions:
Open Item
Close Level
Manage Patch Selection
Change Source
Add New Codeword
Change Target Depot
Copy (analysis)
Show Description of Software
Mark for Copy
Unmark for Copy

Install Software to Local Host

Actions:
Open Item
Close Level
Match What Target Has
Match Patch Selection
Change Source
Add New Codeword
Change Target
Install (analysis)
Show Description of Software
Mark for Install
Unmark for Install
Change Product Location

List Software → **List Depot**   Specify Depot Path

List Installed Software   Specify Host Name

Remove Depot Software → **Remove Depot Software**

Remove Local Host Software

Actions:
Open Item
Close Level
Change Target
Remove (analysis)
Show Description of Software
Mark for Remove
Unmark for Remove

Figure 4-42 Software Management

Copy Software to Depot

The first task to perform under *Copy Software to Depot* is to specify the target depot path. This is the location on your system where software will be stored or managed. Keep in mind that the CD-ROM from which you may be loading software can also be a depot. This is a directory from which your system and other systems can install software. SAM asks whether you would like to use **/var/spool/sw** as the directory of the target depot path. I have selected **/var/spool/swdepot** as the target depot path in the upcoming example. You can use this directory or specify another directory name. SAM then asks for the source host name and source depot path. Using the CD-ROM on the system, we would perform the following steps.

The first step when loading software from CD-ROM is to insert the media and mount the CD-ROM. The directory **/SD_CDROM** should already exist on your HP-UX 11.x system. You can use SAM to mount the CD-ROM for you or do this manually. I issued the following command to mount a CD-ROM at SCSI address 2 on a workstation:

```
$ mount /dev/dsk/c0t2d0 /SD_CDROM
```

The dialog box that appears in SAM, where you specify the source, is shown in Figure 4-43.

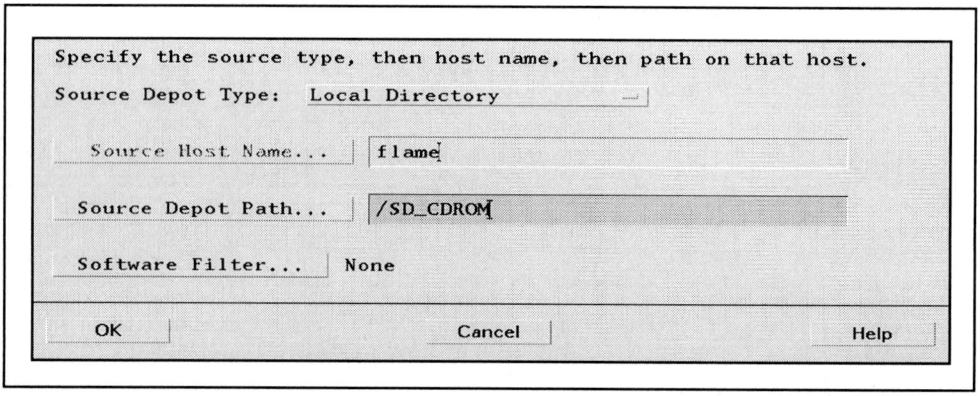

```
Specify the source type, then host name, then path on that host.
Source Depot Type:   Local Directory            ___|

   Source Host Name...  |  flame|

   Source Depot Path...  |  /SD_CDROM|

   Software Filter...  |  None

   OK    |                        Cancel  |                        Help   |
```

Figure 4-43 *Specify Source* Window

At this point, you select the software you wish to copy to the software depot from the source. This is done by highlighting the names you wish to be loaded and selecting *Mark for Copy* from the *Actions* menu and then *Copy* from the *Actions* menu. This places the software in the local depot. Figure 4-44 shows the *Software Selection Window* with the HP C++ Compiler highlighted with a source of **/SD_CDROM** and target depot directory **/var/spool/swdepot**.

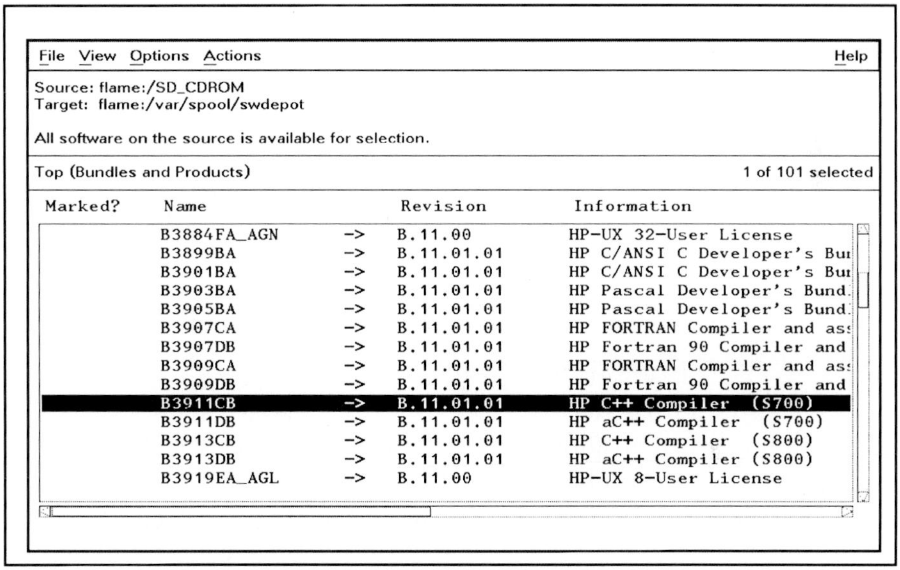

File View Options Actions			Help

Source: flame:/SD_CDROM
Target: flame:/var/spool/swdepot

All software on the source is available for selection.

Top (Bundles and Products)   1 of 101 selected

Marked?	Name		Revision	Information
	B3884FA_AGN	->	B.11.00	HP-UX 32-User License
	B3899BA	->	B.11.01.01	HP C/ANSI C Developer's Bun
	B3901BA	->	B.11.01.01	HP C/ANSI C Developer's Bun
	B3903BA	->	B.11.01.01	HP Pascal Developer's Bund.
	B3905BA	->	B.11.01.01	HP Pascal Developer's Bund.
	B3907CA	->	B.11.01.01	HP FORTRAN Compiler and as
	B3907DB	->	B.11.01.01	HP Fortran 90 Compiler and
	B3909CA	->	B.11.01.01	HP FORTRAN Compiler and as
	B3909DB	->	B.11.01.01	HP Fortran 90 Compiler and
	B3911CB	**->**	**B.11.01.01**	**HP C++ Compiler (S700)**
	B3911DB	->	B.11.01.01	HP aC++ Compiler (S700)
	B3913CB	->	B.11.01.01	HP C++ Compiler (S800)
	B3913DB	->	B.11.01.01	HP aC++ Compiler (S800)
	B3919EA_AGL	->	B.11.00	HP-UX 8-User License

Figure 4-44 *Software Selection* Window

Copy first performs an analysis in which a lot of useful information is produced, such as the amount of disk space in the depot directory both before and after the installation takes place, as shown in Figure 4-45.

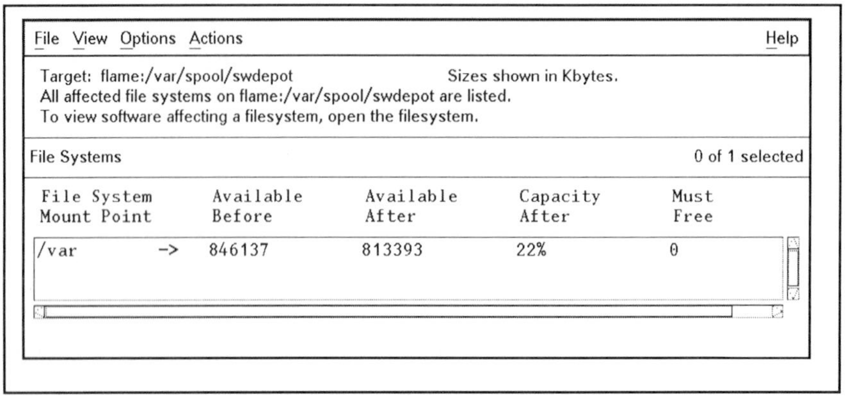

```
 File  View  Options  Actions                                          Help

  Target:  flame:/var/spool/swdepot              Sizes shown in Kbytes.
  All affected file systems on flame:/var/spool/swdepot are listed.
  To view software affecting a filesystem, open the filesystem.

 File Systems                                              0 of 1 selected

   File System      Available       Available      Capacity     Must
   Mount Point      Before          After          After        Free

  /var        ->    846137          813393         22%          0
```

Figure 4-45 *Disk Space Analysis* Window

If you are satisfied with the analysis information, you can load the software. A window showing the status of the installation will appear. It is now in a depot on the hard disk, as opposed to the CD-ROM depot it was loaded from, which this and other systems can access for installing software.

You can select *Save Session As* from the *Actions* menu if you wish to save the list of depots and software.

Manage Patch Selection allows you to add patches to your depot based on a list of available categories. The patches can then be installed based on options you have chosen for that depot. Options include autoselecting patches for the software to be installed, autoselecting patches that will match software on the target, and selecting a patch filter. For example, a patch filter could be set up to allow selection based on whether a patch is critical or whether it fixes system panic situations. You also have the option of setting the new patch rollback feature. This saves previous versions of the patch so that, should a patch be deemed bad, it can be rolled back to the previous good patch. This is different from the HP-UX 10.x release, where you could remove a patch and the previous version of the software would be put back into place. With 11.x, you can keep multiple versions of patches on the system with the ability to roll back several versions.

Install Software to Local Host

Install Software to Local Host is similar to *Copy Software to Local Depot* in that you must specify the Source Host Name and Source Depot Path. The Source Depot Path could be the CD-ROM from which you are loading software, as shown in the previous example as well as the example in Chapter 1, or it could be a directory depot. We just created a directory depot from which software can be installed in the previous example so that we could use that directory rather than the CD-ROM. When that directory name, **/var/spool/swdepot**, is specified as the Source Depot Path, the software in Figure 4-46 is shown in the depot.

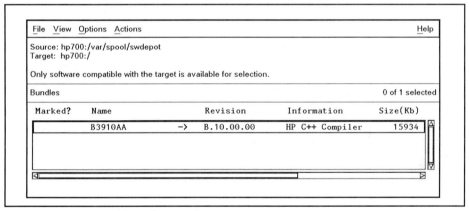

Figure 4-46 Installing from Directory Depot

The HP C++ Compiler is the software we loaded into this directory in the previous example. Before loading software, you should select *Show Description of Software* from the *Actions* menu to see whether a system reboot is required (you may have to scroll down the window to see the bottom of the description). You want to know this before you load software, so that you don't load software that requires a reboot at a time that is inconvenient. Under *Manage Patch Selection* you can select how you want any patches in the depot handled: automatically installed based on new software being installed, or automatically installed based on matching products already on the system. If the latest HP C++ Compiler patches were included in the depot, they could automatically be installed along with the actual software. We can now install this software onto the local host by selecting *Mark for Install* and *Install* from the *Actions* menu.

This installation is complete after only about four minutes when installing from a local disk on the local host. And because a compiler installation has no kernel changes, a system reboot is not required.

List Software

You can select either *List Depot* or *List Installed Software*.

Under *List Depot,* you specify the host and depot path from which to receive a complete list of software. This can be listed at the bundle, product, subproduct, fileset, or file level (these levels are covered in Chapter 1). If you have even a small amount of software installed in a depot, the file level is probably going to be too much detail. Listing HP C++ Compiler we loaded earlier to the fileset level is both manageable to read and informative. The file level is just too much detail.

List Installed Software allows you to list the software installed on your system to the bundle, product, subproduct, fileset, or file level, too. Selecting the bundle level and listing through SAM produces the same output as typing **swlist** at the command line. You can try this on your system to see how the two compare. **swlist** is covered in Chapter 1.

Remove Software

You can use *Remove Depot Software* to remove old or obsolete depots.

We can use the directory depot in **/var/spool/swdepot** we created earlier to delete software. The HP C++ Compiler we loaded in this directory can be highlighted, and then *Mark for Remove* from the *Actions* menu. Selecting *Remove* from the *Actions* menu will remove the software from the directory depot.

Time

The *Time* area of SAM allows you to configure Network Time Protocol, or NTP. NTP is a service that allows you to synchronize the time on all your systems utilizing a Universal Coordinated Time server. For more information on using and configuring NTP, consult the HP-UX manual *Installing and Administering Internet Services.*

NFS Diskless Concepts

Rather than cover NFS diskless as an area to manage, I'm going to deviate from the format found throughout this chapter and instead provide a brief description of NFS Diskless.

This topic was introduced with HP-UX 10.x. Diskless nodes were implemented with Distributed HP-UX (DUX) in HP-UX 9.x and earlier releases. Distributed HP-UX was first introduced in HP-UX 6.0 in 1986 and was successfully used in many HP installations. The new implementation of diskless nodes as of HP-UX 10.x is NFS Diskless. It has many desirable features including the following:

- NFS diskless is the current de facto standard.

- It is not a proprietary solution.

- High-end diskless servers and clients can be symmetric multi-processing systems.

- Many file system types and features are available, such as UNIX File System, Journaled File System, Logical Volume Manager, disk mirroring, etc.

- The System V Release 4 file system layout described throughout this book is implemented. This file system layout is conducive to extensive file sharing, which is used in NFS Diskless.

- Read-only NFS mounts such as **/usr** and **/opt/**<application> are supported.

- Distributed HP-UX functionality such as context-dependent files has been removed.

- Servers can be both Series 700 and Series 800 units.

- The physical link doesn't matter, so servers can use many interfaces such as IEEE 802.3 and FDDI. A server can also assign some diskless systems to one network card, and other systems to other network cards.

- Diskless systems can boot across a gateway, thereby allowing subnets to be used.

- Booting is implemented with standard Boot Protocol (BOOTP) and Trivial File Transfer Protocol (TFTP) protocols.

- Clients can swap to a local disk or swap using NFS to a remote disk.

Many additional features of NFS diskless exist; however, since our focus is on management, let's take a closer look at this. Using SAM, all tasks related to NFS diskless administration can be performed. This means you have a single point of administration for the cluster. You have cluster wide resources, such as printers and file systems, that can be managed from any node in the cluster. You can defer some operations until a later point in time if a node is unreachable. And, of course, you can add and delete clients in SAM.

Using SAM, you get a single point of administration for several NFS Diskless systems. This means that performing an operation in SAM affects all systems in the cluster. The single point of administration areas in SAM include:

- Printers/Plotters

- File Systems

- Users/Groups

- Home Directories

- Electronic Mail

- Backups

Although a great deal could be covered on NFS Diskless and the many improvements in this area over Distributed HP-UX, the key point from an administrative perspective is that SAM provides a central point of administration for NFS Diskless administration. All tasks related to NFS Diskless administration can be performed through SAM.

ENWARE X-station Administration (optional)

If your environment chooses, it can incorporate the use of X-stations on the desktop instead of standalone workstations. ENWARE, an add-on product, supports this environment. ENWARE is not provided as a standard part of SAM, but when you install the ENWARE software on your system, you'll have *ENWARE X-station Administration* as one of your top-level menu picks. While not a standard area of SAM, it makes X-station administration easier. You can perform the following X-station-related functions from within SAM:

1) Add an X-station
2) Remove an X-station
3) Printers, plotters
4) Installation testing and version control
5) XDM Administration

Configuring an X-station in SAM is identical to running **/opt/enware/ lbin/xtadm**.

To add an X-station, you would provide the following information in SAM:

Name
IP address
LAN hardware address

Subnet mask
Default Gateway IP address

Manual Pages for Commands Used in Chapter 4

The following section contains copies of the manual pages of commands used in Chapter 4. This makes for a quick reference for you of commands commonly used throughout your system administration day.

crontab

crontab - Schedule jobs that are executed automatically on a regular basis.

```
crontab(1)                                                              crontab(1)

NAME
     crontab - user job file scheduler

SYNOPSIS

     crontab [file]

     crontab -e

     crontab -l

     crontab -r

DESCRIPTION
     The crontab command manages a crontab file for the user.  You can use
     a crontab file to schedule jobs that are executed automatically by
     cron (see cron(1M)) on a regular basis.  The command has four forms:

              crontab [file]    Create or replace your crontab file by copying
                                the specified file, or standard input if file
                                is omitted or - is specified as file , into the
                                crontab directory, /var/spool/cron/crontabs.
                                The name of your crontab file in the crontab
                                directory is the same as your effective user
                                name.

              crontab -e        Edit a copy of your crontab file, or create an
                                empty file to edit if the crontab file does not
                                exist. When editing is complete, the file will
                                be copied into the crontab directory as your
                                crontab file.

              crontab -l        List your crontab file.

              crontab -r        Remove your crontab file from the crontab
                                directory.

     The entries in a crontab file are lines of six fields each.  The
     fields are separated by spaces or tabs.  The lines have the following
     format:

              minute  hour  monthday  month  weekday  command

     The first five are integer patterns that specify when the sixth field,
     command, should be executed.  They can have the following ranges of
     values:

              minute            The minute of the hour, 0-59

              hour              The hour of the day, 0-23
```

monthday   The day of the month, 1-31

month   The month of the year, 1-12

weekday   The day of the week, 0-6, 0=Sunday

Each pattern can be either an asterisk (*), meaning all legal values, or a list of elements separated by commas. An element is either a number in the ranges shown above, or two numbers in the range separated by a hyphen (meaning an inclusive range). Note that the specification of days can be made in two fields: monthday and weekday. If both are specified in an entry, they are cumulative. For example,

    0   0   1,15   *   1   command

runs command at midnight on the first and fifteenth of each month, as well as every Monday. To specify days in only one field, set the other field to asterisk (*). For example,

    0   0   *   *   1   command

runs command only on Mondays.

The sixth field, command (the balance of a line including blanks in a crontab file), is a string that is executed by the shell at the specified times. A percent character (%) in this field (unless escaped by a backslash (\)) is translated to a newline character, dividing the field into "lines". Only the first "line" (up to a % or end-of-line) of the command field is executed by the shell. Any other "lines" are made available to the command as standard input.

Blank lines and those whose first non-blank character is # will be ignored.

cron invokes the command from the user's HOME directory with the POSIX shell, (/usr/bin/sh). It runs in the c queue (see queuedefs(4)).

cron supplies a default environment for every shell, defining:

    HOME=user's-home-directory
    LOGNAME=user's-login-id
    PATH=/usr/bin:/usr/sbin:.
    SHELL=/usr/bin/sh

Users who desire to have their .profile executed must explicitly do so in the crontab entry or in a script called by the entry.

You can execute crontab if your name appears in the file /var/adm/cron/cron.allow. If that file does not exist, you can use crontab if your name does not appear in the file /var/adm/cron/cron.deny. If only cron.deny exists and is empty, all users can use crontab. If neither file exists, only the root user can use crontab. The allow/deny files consist of one user name per line.

EXTERNAL INFLUENCES
  Environment Variables
    LC_CTYPE determines the interpretation of text within file as single- and/or multi-byte characters.

    LC_MESSAGES determines the language in which messages are displayed.

    If LC_CTYPE or LC_MESSAGES is not specified in the environment or is set to the empty string, the value of LANG is used as a default for each unspecified or empty variable. If LANG is not specified or is set to the empty string, a default of "C" (see lang(5)) is used instead of LANG.

If any internationalization variable contains an invalid setting, crontab behaves as if all internationalization variables are set to "C". See environ(5). EDITOR determines the editor to be invoked when -e option is specified. The default editor is vi.

International Code Set Support
   Single-byte and multi-byte character code sets are supported.

WARNINGS
   Be sure to redirect the standard output and standard error from commands. If this is not done, any generated standard output or standard error is mailed to the user.

FILES
   /var/adm/cron   Main cron directory
   /var/adm/cron/cron.allow   List of allowed users
   /var/adm/cron/cron.deny   List of denied users
   /var/adm/cron/log   Accounting information
   /var/spool/cron/crontabs   Directory containing the crontab files

SEE ALSO
   sh(1), cron(1M), queuedefs(4).

STANDARDS CONFORMANCE
   crontab: SVID2, SVID3, XPG2, XPG3, XPG4

ioscan

ioscan - Scan the system and list results.

```
ioscan(1M)                                                    ioscan(1M)

NAME
     ioscan - scan I/O system

SYNOPSIS
     /usr/sbin/ioscan [-k|-u] [-d driver|-C class] [-I instance] [-H
     hw_path] [-f[-n]|-F[-n]] [devfile]

     /usr/sbin/ioscan -M driver -H hw_path [-I instance]

DESCRIPTION
     ioscan scans system hardware, usable I/O system devices, or kernel I/O
     system data structures as appropriate, and lists the results.  For
     each hardware module on the system, ioscan displays by default the
     hardware path to the hardware module, the class of the hardware
     module, and a brief description.

     By default, ioscan scans the system and lists all reportable hardware
     found.  The types of hardware reported include processors, memory,
     interface cards and I/O devices.  Scanning the hardware may cause
     drivers to be unbound and others bound in their place in order to
     match actual system hardware.  Entities that cannot be scanned are not
     listed.

     In the second form shown, ioscan forces the specified software driver
     into the kernel I/O system at the given hardware path and forces
     software driver to be bound.  This can be used to make the system
     recognize a device that cannot be recognized automatically; for
     example, because it has not yet been connected to the system, does not
     support autoconfiguration, or because diagnostics need to be run on a
     faulty device.

  Options
     ioscan recognizes the following options:

          -C class          Restrict the output listing to those devices
                            belonging to the specified class.  Cannot be
                            used with -d.

          -d driver         Restrict the output listing to those devices
                            controlled by the specified driver.  Cannot be
                            used with -C.

          -f                Generate a full listing, displaying the
                            module's class, instance number, hardware path,
                            driver, software state, hardware type, and a
                            brief description.

          -F                Produce a compact listing of fields (described
                            below), separated by colons. This option
                            overrides the -f option.
```

-H hw_path   Restrict the scan and output listing to those devices connected at the specified hardware path. When used with -M, this option specifies the full hardware path at which to bind the software modules.

-I instance   Restrict the scan and output listing to the specified instance, when used with either -d or -C. When used with -M, specifies the desired instance number for binding.

-k   Scan kernel I/O system data structures instead of the actual hardware and list the results. No binding or unbinding of drivers is performed. The -d, -C, -I, and -H options can be used to restrict listings. Cannot be used with -u.

-M driver   Specifies the software driver to bind at the hardware path given by the -H option. Must be used with the -H option.

-n   List device file names in the output. Only special files in the /dev directory and its subdirectories are listed.

-u   Scan and list usable I/O system devices instead of the actual hardware. Usable I/O devices are those having a driver in the kernel and an assigned instance number. The -d, -C, -I, and -H options can be used to restrict listings. The -u option cannot be used with -k.

The -d and -C options can be used to obtain listings of subsets of the I/O system, although the entire system is still scanned. Specifying -d or -C along with -I, or specifying -H or a devfile causes ioscan to restrict both the scan and the listing to the hardware subset indicated.

Fields

The -F option can be used to generate a compact listing of fields separated by colons (:), useful for producing custom listings with awk. Fields include the module's bus type, cdio, is_block, is_char, is_pseudo, block major number, character major number, minor number, class, driver, hardware path, identify bytes, instance number, module path, module name, software state, hardware type, a brief description, and card instance. If a field does not exist, consecutive colons hold the field's position. Fields are defined as follows:

class   A device category, defined in the files located in the directory /usr/conf/master.d and consistent with the listings output by lsdev (see lsdev(1M)). Examples are disk, printer, and tape.

instance   The instance number associated with the device or card. It is a unique number assigned to a card or device within a class. If no driver is available for the hardware component or an error occurs binding the driver, the kernel will not assign an instance number and a (-1), is listed.

hw path   A numerical string of hardware components, notated sequentially from the bus address to the device address. Typically, the initial number is appended by slash (/), to represent a bus converter (if required by your machine), and

subsequent numbers are separated by periods (.).
Each number represents the location of a hardware
component on the path to the device.

driver   The name of the driver that controls the hardware
                    component. If no driver is available to control
                    the hardware component, a question mark (?) is
                    displayed in the output.

software state The result of software binding.

                    CLAIMED   software bound successfully

                    UNCLAIMED   no associated software found

                    DIFF_HW   software found does not match the
                                     associated software

                    NO_HW   the hardware at this address is no
                                     longer responding

                    ERROR   the hardware at this address is
                                     responding but is in an error state

                    SCAN   node locked, try again later

hardware type Entity identifier for the hardware component. It
                    is one of the following strings:

                    UNKNOWN   There is no hardware associated or
                                     the type of hardware is unknown

                    PROCESSOR   Hardware component is a processor

                    MEMORY   Hardware component is memory

                    BUS_NEXUS   Hardware component is bus converter
                                     or bus adapter

                    INTERFACE   Hardware component is an interface
                                     card

                    DEVICE   Hardware component is a device

bus type   Bus type associated with the node.

cdio   The name associated with the Context-Dependent I/O
                    module.

is_block   A boolean value indicating whether a device block
                    major number exists. A T or F is generated in this
                    field.

is_char   A boolean value indicating whether a device
                    character major number exists. A T or F is
                    generated in this field.

is_pseudo   A boolean value indicating a pseudo driver. A T or
                    F is generated in this field.

block major   The device block major number. A -1 indicates that
                    a device block major number does not exist.

character major

	The device character major number. A -1 indicates that a device character major number does not exist.
minor	The device minor number.
identify bytes	The identify bytes returned from a module or device.
module path	The software components separated by periods (.).
module name	The module name of the software component controlling the node.
description	A description of the device.
card instance	The instance number of the hardware interface card.

RETURN VALUE
    ioscan returns 0 upon normal completion and 1 if an error occurred.

EXAMPLES
    Scan the system hardware and list all the devices belonging to the disk device class.

        ioscan -C disk

    Forcibly bind driver tape1 at the hardware path 8.4.1.

        ioscan -M tape1 -H 8.4.1

AUTHOR
    ioscan was developed by HP.

FILES
    /dev/config
    /dev/*

SEE ALSO
    config(1M), lsdev(1M), ioconfig(4).

kill

kill -Send a signal to a process such as terminate.

```
kill(1)                                                             kill(1)

NAME
      kill - send a signal to a process; terminate a process

SYNOPSIS

      kill [-s signame] pid ...

      kill [-s signum] pid ...

      kill -l

   Obsolescent Versions:
      kill -signame pid ...

      kill -signum pid ...

DESCRIPTION
      The kill command sends a signal to each process specified by a pid
      process identifier.  The default signal is SIGTERM, which normally
      terminates processes that do not trap or ignore the signal.

      pid is a process identifier, an unsigned or negative integer that can
      be one of the following:


          > 0   The number of a process.

          = 0   All processes, except special system processes, whose
                process group ID is equal to the process group ID of the
                sender.

          =-1   All processes, except special system processes, if the user
                has appropriate privileges.  Otherwise, all processes,
                except special system processes, whose real or effective
                user ID is the same as the user ID of the sending process.


          <-1   All processes, except special system processes, whose
                process group ID is equal to the absolute value of pid and
                whose real or effective user ID is the same as the user of
                the sending process.

      Process numbers can be found with the ps command (see ps(1)) and with
      the built-in jobs command available in some shells.

   Options
      kill recognizes the following options:

          -l    (ell)        List all values of signame supported by the
                             implementation.  No signals are sent with this
                             option.  The symbolic names of the signals
                             (without the SIG prefix) are written to
```

standard output, separated by spaces and
newlines.

-s signame   Send the specified signal name. The default is
SIGTERM, number 15. signame can be specified
in upper- and/or lowercase, with or without the
SIG prefix. These values can be obtained by
using the -l option. The symbolic name SIGNULL
represents signal value zero. See "Signal
Names and Numbers" below.

-s signum   Send the specified decimal signal number. The
default is 15, SIGTERM. See "Signal Names and
Numbers" below.

-signame   (Obsolescent.) Equivalent to -s signame.

-signum   (Obsolescent.) Equivalent to -s signum.

Signal Names and Numbers
The following table describes a few of the more common signals that
can be useful from a terminal. For a complete list and a full
description, see the header file <signal.h> and the manual entry
signal(5).

signum	signame	Name	Description
0	SIGNULL	Null	Check access to pid
1	SIGHUP	Hangup	Terminate; can be trapped
2	SIGINT	Interrupt	Terminate; can be trapped
3	SIGQUIT	Quit	Terminate with core dump; can be trapped
9	SIGKILL	Kill	Forced termination; cannot be trapped
15	SIGTERM	Terminate	Terminate; can be trapped
24	SIGSTOP	Stop	Pause the process; cannot be trapped
25	SIGTSTP	Terminal stop	Pause the process; can be trapped
26	SIGCONT	Continue	Run a stopped process

SIGNULL (0), the null signal, invokes error checking but no signal is
actually sent. This can be used to test the validity or existence of
pid.

SIGTERM (15), the (default) terminate signal, can be trapped by the
receiving process, allowing the receiver to execute an orderly
shutdown or to ignore the signal entirely. For orderly operations,
this is the perferred choice.

SIGKILL (9), the kill signal, forces a process to terminate
immediately. Since SIGKILL cannot be trapped or ignored, it is useful
for terminating a process that does not respond to SIGTERM.

The receiving process must belong to the user of the sending process,
unless the user has appropriate privileges.

As a single special case, the continue signal SIGCONT can be sent to
any process that is a member of the same session as the sending
process.

RETURN VALUE
Upon completion, kill returns with one of the following values:

0   At least one matching process was found for each pid
operand, and the specified signal was successfully processed
for at least one matching process.

>0   An error occurred.

EXAMPLES

The command:

        kill 6135

signals process number 6135 to terminate. This gives the process an
opportunity to exit gracefully (removing temporary files, etc.).

The following equivalent commands:

        kill -s SIGKILL 6135
        kill -s KILL 6135
        kill -s 9 6135
        kill -SIGKILL 6135
        kill -KILL 6135
        kill -9 6135

terminate process number 6135 abruptly by sending a SIGKILL signal to
the process. This tells the kernel to remove the process immediately.

WARNINGS

If a process hangs during some operation (such as I/O) so that it is
never scheduled, it cannot die until it is allowed to run. Thus, such
a process may never go away after the kill. Similarly, defunct
processes (see ps(1)) may have already finished executing, but remain
on the system until their parent reaps them (see wait(2)). Using kill
to send signals to them has no effect.

Some non-HP-UX implementations provide kill only as a shell built-in
command.

DEPENDENCIES

This manual entry describes the external command /usr/bin/kill and the
built-in kill command of the POSIX shell (see sh-posix(1)). Other
shells, such as C and Korn (see csh(1) and ksh(1) respectively), also
provide kill as a built-in command. The syntax for and output from
these built-ins may be different.

SEE ALSO

csh(1), ksh(1), ps(1), sh(1), sh-bourne(1), sh-posix(1), kill(2),
wait(2), signal(5).

STANDARDS CONFORMANCE

kill: SVID2, SVID3, XPG2, XPG3, XPG4, POSIX.2

lpstat

lpstat - List the current status of the line printer system.

---

lpstat(1)   lpstat(1)

NAME
     lpstat - report line printer status information

SYNOPSIS

     lpstat [-drst] [-a[list]] [-c[list]] [-o[list]] [-p[list]] [-u[list]]
     [-v[list]] [ID...]

DESCRIPTION
     The lpstat utility writes to standard output information about the
     current status of the line printer system.

     If no arguments are given, lpstat writes the status of all requests
     made to lp by the user that are still in the output queue.

OPTIONS
     The lpstat utility supports the XBD specification, Section 10.2,
     Utility Syntax Guidelines, except the option-arguments are optional
     and cannot be presented as separate arguments.

     Some of the options below can be followed by an optional list that can
     be in one of two forms: a list of items separated from one another by
     a comma, or a quoted list of items separated from one another by a
     comma or one or more blank characters, or combinations of both. See
     EXAMPLES.

     The omission of a list following such options causes all information
     relevant to the option to be written to standard output; for example:

          lpstat -o

     writes the status of all output requests that are still in the output
     queue.

          -a[list]   Write the acceptance status of destinations for
                        output requests. The list argument is a list of
                        intermixed printer names and class names.

          -c[list]   Write the class names and their members. The list
                        argument is a list of class names.

          -d   Write the system default destination for output
                        requests.

          -o[list]   Write the status of output requests. The list
                        argument is a list of intermixed printer names, class
                        names and request IDs.

          -p[list]   Write the status of printers. The list argument is a
                        list of printer names.

          -r   Write the status of the line printer request

                                scheduler.

              -s   Write a status summary, including the status of the
                              line printer scheduler, the system default
                              destination, a list of class names and their members
                              and a list of printers and their associated devices.

              -t   Write all status information.

              -u[list]   Write the status of output requests for users. The
                              list argument is a list of login names.

              -v[list]   Write the names of printers and the pathnames of the
                              devices associated with them. The list argument is a
                              list of printer names.

OPERANDS
     The following operand is supported:

              ID   A request ID, as returned by lp.

STDIN
     Not used.

INPUT FILES
     None.

ENVIRONMENT VARIABLES
     The following environment variables affect the execution of lpstat:

              LANG   Provide a default value for the
                                        internationalisation variables that are
                                        unset or null. If LANG is unset or
                                        null, the corresponding value from the
                                        implementation-specific default locale
                                        will be used. If any of the
                                        internationalisation variables contains
                                        an invalid setting, the utility will
                                        behave as if none of the variables had
                                        been defined.

              LC_ALL   If set to a non-empty string value,
                                        override the values of all the other
                                        internationalisation variables.

              LC_CTYPE   Determine the locale for the
                                        interpretation of sequences of bytes of
                                        text data as characters (for example,
                                        single- as opposed to multi-byte
                                        characters in arguments).

              LC_MESSAGES   Determine the locale that should be used
                                        to affect the format and contents of
                                        diagnostic messages written to standard
                                        error, and informative messages written
                                        to standard output.

              LC_TIME   Determine the format of date and time
                                        strings output when displaying line
                                        printer status information with the -a,
                                        -o, -p, -t, or -u options.

              NLSPATH   Determine the location of message
                                        catalogues for the processing of
                                        LC_MESSAGES.

TZ	Determine the timezone used with date and time strings.

ASYNCHRONOUS EVENTS
    Default.

STDOUT
    The standard output is a text file containing the information
    described in OPTIONS, in an unspecified format.

STDERR
    Used only for diagnostic messages.

OUTPUT FILES
    None.

EXTENDED DESCRIPTION
    None.

EXIT STATUS
    The following exit values are returned:

    0   Successful completion.

    >0   An error occurred.

CONSEQUENCES OF ERRORS
    Default.

APPLICATION USAGE
    The lpstat utility cannot reliably determine the status of print
    requests in all conceivable circumstances. When the printer is under
    the control of another operating system or resides on a remote system
    across a network, it need not be possible to determine the status of
    the print job after it has left the control of the local operating
    system. Even on local printers, spooling hardware in the printer may
    make it appear that the print job has been completed long before the
    final page is printed.

EXAMPLES

    1.   Obtain the status of two printers, the pathnames of two
         printers, a list of all class names and the status of the
         request named HiPri-33:

         lpstat -plaser1,laser4 -v"laser2 laser3" -c HiPri-33

    2.   Obtain user print job status using the obsolescent mixed
         blank and comma form:

         lpstat -u"ddg,gmv, maw"

FUTURE DIRECTIONS
    A version of lpstat that fully supports the XBD specification, Section
    10.2, Utility Syntax Guidelines may be introduced in a future issue.

SEE ALSO
    cancel, lp.

CHANGE HISTORY
    First released in Issue 2.

Issue 3
   The operation of this utility in an 8-bit transparent manner has been
   noted.

   The operation of this utility in an internationalised environment has
   been described.

Issue 4
   Format reorganised.

   Exceptions to Utility Syntax Guidelines conformance noted.

   Internationalised environment variable support mandated.

STANDARDS CONFORMANCE
      lpstat: SVID2, SVID3, XPG2, XPG3, XPG4

lpstat(1)   lpstat(1)

                              HP-UX EXTENSIONS

DESCRIPTION
      Any arguments that are not options are assumed to be request ids (as
      returned by lp). lpstat prints the status of such requests. options
      can appear in any order and can be repeated and intermixed with other
      arguments.

            -i   Inhibit the reporting of remote status.

            -o[list]   Also see the -i option.

            -t   Print all status information. Same as specifying -r,
                          -s, -a, -p, -o. See the -i option.

   Security Restriction
      Only users who have the lp subsystem authorization or the printqueue
      secondary subsystem authorization can view the entire queue.
      Unauthorized users can view only their own jobs whose sensitivity
      levels are dominated by the user's current sensitivity level.

      The allowmacaccess privilege allows viewing jobs at higher sensitivity
      levels.

EXAMPLES
      Check whether your job is queued:

            lpstat

      Check the relative position of a queued job:

            lpstat -t

      Verify that the job scheduler is running:

            lpstat -r

FILES
      /var/spool/lp/*
      /var/adm/lp/*
      /etc/lp/*
      /usr/lib/lp/*

SEE ALSO
      enable(1), lp(1), rlpstat(1M).

STANDARDS CONFORMANCE

```
lpstat: SVID2, SVID3, XPG2, XPG3, XPG4
```

mount

mount - Mount and umount file systems (this is generic man page, there is also a man page for hfs and vxfs.)

```
mount(1M)                                                          mount(1M)

NAME
     mount (generic), umount (generic) - mount and unmount file systems

SYNOPSIS
     /usr/sbin/mount [-l] [-p|-v]

     /usr/sbin/mount -a [-F FStype] [-eQ]

     /usr/sbin/mount [-F FStype] [-eQrV] [-o specific_options]
         {special|directory}

     /usr/sbin/mount [-F FStype] [-eQrV] [-o specific_options]
         special directory

     /usr/sbin/umount [-v] [-V] {special|directory}

     /usr/sbin/umount -a [-F FStype] [-v]

DESCRIPTION
     The mount command mounts file systems.  Only a superuser can mount
     file systems.  Other users can use mount to list mounted file systems.

     The mount command attaches special, a removable file system, to
     directory, a directory on the file tree.  directory, which must
     already exist, will become the name of the root of the newly mounted
     file system.  special and directory must be given as absolute path
     names.  If either special or directory is omitted, mount attempts to
     determine the missing value from an entry in the /etc/fstab file.
     mount can be invoked on any removable file system, except /.

     If mount is invoked without any arguments, it lists all of the mounted
     file systems from the file system mount table, /etc/mnttab.

     The umount command unmounts mounted file systems.  Only a superuser
     can unmount file systems.

   Options (mount)
     The mount command recognizes the following options:

          -a              Attempt to mount all file systems described in
                          /etc/fstab.  All optional fields in /etc/fstab
                          must be included and supported.  If the -F option
                          is specified, all file systems in /etc/fstab with
                          that FStype are mounted.  File systems are not
                          necessarily mounted in the order listed in
                          /etc/fstab.
```

-e	Verbose mode. Write a message to the standard output indicating which file system is being mounted.
-F FStype	Specify FStype, the file system type on which to operate. See fstyp(1M). If this option is not included on the command line, then it is determined from either /etc/fstab, by matching special with an entry in that file, or from file system statistics of special, obtained by statfsdev() (see statfsdev(3C)).
-l	Limit actions to local file systems only.
-o specific_options	
	Specify options specific to each file system type. specific_options is a list of comma separated suboptions and/or keyword/attribute pairs intended for a FStype-specific version of the command. See the FStype-specific manual entries for a description of the specific_options supported, if any.
-p	Report the list of mounted file systems in the /etc/fstab format.
-Q	Prevent the display of error messages that result from an attempt to mount already mounted file systems.
-r	Mount the specified file system as read-only. Physically write-protected file systems must be mounted in this way or errors occur when access times are updated, whether or not any explicit write is attempted.
-v	Report the regular output with file system type and flags; however, the directory and special fields are reversed.
-V	Echo the completed command line, but perform no other action. The command line is generated by incorporating the user-specified options and other information derived from /etc/fstab. This option allows the user to verify the command line.

Options (umount)
The umount command recognizes the following options:

-a	Attempt to unmount all file systems described in /etc/mnttab. All optional fields in /etc/mnttab must be included and supported. If FStype is specified, all file systems in /etc/mnttab with that FStype are unmounted. File systems are not necessarily unmounted in the order listed in /etc/mnttab.
-F FStype	Specify FStype, the file system type on which to operate. If this option is not included on the command line, then it is determined from /etc/mnttab by matching special with an entry in that file. If no match is found, the command fails.
-v	Verbose mode. Write a message to standard output

indicating which file system is being unmounted.

-V   Echo the completed command line, but perform no
                         other action. The command line is generated by
                         incorporating the user-specified options and other
                         information derived from /etc/fstab. This option
                         allows the user to verify the command line.

EXAMPLES
    List the file systems currently mounted:

        mount

    Mount the HFS file system /dev/dsk/c1d2s0 at directory /home:

        mount -F hfs /dev/dsk/c1d2s0 /home

    Unmount the same file system:

        umount /dev/dsk/c1d2s0

AUTHOR
    mount was developed by HP, AT&T, the University of California,
    Berkeley, and Sun Microsystems.

FILES
    /etc/fstab   Static information about the systems
    /etc/mnttab   Mounted file system table

SEE ALSO
    mount_FStype(1M), mount(2), fstab(4), mnttab(4), fs_wrapper(5),
    quota(5).

STANDARDS COMPLIANCE
    mount: SVID3

    umount: SVID3

sam

sam - Start the menu driven System Administration Manager (SAM).

---

sam(1M)   sam(1M)

NAME
     sam - system administration manager

SYNOPSIS

     /usr/sbin/sam [-display display] [-f login] [-r]

DESCRIPTION
     The sam command starts a menu-driven System Administration Manager
     program (SAM) that makes it easy to perform system administration
     tasks with only limited, specialized knowledge of the HP-UX operating
     system. SAM discovers most aspects of a system's configuration
     through automated inquiries and tests. Help menus describe how to use
     SAM and perform the various management tasks. Context-sensitive help
     on the currently highlighted field is always available by pressing the
     F1 function key. Status messages and a log file monitor keep the user
     informed of what SAM is doing.

     Running SAM
     SAM has been tuned to run in the Motif environment, but it can be run
     on text terminals as well. To run SAM in the Motif environment, be
     sure that Motif has been installed on your system, and that the
     DISPLAY environment variable is set to the system name on which the
     SAM screens should be displayed (or use the -display command line
     option).

     Generally, SAM requires superuser (user root) privileges to execute
     successfully. However, SAM can be configured (through the use of
     "Restricted SAM"; see below) to allow subsets of its capabilities to
     be used by non-root users. When Restricted SAM is used, non-root
     users are promoted to root when necessary to enable them to execute
     successfully.

     Options
     sam recognizes the following options.

               -display display   Set the DISPLAY value for the duration of the
                                   SAM session.

               -f login   Execute SAM with the privileges associated
                                   with the specified login. When used in
                                   conjunction with -r, the Restricted SAM
                                   Builder is invoked and initialized with the
                                   privileges associated with the specified
                                   login. You must be a superuser to use this
                                   option. See "Restricted SAM" below for more
                                   information.

               -r   Invoke the Restricted SAM Builder. This
                                   enables the system administrator to provide
                                   limited nonsuperuser access to SAM
                                   functionality. You must be a superuser to

use this option. See "Restricted SAM" below
for more information.

SAM Functional Areas
SAM performs system administration tasks in the following areas:

Auditing and Security (Trusted Systems)

- Set global system security policies

    - Maximum account inactivity period
    - Password generation policies
    - Null password usage and use of password restriction rules

    - Password aging
    - Maximum unsuccessful login attempts
    - Single-user boot authorization
    - Terminal security policies

- Turn the Auditing system on or off

- Set the parameters for the Audit Logs and Size Monitor

- View all or selected parts of the audit logs

- Modify (or view) which users, events, and/or system calls get
  audited

- Convert your system to a Trusted System

- Convert your system to a non-Trusted System

Backup and Recovery

- Interactively back up files to a valid backup device
  (cartridge tape, cartridge tape autochanger, magnetic tape,
  DAT, magneto-optical disk, or magneto-optical disk
  autochanger). The SAM interface is suspended so that you can
  read and/or respond to the interactive messages produced by
  fbackup (see fbackup(1M)).

- Recover files online from a valid backup device. The SAM
  interface is suspended so that you can read/respond to the
  interactive messages produced by frecover (see frecover(1M)).

- Add to, delete from, or view the automated backup schedule.

- Obtain a list of files from a backup tape.

- View various backup and recovery log files.

Disk and File Systems Management

- Add, configure, or unconfigure disk devices. This includes
  hard drives, floppy drives, CD-ROMs, magneto-optical devices,
  and disk arrays.

- Add, modify, or remove local file systems, or convert them to
  long file names.

- Configure HFS or VxFS file systems.

- Remote (NFS) file systems configuration, including:

- Add, modify, or remove remote (NFS) file systems.

- Allow or disallow access by remote systems to local file systems.

- Modify RPC (Remote Procedure Call) services' security.

- Add, remove, or modify device or file system swap.

- Change the primary swap device.

- Add, modify, or remove dump devices.

- Examine, create, extend, or reduce a volume-group pool of disks.

- Create, extend or change number of mirrored copies of a logical volume and associated file system.

- Remove a logical volume or increase its size.

- Split or merge mirrored copies of a logical volume.

- Share or unshare volume groups (only on ServiceGuard clusters running MC/LockManager distributed lock-manager software).

Diskless Cluster Configuration

- Add or remove cluster clients. You can customize the tasks of adding and removing cluster clients by specifying steps to be performed before and/or after SAM does its processing for the task. The Task Customization action leads you through this capability. See "Customizing SAM Tasks" below for more information.

Kernel and Device Configuration

- Change the configuration for I/O device and pseudo drivers.

- Modify operating system parameters.

- Modify dump device configuration in the kernel.

- Minimize kernel and system configuration to reduce memory usage (Series 700 only).

- Add or remove optional subsystems such as NFS, LAN, NS, CD-ROM, etc.

- Generate a new kernel.

Networks/Communications

- Configure one or more LAN cards.

- Configure ARPA services.

- Configure the Network File System (NFS).

- Configure X.25 card or cards and PAD (Packet Assembler/Disassembler) services (if X.25 has been purchased).

Peripheral Devices Management

- Administer the LP spooler or Distributed Print Services and associated printers and plotters (see "Printer and Plotter Management" below).

- Add, modify, or remove the configuration of disk devices.

- Add or remove terminals and modems.

- Configure terminal security policies (Trusted Systems only).

- Lock and unlock terminals (Trusted Systems only).

- Add or remove tape drives.

- Add or remove hardware interface cards and HP-IB instruments.

- View current configuration of peripherals and disk space information.

Printer and Plotter Management
SAM supports two methods for managing printers and plotters:

LP Spooler

- Add and remove local, remote, and networked printers and plotters to/from the LP spooler.

- Enable and disable printers and plotters from printing requests accepted by the LP spooler.

- Accept and reject requests for printers, plotters, and print classes.

- Modify the fence priority of printers and plotters.

- Set the system default print destination.

- Start and stop the LP scheduler.

HP Distributed Print Service (HPDPS)

- Add and remove physical printers (parallel, serial, or network interface and remote printers), logical printers, print queues, spoolers, and supervisors.

- Enable and disable logical printers, print queues, and physical printers to accept print jobs.

- Pause and resume print queues, physical printers, and print jobs.

- Start and stop spoolers and supervisors

- Modify attributes of physical printers, logical printers, print queues, spoolers, and supervisors.

- Remove a single print job or all print jobs assigned to a physical printer, logical printer, print queue, spooler or supervisor.

Process Management

- Kill, stop or continue processes.

- Change the nice priority of processes.

- View the current status of processes.

- Schedule periodic tasks via cron.

- View current periodic (cron) tasks.

- Run performance monitors.

- Display system properties such as: machine model and ID;
  number of installed processors, their version and speed;
  operating-system release version; swap statistics, real,
  physical, and virtual memory statistics; network connection
  information.

Remote Administration

- Configure remote systems for remote administration.

- Execute SAM on systems configured for remote administration.

Routine Tasks

- Shut down the system.

- View and remove large files. Specify size and time-since-
  accessed of large files to display or remove.

- View and remove unowned files. Specify size and time-since-
  accessed of unowned files to display or remove.

- View and remove core files.

- View and trim ASCII or non-ASCII log files. Add or remove
  files from the list of files to monitor. Set recommended size
  for trimming.

User and Group Account Management

- Add, remove, view, and modify user accounts.

- Remove or reassign ownership of files belonging to removed or
  modified user accounts.

- Modify a user account's group membership.

- Set up password aging for a user account.

- Add, remove, view, and modify groups.

- Customize adding and removing users by specifying steps to be
  performed before and/or after SAM does its processing for the
  task. The Task Customization action items in SAM Users and
  Groups leads you through this capability. See "Customizing
  SAM Tasks" below for more information.

- Deactivate and reactivate user accounts.

- Manage trusted system security policies on a per-user basis.
  The policies that can be managed include:

     - Account lifetime
     - Maximum account inactivity period
     - Password generation policies
     - Null password usage and use of password restriction rules

- Maximum password length
- Password aging
- Maximum unsuccessful login attempts
- Generation of admin numbers for new or reactivated
  accounts
- Single-user boot authorization
- Authorized login times

Adding New Functionality to SAM
You can easily add stand-alone commands, programs, and scripts to SAM.
SAM is suspended while the executable program is running. When it
finishes, the SAM interface is restored. You can also write your own
help screen for each menu item you create. To add functionality to
SAM, select the "Add Custom Menu Item" or "Add Custom Menu Group"
action items from the SAM Areas menu. (Note that the new item is
added to the hierarchy that is currently displayed, so you need to
navigate to the desired hierarchy before adding the item.)

Single-Point Administration of NFS Diskless Clusters
SAM provides some special capabilities for managing an NFS diskless
cluster as a single entity.

For printers and file systems, you can use a feature of the "add"
tasks to add a resource to all members of a cluster, making the
printer or file system a "cluster-wide" resource. Not only can the
resource be added to all systems in the cluster in a single task, but
when a cluster-wide resource is selected and a task requested, that
task can be performed automatically on all members of the cluster.

For users/groups and electronic mail, SAM provides the choice between
shared data and private data when the first client is configured.
Choosing shared data results in clients being configured in such a way
that they and the cluster server share such things as /etc/passwd,
/etc/group, and user mailboxes, and such that sendmail is configured
on clients so that all email passes through the server.

Finally, for backups, all publicly-available file systems that belong
to systems in the cluster can be backed up from the cluster server.

Online help in the various SAM areas contains more details about
single-point administration of NFS diskless clusters (for example, the
online help in the Printers/Plotters area provides more information
about managing printers as cluster-wide resources and what it means to
perform a task on a cluster-wide resource).

File System Protection When Removing Users
When removing users or files from a system, there is always the
unfortunate possibility that the wrong user may be removed or that
files belonging to a user who is removed are deleted inadvertently
during the removal process. For example, user bin is the owner of
(from the operating system's perspective) the majority of the
executable commands on the system. Removing this user would obviously
be disastrous. On the other hand, suppose user joe owns all of the
files comprising the test suite for a project. It may be appropriate
to remove joe, but the test suite should be left intact and assigned
to a new owner. SAM provides two features to help protect against
inadvertent removal of users or files when removing users:

    - When prompting for the name of a user to remove from the
      system, SAM checks the name given against a list of names
      specified in the file /etc/sam/rmuser.excl. If the name
      matches one within the file, SAM does not remove the user.

    - When SAM removes a user, all files (or a subset thereof) for
      that user are also removed, unless the ownership is given to
      another user. Before removing a file belonging to the user,

SAM checks to see if the file resides in a path that has been
excluded from removal. SAM uses the file
/etc/sam/rmfiles.excl to determine which paths have been
excluded from removal. So, for example, if the path
/users/joe/test is named in the file, SAM will not remove any
files residing beneath that directory. SAM logs a list of all
files it removes in the file /var/tmp/sam_remove.log.

-   SAM does not remove or reassign any files if the user being
    removed has the same user ID as another user on the system.

Files /etc/sam/rmuser.excl and /etc/sam/rmfiles.excl can be edited to
contain users and directories that you want to exclude from removal by
SAM.

Customizing SAM Tasks
   You can customize the following SAM tasks:

-   Add a New User Account to the System

-   Remove a User Account from the System

-   Add a Cluster Client

-   Remove a Cluster Client

For each of these tasks, you can specify steps you want performed
before and/or after SAM does its processing for the task. Before SAM
performs one of the tasks, it checks to see if a pretask step
(executable file) was defined. If so, SAM invokes the executable,
passes it a set of parameters (see below), and waits for its
completion. You can halt SAM's processing of a task by exiting from
your executable with a nonzero value (for example if an error occurs
during execution of your executable).

After SAM has finished processing, it checks for a posttask step,
performing the same type of actions as for the pretask step.

The executable file must have these characteristics:

-   Must be owned by root.

-   Must be executable only by root, and if writable, only by
    root.

-   Must reside in a directory path where all the directories are
    writable only by owner.

-   The full path name of the executable file must be given in the
    SAM data entry form.

The same parameters are passed from SAM to your program for both the
pretask and posttask steps. Here are the parameters passed for each
task:

-   Add a New User Account to the System

        -l login_name
        -v user_id
        -h home_directory
        -g group
        -s shell
        -p password
        -R real_name
        -L office_location
        -H home_phone

```
     -O office_phone
```

The file /usr/sam/lib/ct_adduser.ex contains an example of how
to process these parameters.

- Remove a User Account From the System

There can be one of three possible parameters, depending on
the option selected in the SAM data entry form. The parameter
can be one of these three:

    -f user_name   Option supplied when all of
                                     user_name's files are being
                                       removed.

    -h user_name   Option supplied when
                                       user_name's home directory and
                                       files below it are being
                                       removed.

    -n new_owner user_name   Option supplied when all of
                                       user_name's files are being
                                       assigned to new_owner.

The file /usr/sam/lib/ct_rmuser.ex contains an example of how
to process these parameters.

- Add a Cluster Client

When adding multiple clients, the customized task is invoked
once for each client. If any pretask command fails (returns
nonzero), the corresponding client is not added.

The parameters are:

    -n client_nodename   Name of the cluster client
                                       being added.

    -i internet_address   Unique network address for the
                                       cluster client, in the form
                                       ddd.ddd.ddd.ddd.

    -s server   Name of the server.

    -h link_level_address   12-character hardware address
                                       associated with the LAN card
                                       in the cluster client.

The file /usr/sam/lib/ct_addnode.ex contains an example of how
to process these parameters. The task customize command is
run with standard output and standard error sent to the SAM
log file.

- Remove a Cluster Client

When removing multiple clients, the customized task is invoked
once for each client. If any pretask command fails (returns
nonzero), the corresponding client is not removed. The format
of the parameter string for this task is:

    -n client_nodename   Name of the cluster client
                                       being removed.

File /usr/sam/lib/ct_rmnode.ex contains an example of how to
process these parameters. The task customize command is run
with standard output and standard error sent to the SAM log

file.

Restricted SAM
   SAM can be configured to provide a subset of its functionality to
   certain users or groups of users. It can also be used to build a
   template file for assigning SAM access restrictions on multiple
   systems. This is done through the Restricted SAM Builder. System
   administrators access the Restricted SAM Builder by invoking SAM with
   the -r option (see "Options" above). In the Builder, system
   administrators may assign subsets of SAM functionality on a per-user
   or per-group basis. Once set up, the -f option (see "Options" above)
   can then be used by system administrators to verify that the
   appropriate SAM functional areas, and only those areas, are available
   to the specified user.

   A nonroot user that has been given Restricted SAM privileges simply
   executes /usr/sbin/sam and sees only those areas the user is
   privileged to access. For security reasons, the "List" and "Shell
   Escape" choices are not provided. (Note that some SAM functional
   areas require the user to be promoted to root in order to execute
   successfully. SAM does this automatically as needed.)

   SAM provides a default set of SAM functional areas that the system
   administrator can assign to other users. Of course, system
   administrators are able to assign custom lists of SAM functional areas
   to users as necessary.

SAM Logging
   All actions taken by SAM are logged into the SAM log file
   /var/sam/log/samlog. The log entries in this file can be viewed via
   the SAM utility samlog_viewer (see samlog_viewer(1M)). samlog_viewer
   can filter the log file by user name, by time of log entry creation,
   and by level of detail.

   The "Options" menu in the SAM Areas Menu enables you to start a log
   file viewer and to control certain logging options. These options
   include whether or not SAM should automatically start a log file
   viewer whenever SAM is executed, whether or not SAM should trim the
   log file automatically, and what maximum log file size should be
   enforced if automatic log file trimming is selected.

VT320 Terminal Support
   Because the VT320 terminal has predefined local functions for keys
   labeled as F1, F2, F3 and F4, users should use following mapping when
   they desire to use function keys:

       HP or Wyse60   VT320 or HP 700/60 in VT320 mode

       F1   PF2 (1)
       F2   PF1 (1)
       F3   spacebar
       F4   PF3 (1)
       F5   F10, [EXIT], F5 (2)
       F6   none
       F7   F18, first unlabeled key to right of
                             Pause/Break (2)
       F8   F19, second unlabeled key to right of
                             Pause/Break (2)

          (1) See the "Configuration: HP 700/60 in DEC mode, or DEC
               terminals with PC-AT-type keyboard" subsection below.

          (2) When using PC-AT keyboard with HP 700/60 in VT320 mode.

Since DEC terminals do not support the softkey menu, that menu is not displayed on those terminals.

Many applications use TAB for forward navigation (moving from one field to another) and shift-TAB for backward navigation. Users having DEC terminals or using terminals in DEC emulation modes such as VT100 or VT320 may note that these terminals/emulators may produce the same character for TAB and shift-TAB. As such, it is impossible for an application to distinguish between the two and both of them are treated as if the TAB key was pressed. This presents an inconvenience to users if they want to go backward. In most cases, they should complete rest of the input fields and get back to the desired field later.

VT100 Terminal Support
  VT100 does not allow the F1-F8 function keys to be configured.
  Therefore, the following keyboard mappings apply to VT100 terminals:

HP or Wyse60	VT100 or HP 700/60 in VT100 mode
F1	PF2 (1)
F2	PF1 (1)
F3	spacebar
F4	PF3, spacebar or PF3, = (1)
F5	Return
F6	none
F7	none
F8	none

    (1) See the "Configuration: HP 700/60 in DEC mode, or DEC
         terminals with PC-AT-type keyboard" subsection below.

See the comments on softkeys and TAB keys in the "VT320 Terminal Support" subsection above.

Configuration: HP 700/60 Terminal in DEC Mode, or DEC Terminal with PC-AT-Type Keyboard
  Customers using the following configuration may want to be aware of the following keyboard difference.

It may be possible for a user with the "HP 700/60 terminal in DEC mode, or DEC terminal with PC-AT-type keyboard" configuration to be told to press function key F1 through F4 to achieve some desired result. For an HP 700/60 terminal in DEC mode or DEC terminals, these functions keys may be mapped onto PF1-PF4 keys. However, the PC-AT-type keyboard does not provide PF1-PF4 keys, as does the DEC/ANSI keyboard.

Key	Maps to
Num Lock	PF1
/	PF2
*	PF3
-	PF4

The Num Lock, /, *, and - keys are located on the keyboard, in a row above the number pad on the right side of the keyboard. Please note that although this keyboard is called a PC-AT-type keyboard, it is supplied by HP. A PC-AT-type keyboard can be recognized by location of ESC key at the left-top of the keyboard.

Wyse60 Terminal Support
  On Wyse60, use the DEL key (located next to Backspace) to backspace.

On an HP 700/60 with a PC-AT-type keyboard in Wyse60 mode, the DEL key
is located in the bottom row on the number pad.

Wyse60 terminals provide a single line to display softkey labels
unlike HP terminals which provide two lines. Sometimes this may
result in truncated softkey labels. For example, the Help on Context
label for F1 may appear as Help on C. Some standard labels for
screen-oriented applications, such as SAM and swinstall are as
follows:

The SAM label:	May appear on the Wyse60 as:
Help On Context	Help On C
Select/Deselect	Select/D
Menubar on/off	Menubar

DEPENDENCIES
     SAM runs in an X Window environment as well as on the following kinds
     of terminals or terminal emulators:

     -   HP-compatible terminal with programmable function keys and
         on-screen display of function key labels.

     -   VT-100 and VT-320

     -   WY30 and WY60

     Depending on what other applications are running concurrently with
     SAM, more swap space may be required. SAM requires the following
     amounts of internal memory:

     8 MB   If using terminal based version of SAM.
     16 MB   If using Motif X Window version of SAM.

     For more detailed information about how to use SAM on a terminal, see
     the System Administration Tasks manual.

AUTHOR
     sam was developed by HP.

FILES
     /etc/sam/custom   Directory where SAM stores user privileges.

     /etc/sam/rmfiles.excl   File containing a list of files and
                              directories that are excluded from removal by
                              SAM.

     /etc/sam/rmuser.excl   File containing a list of users that are
                              excluded from removal by SAM.

     /usr/sam/bin   Directory containing executable files, which
                              can be used outside of any SAM session.

     /usr/sam/help/$LANG   Directory containing SAM language specific
                              online help files.

     /usr/sam/lbin   Directory containing SAM executables, which
                              are intended only for use by SAM and are not
                              supported in any other context.

     /usr/sam/lib   Directory for internal configuration files.

/var/sam	Directory for working space, including lock files (if a SAM session dies, it may leave behind a spurious lock file), preferences, logging, and temporary files.
/var/sam/log/samlog	File containing unformatted SAM logging messages. This file should not be modified by users. Use samlog_viewer to view the contents of this file (see samlog_viewer(1M)).
/var/sam/log/samlog.old	Previous SAM log file. This file is created by SAM when /var/sam/log/samlog is larger than the user specified limit. Use samlog_viewer with its -f option to view the contents of this file (see samlog_viewer(1M)).

SEE ALSO
     samlog_viewer(1M).

     System Administration Tasks
     Installing and Administering ARPA Services
     Installing and Administering LAN/9000
     Installing and Administering NFS Services
     Installing and Administering Network Services
     Installing and Administering X.25/9000
     How HP-UX Works: Concepts for the System Administrator

CHAPTER 5

Introduction to HP-UX
Performance Tools

Where Are Your HP-UX System Resources Going?

In this chapter, I'll cover some techniques for determining how your HP-UX system resources are being used. Once you review the examples in this chapter, you can try some of these techniques on your system(s) to view the way in which system resources are being used. Most of the examples in this chapter use systems running HP-UX 11.x. Some examples use HP-UX 10.x; however, the same principles apply to all releases of HP-UX.

Everyone likes setting up new systems and the excitement of seeing the system run for the first time. With system setup, you get a great deal in return for your investment of time. With an instant ignition system, for instance, you spend a short amount of time in setup and you get a big return - your system is up and running. Similarly, when you perform routine system administration functions with SAM, you spend a short time running SAM and you end up completing a vital task, such as adding a user or performing a system backup.

In Chapter 1, I described a process whereby you spend about two hours unpacking boxes and connecting cables, and then you turn on the power and your system boots. You've done a lot in a short time and it feels great. At this point, it's not even lunch time, and you can justify taking off the rest of the day!

If a new user were to walk up to your desk and ask you for an account, you say that you would be happy to do so but this is a complex process that will take a while. Then you run SAM and in about 30 seconds the new user is added to the system! Again, you're quite pleased with yourself for having done so much so quickly.

In this chapter we get into some of the "gray" areas of system administration. System resource utilization and performance monitoring are less straightforward endeavors than others covered, such as system setup and SAM. You play detective some of the time when determining how systems resources are being used, and sometimes you guess at what is taking place. That's the reason I think this gray part is where the fun begins.

When determining where system resources are going, I often find system administrators dealing with their computer systems as *systems* for the first time. Computer systems are too often thought of as independent components. What may look like the source of a system bottleneck may just be a symptom of some other problem. Keep in mind that components of the system work together; a small problem in one area may manifest itself as a bigger problem in other areas. I'll provide some examples of what to look for throughout this chapter, but keep in mind that your system is indeed unique. You have to consider your environment as you use the tools described here.

Understanding where your HP-UX system resources are going is indeed an art. You have great built-in HP-UX commands such as **iostat** and **vmstat**. Also, some fine performance monitoring tools such as HP Glance-Plus/UX and HP PerfView help you. Which tools you use and how you use them are not as clean and orderly as the topics covered earlier.

Why is it so difficult to determine where your system resources are going if there are so many great tools to assist you? To begin, this is the information age. No one knows better than those of us who deal with information systems that the problem is there is too much information. This can be the problem when you try to determine where your system resources are going. You may end up gathering information about your system in off-hours when it is not in use, thereby getting meaningless results. You may end up with long accounting reports with too much data to digest. You may end up with so many network statistics that a fleet of system administrators wouldn't have time to analyze them, let alone one overworked, albeit enthusiastic, administrator.

Since every system and every network are different, I can't recommend just one approach for determining where your system resources are going. I can recommend, however, that you understand all the tools I cover here and then determine which are best suited for your environment. You may decide that you can get all the information you need from the built-in HP-UX commands. You may, on the other hand, determine that you need the best performance tools available. Once you know what each of these techniques does and does not offer, you will be in a much better position to make this decision.

System Components

Now the big question: *What are the components of your system?* At one time, we viewed the components of a system as:

- **CPU**
- **Memory**
- **I/O**

Well, like all other things in this world, system components have become more complex. All the components of your system work together, or in some cases, against one another. You must, therefore, take an inventory of system components before you can begin to determine how your system resources are being used. Here is a more current list of system components:

1. Applications

- **local** - These applications run locally and don't rely on other systems for either the applications or data.

- **remote** - These are applications that either run remotely or are copied from a remote system to a local system and then run locally. I consider both of these to be remote applications, because an application that has to be copied to the local system before it is run consumes a lot of networking resources, sometimes more than an application that runs remotely would consume.

- **license servers** - Many applications require license servers to be running to ensure that you have a license available for a user who wants to run an application. In a distributed environment, you may have an application with several license servers running, so that if one or two license servers go down, you still have a third license server running. Because you can have many license servers running for many applications, these may be consuming substantial system resources.

2. **Data** - Listing your data as a system resource may be a surprise to you. I think, however, that since most computers and applications are a means to create the data that keeps your company in business, you should indeed consider it a system resource. In some cases, system and database administrators spend many hours planning how data will be stored in order to achieve the fastest response time. In a distributed engineering application, the location and number of data servers can have a major impact on overall system and network performance. In this respect, data is indeed a system resource.

- **local data** - On a local system, consumes primarily system resources.

- **remote data** - On a remote system, consumes resources on the local system, remote system, and network.

3. **Windowing environment and user interface**

- **X, Motif, HP CDE** - You will want to take a close look at the amount of system resources that can be consumed by X, Motif, and HP CDE. Later in this chapter, when we look at programs that are consuming system resources, you will see the substantial impact these programs have.

4. **Networking** - Networking is the perceived or real bottleneck in more and more installations. Because of the increasing demand placed on networking resources by client/server applications and other distributed environments, you need to have an understanding of the amount of networking resources your system is consuming and how busy your network is in general. Because I don't cover such advanced network management tools as HP OpenView in this book, we are going to take a look at the commands you can issue to see how busy the network interface is on a particular system and get an idea of the overall amount of traffic on the network.

5. **CPU** - Of course the CPU is a system resource. I just chose not to list it first because until you know how your system is set up in terms of applications, data, user interface, and so on, it is pointless to start looking at the CPU.

6. **Memory** - Memory is the system resource that I find most often needs to be increased. What sometimes looks to be a shortage of CPU capacity sometimes turns out to be a lack of memory.

7. **Input/Output (I/O)** - The real question with I/O as a system resource is how long does it take to get my applications or data to and from disk. We'll look at various ways to see what kind of I/O activity you have going on.

Commands and Tools for Determining How System Resources Are Being Used

You can take a variety of approaches to determine how system resources are being used. These choices range from quick snapshots that take but a few seconds to create, to long-range capacity planning programs that you may want to run for weeks or months before you even begin to analyze the data they produce. Figure 5-1 shows the level of data produced by some of the possible approaches to determining how your system resources are being consumed.

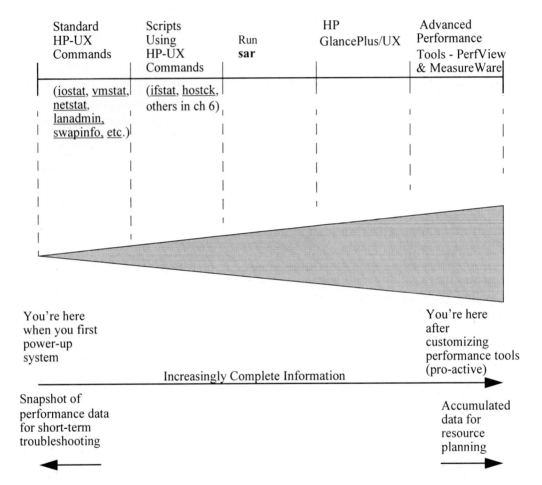

Standard HP-UX Commands	Scripts Using HP-UX Commands	Run **sar**	HP GlancePlus/UX	Advanced Performance Tools - PerfView & MeasureWare
(iostat, vmstat, netstat, lanadmin, swapinfo, etc.)	(ifstat, hostck, others in ch 6)			

You're here when you first power-up system

You're here after customizing performance tools (pro-active)

Increasingly Complete Information

Snapshot of performance data for short-term troubleshooting

Accumulated data for resource planning

Figure 5-1 Methods of Determining How System Resources Are Used

Figure 5-1 shows some commonly used techniques for determining how system resources are being used. We'll cover some of these techniques, including the following:

1. Introducing some standard HP-UX commands that give you information about system resources. These are also embedded in some scripts that are included in Chapter 6, the shell programming chapter.

2. Running **sar**, the system activity reporter.

3. Using the performance monitoring tool HP GlancePlus/UX.

4. Running HP MeasureWare and HP PerfView.

I provide summaries and examples of using many HP-UX commands in this chapter. A great deal more detail can be found in the manual pages for these commands. I provide the full manual pages at the end of this chapter for many of the commands covered.

These approaches are covered in upcoming sections.

Taking Inventory

In an existing computing environment it is essential to first take an inventory of your computing resources before you begin to determine the level of system resources. The minimum you should include in this inventory are the system resources I listed earlier in this chapter (applications, data, user interface, etc.), so you will know how your network is set up before you begin to determine how your system resources are being used.

I will show examples of systems and portions of networks throughout this chapter. In order to show how system resources are being used, it is essential to know the system components you are dealing with, especially if they are scattered among systems in a distributed environment.

With existing networks, this may be a long and painful process, but a process that is well worth the time. A network that has evolved over the course of 20 years will have vast inefficiencies in it that will become apparent immediately upon taking inventory. I have been asked to help improve the performance of such networks, and after taking inventory, I have developed a list of ways to improve the performance of systems without issuing a single HP-UX command! When you see a user's home directory on one system, her application on another, her data on a third, her application's license server on a fourth, and all these systems on different subnets, you can quickly develop ways to improve system performance.

You may find some similarities between the examples I use in this chapter and your own computing environment. In any event, I suggest that you take an inventory of what you have, if you haven't already done so.

There are degrees to which you can take an inventory. You may choose a high-level inventory with little detail that is simply a drawing of your network including systems and major software. A highly detailed inventory, on the other hand, might be a detailed network diagram including all of the hardware components of which each system is comprised and a detailed list of software including what data is located on what disks and so on. The granularity of your inventory depends on what you would like to accomplish. If your goal is to visualize what systems are used for which purpose, then a high-level network diagram may be sufficient. If you need to troubleshoot a disk I/O problem, then you may need to produce a detailed inventory of a system, including what files and directories are located on each disk.

Standard HP-UX Commands

To begin, let's look at some commands you can issue from the HP-UX prompt to give you some information about your system. The commands I'll cover are:

- **iostat**
- **vmstat**
- **netstat**
- **lanadmin**
- **ps**
- **swapinfo**
- **showmount** and **mount**
- **sar**

We'll first look at each of these commands so that you get an understanding of the output produced by each and of how this output may be used. Later in the chapter, we'll then use some of these commands in conjunction with HP GlancePlus/UX to help uncover an interesting performance problem. The HP-UX manual pages for these commands appear at the end of the chapter.

I/O and CPU Statistics with iostat

The **iostat** command gives you an indication of the level of effort the CPU is putting into I/O and the amount of I/O taking place among your disks and terminals. The following example shows the **iostat** command, which will be executed every 10 times at five-second intervals, and associated output from an HP-UX system. The "#" shown is the HP-UX prompt.

```
# iostat 5 10

    device      bps      sps     msps

    c0t6d0        0      0.0      1.0
    c5t4d0        0      0.0      1.0
    c4t5d0        0      0.0      1.0
    c4t5d1        0      0.0      1.0
    c5t4d1        0      0.0      1.0
    c5t4d2        0      0.0      1.0
    c5t4d3        0      0.0      1.0

    c0t6d0        0      0.0      1.0
    c5t4d0       78      5.7      1.0
    c4t5d0        0      0.0      1.0
    c4t5d1      716     50.5      1.0
    c5t4d1        0      0.0      1.0
    c5t4d2        0      0.0      1.0
    c5t4d3        0      0.0      1.0

    c0t6d0        0      0.0      1.0
    c5t4d0      148     12.5      1.0
    c4t5d0        0      0.0      1.0
    c4t5d1      722     58.1      1.0
    c5t4d1        0      0.0      1.0
    c5t4d2       10      1.2      1.0
    c5t4d3        0      0.0      1.0

    c0t6d0        0      0.0      1.0
    c5t4d0      216     15.9      1.0
    c4t5d0        0      0.0      1.0
    c4t5d1      752     62.4      1.0
    c5t4d1        0      0.0      1.0
```

```
c5t4d2       0      0.0      1.0
c5t4d3       0      0.0      1.0

c0t6d0      31      3.8      1.0
c5t4d0     166     12.7      1.0
c4t5d0       0      0.0      1.0
c4t5d1     661     64.8      1.0
c5t4d1       0      0.0      1.0
c5t4d2       0      0.0      1.0
c5t4d3       0      0.0      1.0

c0t6d0      68      8.5      1.0
c5t4d0     184     13.7      1.0
c4t5d0       0      0.0      1.0
c4t5d1     661     65.7      1.0
c5t4d1       0      0.0      1.0
c5t4d2       6      0.6      1.0
c5t4d3       0      0.0      1.0

c0t6d0       2      0.2      1.0
c5t4d0     115      8.3      1.0
c4t5d0       0      0.0      1.0
c4t5d1     197     15.3      1.0
c5t4d1       0      0.0      1.0
c5t4d2      11      1.2      1.0
c5t4d3       0      0.0      1.0

c0t6d0      36      5.1      1.0
c5t4d0     133     14.3      1.0
c4t5d0       0      0.0      1.0
c4t5d1     103     10.1      1.0
c5t4d1       0      0.0      1.0
c5t4d2       0      0.0      1.0
c5t4d3       0      0.0      1.0

c0t6d0      53      5.3      1.0
c5t4d0     108     11.8      1.0
c4t5d0       0      0.0      1.0
c4t5d1      91     10.8      1.0
c5t4d1       0      0.0      1.0
c5t4d2       3      0.4      1.0
c5t4d3       0      0.0      1.0

c0t6d0       0      0.0      1.0
c5t4d0      25      3.5      1.0
c4t5d0       0      0.0      1.0
c4t5d1      31      3.5      1.0
c5t4d1       0      0.0      1.0
```

```
c5t4d2       0      0.0      1.0
c5t4d3       0      0.0      1.0
```

The next **iostat** example includes the **-t** option, which adds terminal and CPU information to the output.

```
# iostat -t 5 5


                               tty     cpu
                       tin tout us  ni  sy   id
                         0    3 17   0   3   80

        device    bps    sps    msps

        c0t6d0      0    0.0     1.0
        c5t4d0      0    0.0     1.0
        c4t5d0      0    0.0     1.0
        c4t5d1      0    0.0     1.0
        c5t4d1      0    0.0     1.0
        c5t4d2      0    0.0     1.0
        c5t4d3      0    0.0     1.0


                               tty     cpu
                       tin tout us  ni  sy   id
                         0    0 30   0  12   58

        device    bps    sps    msps

        c0t6d0      0    0.0     1.0
        c5t4d0     20    2.4     1.0
        c4t5d0      0    0.0     1.0
        c4t5d1     26    2.4     1.0
        c5t4d1      0    0.0     1.0
        c5t4d3      0    0.0     1.0


                               tty     cpu
                       tin tout us  ni  sy   id
                         0    0 36   0  14   51

        device    bps    sps    msps
```

```
c0t6d0        2       0.2       1.0
c5t4d0       33       3.9       1.0
c4t5d0        0       0.0       1.0
c4t5d1       48       4.9       1.0
c5t4d1        0       0.0       1.0
c5t4d2        1       0.2       1.0
c5t4d3        0       0.0       1.0


                                 tty     cpu
                     tin  tout  us   ni   sy   id
                       0     0  25    0   12   64

device      bps     sps     msps

c5t4d0        6      1.0      1.0
c4t5d0        0      0.0      1.0
c4t5d1       17      2.2      1.0
c5t4d1        0      0.0      1.0
c5t4d3        0      0.0      1.0


                                 tty     cpu
                     tin  tout  us   ni   sy   id
                       0     0  31    0   13   56

device      bps     sps     msps

c5t4d0       11      1.4      1.0
c4t5d0        0      0.0      1.0
c4t5d1       14      1.6      1.0
c5t4d1        0      0.0      1.0
c5t4d2        3      0.4      1.0
c5t4d3        0      0.0      1.0
```

Here are descriptions of the reports you receive with **iostat** for terminals, the CPU, and mounted file systems.

For every terminal you have connected (tty), you see a "tin" and "tout," which represent the number of characters read from your terminal and the number of characters written to your terminal, respectively.

For your CPU, you see the percentage of time spent in user mode ("us"), the percentage of time spent running user processes at a low priority called nice ("ni"), the percentage of time spent in system mode ("sy"), and the percentage of time the CPU is idle ("id").

For every locally mounted file system, you receive information on the kilobytes transferred per second ("bps"), number of seeks per second ("sps"), and number of milliseconds per average seek ("msps"). For disks that are NFS-mounted or disks on client nodes of your server, you will not receive a report; **iostat** reports only on locally mounted file systems.

When viewing the output of **iostat**, there are some parameters to take note of.

First, note the time your CPU is spending in the four categories shown. The CPU report is produced with the **-t** option. I have worked on systems with poor performance that the administrator assumed to be a result of a slow CPU when the "id" number was very high, indicating that the CPU was actually idle most of the time. If the CPU is mostly idle, the chances are that the bottleneck is not the CPU but may be I/O, memory, or networking. If the CPU is indeed busy most of the time ("id" is very low), see if any processes are running "nice" (check the "ni" number). It may be that there are some background processes consuming a lot of CPU time that can be changed to run "nice."

Second, compare the milliseconds per average seek ("msps") for all the disks you have mounted. If you have three identical disks mounted, yet the "msps" for one of the disks is substantially higher than the others, then you may be overworking it while the others remain mostly idle. If so, distribute the work load evenly among your disks so that you get as close to the same number of accesses per disk as possible. Note that a slower disk will always have a higher "msps" than a faster disk, so put your most often accessed information on your faster disks. The "msps" for a disk is usually around 20 milliseconds, as in all three disks (1s0, 4s0, and 6s0) in the last example. A CD-ROM would have a much higher msps of approximately 200 milliseconds.

Virtual Memory Statistics with vmstat

vmstat provides virtual memory statistics. It provides information on the status of processes, virtual memory, paging activity, faults, and the breakdown of the percentage of CPU time. In the following example, the output was produced nine times at five-second intervals. The first argument to the **vmstat** command is the interval; the second is the number of times you would like output produced:

```
# vmstat 5 9

procs         memory                     page                        faults          cpu
r  b  w    avm    free   re  at  pi  po  fr  de  sr    in      sy    cs  us sy id
5 240 0 17646    3979    2   0   0   0   0   0   0     0     778   193  17  3 80
4 242 0 16722    4106    0   0   0   0   0   0   0   814   20649   258  89 10  2
4 240 0 16649    4106    0   0   0   0   0   0   0    83   18384   218  91  9  0
4 240 0 16468    4106    0   0   0   0   0   0   0   792   19552   273  89 11  1
5 239 0 15630    4012    9   0   0   0   0   0   0   804   18295   270  93  8 -1
5 241 0 16087    3934    6   0   0   0   0   0   0   920   21044   392  89 10  0
5 241 0 15313    3952   11   0   0   0   0   0   0   968   20239   431  90 10  0
4 242 0 16577    4043    3   0   0   0   0   0   0   926   19230   409  89 10  0
6 238 0 17453    4122    0   0   0   0   0   0   0   837   19269   299  89  9  2
```

You will get more out of the **vmstat** command than you want. Here is a brief description of the categories of information produced by **vmstat**.

Processes are classified into one of three categories: runnable ("r"), blocked on I/O or short-term resources ("b"), or swapped ("w").

Next you will see information about memory. "avm" is the number of virtual memory pages owned by processes that have run within the last 20 seconds. If this number is roughly the size of physical memory minus your kernel, then you are near paging. The "free" column indicates the number of pages on the system's free list. It doesn't mean that the process is finished running and these pages won't be accessed again; it just means that they have not been accessed recently. I suggest that you ignore this column.

Next is paging activity. The first field ("re") is particularly useful. It shows the pages that were reclaimed. These pages made it to the free list but were later referenced and had to be salvaged. Check to see that "re" is a low number. If you are reclaiming pages that were thought to be free by the system, then you are wasting valuable time salvaging these. Reclaiming pages is also a symptom that you are short on memory.

Next you see the number of faults in three categories: interrupts per second, which usually come from hardware ("in"), system calls per second ("sy"), and context switches per second ("cs").

The final output is CPU usage percentage for user ("us"), system ("sy"), and idle ("id"). This is not as complete as the **iostat** output, which also shows **nice** entries.

You want to verify that the runnable processes ("r") value is higher than the blocked ("b") value and the runnable but swapped ("w") processes value. If too many processes are blocked and swapped, your users will get a slower response time. In the example we'll review later in this chapter, you'll see many swapped ("w") processes and no runnable ("r") or blocked ("b") processes, indicating that a great deal of swapping is taking place.

Whenever you see entries in the blocked ("b") or runnable but swapped ("w") columns, you see evidence that processes are standing still. You want to identify the source of the blocked and runnable but swapped processes. The reason will usually be insufficient RAM in your system. Swapped processes are those that have been moved from RAM to disk in an effort to free up RAM for other processes. You may want to look at GlancePlus to do more detailed troubleshooting of memory under the "Memory Detail" screen.

Network Statistics with netstat

netstat provides information related to network statistics. Since network bandwidth has as much to do with performance as the CPU and memory in some networks, you want to get an idea of the level of network traffic you have.

I use two forms of **netstat** to obtain network statistics. The first is **netstat -i**, which shows the state of interfaces that are autoconfigured. Since I am most often interested in getting a summary of lan0, I issue this command. Although **netstat -i** gives a good rundown of lan0, such as the network it is on, its name, and so on, it does not show useful statistical information.

The following diagram shows the output of **netstat -i**:

```
# netstat -i
```

Name	Mtu	Network	Address	Ipkts	Ierrs	Opkts	Oerrs	Col
lan0	1497	151.150	a4410.e.h.c	242194	120	107665	23	19884

netstat doesn't provide as much extraneous information as **iostat** and **vmstat**. Put another way, most of what you get from **netstat** is useful. Here is a description of the nine fields in the **netstat** example:

Name
: The name of your network interface (Name), in this case, "lan0."

Mtu
: The "maximum transmission unit," which is the maximum packet size sent by the interface card.

Network
: The network address of the LAN to which the interface card is connected (151.150).

Address
: The host name of your system. This is the symbolic name of your system as it appears in the **/etc/hosts** file.

Below is the statistical information. Depending on the system you are using, you may not see some of these commands:

Ipkts
: The number of packets received by the interface card, in this case, "lan0."

Ierrs
: The number of errors detected on incoming packets by the interface card.

Opkts
: The number of packets transmitted by the interface card.

Oerrs
: The number of errors detected during the transmission of packets by the interface card.

Col
: The number of collisions that resulted from packet traffic.

netstat provides cumulative data since the node was last powered up; you might have a long elapsed time over which data was accumulated. If you are interested in seeing useful statistical information, you can use **netstat** with different options. You can also specify an interval to report statistics. I usually ignore the first entry since it shows all data since the system was last powered up. This means that the data includes non-prime hours when the system was idle. I prefer to view data at the time the system is working its hardest. This second **netstat** example provides network interface information every five seconds.

```
# netstat -I lan0 5
```

(lan0)-> input		output			(Total)-> input		output		
packets	errs	packets	errs	colls	packets	errs	packets	errs	colls
269841735	27	256627585	1	5092223	281472199	27	268258048	1	5092223
1602	0	1238	0	49	1673	0	1309	0	49
1223	0	1048	0	25	1235	0	1060	0	25
1516	0	1151	0	42	1560	0	1195	0	42
1553	0	1188	0	17	1565	0	1200	0	17
2539	0	2180	0	44	2628	0	2269	0	44
3000	0	2193	0	228	3000	0	2193	0	228
2959	0	2213	0	118	3003	0	2257	0	118
2423	0	1981	0	75	2435	0	1993	0	75

With this example, you get multiple outputs of what is taking place on the LAN interface, including the totals on the right side of the output. As I mentioned earlier, you may want to ignore the first output, since it includes information over a long time period. This may include a time when your network was idle and therefore the data may not be important to you.

You can specify the network interface on which you want statistics reported by using **-I interface**; in the case of the example, it was **-I lan0**. An interval of five seconds was also used in this example.

Analyzing **netstat** statistical information is intuitive. You want to verify that the collisions (Colls) are much lower than the packets transmitted (Opkts). Collisions occur on output from your LAN interface. Every collision your LAN interface encounters slows down the network. You will get varying opinions on what is too many collisions. If your collisions are less than 5 percent of "Opkts," you're probably in good shape and better off spending your time analyzing some other system resource. If this number is high, you may want to consider segmenting your network in some way such as by installing networking equipment between portions of the network that don't share a lot of data.

As a rule of thumb, if you reduce the number of packets you are receiving and transmitting ("Ipkts" and "Opkts"), then you will have less overall network traffic and fewer collisions. Keep this in mind as you plan your network or upgrades to your systems. You may want to have two LAN cards in systems that are in constant communication. That way, these systems have a "private" LAN over which to communicate and do not adversely affect the performance of other systems on the network. One LAN interface on each system is devoted to intrasystem communication. This provides a "tight" communication path among systems that usually act as servers. The second LAN interface is used to communicate with any systems that are usually clients on a larger network.

You can also obtain information related to routing with **netstat** (see Chapter 2). The **-r** option to **netstat** shows the routing tables, which you usually want to know, and the **-n** option can be used to print network addresses as numbers rather than as names. In the following examples, **netstat** is issued with the **-r** option (this will be used when describing the **netstat** output) and the **-rn** options so that you can compare the two outputs.

$ netstat -r

Routing tables

Destination	Gateway	Flags	Refs	Use	Interface	Pmtu
hp700	localhost	UH	0	28	lo0	4608
default	router1	UG	0	0	lan0	4608
128.185.61	system1	U	347	28668	lan0	1500

$ netstat -rn

Routing tables

Destination	Gateway	Flags	Refs	Use	Interface	Pmtu
127.0.0.1	127.0.0.1	UH	0	28	lo0	4608
default	128.185.61.1	UG	0	0	lan0	4608
128.185.61	128.185.61.2	U	347	28668	lan0	1500

With **netstat**, some information is provided about the router, which is the middle entry. The **-r** option shows information about routing but there are many other useful options to this command. Of particular interest in this output is "Flags," which defines the type of routing that takes place. Here are descriptions of the most common flags from the HP-UX manual pages.

1=U	Route to a *network* via a gateway that is the local host itself.
3=UG	Route to a *network* via a gateway that is the remote host.
5=UH	Route to a *host* via a gateway that is the local host itself.
7=UGH	Route to a *host* via a remote gateway that is a host.

The first line is for the local host or loopback interface called **lo0** at address 127.0.0.1 (you can see this address in the **netstat -rn** example). The UH flags indicate the destination address is the local host itself. This class A address allows a client and server on the same host to communicate with one another with TCP/IP. A datagram sent to the loopback interface won't go out onto the network; it will simply go through the loopback.

The second line is for the default route. This entry says to send packets to router1 if a more specific route can't be found. In this case the router has a UG under Flags. Some routers are configured with a U; others, such as the one in this example, with a UG. I've found that I usually end up determining through trial and error whether a U or UG is required. If there is a U in Flags and I am unable to ping a system on the other side of a router, a UG usually fixes the problem.

The third line is for the system's network interface **lan0**. This means to use this network interface for packets to be sent to 128.185.61.

Network Statistics with lanadmin

/usr/sbin/lanadmin provides additional information related to network statistics. When you run **lanadmin,** a menu appears that gives you the option to perform various functions, one of which is to display information related to the LAN interface. The following shows the output of **lanadmin** when this option is selected.

```
# lanadmin

              LOCAL AREA NETWORK ONLINE ADMINISTRATION, Version 1.0
                          Wed, May 6  16:03:53

                    Copyright 1994 Hewlett Packard Company.
                          All rights are reserved.

Test Selection mode.

        lan      = LAN Interface Administration
        menu     = Display this menu
        quit     = Terminate the Administration
        terse    = Do not display command menu
        verbose  = Display command menu

Enter command: lan

LAN Interface test mode. LAN Interface Net Mgmt ID = 4

        clear    = Clear statistics registers
        display  = Display LAN Interface status and statistics registers
        end      = End LAN Interface Administration, return to Test Selection
        menu     = Display this menu
        nmid     = Network Management ID of the LAN Interface
        quit     = Terminate the Administration, return to shell
        reset    = Reset LAN Interface to execute its selftest

Enter command: display
                        LAN INTERFACE STATUS DISPLAY
                          Wed, May 6  16:03:57

Network Management ID              = 4
Description                        = lan1 Hewlett-Packard 10/100Base-TX Half-Duplex
 Hw Rev 0
Type (value)                       = ethernet-csmacd(6)
MTU Size                           = 1500
Speed                              = 10000000
Station Address                    = 0x80009d91067
Administration Status (value)      = up(1)
Operation Status (value)           = down(2)
Last Change                        = 0
Inbound Octets                     = 0
Inbound Unicast Packets            = 0
Inbound Non-Unicast Packets        = 0
Inbound Discards                   = 0
Inbound Errors                     = 0
Inbound Unknown Protocols          = 0
Outbound Octets                    = 0
Outbound Unicast Packets           = 0
Outbound Non-Unicast Packets       = 0
Outbound Discards                  = 0
Outbound Errors                    = 0
Outbound Queue Length              = 0
Specific                           = 655367

Press <Return> to continue
```

```
Ethernet-like Statistics Group

Index                          = 4
Alignment Errors               = 0
FCS Errors                     = 0
Single Collision Frames        = 0
Multiple Collision Frames      = 0
Deferred Transmissions         = 0
Late Collisions                = 0
Excessive Collisions           = 0
Internal MAC Transmit Errors   = 0
Carrier Sense Errors           = 0
Frames Too Long                = 0
Internal MAC Receive Errors    = 0


LAN Interface test mode. LAN Interface Net Mgmt ID = 4

        clear    = Clear statistics registers
        display  = Display LAN Interface status and statistics registers
        end      = End LAN Interface Administration, return to Test Selection
        menu     = Display this menu
        nmid     = Network Management ID of the LAN Interface
        quit     = Terminate the Administration, return to shell
        reset    = Reset LAN Interface to execute its selftest

Enter command: quit
#
```

lanadmin gives more detailed information about the LAN interface than **netstat**. The type of interface, Maximum Transfer Unit (MTU), speed, administration and operation status (a quick way to see whether your interface is up), and the LAN interface address in hex. The hex address is often used when access codes are generated for application software or for generating client kernels.

lanadmin also gives much more detailed error information. Although any error slows down your network, having more detailed information on the types of errors and collisions may be helpful in troubleshooting a problem.

With **lanadmin**, you can also "reset" the network interface an option that is sometimes helpful when the network interface doesn't seem to be working, such as when the LAN interface does not **ping** itself.

Check Processes with ps

To find the answer to "What is my system doing?," use **ps -ef**. This command provides information about every running process on your system. If, for instance, you want to know whether NFS is running, you simply type **ps -ef** and look for NFS daemons. Although **ps** tells you every process that is running on your system, it doesn't provide a good summary of the level of system resources being consumed. The other commands I have covered to this point are superior resource assessment commands. On the other hand, I would guess that **ps** is the most often issued system administration command. There are a number of options you can use with **ps**. I normally use **e** and **f**, which provide information about every ("**e**") running process and lists this information in full ("**f**"). The following example is a partial **ps -ef** listing.

```
# ps -ef
```

```
  UID    PID  PPID C  STIME   TTY   TIME    COMMAND
  root     0     0  0  Mar  9   ?   107:28 swapper
  root     1     0  0  Mar  9   ?     2:27 init
  root     2     0  0  Mar  9   ?    14:13 vhand
  root     3     0  0  Mar  9   ?   114:55 statdaemon
  root     4     0  0  Mar  9   ?     5:57 unhashdaemon
  root     7     0  0  Mar  9   ?   154:33 ttisr
  root    70     0  0  Mar  9   ?     0:01 lvmkd
  root    71     0  0  Mar  9   ?     0:01 lvmkd
  root    72     0  0  Mar  9   ?     0:01 lvmkd
  root    13     0  0  Mar  9   ?     9:54 vx_sched_thread
  root    14     0  0  Mar  9   ?     1:54 vx_iflush_thread
  root    15     0  0  Mar  9   ?     2:06 vx_ifree_thread
  root    16     0  0  Mar  9   ?     2:27 vx_inactive_cache_thread
  root    17     0  0  Mar  9   ?     0:40 vx_delxwri_thread
  root    18     0  0  Mar  9   ?     0:33 vx_logflush_thread
  root    19     0  0  Mar  9   ?     0:07 vx_attrsync_thread
                           .
                           .
                           .
  root    69     0  0  Mar  9   ?     0:09 vx_inactive_thread
  root    73     0  0  Mar  9   ?     0:01 lvmkd
  root    74     0 19  Mar  9   ?  3605:29 netisr
  root    75     0  0  Mar  9   ?     0:18 netisr
  root    76     0  0  Mar  9   ?     0:17 netisr
  root    77     0  0  Mar  9   ?     0:14 netisr
  root    78     0  0  Mar  9   ?     0:48 nvsisr
  root    79     0  0  Mar  9   ?     0:00 supsched
  root    80     0  0  Mar  9   ?     0:00 smpsched
  root    81     0  0  Mar  9   ?     0:00 smpsched
  root    82     0  0  Mar  9   ?     0:00 sblksched
  root    83     0  0  Mar  9   ?     0:00 sblksched
  root    84     0  0  Mar  9   ?     0:00 strmem
  root    85     0  0  Mar  9   ?     0:00 strweld
  root  3730     1  0 16:39:22 console  0:00 /usr/sbin/getty console console
  root   404     1  0  Mar  9   ?     3:57 /usr/sbin/swagentd
oracle   919     1  0 15:23:23  ?     0:00 oraclegprd (LOCAL=NO)
  root   289     1  2  Mar  9   ?    78:34 /usr/sbin/syncer
  root   426     1  0  Mar  9   ?     0:10 /usr/sbin/syslogd -D
  root   576     1  0  Mar  9   ?     0:00 /usr/sbin/portmap
  root   429     1  0  Mar  9   ?     0:00 /usr/sbin/ptydaemon
  root   590     1  0  Mar  9   ?     0:00 /usr/sbin/biod 4
  root   442     1  0  Mar  9   ?     0:00 /usr/lbin/nktl_daemon 0 0 0 0 0 1 -2
oracle  8145     1  0 12:02:48  ?     0:00 oraclegprd (LOCAL=NO)
```

```
root     591     1   0   Mar   9   ?     0:00 /usr/sbin/biod 4
root     589     1   0   Mar   9   ?     0:00 /usr/sbin/biod 4
root     592     1   0   Mar   9   ?     0:00 /usr/sbin/biod 4
root     604     1   0   Mar   9   ?     0:00 /usr/sbin/rpc.lockd
root     598     1   0   Mar   9   ?     0:00 /usr/sbin/rpc.statd
root     610     1   0   Mar   9   ?     0:16 /usr/sbin/automount -f /etc/auto_master
root     638     1   0   Mar   9   ?     0:06 sendmail: accepting connections
root     618     1   0   Mar   9   ?     0:02 /usr/sbin/inetd
root     645     1   0   Mar   9   ?     5:01 /usr/sbin/snmpdm
root     661     1   0   Mar   9   ?    11:28 /usr/sbin/fddisubagtd
root     711     1   0   Mar   9   ?    30:59 /opt/dce/sbin/rpcd
root     720     1   0   Mar   9   ?     0:00 /usr/sbin/vtdaemon
root     867   777   1   Mar   9   ?     0:00 <defunct>
 lp      733     1   0   Mar   9   ?     0:00 /usr/sbin/lpsched
root     777     1   0   Mar   9   ?     8:55 DIAGMON
root     742     1   0   Mar   9   ?     0:15 /usr/sbin/cron
oracle  7880     1   0 11:43:47  ?     0:00 oraclegprd (LOCAL=NO)
root     842     1   0   Mar   9   ?     0:00 /usr/vue/bin/vuelogin
oracle  5625     1   0 07:00:14  ?     0:01 ora_smon_gprd
root     781     1   0   Mar   9   ?     0:00 /usr/sbin/envd
root     833   777   0   Mar   9   ?     0:00 DEMLOG   DEMLOG;DEMLOG;0;0;
root     813     1   0   Mar   9   ?     0:00 /usr/sbin/nfsd 4
root     807     1   0   Mar   9   ?     0:00 /usr/sbin/rpc.mountd
root     815   813   0   Mar   9   ?     0:00 /usr/sbin/nfsd 4
root     817   813   0   Mar   9   ?     0:00 /usr/sbin/nfsd 4
root     835   777   0   Mar   9   ?     0:13 PSMON   PSMON;PSMON;0;0;
```

Here is a brief description of the headings:

UID	The user ID of the process owner.
PID	The process ID. (You can use this number to kill the process.)
PPID	The process ID of the parent process.
C	Process utilization for scheduling.
STIME	Start time of the process.
TTY	The controlling terminal for the process.
TIME	The cumulative execution time for the process.
COMMAND	The command name and arguments.

ps gives a quick profile of the processes running on your system. If you issue the **ps** command and find that a process is hung, you can issue the **kill** command. **kill** is a utility that sends a signal to the process you identify. The most common signal to send is "SIGKILL" which terminates the process. There are other signals you can send to the process, but SIGKILL is the most common. As an alternative to sending the signal, you could send the corresponding signal number. The **kill** described here is **/usr/bin/**

kill or **kill** from the default POSIX shell in HP-UX. The other shells also have **kill** commands. A list of signal numbers and corresponding signals is shown next.

Signal number	Signal
0	SIGNULL
1	SIGHUP
2	SIGINT
3	SIGQUIT
9	SIGKILL
15	SIGTERM
24	SIGSTOP
25	SIGTSTP
26	SIGCONT

To kill the last process shown in this **ps** example, you would issue the following command:

```
$ kill -9 234
     |    |   |
     |    |   |> process id (PID)
     |    |> signal number
     |> kill command to terminate the process
```

Show Remote Mounts with showmount

showmount is used to show all remote systems (clients) that have mounted a local file system. **showmount** is useful for determining the file systems that are most often mounted by clients with NFS. The output of **showmount** is particularly easy to read because it lists the host name and the directory that was mounted by the client.

NFS servers often end up serving many NFS clients that were not originally intended to be served. This situation ends up consuming additional HP-UX system resources on the NFS server, as well as additional network bandwidth. Keep in mind that any data transferred from an NFS server to an NFS client consumes network bandwidth and in some cases may be a substantial amount of bandwith if large files or applications are being transferred from the NFS server to the client. The following example is a partial output of **showmount** taken from a system that is used as an example later in this chapter.

```
# showmount -a

hp100.ct.mp.com:/applic

hp101.ct.mp.com:/applic

hp102.cal.mp.com:/applic

hp103.cal.mp.com:/applic

hp104.cal.mp.com:/applic

hp105.cal.mp.com:/applic

hp106.cal.mp.com:/applic

hp107.cal.mp.com:/applic

hp108.cal.mp.com:/applic

hp109.cal.mp.com:/applic

hp100.cal.mp.com:/usr/users

hp101.cal.mp.com:/usr/users

hp102.cal.mp.com:/usr/users

hp103.cal.mp.com:/usr/users

hp104.cal.mp.com:/usr/users

hp105.cal.mp.com:/usr/users

hp106.cal.mp.com:/usr/users

hp107.cal.mp.com:/usr/users

hp108.cal.mp.com:/usr/users

hp109.cal.mp.com:/usr/users
```

The three following options are available to the **showmount** command:

-a prints output in the format "name:directory," as shown above.
-d lists all the local directories that have been remotely
     mounted by clients.
-e prints a list of exported file systems.

The following are examples of **showmount -d** and **showmount -e**.

 # showmount -d

/applic

/usr/users

/usr/oracle

/usr/users/emp.data

/network/database

/network/users

/tmp/working

 # showmount -e

export list for server101.cal.mp.com

/applic

/usr/users

/cdrom

Show Swap with swapinfo

If your system has insufficient main memory for all of the information it needs to work with, it will move pages of information to your swap area or swap entire processes to your swap area. Pages that were most recently used are kept in main memory and those not recently used will be the first moved out of main memory.

I find that many system administrators spend an inordinate amount of time trying to determine what is the right amount of swap space for their system. This is *not* a parameter you want to leave to a rule of thumb. You can get a good estimate of the amount of swap you require by considering the following three factors:

1. How much swap is recommended by the application(s) you run? Use the swap size recommended by your applications. Application vendors tend to be realistic when recommending swap space. There is sometimes competition among application vendors to claim the lowest memory and CPU requirements in order to keep the overall cost of solutions as low as possible, but swap space recommendations are usually realistic.

2. How many applications will you run simultaneously? If you are running several applications, sum the swap space recommended for each application you plan to run simultaneously. If you have a database application that recommends 200 MBytes of swap and a development tool that recommends 100 MBytes of swap, then configure your system with 300 MBytes of swap minimum.

3. Will you be using substantial system resources on periphery functionality such as NFS? The nature of NFS is to provide access to file systems, some of which may be very large, so this may have an impact on your swap space requirements.

You can view the amount of swap being consumed on your system with **swapinfo**. The following is an example output of **swapinfo**.

```
# swapinfo

              Kb       Kb       Kb   PCT  START/      Kb
TYPE       AVAIL     USED     FREE  USED  LIMIT RESERVE  PRI  NAME
dev        49152    10532    38620   21%      0       -    1  /dev/vg00/lvol2
dev       868352    10888   759160    1%      0       -    1  /dev/vg00/lvol8
reserve        -   532360  -532360
memory    816360   469784   346576   58%
```

Following is a brief overview of what **swapinfo** gives you.

In the previous example, the "TYPE" field indicated whether the swap was "dev" for device, "reserve" for paging space on reserve, or "memory," which is RAM that can be used to hold pages if all the paging areas are in use.

"Kb AVAIL" is the total swap space available in 1024-byte blocks. This includes both used and unused swap.

"Kb USED" is the current number of 1024-byte blocks in use.

"Kb FREE" is the difference between "Kb AVAIL" and "Kb USED."

"PCT USED" is the "Kb USED" divided by "Kb AVAIL."

"START/LIMIT" is the block address of the start of the swap area.

"Kb RESERVE" is "-" for device swap or the number of 1024-byte blocks for file system swap.

"PRI" is the priority given to this swap area.

"NAME" is the device name for the swap device.

You can also issue the **swapinfo** command with a series of options. Here are some of the options you can include:

-m to display output of **swapinfo** in MBytes rather than in 1024-byte blocks.

-d prints information related to device swap areas only.

-f prints information about file system swap areas only.

sar: The System Activity Reporter

sar is another HP-UX command for gathering information about activities on your system. You can gather data over an extended time period with **sar** and later produce reports based on the data. The following are some useful options to **sar,** along with examples of reports produced with these options where applicable.

sar -o   Save data in a file specified by "o." After the file name, you would usually also enter the time interval for samples and the number of samples. The following example shows saving the binary data in file **/tmp/sar.data** at an interval of 60 seconds 300 times:

```
# sar -o /tmp/sar.data 60 300
```

The data in **/tmp/sar.data** can later be extracted from the file.

sar -f   Specify a file from which you will extract data.

sar -u   Report CPU utilization with headings %usr, %sys, %wio, %idle with some processes waiting for block I/O, %idle. This report is similar to the **iostat** and **vmstat** CPU reports. You extract the binary data saved in a file to get CPU information as shown in the following example. The following is a **sar -u** example:

```
# sar -u -f /tmp/sar.data


HP-UX system1 B.10.20 A 9000/859     04/28

12:52:04     %usr     %sys     %wio     %idle
12:53:04      62        4        5       29
12:54:04      88        5        3        4
12:55:04      94        5        1        0
12:56:04      67        4        4       25
12:57:04      59        4        4       32
12:58:04      61        4        3       32
12:59:04      65        4        3       28
13:00:04      62        5       16       17
13:01:04      59        5        9       27
13:02:04      71        4        3       22
13:03:04      60        4        4       32
13:04:04      71        5        4       20
13:05:04      80        6        8        7
13:06:04      56        3        3       37
13:07:04      57        4        4       36
13:08:04      66        4        4       26
13:09:04      80       10        2        8
13:10:04      73       10        2       15
13:11:04      64        6        3       28
13:12:04      56        4        3       38
13:13:04      55        3        3       38
13:14:04      57        4        3       36
13:15:04      70        4        5       21
13:16:04      65        5        9       21
13:17:04      62        6        2       30
13:18:04      60        5        3       33
13:19:04      77        3        4       16
13:20:04      76        5        3       15
                        .
                        .
                        .
14:30:04      50        6        6       38
14:31:04      57       12       19       12
14:32:04      51        8       20       21
14:33:04      41        4        9       46
14:34:04      43        4        9       45
14:35:04      38        4        6       53
14:36:04      38        9        7       46
14:37:04      46        3       11       40
14:38:04      43        4        7       46
14:39:04      37        4        5       54
```

```
14:40:04          33          4          5          58
14:41:04          40          3          3          53
14:42:04          44          3          3          50
14:43:04          27          3          7          64

Average           57          5          8          30
```

sar -b   Report buffer cache activity. A database application such as Oracle would recommend that you
use this option to see the effectiveness of buffer
cache use. You extract the binary data saved in a
file to get CPU information, as shown in the following example:

sar -b -f /tmp/sar.data

```
HP-UX system1 B.10.20 A 9000/859    04/28

12:52:04 bread/s lread/s %rcache bwrit/s lwrit/s %wcache pread/s pwrit/s
12:53:04       5     608      99       1      11      95       0       0
12:54:04       7     759      99       0      14      99       0       0
12:55:04       2    1733     100       4      24      83       0       0
12:56:04       1     836     100       1      18      96       0       0
12:57:04       0     623     100       2      21      92       0       0
12:58:04       0     779     100       1      16      96       0       0
12:59:04       0    1125     100       0      14      98       0       0
13:00:04       2    1144     100       9      89      89       0       0
13:01:04      10     898      99      11      76      86       0       0
13:02:04       0    1156     100       0      14      99       0       0
13:03:04       1     578     100       2      22      88       0       0
13:04:04       5    1251     100       0      12      99       0       0
13:05:04       3    1250     100       0      12      97       0       0
13:06:04       1     588     100       0      12      98       0       0
13:07:04       1     649     100       2      15      86       0       0
13:08:04       1     704     100       2      15      86       0       0
13:09:04       1    1068     100       0      18     100       0       0
13:10:04       0     737     100       1      44      99       0       0
13:11:04       0     735     100       1      13      95       0       0
13:12:04       0     589     100       1      15      93       0       0
13:13:04       0     573     100       0      16      99       0       0
13:14:04       1     756     100       1      16      91       0       0
13:15:04       1    1092     100       9      49      81       0       0
13:16:04       2     808     100       6      82      93       0       0
13:17:04       0     712     100       1       9      93       0       0
13:18:04       1     609     100       0      13      97       0       0
13:19:04       1     603     100       0      10      99       0       0
13:20:04       0    1127     100       0      14      98       0       0
                          .
                          .
```

```
14:30:04      2      542    100      1      22      94      0      0
14:31:04     10      852     99     12     137      92      0      0
14:32:04      2      730    100     10     190      95      0      0
14:33:04      4      568     99      2      26      91      0      0
14:34:04      4      603     99      1      13      91      0      0
14:35:04      1      458    100      1      13      89      0      0
14:36:04     13      640     98      1      24      98      0      0
14:37:04     21      882     98      1      18      95      0      0
14:38:04      7      954     99      0      19      98      0      0
14:39:04      3      620    100      1      11      94      0      0
14:40:04      3      480     99      2      15      85      0      0
14:41:04      1      507    100      0       9      98      0      0
14:42:04      1     1010    100      1      10      91      0      0
14:43:04      5      547     99      1       9      93      0      0

Average       3      782    100      3      37      91      0      0
```

sar -d   Report disk activity. You get the device name, percent that the device was busy, average number of requests outstanding for the device, number of data transfers per second for the device, and other information. You extract the binary data saved in a file to get CPU information, as shown in the following example:

```
# sar -d -f /tmp/sar.data


HP-UX system1 B.10.20 A 9000/859     04/28

12:52:04    device    %busy    avque    r+w/s    blks/s    avwait    avserv
12:53:04    c0t6d0      0.95     1.41        1        10     16.76     17.28
            c5t4d0    100.00     1.03       20       320      8.36     18.90
            c4t5d1     10.77     0.50       13       214      5.02     18.44
            c5t4d2      0.38     0.50        0         3      4.61     18.81
12:54:04    c0t6d0      0.97     1.08        1        11     10.75     14.82
            c5t4d0    100.00     1.28       54       862      9.31     20.06
            c4t5d1     12.43     0.50       15       241      5.21     16.97
            c5t4d2      0.37     0.50        0         3      3.91     18.20
12:55:04    c0t6d0      1.77     1.42        1        22     13.32     14.16
            c5t4d0    100.00     0.79       26       421      8.33     16.00
            c4t5d1     14.47     0.51       17       270      5.30     13.48
```

	c5t4d2	0.72	0.50	0	7	4.82	15.69
12:56:04	c0t6d0	1.07	21.57	1	22	72.94	19.58
	c5t4d0	100.00	0.60	16	251	6.80	13.45
	c4t5d1	8.75	0.50	11	177	5.05	10.61
	c5t4d2	0.62	0.50	0	6	4.79	15.43
12:57:04	c0t6d0	0.78	1.16	1	9	13.53	14.91
	c5t4d0	100.00	0.66	15	237	7.60	13.69
	c4t5d1	9.48	0.54	13	210	5.39	13.33
	c5t4d2	0.87	0.50	1	10	4.86	14.09
12:58:04	c0t6d0	1.12	8.29	1	17	54.96	14.35
	c5t4d0	100.00	0.60	11	176	7.91	14.65
	c4t5d1	5.35	0.50	7	111	5.23	10.35
	c5t4d2	0.92	0.50	1	10	4.63	16.08
12:59:04	c0t6d0	0.67	1.53	1	8	18.03	16.05
	c5t4d0	99.98	0.54	11	174	7.69	14.09
	c4t5d1	3.97	0.50	5	83	4.82	9.54
	c5t4d2	1.05	0.50	1	11	4.69	16.29
13:00:04	c0t6d0	3.22	0.67	3	39	8.49	16.53
	c5t4d0	100.00	0.60	65	1032	8.46	14.83
	c4t5d1	21.62	0.50	31	504	5.30	8.94
	c5t4d2	6.77	0.50	5	78	4.86	14.09
13:01:04	c0t6d0	4.45	3.08	5	59	25.83	11.49
	c5t4d0	100.00	0.65	42	676	7.85	14.52
	c4t5d1	21.34	0.55	30	476	5.87	18.49
	c5t4d2	4.37	0.50	3	51	5.32	13.50
		.					
		.					
		.					
14:42:04	c0t6d0	0.53	0.83	0	7	12.21	16.33
	c5t4d0	100.00	0.56	7	107	6.99	14.65
	c4t5d1	6.38	0.50	7	113	4.97	15.18
	c5t4d2	0.15	0.50	0	2	4.53	16.50
14:43:04	c0t6d0	0.52	0.92	0	7	11.50	15.86
	c5t4d0	99.98	0.92	17	270	8.28	18.64
	c4t5d1	10.26	0.50	9	150	5.35	16.41
	c5t4d2	0.12	0.50	0	1	5.25	14.45
Average	c0t6d0	1.43	108.80	2	26	0.00	14.71
Average	c5t4d0	100.00	0.74	25	398	7.83	-10.31
Average	c4t5d1	19.11	0.51	25	399	5.26	-13.75
Average	c5t4d2	1.71	0.53	1	21	5.29	13.46

sar -q   Report average queue length. You may have a
problem any time the run queue length is greater
than the number of processors on the system.

```
# sar -q -f /tmp/sar.data
```

```
HP-UX system1 B.10.20 A 9000/859     04/28

12:52:04 runq-sz %runocc swpq-sz %swpocc
12:53:04    1.1      20     0.0       0
12:54:04    1.4      51     0.0       0
12:55:04    1.3      71     0.0       0
12:56:04    1.1      22     0.0       0
12:57:04    1.3      16     0.0       0
12:58:04    1.1      14     0.0       0
12:59:04    1.2      12     0.0       0
13:00:04    1.2      21     0.0       0
13:01:04    1.1      18     0.0       0
13:02:04    1.3      20     0.0       0
13:03:04    1.2      15     0.0       0
13:04:04    1.2      20     0.0       0
13:05:04    1.2      43     0.0       0
13:06:04    1.1      14     0.0       0
13:07:04    1.2      15     0.0       0
13:08:04    1.2      26     0.0       0
13:09:04    1.5      38     0.0       0
13:10:04    1.5      30     0.0       0
13:11:04    1.2      23     0.0       0
13:12:04    1.3      11     0.0       0
13:13:04    1.3      12     0.0       0
13:14:04    1.4      16     0.0       0
13:15:04    1.4      27     0.0       0
13:16:04    1.5      20     0.0       0
13:17:04    1.3      21     0.0       0
13:18:04    1.1      15     0.0       0
13:19:04    1.2      19     0.0       0
13:20:04    1.4      22     0.0       0
                      .
                      .
                      .
14:30:04    1.5       5     0.0       0
14:31:04    1.6      12     0.0       0
```

```
14:32:04      1.4        9        0.0         0
14:33:04      1.1        6        0.0         0
14:34:04      1.3        3        0.0         0
14:35:04      1.1        4        0.0         0
14:36:04      1.2        6        0.0         0
14:37:04      1.4        5        0.0         0
14:38:04      1.2       10        0.0         0
14:39:04      1.3        4        0.0         0
14:40:04      1.1        3        0.0         0
14:41:04      1.6        3        0.0         0
14:42:04      1.1        4        0.0         0
14:43:04      1.3        1        0.0         0

Average       1.3       17        1.2         0
```

sar -w   Report system swapping activity.


```
# sar -w -f /tmp/sar.data
```


```
HP-UX system1 B.10.20 A 9000/859     04/28

12:52:04 swpin/s bswin/s swpot/s bswot/s pswch/s
12:53:04    1.00     0.0    1.00     0.0     231
12:54:04    1.00     0.0    1.00     0.0     354
12:55:04    1.00     0.0    1.00     0.0     348
12:56:04    1.00     0.0    1.00     0.0     200
12:57:04    1.00     0.0    1.00     0.0     277
12:58:04    1.00     0.0    1.00     0.0     235
12:59:04    1.02     0.0    1.02     0.0     199
13:00:04    0.78     0.0    0.78     0.0     456
13:01:04    1.00     0.0    1.00     0.0     435
13:02:04    1.02     0.0    1.02     0.0     216
13:03:04    0.98     0.0    0.98     0.0     204
13:04:04    1.02     0.0    1.02     0.0     239
13:05:04    1.00     0.0    1.00     0.0     248
13:06:04    0.97     0.0    0.97     0.0     170
13:07:04    1.00     0.0    1.00     0.0     166
13:08:04    1.02     0.0    1.02     0.0     209
13:09:04    0.98     0.0    0.98     0.0     377
13:10:04    1.00     0.0    1.00     0.0     200
```

13:11:04	1.00	0.0	1.00	0.0	192
13:12:04	0.87	0.0	0.87	0.0	187
13:13:04	0.93	0.0	0.93	0.0	172
13:14:04	1.00	0.0	1.00	0.0	170
13:15:04	1.00	0.0	1.00	0.0	382
13:16:04	1.00	0.0	1.00	0.0	513
13:17:04	1.00	0.0	1.00	0.0	332
13:18:04	1.00	0.0	1.00	0.0	265
13:19:04	1.02	0.0	1.02	0.0	184
13:20:04	0.98	0.0	0.98	0.0	212

.
.
.

14:30:04	0.00	0.0	0.00	0.0	301
14:31:04	0.00	0.0	0.00	0.0	566
14:32:04	0.00	0.0	0.00	0.0	539
14:33:04	0.00	0.0	0.00	0.0	400
14:34:04	0.00	0.0	0.00	0.0	242
14:35:04	0.00	0.0	0.00	0.0	286
14:36:04	0.00	0.0	0.00	0.0	295
14:37:04	0.00	0.0	0.00	0.0	249
14:38:04	0.00	0.0	0.00	0.0	300
14:39:04	0.00	0.0	0.00	0.0	296
14:40:04	0.00	0.0	0.00	0.0	419
14:41:04	0.00	0.0	0.00	0.0	234
14:42:04	0.00	0.0	0.00	0.0	237
14:43:04	0.00	0.0	0.00	0.0	208
Average	0.70	0.0	0.70	0.0	346

timex to Analyze a Command

If you have a specific command you want to find out more about, you can use **timex**, which reports the elapsed time, user time, and system time spent in the execution of a command you specify.

HP GlancePlus/UX

Using HP-UX commands to get a better understanding of what your system is doing requires you to do a lot of work. In the first case, issuing HP-UX commands gives you the advantage of obtaining data about what is taking place on your system that very second. Unfortunately, you can't always issue additional commands to probe deeper into an area, such as a process, about which you want to know more.

Now I'll describe another technique - a tool that can help get useful data in real time, allow you to investigate a specific process, and not bury you in reports. This tool is HP GlancePlus/UX (GlancePlus).

GlancePlus can be run in character mode, with the **glance** command, or in Motif mode, with the **gpm** command. I chose to use the character-based version of GlancePlus because this will run on any display, either graphics- or character-based, and the many colors used by the Motif version of GlancePlus do not show up well in a book. My examples are displayed much more clearly in the book when using the character mode. I recommend that you try both versions of GlancePlus to see which you prefer.

The following is a list of important directories in the **/opt/perf** directory related to GlancePlus:

ReleaseNotes	Files related to installation, error messages, Readme files, and so on.
bin	Executable files.
help	Help files.
lib	Libraries, message catalogs, version files, and so on.
man	Manual pages.
newconfig	Installation files, default **parm** file, and so on.
paperdocs	Documents suitable for printing.

In addition to these directories, the following directory in **/var/opt** is important to GlancePlus:

perf   Contains **parm** file and other files.

Many of the files in these directories will be useful to you as you learn GlancePlus. The help files and man pages will be useful immediately. The configuration files in these directories are not used in the upcoming examples. You may, however, use many of the files in these directories as you become more expert with GlancePlus. The **parm** file, for instance, gives you control over a lot of what takes place in GlancePlus. I do not cover modifying the **parm** file or any other files.

The system used in the examples is a V-class with eight processors, 4 GBytes of RAM, and a substantial amount of EMC Symmetrix disk connected to it.

Figure 5-2 shows one of several interactive screens of GlancePlus. This one is the *Process List* screen, also referred to as the *Global* screen. This is the default screen when bringing up GlancePlus.

Two features of the screen shown in Figure 5-2 are worth noticing immediately:

1. Four histograms at the top of the screen give you a graphical representation of your CPU, Disk, Memory, and Swap Utilization in a format much easier to assimilate than a column of numbers.

2. The "Process Summary" has columns similar to **ps -ef** with which many system administrators are familiar and comfortable. Glance-Plus, however, gives you the additional capability of filtering out processes that are using very few resources by specifying thresholds.

Using GlancePlus, you can take a close look at your system in many areas, including the following:

- Process List
- CPU Report
- Memory Report
- Swap Space
- Disk Report
- LAN Detail
- NFS by System
- PRM Summary (Process Resource Manager)
- I/O by File System
- I/O by Disk
- I/O by Logical Volume
- System Tables

Figure 5-2 is a GlancePlus screen shot.

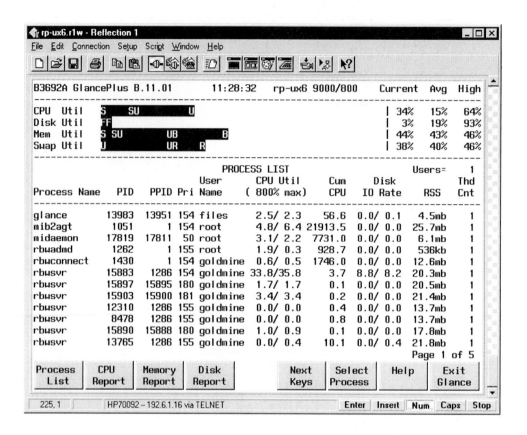

Figure 5-2 HP GlancePlus/UX *Process List* Screen Shot

Since the *Process List* shown in the example tells you where your system resources are going at the highest level, I'll start my description here. I am using a terminal emulator on my portable computer to display Glance-Plus. I find that many system administrators use a PC and a terminal emulator to perform HP-UX management functions. Keep in mind that the information shown on this screen can be updated at any interval you choose. If your system is running in a steady-state mode, you may want to have a long interval since you don't expect things to much change. On the other hand, you may have a dynamic environment and want to see the histograms and other information updated every few seconds. In either case, you can change the update interval to suit your needs. You can use the function keys at the bottom of the screen to go into other functional areas.

Process List Description

The *Process List* screen provides an overview of the state of system resources and active processes.

The top section of the screen (the histogram section) is common to the many screens of GlancePlus. The bottom section of the screen displays a summary of active processes.

Line 1 provides the product and version number of GlancePlus, the time, name of your system, and system type. In this case, we are running version 11.01 of GlancePlus.

Line 3 provides information about the overall state of the CPU. This tends to be the single most important piece of information that administrators want to know about their system - Is my CPU overworked?

The CPU Utilization bar is divided into the following parts:

1. "S" indicates the amount of time spent on "system" activities such as context switching and system calls.

2. "N" indicates the amount of time spent running "nice" user processes (those run at a low priority).

3. "U" indicates the amount of time spent running user processes.

4. "R" indicates real-time processes.

5. "A" indicates the amount of time spent running processes at a negative "nice" priority.

The far right of line 3 shows the percentage of CPU utilization. If your system is "CPU-Bound," you will consistently see this number near 100 percent. You get statistics for Current, Average (since analysis was begun), and High.

Line 4 shows Disk Utilization for the busiest mounted disk. This bar indicates the percentage of File System and Virtual Memory disk I/O over the update interval. This bar is divided into two parts:

1. "F" indicates the amount of file system activity of user reads and writes and other non-paging activities.

2. "V" indicates the percentage of disk I/O devoted to paging virtual memory.

The Current, Avg, and High statistics have the same meaning as in the CPU Utilization description.

Line 5 shows the system memory utilization. This bar is divided into three parts:

1. "S" indicates the amount of memory devoted to system use.

2. "U" indicates the amount of memory devoted to user programs and data.

3. "B" indicates the amount of memory devoted to buffer cache.

The Current, Avg, and High statistics have the same meaning as in the CPU Utilization description.

Line 6 shows swap space information, which is divided into two parts:

1. "R" indicates reserved but not in use.

2. "U" indicates swap space in use.

All three of these areas (CPU, Memory, and Disk) may be further analyzed by using the F2, F3, and F4 function keys, respectively. Again, you may see different function keys, depending on the version of GlancePlus you are running. When you select one of these keys, you move from the *Process List* screen to a screen that provides more in-depth functions in the selected area. In addition, more detailed screens are available for many other system areas. Since most investigation beyond the *Process List* screen takes place on the CPU, Memory, and Disk screens, I'll describe these in more detail shortly.

The bottom of the *Process List* screen shows the active processes running on your system. Because there are typically many processes running on an HP-UX system, you may want to consider using the **o** command to set a threshold for CPU utilization. If you set a threshold of 5 percent, for instance, then only processes that exceed the average CPU utilization of 5 percent over the interval will be displayed. There are other types of thresholds that can be specified such as the amount of RAM used (Resident Size). If you specify thresholds, you see only the processes you're most interested in, that is, those consuming the greatest system resources.

There is a line for each active process that meets the threshold requirements you defined. There may be more than one page of processes to display. The message in the bottom-right corner of the screen indicates which page you are on. You can scroll forward to view the next page with **f** and backwards with **b**. Usually only a few processes consume most of your system resources, so I recommend setting the thresholds so that only one page of processes is displayed. There are a whole series of commands you can issue in GlancePlus. The final figure in this section shows the commands recognized by GlancePlus.

Here is a brief summary of the process headings:

Process Name   The name or abbreviation used to load the executable program.

PID   The process identification number.

PPID   The PID of the parent process.

Pri   The priority of the process. The lower the number, the higher the priority. System-level processes usually run between 0 and 127. Other processes usually run between 128 and 255. "Nice" processes are those with the lowest priority and will have the largest number.

User Name   Name of the user who started the process.

CPU Util   The first number is the percentage of CPU utilization that this process consumed over the update interval. Note that this is 800% maximum for our 8 processor V-class system. The second number is the percentage of CPU utilization that this process consumed since GlancePlus was invoked. I'm skeptical of using GlancePlus, or any other HP-UX command, to get data over an extended period. I rarely use the second number under this heading. If you have been using GlancePlus for some time but only recently started a process that consumes a great deal of CPU, you may find that the second number is very low. The reason is that the process you are analyzing has indeed consumed very little of the CPU since GlancePlus was invoked, despite being a highly CPU-intensive process.

Cum CPU   The total CPU time used by the process. GlancePlus
                 uses the "midaemon" to gather information. If the
                 midaemon started before the process, you will get an
                 accurate measure of cumulative CPU time used by the
                 process. The **midaemon** is started by the **/etc/rc.con-
                 fig.d/mwa** script at bootup by default, so you start
                 gathering information on all processes as soon as the
                 system is booted.

Disk IO Rate   The first number is the average disk I/O rate per sec-
                 ond over the last update interval. The second number is
                 the average disk I/O rate since GlancePlus was started
                 or since the process was started. Disk I/O can mean a
                 lot of different things. Disk I/O could mean taking
                 blocks of data off the disk for the first time and putting
                 them in RAM, or it could be entirely paging and swap-
                 ping. Some processes will simply require a lot more
                 Disk   I/O than others. When this number is very high,
                 however, take a close look at whether or not you have
                 enough RAM.

RSS Size   The amount of RAM in KBytes that is consumed by
                 the process. This is called the Resident Size. Every-
                 thing related to the process that is in RAM is included
                 in this column, such as the process's data, stack, text,
                 and shared memory segments. This is a good column
                 to inspect. Since slow systems are often erroneously
                 assumed to be CPU-bound, I always make a point of
                 looking at this column to identify the amount of RAM
                 that the primary applications are using. This is often
                 revealing. Some applications use a small amount of
                 RAM but use large data sets, a point often overlooked
                 when RAM calculations are made. This column shows
                 all the RAM your process is currently using.

Block On   The reason the process was blocked (unable to run). If
                 the process is currently blocked, you will see why. If
                 the process is running, you will see why it was last
                 blocked. There are many reasons a process could be

blocked. After *Thd Cnt* is a list of the most common reasons for the process being blocked.

Thd Cnt   The total number of threads for this current process.

Abbreviation	Reason for the Blocked Process
CACHE	Waiting for a cache buffer to become available
DISK	Waiting for a disk operation to complete
DUX	Waiting for a diskless transfer to complete
INODE	Waiting for an inode operation to complete
IO	Waiting for a non-disk I/O to complete
IPC	Waiting for a shared memory operation to complete
LAN	Waiting for a LAN operation to complete
MBUF	Waiting for a memory buffer
MESG	Waiting for a message queue operation to complete
NFS	Waiting for an NFS request to complete
PIPE	Waiting for data from a pipe
PRI	Waiting because a higher-priority process is running
RFA	Waiting for a Remote File Access to complete
SEM	Waiting for a semaphore to become available
SLEEP	Waiting because the process called **sleep** or **wait**
SOCKT	Waiting for a socket operation to complete
SYS	Waiting for system resources
TERM	Waiting for a terminal transfer
VM	Waiting for a virtual memory operation to complete
OTHER	Waiting for a reason GlancePlus can't determine

CPU Report Screen Description

If the *Process List* screen indicates that the CPU is overworked, you'll want to refer to the *CPU Report* screen shown in Figure 5-3. It can provide useful information about the seven types of states that GlancePlus reports.

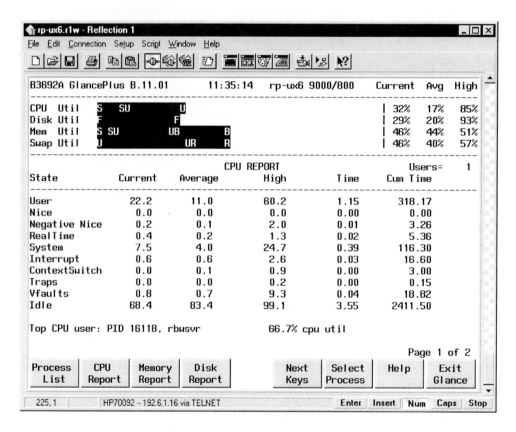

Figure 5-3 HP GlancePlus/UX *CPU Report* Screen Shot

For each of the seven types of states there are columns that provide additional information. Following is a description of the columns:

Current	Displays the percentage of CPU time devoted to this state over the last time interval.

Average	Displays the average percentage of CPU time spent in this state since GlancePlus was started.
High	Displays the highest percentage of CPU time devoted to this state since GlancePlus was started.
Time	Displays the CPU time spent in this state over the last interval.
Cum Time	Displays the total amount of CPU time spent in this state since GlancePlus was started.

A description of the seven states follows:

User	CPU time spent executing user activities under normal priority.
Nice	CPU time spent running user code in nice mode.
Negative Nice	CPU time spent running code at a high priority.
Realtime	CPU time spent executing real-time processes that run at a high priority.
System	CPU time spent executing system calls and programs.
Interrupt	CPU time spent executing system interrupts. A high value here may indicate of a lot of I/O, such as paging and swapping.
ContSwitch	CPU time spent context switching between processes.
Traps	CPU time spent handling traps.
Vfaults	CPU time spent handling page faults.
Idle	CPU time spent idle.

The *CPU Report* screen also shows your system's run queue length or load average. This would be displayed on the second page of the *CPU Report* screen. The current, average, and high values for the number of runnable processes waiting for the CPU are shown. You may want to get a gauge of your system's run queue length when the system is mostly idle and compare these numbers with those you see when your system is in normal use.

The final area reported on the *CPU Report* screen is load average, system calls, interrupts, and context switches. I don't inspect these too closely, because if one of these is high, it is normally the symptom of a problem and not the cause of a problem. If you correct a problem, you will see these numbers reduced.

You can use GlancePlus to view all the CPUs in your system, as shown in Figure 5-4. This is an eight-processor V-class system.

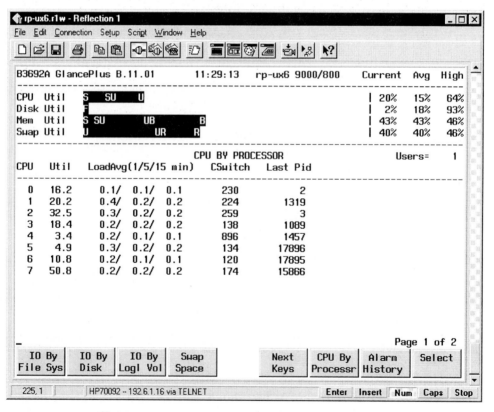

Figure 5-4 *All CPUs* Screen in GlancePlus

Memory Report Screen Description

The *Memory Report* Screen shown in Figure 5-5 provides information on several types of memory management events. The statistics shown are in the form of counts, not percentages. You may want to look at these counts for a mostly idle system and then observe what takes place as the load on the system is incrementally increased. My experience has been that many more memory bottlenecks occur than CPU bottlenecks, so you may find this screen revealing.

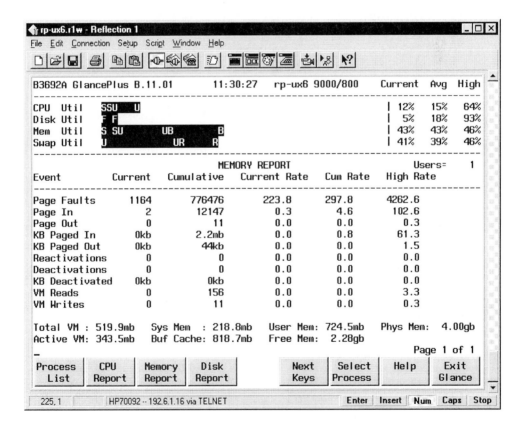

Figure 5-5 HP GlancePlus/UX *Memory Report* Screen Shot

The following five statistics are shown for each memory management event:

Current	The number of times an event occurred in the last interval. The count changes if you update the interval, so you may want to select an interval you are comfortable with and stick with it.
Cumulative	The sum of all counts for this event since Glance-Plus started.
Current Rate	The number of events per second.
Cum Rate	The sum of events.
High Rate	The highest rate recorded.

Following are brief descriptions of the memory management events for which the statistics are provided:

Page Faults	A fault takes place when a process tries to access a page that is not in RAM. The virtual memory of the system will handle the "page in." Keep in mind that the speed of the disk is much slower than RAM, so there is a large performance penalty for the page in.
Page In/Page Out	Pages of data moved from virtual memory (disk) to physical memory (page in) or vice versa.
KB Paged In	The amount of data paged in because of page faults.
KB Paged Out	The amount of data paged out to disk.
Reactivations and Deactivations	
	The number of processes swapped in and swapped out of memory. A system low on RAM will spend a lot of time swapping processes in and out of RAM. If a lot of this type of swapping is taking place, you may see high CPU utilization and see some other statistics go up as well. These may only be symptoms that a lot of swapping is

taking place. You may see Reactivations and Deactivations.

KB Reactivated	The amount of information swapped into RAM as a result of processes having been swapped out earlier due to insufficient RAM. You may see KB Reactivated.
KB Deactivated	The amount of information swapped out when processes are moved to disk. You may see KB Deactivated.
VM Reads	The total count of the number of physical reads to disk. The higher this number, the more often your system is going to disk.
VM Writes	The total count of the number of physical writes to disk.

The following values are also on the Memory screen:

Total VM	The amount of total virtual memory used by all processes.
Active VM	The amount of virtual memory used by all active processes.
Sys Mem	The amount of memory devoted to system use.
Buf Cache Size	The current size of buffer cache.
User Mem	The amount of memory devoted to user use.
Free Memory	The amount of RAM not currently allocated for use.
Phys Memory	The total RAM in your system.

This screen gives you a lot of information about how your memory subsystem is being used. You may want to view some statistics when your system is mostly idle and when it is heavily used and compare the two. Some good numbers to record are "Avail Memory" (to see whether you have any free RAM under either condition) and "Total VM" (to see how much virtual memory has been allocated for all your processes). A system that is RAM rich will have available memory; a system that is RAM-poor will allocate a lot of virtual memory.

Disk Report Screen Description

The *Disk Report* screen appears in Figure 5-6. You may see groupings of "local" and "remote" information.

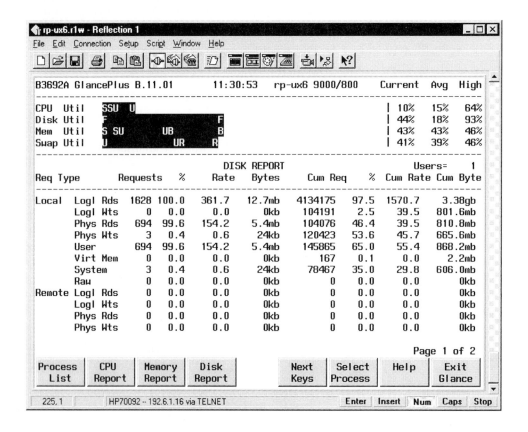

Figure 5-6   HP GlancePlus/UX *Disk Report* Screen Shot

There are eight disk statistics provided for eight events related to logical and physical accesses to all the disks mounted on the local system. These events represent all the disk activity taking place on the system.

Here are descriptions of the eight disk statistics provided:

Requests   The total number of requests of that type over the last interval.

%   The percentage of this type of disk event relative to other types.

Rate   The average number of requests of this type per second.

Bytes   The total number of bytes transferred for this event over the last interval.

Cum Req   The cumulative number of requests since Glance-Plus started.

%   The relative percentage of this type of disk event since GlancePlus started.

Cum Rate   The sum of requests.

Cum Bytes   The total number of bytes transferred for this type of event since GlancePlus started.

Next are descriptions of the disk events for which these statistics are provided, which may be listed under "Local" on your system:

Logl Rds and Logl Wts

                The number of logical reads and writes to a disk. Since disks normally use memory buffer cache, a logical read may not require physical access to the disk.

Phys Rds   The number of physical reads to the disk. These physical reads may be due to either file system logical reads or to virtual memory management.

Phys Wts	The number of physical writes to the disk. This may be due to file system activity or virtual memory management.
User	The amount of physical disk I/O as a result of user file I/O operations.
Virtual Mem	The amount of physical disk I/O as a result of virtual memory management activity.
System	The amount of physical disk I/O as a result of system calls.
Raw	The amount of raw mode disk I/O.

A lot of disk activity may also take place as a result of NFS mounted disks. Statistics are provided for "Remote" disks as well.

Disk access is required on all systems. The question to ask is: What disk activity is unnecessary and slowing down my system? A good place to start is to compare the amount of "User" disk I/O with "Virtual Mem" disk I/O. If your system is performing much more virtual memory I/O than user I/O, you may want to investigate your memory needs.

GlancePlus Summary

In addition to the Process List, or Global, screen and the CPU, Memory, and Disk screens described earlier, there are many other useful screens including the following:

Swap Space	Shows details on all swap areas. May be called by another name in other releases.
Netwk By Intrface	Gives details about each LAN card configured on your system. This screen may have another name in other releases.
NFS Global	Provides details on inbound and outbound NFS mounted file systems. May be called by another name in other releases.

Select Process   Allows you to select a single process to investigate. May be called by another name in other releases.

I/O By File Sys   Shows details of I/O for each mounted disk partition.

I/O By Disk   Shows details of I/O for each mounted disk.

I/O By Logl Vol   Shows details of I/O for each mounted logical volume.

System Tables   Shows details on internal system tables.

Process Threshold   Defines which processes will be displayed on the Process List screen. May be called by another name, such as Global screen, in other releases.

As you can see, while I described the four most commonly used screens in detail, you can use many others to investigate your system further.

There are also many commands you can issue within GlancePlus. Figures 5-7 and 5-8 show the *Command List* screens in GlancePlus.

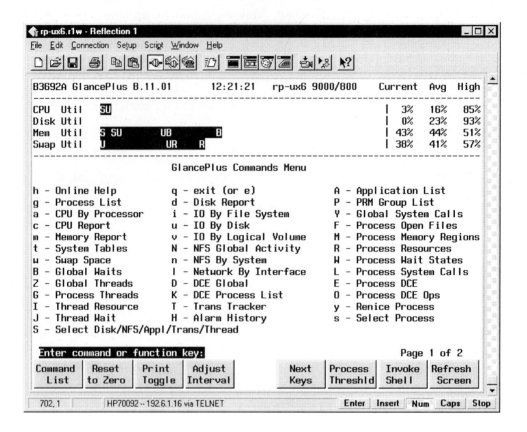

Figure 5-7   HP GlancePlus/UX *Command List* Screen1

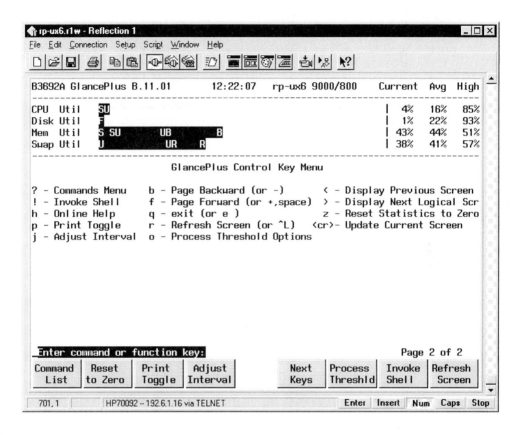

Figure 5-8   HP GlancePlus/UX *Command List* Screen2

What Should I Look for When Using GlancePlus?

Since GlancePlus provides a graphical representation of the way in which your system resources are being used, the answer is simple: See which bars have a high "Avg" utilization. You can then probe further into the process(es) causing this high utilization. If, for instance, you find that your memory is consistently 99 percent utilized, press the F3 function key and have GlancePlus walk you through an investigation of which of your applications and users are memory hogs.

Similarly, you may be surprised to find that GlancePlus shows low utilization of your CPU or other system resources. Many slow systems are assumed to be CPU-bound. I have seen GlancePlus used to determine that a system is in fact memory-bound, resulting in a memory upgrade instead of a CPU upgrade.

The difference between using GlancePlus to determine the level of CPU resources being used and the first two approaches given in this chapter is that GlancePlus takes out a lot of the guesswork involved. If you are going to justify a system upgrade of some type to management, it is easier to do this with the hard and fast data GlancePlus provides, than the detective work you may need to do with HP-UX commands.

Use the GlancePlus screens I showed you to look for the following bottlenecks:

1. CPU Bottleneck
   Use the "Global Screen" and "CPU Detail Screen" to identify these common CPU bottleneck symptoms:

   - Low CPU idle time. Greater than 85% CPU utilization for an extended period of time is high.

   - High CPU utilization in system mode. Greater than 10% utilization in system mode means that a substantial amount of time is spent handling system tasks.

   - High interrupt time. Greater than 10% interrupt time is high.

   - High context switching. Greater than 5% spent context switching is high.

2. Memory Bottleneck
   Use the "Global Screen," "Memory Screen," and "Tables Screen" to identify these common Memory bottleneck symptoms:

   - High swapping activity.

   - High paging activity. Greater than 5 page outs per second is high.

   - Little or no free memory available. Greater than 80% memory utilization for an extended period is high.

- High CPU usage in System mode.

3. Disk Bottleneck
   Use "Global Screen," "Disk I/O Screen," and others to identify these common Disk Bottleneck symptoms:

   - High disk activity.

   - High idle CPU time waiting for I/O requests to complete.

   - Long disk queues.

The best approach to take for understanding where your system resources are going is to become familiar with all three techniques described in this chapter. You can then determine which information is most useful to you.

The most important aspect of this process is to regularly issue commands and review accounting data so that small system utilization problems don't turn into catastrophes and adversely affect all your users.

You may need to go a step further with more sophisticated performance tools. HP can help you identify more sophisticated tools based on your needs.

HP MeasureWare and HP PerfView

We'll use HP MeasureWare Agent and HP PerfView together to take a look at the performance of a system.

The MeasureWare agent is installed on individual systems throughout a distributed environment. It collects resource and performance measurement data on the individual systems. The PerfView management console, which you would typically install on a management system, is then used to display the historical MeasureWare data. You could also set alarms that are set off by exception conditions using the MeasureWare agent. For instance, if the MeasureWare agent detects an exception condition, such as CPU utilization greater than 90%, it produces an alarm message. The alarm messages are then displayed with PerfView. We're going to use the PerfView

Analyzer in our upcoming examples; however, PerfView consists of the following three components:

Monitor   Provides alarm monitoring capability by accept-
                      ing alarms from MeasureWare and displays
                      alarms. This is not part of the base PerfView
                      product.

Planner   Provides forecasting capability by extrapolating
                      MeasureWare data for forecasts. This is not part
                      of the base PerfView product.

Analyzer   Analyzes MeasureWare data from multiple sys-
                      tems and displays data. You can view the data
                      from multiple systems simultaneously. This is the
                      base product.

The following is a list of important directories in the **/opt/perf** directory related to MeasureWare and PerfView:

ReleaseNotes   Files related to installation, error messages,
                     Readme files, and so on.

bin   Executable files.

help   Help files.

include   Transaction Tracker include file.

lib   Libraries, message catalogs, version files, and so
                     on.

man   Manual pages.

newconfig   Installation files, default **parm** and **alarmdef** file,
                     and so on.

paperdocs   Documents suitable for printing.

In addition to these directories, the following directories in **/var/opt/ perf** are important to MeasureWare and PerfView:

perf	Contains **parm**, **alarmdef** files, and other files.
datafiles	Contain *log* files and other files.

In our example, we will be working with a single system. We'll take the MeasureWare data, collected over roughly a one-week period, and display some of it. In this example, we won't take data from several distributed systems and we'll use only one server in the example.

HP MeasureWare Agent produces log files that contain information about the system resource consumption. The longer HP MeasureWare Agent runs, the longer it records data in the log files. I am often called to review systems that are running poorly to propose system upgrades. I usually run HP MeasureWare Agent for a minimum of a week so that I obtain log information over a long enough period of time to obtain useful data. For some systems, this time period is months. For other systems with a regular load, a week may be enough time.

After installing MeasureWare and PerfView with Software Distributor, you must start the MeasureWare Agent. The installation and configuration guide for MeasureWare provides complete instructions for this process. To start the MeasureWare Agent from the command line, you would simply issue the following command:

```
# /opt/perf/bin/mwa start
```

To ensure that mwa starts every time the system boots, you would edit the file **/etc/rc.config.d/mwa** and change:

```
MWA_START=0
```

to

```
MWA_START=1
```

I installed MeasureWare and PerfView on a system that had periods of slow response time for the users. The default installation location for these performance tools is **/opt/perf**. The log files produced by Measure-Ware go into **/var/opt/perf/datafiles**. MeasureWare uses a file called **parm** that allows you to specify the information you wish to log. There is a default **parm** file that is usually sufficient for getting started. In addition, the **/opt/perf/newconfig/parm.examples** file provides several application-related examples that can be useful. I normally start out using the default **parm** file, called **/var/opt/perf/parm**, when I first begin monitoring a system. You can easily modify this file to suit your future needs after you begin using PerfView.

After having run MeasureWare for a week, I invoked PerfView (using **/opt/perf/bin/pv**) to see the level of system resource utilization that took place over the week. The graphs we'll review are CPU, Memory, and Disk. Figure 5-9 shows *Global CPU Summary* for the week.

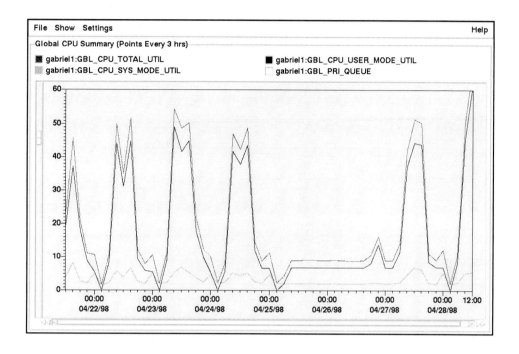

Figure 5-9 HP PerfView *Global CPU Summary*

You can adjust every imaginable feature of this graph with Perf-
View. Unfortunately, the color in this graph is lost in the book. The colors used make it easy to discern the parameters when viewing the graph
on the computer screen. Total CPU utilization is always the top point in
the graph and it is the sum of system and user mode utilization.

Figure 5-9 shows classic CPU utilization with prime hours reflecting
high CPU utilization and non-prime hours reflecting low CPU utilization.
In some respects, however, this graph can be deceiving. Because there is
a data point occurs every three hours, hence the eight ticks per 24-hour
period, you don't get a view of the actual CPU utilization during a much
smaller window of time. We can't, for instance, see precisely what time
in the morning the CPU becomes heavily used. We can see that it is
between the second and third tick, but this is a long time period - between
6:00 and 9:00 am. The same lack of granularity is true at the end of the
day. We see a clear fall-off in CPU utilization between the fifth and sev-

enth ticks, but this does not give us a well defined view. Figure 5-10 shows CPU utilization during a much shorter time window.

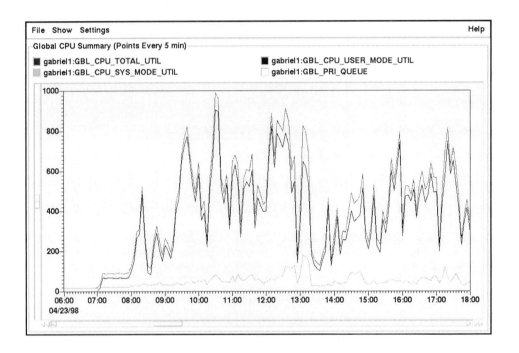

Figure 5-10 HP PerfView *Global CPU Summary* - Short Time Period

Figure 5-10 shows a finer granularity of CPU utilization during the shorter time window. The much finer granularity of this window makes clear the activity spikes that occur throughout the day. For instance, a clear login spike occurs at 8:30 am.

Memory utilization can also be graphed over the course of the week, as shown in Figure 5-11.

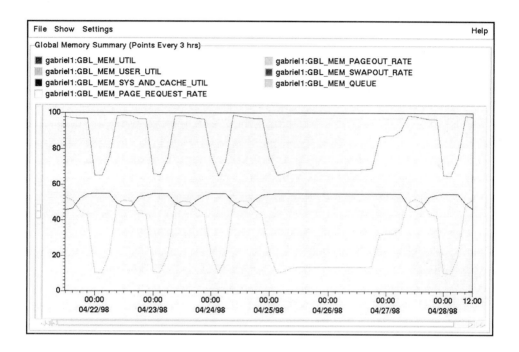

Figure 5-11 HP PerfView *Global Memory Summary*

The user memory utilization is the bottom graph, which roughly corresponds to the CPU utilization shown earlier. User memory utilization is low during non-prime hours and high during prime hours.

System memory utilization is the middle graph, which remains fairly steady throughout the week.

Total memory utilization is always the top point in the graph, and it is the sum of system and user utilization. It rises and drops with user utilization because system memory utilization remains roughly the same.

The three-hour interval between data points on this graph may not give us the granularity we require. Figure 5-12 shows memory utilization during a much shorter time window.

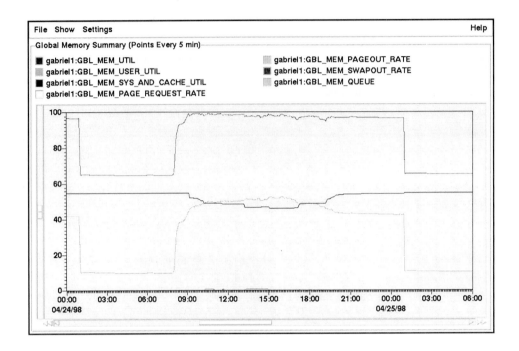

Figure 5-12 HP PerfView *Global Memory Summary* - Short Time Period

Figure 5-12 shows a finer granularity of memory utilization during the shorter time window. You can now see precisely how memory utilization is changing over roughly one day.

Disk utilization can also be graphed over the course of the week, as shown in Figure 5-13.

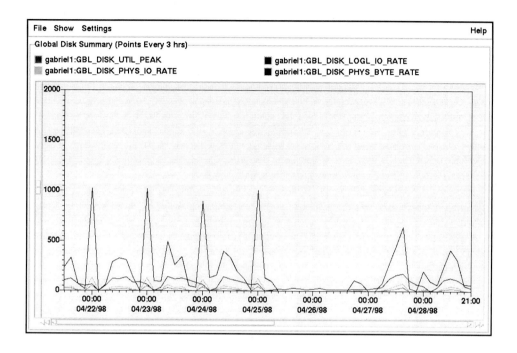

File Show Settings   Help

Global Disk Summary (Points Every 3 hrs)

■ gabriel1:GBL_DISK_UTIL_PEAK   ■ gabriel1:GBL_DISK_LOGL_IO_RATE
■ gabriel1:GBL_DISK_PHYS_IO_RATE   ■ gabriel1:GBL_DISK_PHYS_BYTE_RATE

Figure 5-13 HP PerfView *Global Disk Summary*

Like the CPU and memory graph, this is an entire week of disk usage. Since many spikes occur on this graph, we would surely want to view and analyze much shorter time windows.

Figure 5-14 shows disk utilization during a much shorter time window.

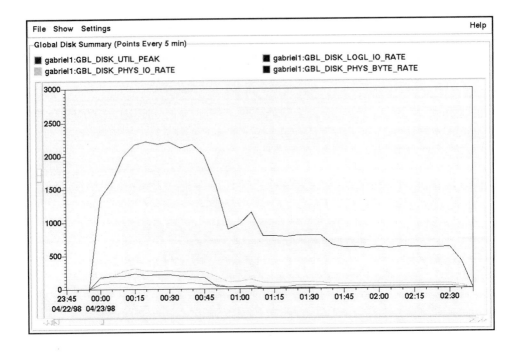

Figure 5-14 HP PerfView *Global Disk Summary* - Short Time Period

This much shorter time window, of roughly three hours, shows a lot
more detail. There are tremendous spikes in disk activity in the middle of
the night. This could take place for a variety of reasons, including batch
job processing or system backup.

You are not limited to viewing parameters related to only one system
resource at a time. You can also view the way many system resources are
used simultaneously, as shown in Figure 5-15.

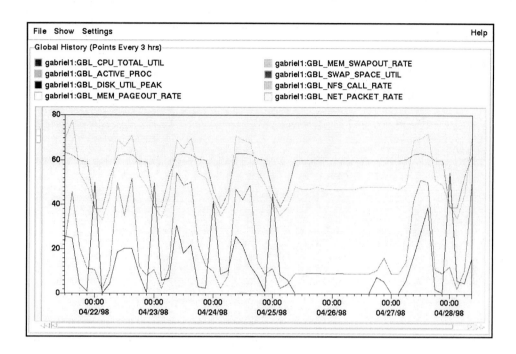

Figure 5-15 HP PerfView *Global Summary*

Many system resources are present on this graph, including cpu, disk, and memory. You would surely want to view a much shorter time period when displaying so many system resources simultaneously.

Figure 5-16 shows the same parameters during a much shorter time window.

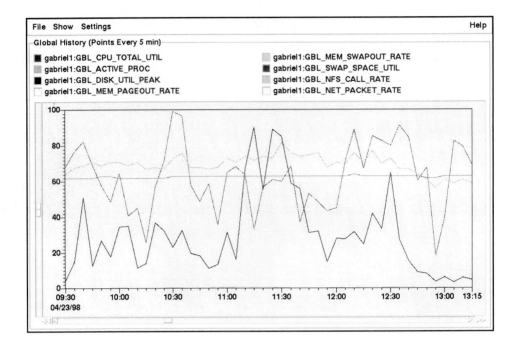

Figure 5-16 HP PerfView *Global Summary* - Short Time Period

Figure 5-16 shows a finer granularity of the utilization of many system resources during the shorter time window. You can now view the
ways in which various system resources are related to other system
resources.

You can find the status of PerfView running on your system with a
useful command called **perfstat**. The following example shows issuing
the **perfstat** command with the **-?** option to see all perfstat options:

```
# perfstat -?

usage: perfstat [options]

Unix option   Function
-----------   --------
    -?        List all perfstat options.
    -c        Show system configuration information.
    -e        Search for warnings and errors from
                 performance tool status files.
```

```
    -f          List size of performance tool status files.
    -p          List active performance tool processes.
    -t          Display last few lines of performance tool
                   status files.
    -v          List version strings for performance tool files.
    -z          Dump perfstat info to a file and tar tape.
```

Using the **-c** option, you get information about your system configuration, as shown in the following listing:

```
# perfstat -c

***************************************************************
** perfstat for rp-ux6 on Fri May 15 12:20:06 EDT
***************************************************************

system configuration information:

uname -a: HP-UX ux6 B.11.00 E 9000/800 71763 8-user license

mounted file systems with disk space shown:
Filesystem             kbytes      used     avail %used Mounted on
/dev/vg00/lvol3         86016     27675     54736   34% /
/dev/vg00/lvol1         67733     44928     16031   74% /stand
/dev/vg00/lvol8        163840     66995     90927   42% /var
/dev/vg00/lvol7        499712    358775    132155   73% /usr
/dev/rp06vgtmp/tmp    4319777   1099297   3134084   26% /tmp
/dev/vg00/lvol6        270336    188902     76405   71% /opt
/dev/vgroot1/var       640691     15636    605834    3% /newvar
/dev/vgroot1/usr       486677    356866    115210   76% /newusr
/dev/vgroot1/stand      67733     45109     15850   74% /newstand
/dev/vgroot1/root       83733     21181     54178   28% /newroot
/dev/vgroot1/opt       263253    188109     67246   74% /newopt
/dev/vg00/lvol5         20480      1109     18168    6% /home


LAN interfaces:
Name     Mtu      Network       Address       Ipkts      Opkts
lo0      4136     127.0.0.0     localhost     7442       7442
lan0     1500     192.60.11.0   rp-ux6        7847831    12939169


************** (end of perfstat -c output) ****************
```

Using the **-f** option shows the size of the performance tools status files, as shown in the following listing:

```
# perfstat -f

***************************************************************
** perfstat for ux6 on Fri May 15 12:20:08 EDT
***************************************************************

ls -l list of performance tool status files in /var/opt/perf:

-rw-rw-rw-   1 root        root      7812 May 10 19:35 status.alarmgen
-rw-r--r--   1 root        root         0 May 10 02:40 status.mi
-rw-rw-rw-   1 root        root      3100 May 10 02:40 status.perflbd
-rw-rw-rw-   1 root        root      3978 May 10 02:40 status.rep_server
-rw-r--r--   1 root        root      6079 May 11 23:30 status.scope
-rw-r--r--   1 root        root         0 Mar 31 07:26 status.ttd

************* (end of perfstat -f output) ****************
```

Using the **-v** option shows the version strings for the performance tools running, as shown in the following listing:

```
# perfstat -v

***************************************************************
** perfstat for ux6 on Fri May 15 12:20:08 EDT
***************************************************************

listing version strings for performance tool files:

NOTE:   The following software version information can be compared
with the version information shown in the /opt/perf/ReleaseNotes
file(s).

MeasureWare executables in the directory /opt/perf/bin
         scopeux  C.01.00      12/17/97 HP-UX 11.0+
             ttd  A.11.00.15   12/15/97 HP-UX 11.00
         perflbd  C.01.00      12/17/97 HP-UX 11.0+
        alarmgen  C.01.00      12/17/97 HP-UX 11.0+
       agdbserver  C.01.00     12/17/97 HP-UX 11.0+
          agsysdb  C.01.00     12/17/97 HP-UX 11.0+
      rep_server  C.01.00      12/17/97 HP-UX 11.0+
         extract  C.01.00      12/17/97 HP-UX 11.0+
         utility  C.01.00      12/17/97 HP-UX 11.0+
             mwa  A.10.52      12/05/97
        perfstat  A.11.01      11/19/97
          dsilog  C.01.00      12/17/97 HP-UX 11.0+
         sdlcomp  C.01.00      12/17/97 HP-UX 11.0+
          sdlexpt  C.01.00     12/17/97 HP-UX 11.0+
```

```
             sdlgendata  C.01.00      12/17/97 HP-UX 11.0+
                sdlutil  C.01.00      12/17/97 HP-UX 11.0+

Measureware libraries in the directory /opt/perf/lib
             libmwa.sl  C.01.00       12/17/97 HP-UX 11.0+
             libarm.a   A.11.00.15    12/15/97 HP-UX 11.00
             libarm.sl  A.11.00.15    12/15/97 HP-UX 11.00

Measureware metric description file in the directory /var/opt/perf
           metdesc  C.01.00      12/17/97

All critical MeasureWare files are accessible

     libnums.sl  B.11.00.15   12/15/97 HP-UX 11.00
       midaemon  B.11.00.15   12/15/97 HP-UX 11.00
         glance  B.11.01      12/16/97 HP-UX 11.00
            gpm  B.11.01      12/16/97 HP-UX 11.00

************* (end of perfstat -v output) ****************
```

Using Some of the Performance Tools in a Benchmark

I've worked on a lot of benchmarks over the years. This section contains several examples of system resource utilization from a benchmark. Many of these are useful for characterizing the performance of systems in general, not just during benchmarks.

Before getting any performance information when evaluating a system, you need to understand its configuration. I always issue several commands to get a snapshot of a system, including **bdf, vgdisplay, lvdisplay, dmesg, ioscan,** and **swapinfo**. Three of the most revealing are **bdf, dmesg** and **ioscan**, which follow:

```
$ bdf
Filesystem           kbytes     used     avail %used Mounted on
/dev/vg00/lvol3     1370353    24131   1209186    2% /
/dev/vg00/lvol1       99669    15350     74352   17% /stand
/dev/vg00/lvol7      577144   156584    362845   30% /var
/dev/vg00/lvol6      398869   276426     82556   77% /usr
/dev/vg00/lvol5      398869   266859     92123   74% /opt
/dev/dsk/c4t4d0     4103198  1624039   2068839   44% /opt/oracle
/dev/vg00/lvol4      199381     1086    178356    1% /home
/dev/dsk/c4t3d0     4103198  2722615    970263   74% /backdb
```

```
$ dmesg

Feb  6 15:25
vuseg=15a87000
  inet_clts:ok  inet_cots:ok 8 ccio
8/0 c720
8/0.0 tgt
8/0.0.0 sdisk
8/0.0.1 sdisk
8/0.0.2 sdisk
8/0.0.3 sdisk
8/0.0.4 sdisk
8/0.0.5 sdisk
8/0.0.6 sdisk
8/0.7 tgt
8/0.7.0 sctl
8/4 c720
8/4.0 tgt
8/4.0.0 sdisk
8/4.0.1 sdisk
8/4.0.2 sdisk
8/4.0.3 sdisk
8/4.0.4 sdisk
8/4.0.5 sdisk
8/4.0.6 sdisk
8/4.7 tgt
8/4.7.0 sctl
8/8 c720
8/8.0 tgt
8/8.0.0 sdisk
8/8.0.1 sdisk
8/8.0.2 sdisk
8/8.0.3 sdisk
8/8.0.4 sdisk
8/8.0.5 sdisk
8/8.0.6 sdisk
8/8.7 tgt
8/8.7.0 sctl
8/12 c720
8/12.0 tgt
8/12.0.0 sdisk
8/12.0.1 sdisk
8/12.0.2 sdisk
8/12.0.3 sdisk
8/12.0.4 sdisk
8/12.0.5 sdisk
8/12.0.6 sdisk
8/12.7 tgt
8/12.7.0 sctl
10 ccio
10/0 c720
10/0.3 tgt
10/0.3.0 sdisk
10/0.4 tgt
10/0.4.0 sdisk
10/0.5 tgt
```

```
10/0.5.0 sdisk
10/0.6 tgt
10/0.6.0 sdisk
10/0.7 tgt
10/0.7.0 sctl
10/4 bc
10/4/0 mux2
10/8 c720
10/8.0 tgt
10/8.0.0 sdisk
10/8.0.1 sdisk
10/8.0.2 sdisk
10/8.0.3 sdisk
10/8.0.4 sdisk
10/8.0.5 sdisk
10/8.0.6 sdisk
10/8.7 tgt
10/8.7.0 sctl
10/12 bus_adapter
10/12/5 c720
10/12/5.0 tgt
10/12/5.0.0 stape
10/12/5.2 tgt
10/12/5.2.0 sdisk
10/12/5.7 tgt
10/12/5.7.0 sctl
10/12/6 lan2
10/12/0 CentIf
ps2_readbyte_timeout: no byte after 500 uSec
ps2_readbyte_timeout: no byte after 500 uSec
10/12/7 ps2
10/16 bc
10/16/12 fddi
32 processor
34 processor
36 processor
38 processor
49 memory
Networking memory for fragment reassembly is restricted
to 358293504 bytes
Logical volume 64, 0x3 configured as ROOT
Logical volume 64, 0x2 configured as SWAP
Logical volume 64, 0x2 configured as DUMP
    Swap device table:  (start & size given in 512-byte blocks)
        entry 0 - major is 64, minor is 0x2; start = 0,size = 2097152
WARNING: Insufficient space on dump device to save full
        crashdump.
    Only 1073741824 of 4026532864 bytes will be saved.
    Dump device table:  (start & size given in 1-Kbyte blocks)
        entry 0 - major is 31, minor is 0x46000; start = 105312,size = 1048576
netisr real-time priority reset to 100
Starting the STREAMS daemons.
    9245XB HP-UX (B.10.20) #1: Sun Jun  9 06:31:19 PDT 1996

Memory Information:
    physical page size = 4096 bytes, logical page size =
    4096 bytes
    Physical: 3932160 Kbytes, lockable: 3036260 Kbytes,available: 3481700 Kbytes
```

```
$ ioscan

H/W Path      Class               Description
==================================================
              bc
8             bc                  I/O Adapter
8/0               ext_bus         GSC add-on Fast/Wide SCSI Interface
8/0.0                 target
8/0.0.0                   disk    EMC      SYMMETRIX
8/0.0.1                   disk    EMC      SYMMETRIX
8/0.0.2                   disk    EMC      SYMMETRIX
8/0.0.3                   disk    EMC      SYMMETRIX
8/0.0.4                   disk    EMC      SYMMETRIX
8/0.0.5                   disk    EMC      SYMMETRIX
8/0.0.6                   disk    EMC      SYMMETRIX
8/0.7                 target
8/0.7.0                   ctl     Initiator
8/4               ext_bus         GSC add-on Fast/Wide SCSI Interface
8/4.0                 target
8/4.0.0                   disk    EMC      SYMMETRIX
8/4.0.1                   disk    EMC      SYMMETRIX
8/4.0.2                   disk    EMC      SYMMETRIX
8/4.0.3                   disk    EMC      SYMMETRIX
8/4.0.4                   disk    EMC      SYMMETRIX
8/4.0.5                   disk    EMC      SYMMETRIX
8/4.0.6                   disk    EMC      SYMMETRIX
8/4.7                 target
8/4.7.0                   ctl     Initiator
8/8               ext_bus         GSC add-on Fast/Wide SCSI Interface
8/8.0                 target
8/8.0.0                   disk    EMC      SYMMETRIX
8/8.0.1                   disk    EMC      SYMMETRIX
8/8.0.2                   disk    EMC      SYMMETRIX
8/8.0.3                   disk    EMC      SYMMETRIX
8/8.0.4                   disk    EMC      SYMMETRIX
8/8.0.5                   disk    EMC      SYMMETRIX
8/8.0.6                   disk    EMC      SYMMETRIX
8/8.7                 target
8/8.7.0                   ctl     Initiator
8/12              ext_bus         GSC add-on Fast/Wide SCSI Interface
8/12.0                target
8/12.0.0                  disk    EMC      SYMMETRIX
8/12.0.1                  disk    EMC      SYMMETRIX
8/12.0.2                  disk    EMC      SYMMETRIX
8/12.0.3                  disk    EMC      SYMMETRIX
8/12.0.4                  disk    EMC      SYMMETRIX
8/12.0.5                  disk    EMC      SYMMETRIX
8/12.0.6                  disk    EMC      SYMMETRIX
8/12.7                target
8/12.7.0                  ctl     Initiator
10            bc                  I/O Adapter
10/0              ext_bus         GSC built-in Fast/Wide SCSI Interface
10/0.3                target
10/0.3.0                  disk    SEAGATE ST15150W
10/0.4                target
10/0.4.0                  disk    SEAGATE ST15150W
10/0.5                target
10/0.5.0                  disk    SEAGATE ST15150W
```

```
10/0.6              target
10/0.6.0               disk        SEAGATE ST15150W
10/0.7              target
10/0.7.0               ctl         Initiator
10/4         bc                    Bus Converter
10/4/0              tty            MUX
10/8         ext_bus               GSC add-on Fast/Wide SCSI Interface
10/8.0              target
10/8.0.0               disk        EMC       SYMMETRIX
10/8.0.1               disk        EMC       SYMMETRIX
10/8.0.2               disk        EMC       SYMMETRIX
10/8.0.3               disk        EMC       SYMMETRIX
10/8.0.4               disk        EMC       SYMMETRIX
10/8.0.5               disk        EMC       SYMMETRIX
10/8.0.6               disk        EMC       SYMMETRIX
10/8.7              target
10/8.7.0               ctl         Initiator
10/12        ba                    Core I/O Adapter
10/12/0             ext_bus        Built-in Parallel Interface
10/12/5             ext_bus        Built-in SCSI
10/12/5.0              target
10/12/5.0.0               tape     HP        C1533A
10/12/5.2              target
10/12/5.2.0               disk     TOSHIBA CD-ROM XM-5401TA
10/12/5.7              target
10/12/5.7.0               ctl      Initiator
10/12/6             lan            Built-in LAN
10/12/7             ps2            Built-in Keyboard/Mouse
10/16        bc                    Bus Converter
10/16/12            lan            HP J2157A - FDDI Interface
32           processor             Processor
34           processor             Processor
36           processor             Processor
38           processor             Processor
49           memory                Memory


$ ioscan -funC disk

Class     I  H/W Path     Driver     S/W State H/W Type  Description
=======================================================================
disk      5  8/0.0.0      sdisk      CLAIMED    DEVICE     EMC      SYMMETRIX
                         /dev/dsk/c0t0d0   /dev/rdsk/c0t0d0
disk      6  8/0.0.1      sdisk      CLAIMED    DEVICE     EMC      SYMMETRIX
                         /dev/dsk/c0t0d1   /dev/rdsk/c0t0d1
disk      7  8/0.0.2      sdisk      CLAIMED    DEVICE     EMC      SYMMETRIX
                         /dev/dsk/c0t0d2   /dev/rdsk/c0t0d2
disk      8  8/0.0.3      sdisk      CLAIMED    DEVICE     EMC      SYMMETRIX
                         /dev/dsk/c0t0d3   /dev/rdsk/c0t0d3
disk      9  8/0.0.4      sdisk      CLAIMED    DEVICE     EMC      SYMMETRIX
                         /dev/dsk/c0t0d4   /dev/rdsk/c0t0d4
disk     10  8/0.0.5      sdisk      CLAIMED    DEVICE     EMC      SYMMETRIX
                         /dev/dsk/c0t0d5   /dev/rdsk/c0t0d5
disk     11  8/0.0.6      sdisk      CLAIMED    DEVICE     EMC      SYMMETRIX
                         /dev/dsk/c0t0d6   /dev/rdsk/c0t0d6
disk     12  8/4.0.0      sdisk      CLAIMED    DEVICE     EMC      SYMMETRIX
                         /dev/dsk/c1t0d0   /dev/rdsk/c1t0d0
disk     13  8/4.0.1      sdisk      CLAIMED    DEVICE     EMC      SYMMETRIX
```

```
                                    /dev/dsk/c1t0d1    /dev/rdsk/c1t0d1
disk    14  8/4.0.2     sdisk       CLAIMED   DEVICE      EMC      SYMMETRIX
                                    /dev/dsk/c1t0d2    /dev/rdsk/c1t0d2
disk    15  8/4.0.3     sdisk       CLAIMED   DEVICE      EMC      SYMMETRIX
                                    /dev/dsk/c1t0d3    /dev/rdsk/c1t0d3
disk    16  8/4.0.4     sdisk       CLAIMED   DEVICE      EMC      SYMMETRIX
                                    /dev/dsk/c1t0d4    /dev/rdsk/c1t0d4
disk    17  8/4.0.5     sdisk       CLAIMED   DEVICE      EMC      SYMMETRIX
                                    /dev/dsk/c1t0d5    /dev/rdsk/c1t0d5
disk    18  8/4.0.6     sdisk       CLAIMED   DEVICE      EMC      SYMMETRIX
                                    /dev/dsk/c1t0d6    /dev/rdsk/c1t0d6
disk    19  8/8.0.0     sdisk       CLAIMED   DEVICE      EMC      SYMMETRIX
                                    /dev/dsk/c2t0d0    /dev/rdsk/c2t0d0
disk    20  8/8.0.1     sdisk       CLAIMED   DEVICE      EMC      SYMMETRIX
                                    /dev/dsk/c2t0d1    /dev/rdsk/c2t0d1
disk    21  8/8.0.2     sdisk       CLAIMED   DEVICE      EMC      SYMMETRIX
                                    /dev/dsk/c2t0d2    /dev/rdsk/c2t0d2
disk    22  8/8.0.3     sdisk       CLAIMED   DEVICE      EMC      SYMMETRIX
                                    /dev/dsk/c2t0d3    /dev/rdsk/c2t0d3
disk    23  8/8.0.4     sdisk       CLAIMED   DEVICE      EMC      SYMMETRIX
                                    /dev/dsk/c2t0d4    /dev/rdsk/c2t0d4
disk    24  8/8.0.5     sdisk       CLAIMED   DEVICE      EMC      SYMMETRIX
                                    /dev/dsk/c2t0d5    /dev/rdsk/c2t0d5
disk    25  8/8.0.6     sdisk       CLAIMED   DEVICE      EMC      SYMMETRIX
                                    /dev/dsk/c2t0d6    /dev/rdsk/c2t0d6
disk    26  8/12.0.0    sdisk       CLAIMED   DEVICE      EMC      SYMMETRIX
                                    /dev/dsk/c3t0d0    /dev/rdsk/c3t0d0
disk    27  8/12.0.1    sdisk       CLAIMED   DEVICE      EMC      SYMMETRIX
                                    /dev/dsk/c3t0d1    /dev/rdsk/c3t0d1
disk    28  8/12.0.2    sdisk       CLAIMED   DEVICE      EMC      SYMMETRIX
                                    /dev/dsk/c3t0d2    /dev/rdsk/c3t0d2
disk    29  8/12.0.3    sdisk       CLAIMED   DEVICE      EMC      SYMMETRIX
                                    /dev/dsk/c3t0d3    /dev/rdsk/c3t0d3
disk    30  8/12.0.4    sdisk       CLAIMED   DEVICE      EMC      SYMMETRIX
                                    /dev/dsk/c3t0d4    /dev/rdsk/c3t0d4
disk    31  8/12.0.5    sdisk       CLAIMED   DEVICE      EMC      SYMMETRIX
                                    /dev/dsk/c3t0d5    /dev/rdsk/c3t0d5
disk    32  8/12.0.6    sdisk       CLAIMED   DEVICE      EMC      SYMMETRIX
                                    /dev/dsk/c3t0d6    /dev/rdsk/c3t0d6
disk     0  10/0.3.0    sdisk       CLAIMED   DEVICE      SEAGATE  ST15150W
                                    /dev/dsk/c4t3d0    /dev/rdsk/c4t3d0
disk     1  10/0.4.0    sdisk       CLAIMED   DEVICE      SEAGATE  ST15150W
                                    /dev/dsk/c4t4d0    /dev/rdsk/c4t4d0
disk     2  10/0.5.0    sdisk       CLAIMED   DEVICE      SEAGATE  ST15150W
                                    /dev/dsk/c4t5d0    /dev/rdsk/c4t5d0
disk     3  10/0.6.0    sdisk       CLAIMED   DEVICE      SEAGATE  ST15150W
                                    /dev/dsk/c4t6d0    /dev/rdsk/c4t6d0
disk    33  10/8.0.0    sdisk       CLAIMED   DEVICE      EMC      SYMMETRIX
                                    /dev/dsk/c5t0d0    /dev/rdsk/c5t0d0
disk    34  10/8.0.1    sdisk       CLAIMED   DEVICE      EMC      SYMMETRIX
                                    /dev/dsk/c5t0d1    /dev/rdsk/c5t0d1
disk    35  10/8.0.2    sdisk       CLAIMED   DEVICE      EMC      SYMMETRIX
                                    /dev/dsk/c5t0d2    /dev/rdsk/c5t0d2
disk    36  10/8.0.3    sdisk       CLAIMED   DEVICE      EMC      SYMMETRIX
                                    /dev/dsk/c5t0d3    /dev/rdsk/c5t0d3
disk    37  10/8.0.4    sdisk       CLAIMED   DEVICE      EMC      SYMMETRIX
                                    /dev/dsk/c5t0d4    /dev/rdsk/c5t0d4
disk    38  10/8.0.5    sdisk       CLAIMED   DEVICE      EMC      SYMMETRIX
```

```
                              /dev/dsk/c5t0d5   /dev/rdsk/c5t0d5
        disk    39  10/8.0.6    sdisk      CLAIMED   DEVICE    EMC       SYMMETRIX
                              /dev/dsk/c5t0d6   /dev/rdsk/c5t0d6
        disk     4  10/12/5.2.0 sdisk      CLAIMED   DEVICE    TOSHIBA CD-ROM XM-5401TA
                              /dev/dsk/c6t2d0   /dev/rdsk/c6t2d0
```

You can see from the **ioscan** outputs that this system has a lot of disk capacity. For the first part of this benchmark, from which the data in this section of the book comes, the disk is used minimally. In subsequent parts of the benchmark there is a lot of disk I/O.

Notice that the first **ioscan** shows both a built-in lan and a Fiber Distributed Data Interface (FDDI). The FDDI is used as a high-speed connection between two systems used in the benchmark.

After initiating the benchmark, I invoked HP GlancePlus/UX to begin characterizing the performance of the system. After a little hopping around in GlancePlus to get a feel for the system, I quickly stumbled across a potential problem. Figure 5-17 shows a GlancePlus screen that clearly identifies that the FDDI is nearly unused at a critical point in the benchmark when it should be heavily used.

```
B3692A GlancePlus B.10.12        11:34:29     Sut26 9000/889      Current   Avg   High
-------------------------------------------------------------------------------------
CPU   Util  S     SAU                              U          | 71%    27%   100%
Disk  Util  F  F                                              |  5%     1%    21%
Mem   Util  S    SU                                     UB     | 78%    69%    78%
Swap  Util  U                                   UR           R| 88%    76%    88%
Network------------------------------------------------------------------------------
                        NETWORK BY INTERFACE                    Users=    3

Interface  Network Type   Packets In   Packets Out   Collisions      Errors

ni0        Serial         0.0/   0.0    0.0/    0.0   0.0/   0.0    0.0/   0.0
ni1        Serial         0.0/   0.0    0.0/    0.0   0.0/   0.0    0.0/   0.0
lo0        Loop           0.0/   5.0    0.0/    5.0   0.0/   0.0    0.0/   0.0
lan1       Lan            0.1/   0.0    0.1/    0.0   0.0/   0.0    0.0/   0.0
lan0       Lan          986.4/ 237.0 1009.6/  251.8  11.1/   1.8    0.0/   0.0




                                                          Page 1 of 1
-------------------------------------------------------------------------------------
|  IO By  |  IO By  |  IO By  | Swap  |   hpterm   |  Next  | Select |Netwk By| System
| File Sys|  Disk   |Logl Vol| Space |            |  Keys  |Process |Intrface| Tables
```

Figure 5-17 HP GlancePlus/UX Showing lan Activity

lan1 is the FDDI over which very few packets are being transferred. Since there should be extensive data being transferred over the FDDI at this point in the benchmark, it was clear there was a problem with the benchmark software configuration. I then issued the following **netstat** command to indeed confirm that the interface is unused:

```
$ netstat -I lan1 5
```

(lan1)-> input		output			(Total)-> input		output		
packets	errs	packets	errs	colls	packets	errs	packets	errs	colls
3880	0	3881	0	0	598018	2	329555	0	1654
2	0	2	0	0	2736	0	3152	0	12
0	0	0	0	0	4997	0	5364	0	42
0	0	0	0	0	4443	0	5263	0	41
0	0	0	0	0	3822	0	4790	0	37
0	0	0	0	0	6061	0	6977	0	29
0	0	0	0	0	5468	0	6483	0	48
2	0	2	0	0	4718	0	5614	0	45
0	0	0	0	0	6135	0	6808	0	43
0	0	0	0	0	6136	0	6887	0	50
0	0	0	0	0	4872	0	5847	0	33
0	0	0	0	0	4673	0	5660	0	30
0	0	0	0	0	6021	0	6831	0	68
2	0	2	0	0	5450	0	6180	0	69
0	0	0	0	0	4208	0	4836	0	35
0	0	0	0	0	3351	0	4083	0	19
0	0	0	0	0	4972	0	5836	0	47
0	0	0	0	0	6381	0	7163	0	52
0	0	0	0	0	5094	0	6146	0	36
2	0	2	0	0	5281	0	6196	0	42

The low input and output packets in this **netstat** output confirm that the FDDI was not used as the source of the extensive data transfer during the benchmark. The problem was easy to fix. The FDDI had not been specified as the interface through which information was to be transferred during the benchmark.

After fixing this problem and the benchmark resumed, I began to view additional performance information. I like to bring up a global Glance screen when I start looking at a system, as shown in Figure 5-18.

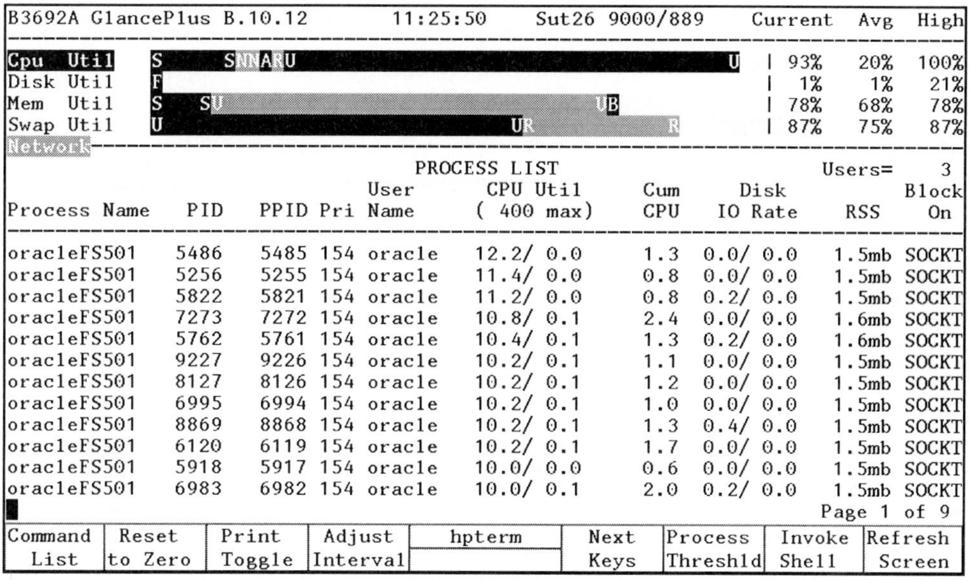

```
B3692A GlancePlus B.10.12        11:25:50      Sut26 9000/889     Current   Avg   High
-----------------------------------------------------------------------------------------
Cpu  Util  S    SNNARU                                     U  | 93%    20%   100%
Disk Util  F                                                  |  1%     1%    21%
Mem  Util  S  SU                                    UB        | 78%    68%    78%
Swap Util  U                            UR              R     | 87%    75%    87%
Network-----------------------------------------------------------------------------------
                                  PROCESS LIST                       Users=    3
                          User     CPU Util       Cum      Disk              Block
Process Name    PID   PPID Pri Name   ( 400 max)    CPU    IO Rate     RSS     On
-----------------------------------------------------------------------------------------
oracleFS501    5486   5485 154 oracle  12.2/ 0.0    1.3    0.0/ 0.0   1.5mb  SOCKT
oracleFS501    5256   5255 154 oracle  11.4/ 0.0    0.8    0.0/ 0.0   1.5mb  SOCKT
oracleFS501    5822   5821 154 oracle  11.2/ 0.0    0.8    0.2/ 0.0   1.5mb  SOCKT
oracleFS501    7273   7272 154 oracle  10.8/ 0.1    2.4    0.0/ 0.0   1.6mb  SOCKT
oracleFS501    5762   5761 154 oracle  10.4/ 0.1    1.3    0.2/ 0.0   1.6mb  SOCKT
oracleFS501    9227   9226 154 oracle  10.2/ 0.1    1.1    0.0/ 0.0   1.5mb  SOCKT
oracleFS501    8127   8126 154 oracle  10.2/ 0.1    1.2    0.0/ 0.0   1.5mb  SOCKT
oracleFS501    6995   6994 154 oracle  10.2/ 0.1    1.0    0.0/ 0.0   1.5mb  SOCKT
oracleFS501    8869   8868 154 oracle  10.2/ 0.1    1.3    0.4/ 0.0   1.5mb  SOCKT
oracleFS501    6120   6119 154 oracle  10.2/ 0.1    1.7    0.0/ 0.0   1.5mb  SOCKT
oracleFS501    5918   5917 154 oracle  10.0/ 0.0    0.6    0.0/ 0.0   1.5mb  SOCKT
oracleFS501    6983   6982 154 oracle  10.0/ 0.1    2.0    0.2/ 0.0   1.5mb  SOCKT
■                                                                Page 1 of 9
-----------------------------------------------------------------------------------------
Command  Reset   Print   Adjust       hpterm      Next  Process   Invoke Refresh
 List  to Zero  Toggle Interval                   Keys Threshld  Shell   Screen
```

Figure 5-18 HP GlancePlus/UX Global Screen

The processes shown in the Global screen are sorted by the amount of CPU consumed. The many "oracleFS501" processes shown are being run by the benchmark program.

It seems clear from Figure 5-18 that the CPU may turn out to be the bottleneck of this portion of the benchmark. The user processes "oracleFS501" are consuming a great deal of system resources. The first of these processes, for instance, is consuming 12.2% out of a total of 400% of CPU resources. You see 400% CPU resources because there are four CPUs in the system times 100% per CPU.

Figure 5-19 shows more detail related to the CPUs of the system.

```
B3692A GlancePlus B.10.12        14:51:51     Sut26 9000/889    Current  Avg  High
--------------------------------------------------------------------------------
Cpu  Util  S  SARU                                         U |100%   89%  100%
Disk Util  F                                                 |  1%    2%    5%
Mem  Util  S  SU                                    UB       | 80%   80%   80%
Swap Util  U                              UR          R      | 91%   91%   91%
Network--------------------------------------------------------------------------
                              CPU REPORT                      Users=    5
State          Current      Average         High       Time    Cum Time
--------------------------------------------------------------------------------
User            91.3         75.3           94.1       4.85      923.23
Nice             0.0          0.0            0.4       0.00        0.03
Negative Nice    0.8          0.9            5.2       0.04       10.79
RealTime         0.6          0.8            2.1       0.03        9.99
System           4.1          7.1           15.3       0.22       86.85
Interrupt        1.7          2.2            3.9       0.09       27.26
ContextSwitch    1.3          2.4            5.8       0.07       29.91
Traps            0.2          0.4            1.0       0.01        5.32
Vfaults          0.0          0.0            0.7       0.00        0.40
Idle             0.0         10.8           62.7       0.00      132.66

Top CPU user: PID 14246, oracleFS501B03      14.5% cpu util

█                                                          Page 1 of 2
--------------------------------------------------------------------------------
Process  | CPU    | Memory | Disk   | hpterm   | Next  | Appl | Help | Exit
List     | Report | Report | Report |          | Keys  | List |      | Glance
```

Figure 5-19 HP GlancePlus/UX CPU Screen

Figure 5-19 shows that user processes are consuming the vast majority of CPU resources, which is exactly what I expected at this point in the benchmark. In addition, 91.3% of the CPU is consumed by user processes and only 4.1% by system processes. At this point I feel the system is running efficiently.

Prior to starting the benchmar, I started **sar** accumulating data at an interval of 60 seconds in the file **sar.data**. This is a binary file from which important performance data can be later extracted. The command used to save the binary performance information in an output file is shown below:

```
# sar -o /tmp/sar.data 60 300
```

We can now view the CPU-related information collected by **sar**. **sar** is useful for showing the historical CPU data. In this case, the historical data consists of one-minute intervals. In the following example, you can see that the CPU started out mostly idle in this benchmark and then worked its way up to a high level of utilization beginning at 13:39:43.

```
$ sar -b -f sar.data

HP-UX Sut26 B.10.20 U 9000/889   12/05/97

13:01:43   %usr   %sys   %wio  %idle
13:02:43    1      1      0     98
13:03:43    1      1      0     98
13:04:43    1      1      0     98
13:05:43    1      1      0     98
13:06:43    1      1      0     98
13:07:43    1      1      0     98
13:08:43    1      1      0     97
13:09:43   18      3      2     77
13:10:43   16      2      1     81
13:11:43    1      1      0     98
13:12:43    1      1      0     98
13:13:43    1      1      0     98
13:14:43    1      1      0     98
13:15:43    1      1      0     97
13:16:43    1      1      0     98
13:17:43    1      1      0     98
13:18:43    1      1      0     98
13:19:43    1      1      0     98
13:20:43    3      1      0     96
13:21:43    5      1      0     94
13:22:43    1      1      0     98
13:23:43    1      1      0     98
13:24:43    1      1      0     98
13:25:43    1      1      0     98
13:26:43    1      1      0     98
13:27:43    1      1      0     98
13:28:43    1      1      0     98
13:29:43    1      1      0     98
13:30:43    1      1      0     97
13:31:43    1      1      0     98
13:32:43    1      1      0     98
13:33:43    1      1      0     98
13:34:43    1      1      0     98
13:35:43    1      1      0     98
13:36:43    1      0      0     99
13:37:43    0      0      0     99
13:38:43    1      0      0     99
13:39:43   35      4      0     61
13:40:43   76      9      0     15
13:41:43   76      9      0     15
13:42:43   71      8      0     21
13:43:43   84     10      0      5
13:44:43   80     13      0      7
13:45:43   60      6      0     34
13:46:43   63      6      0     30
```

13:47:43	77	8	0	15
13:48:43	85	11	0	4
13:49:43	82	11	0	8
13:50:43	80	9	0	11
13:51:43	60	5	0	34
13:52:43	80	8	0	12
13:53:43	84	10	0	6
13:54:43	72	7	0	21
13:55:43	81	9	0	10
13:56:43	76	8	0	16
13:57:43	70	7	0	23
13:58:43	76	7	0	17
13:59:43	76	8	0	16
14:00:43	74	7	0	19
14:01:43	76	8	0	16
14:02:43	78	8	0	13
14:03:43	77	8	0	15
14:04:43	81	9	0	9
14:05:43	69	7	0	24
14:06:43	76	8	0	16
14:07:43	79	8	0	13
14:08:43	70	7	0	23
14:09:43	80	8	0	11
14:10:43	75	8	0	17
14:11:43	70	7	0	22
14:12:43	77	8	0	15
14:13:43	78	8	0	14
14:14:43	72	7	0	21
14:15:43	79	8	0	12
14:16:43	82	8	0	10
14:17:43	79	8	0	13
14:18:43	78	7	0	15
14:19:43	80	8	0	11
14:20:43	79	8	0	13
14:21:43	73	8	0	18
14:22:43	79	9	0	12
14:23:43	81	9	0	9
14:24:43	78	9	0	13
14:25:43	73	8	0	18
14:26:43	68	8	0	23
14:27:43	67	8	0	25
Average	44	5	0	51

This **sar** output shows the trend of CPU utilization. The earlier GlancePlus screen shot showing very high CPU utilization was taken at a time of peak CPU utilization during the benchmark.

In addition to the CPU, memory was considered a key component in this benchmark run. Figure 5-20 is a GlancePlus memory screen shot.

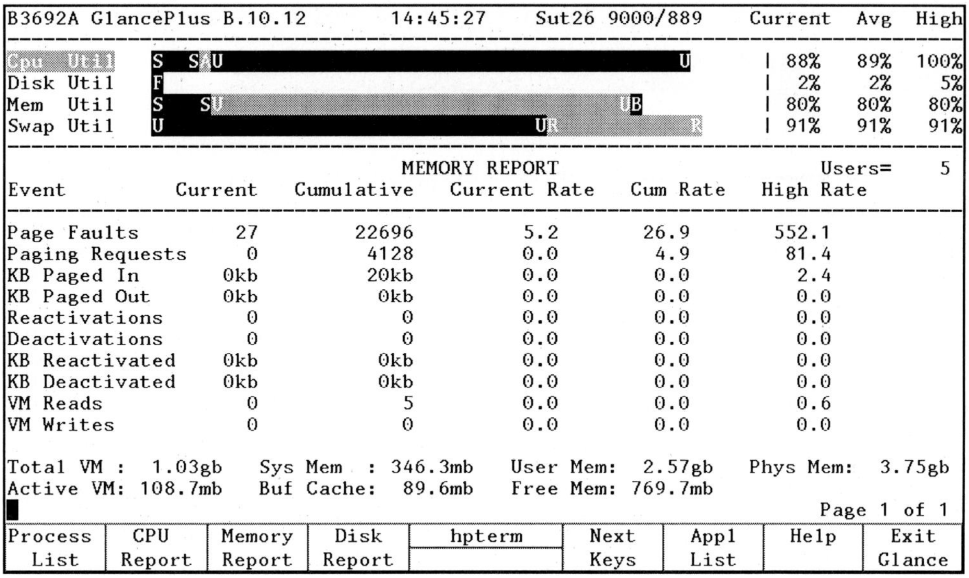

```
B3692A GlancePlus B.10.12        14:45:27      Sut26 9000/889      Current   Avg   High
------------------------------------------------------------------------------
Cpu  Util    S   S U                                        U    | 88%   89%   100%
Disk Util    F                                                    | 2%    2%    5%
Mem  Util    S   S U                                       UB    | 80%   80%   80%
Swap Util    U                                           UR   R  | 91%   91%   91%
------------------------------------------------------------------------------
                              MEMORY REPORT                         Users=   5
Event            Current   Cumulative   Current Rate   Cum Rate   High Rate
------------------------------------------------------------------------------
Page Faults         27       22696          5.2          26.9       552.1
Paging Requests      0        4128          0.0           4.9        81.4
KB Paged In        0kb        20kb          0.0           0.0         2.4
KB Paged Out       0kb         0kb          0.0           0.0         0.0
Reactivations        0           0          0.0           0.0         0.0
Deactivations        0           0          0.0           0.0         0.0
KB Reactivated     0kb         0kb          0.0           0.0         0.0
KB Deactivated     0kb         0kb          0.0           0.0         0.0
VM Reads             0           5          0.0           0.0         0.6
VM Writes            0           0          0.0           0.0         0.0

Total VM :  1.03gb    Sys Mem  : 346.3mb    User Mem:  2.57gb    Phys Mem:  3.75gb
Active VM: 108.7mb    Buf Cache:  89.6mb    Free Mem: 769.7mb
                                                                     Page 1 of 1
------------------------------------------------------------------------------
Process  | CPU    | Memory | Disk   |   hpterm  | Next  | Appl | Help  | Exit
List     | Report | Report | Report |           | Keys  | List |       | Glance
```

Figure 5-20   HP GlancePlus/UX Memory Screen

This screen shows the memory utilization at a steady 80%. The physical memory in the system is 3.75 GBytes, of which roughly 769 MBytes is free. Although 80% is high memory utilization there is still enough free memory at this point in the benchmark to point back to the CPU as the bottleneck.

The disk was not expected to be a factor during the benchmark. Only in the first stage of the benchmark, when a database of roughly 100 GBytes was built, was there high disk utilization. A large Symmetrix® disk bank was included to hold this 100 GByte database for a subsequent step in the benchmark when substantially more data and disk activity was to take place. Figure 5-21 shows some **uncompress** processes that ran early in the benchmark, consuming a lot of CPU and very high disk utilization as the database is created. As soon as the database was created and the benchmark began, the disk utilization dropped back to a very low level.

```
B3692A GlancePlus B.10.12        09:41:18    Sut26 9000/889   Current  Avg  High
--------------------------------------------------------------------------------
Cpu  Util  S              SRU                         U    | 90%   89%   97%
Disk Util  F                                           F   | 99%   96%  100%
Mem  Util  S   SUBB                                        | 13%   13%   13%
Swap Util  UR   R                                         | 13%   13%   13%
--------------------------------------------------------------------------------
                                PROCESS LIST                    Users=    3
                               User     CPU Util    Cum    Disk          Block
Process Name    PID   PPID Pri Name   ( 400 max)    CPU  IO Rate    RSS     On
--------------------------------------------------------------------------------
uncompress     1407   1375 149 root    20.8/18.0   211.7 39.6/26.5  732kb CACHE
uncompress     1408   1375 154 root    16.1/18.8   222.0 20.3/29.1  732kb PIPE
uncompress     1416   1375 154 root    15.8/10.0   117.4 12.9/ 2.5  780kb PIPE
uncompress     1412   1375 241 root    15.4/11.6   136.8 17.4/ 7.2  740kb  PRI
uncompress     1410   1375 154 root    15.0/ 8.5   100.2 15.2/ 2.8  740kb PIPE
uncompress     1419   1375 149 root    14.2/11.1   130.8 17.2/ 8.0  756kb CACHE
uncompress     1427   1375 154 root    13.2/11.5   135.7 13.9/10.0  756kb PIPE
uncompress     1421   1375 154 root    12.5/11.2   132.5  5.0/ 3.8  764kb PIPE
midaemon       1489   1488  50 root    10.7/10.4   122.9  0.0/ 0.0  2.1mb SYSTM
uncompress     1420   1375 154 root     9.7/ 8.9   104.4  1.7/ 0.0  772kb PIPE
uncompress     1413   1375 154 root     9.3/ 8.8   103.7  3.5/ 3.1  740kb PIPE
uncompress     1423   1375 241 root     9.3/ 9.3   110.2  9.4/ 4.0  756kb  PRI
                                                             Page 1 of 5
--------------------------------------------------------------------------------
Process | CPU    | Memory | Disk   | hpterm  | Next  | Appl | Help | Exit
List    | Report | Report | Report |         | Keys  | List |      | Glance
```

Figure 5-21 HP GlancePlus/UX Showing High Disk Utilization as the Database Is Built

The first **uncompress** process is consuming 20% of the CPU (there is 400% CPU available) while the disk is 99% utilized. Since creating the database was preparation for running the benchmark and not the benchmark itself, this high disk utilization was not a concern to me.

The following **sar** output confirms the low disk utilization during the majority of the benchmark. Only a few minutes of data are included in this example, because the output is lengthy due to the many disks on the system.

```
$ sar -d -f sar.data


HP-UX Sut26 B.10.20 U 9000/889    12/05/97

10:38:35   device   %busy   avque   r+w/s   blks/s   avwait   avserv
10:39:35   c4t6d0    0.25    2.74      0        5     20.39    13.31
           c0t0d0    0.18    2.98      0        6     21.93     9.64
           c0t0d1    0.20    3.28      0        7     22.99     9.22
           c0t0d2    0.18    3.06      0        7     22.35     8.92
           c0t0d3    0.17    1.56      0        5     13.68     9.97
           c0t0d4    0.18    2.24      0        6     17.69     9.68
           c1t0d0    0.23    3.13      0        7     22.37     9.61
           c1t0d1    0.20    1.46      0        5     12.78     7.50
           c1t0d2    0.22    3.66      0        7     25.62     9.39
           c1t0d3    0.20    2.66      0        7     21.37     9.44
           c1t0d4    0.23    3.09      0        8     24.15     9.23
           c2t0d0    0.27    3.43      0        7     32.70    11.81
           c2t0d1    0.25    2.40      0        5     24.01    14.10
           c2t0d2    0.23    3.41      0        6     31.27    12.48
           c2t0d3    0.23    2.25      0        5     22.13    13.98
           c2t0d4    0.22    1.75      0        4     15.92    13.92
           c3t0d0    0.20    2.80      0        6     19.83     9.51
           c3t0d1    0.20    3.61      0        7     25.34     9.09
           c3t0d2    0.17    2.10      0        4     20.18    10.86
           c3t0d3    0.20    3.39      0        7     23.76     9.11
           c3t0d4    0.17    1.55      0        6     12.27     8.59
           c5t0d0    0.27    2.74      0        7     25.36    12.55
           c5t0d1    0.32    4.67      1        8     39.51    12.01
           c5t0d2    0.28    2.33      0        6     23.27    13.04
           c5t0d3    0.22    2.89      0        5     28.31    13.58
           c5t0d4    0.25    2.93      0        6     28.25    12.62
           c4t4d0    0.32    1.50      0        6     14.46    11.12
10:40:35   c4t6d0    0.13    0.80      0        2      8.44    12.88
           c0t0d0    0.18    2.00      0        7     16.02     8.32
           c0t0d1    0.17    2.55      0        5     18.06     9.88
           c0t0d2    0.15    2.39      0        5     19.05     9.82
           c0t0d3    0.17    3.37      0        6     23.79     8.64
           c0t0d4    0.15    1.67      0        5     14.17     9.78
           c1t0d0    0.17    1.79      0        6     15.08     8.00
           c1t0d1    0.15    2.73      0        6     21.91     8.27
           c1t0d2    0.18    1.83      0        6     14.52     6.94
           c1t0d3    0.13    3.00      0        5     21.38     8.72
           c1t0d4    0.12    1.43      0        4     13.37     9.25
           c2t0d0    0.20    1.50      0        5     15.43    10.87
           c2t0d1    0.20    3.05      0        5     29.09    11.74
           c2t0d2    0.20    1.90      0        4     17.37    13.70
           c2t0d3    0.22    2.13      0        5     21.91    12.16
           c2t0d4    0.20    2.79      0        5     29.60    13.22
           c3t0d0    0.17    2.03      0        5     17.48     9.27
           c3t0d1    0.17    2.85      0        5     21.18     9.81
           c3t0d2    0.13    1.74      0        5     14.00     9.17
           c3t0d3    0.15    1.87      0        5     15.87     9.18
           c3t0d4    0.17    1.93      0        6     16.30     8.47
           c5t0d0    0.22    1.80      0        5     19.61    12.06
           c5t0d1    0.17    1.90      0        4     17.66    12.84
           c5t0d2    0.20    1.60      0        5     17.52    11.59
```

	c5t0d3	0.20	2.18	0	5	20.64	12.26
	c5t0d4	0.13	1.19	0	3	11.34	11.42
	c4t4d0	0.25	0.85	0	5	7.63	11.82
10:41:35	c4t6d0	0.17	0.93	0	4	11.06	12.21
	c1t0d2	0.03	0.50	0	1	5.21	0.83
	c3t0d1	0.02	0.50	0	1	4.74	0.91
	c4t4d0	0.23	0.86	0	5	8.19	11.09
10:42:35	c4t6d0	0.35	1.46	0	7	14.39	16.72
	c0t0d0	0.13	0.94	0	4	9.45	8.67
	c0t0d1	0.17	2.92	0	7	20.85	7.62
	c0t0d2	0.13	2.14	0	4	18.03	9.96
	c0t0d3	0.13	1.44	0	4	12.33	9.42
	c0t0d4	0.15	2.75	0	5	19.55	9.23
	c1t0d0	0.18	2.12	0	6	15.90	7.89
	c1t0d1	0.18	3.12	0	6	22.67	9.11
	c1t0d2	0.13	2.26	0	4	17.11	7.49
	c1t0d3	0.15	1.78	0	5	14.21	9.26
	c1t0d4	0.15	3.13	0	5	22.44	9.00
	c2t0d0	0.17	1.50	0	4	15.58	12.07
	c2t0d1	0.22	1.50	0	5	19.07	13.46
	c2t0d2	0.20	2.21	0	5	22.28	12.85
	c2t0d3	0.18	2.33	0	5	19.62	11.80
	c2t0d4	0.20	2.13	0	5	20.22	12.65
	c3t0d0	0.13	1.12	0	4	12.33	9.02
	c3t0d1	0.10	1.17	0	4	10.22	7.69
	c3t0d2	0.15	2.09	0	6	15.86	7.54
	c3t0d3	0.10	1.50	0	4	12.48	8.43
	c3t0d4	0.12	0.86	0	4	7.80	8.93
	c5t0d0	0.17	1.95	0	5	16.64	10.50
	c5t0d1	0.18	1.81	0	4	15.79	12.00
	c5t0d2	0.20	1.79	0	5	18.02	12.03
	c5t0d3	0.15	2.04	0	3	20.00	13.35
	c5t0d4	0.17	1.25	0	4	13.22	12.45
	c4t4d0	0.25	0.80	0	5	8.13	11.92
10:43:35	c4t6d0	0.40	1.61	1	9	15.81	13.47
	c0t0d0	0.12	1.79	0	4	13.80	9.13
	c0t0d1	0.12	1.86	0	3	15.52	10.17
	c0t0d2	0.13	2.22	0	5	17.55	9.02
	c0t0d3	0.13	1.62	0	5	12.87	8.48
	c0t0d4	0.13	2.34	0	5	17.77	8.50
	c1t0d0	0.17	2.50	0	5	18.74	9.42
	c1t0d1	0.13	1.71	0	4	15.45	10.46
	c1t0d2	0.17	2.09	0	5	16.18	6.74
	c1t0d3	0.13	1.63	0	4	14.21	9.82
	c1t0d4	0.15	1.91	0	5	16.92	9.58
	c2t0d0	0.22	3.67	0	6	33.16	10.62
	c2t0d1	0.17	2.50	0	4	21.72	12.61
	c2t0d2	0.20	2.74	0	6	26.35	11.46
	c2t0d3	0.17	1.50	0	3	18.71	13.43
	c2t0d4	0.18	1.61	0	5	15.70	11.24
	c3t0d0	0.15	3.00	0	6	20.56	7.90
	c3t0d1	0.10	1.00	0	3	8.48	8.13
	c3t0d2	0.13	1.79	0	5	14.48	8.80
	c3t0d3	0.13	1.91	0	5	14.55	8.78
	c3t0d4	0.15	1.97	0	5	15.41	9.28
	c5t0d0	0.23	2.89	0	6	26.02	11.70
	c5t0d1	0.17	1.75	0	4	17.14	12.56
	c5t0d2	0.18	2.00	0	4	21.24	13.44

```
          c5t0d3    0.22    2.22      0      5   23.23  13.29
          c5t0d4    0.20    2.50      0      5   26.82  13.61
          c4t4d0    0.48    0.82      1      8    8.48  12.50
```

I expected, as this benchmark progressed, that the run queue would grow and later recede. The following **sar** output confirms this expectation:

```
$ sar -q -f sar.data


HP-UX Sut26 B.10.20 U 9000/889      12/05/97

10:38:35 runq-sz %runocc swpq-sz %swpocc
10:39:35    0.0       0    0.0       0
10:40:35    0.0       0    0.0       0
10:41:35    1.0       1    0.0       0
10:42:35    1.0       1    0.0       0
10:43:35    0.0       0    0.0       0
10:44:35    0.0       0    0.0       0
10:45:35    0.0       0    0.0       0
10:46:35    0.0       0    0.0       0
10:47:35    0.0       0    0.0       0
10:48:35    0.0       0    0.0       0
10:49:35    1.0       0    0.0       0
10:50:35    0.0       0    0.0       0
10:51:35    0.0       0    0.0       0
10:52:35    0.0       0    0.0       0
10:53:35    0.0       0    0.0       0
10:54:35    0.0       0    0.0       0
10:55:35    0.0       0    0.0       0
10:56:35    0.0       0    0.0       0
10:57:35    1.0       2    0.0       0
10:58:35    0.0       0    0.0       0
10:59:35    1.0       2    0.0       0
11:00:35    0.0       0    0.0       0
11:01:35    1.0       2    0.0       0
11:02:35    0.0       0    0.0       0
11:03:35    1.0       0    0.0       0
11:04:35    0.0       0    0.0       0
11:05:35    1.0       2    0.0       0
11:06:35    1.0       0    0.0       0
11:07:35    1.0       0    0.0       0
11:08:35    1.0       2    0.0       0
11:09:35    1.0       2    0.0       0
```

11:10:35	1.0	0	0.0	0
11:11:35	1.0	0	0.0	0
11:12:35	1.0	2	0.0	0
11:13:35	0.0	0	0.0	0
11:14:35	0.0	0	0.0	0
11:15:35	1.0	0	0.0	0
11:16:35	8.1	21	0.0	0
11:17:35	7.4	72	0.0	0
11:18:35	3.8	44	0.0	0
11:19:35	6.7	72	0.0	0
11:20:35	8.1	92	0.0	0
11:21:35	10.6	88	0.0	0
11:22:35	13.0	90	0.0	0
11:23:35	6.7	47	0.0	0
11:24:35	7.4	71	0.0	0
11:25:35	6.7	83	0.0	0
11:26:35	8.5	65	0.0	0
11:27:35	8.6	88	0.0	0
11:28:35	5.3	69	0.0	0
11:29:35	5.9	58	0.0	0
11:30:35	4.0	43	0.0	0
11:31:35	7.9	86	0.0	0
11:32:35	7.3	84	0.0	0
11:33:35	5.6	59	0.0	0
11:34:35	6.2	47	0.0	0
11:35:35	7.3	23	0.0	0
11:36:35	0.0	0	0.0	0
11:37:35	0.0	0	0.0	0
11:38:35	0.0	0	0.0	0
Average	7.5	22	0.0	0

The *runq-sz* column shows the average length of the run queue for the one-minute period. The *%runocc* column shows the percentage of time that the run queues were occupied by a process. The higher these numbers, the more activity is taking place on the system.

Beginning at 11:16:35 in this file, the run queue length begins to increase dramatically. As in the other examples, there is a time period in the benchmark when simulated users are logging on to the system, an activity that does not consume much CPU. When the users are finally logged onto the system and simulated updates to the database begin, the CPU load increases and the run queue length increases.

In general, the performance characteristics of this benchmark are what were expected. Because the system is running efficiently, the focus of improving performance was not system-related but application-related. A substantial amount of database tuning was performed to help reduce the load on the CPU.

A Real-Life Performance Problem

It's true that networks "grow a life of their own" over the years. Many of my customers started out with innocent, self-contained, manageable networks 10 years ago that have now turned into monsters. What happened? Well, first, the number of computers grew from 10 to 100. Then the number of applications grew from 2 to 20 when other departments started sharing the same network. Then the data used by the applications grew from 5 MBytes to 200 MBytes. Then more sophisticated technology such as NFS became part of the network.

What if you're asked to improve the performance of an application? The application now takes several hours to complete its run. You are asked to assess the existing system resources (CPU, memory, disk, etc.) and make recommendations for how system resources should be expanded to reduce the completion time of this run. Almost invariably, people assume that a bigger something (CPU, memory, disk, etc.) is what is required to improve system performance.

Let's walk through the process of improving the performance of a specific computer running a specific application in a distributed environment.

First Things First - Taking Inventory

If indeed your network has grown or you are unfamiliar with the components of the network, the first step is to take an inventory. To begin, you want to know what systems run what applications, where data is stored, and where home directories are located. I like to call this a "functional" inventory. "Functional" in this case means that you don't know every detail of every component but you know the flow of data on the network and where it is located. Figure 5-22 is a greatly simplified version of a real functional network diagram. It is highly simplified because the original just won't fit in this book.

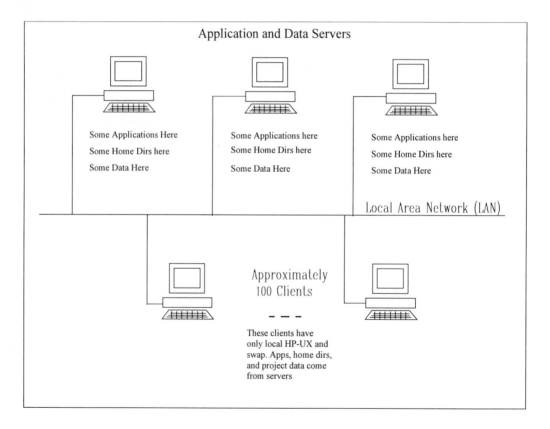

Figure 5-22   A Simplified Network Diagram

This network is set up in such a way that when a user logs in to a client, a home directory is accessed on one of the servers. If a user invokes an application, then the application and project data are copied to the local system. This means that you can expect a lot of network activity initially, but after the application and data are copied to the local system, everything is running on the local system so network activity is low.

This is a simplified network diagram so you can't see the vast number of applications and data spread over these servers. Before we even begin looking at the specific application we want to improve the performance of, you might look at this network diagram and question the amount of redundancy. There are three servers performing basically the same functions. It may make sense to consolidate some of this functionality onto one big server. Having functionality spread over several servers is a characteristic I see when networks have grown over many years. To appreciate the amount of mounting that client systems perform on the server disks, you can use the **showmount** command. The following *partial* **showmount** output (also used earlier in this chapter as an example) on one of the servers gives you an idea of the number of NFS mounted directories on the server:

```
# showmount -a

hp100.ct.mp.com:/applic

hp101.ct.mp.com:/applic

hp102.cal.mp.com:/applic

hp103.cal.mp.com:/applic

hp104.cal.mp.com:/applic

hp105.cal.mp.com:/applic

hp106.cal.mp.com:/applic

hp107.cal.mp.com:/applic

hp108.cal.mp.com:/applic

hp109.cal.mp.com:/applic

hp100.cal.mp.com:/usr/users

hp101.cal.mp.com:/usr/users
```

```
# showmount -a
```

hp102.cal.mp.com:/usr/users

hp103.cal.mp.com:/usr/users

hp104.cal.mp.com:/usr/users

hp105.cal.mp.com:/usr/users

hp106.cal.mp.com:/usr/users

hp107.cal.mp.com:/usr/users

hp108.cal.mp.com:/usr/users

hp109.cal.mp.com:/usr/users

This is a small fraction of the overall **showmount** output. As described earlier in this chapter, **showmount** has three options:

-a prints output in the format "name:directory," as shown above.
-d lists all the local directories that have been remotely
   mounted by clients.
-e prints a list of exported file systems.

Although consolidating information may indeed improve overall efficiency, the original objective is to improve the performance of application runs on client systems. Consolidating home directories and other such improvements might make system administration more efficient, but there is no guarantee this will improve performance. Instead, we want to characterize the application on the client and see how system resources are being used.

Characterize Application

Since the application is taking a long time to run, we need to find the source of the bottleneck. This can be an undersized CPU, lack of memory, or a variety of other problems. We can start by viewing virtual memory with **vmstat**. The following **vmstat** output was produced every five seconds a total of 15 times during an application run:

#vmstat 5 15:

procs			memory		page							faults			cpu		
r	b	w	avm	free	re	at	pi	po	fr	de	sr	in	sy	cs	us	sy	id
0	0	19	9484	91	0	0	0	0	0	0	0	65	84	20	7	0	93
0	0	22	10253	68	0	0	0	0	0	0	0	214	939	127	72	7	21
0	0	25	10288	90	0	0	0	0	0	0	9	289	988	152	73	5	22
0	0	25	10300	89	0	0	0	0	0	0	9	325	820	151	76	3	21
0	0	24	10298	90	0	0	0	0	0	0	2	139	629	94	94	4	2
0	0	21	9889	86	0	0	0	0	0	0	1	189	782	111	72	5	23
0	0	20	9886	77	0	0	0	0	0	0	0	220	998	135	73	5	22
0	0	21	10274	77	0	0	0	0	0	0	0	220	723	124	69	3	28
0	0	22	10285	73	0	0	0	0	0	0	0	265	606	94	90	3	7
0	0	22	10291	69	0	0	0	0	0	0	0	156	872	122	71	5	24
0	0	20	10292	60	0	0	0	0	0	0	0	192	989	139	72	5	23
0	0	21	9913	257	0	0	0	0	0	0	1	282	736	118	81	2	17
0	0	22	9915	257	0	0	0	0	0	0	9	209	596	84	89	5	6
0	0	22	10699	237	0	0	0	0	0	3	7	165	945	117	70	7	23
0	0	21	10211	229	0	0	0	0	0	3	1	331	677	127	71	5	24

From this example, you can see that runnable ("r") and blocked ("b") processes are zero, but swapped ("w") processes are roughly 20 for each five-second interval. This is indicative of a system that has a severe memory shortage. Note also that the active virtual memory ("avm") is around 10,000 blocks which is roughly 40 MBytes:

$$10,000 blocks \times 4,096 bytes per block = 40 MBytes$$

With this amount of active virtual memory and swapped processes, you would expect to see a great deal of disk activity. The next logical step would be to run **iostat** and see whether indeed a great deal of disk activity is taking place. **iostat** was run five times at five-second intervals to produce the following output:

 # iostat 5 5

	tty			cpu		
tin	tout		us	ni	sy	id
0	1		6	0	0	93

/dev/*dsk/c2076d*s*

bps	sps	msps
2	0.3	0.0

	tty			cpu		
tin	tout		us	ni	sy	id
0	73		72	0	5	23

/dev/*dsk/c2076d*s*

bps	sps	msps
17	0.6	0.0

	tty			cpu		
tin	tout		us	ni	sy	id
0	97		85	0	4	11

/dev/*dsk/c2076d*s*

bps	sps	msps
1	0.2	0.0

	tty			cpu		
tin	tout		us	ni	sy	id
0	66		87	0	3	10

/dev/*dsk/c2076d*s*

bps	sps	msps
0	0.0	0.0

tty		cpu			
tin	tout	us	ni	sy	id
0	55	73	0	5	22

/dev/*dsk/c2076d*s*

bps	sps	msps
5	1.2	0.0

This looks to be very low disk access, as indicated by a low number of blocks per second ("bps") and seeks per second ("sps") for a system that has a high number of swapped processes.

The next step is to see how HP GlancePlus/UX characterizes this system. In particular, I am interested in the level of disk activity taking place. Figure 5-23 is a GlancePlus Memory Detail screen shot of this system.

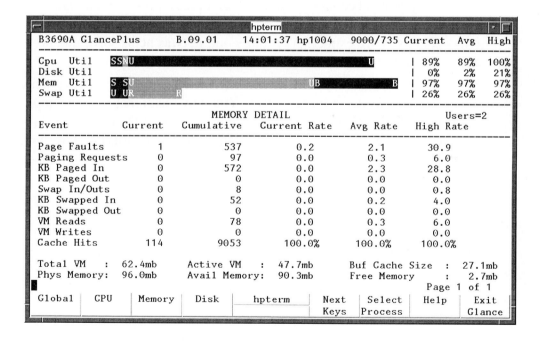

Figure 5-23 HP GlancePlus/UX Memory Detail Screen Shot with Over 40 MBytes of Virtual Memory

This GlancePlus screen shot shows data that corresponds to the information that **vmstat** and **iostat** provided. Here are some of the pieces of information provided by **vmstat**, **iostat**, and this GlancePlus screen shot:

- The CPU utilization is around 90 percent as reported by **vmstat**, **iostat**, and GlancePlus.

- Memory utilization is 97 percent.

- Active virtual memory is over 40 MBytes as reported by **vmstat** (remember the 10,000 blocks x 4 KByte blocks) and GlancePlus (the GlancePlus results are somewhat higher because I opened up several additional windows in HP CDE).

- Disk activity is 0 percent as reported by both **iostat** and GlancePlus!

This system is becoming somewhat of a puzzle. If there is a high level of active virtual memory and a lot of swapped processes, where is the massive disk activity we expect? As it turns out, **netstat** helps solve this problem.

At this point, the system should be running its application and not relying on other systems for resources. You may recall that both the application and data have been copied to the local system, so there is no need for other systems to play a part in this application run. As it turns out, however, **netstat** tells us otherwise. The following **netstat** example was obtained while the application was running:

```
# netstat -I lan0 5
```

input		(lan0)	output	
packets	errs	packets	errs	colls
8792739	120618	106184	0	1522
425	5	383	0	3
220	0	191	0	1
352	1	191	0	3

 # netstat -I lan0 5

input		(lan0)	output	
packets	errs	packets	errs	colls
439	1	380	0	1
296	0	193	0	1
274	2	194	0	2
446	1	373	0	6
394	0	216	0	2
329	1	191	0	0
502	5	304	0	5
362	4	268	0	3
267	1	198	0	1

This output shows that every five seconds there are around 200 input packets and 200 output packets at this network interface. That is a substantial amount of network traffic for a system that should be running in stand-alone mode at this point. Figure 5-24 is a GlancePlus screen shot showing the "LAN" screen.

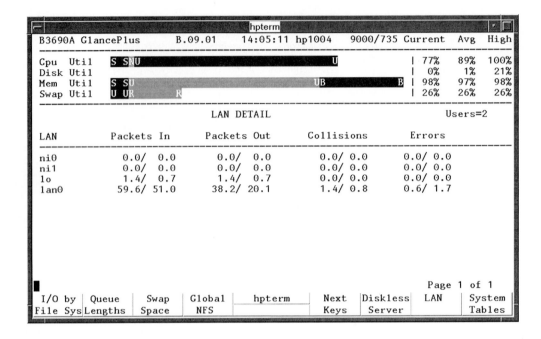

Figure 5-24 HP GlancePlus/UX Network Detail Screen Showing Network
Traffic Similar to **netstat**

This screen shot shows the number of packets in and packets out for lan0. Even though the update interval for GlancePlus is five seconds, the same interval as the **netstat** output, GlancePlus updates the packets in and packets out every second. If you take the 200 packets in and out that **net-stat** reported every five seconds and divide by five, you get the 40 packets in and out shown by GlancePlus! This number can be confusing if you use an interval for **netstat** other than one second and attempt to compare this with the results you get with GlancePlus. The following **netstat** output is for a one-second interval. With this example, you can easily see the corresponding numbers that both **netstat** and GlancePlus are supplying for packets in and packets out.

 # netstat -I lan0 1

input		(lan0)	output	
packets	errs	packets	errs	colls
8802612	120672	113251	0	1588
35	1	18	0	0
10	0	31	0	1
19	1	22	0	2
76	1	34	0	1
45	0	24	0	1
20	2	35	0	2
34	1	29	0	1
50	0	61	0	2
39	1	21	0	0
39	5	23	0	0
19	4	34	0	2
20	1	32	0	1

These networking figures make clear the vast amount of virtual memory activity taking place across the network. The application uses the user's home directory as the default location for working files as the application run takes place. Since the functional inventory showed the user's home directory on one of the servers and *not* the local system, we have an explanation for the lack of disk access on the local system and the high level of network activity on the local system. The fact that local swap is not being used on the client is further reinforced by the following **swapinfo** example from the client, which shows that only 4 percent of the swap space on the client is being used (you may recall this example from earlier in the chapter):

swapinfo

TYPE	Kb AVAIL	Kb USED	Kb FREE	PCT USED	START/ LIMIT	Kb RESERVE	PRI	NAME
dev	204505	8401	196104	4%	820534	-	0	/dev/dsk/c201d6s0
hold	0	30724	-30724					

The only remaining piece of the puzzle required to confirm that the server is being used for virtual memory is to run some of the same commands on it. Since the server is not an HP system, I chose to run **netstat** on it to see whether indeed there was a great deal of network activity on the network interface. I found the numbers to be almost identical to the level of network traffic being generated on the HP client. Since there were no other users on this server system and no other activity in general, all of the data supports the fact that the application was using the remote server system as a swap device. The following is the **netstat** output from the server. Notice that the input packets closely match the output packets from the client.

netstat -I ln0 1

input		(ln0)	output	
packets	errs	packets	errs	colls
8802612	120672	113251	0	1588
35	1	33	0	0
42	0	34	0	1
94	1	444	0	0
38	1	34	0	1
56	0	33	0	1
20	2	45	0	0
34	1	29	0	1
22	0	22	0	0

 # netstat -I ln0 1

input		(ln0)	output	
packets	errs	packets	errs	colls
34	1	24	0	0
29	0	23	0	0
19	4	44	0	0
20	1	21	0	1

After becoming comfortable with the output of commands such as **netstat**, you could write your own shell programs to modify their output.

If you would like to modify the output of the HP-UX commands, you can do so with shell programs (covered in Chapter 6). Figure 5-25 is a shell program called **ifstat**, which uses **netstat** and reformats the output. I have shared this program with a number of people who prefer its output to that of **netstat**. You may want to refer to Chapter 6 if you are interested in shell programming.

```
#!/bin/sh
# Program: ifstat
# Usage: ifstat interval interface_to_watch

# This program will not stop until you interrupt it
# (using Ctrl-C or Break).
interval=${1:-5}         # set interval to $1 or 5 if $1 is
                         # not given
interface=${2:-lan0}     # set interface to $2 or lan0 if $2 is
                         # not given
echo "Interface statistic information for $interface:\n"
# The parentheses around the while loop returns all its output
# as one command so it can be easily piped to the awk command.
(while true
do
    netstat -i
    sleep $interval
done ) | \
awk 'BEGIN { printf "%10s%10s%10s%10s%10s\n", "ipkts",
                    "ierrs", "opkts", "oerrs", "collis" ;
            printf "%10s%10s%10s%10s%10s\n", "-----",
                    "-----", "-----", "-----", "------" ;
# Initialize the variables that will hold the previous
# historical statistics.
pipkts=0; pierrs=0; popkts=0; poerrs=0; pcollis=0
}
# Find the line we care about. This is the line that starts
# with the specified interface name.
/^'$interface'/ { ipkts = $5 - pipkts; # current - previous
ierrs = $6 - pierrs;
opkts = $7 - popkts;
oerrs = $8 - poerrs;
collis = $9 - pcollis;

printf "%10d%10d%10d%10d%10d\n", ipkts, ierrs,
opkts, oerrs, collis;

pipkts = $5; pierrs = $6; popkts = $7; poerrs = $8;
pcollis = $9
                }
' # End of the awk program.
```

Figure 5-25 ifstat Script Example

The **ifstat** shell program runs **netstat -i** continuously at a specified number of seconds and displays only the *new* information, not the historical information. This program can be run when you suspect problems such as excess traffic or collisions on your network.

Here is an example run of **ifstat** with an interval of five seconds on the system using the remote server for swap:

```
$ ifstat 5 lan0
Interface statistic information for lan0:
ipkts    ierrs   opkts   oerrs   collis
-----    -----   -----   -----   ------
8963197 122657  215233      0      2899
    435      2     396      0         7
    107      5      13      0         0
    210      5     233      0         0
    321      4     341      0         7
    234      2     292      0         5
    198      1     256      0         2
    300      3     289      0         4
```

By using a swap device local to the client, you would expect the run time of this application to be greatly reduced. After this was done, an example run went from six hours to one hour. We have achieved our goal of greatly reducing the time of the application run without changing the system configuration! We may, however, want to continue to analyze the application to see what system resource(s) we want to change to further reduce the application run-time.

This example clearly shows that you may set out to perform a performance analysis in one direction and end up moving in a completely different direction.

Manual Pages of Some Commands Used in Chapter 5

Many useful commands are in this chapter. I provided a brief description of many of the commands along with some of the examples. The following are the HP-UX manual pages for many of the commands used in the chapter. The manual pages are thorough and provide much more detailed descriptions of each of the commands.

iostat

iostat - Interactively report I/O and CPU statistics.

```
iostat(1)                                                              iostat(1)

NAME
     iostat - report I/O statistics

SYNOPSIS

     iostat [-t] [interval [count]]

DESCRIPTION
     iostat iteratively reports I/O statistics for each active disk on the
     system.  Disk data is arranged in a four-column format:

          Column Heading              Interpretation
            device                    Device name
            bps                       Kilobytes transferred per second
            sps                       Number of seeks per second
            msps                      Milliseconds per average seek

     If two or more disks are present, data is presented on successive
     lines for each disk.

     To compute this information, seeks, data transfer completions, and the
     number of words transferred are counted for each disk.  Also, the
     state of each disk is examined HZ times per second (as defined in
     <sys/param.h>) and a tally is made if the disk is active.  These
     numbers can be combined with the transfer rates of each device to
     determine average seek times for each device.

     With the advent of new disk technologies, such as data striping, where
     a single data transfer is spread across several disks, the number of
     milliseconds per average seek becomes impossible to compute
     accurately. At best it is only an approximation, varying greatly,
     based on several dynamic system conditions.  For this reason and to
     maintain backward compatibility, the milliseconds per average seek (
     msps ) field is set to the value 1.0.

     Options
        iostat recognizes the following options and command-line arguments:

            -t          Report terminal statistics as well as disk
                        statistics.   Terminal statistics include:

                        tin    Number of characters read from terminals.

                        tout   Number of characters written to
                               terminals.
                        us     Percentage of time system has spent in
                               user mode.
                        ni     Percentage of time system has spent in
                               user mode running low-priority (nice)
                               processes.
                        sy     Percentage of time system has spent in
```

                                  system mode.

        id   Percentage of time system has spent idling.

    interval   Display successive lines which are summaries of the last interval seconds. The first line reported is for the time since a reboot and each subsequent line is for the last interval only.

    count   Repeat the statistics count times.

EXAMPLES

Show current I/O statistics for all disks:

```
iostat
```

Display I/O statistics for all disks every 10 seconds until INTERRUPT or QUIT is pressed:

```
iostat 10
```

Display I/O statistics for all disks every 10 seconds and terminate after 5 successive readings:

```
iostat 10 5
```

Display I/O statistics for all disks every 10 seconds, also show terminal and processor statistics, and terminate after 5 successive readings:

```
iostat -t 10 5
```

WARNINGS

Users of iostat must not rely on the exact field widths and spacing of its output, as these will vary depending on the system, the release of HP-UX, and the data to be displayed.

AUTHOR

iostat was developed by the University of California, Berkeley, and HP.

FILES

/usr/include/sys/param.h

SEE ALSO

vmstat(1).

lanadmin

lanadmin - Local Area Network (LAN) administration program.

```
lanadmin(1M)                                                    lanadmin(1M)

NAME
     lanadmin - local area network administration program

SYNOPSIS

     /usr/sbin/lanadmin [-e] [-t]

     /usr/sbin/lanadmin [-a] [-A station_addr] [-m] [-M mtu_size] [-R]
          [-s] [-S speed] NetMgmtID

DESCRIPTION
     The lanadmin program administers and tests the Local Area Network
     (LAN).  For each interface card, it allows you to:

       - Display and change the station address.
       - Display and change the maximum transmission unit (MTU).
       - Display and change the speed setting.
       - Clear the network statistics registers to zero.
       - Display the interface statistics.
       - Reset the interface card, thus executing its self-test.

     For operations other than display, you must have superuser privileges.

     lanadmin reads commands from standard input, writes prompts and error
     messages to standard error, and writes status information to standard
     output.  When the program is run from a terminal, the interrupt key
     (usually ^C) interrupts a currently executing command; the eof key
     (usually ^D) terminates the program.

     lanadmin operates in two modes: Menu Mode (see the first SYNOPSIS
     line) and Immediate Mode (see the second SYNOPSIS line).  If at least
     one -aAmMRsS option is supplied, lanadmin executes in Immediate Mode.
     Otherwise, it executes in Menu Mode.

   Options and Arguments
     lanadmin recognizes the following Immediate Mode options and
     arguments.  At least one -aAmMRsS option and the NetMgmtID argument
     must be supplied.

         NetMgmtID              The Network Management ID number of the LAN
                                interface.  This argument is ignored if none
                                of the -aAmMRsS options is used (Menu Mode).
                                Any options specified after NetMgmtID are
                                ignored.  Appropriate values can be displayed
                                with the lanscan command (see lanscan(1M)).


         -a                     Display the current station address of the
                                interface corresponding to NetMgmtID.

         -A station_addr        Set the new station address of the interface
                                corresponding to NetMgmtID.  The station_addr
```

	must be entered in hex format with a '0x' prefix. You must have superuser privileges.
-m	Display the current MTU size of the interface corresponding to NetMgmtID.
-M mtu_size	Set the new MTU size of the interface corresponding to NetMgmtID. The mtu_size value must be within the link specific range. You must have superuser privileges.
-R	Reset the MTU size of the interface corresponding to NetMgmtID to the default for that link type. You must have superuser privileges.
-s	Display the current speed setting of the interface corresponding to NetMgmtID.
-S speed	Set the new speed setting of the interface corresponding to NetMgmtID. You must have superuser privileges.

lanadmin recognizes the following Menu Mode options. They are ignored if they are given with an Immediate Mode option.

-e	Echo the input commands on the output device.
-t	Suppress the display of the command menu before each command prompt. This is equivalent to the Test Selection Mode terse command. The default is verbose.

Immediate Mode
    In Immediate Mode, you can display the station address, MTU size, and
    link speed of LAN interface NetMgmtID. For certain interfaces, if you
    have superuser privileges you can also modify the station address, MTU
    size, and link speed. See "Options and Arguments" above.

Menu Mode
    In Menu Mode, you can select an interface card, display statistics for
    the selected card, reset the card, and clear the statistics registers.

    Menu Mode accepts either complete command words or unique
    abbreviations, and no distinction is made between uppercase and
    lowercase letters in commands. Multiple commands can be entered on
    one line if they are separated by spaces, tabs, or commas.

    Test Selection Mode Menu

    This menu is entered when Menu Mode is first selected. The available
    Test Selection Mode commands are:

lan	Select the LAN Interface Test Mode menu.
menu	Display the Test Selection Mode command menu.
quit	Terminate the lanadmin program.
terse	Suppress the display of command menus.
verbose	Restore the display of command menus.

    LAN Interface Test Mode Menu

The following commands are available:

clear

Clear the LAN interface network statistics registers to zero. You must have superuser privileges.

display

Display the RFC 1213 MIB II statistics. Depending on the link, the type-specific MIB statistics may also be displayed. For instance, for Ethernet links, the RFC 1398 Ethernet-like statistics are displayed.

end

Return lanadmin to Test Selection Mode.

menu

Display the LAN Interface Test Mode command menu.

nmid

Prompt for a Network Management ID that corresponds to a LAN interface card. It defaults to the first LAN interface encountered in an internal list. Appropriate values can be displayed with the lanscan command (see lanscan(1M)).

quit

Terminate the lanadmin program.

reset

Reset the local LAN interface card, causing it to execute its self-test. Local access to the network is interrupted during execution of reset. You must have superuser privileges.

AUTHOR

lanadmin was developed by HP.

SEE ALSO

netstat(1), lanscan(1M), linkloop(1M), ping(1M), lan(7).

DARPA Requests for Comments: RFC 1213, RFC 1398.

mount

mount - Mount file systems.

---

mount(1M)   mount(1M)

NAME
     mount (generic), umount (generic) - mount and unmount file systems

SYNOPSIS
     /usr/sbin/mount [-l] [-p|-v]

     /usr/sbin/mount -a [-F FStype] [-eQ]

     /usr/sbin/mount [-F FStype] [-eQrV] [-o specific_options]
          {special|directory}

     /usr/sbin/mount [-F FStype] [-eQrV] [-o specific_options]
          special directory

     /usr/sbin/umount [-v] [-V] {special|directory}

     /usr/sbin/umount -a [-F FStype] [-v]

DESCRIPTION
     The mount command mounts file systems. Only a superuser can mount
     file systems. Other users can use mount to list mounted file systems.

     The mount command attaches special, a removable file system, to
     directory, a directory on the file tree. directory, which must
     already exist, will become the name of the root of the newly mounted
     file system. special and directory must be given as absolute path
     names. If either special or directory is omitted, mount attempts to
     determine the missing value from an entry in the /etc/fstab file.
     mount can be invoked on any removable file system, except /.

     If mount is invoked without any arguments, it lists all of the mounted
     file systems from the file system mount table, /etc/mnttab.

     The umount command unmounts mounted file systems. Only a superuser
     can unmount file systems.

     Options (mount)
     The mount command recognizes the following options:

          -a   Attempt to mount all file systems described in
                            /etc/fstab. All optional fields in /etc/fstab
                            must be included and supported. If the -F option
                            is specified, all file systems in /etc/fstab with
                            that FStype are mounted. File systems are not
                            necessarily mounted in the order listed in
                            /etc/fstab.

          -e   Verbose mode. Write a message to the standard
                            output indicating which file system is being
                            mounted.

-F FStype   Specify FStype, the file system type on which to
                       operate. See fstyp(1M). If this option is not
                       included on the command line, then it is
                       determined from either /etc/fstab, by matching
                       special with an entry in that file, or from file
                       system statistics of special, obtained by
                       statfsdev() (see statfsdev(3C)).

-l   Limit actions to local file systems only.

-o specific_options
                       Specify options specific to each file system type.
                       specific_options is a list of comma separated
                       suboptions and/or keyword/attribute pairs intended
                       for a FStype-specific version of the command. See
                       the FStype-specific manual entries for a
                       description of the specific_options supported, if
                       any.

-p   Report the list of mounted file systems in the
                       /etc/fstab format.

-Q   Prevent the display of error messages that result
                       from an attempt to mount already mounted file
                       systems.

-r   Mount the specified file system as read-only.
                       Physically write-protected file systems must be
                       mounted in this way or errors occur when access
                       times are updated, whether or not any explicit
                       write is attempted.

-v   Report the regular output with file system type
                       and flags; however, the directory and special
                       fields are reversed.

-V   Echo the completed command line, but perform no
                       other action. The command line is generated by
                       incorporating the user-specified options and other
                       information derived from /etc/fstab. This option
                       allows the user to verify the command line.

   Options (umount)
     The umount command recognizes the following options:

-a   Attempt to unmount all file systems described in
                       /etc/mnttab. All optional fields in /etc/mnttab
                       must be included and supported. If FStype is
                       specified, all file systems in /etc/mnttab with
                       that FStype are unmounted. File systems are not
                       necessarily unmounted in the order listed in
                       /etc/mnttab.

-F FStype   Specify FStype, the file system type on which to
                       operate. If this option is not included on the
                       command line, then it is determined from
                       /etc/mnttab by matching special with an entry in
                       that file. If no match is found, the command
                       fails.

-v   Verbose mode. Write a message to standard output
                       indicating which file system is being unmounted.

-V   Echo the completed command line, but perform no
                       other action. The command line is generated by

incorporating the user-specified options and other
information derived from /etc/fstab. This option
allows the user to verify the command line.

EXAMPLES
     List the file systems currently mounted:

          mount

     Mount the HFS file system /dev/dsk/c1d2s0 at directory /home:

          mount -F hfs /dev/dsk/c1d2s0 /home

     Unmount the same file system:

          umount /dev/dsk/c1d2s0

AUTHOR
     mount was developed by HP, AT&T, the University of California,
     Berkeley, and Sun Microsystems.

FILES
     /etc/fstab   Static information about the systems
     /etc/mnttab   Mounted file system table

SEE ALSO
     mount_FStype(1M), mount(2), fstab(4), mnttab(4), fs_wrapper(5),
     quota(5).

STANDARDS COMPLIANCE
     mount: SVID3

     umount: SVID3

netstat

netstat - Shows network status.

```
netstat(1)                                                          netstat(1)

NAME
     netstat - show network status

SYNOPSIS

     netstat [-aAn] [-f address-family] [system [core]]
     netstat [-mMnrsv] [-f address-family] [-p protocol] [system [core]]
     netstat [-gin] [-I interface] [interval] [system [core]]

DESCRIPTION
     netstat displays statistics for network interfaces and protocols, as
     well as the contents of various network-related data structures.  The
     output format varies according to the options selected.  Some options
     are ignored when used in combination with other options.

     Generally, the netstat command takes one of the three forms shown
     above:

          -  The first form of the command displays a list of active
             sockets for each protocol.

          -  The second form displays the contents of one of the other
             network data structures according to the option selected.

          -  The third form displays configuration information for each
             network interface.  It also displays network traffic data on
             configured network interfaces, optionally updated at each
             interval, measured in seconds.

     Options are interpreted as follows:

          -a                  Show the state of all sockets, including
                              passive sockets used by server processes.  When
                              netstat is used without any options (except -A
                              and -n), only active sockets are shown.  This
                              option does not show the state of X.25
                              programmatic access sockets.  The option is
                              ignored if the -g, -i, -I, -m, -M, -p, -r, -s
                              or interval option is specified.

          -A                  Show the address of the protocol control block
                              associated with sockets.  This option is used
                              for debugging.  It does not show the X.25
                              programmatic access control blocks.  This
                              option is ignored if the -g, -i, -I, -m, -M,
                              -p, -r, -s or interval option is specified.

          -f address-family   Show statistics or address control block for
                              only the specified address-family.  The
                              following address families are recognized: inet
                              for AF_INET, and unix for AF_UNIX.  This option
                              applies to the -a, -A and -s options.
```

-g	Show multicast information for network interfaces. Only the address family AF_INET is recognized by this option. This option may be combined with the -i option to display both kinds of information. The option is ignored if the -m, -M or -p option is specified.
-i	Show the state of network interfaces. Interfaces that are statically configured into a system, but not located at boot time, are not shown. This option is ignored if the -m, -M or -p option is specified.
-I interface	Show information about the specified interface only. This option applies to the -g and -i options.
-m	Show statistics recorded by network memory management routines. If this option is specified, all other options are ignored.
-M	Show the multicast routing tables. When -s is used with the -M option, netstat displays multicast routing statistics instead. This option is ignored if the -m or -p option is specified.
-n	Show network addresses as numbers. Normally, netstat interprets addresses and attempts to display them symbolically. This option applies to the -a, -A, -i, -r and -v options.
-p protocol	Show statistics for the specified protocol. The following protocols are recognized: tcp, udp, ip, icmp, igmp, arp, and probe. This option is ignored if the -m option is specified.
-r	Show the routing tables. When -v is used with the -r option, netstat also displays the network masks in the route entries. When -s is used with the -r option, netstat displays routing statistics instead. This option is ignored if the -g, -m, -M, -i, -I, -p or interval option is specified.
-s	Show statistics for all protocols. When this option is used with the -r option, netstat displays routing statistics instead. When this option is used with the -M option, netstat displays multicast routing statistics instead. This option is ignored if the -g, -i, -I, -m, -p or interval option is specified.
-v	Show additional routing information. When -v is used with the -r option, netstat also displays the network masks in the route entries. This option only applies to the -r option.

The arguments system and core allow substitutes for the defaults, /stand/vmunix and /dev/kmem.

If no options or only the -A or -n option is specified, netstat displays the status of only active sockets. The display of active and

passive sockets status shows the local and remote addresses, send and
receive queue sizes (in bytes), protocol, and the internal state of
the protocol. Address formats are of the form host.port, or
network.port if the host portion of a socket address is zero. When
known, the host and network addresses are displayed symbolically by
using gethostbyname() and getnetbyname(), respectively (see
gethostbyname(3N) and getnetbyname(3N)). If a symbolic name for an
address is unknown, or if the -n option is specified, the address is
displayed numerically according to the address family. For more
information regarding the Internet ``dot format'', refer to inet(3N).
Unspecified or ``wildcard'' addresses and ports appear as an asterisk
(*).

The interface display provides a table of cumulative statistics
regarding packets transferred, errors, and collisions. The network
addresses of the interface and the maximum transmission unit (MTU) are
also displayed. When the interval argument is specified, netstat
displays a running count of statistics related to network interfaces.
This display consists of a column for the primary interface (the first
interface found during auto-configuration) and a column summarizing
information for all interfaces. To replace the primary interface with
another interface, use the -I option. The first line of each screen
of information contains a summary since the system was last rebooted.
Subsequent lines of output show values accumulated over the preceding
interval.

The routing table display indicates the available routes and their
status. Each route consists of a destination host or network, a
netmask and a gateway to use in forwarding packets. The Flags field
shows whether the route is up (U), whether the route is to a gateway
(G), whether the route is a host or network route (with or without H),
whether the route was created dynamically (D) by a redirect or by Path
MTU Discovery, and whether a gateway route has been modified (M), or
it has been marked doubtful (?) due to the lack of a timely ARP
response.

The Netmask field shows the mask to be applied to the destination IP
address of an IP packet to be forwarded. The result will be compared
with the destination address in the route entry. If they are the same,
then the route is one of the candidates for routing this IP packet.
If there are several candidate routes, then the route with the longest
Netmask field (contiguous 1's starting from the leftmost bit position)
will be chosen. (see routing (7).)

The Gateway field shows the address of the immediate gateway for
reaching the destination. It can be the address of the outgoing
interface if the destination is on a directly connected network.

The Refs field shows the current number of active uses of the route.
Connection-oriented protocols normally hold on to a single route for
the duration of a connection, while connectionless protocols normally
obtain a route just while sending a particular message. The Use field
shows a count of the number of packets sent using the route. The
Interface field identifies which network interface is used for the
route.

The Pmtu and PmtuTime fields apply only to host routes. The Pmtu
field for network and default routes is the same as the MTU of the
network interface used for the route. If the route is created with a
static PMTU value (see route(1M)), the corresponding PmtuTime field
contains the word perm, and the PMTU value permanently overrides the
interface MTU. If the route is created dynamically (D in the Flags
field), the value in the corresponding PmtuTime field is the number of
minutes remaining before the PMTU expires. When the PMTU expires, the
system rediscovers the current PMTU for the route, in case it has
changed. The PmtuTime field is left blank when the PMTU is identical

to the MTU of the interface. An asterisk (*) in the Pmtu field
indicates that user has disabled the PMTU Discovery for the route.

DEPENDENCIES
    X.25:
        -A and -a options do not list X.25 programmatic access information.

AUTHOR
    netstat was developed by the University of California, Berkeley.

SEE ALSO
    hosts(4), networks(4), gethostbyname(3N), getnetbyname(3N),
    protocols(4), route(1M), services(4).

ps

ps - Reports status of processes.

NAME
     ps - report process status

SYNOPSIS

     ps [-adeflP] [-g grplist] [-p proclist] [-R prmgrplist] [-t termlist]
     [-u uidlist]

XPG4 SYNOPSIS
     ps [-aAcdefHjlP] [-C cmdlist] [-g grplist] [-G gidlist] [-n namelist]
     [-o format] [-p proclist] [-R prmgrplist] [-s sidlist] [-t termlist]
     [-u uidlist] [-U uidlist]

DESCRIPTION
     ps prints information about selected processes. Use options to
     specify which processes to select and what information to print about
     them.

   Process Selection Options
     Use the following options to choose which processes should be
     selected.

     NOTE: If an option is used in both the default (standard HP-UX) and
     XPG4 environments, the description provided here documents the default
     behavior. Refer to the UNIX95 variable under EXTERNAL INFLUENCES for
     additional information on XPG4 behavior.

          (none)   Select those processes associated with the current
                        terminal.

          -A   (XPG4 Only.) Select all processes. (Synonym for
                        -e.)

          -a   Select all processes except process group leaders
                        and processes not associated with a terminal.

          -C cmdlist   (XPG4 Only.) Select processes executing a command
                        with a basename given in cmdlist.

          -d   Select all processes except process group leaders.

          -e   Select all processes.

          -g grplist   Select processes whose process group leaders are
                        given in grplist.

          -G gidlist   (XPG4 Only.) Select processes whose real group ID
                        numbers or group names are given in gidlist.

          -n namelist   (XPG4 Only.) This option is ignored; its presence is allowed for standards compliance.

-p proclist	Select processes whose process ID numbers are given in proclist.
-R prmgrplist	Select processes belonging to PRM process resource groups whose names or ID numbers are given in prmgrplist. See DEPENDENCIES.
-s sidlist	(XPG4 Only.) Select processes whose session leaders are given in sidlist. (Synonym for -g).
-t termlist	Select processes associated with the terminals given in termlist. Terminal identifiers can be specified in one of two forms: the device's file name (such as tty04) or if the device's file name starts with tty, just the rest of it (such as 04). If the device's file is in a directory other than /dev or /dev/pty, the terminal identifier must include the name of the directory under /dev that contains the device file (such as pts/5).
-u uidlist	Select processes whose effective user ID numbers or login names are given in uidlist.
-U uidlist	(XPG4 Only.) Select processes whose real user ID numbers or login names are given in uidlist.

If any of the -a, -A, -d, or -e options is specified, the -C, -g, -G, -p, -R, -t, -u, and -U options are ignored.

If more than one of -a, -A, -d, and -e are specified, the least restrictive option takes effect.

If more than one of the -C, -g, -G, -p, -R, -t, -u, and -U options are specified, processes will be selected if they match any of the options specified.

The lists used as arguments to the -C, -g, -G, -p, -R, -t, -u, and -U options can be specified in one of two forms:

- A list of identifiers separated from one another by a comma.

- A list of identifiers enclosed in quotation marks (") and separated from one another by a comma and/or one or more spaces.

Output Format Options
Use the following options to control which columns of data are included in the output listing. The options are cumulative.

(none)	The default columns are: pid, tty, time, and comm, in that order.
-f	Show columns user, pid, ppid, cpu, stime, tty, time, and args, in that order.
-l	Show columns flags, state, uid, pid, ppid, cpu, intpri, nice, addr, sz, wchan, tty, time, and comm, in that order.
-fl	Show columns flags, state, user, pid, ppid, cpu, intpri, nice, addr, sz, wchan, stime, tty, time, and args, in that order.

-c   (XPG4 Only.) Remove columns cpu and nice; replace
                column intpri with columns cls and pri.

-j   (XPG4 Only.) Add columns pgid and sid after
                column ppid (or pid, if ppid is not being
                displayed).

-P   Add column prmid (for -l) or prmgrp (for -f or
                -fl) immediately before column pid. See
                DEPENDENCIES.

-o format   (XPG4 Only.) format is a comma- or space-separated
                list of the columns to display, in the order they
                should be displayed. (Valid column names are
                listed below.) A column name can optionally be
                followed by an equals sign (=) and a string to use
                as the heading for that column. (Any commas or
                spaces after the equals sign will be taken as a
                part of the column heading; if more columns are
                desired, they must be specified with additional -o
                options.) The width of the column will be the
                greater of the width of the data to be displayed
                and the width of the column heading. If an empty
                column heading is specified for every heading, no
                heading line will be printed. This option
                overrides options -c, -f, -j, -l, and -P; if they
                are specified, they are ignored.

-H   (XPG4 Only.) Shows the process hierarchy. Each
                process is displayed under its parent, and the
                contents of the args or comm column for that
                process is indented from that of its parent. Note
                that this option is expensive in both memory and
                speed.

The column names and their meanings are given below. Except where
noted, the default heading for each column is the uppercase form of
the column name.

addr   The memory address of the process, if resident;
                otherwise, the disk address.

args   The command line given when the process was
                created. This column should be the last one
                specified, if it is desired. Only a subset of the
                command line is saved by the kernel; as much of
                the command line will be displayed as is
                available. The output in this column may contain
                spaces. The default heading for this column is
                COMMAND if -o is specified and CMD otherwise.

cls   Process scheduling class, see rtsched(1).

comm   The command name. The output in this column may
                contain spaces. The default heading for this
                column is COMMAND if -o is specified and CMD
                otherwise.

cpu   Processor utilization for scheduling. The default
                heading for this column is C.

etime   Elapsed time of the process. The default heading
                for this column is ELAPSED.

flags   Flags (octal and additive) associated with the process:

```
0    Swapped
1    In core
2    System process
4    Locked in core (e.g., for physical I/O)

10   Being traced by another process
20   Another tracing flag
```

The default heading for this column is F.

intpri   The priority of the process as it is stored
              internally by the kernel. This column is provided
              for backward compatibility and its use is not
              encouraged.

gid   The group ID number of the effective process
              owner.

group   The group name of the effective process owner.

nice   Nice value; used in priority computation (see
              nice(1)). The default heading for this column is
              NI.

pcpu   The percentage of CPU time used by this process
              during the last scheduling interval. The default
              heading for this column is %CPU.

pgid   The process group ID number of the process group
              to which this process belongs.

pid   The process ID number of the process.

ppid   The process ID number of the parent process.

pri   The priority of the process. The meaning of the
              value depends on the process scheduling class; see
              cls, above, and rtsched(1).

prmid   The PRM process resource group ID number.

prmgrp   The PRM process resource group name.

rgid   The group ID number of the real process owner.

rgroup   The group name of the real process owner.

ruid   The user ID number of the real process owner.

ruser   The login name of the real process owner.

sid   The session ID number of the session to which this
              process belongs.

state   The state of the process:

```
0    Nonexistent
S    Sleeping
W    Waiting
R    Running
I    Intermediate
Z    Terminated
```

                              T   Stopped
                              X   Growing

                    The default heading for this column is S.

        stime   Starting time of the process. If the elapsed time
                            is greater than 24 hours, the starting date is
                            displayed instead.

        sz   The size in physical pages of the core image of
                            the process, including text, data, and stack
                            space. Physical page size is defined by
                            _SC_PAGE_SIZE in the header file <unistd.h> (see
                            sysconf(2) and unistd(5)).

        time   The cumulative execution time for the process.

        tty   The controlling terminal for the process. The
                            default heading for this column is TT if -o is
                            specified and TTY otherwise.

        uid   The user ID number of the effective process owner.

        user   The login name of the effective process owner.

        vsz   The size in kilobytes (1024 byte units) of the
                            core image of the process. See column sz, above.

        wchan   The event for which the process is waiting or
                            sleeping; if there is none, a hyphen (-) is
                            displayed.

   Notes
      ps prints the command name and arguments given at the time of the
      process was created. If the process changes its arguments while
      running (by writing to its argv array), these changes are not
      displayed by ps.

      A process that has exited and has a parent, but has not yet been
      waited for by the parent, is marked <defunct> (see zombie process in
      exit(2)).

      The time printed in the stime column, and used in computing the value
      for the etime column, is the time when the process was forked, not the
      time when it was modified by exec*().

      To make the ps output safer to display and easier to read, all control
      characters in the comm and args columns are displayed as "visible"
      equivalents in the customary control character format, ^x.

   EXTERNAL INFLUENCES
      Environment Variables
         UNIX95 specifies to use the XPG4 behavior for this command. The
         changes for XPG4 include support for the entire option set specified
         above and include the following behavioral changes:

            - The TIME column format changes from mmmm:ss to [dd-]hh:mm:ss.

            - When the comm, args, user, and prmgrp fields are included by
              default or the -f or -l flags are used, the column headings of
              those fields change to CMD, CMD, USER, and PRMGRP,
              respectively.

- -a, -d, and -g will select processes based on session rather than on process group.

- The uid or user column displayed by -f or -l will display effective user rather than real user.

- The -u option will select users based on effective UID rather than real UID.

- The -C and -H options, while they are not part of the XPG4 standard, are enabled.

LC_TIME determines the format and contents of date and time strings. If it is not specified or is null, it defaults to the value of LANG.

If LANG is not specified or is null, it defaults to C (see lang(5)).

If any internationalization variable contains an invalid setting, all internationalization variables default to C (see environ(5)).

International Code Set Support
  Single-byte character code sets are supported.

EXAMPLES
  Generate a full listing of all processes currently running on your machine:

      ps -ef

  To see if a certain process exists on the machine, such as the cron clock daemon, check the far right column for the command name, cron, or try

      ps -f -C cron

WARNINGS
  Things can change while ps is running; the picture it gives is only a snapshot in time. Some data printed for defunct processes is irrelevant.

  If two special files for terminals are located at the same select code, that terminal may be reported with either name. The user can select processes with that terminal using either name.

  Users of ps must not rely on the exact field widths and spacing of its output, as these will vary depending on the system, the release of HP-UX, and the data to be displayed.

DEPENDENCIES
  HP Process Resource Manager
    The -P and -R options require the optional HP Process Resource Manager (PRM) software to be installed and configured. See prmconfig(1) for a description of how to configure HP PRM, and prmconf(4) for the definition of "process resource group."

    If HP PRM is not installed and configured and -P or -R is specified, a warning message is displayed and (for -P) hyphens (-) are displayed in the prmid and prmgrp columns.

FILES
  /dev   Directory of terminal device files

  /etc/passwd   User ID information
  /var/adm/ps_data   Internal data structure

SEE ALSO

kill(1), nice(1), acctcom(1M), exec(2), exit(2), fork(2), sysconf(2),
unistd(5).

HP Process Resource Manager: prmconfig(1), prmconf(4) in HP Process
Resource Manager User's Guide.

STANDARDS COMPLIANCE
     ps: SVID2, XPG2, XPG3, XPG4

sar

sar - System activity reporter.

NAME
     sar - system activity reporter

SYNOPSIS

     sar [-ubdycwaqvmAMS] [-o file] t [n]

     sar [-ubdycwaqvmAMS] [-s time] [-e time] [-i sec] [-f file]

DESCRIPTION
     In the first form above, sar samples cumulative activity counters in
     the operating system at n intervals of t seconds. If the -o option is
     specified, it saves the samples in file in binary format. The default
     value of n is 1. In the second form, with no sampling interval
     specified, sar extracts data from a previously recorded file, either
     the one specified by -f option or, by default, the standard system
     activity daily data file /var/adm/sa/sadd for the current day dd. The
     starting and ending times of the report can be bounded via the -s and
     -e time arguments of the form hh[:mm[:ss]]. The -i option selects
     records at sec-second intervals. Otherwise, all intervals found in
     the data file are reported.

     In either case, subsets of data to be printed are specified by option:

          -u   Report CPU utilization (the default); portion of time
               running in one of several modes. On a multi-processor
               system, if the -M option is used together with the -u
               option, per-CPU utilization as well as the average CPU
               utilization of all the processors are reported. If the -M
               option is not used, only the average CPU utilization of all
               the processors is reported:

                    cpu   cpu number (only on a multi-processor
                                 system with the -M option);

                    %usr   user mode;

                    %sys   system mode;

                    %wio   idle with some process waiting for I/O
                                 (only block I/O, raw I/O, or VM
                                 pageins/swapins indicated);

                    %idle   otherwise idle.

          -b   Report buffer activity:

                    bread/s   Number of physical reads per second
                                 from the disk (or other block devices)
                                 to the buffer cache;

bwrit/s	Number of physical writes per second from the buffer cache to the disk (or other block device);
lread/s	Number of reads per second from buffer cache;
lwrit/s	Number of writes per second to buffer cache;
%rcache	Buffer cache hit ratio for read requests e.g., 1 - bread/lread;
%wcache	Buffer cache hit ratio for write requests e.g., 1 - bwrit/lwrit;
pread/s	Number of reads per second from character device using the physio() (raw I/O) mechanism;
pwrit/s	Number of writes per second to character device using the physio() (i.e., raw I/O) mechanism; mechanism.

-d Report activity for each block device, e.g., disk or tape drive. One line is printed for each device that had activity during the last interval. If no devices were active, a blank line is printed. Each line contains the following data:

device	Logical name of the device and its corresponding instance. Devices are categorized into the following four device types:

> disk1 - HP-IB disks (CS/80)
> disk2 - CIO HP-FL disks (CS/80)
> disk3 - SCSI and NIO FL disks
> sdisk - SCSI disks;

%busy	Portion of time device was busy servicing a request;
avque	Average number of requests outstanding for the device;
r+w/s	Number of data transfers per second (read and writes) from and to the device;
blks/s	Number of bytes transferred (in 512-byte units) from and to the device;
avwait	Average time (in milliseconds) that transfer requests waited idly on queue for the device;
avserv	Average time (in milliseconds) to service each transfer request (includes seek, rotational latency, and data transfer times) for the device.

-y Report tty device activity:

rawch/s	Raw input characters per second;
canch/s	Input characters per second processed by canon();
outch/s	Output characters per second;
rcvin/s	Receive incoming character interrupts per second;
xmtin/s	Transmit outgoing character interrupts per second;
mdmin/s	Modem interrupt rate (not supported; always 0).

-c   Report system calls:

scall/s	Number of system calls of all types per second;
sread/s	Number of read() and/or readv() system calls per second;
swrit/s	Number of write() and/or writev() system calls per second;
fork/s	Number of fork() and/or vfork() system calls per second;
exec/s	Number of exec() system calls per second;
rchar/s	Number of characters transferred by read system calls block devices only) per second;
wchar/s	Number of characters transferred by write system calls (block devices only) per second.

-w   Report system swapping and switching activity:

swpin/s	Number of process swapins per second;
swpot/s	Number of process swapouts per second;
bswin/s	Number of 512-byte units transferred for swapins per second;
bswot/s	Number of 512-byte units transferred for swapouts per second;
pswch/s	Number of process context switches per second.

-a   Report use of file access system routines:

iget/s	Number of file system iget() calls per second;

namei/s   Number of file system lookuppn()
              (pathname translation) calls per
              second;

dirblk/s   Number of file system blocks read per
              second doing directory lookup.

-q   Report average queue length while occupied, and percent of
      time occupied. On a multi-processor machine, if the -M
      option is used together with the -q option, the per-CPU run
      queue as well as the average run queue of all the
      processors are reported. If the -M option is not used,
      only the average run queue information of all the
      processors is reported:

cpu   cpu number (only on a multi-processor
              system and used with the -M option)

runq-sz   Average length of the run queue(s) of
              processes (in memory and runnable);

%runocc   The percentage of time the run queue(s)
              were occupied by processes (in memory
              and runnable);

swpq-sz   Average length of the swap queue of
              runnable processes (processes swapped
              out but ready to run);

%swpocc   The percentage of time the swap queue
              of runnable processes (processes
              swapped out but ready to run) was
              occupied.

-v   Report status of text, process, inode and file tables:

text-sz   (Not Applicable);

proc-sz   The current-size and maximum-size of
              the process table;

inod-sz   The current-size and maximum-size of
              the inode table (inode cache);

file-sz   The current-size and maximum-size of
              the system file table;

text-ov   (Not Applicable);

proc-ov   The number of times the process table
              overflowed (number of times the kernel
              could not find any available process
              table entries) between sample points;

inod-ov   The number of times the inode table
              (inode cache) overflowed (number of
              times the kernel could not find any
              available inode table entries) between
              sample points;

file-ov   The number of times the system file
              table overflowed (number of times the
              kernel could not find any available
              file table entries) between sample

points.

-m   Report message and semaphore activities:

      msg/s   Number of System V msgrcv() calls per
                        second;

      sema/s   Number of System V semop() calls per
                        second;

      select/s   Number of System V select() calls per
                        second. This value will only be
                        reported if the "-S" option is also
                        explicitly specified.

-A   Report all data. Equivalent to -udqbwcayvm.

-M   Report the per-processor data on a multi-processor system
      when used with -q and/or -u options. If the -M option is
      not used on a multi-processor system, the output format of
      the -u and -q options is the same as the uni-processor
      output format and the data reported is the average value of
      all the processors.

EXAMPLES

Watch CPU activity evolve for 5 seconds:

    sar 1 5

Watch CPU activity evolve for 10 minutes and save data:

    sar -o temp 60 10

Review disk and tape activity from that period later:

    sar -d -f temp

Review cpu utilization on a multi-processor system later:

    sar -u -M -f temp

WARNINGS

Users of sar must not rely on the exact field widths and spacing of
its output, as these will vary depending on the system, the release of
HP-UX, and the data to be displayed.

FILES

/var/adm/sa/sadd   daily data file, where dd is two digits
                           representing the day of the month.

SEE ALSO

sa1(1M).

STANDARDS CONFORMANCE

sar: SVID2, SVID3

showmount

showmount - Shows all remote mounts.

```
showmount(1M)                                                    showmount(1M)

NAME
     showmount - show all remote mounts

SYNOPSIS

     /usr/sbin/showmount [-a] [-d] [-e] [host]

DESCRIPTION
     showmount lists all clients that have remotely mounted a filesystem
     from host.  This information is maintained by the mountd server on
     host (see mountd(1M)).  The default value for host is the value
     returned by hostname (see hostname(1)).

   Options
     -a   Print all remote mounts in the format

             name:directory

          where hostname is the name of the client, and directory is the
          directory or root of the file system that was mounted.

     -d   List directories that have been remotely mounted by clients.

     -e   Print the list of exported file systems.

WARNINGS
     If a client crashes, executing showmount on the server will show that
     the client still has a file system mounted.  In other words, the
     client's entry is not removed from /etc/rmtab until the client reboots
     and executes:

          umount -a

     Also, if a client mounts the same remote directory twice, only one
     entry appears in /etc/rmtab.  Doing a umount of one of these
     directories removes the single entry and showmount no longer indicates
     that the remote directory is mounted.

AUTHOR
     showmount was developed by Sun Microsystems, Inc.

SEE ALSO
     hostname(1), exportfs(1M), mountd(1M), exports(4), rmtab(4).
```

swapinfo

swapinfo - Reports system paging information.

NAME
     swapinfo - system paging space information

SYNOPSIS

     /usr/sbin/swapinfo [-mtadfnrMqw]

DESCRIPTION
     swapinfo prints information about device and file system paging space.
     (Note: the term `swap' refers to an obsolete implementation of
     virtual memory; HP-UX actually implements virtual memory by way of
     paging rather than swapping. This command and others retain names
     derived from `swap' for historical reasons.)

     By default, swapinfo prints to standard output a two line header as
     shown here, followed by one line per paging area:

```
             Kb      Kb      Kb     PCT    START/  Kb
      TYPE   AVAIL   USED    FREE   USED   LIMIT   RESERVE PRI     NAME
```

     The fields are:

     TYPE   One of:

                dev   Paging space residing on a mass storage device,
                           either taking up the entire device or, if the
                           device contains a file system, taking up the
                           space between the end of the file system and
                           the end of the device. This space is
                           exclusively reserved for paging, and even if it
                           is not being used for paging, it cannot be used
                           for any other purpose. Device paging areas
                           typically provide the fastest paging.

                fs   Dynamic paging space available from a file
                           system. When this space is needed, the system
                           creates files in the file system and uses them
                           as paging space. File system paging is
                           typically slower than device paging, but allows
                           the space to be used for other things (user
                           files) when not needed for paging.

                localfs   File system paging space (see fs above) on a
                           file system residing on a local disk.

                network   File system paging space (see fs above) on a
                           file system residing on another machine. This
                           file system would have been mounted on the
                           local machine via NFS.

                reserve   Paging space on reserve. This is the amount of
                           paging space that could be needed by processes

that are currently running, but that has not
yet been allocated from one of the above paging
areas. See "Paging Allocation" below.

memory   Memory paging area (also known as pseudo-swap).
This is the amount of system memory that can be
used to hold pages in the event that all of the
above paging areas are used up. See "Paging
Allocation" below. This line appears only if
memory paging is enabled.

Kb AVAIL   The total available space from the paging area, in blocks
of 1024 bytes (rounded to nearest whole block if
necessary), including any paging space already in use.

For file system paging areas the value is not necessarily
constant. It is the current space allocated for paging
(even if not currently used), plus the free blocks
available on the file system to ordinary users, minus
RESERVE (but never less than zero). AVAIL is never more
than LIMIT if LIMIT is non-zero. Since paging space is
allocated in large chunks, AVAIL is rounded down to the
nearest full allocation chunk.

For the memory paging area this value is also not
necessarily constant, because it reflects allocation of
memory by the kernel as well as by processes that might
need to be paged.

Kb USED   The current number of 1-Kbyte blocks used for paging in
the paging area. For the memory paging area, this count
also includes memory used for other purposes and thus
unavailable for paging.

Kb FREE   The amount of space that can be used for future paging.
Usually this is the difference between Kb AVAIL and Kb
USED. There could be a difference if some portion of a
device paging area is unusable, perhaps because the size
of the paging area is not a multiple of the allocation
chunk size, or because the tunable parameter maxswapchunks
is not set high enough.

PCT USED   The percentage of capacity in use, based on Kb USED
divided by Kb AVAIL; 100% if Kb AVAIL is zero.

START/LIMIT   For device paging areas, START is the block address on the
mass storage device of the start of the paging area. The
value is normally 0 for devices dedicated to paging, or
the end of the file system for devices containing both a
file system and paging space.

For file system paging areas, LIMIT is the maximum number
of 1-Kbyte blocks that will be used for paging, the same
as the limit value given to swapon. A file system LIMIT
value of none means there is no fixed limit; all space is
available except that used for files, less the blocks
represented by minfree (see fs(4)) plus RESERVE.

RESERVE   For device paging areas, this value is always ``-''. For
file system paging areas, this value is the number of 1-
Kbyte blocks reserved for file system use by ordinary
users, the same as the reserve value given to swapon.

PRI   The same as the priority value given to swapon. This
value indicates the order in which space is taken from the

devices and file systems used for paging. Space is taken
from areas with lower priority values first. priority can
have a value between 0 and 10. See "Paging Allocation"
below.

NAME   For device paging areas, the block special file name whose
                    major and minor numbers match the device's ID. The
                    swapinfo command searches the /dev tree to find device
                    names. If no matching block special file is found,
                    swapinfo prints the device ID (major and minor values),
                    for example, 28,0x15000.

                    For file system swap areas, NAME is the name of a
                    directory on the file system in which the paging files are
                    stored.

Paging Allocation
  Paging areas are enabled at boot time (for device paging areas
  configured into the kernel) or by the swapon command (see swapon(1M)),
  often invoked by /sbin/init.d/swap_start during system initialization
  based on the contents of /etc/fstab. When a paging area is enabled,
  some portion of that area is allocated for paging space. For device
  paging areas, the entire device is allocated, less any leftover
  fraction of an allocation chunk. (The size of an allocation chunk is
  controlled by the tunable parameter swchunk, and is typically 2 MB.)
  For file system paging areas, the minimum value given to swapon
  (rounded up to the nearest allocation chunk) is allocated.

  When a process is created, or requests additional space, space is
  reserved for it by increasing the space shown on the reserve line
  above. When paging activity actually occurs, space is used in one of
  the paging areas (the one with the lowest priority number that has
  free space available, already allocated), and that space will be shown
  as used in that area.

  The sum of the space used in all of the paging areas, plus the amount
  of space reserved, can never exceed the total amount allocated in all
  of the paging areas. If a request for more memory occurs which would
  cause this to happen, the system tries several options:

  1.   The system tries to increase the total space available by
        allocating more space in file system paging areas.

  2.   If all file system paging areas are completely allocated and the
        request is still not satisfied, the system will try to use memory
        paging as described on the memory line above. (Memory paging is
        controlled by the tunable parameter swapmem_on, which defaults to
        1 (on). If this parameter is turned off, the memory line will
        not appear.)

  3.   If memory paging also cannot satisfy the request, because it is
        full or turned off, the request is denied.

  Several implications of this procedure are noteworthy for
  understanding the output of swapinfo:

  -     Paging space will not be allocated in a file system paging area
        (except for the minimum specified when the area is first enabled)
        until all device paging space has been reserved, even if the file
        system paging area has a lower priority value.

  -     When paging space is allocated to a file system paging area, that
        space becomes unavailable for user files, even if there is no
        paging activity to it.

  -     Requests for more paging space will fail when they cannot be satisfied by reserving device, file system, or memory paging, even if some of the reserved paging space is not yet in use. Thus it is possible for more paging space requests to be denied when some, or even all, of the paging areas show zero usage – space in those areas is completely reserved.

- System available memory is shared between the paging subsystem and kernel memory allocators. Thus, the system may show memory paging usage before all available disk paging space is completely reserved or fully allocated.

Options
  swapinfo recognizes the following options:

-m   Display the AVAIL, USED, FREE, LIMIT, and RESERVE values in Mbytes instead of Kbytes, rounding off to the nearest whole Mbyte (multiples of 1024^2). The output header format changes from Kb to Mb accordingly.

-t   Add a totals line with a TYPE of total. This line totals only the paging information displayed above it, not all paging areas; this line might be misleading if a subset of -dfrM is specified.

-a   Show all device paging areas, including those configured into the kernel but currently disabled. (These are normally omitted.) The word disabled appears after the NAME, and the Kb AVAIL, Kb USED, and Kb FREE values are 0. The -a option is ignored unless the -d option is present or is true by default.

-d   Print information about device paging areas only. This modifies the output header appropriately.

-f   Print information about file system paging areas only. This modifies the output header appropriately.

-n   Categorize file system paging area information into localfs areas and network areas, instead of calling them both fs areas.

-r   Print information about reserved paging space only.

-M   Print information about memory paging space only.

     The -d, -f, -n, -r and -M options can be combined. The default is -dfnrM.

-q   Quiet mode. Print only a total "Kb AVAIL" value (with the -m option, Mb AVAIL); that is, the total paging space available on the system (device, file system, reserve, or memory paging space only if -d, -f, -r, or -M is specified), for possible use by programs that want a quick total. If -q is specified, the -t and -a options are ignored.

-w   Print a warning about each device paging area that contains wasted space; that is, any device paging area whose allocated size is less than its total size. This option is effective only if -d is also specified or true by default.

RETURN VALUE
    swapinfo returns 0 if it completes successfully (including if any warnings are issued), or 1 if it reports any errors.

DIAGNOSTICS

swapinfo prints messages to standard error if it has any problems.

EXAMPLES
      List all file system paging areas with a totals line:

            swapinfo -ft

WARNINGS
      swapinfo needs kernel access for some information. If the user does
      not have appropriate privileges for kernel access, swapinfo will print
      a warning and assume that the defaults for that information have not
      been changed.

      Users of swapinfo must not rely on the exact field widths and spacing
      of its output, as these will vary depending on the system, the release
      of HP-UX, and the data to be displayed.

      The information in this manual page about paging allocation and other
      implementation details may change without warning; users should not
      rely on the accuracy of this information.

AUTHOR
      swapinfo was developed by HP.

SEE ALSO
      swapon(1M), swapon(2), fstab(4), fs(4).

vmstat

vmstat - Report process, virtual memory, trap, and CPU activity.

```
vmstat(1)                                                          vmstat(1)

NAME
     vmstat - report virtual memory statistics

SYNOPSIS

     vmstat [-dnS] [interval [count]]

     vmstat -f | -s | -z

DESCRIPTION
     The vmstat command reports certain statistics kept about process,
     virtual memory, trap, and CPU activity.  It also can clear the
     accumulators in the kernel sum structure.

  Options
     vmstat recognizes the following options:

          -d        Report disk transfer information as a separate section,
                    in the form of transfers per second.

          -n        Provide an output format that is more easily viewed on
                    an 80-column display device.  This format separates the
                    default output into two groups: virtual memory
                    information and CPU data.  Each group is displayed as a
                    separate line of output.  On multiprocessor systems,
                    this display format also provides CPU utilization on a
                    per CPU basis.

          -S        Report the number of processes swapped in and out (si
                    and so) instead of page reclaims and address
                    translation faults (re and at).

          interval  Display successive lines which are summaries over the
                    last interval seconds.  If interval is zero, the output
                    is displayed once only.  If the -d option is specified,
                    the column headers are repeated.  If -d is omitted, the
                    column headers are not repeated.

                    The command vmstat 5 prints what the system is doing
                    every five seconds.  This is a good choice of printing
                    interval since this is how often some of the statistics
                    are sampled in the system; others vary every second.

          count     Repeat the summary statistics count times.  If count is
                    omitted or zero, the output is repeated until an
                    interrupt or quit signal is received.  From the
                    terminal, these are commonly ^C and ^\, respectively
                    (see stty(1)).

          -f        Report on the number of forks and the number of pages
                    of virtual memory involved since boot-up.
```

-s   Print the total number of several kinds of paging-
            related events from the kernel sum structure that have
            occurred since boot-up or since vmstat was last
            executed with the -z option.

-z   Clear all accumulators in the kernel sum structure.
            This requires write file access permission on
            /dev/kmem. This is normally restricted to users with
            appropriate privileges.

If none of these options is given, vmstat displays a one-line summary
of the virtual memory activity since boot-up or since the -z option
was last executed.

Column Descriptions
   The column headings and the meaning of each column are:

   procs   Information about numbers of processes in various
                states.

                   r   In run queue

                   b   Blocked for resources (I/O, paging, etc.)

                   w   Runnable or short sleeper (< 20 secs) but
                          swapped

   memory   Information about the usage of virtual and real
                memory. Virtual pages are considered active if they
                belong to processes that are running or have run in
                the last 20 seconds.

                   avm   Active virtual pages

                   free   Size of the free list

   page   Information about page faults and paging activity.
                These are averaged each five seconds, and given in
                units per second.

                   re   Page reclaims (without -S)

                   at   Address translation faults (without -S)

                   si   Processes swapped in (with -S)

                   so   Processes swapped out (with -S)

                   pi   Pages paged in

                   po   Pages paged out

                   fr   Pages freed per second

                   de   Anticipated short term memory shortfall

                   sr   Pages scanned by clock algorithm, per
                          second

faults   Trap/interrupt rate averages per second over last 5 seconds.

            in   Device interrupts per second (nonclock)

            sy   System calls per second

            cs   CPU context switch rate (switches/sec)

cpu   Breakdown of percentage usage of CPU time

            us   User time for normal and low priority processes

            sy   System time

            id   CPU idle

EXAMPLES

The following examples show the output for various command options. For formatting purposes, some leading blanks have been deleted.

1.   Display the default output.

```
vmstat

    procs           memory                    page
            faults        cpu
r    b    w    avm    free   re   at   pi   po   fr   de   sr
     in   sy   cs  us sy id
0    0    0   1158    511    0    0    0    0    0    0    0
    111   18    7   0  0 100
```

2.   Add the disk tranfer information to the default output.

```
vmstat -d

    procs           memory                    page
            faults        cpu
r    b    w    avm    free   re   at   pi   po   fr   de   sr
     in   sy   cs  us sy id
0    0    0   1158    511    0    0    0    0    0    0    0
    111   18    7   0  0 100

Disk Transfers
  device    xfer/sec
  c0t6d0       0
  c0t1d0       0
  c0t3d0       0
  c0t5d0       0
```

3.   Display the default output in 80-column format.

```
vmstat -n

VM
    memory              page                    faults
   avm    free   re   at   pi   po   fr   de   sr    in    sy   cs
  1158     430    0    0    0    0    0    0    0   111    18    7
CPU
     cpu           procs
 us sy id    r    b    w
```

```
   0  0 100   0    0    0
```

4. Replace the page reclaims and address translation faults with
    process swapping in the default output.

vmstat -S

```
      procs              memory                      page
               faults        cpu
   r   b   w     avm    free   si   so   pi   po   fr   de   sr
         in    sy   cs  us sy id
   0   0   0    1158    430    0    0    0    0    0    0    0
        111    18    7   0  0 100
```

5. Display the default output twice at five-second intervals. Note
    that the headers are not repeated.

vmstat 5 2

```
      procs              memory                      page
               faults        cpu
   r   b   w     avm    free   re   at   pi   po   fr   de   sr
         in    sy   cs  us sy id
   0   0   0    1158    456    0    0    0    0    0    0    0
        111    18    7   0  0 100
   0   0   0    1221    436    5    0    5    0    0    0    0
        108    65   18   0  1 99
```

6. Display the default output twice in 80-column format at five-
    second intervals. Note that the headers are not repeated.

vmstat -n 5 2

```
VM
    memory                        page                      faults
   avm    free   re   at    pi   po    fr   de   sr    in    sy   cs
  1221    436    0    0     0    0     0    0    0    111   18    7
CPU
     cpu           procs
  us sy id    r     b    w
   0  0 100    0     0    0
  1221    435    2    0     2    0     0    0    0    109   35   17
   0  1 99    0     0    0
```

7. Display the default output and disk transfers twice in 80-column
    format at five-second intervals. Note that the headers are
    repeated.

vmstat -dn 5 2

```
VM
    memory                        page                      faults
   avm    free   re   at    pi   po    fr   de   sr    in    sy   cs
  1221    435    0    0     0    0     0    0    0    111   18    7
CPU
     cpu           procs
  us sy id    r     b    w
   0  0 100    0     0    0

Disk Transfers
   device    xfer/sec
   c0t6d0         0
```

```
      c0t1d0          0
      c0t3d0          0
      c0t5d0          0

VM
    memory                        page                          faults
    avm   free   re   at    pi   po    fr   de    sr    in    sy    cs
   1219    425    0    0     0    0     0    0     0    111    54    15
CPU
       cpu           procs
  us  sy id   r     b     w
   1   8 92   0     0     0

Disk Transfers
   device     xfer/sec
   c0t6d0          0
   c0t1d0          0
   c0t3d0          0
   c0t5d0          0
```

8. Display the number of forks and pages of virtual memory since boot-up.

```
vmstat -f

24558 forks, 1471595 pages, average=  59.92
```

9. Display the counts of paging-related events.

```
vmstat -s

0 swap ins
0 swap outs
0 pages swapped in
0 pages swapped out
1344563 total address trans. faults taken
542093 page ins
2185 page outs
602573 pages paged in
4346 pages paged out
482343 reclaims from free list
504621 total page reclaims
124 intransit blocking page faults
1460755 zero fill pages created
404137 zero fill page faults
366022 executable fill pages created
71578 executable fill page faults
0 swap text pages found in free list
162043 inode text pages found in free list
196 revolutions of the clock hand
45732 pages scanned for page out
4859 pages freed by the clock daemon
36680636 cpu context switches
1497746186 device interrupts
1835626 traps
87434493 system calls
```

WARNINGS
> Users of vmstat must not rely on the exact field widths and spacing of its output, as these will vary depending on the system, the release of HP-UX, and the data to be displayed.

AUTHOR
> vmstat was developed by the University of California, Berkeley and HP.

FILES
     /dev/kmem

SEE ALSO
     iostat(1).

CHAPTER 6

Common Desktop Environment

Common Desktop Environment

The Common Desktop Environment (CDE) is the direct lineal descendant of the HP Visual User Environment (HP VUE). CDE represents the effort of major UNIX vendors to unify UNIX at the desktop level. Hewlett-Packard's contribution to this effort is HP VUE, its award-winning graphical user environment. HP VUE is the foundation of CDE. This chapter is an introduction to CDE. If you need to fully understand all the nuances of CDE, you'll want to buy *Configuring the Common Desktop Environment* by Charlie Fernandez, Prentice Hall 1995.

Like HP VUE, the CDE is widely used by X terminal and workstation users. The CDE style manager, which every user has access to, makes it easy to customize CDE on an individual user basis. Sooner or later, however, you may want to provide some common denominator of CDE functionality for your users. If, for instance, you have an application that most users will run, you can set up environment variables, prepare drop-down menus, provide suitable fonts, etc., that will make your users more productive. Users can then perform additional customization such as defining file manager characteristics and selecting backgrounds.

To help you thoroughly understand CDE, I'll first cover the following topics:

1. Why a Graphical User Interface (GUI)?

2. The Relationship among X, Motif, and CDE

3. X, Motif, and CDE Configuration Files

4. The Sequence of Events When CDE Starts

5. Customizing CDE

6. CDE and Performance

After the discussion of how CDE works, I'll guide you through making some CDE customizations. These customizations will give you a working basis for making more advanced changes on your own. I'll show you how to make some basic, simple changes such as changing your font, background, and colors and adding an existing action to a subpanel on the front panel. Then we'll advance a little to creating a personalized drop-down menu, a new front panel icon and action, and we'll modify the default printer on the front panel so that it says what printer it is. Finally, we'll get creative and modify your login screen with a new logo and new prompts.

Why a Graphical User Interface (GUI)?

For computers to be used on every desktop, they had to be made easier to use. A new method of accessing computer power was required, one that avoided the command-line prompt, didn't require users to memorize complex commands, and didn't require a working knowledge of technological infrastructures like networking. Not that this information was unimportant; far from it. The information was both too important and too specialized to be of use to the average worker-bee computer user. A knowledge of their applications was all that was important for these users. After all, so the reasoning goes, to drive a car, one doesn't have to be a mechanic, so why should a computer user have to understand computer technology? The graphical user interface (GUI) makes computers accessible to the application end-user.

The diagram below illustrates the relationship among the computer hardware, the operating system, and the graphical user interface. The computer is the hardware platform on the bottom. The operating system, the next layer up, represents a character-based user interface. To control the computer at this level, users must type commands at the keyboard. The next several layers, beginning with the X Window System, represent the graphical user interface. To control the computer at these levels, users manipulate graphical controls with a mouse.

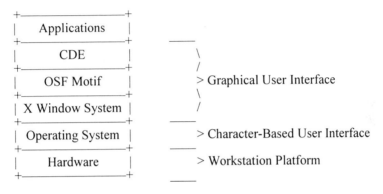

User Interface Components

GUIs replaced memorization with exploration. A user could now use pull-down menus, push buttons, sliding scroll bars, and other direct manipulation to use a computer. Typing operating system commands to perform a function is greatly reduced. With a GUI, it is both easier to learn and easier to use a computer.

Although fairly inexpensive in terms of dollars (CDE is bundled "free" with the operating system), GUIs are not without cost in terms of RAM usage and performance. Despite this performance expense, GUIs have become a permanent part of the computing environment. The benefits of their utility are worth the cost.

Beyond the graphical controls that reduce training, make mundane tasks simpler to do, and generally ease the stress of using a computer, two other benefits of GUIs are worth mentioning: multiple windows per display and client-server topology.

The benefit of multiple windows that GUIs provide is that each window (literally a rectangular area surrounded by a window frame) contains a separate application. The user can work with multiple windows open. CDE goes one step further: Its multiple workspaces allow users to separate application windows by task into specific workspaces. For instance, in a workspace named "Mail," users may have application windows showing the list of incoming electronic mail, a mail message they are currently reading, and a message they are composing for later transmission. In another workspace called "Financials," they could be working on several spreadsheets, each in its own window.

Client-server topology enables the computing resources spread around a network to be accessed efficiently to meet computing needs. In a client-server topology, powerful computers on the network are dedicated to a specific purpose (file management on a file server and running applications on an application server). Users working on less powerful client computers elsewhere on the network access the files or applications remotely. A file server reduces system administration by centralizing file backup, enabling the system administrator to back up only the file server, not each individual client computer. This setup also ensures that files will be backed up at regular intervals. An application server reduces operating costs by reducing the number and size of storage disks required and the size of RAM required on each client computer. A single version of an application resides and runs on the application server and is accessed by multiple users throughout the network.

Although this sounds complicated, the CDE GUI makes it easy. To access a file, users "drag and drop" a file icon from the file manager window. To start an application, users double-click the application icon. To print a file, users drag the file to the icon of the appropriate printer in the front panel and drop it there. Users don't have to know where these files and applications are, what directories they are in, what computers they are on, or how they are accessed. The underlying infrastructure and control you have put in place, along with the power of the GUI, allow users to concentrate on their work and not on the mechanics of their computer.

The Relationship among X, OSF/Motif, and CDE

X, OSF/Motif, and CDE are enabling framework technologies. Taken together, X, Motif, and CDE make up the three graphical layers on top of the operating system and the hardware platform.

The GUI layers provide increasingly richer ease-of-use functions in a progressive series of layers that buffer the end user from the "user hostile" character-based interface of the operating system layer.

The X Window System

The X Window System consists of the following:

- Xlib - Low-level library for programming window manipulation, graphics capabilities such as line drawing and text placement, and controlling display output, mouse and keyboard input, and application network transparency.

- Xt Intrinsics - Higher-level library for programming widgets and gadgets (graphical controls components like menus, scrollbars, and push buttons).

- Display servers - Hardware-specific programs, one per display, that manage the graphical input and output.

- Interclient communication conventions (ICCC) - A manual specifying standards for how X client programs should communicate with each other.

- Configuration files - One configuration file that specifies the default session to start (**sys.x11start**) and another specifying values for resources used to shape the X environment (**sys.Xdefaults**).

Through these mechanisms, X provides the standard upon which the graphical part of the network-oriented, client/server, distributed computing paradigm is based. A knowledge of **Xlib** and the **Xt** Intrinsics is important for programming in X and for programming at the Motif level. For system administrators, however, as long as the display servers work and X client applications are ICCC-compliant, you shouldn't need to delve into the X layer. CDE enables you to view X pretty much as part of "all that underlying technological infrastructure stuff" and focus on developing appropriate configurations of CDE to meet your users' work context.

Motif

Motif consists of the following:

- mwm window manager - Executable program that provides Motif-based window frames, window management, and a workspace menu in the X environment.

- Motif widget toolkit - Higher-level library of widgets and gadgets, the graphical components used to control the user environment.

- Motif style guide - A manual defining the Motif appearance and behavior for programmers.

- Configuration files - The **system.mwmrc** file containing configuration information for the workspace menu and key and button bindings. Resources for the window manager are in **mwm** in the **/usr/lib/X11/app-defaults** directory.

Motif provides the window manager for the end user, the widget toolkit for application developers, and the style guide to help developers design and build proper Motif-conformant applications. As with X, system administrators can view Motif mostly as "programmer's stuff," part of the underlying infrastructure, and focus on developing appropriate CDE configuration files.

CDE

CDE consists of the following, all of which are based on HP VUE 3.0:

- Workspace manager - Executable program that provides Motif-based window frames, window management, a workspace menu, and the front panel.

- File manager - Program that iconically manages files and directories through direct manipulation.

- Style manager - Container of dialog boxes that control elements of the CDE environment, like workspace color and fonts.

- Help manager - Based on the HP Help System, this program provides context-sensitive help text on CDE components.

- Login manager - Daemon-like application that handles login and password verification.

- Session manager - Manager that handles saving and restoring user sessions.

- Application manager - Manager that registers and keeps track of applications in the CDE environment.

- Configuration files - A big bunch, most of which you can avoid dealing with (see below).

Similar to HP VUE, CDE also provides a number of basic, end-user productivity-enhancing applications. In CDE, these include things like a clock showing system time, a calendar showing system date, a datebook/scheduler program for workgroup coordination, and a MIME mailer for sending multimedia electronic mail messages.

In general, CDE provides a graphical environment into which users, or you, their system administrator, can incorporate the software tools needed FOR their work.

X, Motif, and CDE Configuration Files

X, Motif, and CDE all use configuration files to shape their appearance and behavior. Elements of appearance and behavior such as foreground color, keyboard focus policy, or client decoration are resources that can be controlled by values in the appropriate configuration file. In X, Motif, and CDE, the word "resource" has a special meaning. It doesn't refer to vague natural resources or generic system resources, but to specific elements of appearance and behavior. Some examples are the **foreground** resource, the **keyboardFocusPolicy** resource, and the **clientDecoration** resource. For example, foreground color could be black, keyboard focus policy could be explicit, and client decoration could be plus-title (title bar only). These would appear in some appropriate configuration file as the following:

*foreground: black

*keyboardFocusPolicy:explicit

*clientDecoration: +title

Which configuration file these resources appear in depends on the scope of the effect desired (systemwide or individual user) and the graphical interface level being used (X, Motif, or CDE).

X Configuration Files

The X Window System has the following configuration files:

sys.x11start

sys.Xdefaults

system.hpwmrc

X*screens

X*devices

X*pointerkey

By convention, these files are located in the **/usr/lib/X11** directory. In addition, each X client application has its own app-defaults configuration file located, also by convention, in the **/usr/lib/X11/app-defaults** directory. Although six files are listed above, unless you're configuring a workstation for multiple-display screens (X*screens), multiple-input devices (X*devices), or keyboard-only pointer navigation (X*pointerkey), you'll typically need to work with only **sys.x11start**, **sys.Xdefaults**, and **system.hpwmrc**.

The **sys.x11start** file was a script used to start X and X clients before the advent of CDE. System administrators or knowledgeable users modified **sys.x11start** so that the appropriate mix of X clients started "automatically." The **sys.Xdefaults** file was read as X started to obtain values for various appearance and behavior resources. Modifications to **sys.Xdefaults** ensured that the X environment and clients had the proper appearance and behavior. **system.hpwmrc** contained the configuration of the workspace menu and button and key bindings. **system.hpwmrc** has been replaced by the Motif version, **system.mwmrc**.

sys.x11start, **sys.Xdefaults**, and **system.hpwmrc** could be copied to a user's home directory and modified to personalize the user's X environment. These personalized versions, called **.x11start**, **.Xdefaults**, and

.hpwmrc, overrode the systemwide versions, **sys.x11start**, **sys.Xdefaults**, and **system.hpwmrc**.

For more detailed information on X configuration files, see books such as the classic *Using the X Window System* (HP part number B1171-90067).

Motif Configuration Files

Motif added only one new configuration file to the X list: **system.mwmrc**.

By convention, this file is kept with the X configuration files in **/usr/lib/X11**. Actually, this file isn't new; it is the Motif version of **system.hpwmrc,** which simply replaced **system.hpwmrc** in Motif environments.

Where X brought network and interclient communication standards to the graphical user interface, Motif brought a standard for appearance and behavior, the standard originally defined in IBM's System Application Architecture Common User Access (SAACUA), which forms the basis of most PC-based GUIs. Thus, push buttons and scroll bars have a defined look and a defined behavior, and double-clicking always causes the default action to happen.

From a programmer's point of view, the Motif widget toolkit represents quite an advance over programming in "raw" X. From a user's or system administrator's point of view, the Motif user environment is about the same as the X environment, except that the **hpwm** window manager is replaced with the Motif window manager. But because **mwm** is itself a direct lineal descendent of **hpwm**, the way CDE is descended from HP VUE, even this difference is minimal.

CDE Configuration Files

I could point to over 80 files that, in one way or another, contribute to configuring some aspect of CDE. By convention, these files reside in the /**usr/dt** directory. However, if you remove from this list such files as those:

• that configure CDE applications as opposed to the environment itself

- that establish default actions and datatype definitions that, although you will create your own definitions in separate files, you will never modify

- that are CDE working files and should not be customized

- that are more appropriately associated with configuring the UNIX, X, and Motif environments underlying CDE, including the various shell environments then CDE has approximately 19 configuration files, as shown in table 6-1.

table 6-1   CDE CONFIGUATION FILES

* .Xauthority	* sys.font	* Xresources
* .Xdefaults	* sys.resources	* Xservers
* .dtprofile	* sys.sessions	* Xsession
* dtwm.fp	* Xaccess	* Xsetup
* dtwmrc	* Xconfig	* Xstartup
* sys.dtprofile	* Xfailsafe	
* sys.dtwmrc	* Xreset	

Although 19 configuration files are still a lot, don't be alarmed by the number. You won't need to modify many of them, and can ignore a couple you modify once and then forget. You need to understand in depth for periodic modification only one or two, perhaps a systemwide ***.dt** file for custom actions and datatypes or maybe **dtwm.fp**, if you are required to modify the front panel on a regular basis for some reason.

Still, configuring CDE is not something you want to start hacking with without a little preparation and a good idea of what you want to accomplish. All CDE configuration files are pretty well commented, so a good first step is to print the ones you want to modify.

table 6-2 organizes CDE configuration files according to content and the breadth of their influence.

The file **sys.dtwmrc**, like **sys.vuewmrc**, **system.hpwmrc**, and **system.mwmrc** before it, controls the configuration of the workspace manager at the system level. This includes all the following:

Workspace Menu   A menu that displays when mouse button 3 is pressed while the mouse pointer is over the workspace backdrop.

Button Bindings   Definitions of what action happens when a particular mouse button is pressed or released while the mouse pointer is over a particular area (frame, icon, window, or root).

Key Bindings   Definitions of what action happens when a particular key or key sequence is pressed while the mouse pointer is over a particular area (frame, icon, window, or root).

TABLE 6-2   CDE CONFIGURATION FILE INFLUENCE

Nature of Configuration File	Systemwide Influence	User Personal Influence
Environment Variables	sys.dtprofile Xconfig Xsession	.dtprofile
Appearance & Behavior Resources	sys.resources Xconfig Xresources sys.fonts	.Xdefaults
File Types & Action Definitions	misc *.dt files	user-prefs.dt
Client Startup at Login	sys.sessions Xstartup Xsession Xreset Xfailsafe	.xsession sessionetc
Workspace Manager & Front Panel	sys.dtwmrc dtwm.fp	dtwmrc user-prefs.fp
Clients/Servers & Access	Xaccess Xservers	.Xauthority

Unlike previous configuration files, **sys.dtwmrc** does not control the following configuration elements:

Front Panel   The box, usually at the bottom of the workspace, that contains commonly referenced indicators and frequently used graphical controls, including a six-button workspace switch.

Slideup Subpanels Menus that slide up from the front panel at various locations to provide more functionality without consuming more screen space.

Instead, to avoid a massively large and overly complex configuration file, these elements were separated into their own configuration file in CDE, **dtwm.fp**.

Some front panel configuration elements, like the number of workspaces and their arrangement in the workspace switch, are controlled through resources in a **sys.resources**, **dt.resources**, or **.Xdefaults** file. Like other workspace manager configuration files, **sys.dtwmrc** can be copied to a user's home directory, actually to **$HOME/.dt/** as **dtwmrc**, and modified to personalize the user's environment beyond the systemwide configuration of **sys.dtwmrc**.

The **sys.resources** file is one of those files you might modify once, and then never again. The **dt.resources** file is one of those files you won't ever need to modify and so can ignore. The **.Xdefaults** file is one you or your users may modify on occasion. The **sys.resources** file is where you put any non-default resources you want into effect when a brand-new user logs into CDE for the very first time. For example, as system administrator, you may want your users to have a CDE front panel with prenamed workspaces, special colors, particular fonts, or application windows in certain locations. After the first-time login, **sys.resources** is ignored in favor of **dt.resources**. This file, **dt.resources**, resides in **$HOME/.dt/sessions/current** (or **$HOME/.dt/sessions/home** when the home session is restored) and is created automatically by CDE. You can consider it a CDE working file and forget about it. The **.Xdefaults** file is where you or an end user would list X resources specific to the user's personal CDE environment. **sys.resources**, **dt.resources**, and **.Xdefaults** contain a list of resources and their values.

The **sys.sessions** file controls which clients start the very first time a new user logs into CDE. The **dt.sessions** file is to **sys.sessions** as **dt.resources** is to **sys.resources**.

It may be efficient to configure CDE to start particular applications for your users. You would specify these applications in **sys.sessions**. When a new user logs in for the first time, the CDE environment includes the specified clients. At the end of this first session by logging out, the remaining clients would be recorded in **$HOME/.dt/sessions/current** for CDE (**$HOME/.dt/sessions/home** when the home session is restored).

The **sys.dtprofile** file is a template that is automatically copied at first login into each new user's home directory as **.dtprofile. sys.dtprofile** replaces **.profile** or **.login** in the CDE environment (although either **.profile** or **.login** can be sourced in **.dtprofile**). The **.dtprofile** file holds the personal environment variables that would, in a character-based environment, be found in **.profile** or **.login**. Use this separate file to avoid the interference that terminal I/O commands cause to CDE's graphical environment.

The CDE login manager, **dtlogin**, presets the following environment variables to default values:

DISPLAY	The name of the local display
EDITOR	The default text editor
HOME	The user's home directory as specified in **/etc/passwd**
KBD_LANG	The current language of the keyboard
LANG	The current NLS language
LC_ALL	The value of LANG
LC_MESSAGES	The value of LANG
LOGNAME	The user's login name as specified in **/etc/passwd**
MAIL	The default file for mail (usually **/var/mail/$USER**)
PATH	The default directories to search for files and applications
USER	The user name
SHELL	The default shell as specified in **/etc/passwd**
TERM	The default terminal emulation
TZ	The time zone in effect

Variations to these default values belong in each user's **.dtprofile**. Additional environment variables can be added as needed to shape the user's environment to the needs of the work context. Just beware of using commands that cause any terminal I/O.

Like **.dtprofile**, **Xsession** is a shell script that sets user environment variables. The environment variables in **Xsession** apply systemwide. The environment variables in **.dtprofile** apply only to a user's personal environment. Furthermore, since the login manager runs **Xsession** after the X server has started, the variables in **Xsession** are not available to the X server. Variables typically set in **Xsession** include the following:

EDITOR	The default text editor.
KBD_LANG	The language of the keyboard (usually set to the value of $LANG).
TERM	The default terminal emulation.
MAIL	The default file for mail, which is usually **/var/mail/$USER**.
DTHELPSEARCHPATH	The locations to search for CDE help files.
DTAPPSEARCHPATH	The locations to search for applications registered with the CDE application manager.
DTDATABASESEARCHPATH	The locations to search for additional action and datatype definitions.
XMICONSEARCHPATH	The locations to search for additional icons.
XMICONBMSEARCHPATH	Same as above.

As an example, suppose that you are the system administrator for several mixed workstation and X terminal clusters located at a single site. Now suppose that different users you administer have grown accustomed to certain text editors. Some like **vi**, others prefer **emacs**, and a couple wouldn't be caught dead without **dmx**. An easy way to provide each user with his or her favored text editor would be to reset their EDITOR variable to the appropriate value in the individual **.dtprofile** files.

Xconfig contains resources that control the behavior of **dtlogin** and it also provides a place to specify the locations for any other **dtlogin** configuration files you create. The **Xconfig** file works on a systemwide basis, so it's one of those files that you modify only once and then forget. When, during login, **Xconfig** is run, several CDE configuration files get referenced: **Xaccess**, **Xservers**, **Xresources**, **Xstartup**, **Xsession**, **Xreset**, and **Xfailsafe**. Like **Xconfig** itself, most of these files are the type that you modify once when installing CDE and then, unless the network topology changes, you never deal with again.

Xaccess, as the name implies, is a remote display access control file. **Xaccess** contains a list of the host names allowed or denied XDMCP connection access to the local computer. For example, when an X terminal requests login service, **dtlogin** consults the **Xaccess** file to determine whether service should be granted.

The primary use of the **Xservers** file is to list the display screens on the local system that **dtlogin** is responsible for managing. **dtlogin** reads the **Xservers** file and starts an X server for each display listed there. It then starts a child **dtlogin** process to manage the server and display the login screen. Note that **dtlogin** works only locally; **dtlogin** can't start an X server on a remote system or X terminal. For remote display servers, some other mechanism must be used to start the server, which then uses the X Display Management Control Protocol (XDMCP) to request a login screen from **dtlogin**.

The **Xservers** file is another of those files that you may spend some time with initially and then, unless the topography of your network changes, never deal with again. When do you use **Xservers**? When a display doesn't match the default configuration. The default configuration assumes that each system has a single bitmap display and is the system console. X terminals, multiple displays (heads), multiple screens, and Starbase applications all require configuration lines in the **Xservers** file.

The **Xresources** file contains the list of resources that control the appearance and behavior of the login screen. After you substitute your company's logo for the HP logo and change the fonts and colors, you'll probably never have to deal with **Xresources** again (unless your company changes its logo).

Xstartup is a systemwide configuration file executed by the login manager, from which it receives several environment variables:

DISPLAY	The name of the local display.
USER	The login name of the user.

HOME	The user's home directory.
PATH	The value of the **systemPath** resource in **Xconfig**.
SHELL	The value of the **systemShell** resource in **Xconfig**.
XAUTHORITY	The file to access for authority permissions.
TZ	The local time zone.

Because it can execute scripts and start clients on a systemwide basis, **Xstartup** is similar to **sys.sessions**. The difference is that **Xstartup** runs as root. Thus, modifications to **Xstartup** should be reserved for actions like mounting file systems.

Xreset is a systemwide companion script to **Xstartup**. It runs as root and essentially undoes what **Xstartup** put in motion.

The **Xfailsafe** file contains customizations to the standard failsafe session. The failsafe session provides a way to correct improper CDE sessions caused by errors in the login and session configuration files. As such, **Xfailsafe** is something your users are not ever going to use, but you can make your life a little easier with a few judicious customizations.

The **sessionetc** file resides in a user's **.dt/sessions** directory and personalizes that user's CDE session. **sessionetc** handles the starting of additional X clients like **sys.session**, but on a per-user basis, as opposed to systemwide. While **dt.session** also starts clients on a per-user basis, the clients are those of the default or current session. **dt.session** resides in **.dt/session/current**. **sessionetc**, which resides in **.dt/session**, should contain only those clients that are not automatically restored. Typically, these are clients that do not set the **WM_COMMAND** properly, so the session manager can't save or restore them; thus they need to be restarted in **sessionetc**.

The **sys.font** file contains the systemwide, default session font configuration. These default fonts were based on usability studies, so **sys.font** is a file you may never change. However, should you encounter a situation that requires a different mix of fonts on a systemwide basis, this is where you'd change them. Note that the font resources and values mentioned in **sys.font** must match exactly the default font resources specified in the **/usr/dt/app-defaults/C/Dtstyle** file.

CDE has a bunch of files that specify CDE action and data type definitions. All these files end with the file extension ***.dt**. A ***.dt** ("dt" for "desk top") contains both data type and action definitions. The default ***.dt** files are in **/usr/dt/appconfig/types/C** and act on a systemwide basis. Similarly, **user-prefs.dt**, the master copy of which is also located in **/usr/dt/appconfig/types/C**, is used at the personal user level.

The **.Xauthority** file is a user-specific configuration file containing authorization information needed by clients that require an authorization mechanism to connect to the server.

CDE Configuration File Locations

Where CDE looks for particular configuration files depends on the nature of the configuration files, principally what the files configure and how wide their influence is. Table 6-3 shows the location of system and user configuration files based on the nature of the file content:

TABLE 6-3   CDE SYSTEM AND USER CONFIGURATION FILES

Nature of Configuration File	Systemwide Influence	User Personal Influence
Environment Variables	/usr/dt/config/	$HOME/
Appearance & Behavior Resources	/usr/dt/config/C /usr/dt/app-defaults/C	$HOME/.dt/ $HOME/.dt/sessions/current/ $HOME/.dt/sessions/home/
File Types & Action Definitions	/usr/dt/appconfig/ types/C	$HOME/.dt/types
Client Startup at Login	/usr/dt/config/ /usr/dt/config/C	$HOME/.dt/session/ $HOME/.dt/session/current/ $HOME/.dt/session/home/
Workspace Manager	/usr/dt/config	$HOME/.dt/

For each of the default systemwide file locations listed in Table 6-3, a corresponding location exists for custom systemwide configuration files. These custom files should be located in the appropriate subdirectory under **/etc/dt**. The basic procedure is to copy the file you need to customize from **/usr/dt/something** to **/etc/dt/something** and then do your modifications there. For example, to change the default logo in **Xresources**, copy **/usr/dt/**

config/C/Xresources to **/etc/dt/config/C/Xresources**, open **/etc/dt/config/ C/Xresources**, and make your changes.

This is an important point. Files located under **/usr/dt** are considered CDE system files and will be overwritten during updates. Thus any customizations you do there will be lost. Make all modifications to system-wide configuration files in **/etc/dt** and its subdirectories.

How Configuration Files Play Together

From the material covered so far, you've probably concluded correctly that CDE configuration files aren't something to go hacking with without a plan - a well thought out plan. You've probably figured out that the element you want to configure and the breadth of influence you want it to have determine which configuration file you modify.

For instance, if you wanted to set an environment variable, you have a choice of four configuration files: **sys.dtprofile**, **Xconfig**, **Xsession**, and **.dtprofile**. But if you want to set environment variables that affect only a particular user, your choice immediately narrows to a single file, **.dtprofile**.

Now the only remaining piece of the puzzle is to understand the order in which CDE reads its configuration files. When a configuration element (an environment variable, resource, action, or data type) is specified twice but with different values, you obviously want the correct value used and the incorrect value ignored.

The following rules apply:

- For environment variables, the last specified value is used.

- For resources, the last specified value is used. However, this is influenced by specificity. Thus, **emacs*foreground** takes precedence over just ***foreground** for emacs clients, regardless of the order in which the resources were encountered.

- For actions, the first specified is used.

- For datatypes, the first specified is used.

Table 6-4 illustrates which specification is used when CDE reads multiple specifications of configuration elements in its configuration files:

TABLE 6-4 WHAT CDE USES FOR CONFIGURATION

Configuration Element	Element Used
resource	last encountered or most specific
environment	last encountered
action	first encountered
file type	first encountered

Put in terms of scope, a user configuration file overrides a systemwide configuration file. Looking at the order of precedence of just systemwide configuration files, the files in **/etc/dt** have precedence over those in **/usr/dt**, so global custom configurations have precedence over the CDE default configuration. And **$HOME/.dt** files take precedence over those in **/etc/dt.**

For resources, the elements used to specify a GUI's appearance and behavior, CDE sets values according to the following priorities:

1. **Command line** - When you start a client from the command line, options listed on the command line have top priority.

2. **Xresources, .Xdefaults, dt.resources, sys.resources,** - When CDE starts, it reads these resource configuration files to determine the value of X resources to use for the session.

3. **RESOURCE MANAGER** - Resources already in the property **RESOURCE_MANAGER** may affect an application that is just starting.

4. **app-defaults** - Specifies "default" resource values that differ from built-in resource values.

5. **built-in defaults** - Default resources that are "hard coded" have the lowest priority.

Specific resource specifications take precedence over general resource specifications. For example, suppose that you want a certain font in your text entry areas. You could correctly specify a ***FontList** resource in your personal **.Xdefaults** file, only to have it overwritten by an ***XmText*FontList** in an **app-defaults** file. Although **app-defaults** is of lower priority than **.Xdefaults**, the resource specification set there is more specific, so it takes precedence.

For environment variables, CDE sets values according to the following priorities:

1. **$HOME/.dtprofile** - User-specific variables have top priority.

2. **/etc/dt/config/C/Xsession** - Custom systemwide variables not read by X server.

3. **/etc/dt/config/C/Xconfig** - Custom systemwide variables read by X server.

4. **/usr/dt/config/C/Xsession** - Default systemwide variables not read by X server.

5. **/usr/dt/config/C/Xconfig** - Default systemwide variables read by X server.

6. **/usr/dt/bin/dtlogin** - Built-in default variables have the lowest priority.

For datatype and action definitions, CDE looks for **.dt** files according to the following priority:

1. $HOME/.dt/types

2. /etc/dt/appconfig/types/C

3. /usr/dt/appconfig/types/C

Remember, for data types or actions, the first value it finds is the one it uses. So if you just can't get a file type or action to work, check for a duplicate entry earlier in the file or for an entry in a file with higher priority. Note also that the environment variable DTDATABASESEARCH-PATH can be set either in **/etc/dt/config/Xsession** or in **$HOME/.dtprofile** to add directories where CDE can search for file type and action definition information.

Specifying Appearance and Behavior

There are only two tricks to specifying appearance and behavior resources in configuration files. The first is to specify the resource and its value correctly. The second is to specify the resource and value in the correct configuration file.

Two caveats involve colors and fonts. The CDE style manager provides a graphical interface for modifying colors and fonts. However, if you specify an application's color or font directly, this specification will override the ability of the style manager to manage that resource for the application.

Typical ways to specify a color or font directly include the following:

- Type the specification on the command line as a startup option.

- Include the specification in the application's **app-defaults** file.

- Use the **xrdb** utility to add resources for the application to the resource database.

The Sequence of Events When CDE Starts

The following section is a blow-by-blow account of what happens when a user logs into CDE. In this particular account, assume a distributed topology like a diskless cluster. The account begins with the boot of the hub system and nodes in step 1. By step 4, X servers are running on each node and login screens are being displayed. By step 6, the user is logged in. By step 11, the session manager is busy re-creating the user's session.

1. The **dtlogin** executable is started as part of the **init** process that occurs during the system boot sequence on the hub machine and each cluster node.

2. **dtlogin** reads **/usr/dt/config/Xconfig** to get a list of resources with which to configure the login process. This is where **dtlogin** first learns about files like **Xaccess**, **Xservers**, **Xresources**, **Xstartup**, **Xsession**, and **Xreset** and gets the values of a number of appearance and behavior resources.

3. **dtlogin** reads two files in **/usr/dt/config**:

- **Xservers** or the file identified by the **Dtlogin*servers** resource setting in **Xconfig**.

- **Xresources** or the file identified by the **Dtlogin*resources** resource setting in **Xconfig**.

4. **dtlogin** starts an X server and a child **dtlogin** for each local display.

5. Each child **dtlogin** invokes **dtgreet**, the login screen.

6. When a login and password are validated, a child **dtlogin** sets certain environment variables to default values.

7. The child **dtlogin** runs **/usr/dt/config/Xstartup**.

8. The child **dtlogin** runs **/usr/dt/config/Xsession**.

9. **Xsession** runs **dthello**, the copyright screen.

10. **Xsession** reads **$HOME/.dtprofile**, setting any additional environment variables or overwriting those set previously by **dtlogin**.

11. The child **dtlogin** invokes the session manager, **dtsession**.

12. **dtsession** restores the appropriate session. For example, to restore the current session, **dtsession** reads **dt.resources** and **dt.session** in **$HOME/.dt/sessions/current**.

At logout, the reverse happens. The session is saved and **dtlogin** runs **/usr/dt/config/Xreset**. After **Xreset** completes, **dtlogin** again displays the login screen as in step 4.

Customizing CDE

Before you modify any CDE configuration files, first develop a strategy. I know I've mentioned this before, but it's important enough to mention again.

The following questions should get you started:

1. What are your users' needs?

2. Which of those needs can be met by reconfiguring CDE?

3. At what level should these changes be made (systemwide, groups of users, individual users only)?

4. Which CDE files do you need to modify (names and locations)?

5. What are the changes and what is their order within the file?

It's also a good idea to have handy a binder containing man pages for each of the CDE components (for looking up resources and their values) and a copy of each of the CDE configuration files.

The following sections assume that you're making systemwide modifications. To make modifications for individual users, follow the same procedure on the equivalent user's personal file.

Adding Objects to or Removing Objects from the Front Panel

You have two ways to add objects to the CDE front panel:

- Drag and drop them into a slideup subpanel and then make them the default for that subpanel.

- Modify the **/etc/dt/appconfig/types/C/dtwm.fp** configuration file.

To add a control button through drag and drop:

1. Drag the application icon you want as a front panel button from an application manager view and drop the icon onto the installation section (the top section) of the appropriate subpanel.

2. Place the mouse pointer over the icon and press mouse button 3 to display the subpanel menu.

3. Select Copy to Main Panel.

To add a control button by editing the dtwm.fp file:

1. If you haven't already done so, copy **dtwm.fp** from **/usr/dt/app-config/types/C** to **/etc/dt/appconfig/types/C**.

2. Add the new control definition using the format:

```
CONTROL NewControl
{
TYPE              icon
```

```
CONTAINER_NAME  Top
CONTAINER_TYPE  BOX
ICON            NewControlBitmap
PUSH_ACTION     NewControlExecutable
}
```

Note that all control definitions have the following general syntax:

```
KEYWORD value
```

To avoid a lot of typing, it's easiest just to copy an existing definition and insert it where you want your new control to be and then modify it. As you move down the list of control definitions, you're moving from left to right across the front panel (notice the POSITION_HINTS value increases in each definition). So if you want your new control to be to the right of the date on the front panel, you'd insert the control on the line below "date" and add a POSITION_HINTS 3 line to your definition; if you wanted your new control to be to the left of "date," insert the control on the line above "date" with a POSITION_HINTS of 1.

The new control definition can be located anywhere in the list of control definitions. The POSITION_HINTS line keeps it from getting inadvertently bumped to a new position. It's still a good idea to copy an existing definition and avoid extra typing - it reduces the chance of typing mistakes. Don't forget to include the curly braces.

The basic control definition has six parts:

- **CONTROL name** - The definition name. This is the only part of the definition outside the curly braces.

- **TYPE** - The type of control. Several types exist. The most useful for customizing the front panel are probably blank and icon. A blank is useful as a space holder. An icon can start an action or application or be a drop zone.

- **ICON** - The bitmap to display on the front panel. Front panel bitmaps are located in the **/usr/dt/appconfig/icons** directory.

- **CONTAINER_NAME** - The name of the container that holds the control. This must correspond to the name of an actual container listed in **dtwm.fp**.

- **CONTAINER_TYPE** - The type of container that holds the control. This can be **BOX**, **SWITCH**, or **SUBPANEL**, but it must agree with the type of the container name.

- **PUSH_ACTION** - This is what happens when the control button is pushed. **PUSH_ACTION** is just one of several possible actions. For more information, see the **dtwm** man page.

To remove a control button from the front panel, type a pound sign (#) in the leftmost column of the **CONTROL** definition line. The (#) turns the control specification into a comment line.

Changing the Front Panel in Other Ways

In addition to adding or removing buttons, you can shape the front panel in other ways. These other ways use workspace manager resources to modify default values. The following resources relate to the front panel:

- **clientTimeoutInterval** - Length of time the busy light blinks and the pointer remains an hourglass when a client is started from the front panel.

- **geometry** - x and y coordinate location of the front panel.

- **highResFontList** - Font to use on a high-resolution display.

- **lowResFontList** - Font to use on a low-resolution display.

- **mediumResFontList** - Font to use on a medium-resolution display.

- **name** - Name of the front panel to use when multiple front panels are in **dtwm.fp**.

- **pushButtonClickTime** - Time interval distinguishing two single mouse clicks from a double-click (to avoid double launching an application accidently).

- **waitingBlinkRate** - Blink rate of the front panel busy light.

- **workspaceList** - List of workspace names.

- **title** - Title to appear on a workspace button.

Like all other workspace manager resources, these front panel resources have the following syntax:

```
Dtwm*screen*resource: value
```

For example, suppose that instead of the default four workspaces, your users need a front panel with six workspaces named Mail, Reports, Travel, Financials, Projects, and Studio. Further, they prefer a large font and have decided upon New Century Schoolbook 10-point bold. As system administrator, you'd make everyone happy with the following resource specifications:

```
Dtwm*0*workspaceList: One Two Three Four Five Six
Dtwm*0*One*title: Mail
Dtwm*0*Two*title: Reports
Dtwm*0*Three*title: Travel
Dtwm*0*Four*title: Financials
Dtwm*0*Five*title: Projects
Dtwm*0*Six*title: Studio
Dtwm*0*highResFontList:
              -adobe-new century schoolbook-bold-r-normal\
              --10-100-75-75-p-66-iso8859-1
```

The screen designation is usually 0, except for displays capable of both image and overlay planes. The order of screens in the **X*screens** file is what determines the screen number; the first screen, typically the image plane, is designated as 0. Note also the inclusion of workspace names (One, Two, Three, Four, Five, and Six) in the six title resource specifications.

If none of your users have ever logged in, you're in luck. You can add the above lines to **sys.resources**. But since you're probably not that lucky (almost no one is), the easiest way to effect the changes is to use the **EditResources** action to insert the new resource lines into each user's **RESOURCE_MANAGER** property and then restart the workspace manager.

The obvious disadvantage is that you have to physically go to each user's work area and take over the machine for a few minutes. However, on the plus side, the changes are immediate and are automatically saved in the correct **dt.resources** for users who restore their current session. You also avoid having your changes overwritten, which could happen if you modify the right **dt.resources** file at the wrong time, while the user is still logged in.

Have Some Fun Yourself

It's unfortunate, but often true, that users benefit from GUIs, mostly because their system administrator has slogged through a **vi** or **emacs** session editing some configuration file to get things to work as desired. However, anytime you need to edit resources, you can use CDE's drag-and-drop facility to your advantage, enjoy some of the fruits of your labor, and avoid some of the drudgery.

If **dtpad** is the default editor, you can create a file with the resource modifications in it, start the **EditResources** action, and then drop the resource modifications into the resource list that appears in the **EditResources dtpad** window.

If you haven't already played around with **dtpad**, try it. In most cases, you'll probably find it suitable for your users who need a small, fast text editor they can master without learning. **dtpad** has a menu bar with pulldown menus that contain some basic functionality. More important, **dtpad** supports cut-and-paste and drag-and-drop; users don't have to memorize commands but can simply select and manipulate text directly with the mouse.

Adding Things to Slideup Subpanels

Subpanels are defined in **dtwm.fp** after the front panel and front panel control definitions. To associate a subpanel with a front panel control button, the front panel control name is listed as the container name in the subpanel definition.

To add a slideup subpanel to the front panel:

1. Copy the file **/usr/dt/appconfig/types/C/dtwm.fp** to **/etc/dt/appconfig/types/C/dtwm.fp** if you haven't already done so.

2. Decide with which control button the slideup is to be associated.

3. Create the subpanel definition file in **/etc/dt/appconfig/types/C/dtwm.fp**. This will take the following form:

```
SUBPANEL    SubPanelName
{
CONTAINER_NAME  AssociatedFrontPanelControlButton
TITLE   SubPanelTitle
}
```

4. Create subpanel control definitions for the subpanel. These will take the following form:

```
CONTROL   ControlName
{
TYPE   icon
CONTAINER_NAME     SubPanelName
CONTAINER_TYPE     SUBPANEL
ICON   BitmapName
PUSH_ACTION     ActionName
}
```

As with front panel control buttons, it's easier to copy and modify an existing subpanel file than to start from scratch.

Front Panel Animation

Animation for front panel or slideup subpanel drop zones is created by displaying a progressive series of bitmaps. By convention, the bitmaps are in **/usr/dt/appconfig/icons**. The list of bitmaps to display is contained in animation definitions at the end of **dtwm.fp**.

To create an animation sequence for a drop zone:

1. Create a progressive series of bitmaps.

2. Add a list of these bitmap files to the appropriate configuration file using the following syntax:

```
ANIMATION AnimationName
{
 bitmap0
 bitmap1
 bitmap2
 bitmap3
 bitmap4
 bitmap5
}
```

3. Add a line to the appropriate control definition using the syntax:

```
DROP_ANIMATION AnimationName
```

Adding Things to the Workspace Menu

The workspace menu is defined in **sys.dtwmrc**. For one or two changes, you can modify the existing workspace menu. For major changes, it's probably easier to insert an entirely new menu definition in **sys.dtwmrc**.

A menu definition has the following syntax:

```
Menu MenuName
{
  "Menu Name"          f.title
  "Frame"              f.exec /nfs/system1/usr/frame/bin/maker.
  "Second Item"        action
  "Third Item"         action
}
```

The first line specifies the menu name, following the keyword **Menu**. The lines between the curly braces list the items that appear in the menu in their order of appearance; thus the first line is the title as designated by the function **f.title**. The second line is an example of a definition that would start **FrameMaker** on a remote application server in a distributed environment. Numerous other functions exist, approximately 45 in all. For a complete list, see the **dtwmrc** (4) man page.

For users to display the menu, you need to bind the menu definition to a mouse button and a screen location using the action **f.menu MenuName**. For example, if your users want to post the menu by pressing mouse button 3 when the pointer is on the workspace background, you would insert the following line in the Mouse Button Bindings Description section at the end of **sys.dtwmrc**:

```
<Btn3Down> root f.menu MenuName
```

(Actually, it would be easier to modify the line that's already there by exchanging **MenuName** for **DtRootMenu** on the second line.)

Creating Actions and File Types

An action starts a process such as a shell script or an application. An action can be connected to a front panel button to start when the button is pushed. An action can be connected to a front panel drop zone to be performed when a data file is dropped on the drop zone. An action can be associated with an icon in a file manager window so that the action can be started by double-clicking the icon. An action can be associated with a particular data type so that double-clicking the data file icon starts the action and opens the data file.

In addition to setting up a front panel and default session to meet your user's needs, the single most important thing you can do to make computing life easier for the people who depend on you is to create actions and data types.

CDE actions and data types are defined in files that end in **.dt** (for "desk top"). Similar to most other CDE configuration files, ***.dt** files have a systemwide version that can be copied into a user's personal directory and customized for personal use. Most systemwide ***.dt** files are found in **/usr/dt/appconfig/types/C**; personal ***.dt** files are created by copying **user-prefs.dt** from **/usr/dt/appconfig/types/C** to **$HOME/.dt/types**.

The default search path that CDE uses to look for actions and file types includes the following main directories in the order listed:

- $HOME/.dt/types

- /etc/dt/appconfig/types

- /usr/dt/appconfig/types

You can add further directories to the search path using the **DTDATABASESEARCHPATH** environment variable. Insert this environment variable and the new search path into **/usr/dt/config/Xsession** for a systemwide influence. Insert the environment variable and search path into **$HOME/.dtprofile** for individual users.

The following are the recommended locations in which to create an action or file type definition:

- Create a completely new file in the **/etc/dt/appconfig/types** directory. This file will have a systemwide influence. Remember, the file must end with the **.dt** extension.

- Copy **user-prefs.dt** from **/usr/dt/appconfig/types** to the **/etc/dt/appconfig/types** directory and insert the definition there for systemwide use.

- Copy **user-prefs.vf** to **$HOME/.dt/types** and insert the definition there for individual users.

A typical action has the following syntax:

```
ACTION        ActionName
{
 TYPE         type
 keyword      value
 keyword      value
}
```

For example, here's a FrameMaker action:

```
ACTION        FRAME
{
  TYPE        COMMAND
  WINDOW-TYPE NO-STDIO
  EXEC-STRING /nfs/hpcvxmk6/usr/frame/bin/maker
}
```

A typical data type has the following syntax:

```
DATA_ATTRIBUTES            AttributesName
{
  keyword          value
  keyword          value
  ACTIONS          action, action
}
DATA_CRITERIA
{
 DATA_ATTRIBUTES AttributesName
 keyword          value

 keyword          value
}
```

Notice that a data type definition is actually in two parts, an attribute part and a criteria part. The attribute portion of the data type definition specifies the look of the datatype; the criteria portion specifies the behavior of the data type.

For example, here's a file type for FrameMaker files that uses the FRAME action:

```
DATA_ATTRIBUTES      FRAME_Docs
{
  DESCRIPTION        This file type is for FrameMaker documents.
  ICON               makerIcon
  ACTIONS            FRAME
}
DATA_CRITERIA

{

DATA_ATTRIBUTES_NAME   FRAME_Docs

NAME_PATTERN   *.fm

MODE    f

}
```

You can create actions and file types from scratch using these formats. However, the easiest way to create an action is to use the **CreateAction** tool. **CreateAction** is located in the Desktop Applications folder of the Applications Manager and presents you with a fill-in-the-blank dialog box that guides you through creating an **action.dt** file containing the action definition. You can then move this file to the appropriate directory for the range of influence you want the action to have: **/etc/dt/appconfig/types** for a systemwide influence; **$HOME/.dt/types** for individual users.

Using Different Fonts

Although CDE fonts have been carefully selected for readability, you may have valid reasons to prefer other fonts. To make your fonts available systemwide throughout the CDE environment, put them in **/etc/dt/app-defaults/Dtstyle** so that they will appear in the style manager's font dialog box. To make fonts available only for a particular X client application, specify the font in the **app-defaults** file for the application; by convention, this file is located in **/usr/lib/X11/app-defaults**. Just remember, this overrides the fonts in the style manager.

The font dialog box can contain a maximum of seven font sizes. You can adjust this number downward by resetting the value of **Dtstyle*NumFonts** in **/etc/dt/app-defaults/Dtstyle**; however, you can't increase the number higher than seven.

The Font Dialog section of the **Dtstyle** configuration file has seven **SystemFont** resources and seven **UserFont** resources. Again, you can have fewer than seven system and seven user fonts, but you can't have more.

To specify fonts for a particular application, use the ***FontList** resource in the **app-defaults** file for the application.

To modify font resources on an individual-user basis, you can use the **EditResources** action as described in the earlier section "Changing the Front Panel in Other Ways."

CDE and Performance

CDE isn't a monolithic application; it's a set of components layered on top of the operating system, the X Window System, and Motif. Each underlying layer takes its share of RAM before CDE or any other client even starts. Because of the low-level nature of these layers, the RAM they use is hardly ever regained through swapping to disk.

In some cases, operating system overhead and user application requirements restrict the amount of RAM available for a graphical user interface to little more than enough to run a window manager such as Motif. Since the CDE workspace manager and the Motif window manager take roughly the same amount of RAM, users can enjoy an enriched graphical environment with the added value of the CDE's multiple workspaces at essentially no extra RAM cost over running the Motif window manager.

Sample RAM Sizes

Table 6-5 illustrates some sample RAM sizes for HP VUE 3.0. Official numbers for CDE are not available, but should be similar, though a little bigger, than those contained in Table 6-5. The numbers represent working environment RAM and the RAM required after login; during login, a spike in RAM usage occurs as applications and other processes start up. This spike would include, in the case of CDE, starting **dtlogin**, **Xsession**, and **dtsession**. Immediately after login, these clients become inactive and are swapped out, so they don't appear in the working environment numbers.

A word of warning: don't read too much into the numbers. RAM usage numbers vary with the system, the application set, and especially with how the application set is used by each user.

Additionally, kernel size, daemon size, and X server size can vary widely, depending on the configuration and the user. An X server hack may be running an X server stripped down to just 1/2 MByte, the supposed X server ThrashPoint, and get excellent performance. Alternatively, a user with a penchant for large root window bitmaps can quickly swell their X server size to 12 MBytes and still not have reached the RMaxPoint.

TABLE 6-5   SAMPLE HYPOTHETICAL RAM SIZES

Process	ThrashPoint	MTRAM	RMaxPoint
misc daemons	2 MBytes	3 MBytes	5 MBytes
file buffers	1-1/2 MBytes	3-1/4 MBytes	6-1/2 MBytes
kernel	2 MBytes	3 MBytes	5 MBytes
Xserver	1/2 MBytes	2 MBytes	7 MBytes
workspace manager	3/4 MBytes	1 MBytes	1-1/4 MBytes
file manager	1/2 MBytes	3/4 MBytes	2 MBytes
help manager	1/2 MBytes	3/4 MBytes	1 MBytes
style manager	1/2 MBytes	1 MBytes	1 MBytes
hpterm console	1/2 MBytes	3/4 MBytes	1-1/4 MBytes
message server	1/4 MBytes	1/3 MBytes	1/2 MBytes
Total	9 MBytes	16+ MBytes	30-1/2MBytes

The ThrashPoint column shows the typical absolute minimum RAM required to "run" the default HP VUE components, including operating system and X server overhead; however, "run" is a misnomer. The Thrash-Point is when the system just sits there and thrashes, swapping pages in and out of RAM, unable to get enough of an application's code into RAM to execute it before having to swap it out.

The RMaxPoint column shows the other extreme, a reasonable maximum amount of RAM for running the default HP VUE, including operating system and X server overhead. The RMaxPoint is when all code for every process is in RAM, so nothing gets swapped out. The sizes for some items in this column can vary considerably; the kernel hack's kernel size would be smaller; the user with a penchant for big root window bitmaps would have an X server considerably larger.

The MTRAM column shows a typical amount of RAM required to run the default CDE, including operating system and X server overhead. The MTRAM is when a typical user experiences acceptable performance. Acceptable means real-time response to visual controls and drag-and-drop. Again, a caveat: If the user is doing a local compile or working remotely on a heavily loaded network, performance will be worse. If the user is mostly reading email and word processing, performance will be better.

Table 6-5 shows that the typical size of HP VUE (without operating system or X server overhead) is 6^+ MBytes. HP VUE includes the HP VUE managers (the Motif window manager is included in the workspace manager), a console hpterm, and the message server.

For best results with CDE, you better figure a minimum of 24 Mbytes of RAM, with 32 Mbytes or better being preferred.

Tactics for Better Performance

Unless all your users have RAM-loaded powerhouses for systems, you will need to spend some time developing a performance strategy. If you conceive of performance as a bell-shaped curve, satisfaction lies on the leading edge. Your performance strategy should do everything it can to keep your users on the leading edge.

Probably the most logical approach is to start small and grow. In other words, start out with minimal user environments on all the systems on your network. Gradually add software components until you or your users begin to notice performance degradation. Then back off a little. Such an approach might take several weeks or more to evaluate, as you add components and as your users spend several days actually working in the environment to determine the effect of your changes on system performance and their frustration levels.

The most RAM-expensive pieces of CDE are the workspace manager, the session manager, and the file manager. The workspace manager is expensive because portions of it are always in RAM (assuming that you are moving windows around and switching workspaces). The CDE workspace manager is no more expensive than the Motif window manager; if you want a GUI, it's just a price you have to pay. The session manager is expensive only during logout and login, because it saves and restores sessions. The rest of the time, the session manager is dormant and gets swapped out of RAM. Saving your current work session is nice at the end of the day, but it's something to consider giving up if you want to improve your login and logout performance. The file manager is expensive because it wakes up periodically and jumps into RAM to check the status of the file system and update its file manager windows. When it jumps into RAM, it pushes something else out, for example, maybe the desktop publishing program you're using.

Here are some other ideas that you may find useful:

Terminal Emulators   **xterms** are a little less RAM-expensive than **dtterms**. Unless you need the block mode functionality of an **dtterm**, **xterm** might be a better choice for terminal emulation.

Automatic Saves   Some applications automatically save data at periodic intervals. Although this feature can be beneficial, you need to evaluate its effect in light of performance. If the application is central to your users' work, fine, but if not, you might want to disable the automatic save feature.

Scroll Buffers   Large scroll buffers in terminal emulators can be a real convenience, but they can also take up a lot of RAM. Even modestly sized scroll buffers, when multiplied by three or four terminal emulators, consume a lot of RAM.

Background Bitmaps	Avoid large bitmaps; they increase the X server size. Especially avoid switching large bitmaps frequently within a session. If you are hunting for a new background, be sure to restart the X server after you've found the one you want and have included it in the proper **sessionetc** file. The most efficient bitmaps are small ones that can be repeated to tile the background.
Front Panel	Reconfigure the front panel to minimize the number of buttons. Keep just enough to meet user needs. This decreases the workspace manager size in RAM and speeds login and logout.
Pathnames	Whenever possible, use absolute pathnames for bitmap specifications. Although this approach decreases the flexibility of the system, it speeds access time.

Customizing CDE - Personalizing Your Workstation

Now that you have a good understanding as to how CDE works, let's make some changes. This is the fun part - making changes and customizing the system for the entire user community or for each individual user.

As I said at the beginning of the chapter, I'll show you how to make some basic, simple changes such as changing your font, backdrop, and colors and adding an existing action to a subpanel on the front panel. Then we'll advance a little to creating a personalized dropdown menu, a new front panel icon and action, and we'll modify the default printer on the Personal Printers subpanel of the front panel so that it says what printer it is.

Finally, we'll get creative and modify your login screen with a new logo and new prompts.

I'm making a huge assumption that you have installed the Instant Information software on your system. This is the software that lets you access the Instant Information CD that contains the HP-UX manual set, as referred to in Chapter 1. The software is included on the Instant Information CD.

Now let's get started.

Basic Changes - Fonts, Backdrop, Colors, and the Front Panel

Font Size

When we first log in to CDE and the workspace comes up, one of the first things many users change is the size of the font. Initially set to 4, most users want a bigger font. This change. is easy

1. **Click on the Style Manager icon** on the front panel. This brings up the Style Manager.

2. **Highlight 5**.

3. **Click on OK**.

Backdrop and Colors

The Style Manager is also where we can change the backdrop and colors.

1. **Click on Backdrop** and we are presented with a variety of backdrop choices.

2. Once we see one we like, such as Pebbles, we can **click on apply** to change our backdrop. Notice, however, that this changes the backdrop only for the workspace that we are in.

To change the other workspaces, we can either go to them and bring up the Style Manager in that workspace or, since we already have Style Manager up, we can click in the top right corner and access the pull-down menu. From here, we can choose Occupy All Workspaces. Then we can simply go to the other workspaces, and Style Manager is already up and ready for us there. The Backdrop area is the only place we have to worry about moving to other workspaces.

3. To change colors, **click on the Color icon**. We are given a list of different color schemes to choose from. And if one isn't quite to our liking, we can easily modify the color, hue, brightness, and contrast. We can even grab a color from somewhere else, such as an image off the Internet, to include in the color scheme. Once we have the colors we like, we can save the scheme with its own name.

Adding to the Front Panel

The front panel can make life just a little easier for us by putting frequently used items that we put on it. One of the most frequent actions is opening up a terminal window. And although CDE comes with **dtterm** as the default terminal window, we sometimes need to use an **hpterm** or **xterm** window. So let's add them to the Personal Applications subpanel where **dtterm** lives.

1. **Click on the up arrow** of the Personal Applications subpanel so that it pops up.

2. **Click on the Application Manage**r icon where Desktop Applications and Desktop Tools live.

3. **Double click on Desktop_Tools**. Here you will find **Hpterm** and **Xterm**.

4. **Drag and drop the Hpterm** icon from the Desktop_Tools to the Install Icon box at the top of the Personal Applications subpanel.

5. **Drag and drop the Xterm** icon from the Desktop_Tools to the Install Icon box at the top of the Personal Applications subpanel.

That's it! Easy, right? Now if we want **hpterm** to be on the front panel instead of the **dtterm**:

1. **Right click on the Hpterm** icon in the Personal Applications subpanel.

2. **Select Copy To Main Panel**.

Adding Another Workspace

While we're here, let's add another workspace to our system. Users who used VUE were used to having 6 workspaces. CDE comes with a default of 4, but this, too, is easy to change. Let's add one more and call it "Instant Info." We'll assume that this is the window where we'll view Instant Information.

1. **Place the mouse in the Workspace area of the front panel** and **press the right mouse button**.

2. **Select Add Workspace** from the pull-down menu. The workspace "New" has been added.

3. **Right-click on the new workspace labeled "New"** and select **Rename. Type Instant Info** and **press return**.

If we want to delete a Workspace, simply right-click on the Workspace to be removed and then select delete.

Making these kinds of changes is easy, and they help personalize the workspace for the individual user.

More Challenging Changes: Add New Icon and Action to a New Panel Location, Modify Default Printer Label, and Create Dropdown Menu

In this section, we'll tackle making changes to the work environment that must be done manually. First, we'll modify the front panel. We'll actually be modifying the **dtwm.fp** file, which is the front panel. We're going to create an icon specifically for Instant Information and create an action to go with the icon (running the Instant Information program). Then we'll insert that action in the front panel between the Personal Applications sub-panel, where **dtterm**, **xterm** and **hpterm** live, if you added them with me in the previous section, and the **dtmail** icon. Second, we'll further modify the front panel so that the system default printer is labeled so that we know what printer the default is. Our last challenge will be to modifiy the **dtwmrc** file to create a new drop-down menu using the left button of the mouse. The default is for a drop-down menu to appear when you right-click with the mouse over a blank space on the workspace. This menu is the Workspace Menu, which is where you can 1) shuffle among various items that are open on the desktop, 2) restart Workspace Manager, which we'll use to make our changes take effect, and 3) log out of the system, which is the same as the exit button on the front panel. As I said, we're going to create a similar menu for the left button. Our menu will consist of picks to run GlancePlus, the vi editor, and an automatic login to a remote system named systemA.

To give a feel for where all these changes can take place, we're going to make the front panel changes available for one user only. This user will be admin1, and the home location will be **/home/admin1**. We'll make the drop-down menu available for all users. However, be aware that any global changes to the front panel made *after* the user's personal one has been changed won't affect that user's. This is because global changes are put in the **/etc/dt** directory and a specific user's are put in his or her **$HOME/.dt** directory. **$HOME/.dt** takes precedence over **/etc/dt**. If we want all users to get the changes, we'll have to retrofit the new changes into the **$HOME/ .dt** files of the same name. Who says that system administration isn't challenging?

Are you ready to make changes? Let's go!

Creating a New Icon and Action

Creating an icon is a challenging thing. We could use the Icon Editor found under Desktop_Apps in the Application Manager to create a new icon, or we could find a picture we like and use it. One thing to be careful of when pulling in a picture, in order for it to be seen correctly on the front panel, is that it has to be no larger than 32x32 pixels or only a portion of the icon will be displayed. Viewing the picture in the Icon Editor shows you the size of the picture. We may want to search through the application directories for useful icons. For our example, I got lucky and found a 32x32 icon for Instant Information that works fine. The icon was in the **/opt/dynatext/data/bitmaps** directory. The icon is **logoicon.bm**.

1. **Bring up the Icon Editor** from the Desktop_Apps in the Application Manager.

2. **Go to File -> Open**.

3. Enter path or folder name: **/opt/dynatext/data/bitmaps**.

4. Enter file name: **logoicon.bm**

5. Choose **Open**.

We'll see the icon and that it is indeed 32x32. Now we need to save the icon to our own **.dt** directory.

6. **Go to File -> Save As**.

7. Enter path or folder name: **/$HOME/.dt/icons**. For the admin1 user, that would be in **/home/admin1/.dt/icons**.

If we were going to do this globally, we'd put this in **/etc/dt/app-config/types/C**.

8. Leave the file name as is.

9. **Save**.

Now that we have the icon, we need to create an action file and a description file to go with it.

1. **Using either Text Edito**r from the Personal Application subpanel, which brings up dtpad, or using vi or another text editor, enter the following:

```
ACTION instinfo
{
LABEL              instinfo
TYPE               COMMAND
WINDOW_TYPE        NO_STDIO
EXEC_STRING        /opt/dynatext/bin/dynatext
DESCRIPTION        This action starts Instant Information
}
```

The LABEL is the name of the action, the TYPE is a command, the WINDOW_TYPE is none (no standard I/O or NO_STDIO) since the application has its own window, EXEC_STRING is the command to be executed, and the DESCRIPTION is just a description of what this action does. Make sure that the NO_STDIO has an underscore and not a dash and don't forget the last }. I've done both of these and then had fun trying to figure out why the action either didn't appear to exist or, if it did appear, why it wouldn't work.

2. **Save this file as /$HOME/.dt/types/instinfo.dt**. For the admin1 user, that would be **/home/admin1/.dt/types/instinfo.dt**. If this was a global configuration, we'd save the file as **/etc/dt/appconfig/ types/C/instinfo.dt**.

Now that we have an action, we need to create a description file. The contents of this file are irrelevant, but the permissions *must* include executable.

3. Again **using our favorite editor**, enter:

ACTION instinfo
DESCRIPTION This action starts Instant Information

4. **Save this file as /$HOME/.dt/appmanager/instinfo**. For the
   admin1 user, that would be **/home/admin1/.dt/appmanager/**
   instinfo. If this was a global configuration, we'd save the file as
   /etc/dt/appconfig/appmanager/instinfo.

5. Change the permissions to include execute as follows:

chmod 555 /$HOME/.dt/appmanager/instinfo

Now it's time to modify the front panel to include the icon and action
we just created. The front panel file, **dtwm.fp**, is located in the **/usr/dt/**
appconfig/types/C directory. We don't want to overwrite the system file.
We need to copy it locally and then modify it for our use.

1. Copy this to **/$HOME/.dt/types/dtwm.fp**. For the admin1 user,
   that would be:

cp /usr/dt/appconfig/types/C/dtwm.fp   /home/admin1/.dt/types/dtwm.fp

2. **Using our favorite edito**r, we'll modify the local **dtwm.fp** file.

As we look at the file, we notice that it is in the same order as the front
panel is displayed. The clock is the first CONTROL in the file and the first
item on the front panel. Also notice that the POSITION_HINTS is 1. Date
is next and so is POSITION_HINTS 2. What we want to do is put our new
icon and action after POSITION_HINTS 4, the TextEditor CONTROL.

3. Go down just past the } ending CONTROL TextEditor and before
   CONTROL Mail. At this point, **insert the following exactly as**
   shown below. Make sure that the uppercase letters are capitalized
   and the lowercase letters aren't.

```
CONTROL  Info
{
  TYPE                icon
  CONTAINER_NAME      Top
  CONTAINER_TYPE       BOX
  POSITION_HINTS      5
  ICON                logoicon.bm
  LABEL               Instant Info
  PUSH_ACTION         instinfo
}
```

4. Now be careful; this part is tricky. The next items have to have their POSITION_HINTS renumbered. But we are going to **renumber only the next eight items beginning with Mail and ending with Trash**. Instead of 5 through 12, these are going to become 6 through 13.

5. **Save** the file.

Got all that done? Good. Now, let's restart the Workspace Manager. If we did everything right, we'll have a new icon, which, when clicked, will bring up Instant Information.

6. Position the mouse over a blank area on the workspace and press the right mouse button. Select **Restart Workspace Manager**.

A couple of things to remember when creating actions: first and foremost, make sure that the PUSH_LABEL and the file names are the same. That's how they find each other. Make sure that the action file ends with **.dt** and that the description file is executable. If any of these are wrong, the action either won't work or won't show up.

Changing the Default Printer Name Display

If we pop up the Personal Printers subpanel, it shows that we have a default printer configured, but not the name of it. Let's go back into the front panel file, **dtwm.fp**, and change that.

1. Go back into our favorite editor and **edit /$HOME/.dt/types/ dtwm.fp**.

2. Scroll down to CONTROL Printer. You'll see that the LABEL is Default.**Change** or add to that the name of your default printer. Mine is printer a464.

LABEL   Default - a464

3. **Save the file** and **restart Workspace Manager** again. Position the mouse over a blank area on your workspace and press the right mouse button. Select Restart Workspace Manager.

That's it. Pop up the Personal Printers subpanel and now we can see what our default printer really is. Of course, if we change the default, we'll have to change the front panel again. But we know how to do that now, don't we!

Creating a Drop-Down Menu

Okay, let's change gears a bit and create a drop-down menu. This kind of menu comes in handy for those who have a set number of things they do regularly. For instance, a programmer who uses C++, vi, and xdb may have a menu with those items, or a system administrator may have a menu with swinstall, Ignite-UX, and SAM on it. Or those on an expansive network may want a menu of system logins.

We're going to create a simple menu with some of these items. Our menu is going to include running GlancePlus, running the vi editor, and logging into a remote system.

1. First we need a copy of the **/usr/dt/config/C/sys.dtwmrc** file to **/etc/dt/config/C**:

cp /usr/dt/config/C/sys.dtwmrc /etc/dt/config/C/sys.dtwmrc

If we were going to make this a local change for this user only, it would be copied to **/$HOME/.dt** and renamed **dtwmrc**. For the admin1 user, that would be **/home/admin1/.dt/dtwmrc**.

2. Go into our favorite editor and **modify the file**. We're going to add our new menu just after the DtRootMenu entry, which we see on our system as the left mouse button's "Workspace Menu." Add the following, but use a different menu name if you wish:

```
Menu AdminMenu
{
    "Admin1's Menu"        f.title
    "GlancePlus"           f.exec "/opt/perf/bin/gpm"
    "VI Editor"            f.exec "hpterm -e /usr/bin/vi"
    "Login  systemA"       f.exec "hpterm -geometry 80x50+830+0 -sl 200 -bg
DarkOrchid4 -fg white -n SYSTEMA -T SYSTEMA -e remsh systemA &"
}
```

The **f.title** function shows that this is the menu title. **f.exec** means to execute the following string. Notice that GlancePlus does not need a terminal window since it uses its own, whereas vi and the login both need a terminal window to run in. Also, I embellished on the hpterm for the login, making the terminal window very large, with lots of terminal memory, and using specific colors.

Now, let's restart the Workspace Manager and try out our new menu.

3. Position the mouse over a blank area on the workspace and press the right mouse button. Select **Restart Workspace Manager**.

As we can see, creating pull-down menus is easy. And we can easily expand on this by adding menus to our menu. Just make the function **f.menu**, followed by the menu name. We would add the following just after "Admin1's Menu":

"Work Menu"   f.menu   WorkMenu''

And then after the } from the Menu AdminMenu section, add:
Menu WorkMenu
{
.
.
}

Performing these advanced functions really isn't so hard. The hardest part is remembering which directories to put the files in: **/etc/dt** for global changes or **$HOME/.dt** for individual changes.

Creative Changes - Modify the Login Screen

One of the nice things about CDE is the ability to modify so many parts. You can customize individual login accounts or the entire system. By customizing the login screen, you can show those about to log in the name of the system they are accessing, the company logo, and a personalized greeting. These modifications take place in the **Xresources** file.

Changing the Login Messages

1. As we've done already with the **dtwm.fp** and **dtwmrc** files, we will need to copy the system file from **/usr/dt/config** to **/etc/dt/config/ C**.

   cp /usr/dt/config/C/Xresources   /etc/dt/config/C/Xresources

2. **Go into our favorite editor** and bring up the **Xresources** file so we can edit it.

3. **Go to the GREETING area**. Here we'll find the following lines:

!!Dtlogin*greeting.labelString: Welcome to %LocalHost%
!!Dtlogin*greetingpersLabelString: Welcome %s

The first line is the message on the initial login screen. Let's change that so that it welcomes us to our company, ABC, Inc.

1. **Remove the comment notations**. Unlike shell scripts most of us are used to, the Xresources file uses two exclamation points as comment notation. Remove the !!.

2. Next, **modify the "Welcome to %LocalHost%"**. The %Local-Host% variable is replaced with our system name in the login screen. The line should look like this:

   Dtlogin*greeting.labelString: ABC, Inc, Welcomes You to %LocalHost%

3. Next let's **change the second line** to include the department this system is dedicated to: finance. This second line shows what is displayed when we are prompted for our password. The %s variable is our user name. The line should now look like the following:

   Dtlogin*greetingpersLabelString: The Finance Department Welcomes %s

4. **Save the file**.

5. **Now log out and back in**. We should see the changes in the login screen. We didn't need to "reload" the file, since the act of logging out and back in does that.

Changing the Login Picture

Adding a new picture to the login screen is easy if you know one thing. The file has to be a bitmap (.bm) or pixmap (.pm) file. A bitmap file is black and white, and the pixmap file is color. I've tried using other kinds of pictures, but they just don't display. The good news is that these can be imported for other systems for our use, and there are some on our system. To make things simple, we're going to use one already on the system. An HP logo bitmap is in **/usr/lib/X11/bitmap**.

1. Once more, let's go into our favorite editor and modify **/etc/dt/config/C/Xresources**.

2. **Go to the MISC area**. Here we'll find the following lines:

!!Dtlogin*logo*bitmapFile: < bitmap or pixmap file >

3. **Delete the leading !!**, which are the comment designators.

4. **Replace < bitmap or pixmap file >** with the name of the bitmap file using the entire path location. The line should look as follows:

Dtlogin*logo*bitmapFile: /usr/lib/X11/bitmap/HPlogo.bm

5. **Save the file**.

6. **Now log out and back in**. We should see the HPlogo in the login screen. We didn't need to "reload" the file, since the act of logging out and back in does that.

Now that we've seen how easily we can make some simple customizations in CDE for our end users, we should be able to take this knowledge and really make their CDE environments a productive and friendly place to work.

Conclusion

Graphical User Interfaces are here to stay. Although they offer users an easy-to-learn, easy-to-use computing environment, they can make life a little uneasy for system administrators. The default CDE is ready to use, but given its power and flexibility, you will inevitably want to customize the CDE environment for your users' work context and optimum performance. Take the time to develop a good idea of what changes you need to make, the order in which to make them, and exactly where to make them. In so doing, all the power and flexibility of CDE will be open to you.

CHAPTER 7

Shell Programming for System Administrators

Shell Programming

There is much more to a shell than meets the eye. The shell is much more than the command-line interpreter everyone is used to using. UNIX shells actually provide a powerful interpretive programming language as well.

You may be asking yourself, "Why do I need to know about shell programming?" As a system administrator, you will find that many things in your system are controlled using shell programs.

Using shell programs (sometimes called shell scripts), you can build many tools to make your life as an administrator easier. Using shell scripts, you can automate mundane tasks that require several commands to be executed sequentially. You can build new commands to generate reports on system activities or configurations. You could also build scripts that provide shortcuts for executing long or complex command lines.

The shell is one of the most powerful features on any UNIX system. If you can't find the right command to accomplish a task, you can probably build it quite easily using a shell script.

In this chapter, I will show you the basic things you need to know to start programming in the Bourne and C shells. We will be first covering the

Bourne shell (as opposed to the Korn or C shells) because it is the simplest to program and it is a subset of the default HP-UX 10.x shell - the POSIX shell. Once you can program in the Bourne shell, it is easy to adapt to the other available shells, and all Bourne shell programs will run in the POSIX shell. The C shell will then be covered because it is used so widely.

The best way to learn shell programming is by example. Many examples are given in this chapter. Some serve no purpose other than to demonstrate the current topic. Most, however, are useful tools or parts of tools that you can easily expand and adapt into your environment. The examples provide easy-to-understand prompts and output messages. Most examples show what is needed to provide the functionality we are after. They do not do a great deal of error checking. From my experience, however, it only takes a few minutes to get a shell program to do what you want; it can take hours to handle every situation and every error condition. Therefore, these programs are not very dressed up (maybe a sport coat versus a tuxedo). I'm giving you what you need to know to build some useful tools for your environment. I hope you will have enough knowledge and interest by the time we get to the end of this chapter to learn and do more.

All the shell programs in this chapter work with HP-UX 11.x. Although the programs specify the POSIX shell in the first line, they use functionality that would run with the Bourne shell. Many were originally written to work with HP-UX 9.x and the Bourne shell and have been used unmodified with HP-UX 10.x and HP-UX 11.x. This gives an indication of the versatility of shell programming. Although you should always test a shell program when going from one release of HP-UX to the next I think you will be pleasantly surprised how little effort is required to use existing shell programs with new releases of the operating system.

Bourne Shell Programming for System Administrators

Keep in mind that the Bourne shell is a subset of the default POSIX shell. Therefore, any of the topics in this section apply to both the Bourne and POSIX shells. A shell program is simply a file containing a set of commands that you wish to execute sequentially. The file needs to be set with execute permissions so you can execute it just by typing the name of the script.

Two basic forms of shell programs exist:

1. Simple command files - When you have a command line or set of command lines that you use over and over, you can use one simple command to execute them all.

2. Structured programs - The shell provides much more than the ability to "batch" together a series of commands. It has many of the features that any higher-level programming language contains:

   • Variables for storing data

   • Decision-making controls (the **if** and **case** commands)

   • Looping abilities (the **for** and **while** loops)

   • Function calls for modularity

Given these two basic forms, you can build everything from simple command replacements to much larger and more complex data manipulation and system administration tools.

Here is a simple shell script example:

```
#!/usr/bin/sh
# This is a simple shell program that displays today's date
# in a short message.
echo "Today's date is"
date +%x
```

Before we go on, let's take a look at what each line does.

```
#!/usr/bin/sh
```

The different shells (Bourne, Korn, and C) do not use all the same commands. Each has some commands that work differently or don't work at all in other shells. Simple commands like those in this script will work in all shells, but there are many cases where that is not true.

Normally, when you run a shell program, the system tries to execute commands using the same shell you are using for your interactive command lines. The first line makes sure that the system knows that this is a POSIX shell (**/usr/bin/sh**) script so it can start a POSIX shell to execute the commands. Note that the **#!** must be the very first two characters in the file.

If we don't include this line, someone running a shell other than the POSIX shell might have unexpected results when trying to run one of our programs.

As a good practice, you should include **#!shellname** as the first line of every shell program you write. Keep in mind that the default shell in HP-UX 11.x is the POSIX shell. Table 7-1 shows the locations of the most commonly used shells in HP-UX 10.x.

TABLE 7-1   SHELL LOCATIONS

Shell Name	Location
POSIX shell	/usr/bin/sh
C shell	/usr/bin/csh
Bourne shell	/usr/old/bin/sh
Korn shell	/usr/bin/ksh

Note that I claimed I was giving you an example of a Bourne shell program, yet I used **#!/usr/bin/sh**, which corresponds to the path for the POSIX shell. Although I will cover only functionality of the Bourne shell in this chapter, I use the default POSIX shell path, since the Bourne shell is a subset of the POSIX shell.

There is also a POSIX shell with the path **/sbin/sh**. You probably have this POSIX shell entry in your **/etc/passwd** file on an HP-UX 11.x system. This POSIX shell path exists because at the time of boot you may not be able to mount the logical volume **/usr** where the shells are located. **/sbin** is always mounted at boot, so you are guaranteed to have this POSIX shell to use at the time of boot.

Now, getting back to Bourne shell programming, let's look at our example.

```
# This is a simple shell program that displays today's date
# in a short message.
```

These are comments. Everything after a # in a command line is considered a comment. (**#!** on the first line is the one very big exception.)

```
echo "Today's date is"
```

The **echo** command generates prompts and messages in shell programs. See the **echo**(1) manual entry to see all the options available with echo for formatting your output. We commonly enclose the string to be displayed in double quotes. In this case, we did so because we needed to let the shell know that the apostrophe was part of the string and not a single quote that needs a match.

```
date
```

Executes the **date** command.

After we have the commands in the file, we need to make the file executable:

```
$ chmod +x today
```

(The "$" is the default Bourne shell command-line prompt.) Changing the permissions this way makes the file executable by anyone. You will need to do this only once after creating the file. See **chmod**(1) if you need more information on setting permissions.

To execute our new script, we type its name, as shown below:

```
$ today
Today's date is
01/27/99
$
```

Here is a more complex example:

```
#!/usr/bin/sh
# This is a simple shell program that displays the current
# directory name before a long file listing (ll) of that
# directory.
# The script name is myll
echo "Long listing of directory:"
pwd
echo
ll
```

This is what **myll** looks like when it runs:

```
$ myll
Long listing of directory:
/tmp
total 14398
-rw-------  1 gerry  users  47104  Jan 27 21:09 Ex01816
-rw-rw-rw-  1 root   root       0  Jan 27 09:17 test
-rw-r--r--  1 ralph  users  14336  Jan 21 15:05 poetry
-rw-r--r--  1 root   other  66272  Jan 27 10:51 up.log
```

Before we can do more complex shell programs, we need to learn more about some of the programming features built into the shell.

Shell Variables

A shell variable is similar to a variable in any programming language. A variable is simply a name you give to a storage location. Unlike most languages, however, you never have to declare or initialize your variables; you just use them.

Shell variables can have just about any name that starts with a letter (uppercase or lowercase). To avoid confusion with special shell characters (like file name generation characters), keep the names simple and use just letters, numbers, and underscore (_).

To assign values to shell variables, you simply type:

```
name=value
```

Note that there are no spaces before and after the = character.

Following are some examples of setting shell variables from the command line. These examples work correctly.

```
$ myname=ralph
$ HerName=mary
```

This one does not work because of the space after "this":

```
$ his name=norton
his: not found
```

The shell assumes that "his" is a command and tries to execute it. The rest of the line is ignored.

This example contains an illegal character (+) in the name:

```
$ one+one=two
one+one=two: not found
```

A variable must start with a letter:

```
$ 3word=hi
3word=hi: not found
```

Now that we can store values in our variables, we need to know how to use those values. The dollar sign ($) is used to get the value of a variable. Any time the shell sees a $ in the command line, it assumes that the characters immediately following it are a variable name. It replaces the **$variable** with its value. Here are some simple examples using variables at the command line:

```
$ myname=ralph
$ echo myname
myname

$ echo $myname
ralph
$ echo $abc123
```

In the first **echo** command there is no **$**, so the shell ignores the value of the variable **myname**, and **echo** gets **myname** as an argument to be echoed. In the second **echo**, however, the shell sees the **$**, looks up the value of **myname,** and puts it on the command line. Now **echo** sees **ralph** as its argument (not **myname** or **$myname**). The final **echo** statement is similar, except that we have not given a value to **abc123**, so the shell assumes that it has no value and replaces **$abc123** with nothing. Therefore, **echo** has no arguments and echoes a blank line.

There may be times when you want to concatenate variables and strings. This is very easy to do in the shell:

```
$ myname=ralph
$ echo "My name is $myname"
My name is ralph
```

There may be times when the shell can become confused if the variable name is not easily identified in the command line:

```
$ string=dobeedobee
$ echo "$stringdoo"
```

We wanted to display "dobeedobee," but the shell thought that the variable name was stringdoo, which had no value. To accomplish this goal we can use curly braces around the variable name to separate it from surrounding characters:

```
$ echo "${string}doo"
dobeedobeedoo
```

You can set variables in shell programs in the same way, but you would also like to do things such as save the output of a command in a variable so that you can use it later. You may want to ask users a question and read their response into a variable so that you can examine it.

Command Substitution

Command substitution allows us to save the output from a command (**stdout**) into a shell variable. To demonstrate this, let's take another look at how our "today" example can be done using command substitution:

```
#!/usr/bin/sh
d=`date +%x`
echo "Today's date is $d"
```

The back quotes (`) around the **date** command tell the shell to execute **date** and place its output on the command line. The output will then be assigned to the variable **d**.

```
$ today
Today's date is 01/27/99
```

We could also have done this substitution without using the variable **d**. We could have just included the **date** command in the echo string:

```
#!/usr/bin/sh
echo "Today's date is `date +%x`"
```

Reading User Input

The most common way to get information from the user is to prompt him or her and then read the response. The **echo** command is most commonly used to display the prompt; then the **read** command is used to read a line of input from the user (**stdin**). Words from the input line can be assigned to one or several shell variables.

Here is an example with comments to show you how **read** can be used:

```
#!/usr/bin/sh
# program: readtest
echo "Please enter your name: \c" # the \c leaves cursor on
                                  # this line.
read name # there is no $ because we are doing an assignment
          # of whatever the user enters into name.
echo "Hello, $name"
echo "Please enter your two favorite colors: \c"
read color1 color2 # first word entered goes into color1
                   # remainder of line goes into color2
echo "You entered $color2 and $color1"
```

If we ran this program, it would look something like this:

```
$ readtest
Please enter your name: gerry
Hello, gerry
Please enter your two favorite colors: blue green
You entered green and blue
$
```

Notice how the **read** command assigned the two words entered for colors into the two respective color variables. If the user entered fewer words than the read command was expecting, the remaining variables would be set to null. If the user enters too many words, all extra words entered are assigned into the last variable. This is how you can get a whole line of input into one variable. Here's an example of what would happen if you entered more than two colors:

```
$ readtest
Please enter your name: gerry
Hello, gerry
Please enter your two favorite colors: chartreuse orchid blue
You entered orchid blue and chartreuse
$
```

Arguments to Shell Programs

Shell programs can have command-line arguments just like any regular command. Command-line arguments that you use when you invoke your shell program are stored in a special set of variables. These are called the positional parameters.

The first ten words on the command line are directly accessible in the shell program using the special variables **$0-$9**. This is how they work:

$0	The command name
$1	The first argument
$2	The second argument
$3	.
	.
	.
$9	The ninth argument

If you are not sure how many command-line arguments you may get when your program is run, there are two other variables that can help:

$#	The number of command-line arguments
$*	A space-separated list of all the command-line arguments (which does not include the command name).

The variable **$*** is commonly used with the **for** loop (soon to be explained) to process shell script command lines with any number of arguments.

Figure 7-1 illustrates some simple examples of using arguments in our shell programs:

```
#!/usr/bin/sh
# This is a simple shell program that takes one command line
# argument (a directory name) then displays the full pathname
# of that directory before doing a long file listing (ll) on
# it.
#
# The script name is myll
cd $1
echo "Long listing of the `pwd` directory:"
echo
ll
```

Figure 7-1 **myll** Shell Program

If we run **myll** with a directory name, the script changes directory, echoes the message containing the full path name (notice the command substitution), and then executes the **ll** command.

Note that the **cd** in the **myll** program changes only the working directory of the script; it does not affect the working directory of the shell from which we run **myll**.

```
$ myll /tmp
Long listing of the /tmp directory:
total 380
drwxrwxrwx 2 bin     sys     1024 Feb 1 15:01 files
-rw-rw-rw- 1 root    root       0 Feb 1 13:07 ktl_log
-rw-rw-rw- 1 root    root       0 Feb 1 13:07 ntl_lib.log
-rw-rw-rw- 1 root    root     115 Feb 1 13:07 ntl.read
-rw-r--r-- 1 root    other 108008 Feb 2 08:42 database.log
-r-xr--r-- 1 root    other    466 Feb 1 15:29 updist.scr
```

In this case, we could give **myll** no argument and it would still work properly. If we don't provide any command-line arguments, then **$1** will be null, so nothing goes on the command line after **cd**. This will make **cd** take us to our home directory and perform the **ll** there.

If we provide more than one argument, only the first is used and any others are ignored.

If we use a command-line argument, it *must* be a directory name; otherwise, the **cd** command fails and the script terminates with a "bad directory" error message. Later I will show how to test for valid directory and file names so that you can work around potential errors.

A more complex example can be used to build new versions of the **ps** command. Below are two examples that use command-line arguments and command substitution to help you with your process management.

The **psg** shell program in Figure 7-2 is handy for searching through what is typically a long process status listing to find only certain commands or user processes. These examples use **grep**, which finds all lines that contain the pattern you are trying to find.

```
#!/usr/bin/sh
# Program name: psg
# Usage: psg some_pattern
#
# This program searches through a process status (ps -ef)
# listing for a pattern given as the first command line
# argument.
procs=`ps -ef`                       # Get the process listing
head=`echo "$procs" | line`          # Take off the first line (the
                                     # headings)
echo "$head"                         # Write out the headings
echo "$procs" | grep -i $1 | grep -v $0 # Write out lines
       # containing $1 but not this program's command line

# Note that $procs MUST be quoted or the newlines in the ps
# -ef listing will be turned into spaces when echoed. $head
# must also be quoted to preserve any extra white space.
```

Figure 7-2 **psg** Shell Program

Here's what **psg** looks like when it runs. In this example, we want to look at all the Korn shells running on the system.

```
$ psg ksh
   UID    PID   PPID  C  STIME         TTY   TIME   COMMAND
  root   1258   1252  0  18:00:34  ttyp1  0:00   ksh
  root   1347   1346  0  18:03:15  ttyp2  0:01   ksh
 ralph   1733   1732  0  20:06:11  ttys0  0:00   -ksh
```

In this example, we want to see all the processes that **ralph** is running:

```
$ psg ralph
   UID    PID   PPID  C  STIME         TTY   TIME   COMMAND
 ralph   1733   1732  0  20:06:11  ttys0  0:00   -ksh
 ralph   1775   1733  0  20:07:43  ttys0  0:00   vi afile
```

This program also works to find terminal, process ID, parent process ID, start date, and any other information from **ps**.

The **gkill** shell program in Figure 7-3 searches through a **ps -ef** listing for a pattern (just like **psg**); then it kills all listed processes. The examples use the **cut** command, which allows you to specify a range of columns to retain.

```
#!/usr/bin/sh
# Program name: gkill
# Usage: gkill some_pattern
# This program will find all processes that contain the
# pattern specified as the first command line argument then
# kills those processes.
# get the process listing
procs=`ps -ef`
echo "The following processes will be killed:"
# Here we list the processes to kill. We don't kill this
# process
echo "$procs" | grep -i $1 | grep -v $0
# Allow the user a chance to cancel.
echo "\nPress Return to continue Ctrl-C to exit"
# If the user presses Ctrl-C the program will exit.
# Otherwise this read waits for the next return character and
# continue.
read junk
# find the pattern and cut out the pid field
pids=`echo "$procs" | grep -i $1 | grep -v $0 | cut -c9-15`
# kill the processes
kill $pids
```

Figure 7-3 **gkill** Shell Program

If we don't provide any command-line arguments, **grep** issues an error and the program continues. In the next section, we will learn how to check whether **$1** is set and how to gracefully clean up if it's not.

Here is an example of running **gkill**:

```
$ gkill xclock

The following processes will be killed:
  marty 3145 3016 4 15:06:59 ttyp5 0:00 xclock

Press return to continue Ctrl-C to exit

[1] + Terminated                    xclock &
```

Testing and Branching

Decision making is one of the shell's most powerful features. There are two ways to check conditions and branch to a piece of code that can handle that condition.

For example, you may want to ask the user a question and then check whether the answer was yes or no. You may also want to check whether a file exists before you operate on it. In either case, you can use the **if** command to accomplish the task. These shell script segments explain each part of the **if** command:

```
echo "Continue? \c"
read ans
if [ "$ans" = "n" ]
then
        echo "Goodbye"
        exit
fi
```

The **echo** and **read** provide a prompt and response as usual. The **if** statement executes the next command and if it succeeds, it executes any commands between the **then** and the **fi** ("if" spelled backwards).

Note that the **\c** in the **echo** command suppresses the new line that **echo** normally generates. This situation leaves the cursor on the line immediately after the "Continue?" prompt. This is commonly used when prompting for user input.

The **test** command is the most common command to use with the **if** command. The ["$ans" = "n"] is the **test** command. It performs many types of file, string, and numeric logical tests. If the condition is true, the test succeeds.

The syntax of the **test** command requires spaces around the [ ], or you will get a syntax error when the program runs. Also notice the double quotes around the response variable **$ans**. This is a strange anomaly with the **test** command. If the user presses only [[RETURN]] at the prompt without typing any other character, the value of **$ans** will be null. If we didn't have the quote marks around **$ans** in the **test** command, it would look like this when the value of **$ans** was substituted into the test command:

[= "n"]

This would generate a "test: argument expected" error when you run the program. This mistake is very common, and if you ever get this error, you should look for variables in your **test** commands with null values.

Another form of the **if** command is very common. It allows you to do one thing if a condition is met or do something else if not:

```
if [    ]              # if some condition is true
then
                       # do something
else
                       # otherwise do this
fi
```

There are many conditions that the **test** command can test as shown in Table 7-2.

Table **7-2** **test** COMMAND CONDITIONS

STRING TESTS:

["$a" = "string"]	True if $a is equal to "string"
["$a" != "string"]	True if $a is NOT equal to "string"
[-z "$a"]	True if $a is null (zero characters)
[-n "$a"]	True if $a is NOT null

NUMERIC TESTS:

[$x -eq 1]	True if $x is equal to 1
[$x -ne 1]	True if $x is NOT equal to 1
[$x -lt 1]	True if $x is less than 1
[$x -gt 1]	True if $x is greater than 1
[$x -le 1]	True if $x is less than or equal to 1

Table **7-2** **test** COMMAND CONDITIONS

STRING TESTS:

[$x -ge 1]	True if $x is greater than or equal to 1

FILE TESTS:

[-d $file]	True if $file is a directory
[-f $file]	True if $file is a file
[-s $file]	True if $file is a file with > 0 bytes
[-r $file]	True if $file is readable
[-w $file]	True if $file is writable
[-x $file]	True if $file is executable

Tests can be combined using **-a** to logically "AND" the tests together, **-o** to logically "OR" two tests, and **!** to "negate" a test. For example, this test statement is true only if the **$interactive** variable is set to true or if **$file** is a directory:

```
[ "$interactive" = "TRUE" -o -d $file ]
```

This will be used in some upcoming example programs.

Following is a useful extension to the **gkill** program shown earlier. It checks to see that we have exactly one command-line argument before the program will attempt to do the processing. It uses a numeric test and the **$#** variable, which represents the number of command-line arguments. It should be inserted before any other lines of code in the **gkill** example given above.

```
# If we don't have exactly one command-line argument write an
# error and exit.

if [ $# -ne 1 ]
then
    echo "Usage: $0 pattern"
    echo "Some pattern matching the processes to kill must
    echo "be specified"
```

```
      exit 1 # Exit 1 terminates the program and tells the
             # calling shell that we had an error.
fi
```

Some other possible extensions to the **gkill** program might be to:

- Allow the user to specify a signal to use with the **kill** command. For example:
  gkill -9 ralph
  would find all of Ralph's processes and then kill them with **kill -9**.

- Make sure that a valid message is printed if we can't find any processes to kill using the specified pattern.

This same type of command-line check is easily applied to the **psg** program to make sure that you have just exactly one argument representing the pattern to find.

When you are reading user input, you may want to check whether the user entered a value at all. If he or she didn't, you would provide a reasonable default value. This is easily done with a variable modifier.

This example reads answer ("ans") from the user and then checks its value using an **if** command:

```
echo "Do you really want to remove all of your files? \c"
read ans
if [ ${ans:-n} = y ]
then
    rm -rf *
fi
```

The **${ans:-n}** statement checks the value of **$ans**. If a value is in **$ans,** use it in the command line. If the user simply pressed [[RETURN]] at the prompt, **$ans** will be null. In this case, **${ans:-n}** will evaluate to **n** when we do the comparison. Basically, in one small statement, it says, "If the user did not provide an answer, assume that he meant **n**."

Another modifier is often used:

```
${var:=default}
```

It returns the value of **var** if it is set; it returns the default if **var** is not set, and it will also assign the default as the value of **var** for future use.

All of the modifiers available in the Bourne shell are in the **sh** manual entry.

Making Decisions with the case Statement

The **case** statement is another way to make decisions and test conditions in shell programs. It is most commonly used to check for certain patterns in command-line arguments. For example, if you wanted to determine whether the first command-line argument is an option (starts with a -), the **case** statement is the easiest way to do so. The **case** statement is also used to respond to different user input (such as asking the user to select a choice from a menu).

The **case** statement is probably one of the most complicated shell commands because of its syntax:

```
case pattern_to_match in
        pattern1)   cmdA
                    cmdB
                ;;
        pattern2)  cmdC
                ;;
            . . .
       *)  cmdZ
                ;;
esac
```

pattern_to_match is usually a shell variable that you are testing (like a command-line argument or a user response). If **pattern_to_match** matches **pattern1,** then commands **cmdA** and **cmdB** are executed. The **;;** separates this pattern's command list from the next pattern. In all cases, when **;;** is reached, the program jumps to the **esac** (**case** spelled backwards).

If **pattern_to_match** matches **pattern2,** then **cmdC** is executed and we jump to **esac**, the end of the **case** statement.

The * is provided so if **pattern_to_match** did not match anything at all, it will execute **cmdZ**. It's important to have a default action to handle the case where the user types an invalid entry.

For more robust pattern matching,any file name generation characters (*, [ ], ?) can be used to do special pattern matches. There is also a very useful way to check for multiple patterns in one line using the | symbol, which means logical "OR." Here's an example:

```
echo "Do you want to continue? (y/n) \c"
read ans
case $ans in
      y|Y) echo "Continuing"
             . . .

           ;;
      n|N) echo "Done, Goodbye"
           exit
           ;;
      *) echo "Invalid input"
           ;;
esac
```

Here is another example where we are testing to see whether **$1** (the first command-line argument) is a valid option (a character we recognize that begins with a -).

```
case $1 in
        -l | -d) # Perform a listing
                echo "All files in $HOME:\n"
                ll -R $HOME | more
                ;;
        -i) # -i means set an interactive flag to true
            interactive="TRUE"
                ;;
        *)  # Invalid input
            echo "$0: $1 is an invalid option"
            exit 1
            ;;
esac
```

A **case** statement similar to this is used in the **trash** program at the end of this chapter.

Looping

Many times you want to perform an action repeatedly. In the shell, you have two ways to do this:

1. The **for** loop takes a list of items and performs the commands in the loop once for each item in the list.

2. The **while** loop executes some commands (usually the **test** command) if that command executes successfully. (If the test condition is true, then the commands in the loop are executed and then the command is again executed to see whether we should loop again.)

The basic format of the **for** loop is:

```
for var in list_of_items
do
        cmdA
        cmdB
        cmdC
done
```

When the loop starts, the variable **var** has its value set to the first word in the **list_of_items** to loop through. Then the three commands between the **do** and the **done** statements are executed. After the program reaches the **done** statement, it goes back to the top of the loop and assigns **var** to the next item in the list, executes the commands, etc. The last time through the loop, the program continues with the next executable statement after the **done** statement.

The **list_of_items** can be any list of words separated by white space. You can type the words or use variables or command substitution to build the list. For example, let's say that we want to copy a new **.kshrc** file into the home directory of several users. A **for** loop is the easiest way to do this:

```
for name in ralph norton alice edith archie
do
        echo $name
        cp /tmp/.kshrc.new /users/$name/.kshrc
done
```

This example can be extended to copy certain files to several machines using the **rcp** command and verify that they got there using the **remsh** command:

```
for host in neptune jupiter mars earth sun
do
        echo $host
        rcp /etc/passwd /etc/hosts $host:/etc
        rcp /.profile $host:/.profile
        remsh $host ll /etc/passwd /etc/hosts /.profile
done
```

You can also process lists of files in the current directory using command substitution to generate the **list_of_items**:

```
for file in `ls`
do
     if [ -r $file ]
     then
             echo "$file is readable
     fi
done
```

Note that **for file in *** would have done the same thing.

If you have a large list of things you would like to loop through and you don't want to type them on the command line, you can enter them in a file instead. Then, using the **cat** command and command substitution, you can generate the **list_of_items**:

```
for i in `cat important_files`
do
     # do something with each of the files listed in the
     # important_files file.
done
```

The **for** loop, however, is most commonly used to process the list of command line arguments ($*):

```
for name in $*
do
      if [ ! -f $name -a ! -d $name ]
      then
         echo "$name is not a valid file or directory name"
      else
        # do something with the file or directory
      fi
done
```

The **trash** program contains a **for** loop that processes command-line arguments in a similar way.

Figure 7-4 is an example of a program that can be used to customize how SAM adds a user to the system for HP-UX 9.x. It uses a **for** loop and a **case** statement to parse the command line that SAM used to invoke it. This example was adapted from the file **/usr/sam/config/ct_adduser.ex**. It copies a **.kshrc** file and a **.logout** file to the new user's home directory after SAM has added the user to the system. The name of this program should be entered in the "Program to run after adding a user" field of SAM's User Task Customization screen.

```
#! /usr/bin/sh
#
# This script illustrates how to process the parameter string
# from SAM for the "Add a New User Account to the System"
# task.
#
# Iterate through the parameter string and extract the
# arguments.
#

# SAM passes all necessary information to us as command line
# arguments. This chunk of code is provided for you.
for param in $*
do
     case $param in
             -l) login_name=$2; shift 2;;
             -h) home_dir=$2; shift 2;;
             -v) uid=$2; shift 2;;
             -g) group=$2; shift 2;;
             -s) shell=$2; shift 2;;
             -p) password=$2; shift 2;;
             -R) real_name=$2; shift 2;;
             -L) office_loc=$2; shift 2;;
             -H) home_phone=$2; shift 2;;
             -O) office_phone=$2; shift 2;;
     esac
done
#
#
# These are the commands we have to add to copy in a .kshrc
# and a .logout file into the new user's home directory.

# standard.kshrc and standard.logout are just the names of the
# default shell files previously created for every new user.

cp /etc/standard.kshrc $home_dir/.kshrc
cp /etc/standard.logout $home_dir/.logout

exit 0
```

Figure 7-4 newadduser.ex Shell Program

The while Loop

The **while** loop has the following format:

```
while cmd1
do
        cmdA
        cmdB
        cmdC
done
```

cmd1 is executed first. If it executes successfully, then the commands between the **do** and the **done** statements are executed. **cmd1** is then executed again; if successful, the commands in the loop are executed again, etc. When **cmd1** fails, the program jumps past the **done** statement and resumes execution with the next executable statement.

Most of the time, the command executed in place of **cmd1** is the **test** command. You can then perform logical tests as described in the **if** section. If the test succeeds (is true), the commands in the loop are executed and the script tests the condition again. The **while** loop is useful if you have a fixed number of times you want the loop to run or if you want something to happen until some condition is met.

This program displays the primary LAN interface (lan0) statistics using **netstat** ten times, once every 30 seconds:

```
i=1
while [ $i -le 10 ]
do
        netstat -i | grep lan0
        sleep 30
        i=`expr $i + 1`
done
```

The **expr** command is the only way we can do math in the Bourne shell. (The Korn and C shells have some math functions built in). The line

```
expr $i + 1
```

takes the current value of the variable **i** (which must be an integer or the **expr** command will complain) and adds 1 to it, writing the result to standard output (stdout). By using the **expr** command with command substitution, we can capture the result and assign it back into **i**. This is how we increment variables in the shell. The **expr** command can also perform integer subtraction, multiplication, division, remainder, and matching functions. See the **expr** manual entry for all of the details.

The **while** loop can also be used to process command-line arguments one at a time, using the number of command-line arguments and the **shift** command:

```
while [ $# -ne 0 ]
do
    case $1 in
    -*)  # $1 must be an option because it starts with -
         # Add it to the list of options:
         opts="$opts $1"
         ;;
     *)  # $1 must be an argument. Add it to the list of
         # command line arguments:
         args="$args $1"
         ;;
    esac
    shift
done
```

The **shift** command shifts the remaining arguments in **$*** to the left by one position and decrements **$#**. What was the first argument (**$1**) is now gone forever; what was in **$2** is now in **$1**, etc. In the process of shifting command-line arguments, $# is also decremented to accurately reflect the number of arguments left in **$***.

You may want some commands to run until the user stops the program or until some stop condition is met. An infinite **while** loop is the best way to do so. For example, let's say that we are prompting users for some input and we will continue to prompt them until they give us valid input:

```
while true
do
    # prompt users and get their response
    echo "Enter yes or no: \c"
    read ans

    # Check if the response is valid
    if [ "$ans" = "yes" -o "$ans" = "no" ]
    then
```

```
     # If it is valid, stop the looping
     break
 else
     # Otherwise print an error message and try it again
     # from the top of the loop
     echo "Invalid input, try again!\n"
   fi
done
# Now that we have valid input we can process the user's
# request
   .
```

true is a special command that always executes successfully. The loop does not terminate unless the user stops the program by killing it or until a **break** command is executed in the loop. The **break** command will stop the loop.

Shell Functions

As you write shell programs, you will notice that certain sets of commands appear in many places within a program. For example, several times in a script you may check user input and issue an appropriate message if input is invalid. It can be tedious to type the same lines of code in your program numerous times. It can be a nuisance if you later want to change these lines.

Instead, you can put these commands into a shell function. Functions look and act like a new command that can be used inside the script. Here's an example of a basic shell function:

```
# This is a function that may be called from anywhere within
# the program. It displays a standard usage error message
# and then exits the program.

print_usage()
{
    echo "Usage:"
    echo "To trash files: $0 [-i] files_to_trash..."
    echo "Display trashed files: $0 -d"
    echo "Remove all trashed files: $0 -rm"
    echo "Print this message: $0 -help"
    exit 1
}
```

print_usage is now a new command in your shell program. You can use it anywhere in this script.

Shell functions also have their own set of positional parameters (**$1-$9, $#,** and **$***), so you can pass them arguments just like any other command. The only nuance is that **$0** represents the name of the shell program, not the name of the function.

This shell function is used several times in the **trash** program example.

The system startup program **/etc/rc** in HP-UX 9.x is made up of shell functions that are invoked from one of three places in the program, depending on your system configuration. **/etc/rc** is a good example of an advanced shell program. **/sbin/rc** is the startup program in HP-UX 10.x and HP-UX 11.x.

Figure 7-5 is a fairly complex program that exercises all the concepts we have covered so far. It is a **trash** program that removes files from their original locations. Instead of removing them permanently, it places them in a trash can in your home directory. This is a fairly robust program, but I'm sure that you can think of many extensions as you read through it.

```
#!/usr/bin/sh
# Program name: trash
# Usage:
#   To trash files:     trash [-i] file_names_to_trash ...
#   Display trashed files:     trash -d
#   Remove all trashed files: trash -rm
#   Print a help message:      trash -help

# This program takes any number of directory or file name
# arguments. If the argument is a file it will be removed
# from its current place in the file system and placed in the
# user's trash directory ($HOME/.trash). If the argument is a
# directory name the program will ask if the user really
# wants to trash the whole directory.
#
# This program also takes a -i (interactive) option. Like
# the rm command, if the -i is the first argument on the
# command line, the program stops and asks if each file
# named in the remaining arguments should be trashed.

#
# The -d (display) option shows the contents of the
# user's trashed files.
#
# The -help option displays a usage message for the user.
```

Figure 7-5 **trash** Shell Program

```
# The -rm (remove) option interactively
# asks the user if each file or directory in the trash
# directory should be removed permanently.
#
# The -h, -d and -rm options may not be used with
# any other command line arguments.

# Possible extensions:
# - Enhance the -rm option to remove a list of files
# from the trash directory from the command line.
# - Create a program to be run by cron once nightly to empty
# everyone's trash directory.

# This is a function that may be called from anywhere within
# the program. It displays a standard usage error message
# then exits the program.
print_usage()
{
  echo "Usage:"
  echo "To trash files: $0 [-i] file_names_to_trash ..."
  echo "Display trashed files:    $0 -d"
  echo "Remove all trashed files: $0 -rm"
  echo "Print this message:       $0 -help"
exit 1
}
# Make sure we have at least one command line argument before
# we start.
if [ $# -lt 1 ]
then
    print_usage
fi

# If this flag is true then we need to do interactive
# processing.
interactive="FALSE"

# This is the name of the trash can.
trash_dir="$HOME/.trash"

# Make sure the trash directory exists before we go any
# further.
if [ ! -d $trash_dir ]
then
    mkdir $trash_dir
fi
# Sort out the command line arguments.
case $1 in
   -help) # Print a help message.
      print_usage
      ;;
```

Figure 7-5 **trash** Shell Program (Continued)

```
-d | -rm) # a -d or -rm were given
      # If it was not the only command-line argument
      # then display a usage message and then exit.
      if [ $# -ne 1 ]
      then
           print_usage
      fi

      # Otherwise do the task requested.
      if [ $1 = "-d" ]
      then
            echo "The contents of $trash_dir:\n"
            ll -R $trash_dir | more
      else
            # remove all files from the trash directory
            rm -rf $trash_dir/*
            # get any dotfiles too
            rm -rf $trash_dir/.[!.]*
      fi

      # Now we can exit successfully.
      exit 0
      ;;
-i) # If the first argument is -i ask about each file as it
      # is processed.
      interactive="TRUE"
      # Take -i off the command line so we know that the
      # rest of the arguments are file or directory names.

      shift

      ;;

  -*) # Check for an option we don't understand.
      echo "$1 is not a recognized option."
      print_usage
      ;;
      esac

# Just for fun we'll keep a count of the files that were
# trashed.
count=0

for file in $*
do
  # First make sure the file or directory to be renamed exists.
  # If it doesn't, add it to a list of bad files to be written
  # out later. Otherwise process it.
  if [ ! -f $file -a ! -d $file ]
  then
       bad_files="$bad_files $file"
  else
# If we are in interactive mode ask for confirmation
# on each file. Otherwise ask about directories.
```

Figure 7-5   trash Shell Program (Continued)

```
if [ "$interactive" = "TRUE" -o -d $file ]
then
    # Ask the user for confirmation (default answer is no).
    if [ -d $file ]
    then
        echo "Do you want to trash the dir $file ? (y/n) n\b\c"
    else
        echo "Do you really want to trash $file ? (y/n) n\b\c"
    fi
    read doit

    # If they answered y then do the move.
    # Otherwise print a message that the file was not touched.
    if [ "${doit:-n}" = y ]
    then
        mv -i $file $trash_dir
        echo "$file was trashed to $trash_dir"
        count=`expr $count + 1`
    else
        echo "$file was not trashed"
    fi

  else # We are not in interactive mode, so just do it.
        mv -i $file $trash_dir count=`expr
        $count + 1`
  fi
fi
done

echo "$0: trashed $count item(s)"

if [ -n "$bad_files" ]
then
    echo "The following name(s) do not exist and \c"
    echo "could not be trashed:"
    echo "$bad_files"
fi

exit 0
```

Figure 7-5   **trash** Shell Program (Continued)

awk in Shell Programs

awk is a very powerful symbolic programming language. A *what*?

Simply stated, **awk** searches for patterns in lines of input (from **stdin** or from a file). For each line that matches the specified pattern, it can perform some very complex processing on that line. The code to actually process matching lines of input is a cross between a shell script and a C program.

Data manipulation tasks that would be very complex with combinations of **grep**, **cut,** and **paste** are very easily done with **awk**. Since **awk** is a programming language, it can also perform mathematical operations or check the input very easily. (Shells don't do math very well). It can even do floating-point math. (Shells deal only with integers and strings).

The basic form of an **awk** program looks like:

```
awk '/pattern_to_match/ { program to run }' input_file_names
```

Notice that the whole program is enclosed in single quotes. If no input file names are specified, **awk** reads from **stdin** (as from a pipe).

The **pattern_to_match** must appear between the / characters. The pattern is actually called a *regular expression*. Some common regular expression examples are shown in the examples.

The program to execute is written in **awk** code, which looks something like C. The program is executed whenever a line of input matches the **pattern_to_match**. If **/pattern_to_match/** does not precede the program in { }, then the program is executed for every line of input.

awk works with fields of the input lines. Fields are words separated by white space. The fields in **awk** patterns and programs are referenced with $, followed by the field number. For example, the second field of an input line is **$2**. If you are using an **awk** command in your shell programs, the fields (**$1**, **$2**, etc.) are not confused with the shell script's positional parameters, because the **awk** variables are enclosed in single quotes so the shell ignores them.

But let's not talk about it! Let's see some examples.

This simple example lists just the terminals that are active on your system (the terminal name is the second field of a **who** listing):

```
who | awk '{ print $2 }'
```

Note that **cut** could have done this task also, but you would have had to know exactly which columns the terminal name occupied in the **who** output, as shown below:

```
who | cut -c12-20
```

If the user or terminal name is longer than normal in any line, this command will not work. The **awk** example will work because it looks at fields, not columns.

In our **gkill** example, we used **grep** and **cut** to find the process IDs of the processes to kill:

```
procs='ps -ef'
procs_to_kill='echo "$procs" | grep -i $1'
pids='echo "$procs_to_kill" | cut -c9-15'
```

These three complex commands can be replaced with one **awk** command:

```
pids='ps -ef | awk '/'$1'/ { print $2 } ' '
```

The **$1** is actually outside the single quotes, so it is interpreted by the shell as the first command-line argument.

The **llsum** program shown in Figure 7-6 is a more complex example. A few things to note:

- **BEGIN** is a special pattern that means execute the **awk** program in {} before the first line of input. It is usually used for initializing variables and printing headers on the output.

- **END** is used after the last line of input, generally for summarizing the input.

- **printf** is a formatted print statement, as in C. The first argument is a format string containing what you want to print. It contains special characters for printing different things, such as:
  %s means we are printing a string.
  %d means we are printing an integer.
  %f means we are printing a floating-point number.

- The **$1 ~ /pattern/** says: IF the first field matches the pattern, then do the program in {}.

```
#!/usr/bin/sh
# Program: llsum
# Usage: llsum files_or_directories_to_summarize
#
# Displays a truncated long listing (ll) and displays size
# statistics of the files in the listing.
# A sample long listing for reference. Notice that the first
# line of output is less than 8 fields long and is not
# processed.
# ll
# total 46
# drwxrwxrwx 2  gerry aec 24        Mar 21 18:25  awk_ex
# crw--w--w- 1  root  sys 0 0x000000 Mar 22 15:32  /dev/con
#
# awk field numbers:
#      $1      $2 $3    $4  $5          $6  $7  $8    $9
ll $* | \
awk ' BEGIN { x=i=0; printf "%-16s%-10s%8s%8s\n",\
                "FILENAME","OWNER","SIZE","TYPE" }

# Print out the owner, size, and type. Then sum the size.
$1 ~ /^[-dlps]/  { # line format for normal files
          printf "%-16s%-10s%8d",$9,$3,$5
          x = x + $5
          i++
          }
# If the line starts with a - it's a regular file; d is
# directory, etc.
 $1 ~ /^-/ { printf "%8s\n","file" } # standard file types
 $1 ~ /^d/ { printf "%8s\n","dir" }
 $1 ~ /^l/ { printf "%8s\n","link" }
 $1 ~ /^p/ { printf "%8s\n","pipe" }
 $1 ~ /^s/ { printf "%8s\n","socket" }
 $1 ~ /^[bc]/ {          # line format for device files
          printf "%-16s%-10s%8s%8s\n",$10,$3,"","dev"
          }
END
{ printf "\nThese files occupy %d bytes (%.4f Mbytes)\n",\
 x, x / (1024*1024)
    printf "Average file size is %d bytes\n", x/i
}' | \
more # Pipe the output through the more command so it will
    # page.
```

Figure 7-6 **llsum** Shell Program

The following is an example of running **llsum**:

```
$ llsum /home/tomd
FILENAME            OWNER         SIZE    TYPE

.Xauthority         tomd            49    file
.cshrc              tomd           818    file
.dt                 tomd          1024     dir
.dtprofile          tomd          3971    file
.exrc               tomd           347    file
.login              tomd           377    file
.mosaic-global      tomd          6988    file
.mosaic-hotlist     tomd            38    file
.mosaic-personal    tomd          1024     dir
.mosaicpid          tomd             5    file
.profile            tomd           382    file
.sh_history         tomd           426    file
700install          tomd        368640    file
Install.mosaic      tomd          6762    file
README.mosaic       tomd          7441    file
README.ninstall     tomd         24354    file
krsort              tomd         34592    file
krsort.c            tomd          3234    file
krsort.dos          tomd         32756    file
krsort.q            tomd          9922    file
krsortorig.c        tomd          3085    file
print.xwd           tomd         44786    file
qsort               tomd         33596    file
qsort.c             tomd          4093    file
qsort.test          tomd          5503    file
qsorttest.q         tomd          4097    file
qsorttest.q         tomd          9081    file
test.xwd            tomd        589291    file

The files listed occupy 1196682 bytes (1.1412 Mbytes)
Average file size is 4738 bytes

$
```

     awk can also be very useful for summarizing data from standard monitoring commands like **netstat** and **vmstat,** as in the program in Figure 7-7.

```
#!/usr/bin/sh
# Program: ifstat
# Usage: ifstat interval interface_to_watch

# This program will not stop until you interrupt it
# (using Ctrl-C or Break).

interval=${1:-5}      # set interval to $1 or 5 if $1 is
                      # not given
interface=${2:-lan0}  # set interface to $2 or lan0 if $2 is
                      # not given

echo "Interface statistic information for $interface:\n"
# The parentheses around the while loop returns all its output
# as one command so it can be easily piped to the awk command.
(while true
do
    netstat -i
    sleep $interval
done ) | \

awk 'BEGIN { printf "%10s%10s%10s%10s%10s\n", "ipkts",
                    "ierrs", "opkts", "oerrs", "collis" ;
            printf "%10s%10s%10s%10s%10s\n", "-----",
                    "-----", "-----", "-----", "------" ;
# Initialize the variables that will hold the previous
# historical statistics.
pipkts=0; pierrs=0; popkts=0; poerrs=0; pcollis=0
}

# Find the line we care about. This is the line that starts
# with the specified interface name.

/^'$interface'/ { ipkts = $5 - pipkts; # current - previous
ierrs = $6 - pierrs;
opkts = $7 - popkts;
oerrs = $8 - poerrs;
collis = $9 - pcollis;

printf "%10d%10d%10d%10d%10d\n", ipkts, ierrs,
opkts, oerrs, collis;

pipkts = $5; pierrs = $6; popkts = $7; poerrs = $8;
pcollis = $9
                }
' # End of the awk program.
```

Figure 7-7 **ifstat** Shell Program

netstat -i shows input and output packet statistics since the system was last booted or since the LAN interface was last reset. Unfortunately, the numbers can be very large after the system runs for a few days. The **ifstat** shell program runs **netstat -i** continuously for a specified number of seconds and displays only the *new* information, not the historical information. This program can be run when you suspect problems such as excess traffic or collisions on your network.

Here is an example run of **ifstat** with an interval of five seconds:

```
$ ifstat 5
Interface statistic information for lan0:
ipkts ierrs opkts oerrs collis
----- ----- ----- ----- ------
 2234    15  2112    12     65
 1560    18  1480    11     44
                 .
                 .
                 .
```

These values reflect the current activity. They do not contain the history of packets since the system booted.

Some trivia to wow your friends with at your next cocktail party: **awk** is the first letter of the last names of its authors: Alfred Aho, Peter Weinberger, and Brian Kernighan.

Some Example Scripts with LVM and Ignite/UX

Now that we've covered many shell programming techniques, let's take a look at three shell programs that employ Logical Volume Manager (LVM) and Ignite/UX.

First, let me preface this section by saying that these are shell programs designed for a specific HP-UX installation. You could not use these programs without modifying them to suit your needs. They do, however, act as a good example of the type of programs you could craft to meet your specific needs.

The first shell program is an Ignite-UX script that removes all system-specific information so that a tape can be produced from which other systems can be loaded. The specific Ignite-UX functionality that is used by this script is the ability to produce a system recovery tape using the **make_recovery** command. The system recovery tape aspect of Ignite-UX is covered in Chapter 9. This program was used by a company that needed to send tapes out to many locations around the world for initial system load. After the initial system load took place, the system-specific information such as IP address could be manually added to the system. The first part of this program has all of the subroutines. The main program that calls the subroutines and runs the **make_recovery** command are at the end of the program. ADD is the application running on the system to be replicated. You could substitute a subroutine to verify that your application is not running prior to creating your system recovery tape. Figure 7-8 is the listing of the shell program called **preignite**.

```
#!/sbin/sh
#set -x
# pre-ignite script
#
# NOTE: This script will get the ADD system it is run
#                         on ready to have an IgniteUX recovery tape
#                         created on it.
#
#                         It will:
#                         1. Warn users of the impending shutdown
#                         2. Stop all ADD related processes
#                         3. Unconfigure DNS and NFS, stop processes
#                         4. Remove ip address of LAN 0 (built in)
#                         5. Remove hostname of server
#                         6. Undo mirroring
#                         7. Initiate make_recovery -A
#
#                         NOTE: YOU MUST BE ROOT TO RUN THIS SCRIPT
#
########################################################
#

warn_users() {          #send system users a simple message
                        echo " Sending 5 minute warning to all users to log off."
                        wall /usr/contrib/wallmesg
                        }

check_all() {           #are all necessary files available?
                        #check before beginning any configuration
                        #changes to avoid leaving the system
                        #in an intermediate state.
                        rval=0
                        # Is ADD running ?
                        echo " Checking to see if ADD processes running on this server"
                        if [ ! -f /home/add/header.add ]
                        then {
                        echo " ADD is not running."
                        rval=1
                        }
                        fi
```

Figure 7-8 **preignite** Shell Program to Remove System-Specific Information

```
# are all  files available for the DNS reconfiguration?
echo " Checking for inetd.sec"
if [ ! -f /usr/contrib/DNS_files/inetd.sec.other ]
then
{
rval=1
echo " /usr/contrib/DNS_files/inetd.sec.other not available"
}
fi


echo " Checking for nsswitch.conf"
if [ ! -f /usr/contrib/DNS_files/nsswitch.conf.other ]
then
{
rval=1
echo " /usr/contrib/DNS_files/nsswitch.other not available"
}
fi


echo " Checking for resolv.conf"
if [ ! -f /etc/resolv.conf ]
then
{
rval=1
echo "Could not remove /etc/resolv.conf, not on system"
}
fi


echo " Checking for exports file"
if [ ! -f /etc/exports ]
then
{
rval=1
echo "/etc/exports not on system; could not be removed."
}
fi


echo " checking for auto_master"
if [ ! -f /usr/contrib/NFS_files/auto_master.other ]
then
{
rval=1
echo "/usr/contrib/NFS_files/auto_master.other not available."
}
fi


echo " Checking for nfsconf"
if [ ! -f /usr/contrib/NFS_files/nfsconf.other ]
then
{
rval=1
echo "/usr/contrib/NFS_files/nfsconf.other not available"
}
fi


echo " Checking for netconf"
if [ ! -f /usr/contrib/network_files/netconf.other ]
then
{
rval=1
echo "/usr/contrib/network_files/netconf.other not available."
}
fi


echo " Checking for hosts"
```

Figure 7-8 **preignite** Shell Program to Remove System-Specific Information

```
                              if [ ! -f /usr/contrib/network_files/hosts.other ]
                              then
                              {
                              rval=1
                              echo " /usr/contrib/network_files/hosts.other not available."
                              }
                              fi

                              echo " Checking for passwd"
                              if [ ! -f /usr/contrib/network_files/passwd.other ]
                              then
                              {
                              rval=1
                              echo " /usr/contrib/network_files/passwd.other not available."
                              }
                              fi
                              } # end check_all
stop_ADD() {                  #put add application commands in to stop all processes
                              echo " Shutting down ADD ... "
                              echo " Please wait for 'shutdown completed' message"
                              su - adduser -c /home/add/addend
                              while [ -f /home/add/header.add ]
                              do
                              sleep 2
                              print -n '.'
                              done
                              print ''
                              sleep 6
                              rm /data/*
                              } #stop_ADD

DNS_down() {                  # Put config files inplace to run without DNS
                              echo " Replacing configuration files to run without"
                              echo "Domain Name Service (DNS)"

                              cp /usr/contrib/DNS_files/inetd.sec.other /usr/contrib/DNS_files/
inetd.sec

                              HNAME=`uname -n`
                              print 'dtspc    allow    127.0.0.1    '$HNAME >> /usr/contrib/
DNS_files/inetd.sec
                              print 'spc      allow    127.0.0.1    '$HNAME >> /usr/contrib/
DNS_files/inetd.sec
                              print 'mserve   allow    127.0.0.1    '$HNAME >> /usr/contrib/
DNS_files/inetd.sec

                              cp /usr/contrib/DNS_files/inetd.sec /var/adm/inetd.sec

                              cp /usr/contrib/DNS_files/nsswitch.conf.other /etc/nsswitch.conf

                              rm /etc/resolv.conf

                              echo "DNS reconfiguration done."

                              } # end DNS down
#
#
NFS_down() { #Undoing the NFS configration, stopping daemons unmounting filesystems

                              rm /etc/exports

                              cp /usr/contrib/NFS_files/auto_master.other /etc/auto_master

                              # if unconfigured successfully, stop nfs services before igniting
                              /sbin/init.d/nfs.server stop
                              /sbin/init.d/nfs.client stop
                              /sbin/init.d/nfs.core stop

                              cp /usr/contrib/NFS_files/nfsconf.other /etc/rc.config.d/nfsconf
                              echo "NFS daemons stopped."
```

Figure 7-8 preignite Shell Program to Remove System-Specific Information

```
                              echo "System reconfigured for no NFS services."

                              } #end NFS_down

remove_ip() {                 #copy the vanilla version of the /etc/rc.config.d/netconf file
                              # into place. This will remove the system's hostname and
                              # all ip addresses and connections

                              cp /usr/contrib/network_files/netconf.other /etc/rc.config.d/net-
conf

                              cp /usr/contrib/network_files/hosts.other /etc/hosts

                              cp /usr/contrib/network_files/passwd.other /etc/passwd

                              } # end remove_ip
remove_mirrors()    #split all the  mirrored volumes prior to make_recovery
                              {
                              /usr/contrib/bin/remove_mirror_add;
                              }
####################################################################

#main

check_all                     #check to see that all required files are available

if (( rval != 0 ))
                              then
                              {
                              echo " Some files were missing. Configuration could not proceed"
                              }
                              else

                              {
echo "                        Beginning the pre-Ignite process on this server:"

echo "                        1. Warn users of the impending shutdown"
                              warn_users;
echo "                          Waiting five minutes before continuing pre-ignite process ..."
                              sleep 30
echo "                        2. Stop all ADD related processes and remove server"
echo "                           specific files";sleep 3
                              stop_ADD;
echo "                        3. Unconfigure DNS";sleep 3
                              DNS_down;
echo "                        4. Unconfigure NFS";sleep 3
                              NFS_down;
echo "                        5. Remove hostname, ip addresses from server";sleep 3
                              remove_ip;
echo "                        6. Remove mirrors from server prior to creating Ignite tape";sleep
3
                              remove_mirrors;
echo "                        7. Create Ignite tape";sleep 2
echo " "
echo "                        Check that there is an unprotected 4mm DAT "
echo "                        tape in the internal drive"
echo "                        Please hit y followed by ENTER when "
echo "                        you are ready to build the tape"
                              read KYBDHIT
                              if [[ $KYBDHIT =  "y" ||  $KYBDHIT = "Y" ]]
                              then
                              make_recovery -A
                              fi
                              }
                              fi # end if rval !=0
```

Figure 7-8 **preignite** Shell Program to Remove System-Specific Information

The second shell program removes mirroring on a system. This script was also written for a specific system in a specific installation, so you would have to modify it for use in your environment. This script employs many LVM-related commands, as well as **sed**. Figure 7-9 is the listing of the shell program called **remove**.

```
#!/usr/bin/sh
###########################################################
#
#                remove_mirror_add - Deletes bootable mirrored disk
#
###########################################################

Root_Disk="/dev/rdsk/c0t6d0"
Mirror_Disk="/dev/rdsk/c1t6d0"
vol_sequence="1 2 4 3 5 6 7 8 9 10"

answer="n";
echo "This script will REMOVE MIRRORS on ${Mirror_Disk}"
echo "Do you wish to continue? [y/n]"
read answer;
                  if [ $answer = "y" -o $answer = "yes" ]
then
{
echo "Removing Bootable Mirrored Disk ${Mirror_Disk} from `hostname` on \n`date`"| tee
-a /var/tmp/lvm.log


                  /usr/sbin/diskinfo ${Mirror_Disk} >> /var/tmp/lvm.log 2>&1
                  status=$?

                  if [ $status != 0 ]
        then
            echo "Cannot open ${Mirror_Disk} ABORTING $0"
                    exit $status
        fi

vgdisplay -v /dev/vg00 >> /var/tmp/lvm.log 2>&1
pvdisplay -v `echo ${Root_Disk}|sed 's/rdsk/dsk/'` >> /var/tmp/lvm.log 2>&1
pvdisplay -v `echo ${Mirror_Disk}|sed 's/rdsk/dsk/'` >> /var/tmp/lvm.log 2>&1

for vol_number in `echo $vol_sequence`
do
echo "Removing Mirror lvol${vol_number}" | tee -a /var/tmp/lvm.log
lvreduce -m 0 /dev/vg00/lvol${vol_number} `echo ${Mirror_Disk}|sed 's/rdsk/dsk/'` >> /
var/tmp/lvm.log 2>&1
status=$?
if [ $status != 0 ]
then
  echo "Failed to remove mirror of lvol${vol_number} \nABORTING $0:$status"
     exit $status
fi

done

echo "Removing second drive ${Mirror_Disk} from the Root Volume Group" | tee -a /var/
tmp/lvm.log
vgreduce /dev/vg00 `echo ${Mirror_Disk}|sed 's/rdsk/dsk/'` >> /var/tmp/lvm.log 2>&1
status=$?
if [ $status != 0 ]
then
  echo "Failed to remove mirror disk ${Mirror_Disk} \nABORTING $0:$status"
     exit $status
fi

}
else
                  echo "Exiting $0\n"
                  exit
fi
```

Figure 7-9 **remove** Shell Program to Remove Mirror

The third shell program adds mirroring to a system. This shell program runs after the system recovery tape created earlier is loaded onto the system. This program takes a second disk, which will be used to mirror the first disk, make it bootable, and mirror all the logical volumes from the first disk. Figure 7-10 is the listing of the shell program called **create**.

```
#!/usr/bin/sh
#########################################################
#
#       create_mirror_add - Creates bootable mirrored disk
#
#########################################################
Root_Disk="/dev/rdsk/c0t6d0"
Mirror_Disk="/dev/rdsk/c1t6d0"
vol_sequence="1 2 4 3 5 6 7 8 9 10"

check_disk()
                            {
                            /usr/sbin/diskinfo $1 >> /var/tmp/lvm.log 2>&1
                            status=$?

                            if [ $status != 0 ]
                              then
                                echo "Cannot open ${Mirror_Disk} ABORTING $0"
                                exit $status
                            fi
                            }

check_for_existing_mirror()
 {
 for vol_number in `echo $vol_sequence`
 do
    {
      mirror=`lvdisplay /dev/vg00/lvol${vol_number} | awk '/Mirror copies/ {print $3}'`
        if [ $mirror != 0 ]
                            then
                                echo "lvol${vol_number} has already been mirrored!\nABORTING
$0"|tee -a /var/tmp/lvm.log
                                exit 1;
                            fi
    }
  done
 }

save_config()
{
 echo "Pre-Mirror LVM Configuration 'hostname' \n'date'" >> /var/tmp/lvm.log
 vgdisplay -v /dev/vg00 >> /var/tmp/lvm.log 2>&1
 pvdisplay -v `echo ${Root_Disk}|sed 's/rdsk/dsk/'` >> /var/tmp/lvm.log 2>&1
}

format_disk()
{
    echo "Adding Bootable Mirrored Disk $1 to `hostname` on \n`date`"| tee -a /var/tmp/lvm.log
    echo "Creating Volume Group Headers" | tee -a /var/tmp/lvm.log
    pvcreate -f -B ${Mirror_Disk} >> /var/tmp/lvm.log 2>&1
    echo "Creating Boot Area" | tee -a /var/tmp/lvm.log
    mkboot -a "hpux -lq (;0)/stand/vmunix" ${Root_Disk} >> /var/tmp/lvm.log 2>&1
    mkboot -b /usr/lib/uxbootlf -l ${Mirror_Disk} >> /var/tmp/lvm.log 2>&1
    mkboot -a "hpux -lq (;0)/stand/vmunix" ${Mirror_Disk} >> /var/tmp/lvm.log 2>&1
    echo "Adding second drive ${Mirror_Disk} to the Root Volume Group" | tee -a /var/tmp/lvm.log
    vgextend /dev/vg00 `echo ${Mirror_Disk}|sed 's/rdsk/dsk/'` >> /var/tmp/lvm.log 2>&1
}
```

Figure 7-10   **create** Shell Program to Add Mirror

```
create_mirror()
{
 for vol_number in `echo $vol_sequence`
 do
     echo "Mirroring lvol${vol_number}" | tee -a /var/tmp/lvm.log
     lvextend -m 1 /dev/vg00/lvol${vol_number} `echo ${Mirror_Disk}|sed 's/rdsk/dsk/'` >> /var/
tmp/lvm.log 2>&1
 done
}

answer="n";
echo "This script will Mirror ${Root_Disk} to ${Mirror_Disk}"
echo "Do you wish to continue? [y/n]"
read answer;

if [ $answer = "y" -o $answer = "yes" ]
then
    {
                          check_disk ${Mirror_Disk};
                          check_for_existing_mirror;
                          save_config;
                          format_disk;
                          create_mirror;

    }
else

                          echo "Exiting $0\n"
                          exit
fi
```

Figure 7-10 **create** Shell Program to Add Mirror

C Shell Programming for System Administrators

(Much of the material in this section is from *The Unix C Shell Field Guide* by Gail Anderson and Paul Anderson, Prentice Hall, ISBN 013937468X.)

The C shell is similar to the Bourne and POSIX shells covered earlier, in that it provides a user interface to HP-UX. You can use the C shell in the following three ways:

- Interactively type commands on the command line.

- Group commonly executed sets of commands into command files that you can execute by typing the name of the file.

- Create C shell programs (usually called shell scripts) using the structured programming techniques of the C shell.

These three techniques are listed in the order in which you'll probably use them. First, you log in and use interactive commands. Then you group together commonly used commands and execute them with a single command. Finally, you may want to create sophisticated shell scripts.

For this reason, I'll describe these aspects of the C shell in the order in which they are listed. Under the interactive description, I'll also cover the C shell environment and startup programs associated with the C shell.

The path for the C shell, **csh**, used in all of the examples is **/usr/bin/ csh**. A table showing all the shell paths was included early in this   chapter.

Issuing Commands

The first activity you perform after you log in to the system is to issue commands at the prompt. A command you may want to issue immediately is **ll**. Here is what I see on my system after executing this:

```
sys1 5: ll -a
total 22
drwxr-xr-x  3 cshtest home 1024 Nov 1 11:02 .
dr-xr-xr-x 12 bin     bin  1024 Nov 1 11:01 ..
-rw-r--r--  1 cshtest home  818 Nov 1 11:01 .cshrc
drwxr-xr-x  4 cshtest home 1024 Nov 1 11:43 .dt
-rwxr-xr-x  1 cshtest home 3971 Nov 1 11:02 .dtprofile
-rw-r--r--  1 cshtest home  347 Nov 1 11:01 .exrc
-rw-r--r--  1 cshtest home  377 Nov 1 11:01 .login
-rw-r--r--  1 cshtest home  382 Nov 1 11:01 .profile
sys1  6:
```

The C shell prompt consists of system name (**sys1**) followed by the command number and a colon. I'll cover the prompt shortly.

ll shows two files related to the C shell in this user area:

.cshrc and **.login**

Figure 7-11 is the contents of **.cshrc**.

```
# .cshrc for C shell
#
# Default user .cshrc file (/usr/bin/csh initialization).

# Usage:  Copy this file to a user's home directory
# then customize it and test.  It is run by csh each
# time it starts up.

# Set up default command search path:
#
# (For security, this default is a minimal set.)

    Set path=( /bin /usr/bin )

# Set up C shell environment:
    if   ( $?prompt ) then # shell is interactive.
      set history  = 20     # previous commands to remember.
      set savehist = 20     # number to save across sessions.
      set system = `hostname`       # name of this system.
      set prompt =  "$system \!: "   # command prompt.

      # Sample alias:

      alias    h    history

      # More sample aliases, commented out by default:

      #alias    d    dirs
      #alias    pd   pushd
      #alias    pd2  pushd +2
      #alias    po   popd
      #alias    m    more
    endif
```

Figure 7-11 Sample **.cshrc**

Figure 7-12 shows the contents of **.login**:

```
# .login for C shell

# @(#) $Revision:   64.2   $

# Default user .login file ( /usr/bin/csh initialization)

# Set up the default search paths:
set path=(/bin /usr/bin /usr/contrib/bin /usr/local/bin.)

#set up the terminal
eval 'tset -s -Q -m ' :?hp' '
stty erase "^H" kill "^U" intr "^C" eof "^D" susp "^Z"  hupcl
    ixon ixoff tostop
tabs

# Set up shell environment:
set noclobber
set history=20
```

Figure 7-12 Sample **.login**

The .cshrc File

The **.cshrc** is the first file read and executed by the C shell when you log in. You can modify the **.cshrc** file to specify the command-line prompt you wish to use, initialize the history list, and define aliases. The following are descriptions of the way the **.cshrc** file, shown in Figure 7-11, defines these.

Initialize History List in .cshrc

The C shell can keep a history list of the commands you have issued. If you wish to reissue a command or view a command you earlier issued, you can use the history list.

The commands issued are referred to by number so it is helpful to have a number appear at the command prompt. The following line in **.cshrc** provides a number following the system name:

```
set prompt = "$system \!: "

sys1 1:
```

We will get into shell and environment variables shortly, but for now it is sufficient to know that **$system** corresponds to system name "sys1."

You can specify any number of commands of which you want to keep a history. The following line in **.cshrc** sets the history list to 20:

```
set history = 20
```

If you were to now issue a series of commands, you could view these. If we had issued five commands since login, we could view these with **history**, as shown:

```
sys1 6: history
        1    ll
        2    whoami
        3    cd /tmp
        4    pwd
        5    cat database.log
```

All these commands (**ll, whoami, cd /tmp, pwd, cat database.log**) are in the history list with their corresponding numbers. You can repeat the

last command with **!!**, the second command with **!2**, and the last command
that started with "c" with **!c**. After issuing the commands, you could do the
following:

```
sys1    7:!!
            cat database.log


sys1    8:!2
            whoami


sys1    9:!c
            cat database.log
```

Table 7-3 includes some of the more commonly used history list recall
commands.

TABLE 7-3   RECALLING FROM HISTORY LIST

Command	Description	Example
!N	Issue command **N**	**!2**
!!	Issue last command	**!!**
!-N	Issue **Nth** command from last command issued	**!-N**
!str	Issue last command starting with **str**	**!c**
!?str?	Issue last command that had **str** anyplace in command line	**!?cat?**
!{str}str2	Append **str2** to last command with **str1**	**!{cd} /tmp**
^str1^str2^	Substitute **str2** for **str1** in last command	**^cat^more^**

Aliases in .cshrc

An alias is a name that you select for a frequently used command or series of commands. You can use the **.cshrc** file as a place where your aliases are stored and read every time you log in. You can also define aliases at the command-line prompt, but these will be cleared when you log out.

Here is an example of a useful alias:

```
sys1 1: alias h history
sys1 2: h
        history
```

Every time you type **h**, the history command is executed. You can obtain a list of aliases that you currently have active by issuing the alias command. You can also alias a set of commands as shown:

```
sys1 3:alias procs 'echo "Number of processes are: \c";
ps -ef | wc -l'
                        # single quote on outside
                        # double quote on inside
```

When you run **procs**, you see the following:

```
sys1 4: procs
        Number of processes are: 44
```

A lot of quoting is taking place in this command line. To understand what is taking place on this line, Table 7-4 will help.

TABLE 7-4 SHELL QUOTING

Character(s)	Description
'cmd'	Single quote means take string character literally
"str"	Double quote means allow command and variable substitution
\c	Escape character that prevents everything following it from printing including new line
'str'	Grave means execute command and substitute output

Applying Table 7-4 to the earlier **procs** alias, we can see what this alias is comprised of. The alias begins with a single quote, which means execute the command(s) within the single quotes. The first command is the **echo** command, which uses double quotes to specify the characters to **echo**. Embedded in the double quotes is the escape character **\c**, which prevents a new line from being printed. The semicolons separate commands. **ps** is then run to produce a list of processes and the output is piped (|) to word count (**wc**), which produces a count of the number of lines.

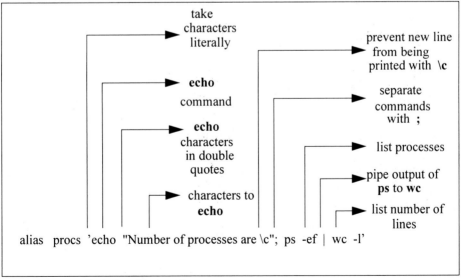

take
characters
literally

prevent new line
from being
printed with **\c**

echo
command

separate
commands
with ;

echo
characters
in double
quotes

list processes

characters to
echo

pipe output of
ps to **wc**

list number of
lines

alias procs 'echo "Number of processes are \c"; ps -ef | wc -l'

Figure 7-13 Quoting Example

As you can see in Figure 7-13, some of the quoting becomes tricky. An understanding of quoting is important if you wish to modify and reuse existing shell scripts or craft your own. A few other aliases you may want to try out are:

```
alias psf 'ps -ef | more'
alias psg 'ps -ef | grep -i'
alias lsf 'lsf -aq'
```

The .login File

The **.login** file is read after the **.cshrc** file. There are only two issues related to the setup present in the example shown. The first is the **tset** command, which sets the **TERM** environment variable. The **eval** preceding **tset** means that the C shell will execute **tset** and its arguments without creating a child process. This allows **tset** to set environment variables in the current shell instead of a subshell, which would be useless. The **stty** command is used to set terminal I/O options. The two set commands are used to define shell variables, which I'll describe shortly. The **noclobber** does not permit redirection to write over an existing file. If you try to write over an existing file, such as **/tmp/processes** below, you will receive a message that the file exists:

```
sys1   1:  ps  -ef  > /tmp/processes
           /tmp/processes:  File exists
```

The ">" means to take the output of **ps** and rather than write it to your screen, it will be written to **/tmp/processes**. The file **/tmp/processes** will not be written over, however, with the output of **ps -ef**, because **/tmp/processes** already exists and an environment variable called **noclobber** has been set. If **noclobber** is set, then redirecting output to this file will not take place. This is a useful technique for preventing existing files from being accidently overwritten. There are many forms of redirection that you'll find useful. Table 7-5 shows some commonly used forms of redirection.

TABLE 7-5 COMMONLY USED REDIRECTION FORMS

Command	Example	Description
<	**wc -l < .login**	Standard input redirection: execute **wc** (word count) and list number of lines (**-l**) in **.login**
>	**ps -ef > /tmp/processes**	Standard output redirection: execute **ps** and send output to file **/tmp/processes**
>>	**ps -ef >> /tmp/processes**	Append standard output: execute **ps** and append output to the end of file **/tmp/processes**
>!	**ps -ef >! /tmp/processes**	Append output redirection and override **noclobber**: write over **/tmp/processes** even if it exists
>>!	**ps -ef >>! /tmp/processes**	Append standard output and override **noclobber**: append to the end of **/tmp/processes**

Shell and Environment Variables

You are indeed special to your HP-UX system. Information about your user environment in the C shell is stored in shell variables and environment variables. You can view shell variables with the **set** command and environment variables with the **env** command, as shown below:

```
sys1 1:  set
argv         ()
autologout   60
cwd          /home/cshtest
history      20
home         /home/cshtest
path         (/bin /usr/bin)
prompt       sys1 !:
savehist     20
shell        /usr/bin/csh
status       0
```

```
system        sys1
term          hpterm
user          cshtest
sys1          2


sys1   6:   env
DEMO_HOME=/demo7100
PATH=/usr/bin
EDITOR=/usr/dt/bin/dtpad
LOGNAME=cshtest
MAIL=/var/mail/cshtest
USER=cshtest
DISPLAY=sys1:0.0
SHELL=/usr/bin/csh
HOME=/home/cshtest
TERM=hpterm
TZ=EST5EDT
PWD=/home/cshtest
WINDOWID=8388625
COMUMNS=81
LINES=37
sys1   7:
```

Shell variables are defined using **set**. We saw in the **.cshrc** file earlier that the **history** shell variable is set with:

set history = 20

Environment variables are defined with **setenv,** as shown below:

setenv EDITOR vi

Applications often use environment variables for their operation.

File Name Expansion

Before we can cover shell programming, I want to take a look at file name expansion. As the system administrator (or a system user manipulating files), you will surely be preparing shell scripts that deal with file names. An overview of file name expansion is useful to ensure that you're comfortable with this topic before you start writing shell scripts.

Table 7-6 lists some common file name expansion and pattern matching.

TABLE 7-6   FILE NAME EXPANSION AND PATTERN MATCHING

Character(s)	Example	Description
*	1) **ls *.c**	Match zero or more characters
?	2) **ls conf.?**	Match any single character
[list]	3) **ls conf.[co]**	Match any character in list
[lower-upper]	4) **ls libdd.9873[5-6].sl**	Match any character in range
str{str1,str2,str3,...}	5) **ls ux*.{700,300}**	Expand str with contents of {}
~	6) **ls -a ~**	Home directory
~username	7) **ls -a ~gene**	Home directory of username

The following descriptions of the examples shown in Table 7-6 are more detailed.

1. To list all files in a directory that end in ".**c**," you could do the following:

```
sys1 30:  ls *.c
          conf. SAM.c  conf.c
```

2. To find all the files in a directory named "conf" with an extension of one character, you could do the following:

```
sys1 31:   ls conf.?
           conf.c   conf.o   conf.1
```

3. To list all the files in a directory named "conf" with only the extension "**c**" or "**o**," you could do the following:

```
sys1 32:   ls conf.{co}
           conf.c   conf.o
```

4. To list files with similar names but a field that covers a range, you could do the following:

```
sys1 46:   ls libdd9873[5-6].sl
           libdd98735.sl   libdd98736.sl
```

5. To list files that start with "**ux**" and have the extension "300" or "**700**," you could do the following:

```
sys1 59:   ls ux*.{700,300}
           uxbootlf.700   uxinstfs.300   unistkern.300
           unistkern.700 unistlf.700
```

6. To list the files in your home directory, you could use ~:

```
sys1 62:   ls -a ~
           .           .cshrc.org  .login       .shrc.org
           ..          .exrc       .login.org   .dt
           .chsrc      .history    .profile     .dtprofile
```

7. To list the files in the home directory of a user, you can do the following:

```
sys1 65:   ls -a ~gene
           .           .history     .dt         splinedat
           ..          .login       .dtprofile  trail.txt
           .chsrc      .login.org   ESP-File    under.des
           .cshrc.org  .profile     Mail        xtra.part
           .exrc       .shrc.org    opt
```

Many of these techniques are useful when writing shell scripts, so it is a good idea to become familiar with file name expansion.

umask and Permissions

An additional topic to cover before shell programming techniques is file permissions and the way they relate to **umask**. This is important because you will write some shell programs anyone can use and others that you will want only a limited number of users, possibly just the system administrator, to use. **umask** is used to specify permission settings for new files and directories.

Let's start with an example of a long listing of a file:

```
sys1 1: ll script1
-rwxr-xr-x  1  marty  users  120 Jul 26 10:20 script1
```

The access rights for this file are defined by the position of read (r), write (w), and execute (x) when the **ll** command is issued. Figure 7-14 shows the three groups of three access rights for this file.

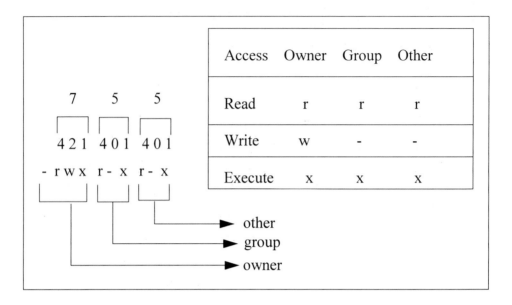

Figure 7-14 Example of File Permissions

The owner of this file has read, write, and execute permissions on the file. The group to which the user belongs has read and execute permissions, and others also have read and execute permissions. The permissions on this file can be specified by the octal sum of each field, which is 755.

What happens if you craft a new shell script or any new file? What permission settings will exist? You will want to execute the shell script, so you will need execute permission for the file. You can use **umask** to define the defaults for all your new files and directories.

You can view your umask with the following command:

```
sys1 2: umask
```

You can set the **umask** in **.cshrc** to define permission settings for new files and directories. The **umask** is used to *disable* access. You start with a **umask** and use the fields to disable some level of access. The **umask** command uses three octal fields. The fields are the sum of the access codes for user, group, and other, as shown in Figure 7-15.

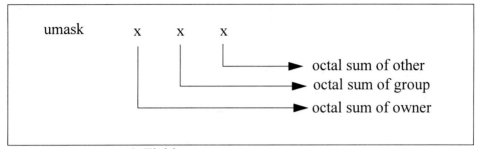

Figure 7-15   umask Fields

The *complement* of the umask field is "*anded*" with the default setting to change the **umask**. If you wanted to remove write permissions of files in Figure 7-16 for "group" and "other," you would assign a **umask** of 022, as shown.

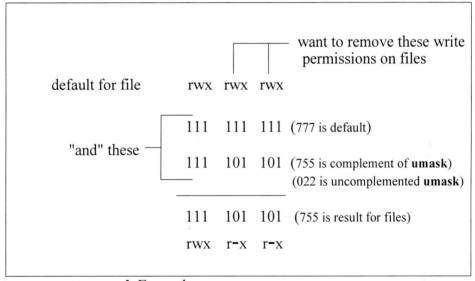

Figure 7-16   umask Example

umask 022 changes the file permissions to 755 in this example.

If you create a new file (**script2**) for your shell script, you may need to make it executable with the **chmod** command. If a file has permissions of

666 (rw-rw-rw-) and you wish to give the owner execute permission, you would issue the following command:

```
sys1 3: chmod 766 script2
```

C Shell Programming

Now that I have covered many of the basics of the C shell, I'll go into some techniques that can be used to write shell programs. I'll cover each shell programming technique briefly and use basic examples to help reinforce each technique. Eventually I'll provide some sophisticated shell programs, which you can modify and build on to meet your specific requirements. In all the following shell programs, any line beginning with a "#" is a comment. This statement is true except for the very first line of a shell program in which the shell the script is written for is executed. In all the following programs, the C shell is executed with **#!/usr/bin/csh**.

Command Substitution

The shell variables earlier covered can be used to save the output from a command. You can then use these variables when issuing other commands. The following shell program executes the **date** command and saves the results in the variable **d**. The variable **d** is then used within the **echo** command:

```
# program "today" which provides the date
set d 'date +%x'
echo "Today's date is $d"
```

When we run **today**, the following is produced:

```
sys1 1: today
        Today's date is 02/15/99
```

The "+%x" in the above example produces the current date. Command substitution of this type is used in several upcoming shell scripts.

Reading User Input

There are two commonly used ways to read user input to shell programs. The first is to prompt the user for information, and the second is to provide arguments to shell programs.

To begin, I'll cover prompting a user for information. A character, word, or sentence can be read into a variable. The following example first shows prompting the user for a word, and then a sentence:

```
#!/usr/bin/csh
echo "Please inter your name: \c"
set name = $<
echo "hello, $name"
echo "Please enter your favorite quote: \c"
set quote = $<
echo "Your favorite quote is:"
echo $quote
```

Here is an example of running this program:

```
sys1 1: userinput
        Please enter your name: marty
        Hello, marty
        Please enter your favorite quote: Creating is
        the essence of life.
        Your favorite quote is:
        Creating is the essence of life.
```

Using this technique, you can prompt a user for information in a shell program. This technique will be used in an upcoming program.

You can also enter command-line arguments. When you type the name of the shell script, you can supply arguments that are saved in the variables $1 through $9. The first ten words on the command line are directly accessible in the shell program using the special variables $0-$9. This is how they work:

$0	The command name
$1	The first argument
$2	The second argument
$3	.
	.
	.
$9	The ninth argument

If you are not sure how many command-line arguments you may get when your program is run, two other variables can help:

$#	The number of command-line arguments
$*	A space-separated list of all the command-line arguments (which does *not* include the command name).

The variable $* is commonly used with a **for** loop (soon to be explained) to process shell script command lines with any number of arguments.

The following script changes to the specified directory ($1) and searches for the specified pattern ($2) in the specified file ($3):

```
#!/usr/bin/csh
# search
# Usage: search directory pattern file
        echo " "
        cd $1# change to search dir and
        grep -n "$2" $3# search for $2 in $3
        echo " " # print line
endif
```

grep is used to search a file for a pattern and print the line in which the pattern was found. **awk** (which will be used later) can be used to pick out a specific field within a line.

Here is an example run of the **search** program:

```
sys1 1: search  /home/cshtest  path  .login

        7:# Set up the default search paths:
        8:set path=(/usr/bin /usr/contrib/bin
            /usr/local/bin)
```

Testing and Branching

Your shell programs can perform many kinds of decision making. **if** provides the flexibility to make decisions and take the appropriate action. Let's expand the search script to verify that the minimum number of arguments (3) is provided:

```
#!/usr/bin/csh
# search
# Usage: search directory pattern files

if ($#argv < 3) then        # if < 3 args provided

    echo "Usage: search directory pattern files"
                                # then print Usage
else
    echo " "                    # else print line and
    cd $1                       # change to search dir and
    grep -n "$2" $3             # search for $2 in $3
    echo " "                    # print line
endif
```

Here are four commonly used forms of **if**:

1)   if (expression) command

2)   if (expression) then
                             command(s)
           endif

3)   if (expression) then
                             command(s)
                 else
                             command(s)
           endif

4)   if (expression) then
                             command(s)
                 [else if expression) then
                           command(s)]

                      .
                      .
                      .

                [else
                             command(s)]
           endif

Many operators can be used in the C shell to compare integer values, such as the < used in the previous example. Here is a list of operators:

>	greater than
<	less than
>=	greater than or equal to
<=	less than or equal to
==	equal to
!=	not equal to

Looping

The C shell supports a number of techniques to support looping, including:

1) The **foreach** loop, which takes a list of items and performs the commands in the loop once for each item in the list.

2) The **while** loop, which executes a command (such as the **test** command) if the command executes successfully.

The format of the **foreach** loop is:

```
foreach name (list)
          command(s)
end
```

The following example uses a **foreach** loop to test whether or not the systems in the **/etc/hosts** file are connected to the local host:

```
#!/usr/bin/csh
#Program name: csh_hostck

#This program will test connectivity to all other hosts in
#your network listed in your /etc/hosts file.

# It uses the awk command to get the names from the hosts file
#and the ping command to check connectivity.

#Note that we use /usr/bin/echo because csh echo doesn't sup-
port #escape chars like \t or \c which are used in        the
#foreach #loop.

#Any line in /etc/hosts that starts with a number represents
#a host entry. Anything else is a comment or a blank line.

#Find all lines in /etc/hosts that start with a number and
#print the second field (the hostname).

set hosts=`awk '/^[1-9]/ { print $2 }' /etc/hosts`
                # grave on outside, single quote on inside

    /usr/bin/echo "Remote host connection status:"
```

```
foreach sys ($hosts)
    /usr/bin/echo "$sys - \c"
                        # send one 64 byte packet and look for
                        # the"1 packets received" message in
                        # the output that indicates success.

        ping $sys 64 1 | grep "1 packets received" > /dev/null
        if ( $status == 0 ) then
                echo "OK"
        else
                echo "DID NOT RESPOND"
        endif
end
```

The crazy-looking line with **awk** is used to obtain the name of remote hosts from the **/etc/hosts** file. The **foreach** loop takes all of the items in the list (the hosts in this case) and checks the status of each.

You could use the **while** loop to execute commands for some number of iterations. The **while** loop is in the following format:

```
while (expression)
                command(s)
    end
```

The following example executes the HP-UX 9.x version of **netstat**, and prints out the heading once and the status of lan0 nine times:

```
#!/usr/bin/csh
# program to run netstat every at specified interval
# Usage: netcheck interval

set limit=9              # set limit on number times
                        # to run netstat

echo " "
netstat -i | grep Name   # print netstat line with headings
set count=0
while ($count<$limit)    # if limit hasn't reached
                        # limit run netstat
        netstat -i | grep lan0
        sleep $1         # sleep for interval
                        # specified on command line
        @ count++        # increment limit
```

```
end
echo "count has reached $limit, run netcheck again to see lan0
status"
```

The following is an example run of the program:

```
sys1 1: netcheck 2
Name   Mtu   Network    Address Ipkts Ierrs Opkts Oerrs Coll
lan0* 1500 none       none    0     0     0     0     0
lan0* 1500 none       none    0     0     0     0     0
lan0* 1500 none       none    0     0     0     0     0
lan0* 1500 none       none    0     0     0     0     0
lan0* 1500 none       none    0     0     0     0     0
lan0* 1500 none       none    0     0     0     0     0
lan0* 1500 none       none    0     0     0     0     0
lan0* 1500 none       none    0     0     0     0     0
lan0* 1500 none       none    0     0     0     0     0
count has reached 9, run netcheck again to see lan0 status
```

This program increments the expression with:

@ count++

If the expression is true, then the command(s) will execute. The **@count++** is an assignment operator in the form of:

@ variable_name operator expression

In this case, the variable is first assigned with "=" and is later auto incremented (++). A number of operations can be performed on the variable as described in Table 7-7.

TABLE 7-7   ASSIGNMENT OPERATORS

Operation	Symbol	Example with count = 100	Result
store value	=	@count=100	100
auto increment	++	@count++	101
auto decrement	--	@count--	99
add value	+=	@count+=50	150
subtract value	-=	@count-=50	50
multiply by value	*=	@count*=2	200
divide by value	/=	@count/2	50

There are also comparison operators, such as the "<" used in the example, as well as arithmetic, bitwise, and logical operators. As you craft more and more shell scripts, you will want to use all of these operators.

There are a set of test conditions related to files that are useful when writing shell scripts that use files. Using the format **- operator filename**, you can use the tests in Table 7-8.

TABLE 7-8   OPERATOR FILENAME TESTS

Operator	Meaning
r	read access
w	write access
x	execute access
o	ownership
z	zero length
f	file, not a directory
d	directory, not a file

The following program (**filetest**) uses these operators to test the file **.login**. Since **.login** is not executable, of zero length, or a directory, I would expect **filetest** to find these false.

Here is a long listing of **.login**:

```
sys1 1:  ll .login
-rw-r--r-- 1 cshtest  users 382 Nov 30 18:24 .login
```

This listing is of the shell script **filetest**:

```
#  Program to test file $1

if (-e $1) then
    echo "$1 exists"
    else
    echo "$1 does not exist"
endif

if (-z $1) then
    echo "$1 is zero length"
    else
    echo "$1 is not zero length"
endif

if (-f $1) then
    echo "$1 is a file"
    else
    echo "$1 is not a file"
endif

if (-d $1) then
    echo "$1 is a directory"
    else
    echo "$1 is not a directory"
endif

if (-o $1) then
    echo "you own $1 "
    else
```

```
        echo "you don't own $1 "
endif

if (-r $1) then
     echo "$1 is readable"
     else
     echo "$1 is not readable"
endif

if (-w $1) then
     echo "$1 is writable"
     else
     echo "$1 is not writable"
endif

if (-x $1) then
     echo "$1 is executable"
     else
     echo "$1 is not executable"
endif
```

Here is the output of **filetest** using **.login** as input:

```
sys1 2: filetest .login
     .login exists
     .login is not of zero length
     .login is a file
     .login is not a directory
      you own .login
     .login is readable
     .login is writable
     .login is not executable
```

Decision Making with switch

You can use **switch** to make decisions within a shell program. You can use **switch** to test command-line arguments or interactive input to shell programs (as in the upcoming example). If, for example, you wanted to create a menu in a shell program and you needed to determine which option a user selected when running this shell program, you could use **switch**.

The syntax of **switch** looks like the following:

switch (pattern_to_match)

        case pattern1
            commands
            breaksw

        case pattern2
            commands
            breaksw

        case pattern 3
            commands
            breaksw

       default
            commands
            breaksw
endsw

pattern_to_match is the user input that you are testing, and if it is equal to **pattern1,** then the commands under **pattern1** are executed. If **pattern_to_match** and **pattern2** are the same, then the commands under **pattern2** will be executed, and so on. If there is no match between **pattern_to_match** and one of the case statement patterns, then the default is executed. The following example uses **switch**:

```
#!/usr/bin/csh
# Program pickscript to run some of
# the C shell scripts we've created
```

```
# Usage: pickscript

echo " -------------------------------------------"
echo "                    Sys Admin Menu                    "
echo "-------------------------------------------"
echo " "
echo " 1                 netcheck for network interface    "
echo " "
echo " 2                 hostck to check connection         "
echo "                   to hosts in /etc/hosts             "
echo " "
echo " -------------------------------------------"
echo " "
echo " Please enter your selection -> \c"

set pick = $<       # read input which is number of script
echo " "
switch ($pick)      # and assign to variable pick

    case 1           # if 1 was selected execute this
        $HOME/cshscripts/netcheck 5
        breaksw

    case 2           # if 2 was selected execute this
        $HOME/cshscripts/hostck
        breaksw
    default
        echo "Please select 1 or 2 next time"
    breaksw

endsw
```

Debugging C Shell Programs

When you begin C shell programming, you'll probably make a lot of simple syntax-related errors. You can have the C shell check the syntax of your program without executing it, using the **-n** option to **csh**. I also use the **-v** option to produce a verbose output. This can sometimes lead to too much information, so I start with **-v** and if there is too much feedback, I eliminate it.

The following example is the earlier **search** program expanded to include a check that three arguments have been provided. When checking to see that **$#argv** is equal to 3, I left off the left parenthesis. Here is the listing of the program and a syntax check showing the error:

```
sys 1 1: cat search
#!/usr/bin/csh
# search
# Usage: search directory pattern files

if ($#argv != 3 then        # if < 3 args provided
        echo "Usage: search directory pattern files"
                            # then print Usage
else
        echo " "            # else print line and
        cd $1               # change to search dir and
        grep -n "$2" $3     # search for $2 in $3
        echo " "            # print line
endif


sys 1 2: csh -nv search
        if ( $#argv != 3 then
        Too many ('s
```

The **csh -nv** has done a syntax check with verbose output. First, the line in question is printed, and then an error message that tells you what is wrong with the line. In this case it is clear that I have left off the left parenthesis.

After fixing the problem, I can run the program with **-x**, which causes all commands to be echoed immediately before execution. The following example shows a run of the search program:

```
sys1 1: csh -xv ./search cwd grep hostck

if ( $#argv != 3 ) then
if ( 3 != 3 ) then

echo " "
echo

cd $1
cd cwd
~/cshscripts
grep -n "$2" $3
grep -n grep hostck
22:/etc/ping $sys 64 1 | grep "1 packets received" >
   /dev/null
echo " "
echo

endif
endif
```

You can follow what is taking place on a line-by-line basis. The line beginning with 22 is the line in the file **hostck** that has **grep** in it, that is, the output you would receive if the program had been run without the **-xv** options.

I would recommend performing the syntax check (**-n**) with a new shell program and then echoing all commands with the **-x** option only if you get unexpected results when you run the program. The debugging options will surely help you at some point when you run into problems with the shell programs you craft.

How Long Does It Take?

You can use the **time** command to see a report of the amount of **time** your shell program takes to run. When you issue the time command, you get a report in the format shown in Figure 7-17.

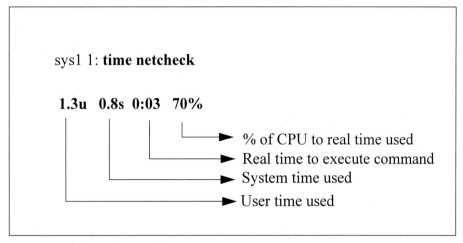

sys1 1: **time netcheck**

1.3u 0.8s 0:03 70%

% of CPU to real time used
Real time to execute command
System time used
User time used

Figure 7-17 **time** Example

Because some of the scripts you write may consume a substantial amount of system resources, you may want to consider investigating some of the job control capabilities of the C shell. The simplest job control you can use is to run scripts in the background so that the priority of the script is low. By issuing the script name followed by the **&,** you will run the script in the background. If you run several scripts in the background, you can get the status of these by issuing the **jobs** command. This is a more advanced C shell topic, but depending on the level of complexity of scripts you write, you may want to look into job control.

Manual Pages for Commands Used in Chapter 7

The following section contains copies of the manual pages of commands used in creating the shell programs in this chapter. This makes for a quick reference as you expand on these programs and create your own shell programs.

awk

awk - Scan input file looking for patterns.

---

awk(1)   awk(1)

NAME
     awk - pattern-directed scanning and processing language

SYNOPSIS
     awk [-Ffs] [-v var=value] [program | -f progfile ...] [file ...]

DESCRIPTION
     awk scans each input file for lines that match any of a set of
     patterns specified literally in program or in one or more files
     specified as -f progfile. With each pattern there can be an
     associated action that is to be performed when a line in a file
     matches the pattern. Each line is matched against the pattern portion
     of every pattern-action statement, and the associated action is
     performed for each matched pattern. The file name - means the
     standard input. Any file of the form var=value is treated as an
     assignment, not a filename. An assignment is evaluated at the time it
     would have been opened if it were a filename, unless the -v option is
     used.

     An input line is made up of fields separated by white space, or by
     regular expression FS. The fields are denoted $1, $2, ...; $0 refers
     to the entire line.

   Options
     awk recognizes the following options and arguments:

          -F fs   Specify regular expression used to separate
                        fields. The default is to recognize space and tab
                        characters, and to discard leading spaces and
                        tabs. If the -F option is used, leading input
                        field separators are no longer discarded.

          -f progfile   Specify an awk program file. Up to 100 program
                        files can be specified. The pattern-action
                        statements in these files are executed in the same
                        order as the files were specified.

          -v var=value Cause var=value assignment to occur before the
                        BEGIN action (if it exists) is executed.

   Statements
     A pattern-action statement has the form:

          pattern { action }

     A missing { action } means print the line; a missing pattern always
     matches. Pattern-action statements are separated by new-lines or
     semicolons.

     An action is a sequence of statements. A statement can be one of the following:

```
if(expression) statement [else statement]
while(expression) statement
for(expression;expression;expression) statement
for(var in array) statement
do statement while(expression)
break
continue
{[statement ...]}
expression                    # commonly var=expression
print[expression-list] [> expression]
printf format [, expression-list] [> expression]
return [expression]
next            # skip remaining patterns on this input line.
delete array [expression]        # delete an array element.
exit [expression]      # exit immediately; status is expression.
```

Statements are terminated by semicolons, newlines or right braces. An
empty expression-list stands for $0. String constants are quoted
(""), with the usual C escapes recognized within. Expressions take on
string or numeric values as appropriate, and are built using the
operators +, -, *, /, %, ^ (exponentiation), and concatenation
(indicated by a blank). The operators ++, --, +=, -=, *=, /=, %=, ^=,
**=, >, >=, <, <=, ==, !=, and ?: are also available in expressions.
Variables can be scalars, array elements (denoted x[i]) or fields.
Variables are initialized to the null string. Array subscripts can be
any string, not necessarily numeric (this allows for a form of
associative memory). Multiple subscripts such as [i,j,k] are
permitted. The constituents are concatenated, separated by the value
of SUBSEP.

The print statement prints its arguments on the standard output (or on
a file if >file or >>file is present or on a pipe if |cmd is present),
separated by the current output field separator, and terminated by the
output record separator. file and cmd can be literal names or
parenthesized expressions. Identical string values in different
statements denote the same open file. The printf statement formats
its expression list according to the format (see printf(3)).

Built-In Functions
  The built-in function close(expr) closes the file or pipe expr opened
  by a print or printf statement or a call to getline with the same
  string-valued expr. This function returns zero if successful,
  otherwise, it returns non-zero.

  The customary functions exp, log, sqrt, sin, cos, atan2 are built in.
  Other built-in functions are:

```
blength[([s])]    Length of its associated argument (in bytes)
                  taken as a string, or of $0 if no argument.

length[([s])]     Length of its associated argument (in characters)
                  taken as a string, or of $0 if no argument.

rand()            Returns a random number between zero and one.

srand([expr])     Sets the seed value for rand, and returns the
                  previous seed value.  If no argument is given,
                  the time of day is used as the seed value;
                  otherwise, expr is used.

int(x)            Truncates to an integer value

substr(s, m[, n]) Return the at most n-character substring of s
                  that begins at position m, numbering from 1.  If
```

n is omitted, the substring is limited by the
length of string s.

index(s, t)   Return the position, in characters, numbering
                   from 1, in string s where string t first occurs,
                   or zero if it does not occur at all.

match(s, ere)   Return the position, in characters, numbering
                   from 1, in string s where the extended regular
                   expression ere occurs, or 0 if it does not. The
                   variables RSTART and RLENGTH are set to the
                   position and length of the matched string.

split(s, a[, fs]) Splits the string s into array elements a[1],
                   a[2], ..., a[n], and returns n. The separation
                   is done with the regular expression fs, or with
                   the field separator FS if fs is not given.

sub(ere, repl [, in])
                   Substitutes repl for the first occurrence of the
                   extended regular expression ere in the string in.
                   If in is not given, $0 is used.

gsub   Same as sub except that all occurrences of the
                   regular expression are replaced; sub and gsub
                   return the number of replacements.

sprintf(fmt, expr, ...)
                   String resulting from formatting expr ...
                   according to the printf(3S) format fmt

system(cmd)   Executes cmd and returns its exit status

toupper(s)   Converts the argument string s to uppercase and
                   returns the result.

tolower(s)   Converts the argument string s to lowercase and
                   returns the result.

The built-in function getline sets $0 to the next input record from
the current input file; getline < file sets $0 to the next record from
file. getline x sets variable x instead. Finally, cmd | getline
pipes the output of cmd into getline; each call of getline returns the
next line of output from cmd. In all cases, getline returns 1 for a
successful input, 0 for end of file, and -1 for an error.

Patterns

Patterns are arbitrary Boolean combinations (with ! || &&) of regular
expressions and relational expressions. awk supports Extended Regular
Expressions as described in regexp(5). Isolated regular expressions
in a pattern apply to the entire line. Regular expressions can also
occur in relational expressions, using the operators ~ and !~. /re/
is a constant regular expression; any string (constant or variable)
can be used as a regular expression, except in the position of an
isolated regular expression in a pattern.

A pattern can consist of two patterns separated by a comma; in this
case, the action is performed for all lines from an occurrence of the
first pattern though an occurrence of the second.

A relational expression is one of the following:

```
expression matchop regular-expression
expression relop expression
expression in array-name
(expr,expr,...) in array-name
```

where a relop is any of the six relational operators in C, and a
matchop is either ~ (matches) or !~ (does not match). A conditional
is an arithmetic expression, a relational expression, or a Boolean
combination of the two.

The special patterns BEGIN and END can be used to capture control
before the first input line is read and after the last. BEGIN and END
do not combine with other patterns.

Special Characters
The following special escape sequences are recognized by awk in both
regular expressions and strings:

Escape	Meaning
\a	alert character
\b	backspace character
\f	form-feed character
\n	new-line character
\r	carriage-return character
\t	tab character
\v	vertical-tab character
\nnn	1- to 3-digit octal value nnn
\xhhh	1- to n-digit hexadecimal number

Variable Names
Variable names with special meanings are:

FS	Input field separator regular expression; a space character by default; also settable by option -Ffs.
NF	The number of fields in the current record.
NR	The ordinal number of the current record from the start of input. Inside a BEGIN action the value is zero. Inside an END action the value is the number of the last record processed.
FNR	The ordinal number of the current record in the current file. Inside a BEGIN action the value is zero. Inside an END action the value is the number of the last record processed in the last file processed.
FILENAME	A pathname of the current input file.
RS	The input record separator; a newline character by default.
OFS	The print statement output field separator; a space character by default.
ORS	The print statement output record separator; a newline character by default.
OFMT	Output format for numbers (default %.6g). If the value of OFMT is not a floating-point format specification, the results are unspecified.
CONVFMT	Internal conversion format for numbers (default %.6g). If the value of CONVFMT is not a floating-point format specification, the results are unspecified.

SUBSEP	The subscript separator string for multi-dimensional arrays; the default value is " 34"
ARGC	The number of elements in the ARGV array.
ARGV	An array of command line arguments, excluding options and the program argument numbered from zero to ARGC-1.
	The arguments in ARGV can be modified or added to; ARGC can be altered. As each input file ends, awk will treat the next non-null element of ARGV, up to the current value of ARGC-1, inclusive, as the name of the next input file. Thus, setting an element of ARGV to null means that it will not be treated as an input file. The name - indicates the standard input. If an argument matches the format of an assignment operand, this argument will be treated as an assignment rather than a file argument.
ENVIRON	Array of environment variables; subscripts are names. For example, if environment variable V=thing, ENVIRON["V"] produces thing.
RSTART	The starting position of the string matched by the match function, numbering from 1. This is always equivalent to the return value of the match function.
RLENGTH	The length of the string matched by the match function.

Functions can be defined (at the position of a pattern-action statement) as follows:

```
function foo(a, b, c) { ...; return x }
```

Parameters are passed by value if scalar, and by reference if array name. Functions can be called recursively. Parameters are local to the function; all other variables are global.

Note that if pattern-action statements are used in an HP-UX command line as an argument to the awk command, the pattern-action statement must be enclosed in single quotes to protect it from the shell. For example, to print lines longer than 72 characters, the pattern-action statement as used in a script (-f progfile command form) is:

```
length > 72
```

The same pattern action statement used as an argument to the awk command is quoted in this manner:

```
awk 'length > 72'
```

EXTERNAL INFLUENCES
  Environment Variables
    LANG   Provides a default value for the internationalization
                    variables that are unset or null. If LANG is unset or
                    null, the default value of "C" (see lang(5)) is used.
                    If any of the internationalization variables contains
                    an invalid setting, awk will behave as if all
                    internationalization variables are set to "C". See
                    environ(5).

LC_ALL   If set to a non-empty string value, overrides the
                  values of all the other internationalization variables.

LC_CTYPE   Determines the interpretation of text as single and/or
                  multi-byte characters, the classification of characters
                  as printable, and the characters matched by character
                  class expressions in regular expressions.

LC_NUMERIC   Determines the radix character used when interpreting
                  numeric input, performing conversion between numeric
                  and string values and formatting numeric output.
                  Regardless of locale, the period character (the
                  decimal-point character of the POSIX locale) is the
                  decimal-point character recognized in processing awk
                  programs (including assignments in command-line
                  arguments).

LC_COLLATE   Determines the locale for the behavior of ranges,
                  equivalence classes and multi-character collating
                  elements within regular expressions.

LC_MESSAGES   Determines the locale that should be used to affect the
                  format and contents of diagnostic messages written to
                  standard error and informative messages written to
                  standard output.

NLSPATH   Determines the location of message catalogues for the
                  processing of LC_MESSAGES.

PATH   Determines the search path when looking for commands
                  executed by system(cmd), or input and output pipes.

In addition, all environment variables will be visible via the awk
variable ENVIRON.

International Code Set Support
    Single- and multi-byte character code sets are supported except that
    variable names must contain only ASCII characters and regular
    expressions must contain only valid characters.

DIAGNOSTICS
    awk supports up to 199 fields ($1, $2, ..., $199) per record.

EXAMPLES
    Print lines longer than 72 characters:

        length > 72

    Print first two fields in opposite order:

        { print $2, $1 }

    Same, with input fields separated by comma and/or blanks and tabs:

        BEGIN { FS = ",[\t]*|[\t]+" }
              { print $2, $1 }

    Add up first column, print sum and average:

                  { s += $1 }"
        END   { print "sum is", s, " average is", s/NR }

    Print all lines between start/stop pairs:

        /start/, /stop/

Simulate echo command (see echo(1)):

```
    BEGIN   {                              # Simulate echo(1)
            for (i = 1; i < ARGC; i++) printf "%s ", ARGV[i]
            printf "\n"
            exit }
```

AUTHOR
    awk was developed by AT&T, IBM, OSF, and HP.

SEE ALSO
    lex(1), sed(1).
    A. V. Aho, B. W. Kernighan, P. J. Weinberger: The AWK Programming
    Language, Addison-Wesley, 1988.

STANDARDS CONFORMANCE
    awk: SVID2, SVID3, XPG2, XPG3, XPG4, POSIX.2

csh

csh - Command language interpreter.

---

csh(1)   csh(1)

NAME
     csh - a shell (command interpreter) with C-like syntax

SYNOPSIS

     csh [-cefinstvxTVX] [command_file] [argument_list ...]

DESCRIPTION
     csh is a command language interpreter that incorporates a command
     history buffer, C-like syntax, and job control facilities.

  Command Options
     Command options are interpreted as follows:

          -c   Read commands from the (single) following argument
                    which must be present. Any remaining arguments are
                    placed in argv.

          -e   C shell exits if any invoked command terminates
                    abnormally or yields a non-zero exit status.

          -f   Suppress execution of the .cshrc file in your home
                    directory, thus speeding up shell start-up time.

          -i   Force csh to respond interactively when called from a
                    device other than a computer terminal (such as another
                    computer). csh normally responds non-interactively.
                    If csh is called from a computer terminal, it always
                    responds interactively, regardless of which options are
                    selected.

          -n   Parse but do not execute commands. This is useful for
                    checking syntax in shell scripts. All substitutions
                    are performed (history, command, alias, etc.).

          -s   Take command input from the standard input.

          -t   Read and execute a single line of input.

          -v   Set the verbose shell variable, causing command input
                    to be echoed to the standard output device after
                    history substitutions are made.

          -x   Set the echo shell variable, causing all commands to be
                    echoed to the standard error immediately before
                    execution.

          -T   Disable the tenex features which use the ESC key for
                    command/file name completion and CTRL-D for listing
                    available files (see the CSH UTILITIES section below)

-V   Set the verbose variable before .cshrc is executed so
            that all .cshrc commands are also echoed to the
            standard output.

-X   Set the echo variable before .cshrc is executed so that
            all .cshrc commands are also echoed to the standard
            output.

After processing the command options, if arguments remain in the
argument list, and the -c, -i, -s, or -t options were not specified,
the first remaining argument is taken as the name of a file of
commands to be executed.

COMMANDS
    A simple command is a sequence of words, the first of which specifies
    the command to be executed. A sequence of simple commands separated
    by vertical bar (|) characters forms a pipeline. The output of each
    command in a pipeline becomes the input for the next command in the
    pipeline. Sequences of pipelines can be separated by semicolons (;)
    which causes them to be executed sequentially. A sequence of
    pipelines can be executed in background mode by adding an ampersand
    character (&) after the last entry.

    Any pipeline can be placed in parentheses to form a simple command
    which, in turn, can be a component of another pipeline. Pipelines can
    also be separated by || or && indicating, as in the C language, that
    the second pipeline is to be executed only if the first fails or
    succeeds, respectively.

Jobs
    csh associates a job with each pipeline and keeps a table of current
    jobs (printed by the jobs command) and assigns them small integer
    numbers. When a job is started asynchronously using &, the shell
    prints a line resembling:

        [1] 1234

    indicating that the job which was started asynchronously was job
    number 1 and had one (top-level) process, whose process id was 1234.

    If you are running a job and want to do something else, you can type
    the currently defined suspend character (see termio(7)) which sends a
    stop signal to the current job. csh then normally indicates that the
    job has been `Stopped', and prints another prompt. You can then
    manipulate the state of this job, putting it in the background with
    the bg command, run some other commands, and then eventually bring the
    job back into the foreground with the foreground command fg. A
    suspend takes effect immediately and is like an interrupt in that
    pending output and unread input are discarded when it is typed. There
    is a delayed suspend character which does not generate a stop signal
    until a program attempts to read(2) it. This can usefully be typed
    ahead when you have prepared some commands for a job which you want to
    stop after it has read them.

    A job being run in the background stops if it tries to read from the
    terminal. Background jobs are normally allowed to produce output, but
    this can be disabled by giving the command stty tostop (see stty(1)).
    If you set this tty option, background jobs stop when they try to
    produce output, just as they do when they try to read input. Keyboard
    signals and line-hangup signals from the terminal interface are not
    sent to background jobs on such systems. This means that background
    jobs are immune to the effects of logging out or typing the interrupt,
    quit, suspend, and delayed suspend characters (see termio(7)).

    There are several ways to refer to jobs in the shell. The character %
    introduces a job name. If you wish to refer to job number 1, you can

name it as %1. Just naming a job brings it to the foreground; thus %1
is a synonym for fg %1 , bringing job 1 back into the foreground.
Similarly, typing %1 & resumes job 1 in the background. Jobs can also
be named by prefixes of the string typed in to start them if these
prefixes are unambiguous; thus %ex normally restarts a suspended ex(1)
job, if there is only one suspended job whose name begins with the
string ex. It is also possible to say %?string which specifies a job
whose text contains string, if there is only one such job.

csh maintains a notion of the current and previous jobs. In output
pertaining to jobs, the current job is marked with a + and the
previous job with a -. The abbreviation %+ refers to the current job
and %- refers to the previous job. For close analogy with the syntax
of the history mechanism (described below), %% is also a synonym for
the current job.

csh learns immediately whenever a process changes state. It normally
informs you whenever a job becomes blocked so that no further progress
is possible, but only just before printing a prompt. This is done so
that it does not otherwise disturb your work. If, however, you set
the shell variable notify, csh notifies you immediately of changes in
status of background jobs. There is also a csh built-in command
called notify which marks a single process so that any status change
is immediately reported. By default, notify marks the current
process. Simply type notify after starting a background job to mark
it.

If you try to leave the shell while jobs are stopped, csh sends the
warning message: You have stopped jobs. Use the jobs command to see
what they are. If you do this or immediately try to exit again, csh
does not warn you a second time, and the suspended jobs are terminated
(see exit(2)).

Built-In Commands
    Built-in commands are executed within the shell without spawning a new
    process. If a built-in command occurs as any component of a pipeline
    except the last, it is executed in a subshell. The built-in commands
    are:

        alias
        alias name

        alias name wordlist
                The first form prints all aliases. The second form
                prints the alias for name. The third form assigns the
                specified wordlist as the alias of name. Command and
                file name substitution are performed on wordlist. name
                cannot be alias or unalias.

        bg [%job ...]
                Put the current (job not specified) or specified jobs
                into the background, continuing them if they were
                stopped.

        break   Causes execution to resume after the end of the nearest
                enclosing foreach or while. The remaining commands on
                the current line are executed. Multi-level breaks are
                thus possible by writing them all on one line.

        breaksw Causes a break from a switch, resuming after the endsw.

        case label:
                A label in a switch statement as discussed below.

        cd

```
cd directory_name

chdir
chdir directory_name
          Change the shell's current working directory to
          directory_name.  If not specified, directory_name
          defaults to your home directory.
          If directory_name is not found as a subdirectory of the
          current working directory (and does not begin with /, ./,
          or ../), each component of the variable cdpath is checked
          to see if it has a subdirectory directory_name.  Finally,
          if all else fails, csh treats directory_name as a shell
          variable.  If its value begins with /, this is tried to
          see if it is a directory.
continue
          Continue execution of the nearest enclosing while or
          foreach.  The rest of the commands on the current line
          are executed.
default:
          Labels the default case in a switch statement.  The
          default should come after all other case labels.
dirs      Prints the directory stack; the top of the stack is at
          the left; the first directory in the stack is the current
          directory.
echo wordlist

echo -n wordlist
          The specified words are written to the shell's standard
          output, separated by spaces, and terminated with a new-
          line unless the -n option is specified.

else
end
endif
endsw     See the descriptions of the foreach, if, switch, and
          while statements below.

eval arguments ...
          (Same behavior as sh(1).) arguments are read as input to
          the shell and the resulting command(s) executed.  This is
          usually used to execute commands generated as the result
          of command or variable substitution, since parsing occurs
          before these substitutions.

exec command
          The specified command is executed in place of the current
          shell.

exit
exit (expression)
          csh exits either with the value of the status variable
          (first form) or with the value of the specified
          expression (second form).

fg [%job ...]
          Brings the current (job not specified) or specified jobs
          into the foreground, continuing them if they were
          stopped.

foreach name (wordlist)

     ...
end       The variable name is successively set to each member of
          wordlist and the sequence of commands between this
          command and the matching end are executed.  (Both foreach
          and end must appear alone on separate lines.)
```

The built-in command continue can be used to continue the
loop prematurely; the built-in command break to terminate
it prematurely. When this command is read from the
terminal, the loop is read once, prompting with ? before
any statements in the loop are executed. If you make a
mistake while typing in a loop at the terminal, use the
erase or line-kill character as appropriate to recover.

glob wordlist
     Like echo but no \ escapes are recognized and words are
     delimited by null characters in the output. Useful in
     programs that use the shell to perform file name
     expansion on a list of words.

goto word
     The specified word is file name and command expanded to
     yield a string of the form label. The shell rewinds its
     input as much as possible and searches for a line of the
     form label: possibly preceded by blanks or tabs.
     Execution continues after the specified line.

hashstat
     Print a statistics line indicating how effective the
     internal hash table has been at locating commands (and
     avoiding execs). An exec is attempted for each component
     of the path where the hash function indicates a possible
     hit, and in each component that does not begin with a /.

history [-h] [-r] [n]
     Displays the history event list. If n is given, only the
     n most recent events are printed. The -r option reverses
     the order of printout to be most recent first rather than
     oldest first. The -h option prints the history list
     without leading numbers for producing files suitable for
     the source command.

if (expression) command
     If expression evaluates true, the single command with
     arguments is executed. Variable substitution on command
     happens early, at the same time it does for the rest of
     the if command. command must be a simple command; not a
     pipeline, a command list, a parenthesized command list,
     or an aliased command. Input/output redirection occurs
     even if expression is false, meaning that command is not
     executed (this is a bug).

if (expression1) then

  ...
else if (expression2) then

  ...
else
  ...
endif   If expression1 is true, all commands down to the first
     else are executed; otherwise if expression2 is true, all
     commands from the first else down to the second else are
     executed, etc. Any number of else-if pairs are possible,
     but only one endif is needed. The else part is likewise
     optional. (The words else and endif must appear at the
     beginning of input lines. The if must appear alone on
     its input line or after an else.)

jobs [-l]
> Lists active jobs. The -l option lists process IDs in
> addition to the usual information.

kill % job

kill - sig % job ...

kill pid

kill - sig pid...

kill -l Sends either the TERM (terminate) signal or the specified
> signal to the specified jobs or processes. Signals are
> either given by number or by names (as given in
> /usr/include/signal.h, stripped of the SIG prefix (see
> signal(2)). The signal names are listed by kill -l.
> There is no default, so kill used alone does not send a
> signal to the current job. If the signal being sent is
> TERM (terminate) or HUP (hangup), the job or process is
> sent a CONT (continue) signal as well.

limit[-h][resource][maximum_use]
> Limits the usage by the current process and each process
> it creates not to (individually) exceed maximum_use on
> the specified resource. If maximum_use is not specified,
> then the current limit is displayed; if resource is not
> specified, then all limitations are given.
>
> If the -h flag is specified, the hard limits are used
> instead of the current limits. The hard limits impose a
> ceiling on the values of the current limits. Only the
> superuser can raise the hard limits, but a user can lower
> or raise the current limits within the legal range.
>
> Controllable resources currently include:
>
> addresspace Maximum address space in bytes for a process
>
> coredumpsize Size of the largest core dump that is created
>
> cputime Maximum number of CPU seconds to be used by each
> process
>
> datasize Maximum growth of the data region allowed beyond
> the end of the program text
>
> descriptors Maximum number of open files for each process
>
> filesize Largest single file that can be created
>
> memoryuse Maximum size to which a process's resident set
> size can grow
>
> stacksize Maximum size of the automatically extended stack
> region
>
> The maximum_use argument can be specified as a floating-
> point or integer number followed by a scale factor: k or
> kilobytes (1024 bytes), m or megabytes, or b or blocks (the
> units used by the ulimit system call). For both resource
> names and scale factors, unambiguous prefixes of the names
> can be used. filesize can be lowered by an instance of csh,
> but can only be raised by an instance whose effective user
> ID is root. For more information, refer to the documentation
> for the ulimit system call.

login
     Terminates a login shell, replacing it with an instance of
     /usr/bin/login. This is one way to log off, included for
     compatibility with sh(1).

logout
     Terminates a login shell. Especially useful if ignoreeof is
     set. A similar function, bye, which works for sessions that
     are not login shells, is provided for historical reasons.
     Its use is not recommended because it is not part of the
     standard BSD csh and may not be supported in future
     releases.

newgrp
     Changes the group identification of the caller; for details
     see newgrp(1). A new shell is executed by newgrp so that
     the current shell environment is lost.

nice
nice +number

·nice command

nice +number command
     The first form sets the nice (run command priority) for this
     shell to 4 (the default). The second form sets the priority
     to the given number. The final two forms run command at
     priority 4 and number respectively. The user with
     appropriate privileges can raise the priority by specifying
     negative niceness using nice -number ... command is always
     executed in a sub-shell, and restrictions placed on commands
     in simple if statements apply.

nohup [command]
     Without an argument, nohup can be used in shell scripts to
     cause hangups to be ignored for the remainder of the script.
     With an argument, causes the specified command to be run
     with hangups ignored. All processes executed in the
     background with & are effectively nohuped as described under
     Jobs in the COMMANDS section.

notify [job ...]
     Causes the shell to notify the user asynchronously when the
     status of the current (job not specified) or specified jobs
     changes; normally notification is presented before a prompt.
     This is automatic if the shell variable notify is set.

onintr [-] [label]
     Controls the action of the shell on interrupts. With no
     arguments, onintr restores the default action of the shell
     on interrupts, which action is to terminate shell scripts or
     return to the terminal command input level. If - is
     specified, all interrupts are ignored. If a label is given,
     the shell executes a goto label when an interrupt is
     received or a child process terminates because it was
     interrupted.

     If the shell is running in the background and interrupts are
     being ignored, onintr has no effect; interrupts continue to
     be ignored by the shell and all invoked commands.

popd [+n]
     Pops the directory stack, returning to the new top
     directory. With an argument, discards the nth entry in the
     stack. The elements of the directory stack are numbered

from 0 starting at the top. A synonym for popd, called rd, is provided for historical reasons. Its use is not recommended because it is not part of the standard BSD csh and may not be supported in future releases.

pushd [name] [+n]
   With no arguments, pushd exchanges the top two elements of the directory stack. Given a name argument, pushd changes to the new directory (using cd) and pushes the old current working directory (as in csw) onto the directory stack. With a numeric argument, pushd rotates the nth argument of the directory stack around to be the top element and changes to that directory. The members of the directory stack are numbered from the top starting at 0. A synonym for pushd, called gd, is provided for historical reasons. Its use is not recommended since it is not part of the standard BSD csh and may not be supported in future releases.

rehash
   Causes the internal hash table of the contents of the directories in the path variable to be recomputed. This is needed if new commands are added to directories in the path while you are logged in. This should only be necessary if you add commands to one of your own directories or if a systems programmer changes the contents of one of the system directories.

repeat count command
   The specified command (which is subject to the same restrictions as the command in the one-line if statement above) is executed count times. I/O redirections occur exactly once, even if count is 0.

set
set name

set name=word

set name[index]=word

set name=(wordlist)
   The first form of set shows the value of all shell variables. Variables whose value is other than a single word print as a parenthesized word list. The second form sets name to the null string. The third form sets name to the single word. The fourth form sets the indexth component of name to word; this component must already exist. The final form sets name to the list of words in wordlist. In all cases the value is command and file-name expanded.

   These arguments can be repeated to set multiple values in a single set command. Note, however, that variable expansion happens for all arguments before any setting occurs.

setenv name value
   Sets the value of environment variable name to be value, a single string. The most commonly used environment variables, USER, TERM, and PATH, are automatically imported to and exported from the csh variables user, term, and path; there is no need to use setenv for these.

shift [variable]
   If no argument is given, the members of argv are shifted to the left, discarding argv[1]. An error occurs if argv is not set or has less than two strings assigned to it. When variable is specified, shift performs the same function on

the specified variable.

source [-h] name
    csh reads commands from name. source commands can be
    nested, but if nested too deeply the shell may run out of
    file descriptors. An error in a source at any level
    terminates all nested source commands. Normally, input
    during source commands is not placed on the history list.
    The -h option can be used to place commands in the history
    list without being executing them.

stop [%job ...]
    Stops the current (no argument) or specified jobs executing
    in the background.

suspend
    Causes csh to stop as if it had been sent a suspend signal.
    Since csh normally ignores suspend signals, this is the only
    way to suspend the shell. This command gives an error
    message if attempted from a login shell.

switch (string)

case str1:

  ...

breaksw

  ...

default:

  ...

breaksw

endsw
    Each case label (str1) is successively matched against the
    specified string which is first command and file name
    expanded. The form of the case labels is the Pattern
    Matching Notation with the exception that non-matching lists
    in bracket expressions are not supported (see regexp(5)).
    If none of the labels match before a default label is found,
    the execution begins after the default label. Each case
    label and the default label must appear at the beginning of
    a line. The breaksw command causes execution to continue
    after the endsw. Otherwise, control may fall through case
    labels and default labels as in C. If no label matches and
    there is no default, execution continues after the endsw.

time [command]
    When command is not specified, a summary of time used by
    this shell and its children is printed. If specified, the
    simple command is timed and a time summary as described
    under the time variable is printed. If necessary, an extra
    shell is created to print the time statistic when the
    command completes.

umask [value]
    The current file creation mask is displayed (value not
    specified) or set to the specified value. The mask is given
    in octal. Common values for the mask are 002, which gives
    all permissions to the owner and group and read and execute
    permissions to all others, or 022, which gives all
    permissions to the owner, and only read and execute

permission to the group and all others.

unalias pattern
>All aliases whose names match the specified pattern are discarded. Thus, all aliases are removed by unalias *. No error occurs if pattern does not match an existing alias.

unhash
>Use of the internal hash table to speed location of executed programs is disabled.

unset pattern
>All variables whose names match the specified pattern are removed. Thus, all variables are removed by unset *; this has noticeably undesirable side-effects. No error occurs if pattern matches nothing.

unsetenv pattern
>Removes all variables whose names match the specified pattern from the environment. See also the setenv command above and printenv(1).

wait Waits for all background jobs to terminate. If the shell is interactive, an interrupt can disrupt the wait, at which time the shell prints names and job numbers of all jobs known to be outstanding.

while (expression)

...

end While the specified expression evaluates non-zero, the commands between the while and the matching end are evaluated. break and continue can be used to terminate or continue the loop prematurely. (The while and end must appear alone on their input lines.) If the input is a terminal (i.e., not a script), prompting occurs the first time through the loop as for the foreach statement.

%job Brings the specified job into the foreground.

%job &
>Continues the specified job in the background.

@
@ name=expression

@ name[index]=expression
>The first form prints the values of all the shell variables. The second form sets the specified name to the value of expression. If the expression contains <, >, &, or |, at least this part of the expression must be placed within parentheses. The third form assigns the value of expression to the indexth argument of name. Both name and its indexth component must already exist.

>The operators *=, +=, etc., are available as in C. White space can optionally separate the name from the assignment operator. However, spaces are mandatory in separating components of expression which would otherwise be single words.

>Special postfix ++ and -- operators increment and decrement name, respectively (e.g., @ i++).

Non-Built-In Command Execution
When a command to be executed is not a built-in command, csh attempts

to execute the command via exec(2). Each word in the variable path
names a directory in which the shell attempts to find the command (if
the command does not begin with /). If neither -c nor -t is given,
the shell hashes the names into these directories into an internal table
so that an exec is attempted only in those directories where the
command might possibly reside. This greatly speeds command location
when a large number of directories are present in the search path. If
this mechanism has been turned off (via unhash), or if -c or -t was
given, or if any directory component of path does not begin with a /,
the shell concatenates the directory name and the given command name
to form a path name of a file which it then attempts to execute.

Commands placed inside parentheses are always executed in a subshell.
Thus

    (cd ; pwd)

prints the home directory then returns to the current directory upon
completion, whereas:

    cd ; pwd

remains in the home directory upon completion.

When commands are placed inside parentheses, it is usually to prevent
chdir from affecting the current shell.

If the file has execute permissions but is not an executable binary
file, it is assumed to be a script file, which is a file of data for
an interpreter that is executed as a separate process.

csh first attempts to load and execute the script file (see exec(2)).
If the first two characters of the script file are #!, exec(2) expects
an interpreter path name to follow and attempts to execute the
specified interpreter as a separate process to read the entire script
file.

If no #! interpreter is named, and there is an alias for the shell,
the words of the alias are inserted at the beginning of the argument
list to form the shell command. The first word of the alias should be
the full path name of the command to be used. Note that this is a
special, late-occurring case of alias substitution, which inserts
words into the argument list without modification.

If no #! interpreter is named and there is no shell alias, but the
first character of the file is #, the interpreter named by the $shell
variable is executed (note that this normally would be /usr/bin/csh,
unless the user has reset $shell). If $shell is not set, /usr/bin/csh
is executed.

If no !# interpreter is named, and there is no shell alias, and the
first character of the file is not #, /usr is executed to
interpret the script file.

History Substitutions
    History substitutions enable you to repeat commands, use words from
    previous commands as portions of new commands, repeat arguments of a
    previous command in the current command, and fix spelling or typing
    mistakes in an earlier command.

    History substitutions begin with an exclamation point (!).
    Substitutions can begin anywhere in the input stream, but cannot be
    nested. The exclamation point can be preceded by a backslash to
    cancel its special meaning. For convenience, an exclamation point is
    passed to the parser unchanged when it is followed by a blank, tab,
    newline, equal sign, or left parenthesis. Any input line that

contains history substitution is echoed on the terminal before it is executed for verification.

Commands input from the terminal that consist of one or more words are saved on the history list. The history substitutions reintroduce sequences of words from these saved commands into the input stream. The number of previous commands saved is controlled by the history variable. The previous command is always saved, regardless of its value. Commands are numbered sequentially from 1.

You can refer to previous events by event number (such as !10 for event 10), relative event location (such as !-2 for the second previous event), full or partial command name (such as !d for the last event using a command with initial character d), and string expression (such as !?mic? referring to an event containing the characters mic).

These forms, without further modification, simply reintroduce the words of the specified events, each separated by a single blank. As a special case, !! is a re-do; it refers to the previous command.

To select words from a command, use a colon (:) and a designator for the desired words after the event specification. The words of an input line are numbered from zero. The basic word designators are:

0   First word (i.e., the command name itself).

n   nth word.

^   First argument. (This is equivalent to 1.)

$ Last word.

a-b Range of words from a through b. Special cases are -y, an
     abbreviation for ``word 0 through word y''; and x-, which
     means ``word x up to, but not including, word $''.

*   Range from the second word through the last word.

%   Used with a search sequence to substitute the immediately
     preceding matching word.

The colon separating the command specification from the word designator can be omitted if the argument selector begins with a ^, $, *, -, or %.

After word designator can be followed by a sequence of modifiers, each preceded by a colon. The following modifiers are defined:

h   Use only the first component of a path name by removing all
     following components.

r   Use the root file name by removing any trailing suffix
     (.xxx).

e   Use the file name's trailing suffix (.xxx) by removing the
     root name.

s /l/r
     substitute the value of r for the value l in the indicated
     command.

t   Use only the final file name of a path name by removing all
     leading path name components.

&   Repeat the previous substitution.

p   Print the new command but do not execute it.

q   Quote the substituted words, preventing further
        substitutions.

x   Like q, but break into words at blanks, tabs and newlines.

g   Use a global command as a prefix to another modifier to
        cause the specified change to be made globally. All words
        in the command are changed, one change per word, and each
        string enclosed in single quotes (') or double quotes (") is
        treated as a single word.

Unless preceded by a g, the modification is applied only to the first
modifiable word. An error results if a substitution is attempted and
cannot be completed (i.e., if you ask for a substitution of !11 on a
history buffer containing only 10 commands).

The left hand side of substitutions are strings; not regular
expressions in the sense of HP-UX editors. Any character can be used
as the delimiter in place of a slash (/). Use a backslash to quote a
delimiter character if it is used in the l or r string. The character
& in the right-hand side is replaced by the text from the left. A \
also quotes &. A null l string uses the previous string either from
an l or from a contextual scan string s in !?s?. The trailing
delimiter in the substitution can be omitted if a new-line character
follows immediately, as may the trailing ? in a contextual scan.

A history reference can be given without an event specification (as in
!$). In this case, the reference is to the previous command unless a
previous history reference occurred on the same line, in which case
this form repeats the previous reference. Thus

        !?foo?^ !$

gives the first and last arguments from the command matching ?foo?.

A special abbreviation of a history reference occurs when the first
non-blank character of an input line is a circumflex (^). This is
equivalent to !:s^, providing a convenient shorthand for substitutions
on the text of the previous line. Thus ^lb^lib fixes the spelling of
lib in the previous command.

Finally, a history substitution can be enclosed within curly braces
{ } if necessary to insulate it from the characters which follow.
Thus, after

        ls -ld ~paul

one could execute !{l}a to do

        ls -ld ~paula

while !la would look for a command starting with la.

grep

grep - Search for a pattern.

---

grep(1)   grep(1)

NAME
    grep, egrep, fgrep - search a file for a pattern

SYNOPSIS

  Plain call with pattern
    grep [-E|-F] [-c|-l|-q] [-insvx] pattern [file ...]

  Call with (multiple) -e pattern
    grep [-E|-F] [-c|-l|-q] [-binsvx] -e pattern... [-e pattern] ...
        [file ...]

  Call with -f file
    grep [-E|-F] [-c|-l|-q] [-insvx] [-f pattern_file] [file ...]

  Obsolescent:
    egrep [-cefilnsv] [expression] [file ...]

    fgrep [-cefilnsvx] [strings] [file ...]

DESCRIPTION
    The grep command searches the input text files (standard input
    default) for lines matching a pattern. Normally, each line found is
    copied to the standard output. grep supports the Basic Regular
    Expression syntax (see regexp(5)). The -E option (egrep) supports
    Extended Regular Expression (ERE) syntax (see regexp(5)). The -F
    option (fgrep) searches for fixed strings using the fast Boyer-Moore
    string searching algorithm. The -E and -F options treat newlines
    embedded in the pattern as alternation characters. A null expression
    or string matches every line.

    The forms egrep and fgrep are maintained for backward compatibility.
    The use of the -E and -F options is recommended for portability.

  Options
      -E   Extended regular expressions. Each pattern
                             specified is a sequence of one or more EREs.
                             The EREs can be separated by newline
                             characters or given in separate -e expression
                             options. A pattern matches an input line if
                             any ERE in the sequence matches the contents
                             of the input line without its trailing
                             newline character. The same functionality is
                             obtained by using egrep.

      -F   Fixed strings. Each pattern specified is a
                             sequence of one or more strings. Strings can
                             be separated by newline characters or given
                             in separate -e expression options. A pattern
                             matches an input line if the line contains
                             any of the strings in the sequence. The same

functionality is obtained by using fgrep.

-b   Each line is preceded by the block number on
                    which it was found. This is useful in
                    locating disk block numbers by context.
                    Block numbers are calculated by dividing by
                    512 the number of bytes that have been read
                    from the file and rounding down the result.

-c   Only a count of matching lines is printed.

-e expression   Same as a simple expression argument, but
                    useful when the expression begins with a
                    hyphen (-). Multiple -e options can be used
                    to specify multiple patterns; an input line
                    is selected if it matches any of the
                    specified patterns.

-f pattern_file   The regular expression (grep and grep -E) or
                    strings list (grep -F) is taken from the
                    pattern_file.

-i   Ignore uppercase/lowercase distinctions
                    during comparisons.

-l   Only the names of files with matching lines
                    are listed (once), separated by newlines. If
                    standard input is searched, a path name of -
                    is listed.

-n   Each line is preceded by its relative line
                    number in the file starting at 1. The line
                    number is reset for each file searched. This
                    option is ignored if -c, -b, -l, or -q is
                    specified.

-q   (Quiet) Do not write anything to the standard
                    output, regardless of matching lines. Exit
                    with zero status upon finding the first
                    matching line. Overrides any options that
                    would produce output.

-s   Error messages produced for nonexistent or
                    unreadable files are suppressed.

-v   All lines but those matching are printed.

-x   (eXact) Matches are recognized only when the
                    entire input line matches the fixed string or
                    regular expression.

In all cases in which output is generated, the file name is output if
there is more than one input file. Care should be taken when using
the characters $, *, [, ^, |, (,), and \ in expression, because they
are also meaningful to the shell. It is safest to enclose the entire
expression argument in single quotes ('...').

EXTERNAL INFLUENCES
  Environment Variables
    LANG determines the locale to use for the locale categories when both
    LC_ALL and the corresponding environment variable (beginning with LC_)
    do not specify a locale. If LANG is not specified or is set to the
    empty string, a default of C (see lang(5)) is used.

    LC_ALL determines the locale to use to override any values for locale categories specified by the settings of LANG or any environment variables beginning with LC_.

LC_COLLATE determines the collating sequence used in evaluating regular expressions.

LC_CTYPE determines the interpretation of text as single byte and/or multi-byte characters, the classification of characters as letters, the case information for the -i option, and the characters matched by character class expressions in regular expressions.

LC_MESSAGES determines the language in which messages are displayed.

If any internationalization variable contains an invalid setting, the commands behave as if all internationalization variables are set to C. See environ(5).

International Code Set Support
Single-byte and multi-byte character code sets are supported.

RETURN VALUE
Upon completion, grep returns one of the following values:

0   One or more matches found.
1   No match found.
2   Syntax error or inaccessible file (even if matches were found).

EXAMPLES
In the Bourne shell (sh(1)) the following example searches two files, finding all lines containing occurrences of any of four strings:

```
grep -F 'if
then
else
fi' file1 file2
```

Note that the single quotes are necessary to tell grep -F when the strings have ended and the file names have begun.

For the C shell (see csh(1)) the following command can be used:

```
grep -F 'if\ then\ else\ fi' file1 file2
```

To search a file named address containing the following entries:

```
Ken    112 Warring St.  Apt. A
Judy   387 Bowditch  Apt. 12
Ann    429 Sixth St.
```

the command:

```
grep Judy address
```

prints:

```
Judy   387 Bowditch  Apt. 12
```

To search a file for lines that contain either a Dec or Nov, use either of the following commands:

```
grep -E '[Dd]ec|[Nn]ov' file
```

```
egrep -i 'dec|nov' file
```

Search all files in the current directory for the string xyz:

```
grep xyz *
```

Search all files in the current directory subtree for the string xyz,
and ensure that no error occurs due to file name expansion exceeding
system argument list limits:

```
find . -type f -print |xargs grep xyz
```

The previous example does not print the name of files where string xyz
appears. To force grep to print file names, add a second argument to
the grep command portion of the command line:

```
find . -type f -print |xargs grep xyz /dev/null
```

In this form, the first file name is that produced by find, and the
second file name is the null file.

WARNINGS
   (XPG4 only.) If the -q option is specified, the exit status will be
   zero if an input line is selected, even if an error was detected.
   Otherwise, default actions will be performed.

SEE ALSO
   sed(1), sh(1), regcomp(3C), environ(5), lang(5), regexp(5).

STANDARDS CONFORMANCE
   grep: SVID2, SVID3, XPG2, XPG3, XPG4, POSIX.2

   egrep: SVID2, SVID3, XPG2, XPG3, XPG4, POSIX.2

   fgrep: SVID2, SVID3, XPG2, XPG3, XPG4, POSIX.2
```
```

sh-posix

sh-posix - POSIX conformant command shell.

---

sh-posix(1)   sh-posix(1)

NAME
     sh, rsh - standard and restricted POSIX.2-conformant command shells

SYNOPSIS

     sh [{-|+}aefhikmnprstuvx] [{-|+}o option]... [-c string] arg]...

     rsh [{-|+}aefhikmnprstuvx] [{-|+}o option]... [-c string] [arg]...

Remarks
     This shell is intended to conform to the shell specification of the
     POSIX.2 Shell and Utility standards. Check any standards conformance
     documents shipped with your system for information on the conformance
     of this shell to any other standards.

List of Subheadings in DESCRIPTION

     Shell Invocation   Tilde Substitution   Environment
     Options   Command Substitution   Functions
     rsh Restrictions   Parameter Substitution   Jobs
     Definitions   Blank Interpretation   Signals
     Commands   File Name Generation   Execution
     Simple Commands   Quoting   Command Reentry
     Compound Commands   Arithmetic Evaluation   Command Line Editing
     Special Commands   Prompting   emacs Editing Mode
     Comments   Conditional Expressions vi Editing Mode
     Aliasing   Input/Output

DESCRIPTION
     sh is a command programming language that executes commands read from
     a terminal or a file.

     rsh is a restricted version of sh. See the "rsh Restrictions"
     subsection below.

Shell Invocation
     If the shell is invoked by an exec*() system call and the first
     character of argument zero (shell parameter 0) is dash (-), the shell
     is assumed to be a login shell and commands are read first from
     /etc/profile, then from either .profile in the current directory or
     $HOME/.profile if either file exists, and finally from the file named
     by performing parameter substitution on the value of the environment
     parameter ENV, if the file exists. If the -s option is not present
     and an arg is, a path search is performed on the first arg to
     determine the name of the script to execute. When running sh with
     arg, the script arg must have read permission and any setuid and
     setgid settings will be ignored. Commands are read as described
     below.

     Shell output, except for the output of some of the commands listed in
     the "Special Commands" subsection, is written to standard error (file

descriptor 2).

Options
   The following options are interpreted by the shell when it is invoked.

   -c string   Read commands from string.

   -i   If -i is present or if the shell input and output are
                    attached to a terminal (as reported by tty()), the
                    shell is interactive. In this case SIGTERM is ignored
                    (so that kill 0 does not kill an interactive shell) and
                    SIGINT is caught and ignored (so that wait is
                    interruptible). In all cases, SIGQUIT is ignored by
                    the shell. See signal(5).

   -r   The shell is a restricted shell.

   -s   If -s is present or if no arguments remain, commands
                    are read from the standard input.

   The remaining options and arguments are described under the set
   command in the "Special Commands" subsection.

rsh Restrictions
   rsh is used to set up login names and execution environments where
   capabilities are more controlled than those of the standard shell.
   The actions of rsh are identical to those of sh, except that the
   following are forbidden:

        - Changing directory (see the cd special command and cd(1))
        - Setting the value of SHELL, ENV, or PATH
        - Specifying path or command names containing /
        - Redirecting output (>, >|, <>, and >>)

   The restrictions above are enforced after the .profile and ENV files
   are interpreted.

   When a command to be executed is found to be a shell procedure, rsh
   invokes sh to execute it. Thus, the end-user is provided with shell
   procedures accessible to the full power of the standard shell, while
   being restricted to a limited menu of commands. This scheme assumes
   that the end-user does not have write and execute permissions in the
   same directory.

   These rules effectively give the writer of the .profile file complete
   control over user actions, by performing guaranteed set-up actions and
   leaving the user in an appropriate directory (probably not the login
   directory).

   The system administrator often sets up a directory of commands
   (usually /usr/rbin) that can be safely invoked by rsh. HP-UX systems
   provide a restricted editor red (see ed(1)), suitable for restricted
   users.

Definitions
   metacharacter   One of the following characters:

                      ; & ( ) | < > newline space tab

   blank   A tab or a space.

   identifier   A sequence of letters, digits, or underscores
                      starting with a letter or underscore. Identifiers
                      are used as names for functions and named
                      parameters.

word
: A sequence of characters separated by one or more nonquoted metacharacters.

command
: A sequence of characters in the syntax of the shell language. The shell reads each command and carries out the desired action, either directly or by invoking separate utilities.

special command
: A command that is carried out by the shell without creating a separate process. Except for documented side effects, most special commands can be implemented as separate utilities.

\#
: Comment delimiter. A word beginning with # and all following characters up to a newline are ignored.

parameter
: An identifier, a decimal number, or one of the characters !, #, $, *, -, ?, @, and _. See the "Parameter Substitution" subsection.

named parameter
: A parameter that can be assigned a value. See the "Parameter Substitution" subsection.

variable
: A parameter.

environment variable
: A parameter that is known outside the local shell, usually by means of the export special command.

Commands

A command can be a simple command that executes an executable file, a special command that executes within the shell, or a compound command that provides flow of control for groups of simple, special, and compound commands.

Simple Commands

A simple command is a sequence of blank-separated words that may be preceded by a parameter assignment list. (See the "Environment" subsection). The first word specifies the name of the command to be executed. Except as specified below, the remaining words are passed as arguments to the invoked command. The command name is passed as argument 0 (see exec(2)). The value of a simple-command is its exit status if it terminates normally, or 128+errorstatus if it terminates abnormally (see signal(5) for a list of errorstatus values).

A pipeline is a sequence of one or more commands separated by a bar (|) and optionally preceded by an exclamation mark (!). The standard output of each command but the last is connected by a pipe (see pipe(2)) to the standard input of the next command. Each command is run as a separate process; the shell waits for the last command to terminate. If ! does not precede the pipeline, the exit status of the pipeline is the exit status of the last command in the pipeline. Otherwise, the exit status of the pipeline is the logical negation of the exit status of the last command in the pipeline.

A list is a sequence of one or more pipelines separated by ;, &, &&, or ||, and optionally terminated by ;, &, or |&.

;
: Causes sequential execution of the preceding pipeline. An arbitrary number of newlines can appear in a list, instead of semicolons, to delimit commands.

&
: Causes asynchronous execution of the preceding pipeline (that is, the shell does not wait for that pipeline to

finish).

| Causes asynchronous execution of the preceding command or
pipeline with a two-way pipe established to the parent
shell. The standard input and output of the spawned command
can be written to and read from by the parent shell using
the -p option of the special commands read and print.

&&   Causes the list following it to be executed only if the
preceding pipeline returns a zero value.

|| Causes the list following it to be executed only if the
preceding pipeline returns a nonzero value.

Of these five symbols, ;, &, and |& have equal precedence, which is
lower than that of && and ||. The symbols && and || also have equal
precedence.

Compound Commands
Unless otherwise stated, the value returned by a compound command is
that of the last simple command executed in the compound command. The
; segment separator can be replaced by one or more newlines.

The following keywords are recognized only as the first word of a
command and when not quoted:

!	}	elif	for	then
[[	case	else	function	time
]]	do	esac	if	until
{	done	fi	select	while

A compound command is one of the following.

case word in [[;] [(] pattern [| pattern]...) list ;;]... ; esac

> Execute the list associated with the first pattern that matches
> word. The form of the patterns is identical to that used for
> file name generation (see the "File Name Generation" subsection).
> The ;; case terminator cannot be replaced by newlines.

for identifier [in word ...] ; do list ; done

> Set identifier to each word in sequence and execute the do list.
> If in word ... is omitted, set identifier to each set positional
> parameter instead. See the "Parameter Substitution" subsection.
> Execution ends when there are no more positional parameters or
> words in the list.

function identifier { list ; }
identifier () { list ; }

> Define a function named by identifier. A function is called by
> executing its identifier as a command. The body of the function
> is the list of commands between { and }. See the "Functions"
> subsection.

if list ; then list ; [elif list ; then list ;]... [else list ;] fi

> Execute the if list and, if its exit status is zero, execute the
> first then list. Otherwise, execute the elif list (if any) and,
> if its exit status is zero, execute the next then list. Failing
> that, execute the else list (if any). If no else list or then
> list is executed, if returns a zero exit status.

select identifier [in word ...] ; do list ; done

Print the set of words on standard error (file descriptor 2),
each preceded by a number. If in word ... is omitted, print the
positional parameters instead (see the "Parameter Substitution"
subsection). Print the PS3 prompt and read a line from standard
input into the parameter REPLY. If this line consists of the
number of one of the listed words, set identifier to the
corresponding word, execute list, and repeat the PS3 prompt. If
the line is empty, print the selection list again, and repeat the
PS3 prompt. Otherwise, set identifier to null, execute list, and
repeat the PS3 prompt. The select loop repeats until a break
special command or end-of-file is encountered.

time pipeline

Execute the pipeline and print the elapsed time, the user time,
and the system time on standard error. See also time(1).

until list ; do list ; done

Execute the until list. If the exit status of the last command
in the list is nonzero, execute the do list and execute the until
list again. When the exit status of the last command in the
until list is zero, terminate the loop. If no commands in the do
list are executed, until returns a zero exit status.

while list ; do list ; done

Execute the while list. If the exit status of the last command
in the list is zero, execute the do list and execute the while
list again. When the exit status of the last command in the
while list is nonzero, terminate the loop. If no commands in the
do list are executed, while returns a nonzero exit status.

(list)

Execute list in a separate environment. If two adjacent open
parentheses are needed for nesting, a space must be inserted
between them to avoid arithmetic evaluation.

{ list ; }

Execute list, but not in a separate environment. Note that { is
a keyword and requires a trailing blank to be recognized.

[[expression]]

Evaluate expression and return a zero exit status when expression
is true. See the "Conditional Expressions" subsection for a
description of expression. Note that [[and]] are keywords and
require blanks between them and expression.

Special Commands

Special commands are simple commands that are executed in the shell
process. They permit input/output redirection. Unless otherwise
indicated, file descriptor 1 (standard output) is the default output
location and the exit status, when there are no syntax errors, is
zero.

Commands that are marked with * or ** are treated specially in the
following ways:

1. Variable assignment lists preceding the command remain in
   effect when the command completes.
2. I/O redirections are processed after variable assignments.
3. Errors cause a script that contains them to abort.
4. Words following a command preceded by ** that are in the

format of a variable assignment are expanded with the same
rules as a variable assignment. This means that tilde
substitution is performed after the = sign and word-splitting
and file-name generation are not performed.

* : [arg]...

(colon) Only expand parameters. A zero exit status is returned.

* . file [arg]...

(period) Read and execute commands from file and return. The
commands are executed in the current shell environment. The
search path specified by PATH is used to find the directory
containing file. If any arguments arg are given, they become the
positional parameters. Otherwise, the positional parameters are
unchanged. The exit status is the exit status of the last
command executed.

** alias [-tx] [name[=value]]...

With name=value specified, define name as an alias and assign it
the value value. A trailing space in value causes the next word
to be checked for alias substitution.

With name=value omitted, print the list of aliases in the form
name=value on standard output.

With name specified without =value, print the specified alias.

With -t, set tracked aliases. The value of a tracked alias is
the full path name corresponding to the given name. The value of
a tracked alias becomes undefined when the value of PATH is
reset, but the alias remains tracked. With name=value omitted,
print the list of tracked aliases in the form name=pathname on
standard output.

With -x, set exported aliases. An exported alias is defined
across subshell environments. With name=value omitted, print the
list of exported aliases in the form name=value on standard
output.

Alias returns true unless a name is given for which no alias has
been defined.

bg [job]...

Put the specified jobs into the background. The current job is
put in the background if job is unspecified. See the "Jobs"
subsection for a description of the format of job.

* break [n]

Exit from the enclosing for, select, until, or while loop, if
any. If n is specified, exit from n levels.

cd [-L|-P] [arg]
cd old new

In the first form, change the current working directory (PWD) to
arg. If arg is -, the directory is changed to the previous
directory (OLDPWD).

With -L (default), preserve logical naming when treating symbolic
links. cd -L .. moves the current directory one path component
closer to the root directory.

With -P, preserve the physical path when treating symbolic links.
cd -P .. changes the working directory to the actual parent
directory of the current directory.

The shell parameter HOME is the default arg. The parameter PWD
is set to the current directory.

The shell parameter CDPATH defines the search path for the
directory containing arg. Alternative directory names are
separated by a colon (:). If CDPATH is null or undefined, the
default value is the current directory. Note that the current
directory is specified by a null path name, which can appear
immediately after the equal sign or between the colon delimiters
anywhere else in the path list. If arg begins with a /, the
search path is not used. Otherwise, each directory in the path
is searched for arg. See also cd(1).

The second form of cd substitutes the string new for the string
old in the current directory name, PWD, and tries to change to
this new directory.

command [arg]...

Treat arg as a command, but disable function lookup on arg. See
command(1) for usage and description.

* continue [n]

Resume the next iteration of the enclosing for, select, until, or
while loop. If n is specified, resume at the nth enclosing loop.

echo [arg]...

Print arg on standard output. See echo(1) for usage and
description. See also the print special command.

* eval [arg]...

Read the arguments as input to the shell and execute the
resulting commands. Allows parameter substitution for keywords
and characters that would otherwise be unrecognized in the
resulting commands.

* exec [arg]...

Parameter assignments remain in effect after the command
completes. If arg is given, execute the command specified by the
arguments in place of this shell without creating a new process.
Input/output arguments may appear and affect the current process.
If no arguments are given, modify file descriptors as prescribed
by the input/output redirection list. In this case, any file
descriptor numbers greater than 2 that are opened with this
mechanism are closed when another program is invoked.

* exit [n]

Exit from the shell with the exit status specified by n. If n is
omitted, the exit status is that of the last command executed.
An end-of-file also causes the shell to exit, except when a shell
has the ignoreeof option set. (See the set special command.)

** export [name[=value]]...
** export -p

Mark the given variable names for automatic export to the

environment of subsequently executed commands. Optionally,
assign values to the variables.

With -p, write the names and values of all exported variables to
standard output, in a format with the proper use of quoting, so
that it is suitable for re-input to the shell as commands that
achieve the same exporting results.

```
fc [-r] [-e ename] [first [last]]
fc -l [-nr] [first [last]]
fc -s [old=new] [first]
fc -e - [old=new] [command]
```

List, or edit and reexecute, commands previously entered to an
interactive shell. A range of commands from first to last is
selected from the last HISTSIZE commands typed at the terminal.
The arguments first and last can be specified as a number or
string. A given string is used to locate the most recent
command. A negative number is used to offset the current command
number.

With -l, list the commands on standard output. Without -l,
invoke the editor program ename on a file containing these
keyboard commands. If ename is not supplied, the value of the
parameter FCEDIT (default /usr/bin/ed) is used as the editor.
Once editing has ended, the commands (if any) are executed. If
last is omitted, only the command specified by first is used. If
first is not specified, the default is the previous command for
editing and -16 for listing.

With -r, reverse the order of the commands.

With -n, suppress command numbers when listing.

With -s, reexecute the command without invoking an editor.

The old=new argument replaces the first occurrence of string old
in the command to be reexecuted by the string new.

```
fg [job]...
```

Bring each job into the foreground in the order specified. If no
job is specified, bring the current job into the foreground. See
the "Jobs" subsection for a description of the format of job.

```
getopts optstring name [arg]...
```

Parse the argument list, or the positional parameters if no
arguments, for valid options. On each execution, return the next
option in name. See getopts(1) for usage and description.

An option begins with a + or a -. An argument not beginning with
+ or -, or the argument --, ends the options. optstring contains
the letters that getopts recognizes. If a letter is followed by
a :, that option is expected to have an argument. The options
can be separated from the argument by blanks.

For an option specified as -letter, name is set to letter. For
an option specified as +letter, name is set to +letter. The
index of the next arg is stored in OPTIND. The option argument,
if any, is stored in OPTARG. If no option argument is found, or
the option found does not take an argument, OPTARG is unset.

A leading : in optstring causes getopts to store the letter of an
invalid option in OPTARG, and to set name to ? for an unknown
option and to : when a required option argument is missing.

Otherwise, getopts prints an error message. The exit status is nonzero when there are no more options.

hash [utility]...
hash -r

    Affect the way the current shell environment remembers the locations of utilities. With utility, add utility locations to a list of remembered locations. With no arguments, print the contents of the list. With -r, forget all previously remembered utility locations.

jobs [-lnp] [job]...

    List information about each given job, or all active jobs if job is not specified. With -l, list process IDs in addition to the normal information. With -n, display only jobs that have stopped or exited since last notified. With -p, list only the process group. See the "Jobs" subsection for a description of the format of job.

kill [-s signal] process ...
kill -l
kill [-signal] process ...

    Send either signal 15 (SIGTERM, terminate) or the specified signal to the specified jobs or processes. See kill(1) for usage and description.

    With -l, list the signal names and numbers.

let arg ...
((arg ...))

    Evaluate each arg as a separate arithmetic expression. See the "Arithmetic Evaluation" subsection for a description of arithmetic expression evaluation. The exit status is 0 if the value of the last expression is nonzero, and 1 otherwise.

* newgrp [-] [group]

    Replace the current shell with a new one having group as the user's group. The default group is the user's login group. With -, the user's .profile and $ENV files are also executed. See newgrp(1) for usage and description. Equivalent to exec newgrp arg ....

print [-nprRsu[n]] [arg]...

    The shell output mechanism. With no options or with option - or --, print the arguments on standard output as described in echo(1). See also printf(1).

    With -n, do not add a newline character to the output.

    With -p, write the arguments onto the pipe of the process spawned with |& instead of standard output.

    With -R or -r (raw mode), ignore the escape conventions of echo. With -R, print all subsequent arguments and options other than -n.

    With -s, write the arguments into the history file instead of to standard output.

    With -u, specify a one-digit file descriptor unit number n on

which the output will be placed. The default is 1 (standard
output).

pwd [-L|-P]

Print the name of the current working directory (equivalent to
print -r - $PWD). With -L (the default), preserve the logical
meaning of the current directory. With -P, preserve the physical
meaning of the current directory if it is a symbolic link. See
also the cd special command, cd(1), ln(1), and pwd(1).

read [-prsu[n]] [name?prompt] [name]...

The shell input mechanism. Read one line (by default, from
standard input) and break it up into words using the characters
in IFS as separators. The first word is assigned to the first
name, the second word to the second name, and so on; the
remaining words are assigned to the last name. See also read(1).
The return code is 0, unless an end-of-file is encountered.

With -p, take the input line from the input pipe of a process
spawned by the shell using |&. An end-of-file with -p causes
cleanup for this process so that another process can be spawned.

With -r (raw mode), a \ at the end of a line does not signify
line continuation.

With -s, save the input as a command in the history file.

With -u, specify a one-digit file descriptor unit to read from.
The file descriptor can be opened with the exec special command.
The default value of n is 0 (standard input). If name is
omitted, REPLY is used as the default name.

If the first argument contains a ?, the remainder of the argument
is used as a prompt when the shell is interactive.

If the given file descriptor is open for writing and is a
terminal device, the prompt is placed on that unit. Otherwise,
the prompt is issued on file descriptor 2 (standard error).

** readonly [name[=value]]...
** readonly -p

Mark the given names read only. These names cannot be changed by
subsequent assignment.

With -p, write the names and values of all read-only variables to
standard output in a format with the proper use of quoting so
that it is suitable for re-input to the shell as commands that
achieve the same attribute-setting results.

* return [n]

Cause a shell function to return to the invoking script with the
return status specified by n. If n is omitted, the return status
is that of the last command executed. Only the low 8 bits of n
(decimal 0 to 255) are passed back to the caller. If return is
invoked while not in a function or a . script (see the . special
command), it has the same effect as an exit command.

set [{-|+}abCefhkmnopstuvx] [{-|+}o option]... [{-|+}A name] [arg]...

Set (-) or clear (+) execution options or perform array
assignments (-A, +A). All options except -A and +A can be
supplied in a shell invocation (see the SYNOPSIS section and the

"Shell Invocation" subsection).

Using + instead of - before an option causes the option to be turned off. These options can also be used when invoking the shell. The current list of set single-letter options is contained in the shell variable -. It can be examined with the command echo $-.

The - and + options can be intermixed in the same command, except that there can be only one -A or +A option.

Unless -A or +A is specified, the remaining arg arguments are assigned consecutively to the positional parameters 1, 2, ...

The set command with neither arguments nor options displays the names and values of all shell parameters on standard output. See also env(1).

The options are defined as follows.

-A   Array assignment. Unset the variable name and assign values sequentially from the list arg. With +A, do not unset the variable name first.

-a   Automatically export subsequently defined parameters.

-b   Cause the shell to notify the user asynchronously of background jobs as they are completed. When the shell notifies the user that a job has been completed, it can remove the job's process ID from the list of those known in the current shell execution environment.

-C   Prevent redirection > from truncating existing files. Requires >| to truncate a file when turned on.

-e   Execute the ERR trap, if set, and exit if a command has a nonzero exit status, and is not part of the compound list following a if, until, or while keyword, and is not part of an AND or OR list, and is not a pipeline preceded by the ! reserved word. This mode is disabled while reading profiles.

-f   Disable file name generation.

-h   Specify that each command whose name is an identifier becomes a tracked alias when first encountered.

-k   Place all parameter assignment arguments (not just those that precede the command name) into the environment for a command.

-m   Run background jobs in a separate process group and print a line upon completion. The exit status of background jobs is reported in a completion message. This option is turned on automatically for interactive shells.

-n   Read commands and check them for syntax errors, but do not execute them. The -n option is ignored for interactive shells.

-o   Set an option argument from the following list. Repeat the -o option to specify additional option arguments.

    allexport   Same as -a.
    bgnice   Run all background jobs at a lower priority.

errexit	Same as -e.
emacs	Use a emacs-style inline editor for command entry.
gmacs	Use a gmacs-style inline editor for command entry.
ignoreeof	Do not exit from the shell on end-of-file (eof as defined by stty; default is ^D). The exit special command must be used.
keyword	Same as -k.
markdirs	Append a trailing / to all directory names resulting from file name generation.
monitor	Same as -m.
noclobber	Same as -C.
noexec	Same as -n.
noglob	Same as -f.
nolog	Do not save function definitions in history file.
notify	Same as -b.
nounset	Same as -u.
privileged	Same as -p.
verbose	Same as -v.
trackall	Same as -h.
vi	Use a vi-style inline editor for command entry.
viraw	Process each character as it is typed in vi mode.
xtrace	Same as -x.

-p   Disable processing of the $HOME/.profile file and uses the file /etc/suid_profile instead of the ENV file. This mode is on whenever the effective user ID (group ID) is not equal to the real user ID (group ID). Turning this off causes the effective user ID and group ID to be set to the real user ID and group ID.

-s   Sort the positional parameters.

-t   Exit after reading and executing one command.

-u   Treat unset parameters as an error when substituting.

-v   Print shell input lines as they are read.

-x   Print commands and their arguments as they are executed.

-    Turn off -x and -v options and stop examining arguments for options.

--   Do not change any of the options; useful in setting parameter 1 to a value beginning with -. If no arguments follow this option, the positional parameters are unset.

* shift [n]

Rename the positional parameters from n+1 ... to 1 .... The default value of n is 1. n can be any arithmetic expression that evaluates to a nonnegative number less than or equal to $#.

test [expr]

Evaluate conditional expression expr. See test(1) for usage and description. The arithmetic comparison operators are not restricted to integers. They allow any arithmetic expression. The following additional primitive expressions are allowed:

```
            -L file                 True if file is a symbolic link.
            -e file                 True if file exists.
            file1 -nt file2         True if file1 is newer than file2.
            file1 -ot file2         True if file1 is older than file2.
            file1 -ef file2         True if file1 has the same device and i-node
                                    number as file2.
```

* times

    Print the accumulated user and system times for the shell and for
    processes run from the shell.

* trap [arg] [sig]...

    Set arg as a command that is read and executed when the shell
    receives a sig signal. (Note that arg is scanned once when the
    trap is set and once when the trap is taken.) Each sig can be
    given as the number or name of a signal. Letter case is ignored.
    For example, 3, QUIT, quit, and SIGQUIT all specify the same
    signal. Use kill -l to get a list of signals.

    Trap commands are executed in signal number order. Any attempt
    to set a trap on a signal that was ignored upon entering the
    current shell is ineffective.

    If arg is - (or if arg is omitted and the first sig is numeric),
    reset all traps for each sig to their original values.

    If arg is the null string ('' or ""), each sig is ignored by the
    shell and by the commands it invokes.

    If sig is DEBUG, then arg is executed after each command. If sig
    is ERR, arg is executed whenever a command has a nonzero exit
    code. If sig is 0 or EXIT and the trap statement is executed
    inside the body of a function, the command arg is executed after
    the function completes. If sig is 0 or EXIT for a trap set
    outside any function, the command arg is executed on exit from
    the shell.

    With no arguments, print a list of commands associated with each
    signal name.

** typeset [{-|+}LRZfilrtux[n]] [name[=value]]...
** name=value [name=value]...

    Assign types and a value to a local named parameter name. See
    also the export special command. Parameter assignments remain in
    effect after the command completes. When invoked inside a
    function, create a new instance of the parameter name. The
    parameter value and type are restored when the function
    completes.

    The following list of attributes can be specified. Use + instead
    of - to turn the options off.

        -L Left justify and remove leading blanks from value. If n is
            nonzero, it defines the width of the field; otherwise, it is
            determined by the width of the value of first assignment.
            When name is assigned, the value is filled on the right with
            blanks or truncated, if necessary, to fit into the field.
            Leading zeros are removed if the -Z option is also set. The
            -R option is turned off. Flagged as leftjust n.

        -R Right justify and fill with leading blanks. If n is

nonzero, it defines the width of the field; otherwise, it is determined by the width of the value of first assignment. The field is left-filled with blanks or truncated from the end if the parameter is reassigned. The -L option is turned off. Flagged as rightjust n.

-Z   Right justify and fill with leading zeros if the first nonblank character is a digit and the -L option has not been set. If n is nonzero it defines the width of the field; otherwise, it is determined by the width of the value of first assignment. Flagged as zerofill n plus the flag for -L or -R.

-f   Cause name to refer to function names rather than parameter names. No assignments can be made to the name declared with the typeset statement. The only other valid options are -t (which turns on execution tracing for this function) and -x (which allows the function to remain in effect across shell procedures executed in the same process environment). Flagged as function.

-i   Parameter is an integer. This makes arithmetic faster. If n is nonzero it defines the output arithmetic base; otherwise, the first assignment determines the output base. Flagged as integer [base n].

-l   Convert all uppercase characters to lowercase. The uppercase -u option is turned off. Flagged as lowercase.

-r   Mark any given name as "read only". The name cannot be changed by subsequent assignment. Flagged as readonly.

-t   Tag the named parameters. Tags are user-definable and have no special meaning to the shell. Flagged as tagged.

-u   Convert all lowercase characters to uppercase characters. The lowercase -l option is turned off. Flagged as uppercase.

-x   Mark any given name for automatic export to the environment of subsequently executed commands. Flagged as export.

typeset alone displays a list of parameter names, prefixed by any flags specified above.

typeset - displays the parameter names followed by their values. Specify one or more of the option letters to restrict the list. Some options are incompatible with others.

typeset + displays the parameter names alone. Specify one or more of the option letters to restrict the list. Some options are incompatible with others.

ulimit [-HSacdfnst] [limit]

Set or display a resource limit. The limit for a specified resource is set when limit is specified. The value of limit can be a number in the unit specified with each resource, or the keyword unlimited.

The -H and -S flags specify whether the hard limit or the soft limit is set for the given resource. A hard limit cannot be increased once it is set. A soft limit can be increased up to the hard limit. If neither -H nor -S is specified, the limit applies to both. The current resource limit is printed when limit is omitted. In this case, the soft limit is printed unless

-H is specified. When more than one resource is specified, the
limit name and unit are printed before the value.

If no option is given, -f is assumed.

-a   List all of the current resource limits.
-c   The number of 512-byte blocks in the size of core dumps.
-d   The number of kilobytes in the size of the data area.
-f   The number of 512-byte blocks in files written by child
     processes (files of any size can be read).
-n   The number of file descriptors.
-s   The number of kilobytes in the size of the stack area.
-t   The number of seconds to be used by each process.

umask [-S] [mask]

Set the user file-creation mask mask. mask can be either an
octal number or a symbolic value as described in umask(1). A
symbolic value shows permissions that are unmasked. An octal
value shows permissions that are masked off.

Without mask , print the current value of the mask. With -S,
print the value in symbolic format. Without -S, print the value
as an octal number. The output from either form can be used as
the mask of a subsequent invocation of umask.

unalias name ...
unalias -a

Remove each name from the alias list. With -a, remove all alias
definitions from the current shell execution environment.

unset [-fv] name ...

Remove the named shell parameters from the parameter list. Their
values and attributes are erased. Read-only variables cannot be
unset. With -f, names refer to function names. With -v, names
refer to variable names. Unsetting _, ERRNO, LINENO, MAILCHECK,
OPTARG, OPTIND, RANDOM, SECONDS, and TMOUT removes their special
meaning, even if they are subsequently assigned to.

* wait [job]

Wait for the specified job to terminate or stop, and report its
status. This status becomes the return code for the wait
command. Without job , wait for all currently active child
processes to terminate or stop. The termination status returned
is that of the last process. See the "Jobs" subsection for a
description of the format of job.

whence [-pv] name ...

For each name, indicate how it would be interpreted if used as a
command name. With -v, produce a more verbose report. With -p
do a path search for name, disregarding any use as an alias, a
function, or a reserved word.

Comments
A word beginning with # causes that word and all the following
characters up to a newline to be ignored.

Aliasing
The first word of each command is replaced by the text of an alias, if
an alias for this word has been defined. An alias name consists of
any number of characters excluding metacharacters, quoting characters,

file expansion characters, parameter and command substitution
characters, and =. The replacement string can contain any valid shell
script, including the metacharacters listed above. The first word of
each command in the replaced text, other than any that are in the
process of being replaced, will be tested for additional aliases. If
the last character of the alias value is a blank, the word following
the alias is also checked for alias substitution. Aliases can be used
to redefine special commands, but cannot be used to redefine the
keywords listed in the "Compound Commands" subsection. Aliases can be
created, listed, and exported with the alias command and can be
removed with the unalias command. Exported aliases remain in effect
for subshells but must be reinitialized for separate invocations of
the shell (see the "Shell Invocation" subsection).

Aliasing is performed when scripts are read, not while they are
executed. Therefore, for it to take effect, an alias must be executed
before the command referring to the alias is read.

Aliases are frequently used as a shorthand for full path names. An
option to the aliasing facility allows the value of the alias to be
automatically set to the full path name of the corresponding command.
These aliases are called tracked aliases. The value of a tracked
alias is defined the first time the identifier is read and becomes
undefined each time the PATH variable is reset. These aliases remain
tracked so that the next reference will redefine the value. Several
tracked aliases are compiled into the shell. The -h option of the set
command converts each command name that is an identifier into a
tracked alias.

The following exported aliases are compiled into the shell but can be
unset or redefined:

```
autoload='typeset -fu'
command='command '
functions='typeset -f'
history='fc -l'
integer='typeset -i'
local=typeset
nohup='nohup '
r='fc -e -'
stop='kill -STOP'
suspend='kill -STOP $$'
type='whence -v'
```

Tilde Substitution
    After alias substitution is performed, each word is checked to see if
    it begins with an unquoted tilde (~). If it does, the word up to a /
    is checked to see if it matches a user name in the /etc/passwd file.
    If a match is found, the ~ and the matched login name are replaced by
    the login directory of the matched user. If no match is found, the
    original text is left unchanged. A ~ alone or before a / is replaced
    by the value of the HOME parameter. A ~ followed by a + or - is
    replaced by the value of the parameter PWD and OLDPWD, respectively.
    In addition, tilde substitution is attempted when the value of a
    parameter assignment begins with a ~.

Command Substitution
    The standard output from a command enclosed in parenthesis preceded by
    a dollar sign ($(...)) or a pair of grave accents (`...`) can be used
    as part or all of a word; trailing newlines are removed. In the
    second (archaic) form, the string between the accents is processed for
    special quoting characters before the command is executed. See the
    "Quoting" subsection. The command substitution $(cat file) can be
    replaced by the equivalent but faster $(<file). Command substitution
    of most special commands that do not perform input/output redirection
    are carried out without creating a separate process.

An arithmetic expression enclosed in double parenthesis preceded by a dollar sign ($((...))) is replaced by the value of the arithmetic expression within the double parenthesis. See the "Arithmetic Evaluation" subsection for a description of arithmetic expressions.

sed

sed - Edit files according to a script.

---

sed(1)   sed(1)

NAME
      sed - stream text editor

SYNOPSIS

      sed [-n] script [file ...]

      sed [-n] [-e script] ... [-f script_file] ... [file ...]

DESCRIPTION
      sed copies the named text files (standard input default) to the
      standard output, edited according to a script containing up to 100
      commands. Only complete input lines are processed. Any input text at
      the end of a file that is not terminated by a new-line character is
      ignored.

   Options
      sed recognizes the following options:

           -f script_file
                     Take script from file script_file.

           -e script   Edit according to script. If there is just one -e
                       option and no -f options, the flag -e can be omitted.

           -n   Suppress the default output.

      sed interprets all -escript and -fscript_file arguments in the order
      given. Use caution, if mixing -e and -f options, to avoid
      unpredictable or incorrect results.

   Command Scripts
      A script consists of editor commands, one per line, of the following
      form:

           [address [, address]] function [arguments]

      In normal operation, sed cyclically copies a line of input into a
      pattern space (unless there is something left after a D command),
      applies in sequence all commands whose addresses select that pattern
      space, and, at the end of the script, copies the pattern space to the
      standard output (except under -n) and deletes the pattern space.

      Some of the commands use a hold space to save all or part of the
      pattern space for subsequent retrieval.

   Command Addresses
      An address is either a decimal number that counts input lines
      cumulatively across files, a $ which addresses the last line of input,
      or a context address; that is, a /regular expression/ in the style of

ed(1) modified thus:

- In a context address, the construction \?regular expression?, where ? is any character, is identical to /regular expression/. Note that in the context address \xabc\xdefx, the second x stands for itself, so that the regular expression is abcxdef.

- The escape sequence \n matches a new-line character embedded in the pattern space.

- A period (.) matches any character except the terminal new-line of the pattern space.

- A command line with no addresses selects every pattern space.

- A command line with one address selects each pattern space that matches the address.

- A command line with two addresses selects the inclusive range from the first pattern space that matches the first address through the next pattern space that matches the second (if the second address is a number less than or equal to the line number first selected, only one line is selected). Thereafter the process is repeated, looking again for the first address.

sed supports Basic Regular Expression syntax (see regexp(5)).

Editing commands can also be applied to only non-selected pattern spaces by use of the negation function ! (described below).

Command Functions
In the following list of functions, the maximum number of permissible addresses for each function is indicated in parentheses. Other function elements are interpreted as follows:

text   One or more lines, all but the last of which end with \ to hide the new-line. Backslashes in text are treated like backslashes in the replacement string of an s command, and can be used to protect initial blanks and tabs against the stripping that is done on every script line.

rfile   Must terminate the command line, and must be preceded by exactly one blank.

wfile   Must terminate the command line, and must be preceded by exactly one blank. Each wfile is created before processing begins. There can be at most 10 distinct wfile arguments.

sed recognizes the following functions:

(1)a\
text   Append. Place text on the output before reading next input line.

(2)b label Branch to the : command bearing label. If no label is specified, branch to the end of the script.

(2)c\
text   Change. Delete the pattern space. With 0 or 1 address or at the end of a 2-address range, place text on the output. Start the next cycle.

(2)d	Delete pattern space and start the next cycle.
(2)D	Delete initial segment of pattern space through first new-line and start the next cycle.
(2)g	Replace contents of the pattern space with contents of the hold space.
(2)G	Append contents of hold space to the pattern space.
(2)h	Replace contents of the hold space with contents of the pattern space.
(2)H	Append the contents of the pattern space to the hold space.
(1)i\ text	Insert. Place text on the standard output.
(2)l	List the pattern space on the standard output in an unambiguous form. Non-printing characters are spelled in three-digit octal number format (with a preceding backslash), and long lines are folded.
(2)n	Copy the pattern space to the standard output if the default output has not been suppressed (by the -n option on the command line or the #n command in the script file). Replace the pattern space with the next line of input.
(2)N	Append the next line of input to the pattern space with an embedded new-line. (The current line number changes.)
(2)p	Print. Copy the pattern space to the standard output.
(2)P	Copy the initial segment of the pattern space through the first new-line to the standard output.
(1)q	Quit. Branch to the end of the script. Do not start a new cycle.
(1)r rfile	Read contents of rfile and place on output before reading the next input line.
(2)s/regular expression/replacement/flags	Substitute replacement string for instances of regular expression in the pattern space. Any character can be used instead of /. For a fuller description see ed(1). flags is zero or more of:

	n	n=1-2048 (LINE_MAX). Substitute for just the nth occurrence of regular expression in the pattern space.
	g	Global. Substitute for all non-overlapping instances of regular expression rather than just the first one.
	p	Print the pattern space if a replacement was made and the default output has been suppressed (by the -n option on the command line or the #n command in the script file).
	w wfile	Write. Append the pattern space to wfile if a replacement was made.

(2)t label   Test. Branch to the : command bearing the label if any
              substitutions have been made since the most recent reading
              of an input line or execution of a t. If label is empty,
              branch to the end of the script.

(2)w wfile   Write. Append the pattern space to wfile.

(2)x   Exchange the contents of the pattern and hold spaces.

(2)y/string1/string2/
              Transform. Replace all occurrences of characters in
              string1 with the corresponding character in string2. The
              lengths of string1 and string2 must be equal.

(2)! function
              Don't. Apply the function (or group, if function is {})
              only to lines not selected by the address or addresses.

(0): label   This command does nothing; it bears a label for b and t
              commands to branch to.

(1)=   Place the current line number on the standard output as a
              line.

(2){   Execute the following commands through a matching } only
              when the pattern space is selected. The syntax is:

              { cmd1
              cmd2
              cmd3
                .
                .
                .
              }

(0)   An empty command is ignored.

(0)#   If a # appears as the first character on the first line of
              a script file, that entire line is treated as a comment
              with one exception: If the character after the # is an n,
              the default output is suppressed. The rest of the line
              after #n is also ignored. A script file must contain at
              least one non-comment line.

EXTERNAL INFLUENCES
  Environment Variables
      LANG provides a default value for the internationalization variables
      that are unset or null. If LANG is unset or null, the default value of
      "C" (see lang(5)) is used. If any of the internationalization
      variables contains an invalid setting, sed will behave as if all
      internationalization variables are set to "C". See environ(5).

      LC_ALL If set to a non-empty string value, overrides the values of all
      the other internationalization variables.

      LC_CTYPE determines the interpretation of text as single and/or
      multi-byte characters, the classification of characters as printable,
      and the characters matched by character class expressions in regular
      expressions.

      LC_MESSAGES determines the locale that should be used to affect the
      format and contents of diagnostic messages written to standard error
      and informative messages written to standard output.

      NLSPATH determines the location of message catalogues for the processing of LC_MESSAGES.

International Code Set Support
Single- and multi-byte character code sets are supported.

EXAMPLES
Make a simple substitution in a file from the command line or from a
shell script, changing abc to xyz:

```
sed 's/abc/xyz/' file1 >file1.out
```

Same as above but use shell or environment variables var1 and var2 in
search and replacement strings:

```
sed "s/$var1/$var2/" file1 >file1.out
```

or

```
sed 's/'$var1'/'$var2'/' file1 >file1.out
```

Multiple substitutions in a single command:

```
sed -e 's/abc/xyz/' -e 's/lmn/rst/' file1
```

or

```
sed -e 's/abc/xyz/' \
-e 's/lmn/rst/' \
file1 >file1.out
```

WARNINGS
sed limits command scripts to a total of not more than 100 commands.

The hold space is limited to 8192 characters.

sed processes only text files. See the glossary for a definition of
text files and their limitations.

AUTHOR
sed was developed by OSF and HP.

SEE ALSO
awk(1), ed(1), grep(1), environ(5), lang(5), regexp(5).

sed: A Non-Interactive Streaming Editor tutorial in the Text
Processing Users Guide.

STANDARDS CONFORMANCE
sed: SVID2, SVID3, XPG2, XPG3, XPG4, POSIX.2

CHAPTER 8

HP-UX System Auditing

What Should You Audit?

In this chapter, I'm first going define the aspects of systems that I audit and then give some example scripts you can use as the basis for your own audit program. I have prefaced pretty much every system administration topic I've covered by saying, "Every installation is unique." Having given my standard disclaimer, let me list some areas to audit that apply to virtually every installation. You surely have others that are peculiar to your installation that should be included in an audit of your system(s).

Important Files The first thing any audit program should do is save the most important files on your system. You need to determine what files are important. When I cover this topic, I give a listing of some important files you should consider saving on a regular basis.

Security   Who can shut down your HP-UX system? Who
                        has switched to superuser in the last 24 hours.
                        Have there been any failed attempts to login as
                        root in the last 24 hours? Are there old users in the
                        /etc/password file? Most system administrators
                        can't answer these questions (I know I can't
                        answer them about the system in my office).
                        There are simple security checks you can perform
                        to answer these questions.

Logical Volume Review   One Logical Volume Manager change
                        can have a big impact on your system. I have
                        worked at installations that had several unused
                        disks on their system and the system administra-
                        tor didn't know it! An audit program should docu-
                        ment your existing Logical Volume Manager
                        configuration and perform some checks.

Performance   How is swap set up? If you put two swap sections
                        on one disk, this setup will provide lower perfor-
                        mance. Have you run **sar**, **vmstat**, or **iostat**
                        recently? An audit should include a performance
                        snapshot.

Disk Usage   Who are the disk hogs on your system? There is a
                        command to help you quickly determine this. You
                        don't want old files, especially core files, floating
                        around your system. An audit program should
                        look for these.

Kernel   Was your HP-UX kernel built with your existing
                        /stand/system file? A different **system** file may
                        have been used. Can you use all of your hard-

ware? You may have hardware attached to your system for which you do not have a driver built into your kernel.

System Boot   Does your system boot smoothly? Run **dmesg** to see information produced at the last system boot.

System Crash   See if the directory exists where core files would be placed, and if so, see if there are core files in it.

Printers   Get printer status. Should you encounter a system disaster it will be easier to rebuild your system printers configurations if you have documented your printers.

Patches   Report all patches currently installed on the system.

Networking   Run all networking commands to get a snapshot of what is configured.

These are all worthwhile areas to document and audit. Even if you do not find a single problem with your system, the audit will produce a document providing a snapshot of your system.

Let's take a closer look at some of these areas.

Important Files

In the event of a system catastrophe it would be helpful to have saved all of your important system files. Here is a listing of some files that I have copied from their original locations to **/tmp/IMPORTANT**:

```
-rw-------   1   root   syts       502   Apr   24   19:19   /tmp/IMPORTANT/PATCHES_ONLY

-rw-------   1   root   syts     52561   Apr   24   19:19   /tmp/IMPORTANT/archive.imp

-rw-------   1   root   syts     14317   Apr   24   19:19   /tmp/IMPORTANT/bootptab

-rw-------   1   root   syts      1617   Apr   24   19:19   /tmp/IMPORTANT/hosts

-rw-------   1   root   syts      3653   Apr   24   19:19   /tmp/IMPORTANT/inetd.conf

-rw-------   1   root   syts      1347   Apr   24   19:19   /tmp/IMPORTANT/inittab

-rw-------   1   root   syts      1462   Apr   24   19:19   /tmp/IMPORTANT/lvmrc

-rw-------   1   root   syts     59667   Apr   24   19:19   /tmp/IMPORTANT/lvdisplay.out

-rw-------   1   root   syts      2947   Apr   24   19:19   /tmp/IMPORTANT/netconf

-rw-------   1   root   syts      5707   Apr   24   19:19   /tmp/IMPORTANT/passwd

-rw-------   1   root   syts      2642   Apr   24   19:19   /tmp/IMPORTANT/profile

-rw-------   1   root   syts     75759   Apr   24   19:19   /tmp/IMPORTANT/rc.log

-rw-------   1   root   syts      7779   Apr   24   19:19   /tmp/IMPORTANT/services

-rw-------   1   root   syts       257   Apr   24   19:19   /tmp/IMPORTANT/syslog.conf

-rw-------   1   root   syts       615   Apr   24   19:19   /tmp/IMPORTANT/system

-rw-------   1   root   syts      4996   Apr   24   19:19   /tmp/IMPORTANT/vgdisplay.out

-rw-------   1   root   syts      2061   Apr   24   19:19   /tmp/IMPORTANT/vue

-rw-------   1   root   syts      2061   Apr   24   19:19   /tmp/IMPORTANT/cde
```

Some of these files, like **lvdisplay.out** and **vgdisplay.out**, contain a full listing of the logical volume information for this system. You never know when you will have to rebuild a volume group, and having this information in a file can be handy. Notice also there are several files which contain patch-related information.

Security

Who can shut down the system? The **/etc/shutdown.allow** file has in it a list of those who have permission to shut down a system. Verify only the users you want to shut down a system have entries in this file.

When has the system been shutdown and by whom is in **shutdown-log**. Part of **shutdownlog** with a panic is shown below:

```
16:58 Mon Feb  12,  1996.  Reboot:  (by system1!root)

21:49 Mon Feb  12,  1996.  Reboot:  (by system1!root)

16:46 Tue Feb  13,  1996.  Reboot after panic:  steven:
invalid relocation status

16:28 Sun Mar  24,  1996.  Reboot:  (by system1!root)

17:08 Thu Mar  28,  1996.  Reboot:  (by system1!root)
```

Very few users should be switching to superuser. You may have users that need to make system adjustments in a development environment. In a production environment, however, you should very seldom see a switch to superuser. The **/var/adm/sulog** file has in it all **su** commands issued. All of the following entries have switched from a user name to root.

```
SU 04/22 19:57 - ttyp2 mike-root

SU 04/22 19:57 - ttyp2 mike-root

SU 04/22 19:57 + ttyp2 mike-root

SU 04/23 11:00 + ttyu1 chang-root

SU 04/23 11:12 + ttyu2 denise-root
```

Review of bad login attempts in quick succession, or as root, can be viewed with the **lastb** command. The following example shows several bad login attempts as root:

```
root ttyp6   Tue Apr 16 13:00-13:00 (00:00)

root ttyp6   Tue Apr 16 13:01-13:01 (00:00)

root ttyp6   Tue Apr 16 13:01-13:01 (00:00)

root ttyp6   Tue Apr 16 13:02-13:02 (00:00)

root ttyp6   Tue Apr 16 13:02-13:02 (00:00)

root ttyp6   Tue Apr 16 13:03-13:03 (00:00)

root ttyp6   Tue Apr 16 13:03-13:03 (00:00)

             .

             .

             .
```

Use **pwck** to check the **/etc/passwd** file looking for all types of problems. This command performs a sanity check on the **passwd** file that, although it is not a log file, is an important file that should be monitored closely. The following are two errors in the **passwd** file that were found by running the **pwck** command. The first is a user with a **passwd** entry but with no files on the system. The second is a user with an incorrect home directory name:

```
denise - Login name not found on system

jlance:Hhadsf4353hadsfae:110:20:Joe  Lance,,,:/net/sys1/net/
sys1/home/jlance:/usr/bin/sh
Login directory not found
```

Use **grpck** to check the **/etc/group** file looking for all types of problems.

This command performs a check of the **group** file which must also be carefully monitored. The following example shows a **group** entry in which there are no users present and a group that contains a user for which there is no entry in the **passwd** file:

```
database:10:
        No users in this group

development1:*:200:nadmin,charles,william
        william - Login name not found in password file
```

Logical Volume Review

Check the integrity of the **/etc/lvmtab** file. One way of doing so is to compare **strings lvmtab** with **vgscan -v -p**. In the following example, the output of **strings lvmtab** is used as input to **vgscan** and this yields an unused volume group.

```
# vgscan -v -p

/dev/vgsys
/dev/dsk/c2d0s2
/dev/dsk/c3d0s2

/dev/vgtext
/dev/dsk/c4d0s2
/dev/dsk/c5d0s2
```

```
/dev/vgroot
/dev/dsk/c4d0s2
/dev/dsk/c7d0s2
```

```
The volume group /dev/vg00 was not matched with any
Physical Volumes.
```

```
Scan of the Physical Volumes complete.
```

```
# ll -d /dev/vg*
```

```
drwxrwxrwx  2 root     root    1024 Nov  7  1997 /dev/vg00
drwxrwxrwx  2 root     sys     1024 Jan 20  1997 /dev/vgroot
drwxrwxrwx  2 root     root    1024 Nov  7  1997 /dev/vgsys
drwxrwxrwx  2 root     root    1024 Nov  7  1997 /dev/vgtext
```

The command **ll /dev/vg*** shows four volume groups, only three of which are used. **/dev/vg00** exists but is not in use.

A common problem with a mirrored root volume is that the data is mirrored but there is no boot area on the mirror. This means that if the primary root volume becomes unbootable then you won't be able to boot off the mirror. Identify boot lif areas with **lifls -Clv /dev/rdsk/***. You can also run the **lvlnboot** command to see all disks that are bootable. The following example shows a root disk (c0t6d0) as bootable as well as its mirror (c1t3d0).

```
# lvlnboot -v
```

```
Boot Definitions for Volume Group /dev/vg00:
Physical Volumes belonging in Root Volume Group:

            /dev/dsk/c0t6d0 (10/0.6.0)   -- Boot Disk
            /dev/dsk/c1t3d0 (10/4/4.3.0) -- Boot Disk
```

·

·

I am surprised at the number of times that unused disks are found on a system. The following subroutine of an audit program identifies unused disks with the output of **ioscan** providing input to **pvdisplay**.

```
pvtest ()
{
for me in `ioscan -fkC disk | awk '{print $3}' `
do
     if [ "$me" != "H/W" ]
     then
     echo "\n$PROG>>>>> from ioscan -fkC , check PV info" | tee -a $DESTF
     diskn=`lssf /dev/dsk/* | grep $me | grep 'section 0' | awk '{print $16}'`
       echo "$PROG>>>>> the disk is $diskn" | tee -a $DESTF
       echo "$PROG>>>>> listing first 25 lines by: pvdisplay -v $diskn |\ head -25" |
tee -a $DESTF

     pvdisplay -v $diskn 2>&1 | head -25 | tee -a $DESTF
     fi
done
}
```

Here is the result for a disk that was not identified as part of a volume group:

```
pvdisplay: Couldn't query physical volume "/dev/dsk/c0d0s2":
```

The specified path does not correspond to a physical volume attached to any volume group. This fact means that the disk is physically attached to the system but is not in a volume group.

Performance

Performance is a discipline unto itself. You are not going to perform a detailed performance analysis as part of a system audit. You can get a snapshot of your system that you can later sit down and review, however, which may provide some interesting results.

As part of the audit, you should run the following performance-related commands: **vmstat**, **iostat**, **uptime**, **sar -u** and **sar -b**. The following are examples of running **sar -u** and **sar -b**:

```
# sar -u 5 5


HP-UX system1 B.10.20 A 9000/819     12/24/96


19:08:02    %usr    %sys    %wio    %idle

19:08:07     1       2       1       96
19:08:12     1       1       0       99
19:08:17     0       1       0       99
19:08:22     1       1       0       98
19:08:27     0       1       0       99

Average      1       1       0       98

# sar -b 5 10


HP-UX system1 B.10.20 A 9000/819     12/24/96


19:08:27 bread/s lread/s %rcache bwrit/s lwrit/s %wcache pread/s pwrit/s

19:08:32     0      46     100      0       5      100      0      0
19:08:37     0      28     100      1       4       80      0      0
19:08:42     0      13     100      0       0        0      0      0
19:08:47     0       0       0      0       0        0      0      0
19:08:52     0      37     100      0       0        0      0      0
19:08:57     0       6     100      1       2       50      0      0
19:09:02     0      29     100      0       0        0      0      0
19:09:07     0      27     100      2       4       59      0      0
19:09:12     0      13     100      0       0        0      0      0
19:09:17     0       0       0      0       0        0      0      0

Average      0      20     100      0       2       77      0      0
```

An area that is often overlooked regarding performance is swap space. If swap is properly configured you can get much better performance out of it than if it is inefficiently configured.

Run **swapinfo -at** and **swapinfo -m**. Swap is sometimes added to systems in a random fashion. The following example shows two swap sections on **/dev/dsk/c0t6d0**, which is a bad practice:

```
# swapinfo -at

            Kb       Kb       Kb  PCT  START/       Kb
TYPE      AVAIL     USED     FREE USED  LIMIT RESERVE PRI   NAME          ( disk )

dev      512000       0   512000  0%      0     -      1   /dev/vg00/lvol2   c0t6d0

dev      274432       0   274432  0%      0     -      0   /dev/vg00/lvol8   c0t6d0

dev      262144       0   262144  0%      0     -      0   /dev/vg03/lvol20  c1t4d0

dev      524288       0   524288  0%      0     -      0   /dev/vg02/lvol21  c1t2d0
```

It is not a good practice to put two swap sections on the same disk as has been done with **c0t6d0** in this example. It is better is distribute the load among multiple disks and to have the sections the same size to enhance interleaving swap. This size should also be big enough to hold a core dump.

Disk and File System Information

The first thing you need to know about how your disks are being used is which users are consuming the most space. The following subroutine from an audit program uses the **diskusg** command to determine the disk hogs:

```
#!/usr/bin/ksh
# 1st print stats concerning the disk's file systems
echo "This program produces logical volume statistics and the amount of disk"
echo "space consumed by users on each logical volume. \n"
for fs in `bdf| grep '^/' | awk '{print $1}'`
do
fsys=`fstyp $fs`
echo "\n $printing logical volume stats for $fs using fstyp -v \n"
fstyp -v $fs 2>&1
if [ $fsys = vxfs ]
then
echo "\n finding space consumed per user for logical volume "
echo " $fs with vxdiskusg $fs \n"
/usr/sbin/acct/vxdiskusg $fs 2>&1 | tee -a $DESTF
else
# assume hfs type
echo "\n finding space consumed per user for logical volume "
echo " $fs with diskusg $fs \n"
echo "\nUserID login number of blocks "
echo "------ ------------------- \n"
        /usr/sbin/acct/diskusg $fs 2>&1
fi
done
```

Here is an example of finding hogs for filesystem **/dev/vg00/lvol6** mounted as **/usr**. In this example, *mike* is consuming substantially more space than *jclairmo*.

diskusg /dev/vg00/lvol6

0	root	105254
1	daemon	304
2	bin	375704
5	uucp	882
9	lp	386
101	jclairmo	36
102	mike	43580

Use **find** to search for old and large files, core files, and so on. **find** can be used to uncover such information as large old files, such as those greater than 1MB and older than 120 days, as in the following example:

```
# find / \( -fsonly hfs -o -fsonly vxfs \) -a \( -atime +120 -a -size +1000000c \) -
print |    xargs -nl ll


-rw-------   1 jhowell  users    2150400 Nov  1 00:44 /home/jjersey/acrobat/READ.TAR

-rw-------   1 jhowell  users    3921920 Nov  1 00:44 /home/jjersey/acrobat/HPUXR.TAR
```

The following command can be used to find all core files on your system:

```
find / \( -fsonly hfs -o -fsonly vxfs \) -name core -exec what {} \ ;
```

Kernel, Boot, and Printer Information

This section could almost be called "miscellaneous" because it checks several different areas.

Run **ioscan -fk** to check the kernel. You may find errors such as hardware for which there is no driver installed, as in the following example.

```
Class       I  H/W Path     Driver      S/W State H/W Type Description
=========================================================================
             .
             .
             .
disk        4  10/4/4.1.0   disc3       CLAIMED    DEVICE    HP C2490WD
unknown     -  9            ?           No_Driver
             .
             .
             .
```

The two lines left in this **ioscan** output shows that there is an "unknown" device is at hardware path 9 for which there is no driver installed. Although you don't know what this is and it is probably not serious, this is the purpose of the audit program - to identify any potential problems on your system.

I very seldom watch a system boot yet there can be some revealing information produced at boot time. Running **dmesg** can show problems uncovered at boot such as the following message showing the **/var** logical volume as full:

```
/var
file: table is full
file: table is full
file: table is full
file: table is full
file: table is full
file: table is full
file: table is full
file: table is full
file: table is full
file: table is full
file: table is full
file: table is full
```

```
file: table is full
```

You can determine whether the existing kernel was built with **/stand/ system**. Run **system_prep -s** and compare it to **/stand/system**. The following routine performs this check:

```
#!/bin/ksh
DESTF="$home/audit.ker.out"
export DESTF
{
 /usr/lbin/sysadm/system_prep -s system.tmp
diffs=`diff system.tmp /stand/system`
if [ ! -z "$diffs" ]
then
echo "the system file is different: $diffs"
echo "/stand/vmunix WAS NOT built with /stand/system"
else
echo "/stand/vmunix was built with /stand/system"
fi
}
```

One area of your system that you might have a difficult time rebuilding is printer-related setup. Run the following commands and save the output for future reference:

lpstat -s
lpstat -d
lpstat -t

If you should encounter a system crash, **/var/adm/crash** is used to save the core dump to your file system. The following routine checks whether this directory exists:

```ksh
#!/usr/bin/ksh
echo "\n\n"
echo "The /var/adm/crash directory is needed by savecore in order to save the status"
echo "if a system crash occurs. The coredump can then be copied to a file and"
echo "sent to HP for analysis."
echo "See the savecore manual page to get more information about saving a core dump."

REMEMBERCORE=0
if [ -d /var/adm/crash ]
     then
                    echo "\n\t/var/adm/crash exists \c"
                    if [ -r /var/adm/crash/core.? ]
                    then
                    echo "and contains a dump."
                    echo "\n\tPlease copy the dump in /var/adm/crash to tape."
                    echo "\n\nHere is a listing of the core dump(s) on `hostname`. \n"
                    ll /var/adm/crash/core.?
                    REMEMBERCORE=1
        else
                    echo "and contains NO dump."
     fi

else
                    echo "\n\n WARNING: /var/adm/crash did not exist."
                    echo " use mkdir -p /var/adm/crash "
     fi
```

Patches

Whether or not the appropriate patches are on your system, you need to include an inventory of patches as part of the audit. Patches are difficult to keep up with but are essential to the proper operation of your system. The first few lines of each patch you have installed give a description of the patch, including its number. A good audit program will read this information and save it in a file so that you have this in the directory with your other important files.

Networking

System administrators spend a lot of time setting up networking. If you encountered a system disaster of some type, it would be helpful to have a section that thoroughly documented your networking setup. The following bullet items describe some of the more common areas of networking to check:

- See whether your system is an NFS server and check **/etc/exports** for exported file systems.

- Check **syslog** for errors with the following command:

```
# grep err /var/adm/syslog/syslog.log
```

- Check rpc registration with

```
# rpcinfo -p
```

- Check your system information with DNS.

```
# nslookup $HOSTNAME
```

- Check for the existence of **/etc/resolv.conf**, which would indicate that your system uses DNS.

```
# ll /etc/resolv.conf
```

- View lan devices with

```
# ll /dev/lan*
```

- Check LAN cards by running **lanscan** for all interfaces.

- Check the kernel for LAN card configuration with

```
# ioscan -funC lan
```

- Show routes with

```
# netstat -r
```

- Check for SNA with

```
# snapshownet
```

- Check for uucp with

```
# /usr/lbin/uucp/uucheck -v
```

Auditing your system becomes increasingly more important as you make changes to it. The auditing I have covered in this section does not even address the applications you are running. Having a well-documented system and putting effort into reviewing the audit results will pay dividends in the long run. Fixing the small problems you find as a result of the audit may prevent much bigger problems down the road.

Some Example Scripts

You would ultimately like to have a full audit program that you could run on all your HP-UX systems on a regular basis. The topics I have suggested in this chapter are a good place to start. You may also have additional aspects of your systems that should also be audited periodically.

The following sections contain several short scripts that could be run to get a feel for the type of output you could produce with your audit script. Many such short scripts could then be combined to produce a larger, more comprehensive audit program. The short scripts you craft could be used as subroutines called by a main program.

The following sections show example scripts and the result of having run the scripts. The earlier discussions in this chapter cover the topics of auditing your system, so I do not include much additional explanation in the upcoming sections.

Kernel

The following script, called **audker.sh**, determines whether the existing kernel was built with **/stand/system**. The program runs **system_prep -s** and compares it to the file **/stand/system**.

```
#!/bin/ksh
DESTF="$home/audit.ker.out"
export DESTF
{
 /usr/lbin/sysadm/system_prep -s system.tmp
diffs=`diff system.tmp /stand/system`
if [ ! -z "$diffs" ]
then
echo "the system file is different: $diffs"
echo "/stand/vmunix WAS NOT built with /stand/system"
else
echo "/stand/vmunix was built with /stand/system"
fi
}
```

The following output was received from having run **audker.sh**.

```
# audker.sh

the system file is different: 51a52
> spt0
/stand/vmunix WAS NOT built with /stand/system
```

This output indicates that the original **system** file is different from the **system** file just generated from the currently running kernel. The following listings show both **system** files. The first listing is the original **system** file that includes the *spt0* driver.

The second listing does not include the *spt0* driver, meaning that it is not part of the current HP-UX kernel.

First listing: original system file

```
* Drivers and Subsystems

CentIf
CharDrv
asp
c720
ccio
cdfs
cio_ca0
clone
core
diag0
diag2
disc3
dlpi
dmem
echo
ffs
hpstreams
inet
inet_clts
inet_cots
klog
lan2
lasi
ldterm
lv
lvm
mux2
netdiag1
netman
nfs
ni
pa
pckt
pfail
pipedev
pipemod
ps2
ptem
ptm
pts
sad
sc
scsi1
scsi2
scsi3
sctl
sdisk
sio
spt
spt0                            <---- spt0 driver in old system file
stape
strlog
strpty_included
tape2
```

```
tape2_included
target
timod
tirdwr
tpiso
uipc
vxbase
wsio


* Kernel Device info

dump lvol


* Tunable parameters

dbc_max_pct        10
dbc_min_pct        10
maxswapchunks      1024
maxuprc            100
maxusers           250
msgmax             32768
msgmnb             32768
msgmni             100
msgseg             7168
msgtql             256
nfile              (24*(NPROC+16+MAXUSERS)/10+32+2*(NPTY+NSTRPTY))
npty               250
nstrpty            60
semmni             96
semmns             192
swapmem_on         0
```

Second listing: new system file

```
* Drivers and Subsystems

CentIf
CharDrv
asp
c720
ccio
cdfs
cio_ca0
clone
core
diag0
diag2
disc3
dlpi
dmem
echo
ffs
hpstreams
inet
inet_clts
inet_cots
klog
lan2
lasi
```

```
ldterm
lv
lvm
mux2
netdiag1
netman
nfs
ni
pa
pckt
pfail
pipedev
pipemod
ps2
ptem
ptm
pts
sad
sc
scsi1
scsi2
scsi3
sctl
sdisk
sio
spt                                     <--- spt0 driver not in current kernel
stape
strlog
strpty_included
tape2
tape2_included
target
timod
tirdwr
tpiso
uipc
vxbase
wsio


* Kernel Device info

dump lvol


* Tunable parameters

dbc_max_pct      10
dbc_min_pct      10
maxswapchunks    1024
maxuprc          100
maxusers         250
msgmax           32768
msgmnb           32768
msgmni           100
msgseg           7168
msgtql           256
nfile            (24*(NPROC+16+MAXUSERS)/10+32+2*(NPTY+NSTRPTY))
npty             250
nstrpty          60
semmni           96
semmns           192
swapmem_on       0
```

Disk Information

The following script, called **auddisk.sh**, lists all disks on the system and then provides a detailed description of each disk.

```ksh
#!/bin/ksh

{
echo "The following is a description of disks by ioscan -fkC disk\n"
ioscan -fkC disk
echo "\n\n"
echo "The following is a detailed description of the disks earlier"
        echo "identified by ioscan."

echo "\n\nHardware disk information:\n"
for DEV in `ioscan -funC disk | awk '{print $2}' | \
                grep '\/dev\/rdsk'`
do
IS_THERE=$(/etc/diskinfo $DEV 2>&1)
                        if [ ${IS_THERE%% *} != "diskinfo:" ]
                                then
                                        /etc/diskinfo -v $DEV 2>&1
                        fi
echo "  - - - - - - - - - - - -"
echo ""
done
        }
```

The following output was received from running **auddisk.sh**.

```
# auddisk.sh
```

```
The following is a description of disks by ioscan -fkC disk
```

Class	I	H/W Path	Driver	S/W State	H/W Type	Description	
disk	3	10/0.1.0	sdisk	CLAIMED	DEVICE	SEAGATE	ST32550W
disk	4	10/0.2.0	sdisk	CLAIMED	DEVICE	HP	C2490WD
disk	0	10/0.5.0	sdisk	CLAIMED	DEVICE	SEAGATE	ST32550W
disk	1	10/0.6.0	sdisk	CLAIMED	DEVICE	SEAGATE	ST32550W
disk	9	10/4/12.5.0	disc3	CLAIMED	DEVICE	DGC	C2300WDR5
disk	10	10/4/12.5.1	disc3	CLAIMED	DEVICE	DGC	C2300WDR5
disk	11	10/4/12.6.0	disc3	CLAIMED	DEVICE	DGC	C2300WDR5
disk	12	10/4/12.6.1	disc3	CLAIMED	DEVICE	DGC	C2300WDR5
disk	13	10/8.0.0	sdisk	CLAIMED	DEVICE	HP	C3586A
disk	14	10/8.0.1	sdisk	CLAIMED	DEVICE	HP	C3586A
disk	15	10/8.1.0	sdisk	CLAIMED	DEVICE	HP	C3586A
disk	16	10/8.1.1	sdisk	CLAIMED	DEVICE	HP	C3586A
disk	2	10/12/5.2.0	sdisk	CLAIMED	DEVICE	TOSHIBA	CD-ROM

The following is a detailed description of the disks earlier
identified by ioscan.

Hardware disk information:

SCSI describe of /dev/rdsk/c0t1d0:
                vendor: SEAGATE
            product id: ST32550W
                  type: direct access
                  size: 2082636 Kbytes
      bytes per sector: 512
             rev level: HP07
       blocks per disk: 4165272
           ISO version: 0
          ECMA version: 0
          ANSI version: 2
       removable media: no
       response format: 2
       (Additional inquiry bytes: (32)31 (33)34 (34)34 (35)37 (36)31 (37)30 (38)32
(39)0 (40)0 (41)0 (42)0 (43)0 (44)0 (45)0 (46)0 (47)0 (48)0 (49)0 (50)0 (51)0 (52)0
(53)0 (54)0 (55)0 (56)0 (57)0 (58)0 (59)0 (60)0 (61)0 (62)0 (63)0 (64)0 (65)0 (66)0
(67)0 (68)0 (69)0 (70)0 (71)0 (72)0 (73)0 (74)0 (75)0 (76)0 (77)0 (78)0 (79)0 (80)0
(81)0 (82)0 (83)0 (84)0 (85)0 (86)0 (87)0 (88)0 (89)0 (90)0 (91)0 (92)43 (93)6f (94)70
(95)79 (96)72 (97)69 (98)67 (99)68 (100)74 (101)20 (102)28 (103)63 (104)29 (105)20
(106)31 (107)39 (108)39 (109)35 (110)20 (111)53 (112)65 (113)61 (114)67 (115)61
(116)74 (117)65 (118)20 (119)41 (120)6c (121)6c (122)20 (123)0 (124)3f (125)8e (126)98
(127)0 (128)0 (129)2 (130)0 (131)0 (132)0 (133)0 (134)0 (135)0 (136)0 (137)0 (138)0
(139)0 (140)0 (141)0 (142)0)
        - - - - - - - - - - - - -

SCSI describe of /dev/rdsk/c0t2d0:
                vendor: HP
            product id: C2490WD
                  type: direct access
                  size: 2082636 Kbytes
      bytes per sector: 512
             rev level: 4250
       blocks per disk: 4165272
           ISO version: 0
          ECMA version: 0
          ANSI version: 2
       removable media: no
       response format: 2
        - - - - - - - - - - - - -

SCSI describe of /dev/rdsk/c0t5d0:
                vendor: SEAGATE
            product id: ST32550W
                  type: direct access
                  size: 2082636 Kbytes
      bytes per sector: 512
             rev level: HP06
       blocks per disk: 4165272
           ISO version: 0
          ECMA version: 0
          ANSI version: 2
       removable media: no
       response format: 2
       (Additional inquiry bytes: (32)30 (33)37 (34)32 (35)35 (36)30 (37)36 (38)30
(39)0 (40)0 (41)0 (42)0 (43)0 (44)0 (45)0 (46)0 (47)0 (48)0 (49)0 (50)0 (51)0 (52)0
(53)0 (54)0 (55)0 (56)0 (57)0 (58)0 (59)0 (60)0 (61)0 (62)0 (63)0 (64)0 (65)0 (66)0
(67)0 (68)0 (69)0 (70)0 (71)0 (72)0 (73)0 (74)0 (75)0 (76)0 (77)0 (78)0 (79)0 (80)0
(81)0 (82)0 (83)0 (84)0 (85)0 (86)0 (87)0 (88)0 (89)0 (90)0 (91)0 (92)43 (93)6f (94)70
(95)79 (96)72 (97)69 (98)67 (99)68 (100)74 (101)20 (102)28 (103)63 (104)29 (105)20

(106)31 (107)39 (108)39 (109)35 (110)20 (111)53 (112)65 (113)61 (114)67 (115)61
(116)74 (117)65 (118)20 (119)41 (120)6c (121)6c (122)20 (123)0 (124)3f (125)8e (126)98
(127)0 (128)0 (129)2 (130)0 (131)0 (132)0 (133)0 (134)0 (135)0 (136)0 (137)0 (138)0
(139)0 (140)0 (141)0 (142)0)
            - - - - - - - - - - - - -

                SCSI describe of /dev/rdsk/c0t6d0:
                        vendor: SEAGATE
                    product id: ST32550W
                          type: direct access
                          size: 2082636 Kbytes
              bytes per sector: 512
                     rev level: HP06
               blocks per disk: 4165272
                   ISO version: 0
                  ECMA version: 0
                  ANSI version: 2
               removable media: no
               response format: 2
                (Additional inquiry bytes: (32)31 (33)34 (34)33 (35)33 (36)38 (37)37 (38)32
(39)0 (40)0 (41)0 (42)0 (43)0 (44)0 (45)0 (46)0 (47)0 (48)0 (49)0 (50)0 (51)0 (52)0
(53)0 (54)0 (55)0 (56)0 (57)0 (58)0 (59)0 (60)0 (61)0 (62)0 (63)0 (64)0 (65)0 (66)0
(67)0 (68)0 (69)0 (70)0 (71)0 (72)0 (73)0 (74)0 (75)0 (76)0 (77)0 (78)0 (79)0 (80)0
(81)0 (82)0 (83)0 (84)0 (85)0 (86)0 (87)0 (88)0 (89)0 (90)0 (91)0 (92)43 (93)6f (94)70
(95)79 (96)72 (97)69 (98)67 (99)68 (100)74 (101)20 (102)28 (103)63 (104)29 (105)20
(106)31 (107)39 (108)39 (109)35 (110)20 (111)53 (112)65 (113)61 (114)67 (115)61
(116)74 (117)65 (118)20 (119)41 (120)6c (121)6c (122)20 (123)0 (124)3f (125)8e (126)98
(127)0 (128)0 (129)2 (130)0 (131)0 (132)0 (133)0 (134)0 (135)0 (136)0 (137)0 (138)0
(139)0 (140)0 (141)0 (142)0)
            - - - - - - - - - - - - -

                SCSI describe of /dev/rdsk/c4t5d0:
                        vendor: DGC
                    product id: C2300WDR5
                          type: direct access
                          size: 8146176 Kbytes
              bytes per sector: 512
                     rev level: HP02
               blocks per disk: 16292352
                   ISO version: 0
                  ECMA version: 0
                  ANSI version: 2
               removable media: no
               response format: 2
                (Additional inquiry bytes: (32)41 (33)55 (34)4e (35)41 (36)20 (37)43 (38)4f
(39)4e (40)54 (41)52 (42)4f (43)4c (44)4c (45)45 (46)52 (47)20 (48)20 (49)20 (50)20
(51)0 (52)0 (53)0 (54)0 (55)0 (56)0 (57)0 (58)0 (59)0 (60)0 (61)0 (62)0 (63)0 (64)0
(65)0 (66)0 (67)0 (68)0 (69)0 (70)0 (71)0 (72)0 (73)0 (74)0 (75)0 (76)0 (77)0 (78)0
(79)0 (80)0 (81)0 (82)0 (83)0 (84)0 (85)0 (86)0 (87)0 (88)0 (89)0 (90)0 (91)2 (92)1
(93)6 (94)0 (95)39 (96)34 (97)2d (98)33 (99)31 (100)36 (101)35 (102)2d (103)31 (104)31
(105)30 (106)0 (107)a (108)f5 (109)17 (110)0 (111)35 (112)7 (113)10 (114)0 (115)0
(116)0 (117)0 (118)0 (119)0 (120)0 (121)0 (122)0)
            - - - - - - - - - - - - -

                SCSI describe of /dev/rdsk/c4t5d1:
                        vendor: DGC
                    product id: C2300WDR5
                          type: direct access
                          size: 8146176 Kbytes
              bytes per sector: 512
                     rev level: HP02
               blocks per disk: 16292352
                   ISO version: 0
                  ECMA version: 0
                  ANSI version: 2
               removable media: no

```
                 response format: 2
                 (Additional inquiry bytes: (32)41 (33)55 (34)4e (35)41 (36)20 (37)43 (38)4f
(39)4e (40)54 (41)52 (42)4f (43)4c (44)4c (45)45 (46)52 (47)20 (48)20 (49)20 (50)20
(51)0 (52)0 (53)0 (54)0 (55)0 (56)0 (57)0 (58)0 (59)0 (60)0 (61)0 (62)0 (63)0 (64)0
(65)0 (66)0 (67)0 (68)0 (69)0 (70)0 (71)0 (72)0 (73)0 (74)0 (75)0 (76)0 (77)0 (78)0
(79)0 (80)0 (81)0 (82)0 (83)0 (84)0 (85)0 (86)0 (87)0 (88)0 (89)0 (90)0 (91)2 (92)1
(93)6 (94)0 (95)39 (96)34 (97)2d (98)33 (99)31 (100)36 (101)35 (102)2d (103)31 (104)31
(105)30 (106)0 (107)a (108)f5 (109)17 (110)0 (111)35 (112)7 (113)10 (114)0 (115)0
(116)0 (117)0 (118)0 (119)0 (120)0 (121)0 (122)0 )
                 - - - - - - - - - - - - -


          SCSI describe of /dev/rdsk/c4t6d0:
                      vendor: DGC
                  product id: C2300WDR5
                        type: direct access
                        size: 8146176 Kbytes
            bytes per sector: 512
                   rev level: HP02
             blocks per disk: 16292352
                 ISO version: 0
                ECMA version: 0
                ANSI version: 2
             removable media: no
             response format: 2
                 (Additional inquiry bytes: (32)41 (33)55 (34)4e (35)41 (36)20 (37)43 (38)4f
(39)4e (40)54 (41)52 (42)4f (43)4c (44)4c (45)45 (46)52 (47)20 (48)20 (49)20 (50)20
(51)0 (52)0 (53)0 (54)0 (55)0 (56)0 (57)0 (58)0 (59)0 (60)0 (61)0 (62)0 (63)0 (64)0
(65)0 (66)0 (67)0 (68)0 (69)0 (70)0 (71)0 (72)0 (73)0 (74)0 (75)0 (76)0 (77)0 (78)0
(79)0 (80)0 (81)0 (82)0 (83)0 (84)0 (85)0 (86)0 (87)0 (88)0 (89)0 (90)0 (91)1 (92)0
(93)5 (94)0 (95)39 (96)34 (97)2d (98)33 (99)31 (100)36 (101)35 (102)2d (103)31 (104)31
(105)30 (106)0 (107)35 (108)7 (109)10 (110)0 (111)a (112)f5 (113)17 (114)0 (115)0
(116)0 (117)0 (118)0 (119)0 (120)0 (121)0 (122)0 )
                 - - - - - - - - - - - - -


          SCSI describe of /dev/rdsk/c4t6d1:
                      vendor: DGC
                  product id: C2300WDR5
                        type: direct access
                        size: 8146176 Kbytes
            bytes per sector: 512
                   rev level: HP02
             blocks per disk: 16292352
                 ISO version: 0
                ECMA version: 0
                ANSI version: 2
             removable media: no
             response format: 2
                 (Additional inquiry bytes: (32)41 (33)55 (34)4e (35)41 (36)20 (37)43 (38)4f
(39)4e (40)54 (41)52 (42)4f (43)4c (44)4c (45)45 (46)52 (47)20 (48)20 (49)20 (50)20
(51)0 (52)0 (53)0 (54)0 (55)0 (56)0 (57)0 (58)0 (59)0 (60)0 (61)0 (62)0 (63)0 (64)0
(65)0 (66)0 (67)0 (68)0 (69)0 (70)0 (71)0 (72)0 (73)0 (74)0 (75)0 (76)0 (77)0 (78)0
(79)0 (80)0 (81)0 (82)0 (83)0 (84)0 (85)0 (86)0 (87)0 (88)0 (89)0 (90)0 (91)1 (92)0
(93)5 (94)0 (95)39 (96)34 (97)2d (98)33 (99)31 (100)36 (101)35 (102)2d (103)31 (104)31
(105)30 (106)0 (107)35 (108)7 (109)10 (110)0 (111)a (112)f5 (113)17 (114)0 (115)0
(116)0 (117)0 (118)0 (119)0 (120)0 (121)0 (122)0 )
                 - - - - - - - - - - - - - -


          SCSI describe of /dev/rdsk/c5t0d0:
                      vendor: HP
                  product id: C3586A
                        type: direct access
                        size: 2097152 Kbytes
            bytes per sector: 512
                   rev level: HP02
             blocks per disk: 4194304
                 ISO version: 0
```

```
           ECMA version: 0
           ANSI version: 2
        removable media: no
        response format: 2
    - - - - - - - - - - - - - -


    SCSI describe of /dev/rdsk/c5t0d1:
                 vendor: HP
             product id: C3586A
                   type: direct access
                   size: 10485760 Kbytes
       bytes per sector: 512
              rev level: HP02
        blocks per disk: 20971520
            ISO version: 0
           ECMA version: 0
           ANSI version: 2
        removable media: no
        response format: 2
    - - - - - - - - - - - - - -


    SCSI describe of /dev/rdsk/c5t1d0:
                 vendor: HP
             product id: C3586A
                   type: direct access
                   size: 2097152 Kbytes
       bytes per sector: 512
              rev level: HP02
        blocks per disk: 4194304
            ISO version: 0
           ECMA version: 0
           ANSI version: 2
        removable media: no
        response format: 2
    - - - - - - - - - - - - - -


    SCSI describe of /dev/rdsk/c5t1d1:
                 vendor: HP
             product id: C3586A
                   type: direct access
                   size: 10485760 Kbytes
       bytes per sector: 512
              rev level: HP02
        blocks per disk: 20971520
            ISO version: 0
           ECMA version: 0
           ANSI version: 2
        removable media: no
        response format: 2
    - - - - - - - - - - - - - -


    SCSI describe of /dev/rdsk/c1t2d0:
                 vendor: TOSHIBA
             product id: CD-ROM XM-4101TA
                   type: CD-ROM
                   size: 347936 Kbytes
       bytes per sector: 2048
              rev level: 1084
        blocks per disk: 173968
            ISO version: 0
           ECMA version: 0
           ANSI version: 2
        removable media: yes
        response format: 2
        (Additional inquiry bytes: (32)34 (33)2f (34)31 (35)38 (36)2f (37)39 (38)34
 (39)0 (40)0 (41)0 (42)0 (43)0 (44)0 (45)0 (46)0 (47)0 (48)0 (49)0 (50)0 (51)0 (52)0
```

```
(53)0  (54)0  (55)0  (56)0  (57)0  (58)0  (59)0  (60)0  (61)0  (62)0  (63)0  (64)0  (65)0  (66)0
(67)0  (68)0  (69)0  (70)0  (71)0  (72)0  (73)0  (74)0  (75)0  (76)0  (77)0  (78)0  (79)0  (80)0
(81)0  (82)0  (83)0  (84)0  (85)0  (86)0  (87)0  (88)0  (89)0  (90)0  )
       - - - - - - - - - - - - - -
```

Logical Volume Summary

After viewing the physical disks connected to the system, it would be help-ful to see some summary information on logical volumes including the physical disks to which the logical volumes have been assigned. The fol-lowing script, called **audlvsum.sh**, provides a concise summary of the log-ical volumes on a system.

```ksh
#!/usr/bin/ksh

USAGE="Usage: $0 [-d]"

VOLORDER='y'   #default - sort by logical volume
               #         n = sort by disk

while (( $# > 0 ))
do
  case "$1" in
    -d ) VOLORDER='n'
      ;;
    * ) echo unrecognized option: "$1"
        echo $USAGE
      exit 1
  ;;
  esac
  shift
done

if [ "$VOLORDER" = "y" ]     #determine sorting order based on cmdline option
then
  FINISH=sort
else
  FINISH=cat
fi

# width specifiers to make the output align better
#
# LVMINFO = LV + USE + 6
# DISKINFO = HW + ID + 8
#
typeset -L28 LVMINFO
typeset -L18 LV
typeset -L30 DISKINFO
typeset -L10 ID
typeset -L12 HW
typeset -R9  SZ
typeset -R4  USE FRE

ioscan -f|grep -e disk -e ext_bus|awk '{print $1" "$2" "$3}'|while read LINE
do set $LINE
  TY="$1"
```

```
         if [ "$TY" = "ext_bus" ]
         then
           C="$2"
         else
           HW="$3"
           T="`echo $HW | cut -f 2 -d .`"
           D="`echo $HW | cut -f 3 -d .`"
           INFO="`diskinfo /dev/rdsk/c${C}t${T}d${D}`"
           ID=`echo $INFO | sed -e 's/^.*product id: //' -e 's/ .*$//'`
           PVD="`pvdisplay -v /dev/dsk/c${C}t${T}d${D} 2>&1|sed '/Physical ext/,$d'`"

           DISKINFO="HW $HW  ID $ID"
           if echo $PVD |grep "find the volume group" > /dev/null
           then
             SZ=`echo $INFO | sed -e 's/^.*size: //' -e 's/ .*$//'`
             LVMINFO="Non-LVM disk $SZ KB"
             DEVFILE=" /dev/rdsk/c${C}t${T}d${D}"
             echo "$LVMINFO$DISKINFO$DEVFILE"
             if [ "$VOLORDER" = "n" ]
             then
               echo
             fi
           else
             PE=`echo $PVD | sed -e 's/^.*PE Size[^0-9]*//' -e 's/ .*$//'`
             TOT=`echo $PVD | sed -e 's/^.*Total PE[^0-9]*//' -e 's/ .*$//'`
             FRE=`echo $PVD | sed -e 's/^.*Free PE[^0-9]*//' -e 's/ .*$//'`
             VG=`echo $PVD | sed -e 's/^.*VG Name *//' -e 's/ .*$//'`
             VG=`basename $VG`

             echo "$PVD" | sed '1,/^    LV Name/d' | while read LVINFO
             do
               set $LVINFO
               LV="$VG/`basename $1`"
               FULLLV="/dev/$VG/`basename $1`"   #Version without spaces
               USE="$3"
               LVMINFO="$LV${USE}x${PE}MB"
               SYSUSE=`sed 's/#.*//' < /etc/fstab |
                          grep "$FULLLV[        ]" | awk '{ print $2 }'`
               echo "$LVMINFO$DISKINFO$SYSUSE"
             done
             LV="$VG/UNUSED"
             LVMINFO="$LV${FRE}x${PE}MB"
             echo "$LVMINFO$DISKINFO"
             if [ "$VOLORDER" = "n" ]
             then
               echo
             fi
           fi
         fi
    done | $FINISH
```

I redirected the output of this script to **audlvsum.out**, shown in the following listing. This output produces a lot of useful information, including unused areas of physical volume groups.

```
Non-LVM disk      347936 KB   HW 10/12/5.2.0    ID CD-ROM      /dev/rdsk/c1t2d0
Non-LVM disk     2097152 KB   HW 10/8.1.0       ID C3586A      /dev/rdsk/c5t1d0
Non-LVM disk    10485760 KB   HW 10/8.1.1       ID C3586A      /dev/rdsk/c5t1d1
vg00/UNUSED          0x4MB    HW 10/0.5.0       ID ST32550W
vg00/UNUSED          0x4MB    HW 10/0.6.0       ID ST32550W
vg00/lvol1          12x4MB    HW 10/0.6.0       ID ST32550W    /stand
vg00/lvol2         128x4MB    HW 10/0.6.0       ID ST32550W
vg00/lvol3          25x4MB    HW 10/0.6.0       ID ST32550W    /
vg00/lvol4         256x4MB    HW 10/0.6.0       ID ST32550W    /opt
vg00/lvol5          50x4MB    HW 10/0.6.0       ID ST32550W    /tmp
vg00/lvol6          36x4MB    HW 10/0.6.0       ID ST32550W    /usr
vg00/lvol6         220x4MB    HW 10/0.5.0       ID ST32550W    /usr
vg00/lvol7         188x4MB    HW 10/0.5.0       ID ST32550W    /var
vg00/lvol8         100x4MB    HW 10/0.5.0       ID ST32550W    ...
vg01/UNUSED        256x4MB    HW 10/4/12.5.0    ID C2300WDR5
vg01/UNUSED        256x4MB    HW 10/4/12.6.0    ID C2300WDR5
vg01/UNUSED        327x4MB    HW 10/8.0.0       ID C3586A
vg01/add           125x4MB    HW 10/8.0.0       ID C3586A      /add
vg01/lvol10       1023x4MB    HW 10/4/12.5.0    ID C2300WDR5   /dev01
vg01/lvol10       1023x4MB    HW 10/4/12.6.0    ID C2300WDR5   /dev01
vg01/lvol12        256x4MB    HW 10/4/12.5.0    ID C2300WDR5   /mdd
vg01/lvol12        256x4MB    HW 10/4/12.6.0    ID C2300WDR5   /mdd
vg01/lvol14         59x4MB    HW 10/8.0.0       ID C3586A      /npscm
vg01/lvol14        453x4MB    HW 10/4/12.5.0    ID C2300WDR5   /npscm
vg01/lvol14        453x4MB    HW 10/4/12.6.0    ID C2300WDR5   /npscm
vg03/UNUSED         90x4MB    HW 10/4/12.5.1    ID C2300WDR5
vg03/UNUSED         90x4MB    HW 10/4/12.6.1    ID C2300WDR5
vg03/lvol11       1023x4MB    HW 10/4/12.5.1    ID C2300WDR5   /dev02
vg03/lvol11       1023x4MB    HW 10/4/12.6.1    ID C2300WDR5   /dev02
vg03/lvol31        375x4MB    HW 10/4/12.5.1    ID C2300WDR5   /ccur
vg03/lvol31        375x4MB    HW 10/4/12.6.1    ID C2300WDR5   /ccur
vg03/lvol41        500x4MB    HW 10/4/12.5.1    ID C2300WDR5   /usr/wind
vg03/lvol41        500x4MB    HW 10/4/12.6.1    ID C2300WDR5   /usr/wind
vg04/UNUSED          0x4MB    HW 10/0.1.0       ID ST32550W
vg04/UNUSED          0x4MB    HW 10/0.2.0       ID C2490WD
vg04/lvol1          25x4MB    HW 10/0.2.0       ID C2490WD     /OLDROOT
vg04/lvol2         125x4MB    HW 10/0.2.0       ID C2490WD
vg04/lvol4          88x4MB    HW 10/0.1.0       ID ST32550W    /OLDOPT
vg04/lvol4         125x4MB    HW 10/0.2.0       ID C2490WD     /OLDOPT
vg04/lvol5           6x4MB    HW 10/0.2.0       ID C2490WD     /OLDTMP
vg04/lvol5          19x4MB    HW 10/0.1.0       ID ST32550W    /OLDTMP
vg04/lvol6         215x4MB    HW 10/0.1.0       ID ST32550W    /OLDUSR
vg04/lvol7           2x4MB    HW 10/0.2.0       ID C2490WD     /OLDVAR
vg04/lvol7         186x4MB    HW 10/0.1.0       ID ST32550W    /OLDVAR
vg04/lvol8          67x4MB    HW 10/0.2.0       ID C2490WD
vg04/lvol9         157x4MB    HW 10/0.2.0       ID C2490WD
vg05/UNUSED          0x4MB    HW 10/8.0.1       ID C3586A
vg05/lvol10       2431x4MB    HW 10/8.0.1       ID C3586A      /home
vg05/lvol21        128x4MB    HW 10/8.0.1       ID C3586A      ...
```

Logical Volume Detail

The previous script provided a useful summary of logical volumes. The next useful information to have would be detailed information on the logical volumes of the system. The following script, called **audlvdis.sh**, provides detailed information on the logical volumes connected to a system.

```
#!/usr/bin/ksh
echo "a listing by: lvdisplay -v " >$ARCHDIR/lvdisplay_v.txt
for lv in `vgdisplay -v | grep 'LV Name' | awk '{print $3}'`
do
entry=`bdf | grep $lv`
if [ ! -z "$entry" ]
then
echo "\n$PROG>>>>> $lv IS mounted, line from bdf is:\n$entry"
else
echo "\n$PROG>>>>> $lv IS NOT mounted"
fi
echo "$PROG>>>>> documenting first 30 lines of lvm information \
by: lvdisplay -v $lv | head -30"
echo "the logical volume is:$lv"
lvdisplay -v $lv | head -30
lvdisplay -v $lv >>$ARCHDIR/lvdisplay_v.txt
done
echo "PROG>>>>> archived by lvdisplay -v >$ARCHDIR/lvdisplay_v.txt"
```

I redirected the output of this script to **audlvdis.out**, shown in the following listing. Only the first few logical volumes are listed.

```
        >>>>> /dev/vg00/lvol3 IS mounted, line from bdf is:
        /dev/vg00/lvol3        99669    33110    56592    37% /
        >>>>> documenting first 30 lines of lvm information by: lvdisplay -v /dev/vg00/
lvol3 | head -30
        the logical volume is:/dev/vg00/lvol3
        --- Logical volumes ---
        LV Name                      /dev/vg00/lvol3
        VG Name                      /dev/vg00
        LV Permission                read/write
        LV Status                    available/syncd
        Mirror copies                0
        Consistency Recovery         MWC
        Schedule                     parallel
        LV Size (Mbytes)             100
        Current LE                   25
        Allocated PE                 25
        Stripes                      0
        Stripe Size (Kbytes)         0
        Bad block                    off
        Allocation                   strict/contiguous

        --- Distribution of logical volume ---
        PV Name              LE on PV  PE on PV
        /dev/dsk/c0t6d0        25         25

        --- Logical extents ---
        LE    PV1                    PE1   Status 1
        0000 /dev/dsk/c0t6d0         0140  current
        0001 /dev/dsk/c0t6d0         0141  current
```

```
       0002 /dev/dsk/c0t6d0    0142 current
       0003 /dev/dsk/c0t6d0    0143 current
       0004 /dev/dsk/c0t6d0    0144 current
       0005 /dev/dsk/c0t6d0    0145 current
       0006 /dev/dsk/c0t6d0    0146 current
       0007 /dev/dsk/c0t6d0    0147 current

   >>>>> /dev/vg00/lvol2 IS NOT mounted
   >>>>> documenting first 30 lines of lvm information by: lvdisplay -v /dev/vg00/
lvol2 | head -30
   the logical volume is:/dev/vg00/lvol2
   --- Logical volumes ---
   LV Name                    /dev/vg00/lvol2
   VG Name                    /dev/vg00
   LV Permission              read/write
   LV Status                  available/syncd
   Mirror copies              0
   Consistency Recovery       MWC
   Schedule                   parallel
   LV Size (Mbytes)           512
   Current LE                 128
   Allocated PE               128
   Stripes                    0
   Stripe Size (Kbytes)       0
   Bad block                  off
   Allocation                 strict/contiguous

      --- Distribution of logical volume ---
      PV Name           LE on PV  PE on PV
      /dev/dsk/c0t6d0   128       128

      --- Logical extents ---
      LE     PV1            PE1  Status 1
      0000 /dev/dsk/c0t6d0    0012 current
      0001 /dev/dsk/c0t6d0    0013 current
      0002 /dev/dsk/c0t6d0    0014 current
      0003 /dev/dsk/c0t6d0    0015 current
      0004 /dev/dsk/c0t6d0    0016 current
      0005 /dev/dsk/c0t6d0    0017 current
      0006 /dev/dsk/c0t6d0    0018 current
      0007 /dev/dsk/c0t6d0    0019 current

   >>>>> /dev/vg00/lvol1 IS mounted, line from bdf is:
   /dev/vg00/lvol1    47829   29893   13153   69% /stand
   >>>>> documenting first 30 lines of lvm information by: lvdisplay -v /dev/vg00/
lvol1 | head -30
   the logical volume is:/dev/vg00/lvol1
   --- Logical volumes ---
   LV Name                    /dev/vg00/lvol1
   VG Name                    /dev/vg00
   LV Permission              read/write
   LV Status                  available/syncd
   Mirror copies              0
   Consistency Recovery       MWC
   Schedule                   parallel
   LV Size (Mbytes)           48
   Current LE                 12
   Allocated PE               12
   Stripes                    0
   Stripe Size (Kbytes)       0
   Bad block                  off
   Allocation                 strict/contiguous

      --- Distribution of logical volume ---
      PV Name           LE on PV  PE on PV
      /dev/dsk/c0t6d0   12        12
```

```
    --- Logical extents ---
    LE    PV1                   PE1  Status 1
    0000 /dev/dsk/c0t6d0        0000 current
    0001 /dev/dsk/c0t6d0        0001 current
    0002 /dev/dsk/c0t6d0        0002 current
    0003 /dev/dsk/c0t6d0        0003 current
    0004 /dev/dsk/c0t6d0        0004 current
    0005 /dev/dsk/c0t6d0        0005 current
    0006 /dev/dsk/c0t6d0        0006 current
    0007 /dev/dsk/c0t6d0        0007 current

>>>>> /dev/vg00/lvol6 IS mounted, line from bdf is:
/dev/vg00/lvol6   1025617  605780  317275   66% /usr
>>>>> documenting first 30 lines of lvm information by: lvdisplay -v /dev/vg00/
lvol6 | head -30
    the logical volume is:/dev/vg00/lvol6
    --- Logical volumes ---
    LV Name                     /dev/vg00/lvol6
    VG Name                     /dev/vg00
    LV Permission               read/write
    LV Status                   available/syncd
    Mirror copies               0
    Consistency Recovery        MWC
    Schedule                    parallel
    LV Size (Mbytes)            1024
    Current LE                  256
    Allocated PE                256
    Stripes                     0
    Stripe Size (Kbytes)        0
    Bad block                   on
    Allocation                  strict

        --- Distribution of logical volume ---
        PV Name             LE on PV  PE on PV
        /dev/dsk/c0t6d0     36        36
        /dev/dsk/c0t5d0     220       220

        --- Logical extents ---
        LE    PV1                 PE1  Status 1
        0000 /dev/dsk/c0t6d0      0471 current
        0001 /dev/dsk/c0t6d0      0472 current
        0002 /dev/dsk/c0t6d0      0473 current
        0003 /dev/dsk/c0t6d0      0474 current
        0004 /dev/dsk/c0t6d0      0475 current
        0005 /dev/dsk/c0t6d0      0476 current
        0006 /dev/dsk/c0t6d0      0477 current

>>>>> /dev/vg00/lvol4 IS mounted, line from bdf is:
/dev/vg00/lvol4   1025617  667722  255333   72% /opt
>>>>> documenting first 30 lines of lvm information by: lvdisplay -v /dev/vg00/
lvol4 | head -30
    the logical volume is:/dev/vg00/lvol4
    --- Logical volumes ---
    LV Name                     /dev/vg00/lvol4
    VG Name                     /dev/vg00
    LV Permission               read/write
    LV Status                   available/syncd
    Mirror copies               0
    Consistency Recovery        MWC
    Schedule                    parallel
    LV Size (Mbytes)            1024
    Current LE                  256
    Allocated PE                256
    Stripes                     0
    Stripe Size (Kbytes)        0
```

```
Bad block                    on
Allocation                   strict

   --- Distribution of logical volume ---
   PV Name             LE on PV  PE on PV
   /dev/dsk/c0t6d0     256       256

   --- Logical extents ---
   LE   PV1                 PE1   Status 1
   0000 /dev/dsk/c0t6d0     0165  current
   0001 /dev/dsk/c0t6d0     0166  current
   0002 /dev/dsk/c0t6d0     0167  current
   0003 /dev/dsk/c0t6d0     0168  current
   0004 /dev/dsk/c0t6d0     0169  current
   0005 /dev/dsk/c0t6d0     0170  current
   0006 /dev/dsk/c0t6d0     0171  current
   0007 /dev/dsk/c0t6d0     0172  current
```

Patches

The following script, called **audpatch.sh**, is used to produce a list of patches installed on your system. The program categorizes the patches as well as listing them.

```ksh
#!/bin/ksh


echo "\nThis is a list of patches installed on system `hostname`\n"

swlist > swlist.out

        WORD_COUNT=$(cat swlist.out | grep PHKL | wc -l)
        echo "\n\nNumber of kernel patches on `hostname` is $WORD_COUNT."
echo "\nKernel patches : \n"
        echo " Patch Number \t\t\t\t Revision \t Description"
        cat swlist.out | grep PHKL

        WORD_COUNT=$(cat swlist.out | grep PHCO | wc -l)
        echo "\n\nNumber of command patches on `hostname` is $WORD_COUNT."
echo "\nCommand patches : \n"
        echo " Patch Number \t\t\t\t Revision \t Description"
        cat swlist.out | grep PHCO

        WORD_COUNT=$(cat swlist.out | grep PHNE | wc -l)
        echo "\n\nNumber of network patches on `hostname` is $WORD_COUNT."
echo "\nNetwork patches : \n"
        echo " Patch Number \t\t\t\t Revision \t Description"
        cat swlist.out | grep PHNE

        WORD_COUNT=$(cat swlist.out | grep PHSS | wc -l)
        echo "\n\nNumber of subsystem patches on `hostname` is $WORD_COUNT."
echo "\nSubsystem patches : \n"
        echo " Patch Number \t\t\t\t Revision \t Description"
        cat swlist.out | grep PHSS
```

The following output was received from running **audpatch.sh**:

```
# audpatch.sh


This is a list of patches installed on system hpux1


Number of kernel patches on hpux1 is 25.

Kernel patches :

    Patch Number  Revision              Description
     PHKL_10258   B.10.00.00.AA  exec, ptrace, MMF, large shmem, large buf cache
     PHKL_10443   B.10.00.00.AA  SCSI Passthru driver cumulative patch
     PHKL_10453   B.10.00.00.AA  LVM kernel and pstat cumulative patch
     PHKL_10459   B.10.00.00.AA  cumulative patch for SystemV semaphores, semop()
     PHKL_10464   B.10.00.00.AA  HP-PB SCSI cumulative patch (scsi1/scsi3)
     PHKL_10670   B.10.00.00.AA  disc3/disc30 cumulative patch
     PHKL_7764    B.10.00.00.AA  Data loss when truncating VxFS (JFS) files
     PHKL_7765    B.10.00.00.AA  hpux(1M) for kernels larger than 13 MBytes
     PHKL_7900    B.10.00.00.AA  JFS KI, page fault, deadlock, & setuid fixes
     PHKL_8188    B.10.00.00.AA  B_NDELAY and Zalon chip hang workaround.
     PHKL_8204    B.10.00.00.AA  Fix for system hang during panic
     PHKL_8377    B.10.00.00.AA  Fix vmtrace bug. Release malloc memory.
     PHKL_8656    B.10.00.00.AA  panic with autochanger connected to FW interface
     PHKL_8684    B.10.00.00.AA  Two panics page fault on ICS - sysmemunreserve.
     PHKL_8780    B.10.00.00.AA  panic on GSC/HSC MP machines on kernel semaphore
     PHKL_9076    B.10.00.00.AA  MMF performance, large SHMEM, large buffer cache
     PHKL_9152    B.10.00.00.AA  Performance enhancements for PA-8000 systems.
     PHKL_9156    B.10.00.00.AA  NFS Kernel Cumulative Megapatch
     PHKL_9362    B.10.00.00.AA  Fix panic caused by MP race
     PHKL_9366    B.10.00.00.AA  Data corruption on PA-8000 based systems.
     PHKL_9371    B.10.00.00.AA  Various fixes for unmountable VxFS file systems
     PHKL_9570    B.10.00.00.AA  NFS and VxFS (JFS) cumulative patch
     PHKL_9712    B.10.00.00.AA  VxFS (JFS) patch for "edquota -t"
     PHKL_9724    B.10.00.00.AA  select() system call performance improvement
     PHKL_SP20    B.10.00.00.AA  Unofficial_test_patch


Number of command patches on hpux1 is 11.

Command patches :

    Patch Number  Revision              Description
     PHCO_10016   A.01.20        HP Disk Array Utilities w/AutoRAID Manager
     PHCO_10027   B.10.00.00.AA  libc cumulative patch
     PHCO_10048   B.10.00.00.AA  LVM commands cumulative patch
     PHCO_10175   B.10.00.00.AA  libc year2000 white paper
     PHCO_10295   B.10.00.00.AA  Allows umounting a disabled vxfs snapshot FS
     PHCO_7817    B.10.00.00.AA  fixes LVM maintenance mode HFS fsck error
     PHCO_8549    B.10.00.00.AA  extendfs_hfs fix for large file systems
     PHCO_9228    B.10.00.00.AA  Fbackup(1M) Long User or Group Name Patch
     PHCO_9396    B.10.00.00.AA  Fix for umountable VxFS file systems
```

```
      PHCO_9543      B.10.00.00.AA  Allows umount to unmount a Stale NFS FS
      PHCO_9895      B.10.00.00.AA  Cumulative SAM Patch 4.


   Number of network patches on hpux1 is 6.

   Network patches :

     Patch Number  Revision          Description
      PHNE_10512   B.10.00.00.AA  LAN products cumulative Patch
      PHNE_6190    B.10.00.00.AA  cumulative ocd(1M) patch
      PHNE_8328    B.10.00.00.AA  cumulative telnetd(1M) patch
      PHNE_9060    B.10.00.00.AA  Fix a panic in STREAMS
      PHNE_9107    B.10.00.00.AA  cumulative ARPA Transport patch
      PHNE_9438    B.10.00.00.AA  Cumulative Mux and Pty Patch


   Number of subsystem patches on hpux1 is 12.

   Subsystem patches :

     Patch Number  Revision          Description
      PHSS_7789    C.10.20.02     Predictive Support: SCSISCAN-Switch Log
      PHSS_8490    B.10.00.00.AA  cumulative pxdb patch.
      PHSS_8590    B.10.00.00.AA  third diagnostic patch
      PHSS_8709    B.10.00.00.AA  X11R5/Motif1.2 Development Nov96 Patch
      PHSS_8711    B.10.00.00.AA  X11R6/Motif1.2 Development Nov96 Patch
      PHSS_9096    B.10.00.00.AA  HP C++ core library components (A.10.24)
      PHSS_9356    B.10.00.00.AA  X11R5/Xt/Motif Nov-D Point patch
      PHSS_9400    B.10.00.00.AA  ld(1) cumulative patch
      PHSS_9778    B.10.00.00.AA  X11R6/Xt/Motif Nov96-D Point patch
      PHSS_9803    B.10.00.00.AA  CDE Runtime Mar97 Patch
      PHSS_9855    B.10.00.00.AA  HP C++ (A.10.24) with a correct eh/lib++.a
      PHSS_9977    B.10.00.00.AA  HP aC++ (A.01.02) to fix numerous defects
```

The following is the file **swlist.out** that was produced in the script by running the **swlist** command. You can see that the summary list of patches produced by **audpatch.sh** is much easier to read than this **swlist** output.

```
      # Initializing...
      # Contacting target "hpux1"...
      #
      # Target: hpux1:/
      #

      #
      # Bundle(s):
      #

        2UserDegradeB.10.20            HP-UX 2-User License (For degrading user license
level)
        A3516A_APZA.01.16        HP Disk Array Utilities for Unix (S800)
        B2491A_APZB.10.20        MirrorDisk/UX
        B3191A_APZB.10.20            DCE/9000 Core Services Media and Manuals, Interna-
tional version
        B3193A_APZB.10.20        DCE/9000 Application Development Tools Media and Man-
uals
```

```
        B3395AA_APZB.10.20.02      HP-UX Developer's Toolkit for 10.0 Series 800
        B3519AA_APZB.10.20              DCE/9000 Quickstart Bundle, International version,
Media and Manuals
        B3701AA_APZ_TRYB.10.20.89      Trial HP GlancePlus/UX Pak for s800 10.20
        B3900AA_APZB.10.20.02     HP C/ANSI C Developer's Bundle for HP-UX 10.20 (S800)
        B3912AA_APZB.10.20.02      HP C++ Compiler S800
        B3912BA_APZA.01.00         HP aC++ Compiler S800
        B3919CA_AGLB.10.20         HP-UX 8-User License
        B3920CAB.10.20          HP-UX Media Kit (Reference Only. See Description)
        B4085CBEngC.05.25          English C SoftBench S800 10.x
        B4087CBEngC.05.25          English C++ SoftBench S800 10.x
        B4474EA_APZ7.09            ENWARE X Station Software
        B5050BBEngC.05.25          English SoftBench CM S800 10.x
        DCEProgB.10.20          DCE Programming and Archive Libraries
        DCESystemAdminB.10.20         DCE System Administration Utilities
        GSLDevEnvB.10.20         GSL Starbase/PEX Development Environment
        HPUXEngGS800B.10.20         English HP-UX VUE Runtime Environment
        Integ-LogonB.10.20         Integrated Logon Bundle
        J2559CD.01.08           Hewlett-Packard JetAdmin for Unix Utility
        MiscDiagB.10.20.02         HPUX 10.0 Support Tools Bundle
        OnlineDiagB.10.20.02       HPUX 10.0 Support Tools Bundle
        SoftBenchRefC.05.25         SoftBench 5.0 (Reference Only.  See Description)
        VUE-to-CDE-ToolsB.10.20        VUE to CDE Migration Tools (for all languages)
        #
        # Product(s) not contained in a Bundle:
        #

        LROMB.02.01          HP LaserROM/UX
        OVOPC-UX10-NODA.03.01           OpC Mgd Node SW running on HP-UX 10.0
        PHCO_10016A.01.20          HP Disk Array Utilities w/AutoRAID Manager
        PHCO_10027B.10.00.00.AA  libc cumulative patch
        PHCO_10048B.10.00.00.AA  LVM commands cumulative patch
        PHCO_10175B.10.00.00.AA  libc year2000 white paper
        PHCO_10295B.10.00.00.AA  Allows umounting a disabled vxfs snapshot FS
        PHCO_7817B.10.00.00.AA   fixes LVM maintenance mode HFS fsck error
        PHCO_8549B.10.00.00.AA   extendfs_hfs fix for large file systems
        PHCO_9228B.10.00.00.AA   Fbackup(1M) Long User or Group Name Patch
        PHCO_9396B.10.00.00.AA   Fix for umountable VxFS file systems
        PHCO_9543B.10.00.00.AA   Allows umount to unmount a Stale NFS FS
        PHCO_9895B.10.00.00.AA   Cumulative SAM Patch 4.
        PHKL_10258B.10.00.00.AA  exec, ptrace, MMF, large shmem, large buf cache
        PHKL_10443B.10.00.00.AA  SCSI Passthru driver cumulative patch
        PHKL_10453B.10.00.00.AA  LVM kernel and pstat cumulative patch
        PHKL_10459B.10.00.00.AA  cumulative patch for SystemV semaphores, semop()
        PHKL_10464B.10.00.00.AA  HP-PB SCSI cumulative patch (scsi1/scsi3)
        PHKL_10670B.10.00.00.AA  disc3/disc30 cumulative patch
        PHKL_7764B.10.00.00.AA   Data loss when truncating VxFS (JFS) files
        PHKL_7765B.10.00.00.AA   hpux(1M) for kernels larger than 13 MBytes
        PHKL_7900B.10.00.00.AA   JFS KI, page fault, deadlock, & setuid fixes
        PHKL_8188B.10.00.00.AA   B_NDELAY and Zalon chip hang workaround.
        PHKL_8204B.10.00.00.AA   Fix for system hang during panic
        PHKL_8377B.10.00.00.AA   Fix vmtrace bug. Release malloc memory.
        PHKL_8656B.10.00.00.AA   panic with autochanger connected to FW interface
        PHKL_8684B.10.00.00.AA   Two panics page fault on ICS - sysmemunreserve.
        PHKL_8780B.10.00.00.AA   panic on GSC/HSC MP machines on kernel semaphore
        PHKL_9076B.10.00.00.AA   MMF performance, large SHMEM, large buffer cache
        PHKL_9152B.10.00.00.AA   Performance enhancements for PA-8000 systems.
        PHKL_9156B.10.00.00.AA   NFS Kernel Cumulative Megapatch
        PHKL_9362B.10.00.00.AA   Fix panic caused by MP race
        PHKL_9366B.10.00.00.AA   Data corruption on PA-8000 based systems.
        PHKL_9371B.10.00.00.AA   Various fixes for unmountable VxFS file systems
        PHKL_9570B.10.00.00.AA   NFS and VxFS (JFS) cumulative patch
        PHKL_9712B.10.00.00.AA   VxFS (JFS) patch for "edquota -t"
        PHKL_9724B.10.00.00.AA   select() system call performance improvement
        PHKL_SP20B.10.00.00.AA   Unofficial_test_patch
        PHNE_10512B.10.00.00.AA  LAN products cumulative Patch
```

```
PHNE_6190B.10.00.00.AA   cumulative ocd(1M) patch
PHNE_8328B.10.00.00.AA   cumulative telnetd(1M) patch
PHNE_9060B.10.00.00.AA   Fix a panic in STREAMS
PHNE_9107B.10.00.00.AA   cumulative ARPA Transport patch
PHNE_9438B.10.00.00.AA   Cumulative Mux and Pty Patch
PHSS_7789C.10.20.02      Predictive Support: SCSISCAN-Switch Log
PHSS_8490B.10.00.00.AA   cumulative pxdb patch.
PHSS_8590B.10.00.00.AA   third diagnostic patch
PHSS_8709B.10.00.00.AA   X11R5/Motif1.2 Development Nov96 Patch
PHSS_8711B.10.00.00.AA   X11R6/Motif1.2 Development Nov96 Patch
PHSS_9096B.10.00.00.AA   HP C++ core library components (A.10.24)
PHSS_9356B.10.00.00.AA   X11R5/Xt/Motif Nov-D Point patch
PHSS_9400B.10.00.00.AA   ld(1) cumulative patch
PHSS_9778B.10.00.00.AA   X11R6/Xt/Motif Nov96-D Point patch
PHSS_9803B.10.00.00.AA   CDE Runtime Mar97 Patch
PHSS_9855B.10.00.00.AA   HP C++ (A.10.24) with a correct eh/lib++.a
PHSS_9977B.10.00.00.AA   HP aC++ (A.01.02) to fix numerous defects
```

Software Check

The following script, called **audswchk.sh**, runs the **swverify** command to verify the software installed on your system.

```
#!/usr/bin/ksh
# testing of swverify command
echo " About to verify installed software using swverify"
echo " Please be patient, this can take 10-20 minutes"
swverify -x allow_incompatible=true -x autoselect_dependencies=false \* 1>/dev/
null 2>&1
   begnum=`grep -n 'BEGIN verify AGENT SESSION' /var/adm/sw/swagent.log | \
   tail -1 | cut -d: -f1`
   endnum=`cat /var/adm/sw/swagent.log | wc -l`
   let tailnum=`endnum-begnum`
   if [ "$tailnum" -gt 0 ]; then
   echo "Writing swverify data to file audswchk.out"
   tail -n $tailnum /var/adm/sw/swagent.log >audswchk.out 2>&1
   fi
```

The following output was created from running **audswchk.sh**. In addition to this output file there is also a message written to the screen indicating that it may take some time for this script to complete. The system on which this **audswchk.sh** was run is a smooth-running system with no known errors, yet this output is very long and shows some warnings and errors that could result in serious problems.

```
WARNING: Fileset "VUEHelpDevKit.VUE-HELP-PRG,l=/,r=B.10.20.01" had file
```

```
          warnings.
WARNING:  Directory "/" should have mode "1363" but the actual mode is
          "755".
WARNING:  Directory "/" should have owner,uid "xbuild,3395" but the
          actual owner,uid is "root,0".
WARNING:  Directory "/" should have group,gid "users,20" but the actual
          group,gid is "root,0".
WARNING:  Fileset "VUEHelpDevKit.VUE-PRG-MAN,l=/,r=B.10.20.01" had file
          warnings.
WARNING:  Directory "/" should have mode "555" but the actual mode is
          "755".
WARNING:  Directory "/" should have owner,uid "xbuild,3395" but the
          actual owner,uid is "root,0".
WARNING:  Directory "/" should have group,gid "users,20" but the actual
          group,gid is "root,0".
WARNING:  Directory "/usr" should have owner,uid "root,0" but the actual
          owner,uid is "bin,2".
WARNING:  Directory "/usr" should have group,gid "other,1" but the
          actual group,gid is "bin,2".
WARNING:  Directory "/usr/lib" should have owner,uid "root,0" but the
          actual owner,uid is "bin,2".
WARNING:  Directory "/usr/lib" should have group,gid "other,1" but the
          actual group,gid is "bin,2".
WARNING:  Directory "/usr/lib/X11" should have owner,uid "xbuild,3395"
          but the actual owner,uid is "bin,2".
WARNING:  Directory "/usr/lib/X11" should have group,gid "users,20" but
          the actual group,gid is "bin,2".
WARNING:  Fileset "X11MotifDevKit.IMAKE,l=/,r=B.10.20.02" had file
          warnings.
WARNING:  Directory "/" should have mode "555" but the actual mode is
          "755".
WARNING:  Directory "/" should have group,gid "other,1" but the actual
          group,gid is "root,0".
ERROR:    File "/usr/lib/libXm.a" missing.
ERROR:    Fileset "X11MotifDevKit.MOTIF12-PRG,l=/,r=B.10.20.02" had file
          errors.
WARNING:  Directory "/" should have mode "555" but the actual mode is
          "755".
WARNING:  Directory "/" should have owner,uid "xbuild,3395" but the
          actual owner,uid is "root,0".
WARNING:  Directory "/" should have group,gid "users,20" but the actual
          group,gid is "root,0".
WARNING:  Directory "/usr/dt" should have owner,uid "root,0" but the
          actual owner,uid is "bin,2".
WARNING:  Directory "/usr/dt" should have group,gid "other,1" but the
          actual group,gid is "bin,2".
WARNING:  Directory "/usr/dt/share" should have owner,uid "root,0" but
          the actual owner,uid is "bin,2".
WARNING:  Directory "/usr/dt/share" should have group,gid "other,1" but
          the actual group,gid is "bin,2".
WARNING:  Directory "/usr/dt/share/man" should have owner,uid "root,0"
          but the actual owner,uid is "bin,2".
WARNING:  Directory "/usr/dt/share/man" should have group,gid "other,1"
          but the actual group,gid is "bin,2".
WARNING:  Directory "/usr/share" should have owner,uid "xbuild,3395" but
          the actual owner,uid is "bin,2".
WARNING:  Directory "/usr/share" should have group,gid "users,20" but
          the actual group,gid is "bin,2".
WARNING:  Directory "/usr/share/man/man3.Z" should have owner,uid
          "xbuild,3395" but the actual owner,uid is "bin,2".
WARNING:  Directory "/usr/share/man/man3.Z" should have group,gid
          "users,20" but the actual group,gid is "bin,2".
WARNING:  Fileset "X11MotifDevKit.MOTIF12-PRGMAN,l=/,r=B.10.20.02" had
          file warnings.
WARNING:  Directory "/" should have mode "555" but the actual mode is
          "755".
```

```
WARNING: Directory "/" should have group,gid "other,1" but the actual
         group,gid is "root,0".
WARNING: Fileset "X11MotifDevKit.X11R5-PRG,l=/,r=B.10.20.02" had file
         warnings.
WARNING: Directory "/" should have mode "555" but the actual mode is
         "755".
WARNING: Directory "/" should have group,gid "other,1" but the actual
         group,gid is "root,0".
WARNING: Directory "/usr/newconfig" should have owner,uid "root,0" but
         the actual owner,uid is "bin,2".
WARNING: Directory "/usr/newconfig" should have group,gid "other,1" but
         the actual group,gid is "bin,2".
WARNING: Fileset "X11MotifDevKit.X11R6-PRG,l=/,r=B.10.20.02" had file
         warnings.
WARNING: Directory "/" should have mode "555" but the actual mode is
         "755".
WARNING: Directory "/" should have group,gid "other,1" but the actual
         group,gid is "root,0".
WARNING: Directory "/usr/contrib/lib" should have owner,uid
         "xbuild,3395" but the actual owner,uid is "bin,2".
WARNING: Directory "/usr/contrib/lib" should have group,gid "users,20"
         but the actual group,gid is "bin,2".
WARNING: Fileset "X11MotifDevKit.X11R6-PRG-CTRB,l=/,r=B.10.20.02" had
         file warnings.
WARNING: Directory "/" should have mode "555" but the actual mode is
         "755".
WARNING: Directory "/" should have group,gid "other,1" but the actual
         group,gid is "root,0".
ERROR:   File "/usr/share/man/man3.Z/XHPSSChange.3x" had a different
         mtime than expected.
ERROR:   Fileset "X11MotifDevKit.X11R6-PRG-MAN,l=/,r=B.10.20.02" had
         file errors.

       * Summary of Analysis Phase:
ERROR:       Verify failed Diag-Sys-800.SUP-CORE-800,l=/,r=B.10.20.02
ERROR:       Verify failed OS-Core.CORE-KRN,l=/,r=B.10.20
ERROR:       Verify failed OS-Core.C2400-UTIL,l=/,r=B.10.20
ERROR:       Verify failed OS-Core.Q4,l=/,r=B.10.20
ERROR:       Verify failed LVM.LVM-RUN,l=/,r=B.10.20
ERROR:       Verify failed LVM.LVM-MIRROR-RUN,l=/,r=B.10.20
ERROR:       Verify failed PHKL_10258.PHKL_10258,l=/,r=B.10.00.00.AA
ERROR:       Verify failed PHKL_10464.PHKL_10464,l=/,r=B.10.00.00.AA
ERROR:       Verify failed PHKL_10670.PHKL_10670,l=/,r=B.10.00.00.AA
ERROR:       Verify failed PHKL_SP20.PHKL_SP20,l=/,r=B.10.00.00.AA
ERROR:       Verify failed
         Sup-Tool-Mgr-800.STM-UUT-800-RUN,l=/,r=B.10.20.02
ERROR:       Verify failed UserLicense.08-USER,l=/,r=B.10.20
WARNING:     Verified with warnings ACXX.ACXX,l=/opt/aCC,r=A.01.00
WARNING:     Verified with warnings ACXX.ACXX-HELP,l=/opt/aCC,r=A.01.00
WARNING:     Verified with warnings
         ACXX.ACXX-JPN-E-MAN,l=/opt/aCC,r=A.01.00
WARNING:     Verified with warnings
         ACXX.ACXX-JPN-S-MAN,l=/opt/aCC,r=A.01.00
WARNING:     Verified with warnings ACXX.ACXX-MAN,l=/opt/aCC,r=A.01.00
WARNING:     Verified with warnings ACXX.ACXX-SC,l=/opt/aCC,r=A.01.00
WARNING:     Verified with warnings
         ACXX.ACXX-STDLIB,l=/opt/aCC,r=A.01.00
WARNING:     Verified with warnings
         AudioDevKit.AUDIO-PGMAN,l=/opt/audio,r=B.10.10.00
WARNING:     Verified with warnings
         AudioDevKit.AUDIO-PRG,l=/opt/audio,r=B.10.10.00
WARNING:     Verified with warnings
         C-ANSI-C.C,l=/opt/ansic,r=B.10.20.00
ERROR:       Verify failed C-Plus-Plus.HPCXX,l=/opt/CC,r=B.10.20.00
ERROR:       Verify failed C-Plus-Plus.HPCXX-MAN,l=/opt/CC,r=B.10.20.00
ERROR:       Verify failed CDE.CDE-RUN,l=/,r=B.10.20
```

```
WARNING:       Verified with warnings
          CDEDevKit.CDE-DEMOS,l=/,r=B.10.20.02
WARNING:       Verified with warnings
          CDEDevKit.CDE-HELP-PRG,l=/,r=B.10.20.02
WARNING:       Verified with warnings CDEDevKit.CDE-INC,l=/,r=B.10.20.02
WARNING:       Verified with warnings
          CDEDevKit.CDE-MAN-DEV,l=/,r=B.10.20.02
WARNING:       Verified with warnings CDEDevKit.CDE-PRG,l=/,r=B.10.20.02
WARNING:       Verified with warnings
          COBOLRT.COBRT,l=/opt/cobol,r=B.11.25
WARNING:       Verified with warnings
          COBOLCRT.COBCRT,l=/opt/cobol,r=B.11.25
WARNING:       Verified with warnings
          COBOLDEV.COBDEV,l=/opt/cobol,r=B.11.25
WARNING:       Verified with warnings
          COBOLTBOX.COBTBOX,l=/opt/cobol,r=B.11.25
WARNING:       Verified with warnings
          CustomerServ.CUST-SERV,l=/opt/secustserv,r=C.05.25
WARNING:       Verified with warnings
          CustomerServ.CUST-SERV-J,l=/opt/secustserv,r=C.05.25
ERROR:         Verify failed
          DCE-CoreAdmin.DCE-CORE-DIAG,l=/opt/dce,r=B.10.20
WARNING:       Verified with warnings
          DigitalVideoDK.DVC-PRG,l=/,r=B.10.20.01
WARNING:       Verified with warnings
          DigitalVideoDK.DVC-PRGMAN,l=/,r=B.10.20.01
WARNING:       Verified with warnings
          DigitalVideoDK.DVC-SHLIBS,l=/,r=B.10.20.01
WARNING:       Verified with warnings
          DigitalVideoDK.DVC-SRV,l=/,r=B.10.20.01
WARNING:       Verified with warnings
          DigitalVideoDK.DVIDEO-FILES,l=/,r=B.10.20.01
WARNING:       Verified with warnings
          DigitalVideoDK.DVIDEO-PGMAN,l=/,r=B.10.20.01
WARNING:       Verified with warnings
          DigitalVideoDK.DVIDEO-PRG,l=/,r=B.10.20.01
WARNING:       Verified with warnings
          DigitalVideoDK.VIDEOOUT-PGMAN,l=/,r=B.10.20.01
WARNING:       Verified with warnings
          DigitalVideoDK.VIDEOOUT-PRG,l=/,r=B.10.20.01
WARNING:       Verified with warnings
          DigitalVideoDK.VIDEOOUT-SHLIBS,l=/,r=B.10.20.01
ERROR:         Verify failed ENWARE.HPXT-SUPPL,l=/opt/hpxt/enware,r=7.09
ERROR:         Verify failed ENWARE.HPXT-700RX,l=/opt/hpxt/enware,r=7.09
ERROR:         Verify failed ENWARE.HPXT-AUDIO,l=/opt/hpxt/enware,r=7.09
ERROR:         Verify failed ENWARE.HPXT-CDE,l=/opt/hpxt/enware,r=7.09
ERROR:         Verify failed
          ENWARE.HPXT-CLIENTS,l=/opt/hpxt/enware,r=7.09
ERROR:         Verify failed ENWARE.HPXT-ENVIZE,l=/opt/hpxt/enware,r=7.09
ERROR:         Verify failed ENWARE.HPXT-NFS,l=/opt/hpxt/enware,r=7.09
ERROR:         Verify failed ENWARE.HPXT-FLOPPY,l=/opt/hpxt/enware,r=7.09
ERROR:         Verify failed
          ENWARE.HPXT-HP8FONTS,l=/opt/hpxt/enware,r=7.09
ERROR:         Verify failed
          ENWARE.HPXT-ISOFONTS,l=/opt/hpxt/enware,r=7.09
ERROR:         Verify failed
          ENWARE.HPXT-MISCFONT,l=/opt/hpxt/enware,r=7.09
ERROR:         Verify failed ENWARE.HPXT-MPEG,l=/opt/hpxt/enware,r=7.09
ERROR:         Verify failed
          ENWARE.HPXT-PRINTER,l=/opt/hpxt/enware,r=7.09
ERROR:         Verify failed
          ENWARE.HPXT-SCANNER,l=/opt/hpxt/enware,r=7.09
ERROR:         Verify failed ENWARE.HPXT-TOKN,l=/opt/hpxt/enware,r=7.09
ERROR:         Verify failed ENWARE.HPXT-VT320,l=/opt/hpxt/enware,r=7.09
ERROR:         Verify failed ENWARE.HPXT-XLOCK,l=/opt/hpxt/enware,r=7.09
ERROR:         Verify failed ENWARE.HPXT-XTOUCH,l=/opt/hpxt/enware,r=7.09
```

```
WARNING:      Verified with warnings
          MeasureWare.MWA,l=/opt/perf,r=B.10.20.89
WARNING:      Verified with warnings
          GraphicsPEX5DK.PEX5-EXAMPLES,l=/opt/graphics/PEX5,r=B.10.20
WARNING:      Verified with warnings
          GraphicsPEX5DK.PEX5-HELP,l=/opt/graphics/PEX5,r=B.10.20
WARNING:      Verified with warnings
          GraphicsPEX5DK.PEX5-PRG,l=/opt/graphics/PEX5,r=B.10.20
WARNING:      Verified with warnings
          GraphicsSBaseDK.FAFM-MAN,l=/opt/graphics/starbase,r=B.10.20
WARNING:      Verified with warnings
          GraphicsSBaseDK.FAFM-PRG,l=/opt/graphics/starbase,r=B.10.20
WARNING:      Verified with warnings
          GraphicsSBaseDK.SBDL-DEMO,l=/opt/graphics/starbase,r=B.10.20
WARNING:      Verified with warnings
          GraphicsSBaseDK.SBDL-MAN,l=/opt/graphics/starbase,r=B.10.20
WARNING:      Verified with warnings
          GraphicsSBaseDK.SBDL-PRG,l=/opt/graphics/starbase,r=B.10.20
WARNING:      Verified with warnings
          GraphicsSBaseDK.STAR-DEMO,l=/opt/graphics/starbase,r=B.10.20
WARNING:      Verified with warnings
          GraphicsSBaseDK.STAR-HARDCOPY,l=/opt/graphics/starbase,r=B.10.20

WARNING:      Verified with warnings
          GraphicsSBaseDK.STAR-MAN,l=/opt/graphics/starbase,r=B.10.20
WARNING:      Verified with warnings
          GraphicsSBaseDK.STAR-PRG,l=/opt/graphics/starbase,r=B.10.20
WARNING:      Verified with warnings
          GraphicsSBaseDK.STAR-WEBDOC,l=/opt/graphics/starbase,r=B.10.20
ERROR:        Verify failed
          HPAutoRAID.HPAutoRAID-MAN,l=/opt/hparray,r=A.01.16
ERROR:        Verify failed
          HPAutoRAID.HPAutoRAID-RUN,l=/opt/hparray,r=A.01.16
ERROR:        Verify failed HPNP.HPNP-RUN,l=/opt/hpnp,r=D.01.08
WARNING:      Verified with warnings
          ImagingDevKit.IMAGE-FILES,l=/,r=B.10.20.02
WARNING:      Verified with warnings
          ImagingDevKit.IMAGE-PGMAN,l=/,r=B.10.20.02
WARNING:      Verified with warnings
          ImagingDevKit.IMAGE-PRG,l=/,r=B.10.20.02
ERROR:        Verify failed LSSERV.LSSERV-ADMIN,l=/opt/ifor,r=B.10.20
WARNING:      Verified with warnings
          LSSERV.LSSERV-SERVER,l=/opt/ifor,r=B.10.20
ERROR:        Verify failed OVOPC-UX10-NOD.OVOPC-UX10,l=/,r=A.03.01
ERROR:        Verify failed PHCO_10048.PHCO_10048,l=/,r=B.10.00.00.AA
WARNING:      Verified with warnings SystemAdmin.SAM-HELP,l=/,r=B.10.20
WARNING:      Verified with warnings SystemAdmin.SAM,l=/,r=B.10.20
ERROR:        Verify failed PHSS_8709.PHSS_8709,l=/,r=B.10.00.00.AA
ERROR:        Verify failed PHSS_9855.PHSS_9855,l=/,r=B.10.00.00.AA
WARNING:      Verified with warnings
          SB-BMSFramework.BMS-ENG-A-MAN,l=/opt/softbench,r=C.05.25
WARNING:      Verified with warnings
          SB-BMSFramework.BMS-JPN-E-MAN,l=/opt/softbench,r=C.05.25
WARNING:      Verified with warnings
          SB-BMSFramework.BMS-JPN-E-MSG,l=/opt/softbench,r=C.05.25
WARNING:      Verified with warnings
          SB-BMSFramework.BMS-JPN-S-MAN,l=/opt/softbench,r=C.05.25
WARNING:      Verified with warnings
          SB-BMSFramework.BMS-JPN-S-MSG,l=/opt/softbench,r=C.05.25
WARNING:      Verified with warnings
          SB-BMSFramework.SB-BMS,l=/opt/softbench,r=C.05.25
WARNING:      Verified with warnings
          SB-BMSFramework.SB-BMSFW,l=/opt/softbench,r=C.05.25
ERROR:        Verify failed
          SB-BMSFramework.SB-FONTS,l=/opt/softbench,r=C.05.25
WARNING:      Verified with warnings
```

```
                SB-BMSFramework.SB-MSGCONN,l=/opt/softbench,r=C.05.25
WARNING:        Verified with warnings
                SB-BMSFramework.SBM-ENG-A-MAN,l=/opt/softbench,r=C.05.25
WARNING:        Verified with warnings
                SB-CM.SBCM-CLT,l=/opt/softbench,r=B.01.55
WARNING:        Verified with warnings
                SB-CM.SBCM-ENG-A-HLP,l=/opt/softbench,r=B.01.55
WARNING:        Verified with warnings
                SB-CM.SBCM-ENG-A-MAN,l=/opt/softbench,r=B.01.55
WARNING:        Verified with warnings
                SB-CM.SBCM-GUI,l=/opt/softbench,r=B.01.55
WARNING:        Verified with warnings
                SB-CM.SBCM-J,l=/opt/softbench,r=B.01.55
WARNING:        Verified with warnings
                SB-CM.SBCM-JPN-E-HLP,l=/opt/softbench,r=B.01.55
WARNING:        Verified with warnings
                SB-CM.SBCM-JPN-E-MAN,l=/opt/softbench,r=B.01.55
WARNING:        Verified with warnings
                SB-CM.SBCM-JPN-E-MSG,l=/opt/softbench,r=B.01.55
WARNING:        Verified with warnings
                SB-CM.SBCM-JPN-S-HLP,l=/opt/softbench,r=B.01.55
WARNING:        Verified with warnings
                SB-CM.SBCM-JPN-S-MAN,l=/opt/softbench,r=B.01.55
WARNING:        Verified with warnings
                SB-CM.SBCM-JPN-S-MSG,l=/opt/softbench,r=B.01.55
WARNING:        Verified with warnings
                SB-CM.SBCM-SRV,l=/opt/softbench,r=B.01.55
WARNING:        Verified with warnings
                SB-SoftBenchCore.SB40-LIBS,l=/opt/softbench,r=C.05.25
WARNING:        Verified with warnings
                SB-SoftBenchCore.SB-LSMGR,l=/opt/softbench,r=C.05.25
WARNING:        Verified with warnings
                SB-SoftBenchCore.SB-GNUBIN,l=/opt/softbench,r=C.05.25
ERROR:          Verify failed
                SB-SoftBenchCore.SB-CORE,l=/opt/softbench,r=C.05.25
WARNING:        Verified with warnings
                SB-SoftBenchCore.SB-COMMON,l=/opt/softbench,r=C.05.25
WARNING:        Verified with warnings
                SB-SoftBenchCore.SB-DT,l=/opt/softbench,r=C.05.25
WARNING:        Verified with warnings
                SB-SoftBenchCore.SB-DEMO,l=/opt/softbench,r=C.05.25
WARNING:        Verified with warnings
                SB-SoftBenchCore.SB-ENG-A-MAN,l=/opt/softbench,r=C.05.25
WARNING:        Verified with warnings
                SB-SoftBenchCore.SB-GNUBIN-MAN,l=/opt/softbench,r=C.05.25
WARNING:        Verified with warnings
                SB-SoftBenchCore.SB-GNUSRC,l=/opt/softbench,r=C.05.25
WARNING:        Verified with warnings
                SB-SoftBenchCore.SB-JPN-E-MAN,l=/opt/softbench,r=C.05.25
WARNING:        Verified with warnings
                SB-SoftBenchCore.SB-JPN-E-MSG,l=/opt/softbench,r=C.05.25
WARNING:        Verified with warnings
                SB-SoftBenchCore.SB-JPN-S-MAN,l=/opt/softbench,r=C.05.25
WARNING:        Verified with warnings
                SB-SoftBenchCore.SB-JPN-S-MSG,l=/opt/softbench,r=C.05.25
WARNING:        Verified with warnings
                SB-SoftBenchCore.SB40-EDL,l=/opt/softbench,r=C.05.25
WARNING:        Verified with warnings
                SB-SoftBenchCore.SBL-ENG-A-MAN,l=/opt/softbench,r=C.05.25
WARNING:        Verified with warnings
                SB-CPersonality.SB-ADA,l=/opt/softbench,r=C.05.25
WARNING:        Verified with warnings
                SB-CPersonality.SB-C,l=/opt/softbench,r=C.05.25
WARNING:        Verified with warnings
                SB-CPersonality.SB-CBTC,l=/opt/softbench,r=C.05.25
WARNING:        Verified with warnings
```

```
              SB-CPersonality.SB-DDE,l=/opt/softbench,r=C.05.25
WARNING:      Verified with warnings
              SB-CPersonality.SBC-ENG-A-HLP,l=/opt/softbench,r=C.05.25
WARNING:      Verified with warnings
              SB-CPersonality.SBC-ENG-A-MAN,l=/opt/softbench,r=C.05.25
WARNING:      Verified with warnings
              SB-CPersonality.SBC-JPN-E-HLP,l=/opt/softbench,r=C.05.25
WARNING:      Verified with warnings
              SB-CPersonality.SBC-JPN-E-MAN,l=/opt/softbench,r=C.05.25
WARNING:      Verified with warnings
              SB-CPersonality.SBC-JPN-E-MSG,l=/opt/softbench,r=C.05.25
WARNING:      Verified with warnings
              SB-CPersonality.SBC-JPN-S-HLP,l=/opt/softbench,r=C.05.25
WARNING:      Verified with warnings
              SB-CPersonality.SBC-JPN-S-MAN,l=/opt/softbench,r=C.05.25
WARNING:      Verified with warnings
              SB-CPersonality.SBC-JPN-S-MSG,l=/opt/softbench,r=C.05.25
WARNING:      Verified with warnings
              SB-CXXAdvisor.SB-RLCK,l=/opt/softbench,r=C.05.25
WARNING:      Verified with warnings
              SB-CXXAdvisor.SBA-ENG-A-HLP,l=/opt/softbench,r=C.05.25
WARNING:      Verified with warnings
              SB-CXXAdvisor.SBA-ENG-A-MAN,l=/opt/softbench,r=C.05.25
WARNING:      Verified with warnings
              SB-CXXPersnlty.SB-CBTCXX,l=/opt/softbench,r=C.05.25
WARNING:      Verified with warnings
              SB-CXXPersnlty.SB-CXX,l=/opt/softbench,r=C.05.25
WARNING:      Verified with warnings
              SB-CXXPersnlty.SBX-JPN-E-MSG,l=/opt/softbench,r=C.05.25
WARNING:      Verified with warnings
              SB-CXXPersnlty.SBX-JPN-S-MSG,l=/opt/softbench,r=C.05.25
WARNING:      Verified with warnings
              SB-CobolPersnlty.SB-CBTCOBOL,l=/opt/softbench,r=C.05.25
WARNING:      Verified with warnings
              SB-CobolPersnlty.SB-COBOL,l=/opt/softbench,r=C.05.25
WARNING:      Verified with warnings
              SB-CobolPersnlty.SB-COBOL-J,l=/opt/softbench,r=C.05.25
WARNING:      Verified with warnings
              SB-CobolPersnlty.SBO-ENG-A-HELP,l=/opt/softbench,r=C.05.25
WARNING:      Verified with warnings
              SB-CobolPersnlty.SBO-JPN-E-HELP,l=/opt/softbench,r=C.05.25
WARNING:      Verified with warnings
              SB-CobolPersnlty.SBO-JPN-E-MAN,l=/opt/softbench,r=C.05.25
WARNING:      Verified with warnings
              SB-CobolPersnlty.SBO-JPN-E-MSG,l=/opt/softbench,r=C.05.25
WARNING:      Verified with warnings
              SB-CobolPersnlty.SBO-JPN-S-HELP,l=/opt/softbench,r=C.05.25
WARNING:      Verified with warnings
              SB-CobolPersnlty.SBO-JPN-S-MAN,l=/opt/softbench,r=C.05.25
WARNING:      Verified with warnings
              SB-CobolPersnlty.SBO-JPN-S-MSG,l=/opt/softbench,r=C.05.25
WARNING:      Verified with warnings SW-DIST.SD-FAL,l=/,r=B.10.20
ERROR:        Verify failed VUE.VUE-RUN,l=/,r=B.10.20
WARNING:      Verified with warnings
              VUEHelpDevKit.VUE-HELP-PRG,l=/,r=B.10.20.01
WARNING:      Verified with warnings
              VUEHelpDevKit.VUE-PRG-MAN,l=/,r=B.10.20.01
WARNING:      Verified with warnings
              X11MotifDevKit.IMAKE,l=/,r=B.10.20.02
ERROR:        Verify failed X11MotifDevKit.MOTIF12-PRG,l=/,r=B.10.20.02
WARNING:      Verified with warnings
              X11MotifDevKit.MOTIF12-PRGMAN,l=/,r=B.10.20.02
WARNING:      Verified with warnings
              X11MotifDevKit.X11R5-PRG,l=/,r=B.10.20.02
WARNING:      Verified with warnings
              X11MotifDevKit.X11R6-PRG,l=/,r=B.10.20.02
```

```
WARNING:      Verified with warnings
              X11MotifDevKit.X11R6-PRG-CTRB,l=/,r=B.10.20.02
ERROR:        Verify failed
              X11MotifDevKit.X11R6-PRG-MAN,l=/,r=B.10.20.02
ERROR:    47 of 952 filesets had Errors.
WARNING: 124 of 952 filesets had Warnings.
       * 781 of 952 filesets had no Errors or Warnings.
ERROR:    The Analysis Phase had errors and warnings.  See the above
          output for details.


=======   19:18:13 EDT  END verify AGENT SESSION (pid=21385)
          (jobid=hpux1-0144)
```

Password and Group Check

The following script, called **audpassw.sh**, checks the **/etc/passwd** and **/etc/ group** files, looking for potential problems:

```ksh
#!/usr/bin/ksh

echo    "************************************************************" >
audpasswd.out
    echo  "  This program performs password and group checks on system `hostname`."
>> audpasswd.out
    echo
"************************************************************\n\n\n" >>  aud-
passwd.out
    echo   "Check for multiple root users by using awk on /etc/passwd." >> aud-
passwd.out
    echo  "The following users have a user ID of 0.\n" >> audpasswd.out
    awk -F: '{ if ( $3 == 0 ) print $1 }' /etc/passwd >> audpasswd.out

    echo "\n\nThe following users do not have a password assigned. " >> audpasswd.out
    echo "This could be a serious security problem on the system.\n" >> audpasswd.out
    awk -F: '{ if ( $2 == "" ) print $1 }' /etc/passwd >> audpasswd.out

    echo  "\n\n\nRunning password consistency check using pwck program." >> aud-
passwd.out
    echo "This program prints the password entry and corresponding" >> audpasswd.out
    echo "problem such as login directory not found or bad character" >> aud-
passwd.out
    echo "in login name.\n" >> audpasswd.out
    pwck 2>> audpasswd.out

    echo  "\n\n\nRunning group consistency check using grpck program." >> aud-
passwd.out
    echo "This program prints the group entry and corresponding" >> audpasswd.out
    echo "problem such as invalid GID, login name not in password" >> audpasswd.out
    echo "file, and groups in which there are no users.\n" >> audpasswd.out
    grpck 2>>audpasswd.out
```

This script produces the file **audpasswd.out**. This file has in it several potential user-and group-related problems, such as a user without a password:

```
*******************************************************************
   This program performs password and group checks on system hpux1.
*******************************************************************


   Check for multiple root users by using awk on /etc/passwd.
   The following users have a user ID of 0.

   root
   sam_exec


   The following users do not have a password assigned.
   This could be a serious security problem on the system.

   tburns



   Running password consistency check using pwck program.
   This program prints the password entry and corresponding
   problem such as login directory not found or bad character
   in login name.

   mcohn:2c4hWtfYlRwks:148:101:Mike,Cohn,,:/home/mcohn:/usr/local/bin/tcsh
   Login directory not found

   sam_exec:*:0:1::/home/sam_exec:/usr/bin/sh
   1 Bad character(s) in logname

   opc_op:*:777:77:OpC default operator:/home/opc_op:/usr/bin/ksh
   1 Bad character(s) in logname



   Running group consistency check using grpck program.
   This program prints the group entry and corresponding
   problem such as invalid GID, login name not in password
   file, and groups in which there are no users.



   tty::10:
   Null login name


   users::20:root,testhp,addadm,mflahert,tdolan,clloyd,eschwartz,jperwinc,denise
   denise - Logname not found in password file


   nogroup:*:-2:
   Invalid GID
   Null login name
```

Check for Disk Hogs

With the shell program in this section, you can regularly check both the characteristics of each logical volume as well as the amount of disk space consumed by each user. The following script, called **audhogs.sh**, uses the **fstyp**, **diskusg**, and **vxdiskusg** programs to produce reports:

```ksh
#!/usr/bin/ksh
# 1st print stats concerning the disk's file systems
echo "This program produces logical volume statistics and the amount of disk"
echo "space consumed by users on each logical volume. \n"
for fs in `bdf| grep '^/' | awk '{print $1}'`
do
fsys=`fstyp $fs`
echo "\n $printing logical volume stats for $fs using fstyp -v \n"
fstyp -v $fs 2>&1
if [ $fsys = vxfs ]
then
echo "\n finding space consumed per user for logical volume "
echo " $fs with vxdiskusg $fs \n"
/usr/sbin/acct/vxdiskusg $fs 2>&1 | tee -a $DESTF
else
# assume hfs type
echo "\n finding space consumed per user for logical volume "
echo " $fs with diskusg $fs \n"
echo "\nUserID login number of blocks "
echo "------ -------------------- \n"
        /usr/sbin/acct/diskusg $fs 2>&1
fi
done
```

I redirected the output of this script to **audhogs.out**. This file contains a summary of each logical volume and the amount of disk space on each logical volume consumed by each user. Only the first few logical volumes are shown.

```
This program produces logical volume statistics and the amount of disk
space consumed by users on each logical volume.

   logical volume stats for /dev/vg00/lvol3 using fstyp -v

hfs
f_bsize: 8192
f_frsize: 1024
f_blocks: 99669
f_bfree: 66562
f_bavail: 56595
f_files: 16128
f_ffree: 12525
f_favail: 12525
f_fsid: 1073741827
f_basetype: hfs
```

```
f_namemax: 255
f_magic: 95014
f_featurebits: 1
f_flag: 0
f_fsindex: 0
f_size: 102400

 finding space consumed per user for logical volume
 /dev/vg00/lvol3 with diskusg /dev/vg00/lvol3


UserID login number of blocks
------ ----- --------------

0       root    35014
1001    softcm  2
2       bin     30782
5       uucp    2
9       lp      410
100     adduser 4

  logical volume stats for /dev/vg00/lvol1 using fstyp -v

hfs
f_bsize: 8192
f_frsize: 1024
f_blocks: 47829
f_bfree: 17936
f_bavail: 13153
f_files: 7680
f_ffree: 7654
f_favail: 7654
f_fsid: 1073741825
f_basetype: hfs
f_namemax: 255
f_magic: 95014
f_featurebits: 1
f_flag: 0
f_fsindex: 0
f_size: 49152

 finding space consumed per user for logical volume
 /dev/vg00/lvol1 with diskusg /dev/vg00/lvol1


UserID login number of blocks
------ ----- --------------

0       root    59784
2       bin     2

  logical volume stats for /dev/vg00/lvol7 using fstyp -v

hfs
f_bsize: 8192
f_frsize: 1024
f_blocks: 723288
f_bfree: 431130
f_bavail: 358801
f_files: 351168
f_ffree: 340324
f_favail: 340324
f_fsid: 1073741831
f_basetype: hfs
f_namemax: 255
f_magic: 95014
```

```
f_featurebits: 1
f_flag: 0
f_fsindex: 0
f_size: 770048

finding space consumed per user for logical volume
/dev/vg00/lvol7 with diskusg /dev/vg00/lvol7


UserID login number of blocks
------ ----- --------------

0      root    318706
1      daemon  344
1001   softcm  4696
2      bin     197450
4      adm     1754
5      uucp    38
9      lp      328
100    adduser 2
102    user1   164
103    user2   6
104    user3   2
105    user4   68
107    user5   84
109    user6   288
113    user7   192
115    user8   416
116    user9   112
119    user10  110

        .
        .
        .
```

Ignite-UX Check

Ignite-UX is a product bundled with HP-UX that provides a process to create a bootable system recovery tape. Chapter 9 is devoted to Ignite-UX,
and the shell programming chapter includes some example shell programs
using Ignite-UX commands. In this section, I will first see if Ignite-UX is
loaded on the system. If indeed Ignite-UX is loaded on the system, I'll
check to see whether the **make_recovery** command has been run, which
produces a bootable system recover tape. The final check determines
whether **make_recovery** was run with the "-C" option. This option produces a snapshot of the system and allows us to run **check_recovery** to see
whether any important system files have been modified.

```
#!/bin/sh
{

echo "PROG>>>>> determining if Ignite-UX loaded on system."


igtest=`swlist | grep Ignite`
echo $igtest
if [ -n "$igtest" ]; then
echo "Ignite-UX installed"
else
echo "Ignite-UX is not installed"
fi

echo "PROG>>>>> determining if make_recovery has been run by
                checking for /var/opt/ignite/arch.include."

if [ -f /var/opt/ignite/recovery/arch.include ]; then
echo "make_recovery has been run."
else
echo "make_recovery has not been run."
fi

echo "PROG>>>>> determining if make_recovery was run with the
                -C (for check_recovery) option."

if [ -f /var/opt/ignite/recovery/makrec.last ]; then
echo "make_recovery with -C has been run. We'll now
                run check_recovery."
/opt/ignite/bin/check_recovery 2>&1
else
echo "make_recovery with -C has not been run. We can't
                run check_recovery."
fi

} | tee -a /tmp/IMPORTANT/igtest.out
```

The following output of the script shows that **make_recovery** is loaded and was run with the "-C" option. **check_recovery** was then run, showing that three important system files have changed.

```
PROG>>>>> determining if Ignite-UX loaded on system.
B5725AA B.1.48 HP-UX Installation Utilities (Ignite-UX) Ignite-UX-11-00 B.1.48 HP-UX
Installation Utilities for Installing 11.00 Systems
Ignite-UX installed
PROG>>>>> determining if make_recovery has been run by
                checking for /var/opt/ignite/arch.include.
make_recovery has been run.
PROG>>>>> determining if make_recovery was run with the
                -C (for check_recovery) option.
make_recovery with -C has been run. We'll now
                run check_recovery.

Since the last System Recovery Image was created, the following system
files (or links) have been added to the current system.

  /.rhosts
  /etc/hosts.equiv
  /usr/share/man/cat1.Z/lifcp.1
```

CHAPTER 9

System Recovery with Ignite-UX

System Recovery with Ignite-UX

Ignite-UX is a product bundled with HP-UX 11.x that provides a process to create a bootable system recovery tape. The tape contains a boot area and an operating system archive. Should your root disk fail or corruption of the root disk take place, you can recover using the bootable system recovery tape.

make_recovery is the Ignite-UX tool that is used to create the bootable system recovery tape. You could boot and restore from the system recovery tape and then use your system backup to fully restore the system. If your root disk were to fail, in a non-mirrored environment, you would perform the following steps to recover from the failure:

- Replace the defective root disk.

- Boot from the recovery tape by selecting the tape device.

- Monitor the restoration of the operating system archive from the recovery tape.

- Restore the balance of data on the system with backup information.

The bootable system recovery tape consists of both a Logical Interchange Format (LIF) volume as well as the operating system archive. The LIF volume contains all the components necessary to boot from the tape. The operating system archive contains only the core operating system by default.

You can include additional files in the operating system archive, if you wish using two different techniques. The first is to edit the file **/var/ opt/ignite/recovery/makrec.append** and add to it the file name, directory name, or software distributor product name you wish to include in the operating system archive. The second technique is to run **make_recovery** in preview mode with the **-p** option, manually add files to include and/or exclude from the archive, and resume the **make_recovery** with the **-r** option. The manual pages for **/opt/ignite/bin/make_recovery** and **/opt/ ignite/bin/ignite** appear at the end of this chapter.

You can also determine whether your recovery tape is up-to-date by using the **check_recovery** command. Running **make_recovery** with the -**C** option produces a system recovery status file. **check_recovery** compares the system recovery status file to the current state of the system and produces a list of discrepancies. From this list, you can determine whether or not you should produce another system recovery tape. The manual page for **/opt/ignite/bin/check_recovery** is also included at the end of this chapter.

The recovery feature is only one component of the Ignite-UX product. Ignite-UX provides a means to install systems over the network by either pushing the installation to a client from an Ignite server or pulling the installation from the Ignite server to the client. With Ignite-UX, "golden images" of your standard installation setup can be created and systems can be set up in a matter of minutes by "igniting" them from this image over the network. More information about Ignite-UX can be viewed on the Internet at **http://www.software.hp.com/products/IUX** and read about in the "Configuring an Ignite-UX Server" and "Installing from the Ignite-UX Server" chapters and Appendix C: "Ignite-UX System Administration" of the *Installing HP-UX 11.0 and Upgrading 10.x to 11.0* manual from Hewlett-Packard. The "HP-UX System Recovery" chapter of the same manual gives additional information about the **make_recovery** feature of Ignite-UX.

An Example of Creating a Bootable System Recovery Tape

Now that we have covered the basic components and capabilities of the Ignite-UX recovery process, let's take an example of creating a bootable system recovery tape.

Let's first run **make_recovery** with the **-p** option so that we see the way Ignite-UX reports the information it is including on the tape. I'll also use the **-A** option, which specifies that the entire root volume group is to be included. I sometimes use **make_recovery** to clone identical systems by producing a recovery tape with the **-A** option and then loading the tape on systems that I want to be identical to the original system. You would not use the **-A** option if you have a large root volume group or if you perform normal backups and don't need to include all root volume group information on the recovery tape. In addition to **-p** for preview and **-A** for all, I'll also use the **-v** for verbose option and **-C** to create the system status file in the following preview command example:

```
# make_recovery -p -v -A -C


        *** Previewing only ***
    Option -A specified. Entire Core Volume Group/disk will be backed up.


    *****************************************
    HP-UX System Recovery
    Validating append file
            Done

    File Systems on Core OS Disks/Volume Groups:

            vg name = vg00
            pv_name =  /dev/dsk/c0t5d0

            vg00        /dev/vg00/lvol3      /
            vg00        /dev/vg00/lvol4      /home
            vg00        /dev/vg00/lvol5      /opt
            vg00        /dev/vg00/lvol1      /stand
            vg00        /dev/vg00/lvol6      /tmp
            vg00        /dev/vg00/lvol7      /usr
            vg00        /dev/vg00/lvol8      /var

    Create mount points
     /apps
     /work
     /spill
     /spill2
     /rbdisk01
     /rbdisk02
     /rbdisk03
```

```
/rbdisk04
/rbdisk05
/rbdisk06
/rbdisk07
/rbdisk09
/rbdisk10
/rbdisk11
/rbdisk12
/rbdisk13
/rbdisk14
/rbdisk15
/rbdisk16
/rbdisk17
/rbdisk18
/nfs

        /opt is a mounted directory
          It is in the Core Volume Group
          Mounted at /dev/vg00/lvol5

        /var is a mounted directory
          It is in the Core Volume Group
          Mounted at /dev/vg00/lvol8

Destination = /dev/rmt/0m
Boot LIF location = /var/tmp/uxinstlf.recovery


*****************************************
   Preview only. Tape not created

The /var/opt/ignite/recovery/arch.include file has been created.
This can be modified to exclude known files.
Only delete files or directories that are strictly user created.
The creation of the System Recovery tape can then be
resumed using the -r option.

No further checks will be performed by the commands.
        Cleanup
```

The **arch.include** file has been produced at this point. The following is an abbreviated listing of **arch.include**, showing just the very beginning and very end of the file:

```
/
/lost+found
/etc
/etc/vue
/etc/vue/config
/etc/vue/config/types
/etc/vue/config/types/tools
/etc/vue/config/types/tools/System_Admin
/etc/vue/config/types/tools/System_Admin/FontClientSrvr
/etc/vue/config/types/tools/System_Admin/SetNetworking
/etc/vue/config/types/tools/System_Admin/ShutdownSystem
```

```
/etc/vue/config/types/tools/System_Admin/VerifyPEX
/etc/vue/config/types/tools/System_Admin/VerifyPEX
/etc/vue/config/types/tools/Media

    .
    .
    .

/spp/scripts/tc_standalone
/spp/scripts/sppconsole.old
/spp/unsupported
/spp/unsupported/cbus
/spp/unsupported/clear_pid
/spp/unsupported/ex_shm
/spp/unsupported/rdr_dumper.fw
/spp/unsupported/rdr_formatter
/spp/unsupported/reset_jtag
/spp/unsupported/scan_sram
/users
/users/sppuser
/users/sppuser/.Xdefaults
/users/sppuser/.cshrc
/users/sppuser/.kshrc
/users/sppuser/.login
/users/sppuser/.mwmrc
/users/sppuser/.profile
/users/sppuser/.x11start
/users/sppuser/.x11startlog
/users/sppuser/.sh_history
/users/sppuser/.sw
/users/sppuser/.sw/sessions
/users/sppuser/.sw/sessions/swlist.last
/users/sppuser/.history
/.sh_history
/.profile
/lib
/lib
/bin
/bin
/core
/ignite_10.20.tar
/var/tmp/makrec.lasttmp
/var/opt/ignite/recovery/chkrec.include
/var/opt/ignite/recovery/config.recover
```

On the K-class system, on which this **make_recovery** was performed, the **arch.include** file had over 44,000 lines in it, as shown below:

```
# cat /var/opt/igntite/recovery/arch.include | wc
44142 44146 1730818
```

Now let's resume **make_recovery**, which was running in preview mode, with the **-r** option for resume and the **-v** option for verbose, and **-C** option to create the system status file. **-d** option will not be specified because the default tape device will be used. The **-A** option, which was specified earlier in preview mode, specifies that the entire root volume group is to be included.

```
# make_recovery -r -C -v
make_recovery(306): In Resume mode. Do you wish to continue?y


        *****************************************
        HP-UX System Recovery

        File Systems on Core OS Disks/Volume Groups:

                    vg name = vg00
                    pv_name =  /dev/dsk/c0t5d0

                    vg00        /dev/vg00/lvol3         /
                    vg00        /dev/vg00/lvol4         /home
                    vg00        /dev/vg00/lvol5         /opt
                    vg00        /dev/vg00/lvol1         /stand
                    vg00        /dev/vg00/lvol6         /tmp
                    vg00        /dev/vg00/lvol7         /usr
                    vg00        /dev/vg00/lvol8         /var

          Create mount points
           /apps
           /work
           /spill
           /spill2
           /rbdisk01
           /rbdisk02
           /rbdisk03
           /rbdisk04
           /rbdisk05
           /rbdisk06
           /rbdisk07
           /rbdisk09
           /rbdisk10
           /rbdisk11
           /rbdisk12
           /rbdisk13
           /rbdisk14
           /rbdisk15
           /rbdisk16
           /rbdisk17
           /rbdisk18
           /nfs

              /opt is a mounted directory
```

```
                    It is in the Core Volume Group
                    Mounted at /dev/vg00/lvol5


             /var is a mounted directory
                    It is in the Core Volume Group
                    Mounted at /dev/vg00/lvol8

    Destination = /dev/rmt/0m
    Boot LIF location = /var/tmp/uxinstlf.recovery


    *****************************************
    Creating the configuration file.
            Done
    Modifying the configuration file.
            Done
    Backing up vg configurations
            Volume Group vg00
            Volume Group vg01
            Volume Group vg03
            Volume Group vg02
            Done
    Creating the /var/opt/ignite/recovery/makrec.last file
            Done
    Going to create the tape.
    Processing tape
            Invoking instl_adm -T
            Creating boot LIF
            Done
            Writing boot LIF to tape /dev/rmt/0mn
            Done
            Creating archive - this may take about 30 minutes.
            Done
    System Recovery Tape successfully created.
#
```

A system recovery tape has now been produced. You could now boot from the system recovery tape and restore the entire volume group **vg00** on this system.

Running the check_recovery Command

You can run the **check_recovery** command any time to view the changes that have been made to the system since the last time that the system recovery status file was created with the **-C** option. The following example shows running the **check_recovery** command:

```
# check_recovery
```

Since the last System Recovery Image was created, the following software
product changes have been detected.

```
(Added)       Auxiliary-OptB.11.01.01    Auxiliary Optimizer for HP Languages.
(Added)       OBJCOBOLB.12.50             Object COBOL Developer
```

Since the last System Recovery Image was created, the following system
files (or links) have been added to the current system.

```
/apps/informix7.3/lib/iosm07a.sl
/apps/informix7.3/lib/ipldd07a.sl
/apps/informix7.3/lib/liborb_r.sl
/dev/vg13/lvol01
/dev/vg13/rlvol01
/etc/sam/custom/scjjs.cf
/etc/sam/custom/scrar.cf
/sbin/init.d/flex
/sbin/rc2.d/S989flex
/usr/lib/iosm07a.sl
/usr/lib/iosm07a.sl.980709
/usr/lib/ipldd07a.sl.980709
/usr/lib/liborb_r.sl
/usr/local/adm/bin/user_watch.pl
/usr/local/adm/etc/rept
/usr/local/flexlm/bin/lmcksum
/usr/local/flexlm/bin/lmdiag
/usr/local/flexlm/bin/lmdown
/usr/local/flexlm/bin/lmgrd
/usr/local/flexlm/bin/lmhostid
/usr/local/flexlm/bin/lmremove
/usr/local/flexlm/bin/lmreread
/usr/local/flexlm/bin/lmstat
/usr/local/flexlm/bin/lmswitchr
/usr/local/flexlm/bin/lmutil
/usr/local/flexlm/bin/lmver
/usr/local/flexlm/daemons/HPCUPLANGS
/usr/local/flexlm/licenses/license.dat
/usr/local/flexlm/licenses/license.log
/usr/share/man/cat1.Z/X.1
/usr/share/man/cat1.Z/Xserver.1
/usr/share/man/cat1.Z/grep.1
/usr/share/man/cat1.Z/mwm.1
/usr/share/man/cat1.Z/xhost.1
/usr/share/man/cat1.Z/xset.1
/usr/share/man/cat2.Z/exec.2
```

Since the last System Recovery Image was created, the following system
files (or links) have been deleted from the current system.

```
/dev/vg13/lvol1
/dev/vg13/rlvol1
/stand/build/conf.o
```

Since the last System Recovery Image was created, the following system
files (or links) have been modified on the current system.

```
                              Current              makrec.last
                              -------              -----------
/dev/pty/ttyp2
      permissions            crw-rw-rw-           crw--w----
      uid                    0                    102
      gid                    0                    10
/dev/pty/ttyp3
      permissions            crw--w----           crw-rw-rw-
```

```
                    uid              102                      0
                    gid              10                       0
/dev/pty/ttyp4
                    permissions      crw--w----               crw-rw-rw-
                    gid              10                       0
/dev/pty/ttyp5
                    permissions      crw-rw-rw-               crw--w----
                    uid              0                        102
                    gid              0                        10
/dev/pty/ttyp6
                    permissions      crw-rw-rw-               crw--w----
                    uid              0                        102
                    gid              0                        10
/dev/pty/ttyp8
                    uid              0                        2
                    gid              0                        10
/dev/ttyp2
                    permissions      crw-rw-rw-               crw--w----
                    uid              0                        102
                    gid              0                        10
/dev/ttyp3
                    permissions      crw--w----               crw-rw-rw-
                    uid              102                      0
                    gid              10                       0
/dev/ttyp4
                    permissions      crw--w----               crw-rw-rw-
                    gid              10                       0
/dev/ttyp5
                    permissions      crw-rw-rw-               crw--w----
                    uid              0                        102
                    gid              0                        10
/dev/ttyp6
                    permissions      crw-rw-rw-               crw--w----
                    uid              0                        102
                    gid              0                        10
/dev/ttyp8
                    uid              0                        2
                    gid              0                        10
/etc/MANPATH
                    checksum         1982379524               497249200
/etc/PATH
                    checksum         562953260                2784298760
/etc/SHLIB_PATH
                    checksum         2664385509               241316845
/etc/fstab
                    checksum         3014086519               200239819
/etc/fstab.old
                    checksum         682979636                2528618126
/etc/group
                    checksum         368341889                127908837
/etc/lvmconf/vg13.conf
                    checksum         1522028984               929609311
/etc/lvmconf/vg13.conf.old
                    checksum         1830986219               3891043243
/etc/lvmtab
                    checksum         4141778997               3277790772
/etc/passwd
                    checksum         1661378396               2350540120
/etc/profile
                    checksum         510591831                2645970599
/stand/build/conf.SAM.c
                    checksum         3973853979               4022316306
/stand/build/conf.SAM.o
                    checksum         4142700410               118504989
/stand/build/conf.o.old
                    checksum         2526740160               1129366190
```

```
/stand/build/config.SAM.mk
        checksum            2849240259           1706527948
/stand/build/function_names.c
        checksum            2434797998           1240646943
        permissions         rw-rw-rw-            rw-r--r--
/stand/build/function_names.o
        checksum            3857693076           1165263911
        permissions         rw-rw-rw-            rw-r--r--
/stand/build/space.h
        permissions         rw-rw-rw-            rw-r--r--
/stand/build/tune.h
        checksum            2763942582           2084822502
/stand/dlkm.vmunix.prev/symtab
        checksum            2086890351           1785861028
        permissions         rw-r--r--            rw-rw-rw-
/stand/dlkm.vmunix.prev/system
        checksum            3376707916           2873910478
/stand/dlkm/symtab
        checksum            2368412414           2086890351
        permissions         rw-rw-rw-            rw-r--r--
/stand/dlkm/system
        checksum            2855591959           3376707916
/stand/system
        checksum            4141126356           1910321628
        permissions         rw-rw-rw-            r--r--r--
/stand/system.prev
        checksum            1910321628           253499711
        permissions         r--r--r--            rw-rw-rw-
/stand/vmunix
        checksum            2977157561           2742478025
/stand/vmunix.prev
        checksum            2742478025           3594881120
/usr/lib/ipldd07a.sl
        linkname        /apps/informix7.3/lib/ipldd07a.sl  /apps/informix/
lib/ipldd07a.sl
/usr/local/samba.1.9.18p3/var/locks/browse.dat
        checksum            2594069517           2221092461
/usr/local/samba.1.9.18p3/var/log.nmb
        checksum            4219117043           2190854115
/usr/local/samba.1.9.18p3/var/log.smb
        checksum            2251415300           1791314631
/var/spool/cron/crontabs/root
        checksum            2015828837           1660287231
#
```

This output indicates that many changes have been made to the system, including software additions and system file additions, deletions, and modifications. If **check_recovery** produces any significant changes to the system, you should rerun the **make_recovery** command so that the system recovery tape reflects the current state of your system.

As a result of completing the procedure covered in this section, many files were produced. Some that you may want to take a look at are in the **/var/opt/ignite/recovery** directory shown in the following listing:

```
# cd /var/opt/ignite/recovery
# ll
total 5412
-rw-rw-rw-   1 root      sys       1737051 Jul 13 16:17 arch.include
-rw-rw-rw-   1 root      sys           250 Jul 13 16:12 chkrec.include
-rw-rw-rw-   1 root      sys          4872 Jul 13 16:17 config.recover
-rw-rw-rw-   1 root     sys          4872 Jul 13 16:17 config.recover.prev
-rw-rw-rw-   1 root      sys          1682 Jul 13 16:12 fstab
-rw-rw-rw-   1 root      sys           390 Jul 13 16:29 group.makrec
-r--r--r--   1 root      sys          1971 Jun 25 12:27 makrec.append
-r--r--r--   1 bin       bin          1971 Apr 24 00:32 makrec.append.org
-rw-rw-rw-   1 root      sys       1010844 Jul 13 16:28 makrec.last
-rw-rw-rw-   1 root      sys          2573 Jul 13 16:29 passwd.makrec
```

Manual Pages for Commands Used in Chapter 9

The following section contains copies of the manual pages of Ignite-UX commands used in Chapter 9.

check_recovery

check_recovery - Compare the current system to the system recovery status file created by **make_recovery**.

---

check_recovery(1M)   check_recovery(1M)

NAME
     check_recovery - compare the current system to the System Recovery
     status file created by the last invocation of make_recovery.

SYNOPSIS
     /opt/ignite/bin/check_recovery

DESCRIPTION
     check_recovery compares the current state of the system to the System
     Recovery status file (created by the last invocation of make_recovery)
     to determine if a new System Recovery Tape needs to be created. Only
     Core OS and User Core OS files are validated. Refer to make_recovery
     for an explanation of these terms.

     check_recovery displays all discrepancies found between the current
     system and the status file to stderr. Based on these, the System
     Administrator can then make a determination as to whether a new System
     Recovery Tape needs to be created.

     check_recovery detects the following discrepancies:

   + Additions: A file existing on the current system and not
      listed in the System Recovery status file is a file added to
      the system since the last System Recovery Tape was created.

   + Deletions: A file not existing on the current system and
      listed in the System Recovery status file is a file deleted
      from the system since the last System Recovery Tape was
      created.

   + Modifications: A file existing on the current system but with
      a different "last modification date" is further validated via
      its checksum. If the file's checksum is different from the
      value in the System Recovery status file, then the file has
      been modified.

     check_recovery can be invoked only by a user who has superuser
     privileges.

   Options
     check_recovery has no options.

EXAMPLES

Check the current system to determine whether a new System Recovery
Tape needs to be created.

check_recovery

NOTES
make_recovery must have been previously executed with the -C option to
create the System Recovery status file.

AUTHOR
check_recovery was developed by HP.

FILES
/var/opt/ignite/recovery/makrec.last
System Recovery status file created by
make_recovery during the last System Recovery
archive creation

/var/opt/ignite/recovery/chkrec.include
List of files to be included for validation by
check_recovery

/opt/ignite/recovery/chkrec.exclude
List of files to be excluded for validation by
check_recovery

SEE ALSO
make_recovery(1M).

ignite

ignite - Invoke graphical user interface of Ignite-UX.

ignite(5)   ignite(5)

NAME
     ignite - HP-UX configuration and installation manager

SYNOPSIS
     /opt/ignite/bin/ignite

DESCRIPTION
   Introduction
     ignite is part of the Ignite-UX product, a client-server application
     that provides the ability to configure and install HP-UX systems.
     Ignite-UX is available on all HP-UX 10.XX platforms (with the
     exception of HP-UX 10.00) and supports the installation of all 10.XX
     releases and 10.XX applications.

     The ignite command is the graphical user interface of this client-
     server application. It provides the ability to build software
     configurations and to use these configurations to install HP-UX
     systems.

     Key features:

   + True client-server framework enabling an install session for
     multiple targets to be controlled from a single server.

   + Support of client standalone installation by enabling an
     installation to be controlled from a terminal user interface
     running on the target machine.

   + Support for non-interactive installations initiated from the
     client or server.

   + Support for multiple sources within a single install session.
     This allows end customers to install multiple applications at
     the same time they install the base OS.

   + Support for Software Distributor (SD) and non-SD sources, by
     providing the ability to load SD software, as well as software
     from a non-SD sources (tar, cpio, or pax). One use of this
     feature is the ability to load a system with an OS and
     applications, capture that system into an archive and then use
     that archive to install to multiple targets.

   + Support for user-defined configurations by allowing a system
     administrator to construct a description (configuration) for a
     target system including disk and networking layout, software to
     install, kernel modifications and post-installation
     customizations. Once this configuration has been defined it
     may then be applied to one or more target machines.

+ Support for user-defined customization both by defining what a
  target system should look like and by allowing execution of
  user-supplied scripts at pre-defined points in the installation
  process.

+ Support for saved configurations by enabling a user to modify
  an existing configuration, save these changes, and then quickly
  apply the new configuration to a target system.

+ Support for system manifest creation by providing a simple
  method to capture a snapshot of the currently loaded software
  along with a complete hardware inventory.

Hardware/Software Requirements
    For doing 10.XX loads, the following hardware is required to set up
    either a Series 700 or Series 800 Ignite-UX server. If a Series 800
    Ignite-UX server is set up, it needs a graphics display or the display
    can be redirected to another X(1) windows system. The redirection is
    accomplished by setting the DISPLAY environment variable. For
    example, in the Korn Shell or Posix Shell you would type: export
    DISPLAY=hpfcdn:0.0

    Ignite-UX server requirements:

+ A Series 700/800 system running HP-UX 10.XX.

+ An X11 display server (workstation, X-terminal, PC running an
   X server, etc). Can be the same system as above.

+ Sufficient disk space to load Ignite-UX, and any software
  depots and/or archives to be used during the install.

+ Access to the Ignite-UX tool set.The tool set can be loaded
  onto any 10.XX system.

+ Tape/CD-ROM in order to load Ignite-UX and any software depots
  you plan to distribute onto the server.

+ Network access to any clients to be installed. Client and
  Server must be on the same subnet if you plan to do the initial
  boot of the client over the network.

Server Setup: Overview
1. Install HP-UX 10.XX.

2. Install Ignite-UX tools and data.

3. Set up core software.

4. Add additional applications (optional).

5. Run ignite to complete the configuration and to start the
    process.

    Note: All operations are executed as "root" on the Ignite-UX
    server.Except where noted, all commands referenced here are
    located in /opt/ignite/bin.

Server Setup: Details
  1. Install HP-UX 10.XX
Refer to the manual for instructions on how to update a system to
HP-UX 10.XX.

   2. Install Ignite-UX Software
The Ignite-UX tool-set is contained on the HP-UX application set
of CD-ROMs.The software bundles are named as such: Ignite-UX-
10-01, Ignite-UX-10-10, Ignite-UX-10-20, etc. Each software
bundle contains the Ignite-UX tools plus the data files required
for support of the particular HP-UX release indicated by the
bundle name. You may load one or more of the Ignite-UX-10-XX
bundles onto your server depending on which releases of HP-UX you
plan on installing onto clients.

The Ignite-UX product replaces the capability previously supplied
by the NetInstall bundle that came with HP-UX releases 10.01,
10.10 and 10.20. Loading one of the Ignite-UX software bundles
will cause the NetInstall bundle to be automatically removed.

Once the application CD-ROM containing Ignite-UX has been
mounted, you may use the swinstall command to load the desired
Ignite-UX bundles. For example, the command below would load the
support needed for installing HP-UX 10.20 onto clients:

swinstall -s /cdromIgnite-UX-10-20

   3. Set up "core" HP-UX software
Before Ignite-UX can be used, you must configure the software for
it to load onto the clients. Since both SD sources and archive
(non-SD) sources (tar, cpio, or pax) may be used, both cases will
be considered separately below.

   For SD OS software:
For Ignite-UX to use an SD source, you must have a
registered SD depot available, and an Ignite-UX
configuration file generated from that depot.

If you already have an SD depot containing the core HP-UX
software, then you can enable Ignite-UX to access it by
using the make_config and manage_index commands. If you do
not already have a depot available, you may want to use the
add_release command to lead you though copying the software
from the distribution media into a depot and then
configuring Ignite-UX to use it. Both methods are outlined
below.

   Enabling (or updating) an existing depot
   If you already have an SD depot available, or if you
   have made changes to a depot that Ignite-UX knows
   about, then you can use the make_config and
   manage_index commands to generate a configuration file
   that Ignite-UX will use in accessing the depot. For
   example:
   make_config -s server:/depot_700 \
 -c /var/opt/ignite/data/Rel_B.10.20/core_700
   manage_index -a -f /var/opt/ignite/data/Rel_B.10.20/core_700

   If at a later time, you modify the contents of a depot
   (you use swcopy to add software, for example), then the
   same make_config step will need to be rerun in order
   for Ignite-UX to be aware of the modifications.

   Note: The make_config command only operates on software
   that is contained in a bundle. If you have a depot
   that has products not in a bundle, then you can run the
   make_bundles command on the depot prior to running
   make_config.

Using add_release to do it all
     If you need to copy the core HP-UX software off the
     distribution media into a depot, and configure Ignite-
     UX to use it, then the add_release command can be used
     to lead you though all the steps.

     To run add_release to see what it would do and not
     actually modify anything, you can specify the -p option
     (preview mode).

     For example:
     /opt/ignite/bin/add_release -s /dev/dsk/c0t2s0 -p

     To use a depot other than /dev/rmt/0m to read the
     software, you can specify it with the -s option.

     For example:
     /opt/ignite/bin/add_release -s jupiter:/depot/s700_10.XX_final

   For non-SD (archive) OS software:
Ignite-UX has the capability of loading a system from an
archive image taken from a system that represents your
standard configuration. This method gives significantly
faster install times, but may not be as flexible as using an
SD source.

You will first need to generate the archive image of a
system in the desired state. It is recommended that the
/opt/ignite/data/scripts/make_sys_image script be used to
accomplish this task.

Once an archive image is created, then a configuration file
that represents the location and attributes of that image
must be created before Ignite-UX can use it.

A sample of a config file that can be used with a core
archive can be found at:
/opt/ignite/data/examples/core.cfg

The comments in this example file describe where to copy the
file and what to change in the file to make it reference
your archive and to work in your environment.

   4. Add additional applications (optional)
   If you have other software that you would like to have loaded
   during the system installation then you can create configuration
   files similar to what was done for the core-OS software by using
   make_config and manage_index or by using an example configuration
   file and modifying it.

   For SD application software
Run the following commands for each depot you plan to load
SD software from during the installation. The make_config
command only handles SD software which is packaged in bundle
form. If the SD depot you want to use has software not
contained in a bundle (for example: a collection of
patches), then the make_bundles command may be used to
create bundles in the depot.

If the contents are not 700/800 specific then the
make_config -a[78]00 option should not be used.

For example, to make a depot containing patches available:
make_bundles /depots/s700_10.20_patches

make_config -s hpfcxxx.hp.com:/depots/s700_10.20_patches

```
-a 700 -c /opt/ignite/data/Rel_B.10.20/patches_700_cfg
```

```
manage_index -a -f /opt/ignite/data/Rel_B.10.20/patches_700_cfg
```

For example, to make a depot containing compilers available
which are already in bundles (no need to use make_bundles):
```
make_config -s hpfcxxx.hp.com:/depots/compiler
 -c /opt/ignite/data/Rel_B.10.XX/compilers_cfg
```

```
manage_index -a -f /opt/ignite/data/Rel_B.10.XX/compilers_cfg
```

The depot server (in this example hpfcxxx) should be
replaced with the server you have the SD software on. The
make_bundles script must be run on the same system where the
depot exists. If the depot is not on the Ignite-UX server,
you may need to copy the make_bundles script to the depot
server and run it there.

Note: The make_config command will need to be re-run each
time new software is added or modified in the depots.

make_config constructs Ignite-UX config files which
correspond to SD depots. When an SD depot is used as part
of the Ignite-UX process, it must have a config file which
describes the contents of the depot to Ignite-UX. This
command can automatically construct such a config file given
the name of an SD depot to operate on.This command should
be run when adding or changing a depot which will be used by
Ignite-UX.

manage_index is used to manipulate the /var/opt/ignite/INDEX
file. This utility is primarily called by other Ignite-UX
tools but can also be called directly.

    For non-SD application software:
If the source is not an "SD" depot, the make_config command
is not applicable. You will need to create a unique config
file that includes the non-SD software. A sample of a
config file that does a non-core archive can be found at:

/opt/ignite/data/examples/noncore.cfg

The comments in this example file describe where to copy the
file and what to change in the file to make it reference
your archive and to work in your environment.

    5. Run ignite to complete the configuration and to start the process
    On the Series 700 server run: /opt/ignite/bin/ignite. This will start
    the Ignite-UX server program.

    Complete the Configuration:
  When the GUI display titled "Ignite-UX" appears, do the following
  in that window:

  a)Choose Options: Server Configuration

  b)Look over both the Server Options and the Session Options to
see if they are suitable.

    About the Screen: 'Add Booting IP Addresses':

  Booting Clients: xx.xx.xx.xx to xx.xx.xx.xx
These IP addresses are used to initially boot the target
systems. They are used until the system is assigned one of
the DHCP-assigned addresses. One address is required for

each simultaneous boot. Typically one to three are needed, depending on the usage.

DHCP Addresses: xx.xx.xx.xx to xx.xx.xx.xx
These IP addresses are used during the OS download and application loading. These addresses are in use for most of the Ignite-UX download to a target machine.

One address is required for each simultaneous download. You should set more, if the addresses are assigned permanently.

DHCP Class ID:
The unique name for the DHCP server that serves these DHCP Addresses. Not necessarily the install server.

If you will not be using the install server as the DHCP server, then either do not set class ID at all, or you need to know what the client ID is set to on your real DHCP server.

Do not apply the class ID unless you are configuring the install server to be a DHCP server.

DHCP Addresses are temporary:
If these DHCP Addresses are only used for doing installs, and the clients will get reassigned new addresses when deployed. Keep this field set.

If you want to set up the Ignite-UX server as a departmental DHCP server, in which case the IP address leases are permanent, and isolated to the department's DHCP server, set this field to false.

Boot the S700 or S800 client system that supports network boot: If the system you plan to install is running HP-UX version 9.X or 10.X, then you can use the bootsys command to remotely reboot the client to run Ignite-UX.

If the client system is new, or disabled such that bootsys cannot be used, then you can boot it over the network (note, that currently the only S800 systems that are capable of network boot are the K and D class systems).

To do a network boot, Go to the console for that client and enter the appropriate command. (You will find the exact boot ROM commands for your system in

In general:

1)   Stop the auto-boot by pressing <escape>.

2)   For older Series 700s (non-bootp), type the following:

     search lan

     It will typically require three searches for the server to be found and listed, on older Series 700s.

     Boot the client either by using the index displayed in the search or by using the following:

     boot lan.080009-XXXYYY

3)   For newer Series 700s, type the following to search for servers on your network. If you already know the server's IP address, or you are on a S800 (K and D class) that do not

```
support the search command, then just issue the boot command
below:

search lan install

Note: Some C-class systems had a firmware defect such that
the search lan install install does not display any servers.
However, doing an explicit boot using the server's IP address
works correctly. A firmware upgrade is available for systems
with this defect.

Choose the preferred boot server (if you have more than one)
and enter the following:

boot lan.IP-Address install

If only one server appears in the listing, just type the
following:

boot lan install

If the client cannot find the server, check the following
items:

+ Client is on the same subnet as the server.

+ Any instl_bootd errors in /var/adm/syslog/syslog.log.
```

+ Your /var/adm/inetd.sec file to make sure that IP address
0.0.0.0 is not being disallowed for the instl_boots
service.

+ If /etc/services comes from NIS, make sure that the NIS
server has instl_boot* entries.

```
    + rbootd is running.

Booting a system remotely using bootsys:
    If a system you need to reinstall is up and running HP-UX 9.X or 10.X
    and available on the network, then you can use the bootsys command
    from the server to cause the client system to boot Ignite-UX.  Using
    the bootsys command has the advantages of:

+ Can be done remotely from the Ignite-UX server.  Does not
  require access to the client console.

+ It is able to boot S800's that are not capable of a network
  boot.

+ It allows booting clients that are on different subnets (since
  it is not really doing a true network boot).

+ The bootsys command may also be used to schedule installations
  to happen at a later time by calling it from at or cron.

The bootsys command has options to initiate an automated
installation (-a), or an installation controlled from the ignite
user interface (-w).

Booting a system from customer-created install
    An install image used to boot a system can be created using
    make_medialif.  When transferred to physical media, it can be used to:

+ Automatically load an archive image also stored on the media
  without intervention.
```

+ Initiate an install from an Ignite-UX server. The install can
  be either automated or interactive.

    This is a way for shipping user-customized install media to remote
    sites. See make_medialif(1M) for more information.

Start the Installation:
    After the client is booted, its icon should appear on the ignite
    interface. If the server has not been set up completely, or if the
    client could not obtain enough networking parameters via DHCP, then
    the client may require interaction on the client console.

    After the client icon appears on the server screen, select it by
    clicking on the icon for that client. Use the Actions menu to select a
    task for the selected client. The first task would be to choose
    "Install Client". Then choose "New Install".

    During the installation, choose a configuration file for this
    installation. Clients will be installed per the description given in
    the configuration file. If you want to reuse this configuration, save
    the file.

    Once installation is proceeding, check the client's status on the
    server.

    When the installation completes, you can print a manifest, and either
    save the client's data in a history directory or remove the client and
    its data from the server.

    Refer to the online help: "Ignite-UX Concepts", or "Getting Started"
    for more information.

Standalone Installation
    The standalone type of installation is invoked by booting the system
    from the network, as described in the previous section, or by booting
    from the Ignite-UX media. After choosing "Install HP-UX", select
    "Local interaction at console, installing from network server" on the
    next screen.

    Or if you are installing from media, select "Media installation, with
    user interaction at local console".

    A basic interface, "wizard mode" can be chosen at this point. This
    will direct you though the required system setup steps. This mode is
    for the novice user, and proceeds though a more limited set of
    configuration steps, while giving you recommended choices based on
    your system's hardware.

    Additionally, a more sophisticated interface can be selected if the
    user needs to modify the filesystem configuration, or would like to
    set the system hostname and networking parameters prior to completing
    the installation.

    If you find that you have selected the wrong interface to accomplish
    your task, you may use the "Cancel" button which will allow you to
    switch to the other interface mode.

    The standalone installation uses an ASCII (TUI) interface, and
    requires a keyboard for navigation.

    The following keys can be used to navigate in the various screens:

+ <return> and <space> keys select an item

+ <tab> key moves to the next item on the screen.

+ <right> arrow and <down> arrow keys cycle to the next item in
  the "Tab Group"

  A Tab Group is defined as all of the selectable options within
  an area of the screen defined by dotted lines. To move to the
  next Tab Group, the <tab> key must be used.

+ <left> arrow and <up> arrow keys cycle to the previous item in
  the Tab Group. To move to the next Tab Group, the <tab> key
  must be used.

+ Additionally, any key with an underlined character, can be
  chosen by typing that underlined character.

  Manifest Generation
      Included in the Ignite-UX tool set is a command: print_manifest(1M).
      This utility prints a formatted ascii system manifest to stdout.The
      manifest includes information on hardware and software installed and
      configured on the system. It gathers information about the system
      every time it is run.

      ignite can display and/or print the manifest of a just-installed
      system with the action "View/Print Manifest". If the client's data is
      moved to history, that data includes both the client's manifest and
      config file. Both these files can be recalled at a later time.

EXTERNAL INPUTS AND INFLUENCES
    Default Options:
        The server maintains a defaults file, ignite.defs, located at
        /var/opt/ignite/server/ignite.defs. This file contains a subset of
        the values that are entered on the Server Configuration screen.

        The following values and their defaults are shipped in the Ignite-UX
        product:

        client_timeout:30
        Time (in mins) until the client is declared hung.

        halt_when_done:false
        Halt the client after installation rather than reboot to invoke
        set_parms.

        ignite_welcome:true
        Show the server's welcome screen.

        itool_welcome:true
        Ask for customer information during client installation.

        new_client_notification:true
        Asks whether the user be notified when new clients boot.

    Locking
        In order to allow multiple ignite sessions to run concurrently with
        the currently installing process, ignite will lock a client during a
        New Install or a Repeat Install.This lock is tested in the actions:
        New Install, Repeat Installation, Stop Client and Remove Client.
        The lock is removed when the client is stopped or COMPLETE. For
        stopped clients, it is possible for someone, other than the installer,
        to remove them. For COMPLETE clients, it is possible for someone,
        other than the installer, to remove them or move them to history.

RETURN VALUES
    ignite returns the following values:

    0ignite completed successfully.

lignite failed.

DIAGNOSTICS
   Logging:
      All major events are logged to the server logfile located at
      /var/opt/ignite/logs/server.

FILES
      /opt/ignite/bin
   Contains Ignite-UX commands.

      /opt/ignite/lbin
   Contains Ignite-UX commands used by other commands.

      /var/opt/ignite/depots
   Contains the software depots used by Ignite-UX.

      /var/opt/ignite/logs
   Contains logfiles for each command.

      /var/opt/ignite/clients
   Contains the per-client directories.

      /var/opt/ignite/server
   Contains the file ignite.defs (server defaults).

AUTHOR
      Ignite-UX was developed by the Hewlett-Packard Company.

SEE ALSO
      add_release(1M), archive_impact(1M), bootsys(1M), instl_adm(1M),
      instl_adm(4), instl_bootd(1M), make_bundles(1M), make_config(1M),
      make_depots(1M), make_medialif(1M), manage_index(1M),
      print_manifest(1M), remove_release(1M), save_config(1M), sd(5),
      setup_server(1M).

make_recovery

make_recovery - Create an Ignite-UX system recovery tape.

```
make_recovery(1M)                                    make_recovery(1M)


NAME
     make_recovery - create the System Recovery Tape

SYNOPSIS
     /opt/ignite/bin/make_recovery [-AprvC] [-d destination] [-b
boot_destination]

DESCRIPTION
     make_recovery creates the System Recovery Tape. This tape can be used
     to:

  restore a non-bootable system with little or no human
  intervention.

  restore a system in the event of a hardware failure of the root
  disk or volume group when a disk has to be replaced.

  Clone the software from one system to another.

  Convert from hfs to vxfs file systems.

  Modify root file system size.

  Modify primary swap space allocation.

     It makes use of the installation technology provided by the Ignite-UX
     product, and can be considered a "customized" installation media. A
     system can be recovered by booting and installing from the tape
     without user intervention. All information regarding disk
     configuration, software, and system identity is stored on the tape at
     the time that make_recovery is executed.

     The System Recovery tape consists of a Boot Image, followed by an
     archive of system files that comprise a "Minimum Core OS". Minimum
     Core OS is defined as: /stand, /sbin, /dev, /etc, and subsets of /usr,
     /opt and /var that are required during the install process. The
     devices or volume groups that correspond to the file
     systems/directories /, /dev, /etc, /sbin, /stand and /usr are
     considered "Core" devices/volume groups. These devices or volume
     groups are recreated during the recovery process. All non-OS data on
     these devices or volume groups would be removed unless specifically
     appended to the recovery tape (as described below).

     Since non-core Applications reside in /opt /<application> and system
     dynamic files such as administration files, data bases etc. reside in
```

/var, these file systems have not been considered part of the Minimum Core OS.

If these reside in the "Core" disk/volume group, they will be recreated during the recovery installation process and the data must be recovered. The data can be included in the archive by using the -A option (described below). In that case, if the system has to be recovered, then these directories will be recreated by the install process, and the data will be recovered from the archive. Alternatively, the data can be recovered from normal backups if the -A option is not used while creating the recovery tape.

Any file system that resides in a "non-Core" disk/volume group will not be recreated by the install process. The original file system will be remounted after final re-boot and the data will be preserved.

make_recovery provides a mechanism for the user to include user specified non-system files in the archive via the /var/opt/ignite/recovery/makrec.append file. These are limited to files or directories that belong to file systems in the "Core" devices/volume groups, /opt and /var.

make_recovery also provides a mechanism for the user to exclude selected files from the archive via the -p and -r options.

Non-Core File Systems, which are not on the Core device/volume groups are expected to be backed up and recovered using normal backup utilities.

The System Recovery tape is only as good as the last time it was created.The tape should be recreated if the software, hardware, patches, etc. on the system are changed. The check_recovery command can be used to determine if the system has changed enough that the tape needs to be recreated.

To recover a failed system disk or volume group, the user would
- mount the System Recovery tape on the tape drive
- boot the system
- interrupt the boot sequence to redirect it to the tape drive
- elect no intervention with ISL
- allow the install process to complete.

To clone a system disk or volume group, the user would
- mount the System Recovery tape on the tape drive
- boot the system
- interrupt the boot sequence to redirect it to the tape drive
- Cancel the non-interactive installation by hitting the return key when the following messages are displayed:

WARNING: The configuration information calls for a non-interactive installation.

Press <Return> within 10 seconds to cancel batch-mode installation:

- The "Ignite-UX Welcome" screen will be presented.

As a "customized" installation is being performed, select the option
[Install HP-UX]
   and then the option
[   ] Advanced Installation (recommended for disk and filesystem management)
   Then configure/change disks, file systems, hostname, IP address, timezone, root password, DNS server, gateway information. These

can also be configured by using /etc/set_parms after the system
has been finally re-booted.
- allow the install process to complete.

The System Recovery tape can be used to clone the software on a system
on to another system, with manual configuration to be performed by the
user during the interactive installation.

Progress and errors are logged to /var/opt/ignite/logs/makrec.log1.

make_recovery requires superuser privilege.

Options
make_recovery recognizes the following options:

-A Specifies that the entire root disk/volume group
is to be included in the System Recovery tape.
This creates a complete bootable backup of the
disk or volume group.

In the case of large root disks or volume groups,
or when other utilities are used for normal
backups, this option should not be used. Instead,
the default minimum core OS should be backed up,
to recover a minimum system, and then the full
recovery should be done from the backups.

-p Previews what processing would take place, without
actually creating the tape. This is a way of
verifying /var/opt/ignite/recovery/makrec.append,
and getting /var/opt/ignite/recovery/arch.include
created. The latter file determines what goes into
the archive. This file can be edited to exclude
some files/directories from the archive if desired
by deleting them from the file. Only files or
directories that are known to be user created
should be deleted. No further checks are done by
make_recovery. The creation of the System
Recovery tape can then be resumed using the -r
option.

-r Resumes creation of the System Recovery tape after
the -p option has been used to create
/var/opt/ignite/recovery/arch.include, and it has
been possibly edited. If the -A and -r options
are both used, the -A option will override the -r
option, and the entire root disk/volume group will
be backed up.

-v Specifies verbose mode that displays progress
messages.

-d destination Specifies the device file of a DDS tape drive
where the System Recovery Tape is to be created.
A no-rewind device file is required. The default
is /dev/rmt/0mn.

-b destination Specifies the location where the boot LIF volume
is to be assembled, before it is written out to
tape. 32Mb is required. The default location is
/var/tmp/uxinstlf.recovery.

-C Create the System status file
/var/opt/ignite/recovery/makrec.last. This file
reflects the current state of the system. It
contains the names, dates of last modification,

and checksums of all the files on the tape that
are considered "Core OS" files. It may also
contain the file information for the user files
specified in the
/var/opt/ignite/recovery/makrec.append file if the
file exists. This option would be used if the user
plans to use check_recovery to determine if the
system has been changed such that the System
Recovery tape needs to be recreated.

> The /var/opt/ignite/recovery/makrec.append file is provided for the
> user to append selected data files to the archive. This has the
> format:
>
> ** User Core OS **
> file: filename
> file: filename
> file: filename
> dir: dirname
> product: productname
> ** User Data **
> file: filename
> file: filename
> product: productname
> dir: dirname
>
> The headers ** User Core OS ** and ** User Data ** are fixed form. The
> files/directories listed in the ** User Core OS ** section are
> considered Users system files, and are appended to the System Recovery
> archive, as well as to the /var/opt/ignite/recovery/makrec.last file,
> which is used by the check_recovery command for system validation.
>
> The files/directories listed in the ** User Data ** section are not
> considered system files, and while they are appended to the archive,
> they are not validated by check_recovery.
>
> Adding unnecessary files/directories to the ** User Core OS ** section
> indiscriminately will significantly increase the amount of time
> required for both tape generation and check_recovery execution, and is
> not advised.
>
> The product tag is provided to allow a user to append a backup utility
> to the System Recovery tape. This is limited to utilities that have
> been installed using SD (Software Distributor), and follow the SD
> guidelines.
>
> Lines starting with "#" are treated as comments and ignored. Blank
> lines are also ignored.

EXAMPLES
> To create a Minimum OS System Recovery tape at /dev/rmt/0mn. This
> tape includes only the minimum OS required to boot the system. A
> system recovery from this tape would mean booting from the tape to
> recover the minimum Core OS, and then following up with a user data
> recovery from normal backup media.

 make_recovery

> To create a Minimum OS System Recovery tape at /dev/rmt/c0t1d1BESTn
> (assuming a writable DDS tape is in the drive pointed to by
> /dev/rmt/c0t1d1BESTn.) User data recovery is done as described above.

 make_recovery -d /dev/rmt/c0t1d1BESTn

> To preview the creation of a System Recovery tape at
> /dev/rmt/c0t1d1BESTn (assuming a writable DDS tape is in the drive

pointed to by /dev/rmt/c0t1d1BESTn), review the list of files that will be included in the archive, possibly modify the list, and then subsequently continue the creation.

```
make_recovery -p -d /dev/rmt/c0t1d1BESTn
vi /var/opt/ignite/arch.include
make_recovery -r -d /dev/rmt/c0t1d1BESTn
```

To create a System Recovery tape, at the default device /dev/rmt/0m, and include the entire root disk in the archive.
```
make_recovery -A
```

To create a System Recovery tape that
- includes the entire root file system in the disk,
- adds the file /mnt/fileA as a users system file,
- adds the data directory /mnt/dirB to the archive as non-system data. (assuming that /mnt is mounted on the same volume group as the core File Systems),
- creates the system status file.

Edit the /var/opt/ignite/recovery/makrec.append file to include:

```
** User Core OS **
file: /mnt/fileA
** User Data **
dir: /mnt/dirB
```

Then issue the command:
```
make_recovery -v -C
```

To clone a system, create the System Recovery tape.
```
make_recovery -v -A
```
Install it on the new system. Invoke the user interface by hitting any key during the 10 second interval given for this purpose during the installation. Configure the hostname, IP address, root password etc. using the "system" screen of the user interface.

The installation can be non-interactive if the configuration of the system being installed is the same as that of the original system.

If the system is installed non-interactively, immediately run /etc/set_parms to configure the new hostname, IP address etc for the system. This method is not recommended. (See WARNINGS).

If the configuration of the system being installed is not the same as that of the original system, the normal user interface for installation will be presented, and the user has the opportunity to provide the configuration information via the "system" installation configuration screen.

WARNINGS
make_recovery relies on the Installed Products Database (IPD) to extract files relevant to a product added to the System Recovery tape via the "product" tag in the append file. It is only as reliable as the IPD.Only products installed via SD (Software Distributor) are logged into the IPD. It is also necessary that the SD commands be used to add, modify, remove these products, so that the IPD is correctly updated to reflect these changes. If there is any possibility that the product has been manipulated without using SD, or that the products' installation/configuration scripts are not modifying the IPD reliably, then it is better to set up /var/opt/ignite/recovery/makrec.append with all the filenames for the product as a one time effort.

If the System Recovery tape is used to clone the software on another system, the newly installed system will have the same hostname and IP address as the original system. These should be immediately changed using /etc/set_parms. Introducing a second system into the network with the same hostname or IP address will very possibly disable networking on both systems.

The -p and -r options can be used to exclude some non OS files/directories from the System Recovery archive. These should only be used by knowledgeable System Administrators as excluding required files/directories from the boot tape could render it useless.

On systems that support Large UID/GIDs or Large Files (>2GB), the System Recovery tape should be created for only the Minimum OS, and remaining user data recovered from Normal Backup Media that support these features. make_recovery does not directly support these features since pax (used to generate the archive) does not as yet support them.

make_recovery does not support mirrored disks. V-class systems are not supported at first release.

NOTES

If a non-root disk is corrupted, it should be recovered from normal backups.

The System Recovery tape should be used when the root disk or volume group is corrupted and the system cannot be booted. The install process recreates the disk or volume group from scratch, and no data on the disks is salvaged. The file systems /, /stand, /sbin, /etc and /dev are always mounted on the root volume group, and are always recreated.

/usr is always recreated. If it is mounted on a non-root volume group, that volume group will also be considered Core, and will be recreated.

The entire / file system is not archived by default. This can be done via the append file, or by using the -A option.

If /opt and /var are mounted on the root volume group, these can either be included in the System Recovery archive, or recovered from normal backups after the system is brought up.

/opt and /var tend to grow large, and are occasionally mounted on a separate disk or in a non root volume group. In such cases, it is essential that the user data on these disks should not be "wiped out" during the process of reinstalling the root disk/volume group. Some files from these file systems are required for Ignite-UX processing and make_recovery would automatically include them in the archive. Other files from these file systems can be included in the archive for cloning purposes, but if the same system is being recovered, the files will not be restored onto these file systems. These file systems will be left unaltered.

If the disks on the system have been changed, the install process can detect that the hardware is different, and starts up the install user interface to allow changes to the configuration.If the hardware configuration is the same, the installation can complete non-interactively.

The user can also elect to invoke the user interface by hitting any key during the 10 second interval given for this purpose during the installation. The user can then make configuration choices, but the archives will be recovered in a manner similar to a cold install. The software, data files and so forth will be recovered, but the user will

manually complete the configuration of hostname, IP address, DNS
server, date and time, root password. The /etc/fstab and /etc/hosts
files will have to be re-created. A copy of the original /etc/fstab
file is saved in /var/opt/ignite/recovery/fstab for reference.

Minimum Core OS consists of:
/.profile, /.rhosts,
/dev, /etc, /sbin,

/usr/bin, /usr/sbin,
/usr/lib, /usr/obam,
/usr/sam, /usr/share,
/usr/ccs, /usr/conf,
/usr/lbin, /usr/contrib,
/usr/local, /usr/newconfig

/var/adm/sw, /var/opt/ignite/local/manifest,
/var/adm/cron, /var/spool/cron

The following files/directories are considered part of minimum Core OS
if they exist on the system.

/opt/ignite/bin/print_manifest,
/opt/ignite/share/man/man1m.Z/print_manifest.1m,
/opt/upgrade

All of the above files/directories are included in the archive as
default.

DEPENDENCIES
        make_recovery requires that the following filesets of the Ignite-UX
        product be installed on the system.

        Ignite-UX.BOOT-KERNEL
        Ignite-UX.BOOT-SERVICES
        Ignite-UX.FILE-SRV-release
        Ignite-UX.MGMT-TOOLS
        Ignite-UX.IGNT-ENG-A-MAN

        For 10.x systems, the current patch for pax that fixes problems with
        hardlinks is required.

FILES
        /var/opt/ignite/recovery/makrec.append
User created file for appending
files/directories/products to the System Recovery
archive.

        /var/opt/ignite/logs/makrec.log1
Progress and error log.

        /var/opt/ignite/logs/makrec.log2
Archive content log.

        /var/opt/ignite/recovery/makrec.last
System status file created with the -C option.
This file will be used by check_recovery for
system validation.

        /var/opt/ignite/recovery/arch.include
List of files to be included in the System
Recovery archive.

        /var/opt/ignite/recovery/chkrec.include
List of files that will be validated by
check_recovery.

/var/opt/ignite/recovery/config.recover
File that describes the System configuration.

/var/opt/ignite/recovery/fstab
A copy of the current /etc/fstab file for
reference in case the Interactive mode was used,
causing the /etc/fstab file to be re-created.

/var/tmp/uxinstlf.recovery
Default location for Boot LIF volume creation.

SEE ALSO
check_recovery(1M), save_config(1M), make_medialif(1M), instl_adm(1M),
instl_adm(5), ignite(5), pax(1).

Chapter 10

The vi Editor

The vi Editor

Many UNIX users have a Graphical User Interface (GUI) through which they access their UNIX system. The Common Desktop Environment (CDE) is the most commonly used GUI on UNIX systems. It is based on the X Windows System and Motif, which together provide an advanced windowing environment. There is a chapter in this book devoted to CDE. Most UNIX GUIs provide a graphical editor. Despite the fact that these graphical editors are a standard part of most GUIs, the visual editor, **vi**, still remains the most popular UNIX editor. With many fine graphics-based editors as a standard part of most UNIX GUIs and a plethora of editors available as part of personal computer windowing environments, why am I covering **vi**? The answer is twofold. First, not everyone using a UNIX system has access to a graphics display and may therefore need to know and use **vi**. Since **vi** comes with most UNIX-based systems and is a powerful editor, many new UNIX users end up using and liking it. Second, **vi** has traditionally been thought of as *the* UNIX editor. There are few UNIX users who have not used **vi**. This does not mean that it is everyone's primary editor; however, virtually all UNIX users have had some experience with **vi**.

There is also a line editor called **ed** that comes with many UNIX systems. It is now seldom used because **vi** is a screen editor. Also available is an enhanced version of **ed** called **ex**. **vi** is much more widely used than either of the line editors, so I'll cover only **vi** in this chapter.

I'll cover the *basics* of using **vi** in this chapter. You can experiment with what is covered here, and if you really like it, you can investigate some of the more advanced features of **vi**. A quick reference card summarizing all the **vi** commands covered in this chapter is included with this book.

The following table is a list of tables in this chapter that summarize some of the more commonly used **vi** commands by function:

Table Number	vi Function
Introduction	Modes and Notations in **vi**
1	Starting a **vi** Session
2	Cursor Control Commands in **vi**
3	Adding Text in **vi**
4	Deleting Text in **vi**
5	Changing Text in **vi**
6	Search and Replace in **vi**
7	Copying in **vi**
8	Undo in **vi**
9	Saving Text and Exiting **vi**
10	Options in **vi**
11	Status in **vi**
12	Positioning and Marking in **vi**
13	Joining Lines in **vi**
14	Cursor Placement and Adjusting Screen in **vi**

Table Number	vi Function
15	Shell Escape Commands in **vi**
16	Macros and Abbreviations in **vi**
17	Indenting Text in **vi**
18	Shell Filters in **vi**
19	Pattern Matching in **vi**

Modes Notations

We're first going to cover some of the fundamentals of the operation of **vi** called modes, and then go over some of the notations used in the tables in this chapter.

A feature of **vi** that often confuses new users is that it has modes. When you are in *command mode*, everything you type is interpreted as a command. In *command mode,* you can specify such actions as the location to which you want the cursor to move. When you are in *input mode,* everything you type is information to be added to the file. *Command mode* is the default when you start **vi**. You can move into *command mode* from *input mode* at any time by pressing the *escape* key. You move into *insert mode* from *command mode* by typing one of the *input mode* commands covered shortly.

vi commands don't really have a standard form. For this reason, I'll cover common notations. Table 10 - Introduction summarizes modes and commands in **vi**.

TABLE 10- Introduction MODES AND NOTATIONS IN vi

Mode or Notation	Description
Command Mode	You are issuing commands such as moving the cursor or deleting text, rather than inserting or changing text when in command mode. You can switch to insert mode by issuing an insert mode command such as **i** for insert or **a** for add text.
Insert Mode	You are in insert mode when changing or inserting more than one character of text. You can switch to command mode by pressing the *escape* key.
: (colon commands)	Commands that start with a : are completed by pressing the *return* key.
control (^) commands	When a command uses the *control* (^) key, you press and hold down the *control* key and then press the next key that is part of the command. For instance, **^g** means press and hold *control* and then **g** to get the status on the file you are editing.
file for the name of a file	Many commands require you to specify the name of a file. For instance, in the command **vi** *file,* you would substitute the name of the file you wish to edit for *file.*
char for the name of a character	Many commands require you to specify a single character. For instance, in the command **f***char,* you would substitute the character you wish to search for in place of *char.*
cursor_command for a cursor movement command	Many commands require you to specify a cursor command to execute. For instance, in the command **d***cursor_command,* you would substitute for *cursor_command* the command you wish to execute.

Mode or Notation	Description
string for a character string	Many commands require you to specify a character string. For instance, in the command /*string*, you would substitute for *string* the character string for which you wish to search.

Starting a vi Session

Let's jump right in and edit a file. For most of the examples in this chapter, I perform various **vi** commands and capture the results in an X Window. The best way to learn any topic is by example. I not only provide many examples, but I also capture each example in an X Window so you can see the results of each command. From the command line, we type **vi** and the name of the file we wish to edit, in this case **wisdom**.

```
$ vi wisdom
```

We are then editing the file **wisdom** as shown in Figure 10-1. **wisdom** contains a passage from <u>Tao Te Ching</u> or "Book of the Way." We will use this file throughout this chapter.

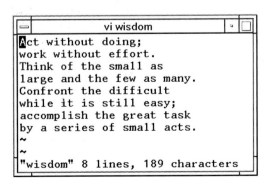

Figure 10-1 Editing the File **wisdom**

The bottom line in Figure 10-1 is the message line in **vi**. After invoking **vi,** the message line indicates the name of the file, the number of lines, and the number of characters in the file. Different messages appear on the message line, depending on the command you issue, as we will see in upcoming examples. If a tilde appears on any lines in the file, as it does in the two lines exist above the message line in **wisdom**, it means that not enough lines to fill up the screen. The cursor is the dark box that appears at line 1 in Figure 10-1.

We can specify several file names and after saving the first file move on to the second file by entering **:n,** and continue going through the list of files in this way. Or we can specify a file and position the cursor on the last line in the file. The default is for the cursor to appear over the first character in the file, as shown in Figure 10-1.

Table 10-1 shows some of the ways we can start a **vi** session.

TABLE 10-1 STARTING A **vi** SESSION

Command	Description
vi *file*	Edit *file.*
vi -r *file*	Edit last saved version of *file* after a crash.
vi -R *file*	Edit *file* in readonly mode.
vi + *n file*	Edit *file* and place cursor at line *n.*
vi + *file*	Edit *file* and place cursor on last line.
vi *file1 file2 file3 ...*	Edit *file1* through *file3,* and after saving changes in *file1,* you can move to *file2* by entering **:n.**
**vi +/*string file*	Edit *file* and place cursor at the beginning of the line containing *string.*

Figure 10-2 shows editing wisdom and placing the cursor at line 5 with the command **vi +5 wisdom**.

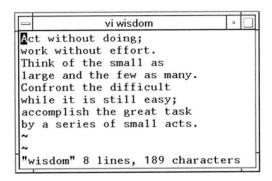

Figure 10-2 Editing the File **wisdom** and Placing Cursor at Line 5 with **vi +5 wisdom**

Figure 10-3 shows editing wisdom and placing the cursor at the last line of the file with the command **vi + wisdom**.

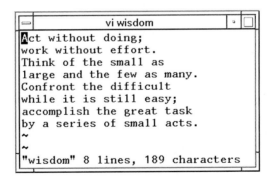

Figure 10-3 Editing the File **wisdom** and Placing Cursor at last line with **vi + wisdom**

Figure 10-4 shows editing wisdom and placing the cursor at the line containing task with **vi +/task wisdom**.

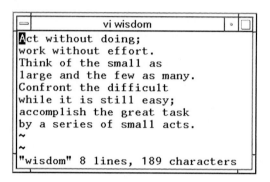

Figure 10-4   Editing the File **wisdom** and Placing Cursor at Line Containing *task* with **vi +/ task wisdom**

Cursor Control Commands

A key skill to develop in **vi** is getting the cursor to the desired position. You do this in *command mode*. You have a variety of ways to move the cursor around the screen. Table 10-2 summarizes some of the more commonly used cursor movements.

TABLE 10-2 CURSOR CONTROL COMMANDS IN **vi**

Command	Cursor Movement
h or **^h**	Move left one character.
j or **^j** or **^n**	Move down one line.
k or **^p**	Move up one line.
l or **space**	Move right one character.

TABLE 10-2 CURSOR CONTROL COMMANDS IN vi

Command	Cursor Movement
G	Go to the last line of the file.
nG	Go to line number n.
G$	Go to the last character in the file.
1G	Go to the first line in the file.
w	Go to the beginning of the next word.
W	Go to the beginning of next word, ignore punctuation.
b	Go to the beginning of the previous word.
B	Go to the start of previous word, ignore punctuation.
L	Go to the last line of the screen.
M	Go to the middle line of the screen.
H	Go to the first line of the screen.
e	Move to the end of the next word.
E	Move to the end of the next word, ignore punctuation.
(	Go to the beginning of the sentence.
)	Go to the end of the sentence.
{	Go to the beginning of the paragraph.
}	Go to the beginning of the next paragraph.
0 or |	Go to the first column in the current line.
n|	Go to column n in the current line.
^ (caret)	Go to the first non-blank character in the current line.
$	Go to the last character in the current line.
+ or *return*	Go to the first character in the next line.
-	Go to the first non-blank character in the previous line.

I know that the fact that you have to remember these commands in order to get the cursor to the desired position may seem a little strange at first, but this is the way **vi** works. Let's use **wisdom** to show how some of these cursor movements work. Figures 10-5 and 10-6 show some cursor movements. Like all of the upcoming figures, Figures 10-5 and 10-6 show **wisdom** before a command is entered on the left and the result after the command is entered on the right. The command issued appears in the middle. Some of the commands in upcoming figures use the *enter* and *escape* keys.

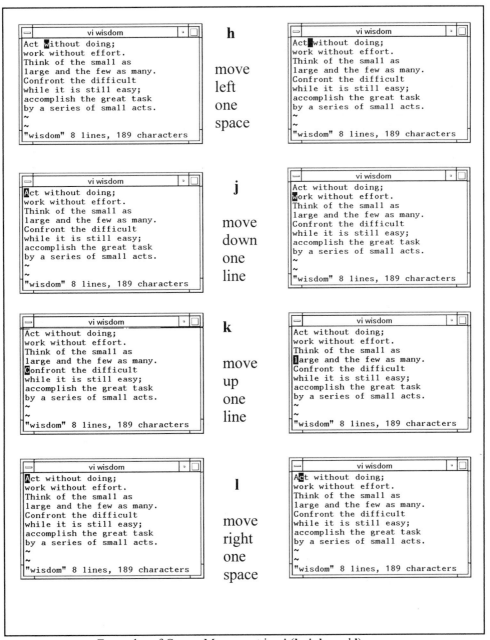

Figure 10-5 Examples of Cursor Movement in **vi** (**h**, **j**, **k**, and **l**)

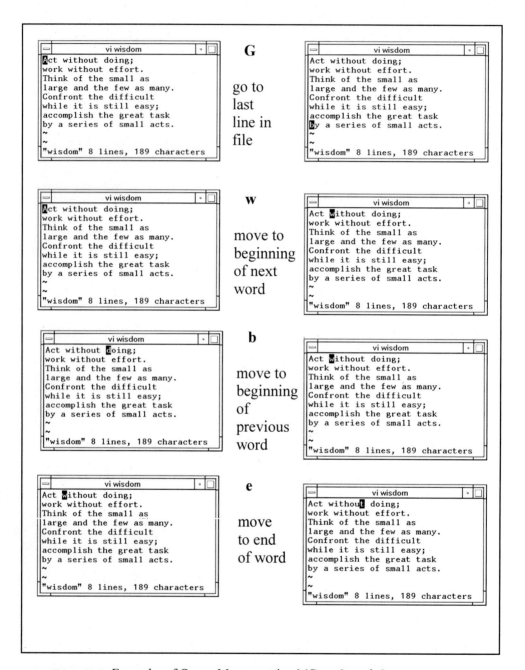

Figure 10-6 Examples of Cursor Movement in **vi** (**G**, **w**, **b**, and **e**)

Adding Text in vi

Now that we know how to move around the cursor, let's do something with it. You need to first learn about cursor movement, since the commands for adding text take place relative to the position of the cursor. Table 10-3 summarizes some commands for adding text.

TABLE 10-3 ADDING TEXT IN **vi**

Command	Insertion Action
a	Append new text after the cursor.
A	Append new text after the end of the current line.
i	Insert new text before the cursor.
I	Insert new text before the beginning of the current line.
o	Open a line below the current line and insert.
O	Open a line above the current line and insert.
:r *file*	Read *file* and insert after the current line.
:nr *file*	Read *file* and insert after line *n*.
escape	Get back to command mode.
^v *char*	Ignore special meaning of *char* when inserting. This is for inserting special characters.

Let's now look at some examples for adding text into **wisdom** in Figure 10-7.

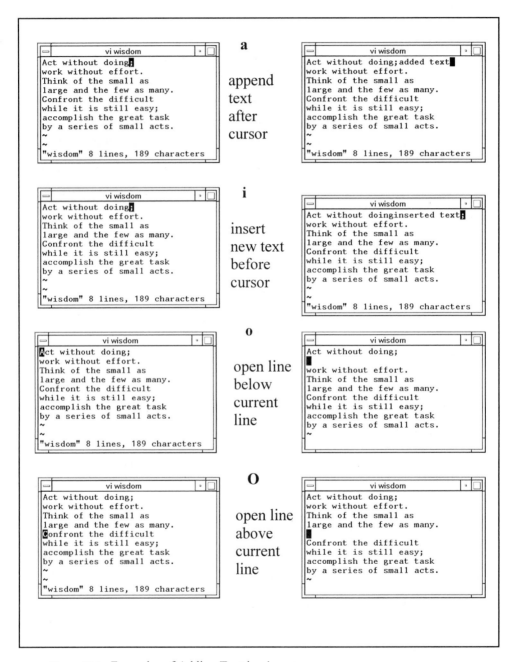

Figure 10-7 Examples of Adding Text in **vi**

Deleting Text in vi

We also need to learn about cursor movement before learning how to delete text, since the commands for deleting text take place relative to the position of the cursor. Table 10-4 summarizes some commands for deleting text.

TABLE 10-4 DELETING TEXT IN vi

Command	Deletion Action
x	Delete the character at the cursor. You can also put a number in front of x to specify the number of characters to delete.
nx	Delete n characters beginning with the current.
X	Delete the previous character. You can also put a number in front of X to specify the number of previous characters to delete.
nX	Delete previous n characters.
dw	Delete to the beginning of the next word.
$n$dw	Delete the next n words beginning with the current.
dG	Delete lines to the end of the file.
dd	Delete the entire line.
$n$dd	Delete n lines beginning with the current.
db	Delete the previous word.
$n$db	Delete the previous n words beginning with the current.
:n,md	Deletes lines n through m.
D or d$	Delete from the cursor to the end of the line.

TABLE 10-4 DELETING TEXT IN vi

Command	Deletion Action
d*cursor_command*	Delete text to the *cursor_command*. **dG** would delete from the current line to the end of the file.
^**h** or *backspace*	While inserting, delete the previous character.
^**w**	While inserting, delete the previous word.

Let's now look at some examples for deleting text from **wisdom** in Figures 10-8 and 10-9.

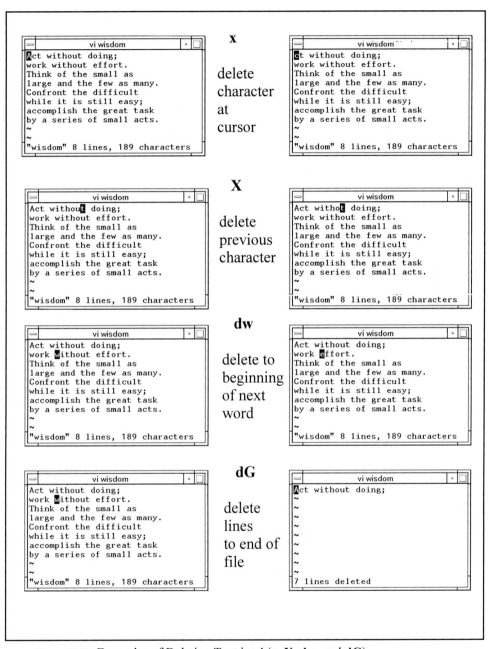

Figure 10-8 Examples of Deleting Text in **vi** (**x**, **X**, **dw**, and **dG**)

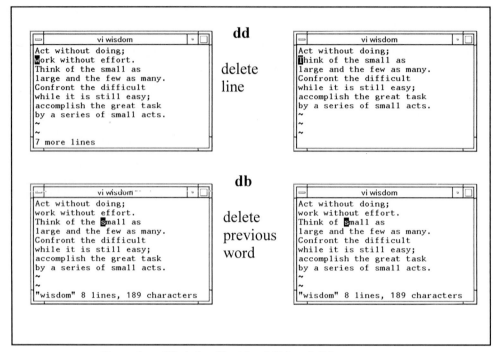

Figure 10-9 Examples of Deleting Text in **vi** (**dd** and **db**)

Changing Text in vi

Okay, you've added text and deleted text and now you want to change text. **vi** isn't so bad so far, is it? Table 10-5 summarizes some commands for changing text.

TABLE 10-5 CHANGING TEXT IN **vi**

Command (Preceding these commands with a number repeats the commands any number of times.)	Replacement Action
r*char*	Replace the current character with *char*.
R*text escape*	Replace the current characters with *text* until *escape* is entered.
s*text escape*	Substitute *text* for the current character.
S or **cc***text escape*	Substitute *text* for the entire line.
cw*text escape*	Change the current word to *text*.
C*text escape*	Change the rest of the current line to *text*.
cG *escape*	Change to the end of the file.
c*cursor_cmd* **text** *escape*	Change to *text* from the current position to *cursor_cmd*.

Let's now look at some examples of replacing text from **wisdom** in Figures 10-10 and 10-11.

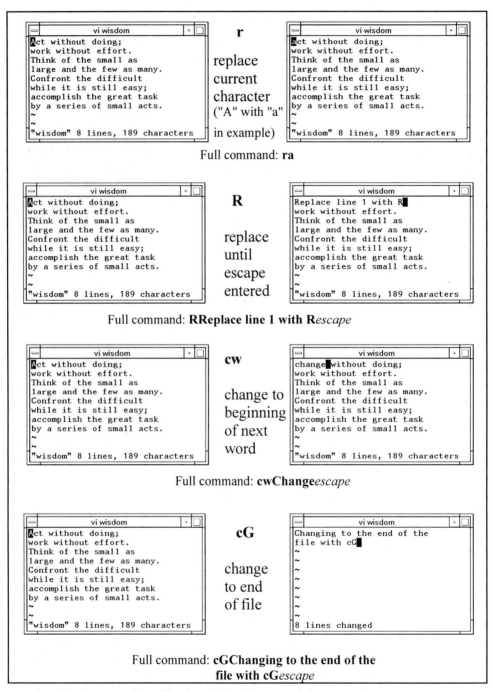

Figure 10-10   Examples of Changing Text in **vi** (**r**, **R**, **cw**, and **cG**)

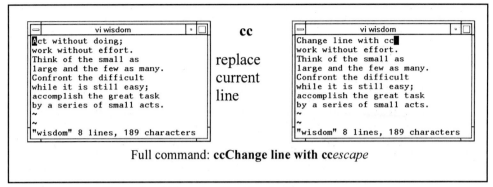

Full command: **ccChange line with cc***escape*

Figure 10-11 Example of Changing Text in **vi** with **cc**

Search and Replace in vi

You have a lot of search and replace functionality in **vi**. Table 10-6 summarizes some of the more common search-and-replace functionality in **vi**.

TABLE 10-6 SEARCH AND REPLACE IN **vi**

Command	Search and Replace Action
/*text*	Search for ***text*** going forward into the file.
?*text*	Search for ***text*** going backward into the file.
n	Repeat the search in the same direction as the original search.
N	Repeat the search in the opposite direction as the original search.
f*text*	Search for *text* going forward in the current line.
F*text*	Search for *text* going backward in the current line.
t*text*	Search for *text* going forward in the current line and stop at the character before *text*.

TABLE 10-6 SEARCH AND REPLACE IN **vi**

Command	Search and Replace Action
T_text_	Search for _text_ going backward in the current line to character after _text_.
:set ic	Ignore case when searching.
:set noic	Make searching case-sensitive.
:s/_oldtext_/_newtext_/	Substitute _newtext_ for _oldtext_.
:_m,n_**s**/_oldtext_/_newtext_/	Substitute _newtext_ for _oldtext_ in lines _m_ through _n_.
&	Repeat the last **:s** command.
:g/_text1_/**s**/_text2_/_text3_	Find line containing _text1_, replace _text2_ with _text3_.
:g/_text_/_command_	Run _command_ on all lines that contain _text_.
:v/_text_/_command_	Run _command_ on all lines that do not contain _text_.

Let's now look at some examples of searching and replacing text in **wisdom** in Figure 10-12.

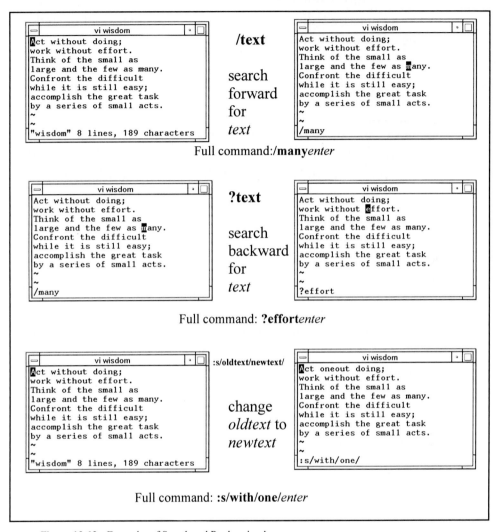

Figure 10-12   Examples of Search and Replace in **vi**

You can perform advanced searches with **:g** and **:v**. You can find and display all the lines in a file containing **while** with the following command:

```
:g/while/p
```

The /**p** in this command line is the print command used with the **ex** editor. You could find all the lines in the file that contain **while** and delete those lines with the following command:

```
:g/while/d
```

You can also specify the specific line numbers for which you want the search to take place. The following command finds all the lines between 10 and 20 that contain **while** and prints the line number on which they appear:

```
:10,20g/while/nu
```

:**g** runs a command on the lines that contain the text for which we are searching, and :**v** runs a command on the lines that do not contain the specified text. The following three commands act on the lines that do not contain **while**, in the same way that the previous three act on the lines that do contain **while**.

```
:v/while/p
```

```
:v/while/d
```

```
:10,20v/while/nu
```

The first command prints lines that do not contain **while**. The second command deletes the lines on which **while** does not appear. The third command prints the line number between 10 and 20 on which **while** does not appear.

Copying Text in vi

You can copy text in **vi**. Some commands for copying are shown in Table 10-7.

TABLE 10-7 COPYING IN vi

Command	Copy Action
yy	Yank the current line.
nyy	Yank **n** lines.
p (lower case)	Put the yanked text after the cursor.
p (upper case)	Put the yanked text before the cursor.
*"(a-z)n***yy**	Copy *n* lines into the buffer named in parentheses. Omit *n* for the current line.
*"(a-z)n***dd**	Delete *n* lines into the buffer named in parenthesis. Omit *n* for the current line.
*"(a-z)***p**	Put lines named in the buffer in parentheses after current line.
*"(a-z)***P**	Put lines named in the buffer in parentheses before the current line.

Let's now look at some examples of copying text in **wisdom** in Figure 10-13.

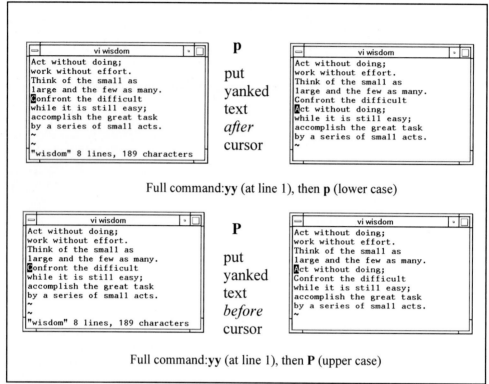

Figure 10-13   Copying in vi

Undo and Repeat in vi

You can easily undo changes in **vi** with the commands shown in Table 10-8.

Table 10-8 UNDO IN vi

Command	Undo Action
u	Undo the last change.
U	Undo all changes to the current line.
. (period)	Repeat the last change.
, (comma)	Repeat, in reverse direction, last **f**, **F**, **t**, or **T** search command.
; (semi-colon)	Repeat last **f**, **F**, **t**, or **T** search command.
"np	Retrieve the last nth delete (a limited number of deletes are in the buffer, usually nine).
n	Repeat last **/** or **?** search command.
N	Repeat, in reverse direction, last **/** or **?** search command.

Save Text and Exit vi

You have a number of different ways to save files and exit **vi**, some of which are summarized in Table 10-9.

TABLE 10-9 SAVING TEXT AND EXITING vi

Command	Save and/or Quit Action
:w	Save the file but don't exit **vi**.

TABLE 10-9 SAVING TEXT AND EXITING **vi**

Command	Save and/or Quit Action
:**w** *file*	Save changes in *file* but don't quit **vi**.
:**wq** or **ZZ** or :**x**	Save the file and quit **vi**.
:**q!**	Quit **vi** without saving the file.
:**e!**	Re-edit the file discarding changes since the last write.

Options in vi

There are many options you can set and unset in **vi**. To set an option, you type :**set** *option.* To unset an option, you type :**set no***option.* Table 10-10 summarizes some of the more commonly used options.

TABLE 10-10 OPTIONS IN **vi**

Option	Action
:**set all**	Print all options.
:**set no***option*	Turn off *option*.
:**set nu**	Prefix lines with line number.
:**set showmode**	Show whether input or replace mode.
:**set noic**	Ignore case when searching.
:**set list**	Show tabs (^I) and end of line ($).

TABLE 10-10 OPTIONS IN **vi**

Option	Action
:set ts=8	Set tab stops for text input.
:set window=*n*	Set number of lines in a text window to *n*.

Let's now prefix lines with line numbers and show input or replace mode in Figure 10-14.

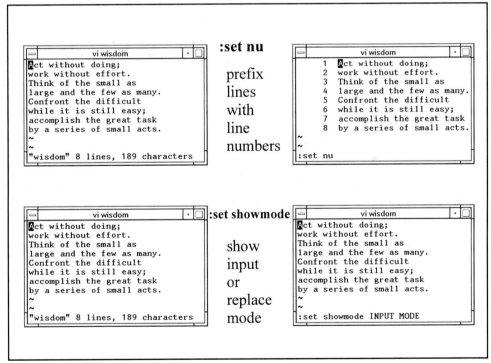

Figure 10-14 Options in **vi**

Many additional options are available beyond those in Table 10-10. The following is a list of options produced on a UNIX system from the **:set all** command. You should issue this command when in **vi** to see the options available to you.

```
:set all
noautoindent
autoprint
noautowrite
nobeautify
directory=/var/tmp
nodoubleescape
noedcompatible
noerrorbells
noexrc
flash
hardtabs=8
noignorecase
keyboardedit
nokeyboardedit!
nolisp
nolist
magic
mesg
nomodelines
nonumber
nonovice
nooptimize
paragraphs=IPLPPPQPP LIpplpipnpbp
prompt
noreadonly
redraw
remap
report=5
scroll=11
```

```
sections=NHSHH HUuhsh+c
shell=/sbin/sh
shiftwidth=8
noshowmatch
noshowmode
noslowopen
tabstop=8
taglength=0
tags=tags /usr/lib/tags
tagstack
term=hp
noterse
timeout
timeoutlen=500
ttytype=hp
warn
window=23
wrapscan
wrapmargin=0
nowriteany
noshowmatch
noshowmode
```

Many of the options are preceded by a "no," indicating that the option is not set. You may want to list your options with **:set all** and then experiment with the options of interest to you to see the effect they will have on your **vi** session.

Status in vi

You can obtain a lot of useful status information with some simple commands in **vi**. You can display current line number, number of lines in the file, file name, and other status information with the commands shown in Table 10-11.

TABLE 10-11 STATUS IN vi

Option	Action
:.=	Print the current line number.
:=	Print the number of lines in the file.
^g	Show the file name, current line number, total lines in the file, and percent of file location.
:l	Use the letter "l" to display various special characters such as tab and newline.

Section Positioning and Placing Marks in Text

You can define sections of text to which you can move as well as mark text with characters and move to those marks. Table 10-12 summarizes positioning and marking in **vi**.

TABLE 10-12 POSITIONING AND MARKING IN **vi**

Option	Action
{	Insert { in first column to define section.
[[	Go back to beginning of section.
]]	Forward to beginning of next section.
m*(a-z)*	Mark current position with a letter such as **mz** for mark *z*.
'*(a-z)*	Move cursor to specified mark such as '**z** for move to *z*.

Joining Lines in vi

You can join one or more lines in **vi** using the commands shown in Table 10-13.

TABLE 10-13 JOINING LINES IN **vi**

Option	Action
J	Join the next line to the end of the current line.
*n***J**	Join the next *n* lines.

Cursor Placement and Adjusting the Screen

You can place the cursor anyplace in your file and adjust the screen in a variety of ways using the commands shown in Table 10-14.

TABLE 10-14 CURSOR PLACEMENT AND ADJUSTING THE SCREEN IN **vi**

Option	Action
H	Move cursor to top line of the screen.
*n*H	Move cursor to *n* line from the top of the screen.
M	Move cursor to the middle of the screen.
L	Move cursor to the bottom line of the screen.
*n*L	Move cursor to line *n* from the bottom of the screen.
^e (control-e)	Move screen up one line.
^y	Move screen down one line.
^u	Move screen up one-half page.
^d	Move screen down one-half page.
^b	Move screen up one page.
^f	Move screen down one page.
^l (letter l)	Redraw screen.
z - *return*	Make current line the top of screen.
*n*z - *return*	Make *n* line the top of screen.
z.	Make current line the middle line.
*n*z.	Make line *n* the middle line on screen.
z-	Make current line the bottom line.
*n*z-	Make line *n* the bottom line on screen.

Shell Escape Commands

You can run a UNIX command without exiting **vi** by using shell escape commands. You could do something as simple as start a sub-shell with the **:sh** command. You could also run a command outside the file you are editing without exiting **vi**. Table 10-15 describes shell escape commands.

TABLE 10-15 SHELL ESCAPE COMMANDS IN vi

Option	Action
:! *command*	Execute shell command *command* such as **:! ls**.
:!!	Execute last shell command.
:r! *command*	Read and insert output from *command*, such as **:r! ls** to run **ls** and read contents.
:w !*command*	Send currently edited file to *command* as standard input and execute *command*, such as **:w ! grep all**.
:cd *directory*	Change the current working directory to *directory*.
:sh	Start a sub-shell and use **^d** (control-d) to return to **vi**.
:so *file*	Read and execute commands in the shell program *file*.

An example of using **:w** would be to send the file **wisdom** as standard input to **grep** looking for all lines that contain **all**, as in the following example:

:w ! grep all
Think of the small as
by a series of small acts.

You can issue the **:so** command to read and execute the commands in a file. Issuing the following command when in **vi** would run the commands in the file **file_with_commands**:

:so file_with_commands

This file contains the following two commands:

:set nu
:g/all/p

When we issue the earlier **:so** command, line numbers are shown with the **:set nu** command and the following lines containing *all* are printed:

Think of the small as
by a series of small acts.

Macros and Abbreviations

You are not limited to issuing individual **vi** commands. You can define strings of **vi** commands and define a key corresponding to this string that you can recall. When defining the keys for your macros, you can't use the following: **K V g q v * =** and function keys. There are also control keys you can't use, so stay away from control keys in general. Table 10-16 shows macros and abbreviations.

TABLE 10-16 MACROS AND ABBREVIATIONS IN vi

Option	Action
:map *key command_seq*	Define *key* to run *command_seq,* such as **:map e ea** to append text whenever you use **e** to move to the end of a word.
:map	Display all defined macros on the status line.
:umap *key*	Remove the macro for *key.*
:ab *string1 string2*	Define an abbreviation such that when *string1* is inserted, replace it with *string2.* When inserting text type *string1,* press *escape* key and *string2* will be inserted.
:ab	Display all abbreviations.
:cd *directory*	Change the current working directory to *directory.*
:una *string*	Unabbreviate *string.*
	Avoid control keys, symbols, and don't use characters: **K V g q v** * = and function keys.

An example of using the map command would be to automatically add text when you move to the end, as shown with the following map command:

:map e ea

This command maps **e** to **ea**. When you go to the end of the next word with **e**, you are also placed in insert mode with **a** so that you can append new text immediately after the end of the word.

You can also abbreviate long sequences with **ab**. For instance, you could abbreviate *system administration* with *sa* with the following command:

:ab sa system administration

Now whenever you insert text, type *sa*, and then press the *escape* key to complete the insert, the string *system administration* appears. *sa* is and abbreviation for *system administration.*

Indenting Text

You can indent text a variety of different ways. Table 10-17 shows some of the more commonly used indenting commands.

TABLE 10-17 INDENTING TEXT IN vi

Option	Action
^i (control i) or *tab*	While inserting text, insert on shift width. Shift width can be defined.
:set ai	Turn on auto-indentation.
:set sw=*n*	Set shift width to *n* characters.
n<<	Shift *n* lines left by one shift width.
n>>	Shift *n* lines right by one shift width. For example, **3>>** shifts the next three lines right by one shift width.

Before you adjust the shift width, you may want to issue **:set all** in order to see the current number of characters to which the shift width is set. It is usually eight characters by default. To set shift width to 16 characters you would issue the following command:

:set sw=16

You can then shift over the next three lines to the right by 16 characters each, with the following command:

3>>

The next three lines will then be shifted right by 16 characters.

Shell Filters

You can send information from the file you are editing to a command and then replace the original text with the output of the command. Table 10-18 shows a shell filter.

TABLE 10-18 SHELL FILTERS IN **vi**

Option	Action
!cursor_command command	Send text from the current position to that described by *cursor_command* to the shell *command.* For example, use **!} grep admin** to take text from the current position to the end of the paragraph, run this text through **grep** looking for the word *admin*, and replace existing text with the output of **grep**.

Pattern Matching

Pattern matching allows you to find patterns within the file you are editing. You can then perform functions such as changing what you have found in some way. Table 10-19 shows some of the most common pattern matching commands.

TABLE 10-19 PATTERN MATCHING IN **vi**

Option	Action
^ (caret)	Match the beginning of the line. To search for **Think** at only the beginning of the line, you would use: **/^Think** You can use this in combination with **$**, which matches to the end of the line, to delete all blank lines with: **:g/^$/d**.

TABLE 10-19 PATTERN MATCHING IN **vi**

Option	Action
$	Match end of line. To match **last.** only when it is followed by a newline character, you would use: **/last.$**
.	Match any single character.
\\<	Match beginning of word.
\\>	Match end of word.
[*string*]	Match any single character in *string*. To find **mp**, **mP**, **Mp**, or **MP**, use: **/[mM][pP]** Change all occurrences of **input** or **Input** to **INPUT** with: **:%s/[Ii]nput/INPUT/g**
[^*string*]	Match any character not in *string*.
[*a-p*]	Match any character between *a* and *p*.
*	Match zero or more occurrences of previous character in expression.
\\	Escape meaning of next character. To search for [, use the following: Λ[
\\\\	Escape the \\ character.

You may find pattern matching a little confusing when you first start to use it so I'll use several simple examples to get you started. Keep in mind that many of the pattern-matching techniques described here also work outside **vi** in your shell.

Matching a Set

We'll begin with the *square bracket operator*. To match any of the single characters **m**, **f**, or **p**, you would use the following:

/[mfp]

A common pattern to match would be a word with the first letter in the word either uppercase or lowercase. To match **input** or **Input**, you would use the following:

/[Ii]nput

Once you match either **Input** or **input**, you could then change it to **INPUT** with the following command:

:%s/[Ii]nput/INPUT/g

You can use sequences of expressions to search for more than one character, as shown in the following example:

/[mM][pP]

This sequence will match **mp**, **mP**, **Mp**, or **MP**. You are, in effect, searching for any of the four two-character strings.

Matching a Range

You can also use the square bracket operator to match single characters within a range. To find an occurrence of any digit in a file, you could use either of the two following square bracket searches:

/[0123456789]

or

/[0-9]

The hyphen denotes a range within the square bracket. To find any character, either uppercase or lowercase, you could use the following:

/[a-zA-Z]

To search for characters that normally have a special meaning, such as **[**, you can ignore, or escape, the special meaning by preceding the special character with a \ (backslash). To search for **[** in **vi**, for instance, you would use the following sequence:

/\[

This search will find the first occurrence of **[**.

Beginning and End of Line Search

You can specify that you wish your pattern match to take place at only the beginning or end of a line. To specify a beginning of the line pattern match, use the ^ (caret) preceding your desired pattern, as shown in the following example:

/^Think

This will match **Think** only when it appears at the beginning of a line. To specify an end of the line pattern match, use a **$** (dollar sign) following your desired pattern, as shown in the following example:

/last.$

This will match **last.** only when it is followed by a newline.

Manual Pages for Commands Used in Chapter 10

The following section contains copies of the manual pages for **vi**.

vi

vi - Run visual editor.

---

vi(1)   vi(1)

NAME
       vi, view, vedit - screen-oriented (visual) text editor

SYNOPSIS

       vi [-] [-l] [-r] [-R] [-t tag] [-v] [-V] [-wsize] [-x] [+command] [file
       ...]

   XPG4 Synopsis
       vi [-rR] [-c command] [-t tag] [-w size] [file ...]

   Obsolescent Options
       vi [-rR] [+command] [-t tag] [-w size] [file ...]

       view [-] [-l] [-r] [-R] [-t tag] [-v] [-V] [-wsize] [-x] [+command]
       [file ...]

       vedit [-] [-r] [-R] [-l] [-t tag] [-v] [-V] [-wsize] [-x] [+command]
       [file ...]

   Remarks
       The program names ex, edit, vi, view, and vedit are separate
       personalities of the same program. This manual entry describes the
       behavior of the vi/view/vedit personality.

DESCRIPTION
       The vi (visual) program is a display-oriented text editor that is
       based on the underlying ex line editor (see ex(1)). It is possible to
       switch back and forth between the two and to execute ex commands from
       within vi. The line-editor commands and the editor options are
       described in ex(1). Only the visual mode commands are described here.

       The view program is identical to vi except that the readonly editor
       option is set (see ex(1)).

       The vedit program is somewhat friendlier for beginners and casual
       users. The report editor option is set to 1, and the nomagic, novice,
       and showmode editor options are set.

       In vi, the terminal screen acts as a window into a memory copy of the
       file being edited. Changes made to the file copy are reflected in the
       screen display. The position of the cursor on the screen indicates
       the position within the file copy.

       The environment variable TERM must specify a terminal type that is
       defined in the terminfo database (see terminfo(4)). Otherwise, a
       message is displayed and the line-editor is invoked.

       As with ex, editor initialization scripts can be placed in the
       environment variable EXINIT, or in the file .exrc in the current or
       home directory.

Options and Arguments
vi recognizes the following command-line options and arguments:

-               Suppress all interactive-user feedback. This is useful
                when editor commands are taken from scripts.

-l   Set the lisp editor option (see ex(1)). Provides
                indents appropriate for lisp code. The (,), {, }, [[,
                and]] commands in vi are modified to function with
                lisp source code.

-r   Recover the specified files after an editor or system
                crash. If no file is specified, a list of all saved
                files is printed. You must be the owner of the saved
                file in order to recover it (superuser cannot recover
                files owned by other users).

-R   Set the readonly editor option to prevent overwriting a
                file inadvertently (see ex(1)).

-t tag   Execute the tag tag command to load and position a
                predefined file. See the tag command and the tags
                editor option in ex(1).

-v   Invoke visual mode (vi). Useful with ex, it has no
                effect on vi.

-V   Set verbose mode. Editor commands are displayed as
                they are executed when input from a .exrc file or a
                source file (see the source command in ex(1)).

-wsize   Set the value of the window editor option to size. If
                size is omitted, it defaults to 3.

-x   Set encryption mode. You are prompted for a key to
                allow for the creation or editing of an encrypted file
                (see the crypt command in ex(1)).

-c command   (XPG4 only.)

+command   (Obsolescent) Begin editing by executing the specified
                ex command-mode commands. As with the normal ex
                command-line entries, the command option-argument can
                consist of multiple ex commands separated by vertical-
                line commands (|). The use of commands that enter input
                mode in this manner produces undefined results.

file   Specify the file or files to be edited. If more than
                one file is specified, they are processed in the order
                given. If the -r option is also specified, the files
                are read from the recovery area.

(XPG4 only.) If both the -t tag and -c command (or the obsolescent
+command) options are given, the -t tag will be processed first, that
is, the file containing the tag is selected by -t and then the command
is executed.

When invoked, vi is in command mode. input mode is initiated by
several commands used to insert or change text.

In input mode, ESC (escape) is used to leave input mode; however, two
consecutive ESC characters are required to leave input mode if the
doubleescape editor option is set (see ex(1)).

In command mode, ESC is used to cancel a partial command; the terminal

bell sounds if the editor is not in input mode and there is no
partially entered command.

WARNING: ESC completes a "bottom line" command (see below).

The last (bottom) line of the screen is used to echo the input for
search commands (/ and ?), ex commands (:), and system commands (!).
It is also used to report errors or print other messages.

The receipt of SIGINT during text input or during the input of a
command on the bottom line terminates the input (or cancels the
command) and returns the editor to command mode. During command mode,
SIGINT causes the bell to be sounded. In general the bell indicates
an error (such as an unrecognized key).

Lines displayed on the screen containing only a ~ indicate that the
last line above them is the last line of the file (the ~ lines are
past the end of the file). Terminals with limited local intelligence
might display lines on the screen marked with an @. These indicate
space on the screen not corresponding to lines in the file. (These
lines can be removed by entering a ^R, forcing the editor to retype
the screen without these holes.)

If the system crashes or vi aborts due to an internal error or
unexpected signal, vi attempts to preserve the buffer if any unwritten
changes were made. Use the -r command line option to retrieve the
saved changes.

The vi text editor supports the SIGWINCH signal, and redraws the
screen in response to window-size changes.

Command Summary
   Most commands accept a preceding number as an argument, either to give
   a size or position (for display or movement commands), or as a repeat
   count (for commands that change text). For simplicity, this optional
   argument is referred to as count when its effect is described.

   The following operators can be followed by a movement command to
   specify an extent of text to be affected: c, d, y, <, >, !, and =.
   The region specified begins at the current cursor position and ends
   just prior to the cursor position indicated by the move. If the
   command operates on lines only, all the lines that fall partly or
   wholly within this region are affected. Otherwise the exact marked
   region is affected.

   In the following description, control characters are indicated in the
   form ^X, which represents Ctrl-X. Whitespace is defined to be the
   characters space, tab, and alternative space. Alternative space is
   the first character of the ALT_PUNCT item described in langinfo(5) for
   the language specified by the LANG environment variable (see
   environ(5)).

   Unless otherwise specified, the commands are interpreted in command
   mode and have no special effect in input mode.

           ^B   Scroll backward to display the previous window of
                       text. A preceding count specifies the number of
                       windows to go back. Two lines of overlap are kept if
                       possible.

           ^D   Scroll forward a half-window of text. A preceding
                       count gives the number of (logical) lines to scroll,
                       and is remembered for future ^D and ^U commands.

           ^D   (input mode) Backs up over the indentation provided
                       by autoindent or ^T to the next multiple of

shiftwidth spaces. Whitespace inserted by ^T at other than the beginning of a line cannot be backed over using ^D. A preceding ^ removes all indentation for the current and subsequent input lines of the current input mode until new indentation is established by inserting leading whitespace, either by direct input or by using ^T.

^E   Scroll forward one line, leaving the cursor where it is if possible.

^F   Scroll forward to display the window of text following the current one. A preceding count specifies the number of windows to advance. Two lines of overlap are kept if possible.

     (XPG4 only.) The current line is displayed and the cursor is moved to the first nonblank character of the current line or the first character if the line is a blank line.

^G   Print the current file name and other information, including the number of lines and the current position (equivalent to the ex command f).

^H   Move one space to the left (stops at the left margin). A preceding count specifies the number of spaces to back up. (Same as h).

^H   (input mode) Move the cursor left to the previous input character without erasing it from the screen. The character is deleted from the saved text.

^J   Move the cursor down one line in the same column, if possible. A preceding count specifies the number of lines to move down. (Same as ^N and j).

^L   Clear and redraw the screen. Use when the screen is scrambled for any reason.

^M   Move to the first nonwhitespace character in the next line. A preceding count specifies the number of lines to advance.

^N   Same as ^J and j.

^P   Move the cursor up one line in the same column. A preceding count specifies the number of lines to move up (same as k).

^R   Redraw the current screen, eliminating the false lines marked with @ (which do not correspond to actual lines in the file).

^T   Pop the tag stack. See the pop command in ex(1).

^T   (input mode) Insert shiftwidth whitespace. If at the beginning of the line, this inserted space can only be backed over using ^D.

^U   Scroll up a half-window of text. A preceding count gives the number of (logical) lines to scroll, and is remembered for future ^D and ^U commands.

^V   In input mode, ^V quotes the next character to permit the insertion of special characters (including ESC) into the file.

^W   In input mode, ^W backs up one word; the deleted
                characters remain on the display.

^Y   Scroll backward one line, leaving the cursor where it
                is, if possible.

^[Cancel a partially formed command; ^[sounds the bell
                if there is no partially formed command.

                In input mode, ^[terminates input mode. However,
                two consecutive ESC characters are required to
                terminate input mode if the doubleescape editor
                option is set (see ex(1)).

                When entering a command on the bottom line of the
                screen (ex command line or search pattern with \ or
                ?), terminate input and execute command.

                On many terminals, ^[can be entered by pressing the
                ESC or ESCAPE key.

^\   Exit vi and enter ex command mode. If in input mode,
                terminate the input first.

^]   Take the word at or after the cursor as a tag and
                execute the tagMbobC editor command (see ex(1)).

^^   Return to the previous file (equivalent to :ex #).

space   Move one space to the right (stops at the end of the
                line). A preceding count specifies the number of
                spaces to go forward (same as l).

erase   Erase, where erase is the user-designated erase
                character (see stty(1)). Same as ^H.

kill   Kill, where kill is the user-designated kill
                character (see stty(1)). In input mode, kill backs
                up to the beginning of the current input line without
                erasing the line from the screen display.

susp   Suspend the editor session and return to the calling
                shell, where susp is the user-designated process-
                control suspend character (see stty(1)). See ex(1)
                for more information on the suspend editor command.

!   An operator that passes specified lines from the
                buffer as standard input to the specified system
                command, and replaces those lines with the standard
                output from the command. The ! is followed by a
                movement command specifying the lines to be passed
                (lines from the current position to the end of the
                movement) and then the command (terminated as usual
                by a return). A preceding count is passed on to the
                movement command after !.

                Doubling ! and preceding it by count causes that
                many lines, starting with the current line, to be
                passed.

"   Use to precede a named buffer specification. There
                are named buffers 1 through 9 in which the editor
                places deleted text. The named buffers a through z

are available to the user for saving deleted or
yanked text; see also y, below.

$ Move to the end of the current line. A preceding
count specifies the number of lines to advance (for
example, 2$ causes the cursor to advance to the end
of the next line).

%   Move to the parenthesis or brace that matches the
parenthesis or brace at the current cursor position.

&   Same as the ex command & (that is, & repeats the
previous substitute command).

'   When followed by a ', vi returns to the previous
context, placing the cursor at the beginning of the
line. (The previous context is set whenever a
nonrelative move is made.) When followed by a letter
a-z, returns to the line marked with that letter (see
the m command), at the first nonwhitespace character
in the line.

When used with an operator such as d to specify an
extent of text, the operation takes place over
complete lines (see also `).

`          When followed by a `, vi returns to the previous
context, placing the cursor at the character position
marked (the previous context is set whenever a
nonrelative move is made). When followed by a letter
a z, returns to the line marked with that letter (see
the m command), at the character position marked.

When used with an operator such as d to specify an
extent of text, the operation takes place from the
exact marked place to the current position within the
line (see also ').

[[Back up to the previous section boundary. A section
is defined by the value of the sections option.
Lines that start with a form feed (^L) or { also stop
[[.

If the option lisp is set, the cursor stops at each (
at the beginning of a line.

]]   Move forward to a section boundary (see [[).

^   Move to the first nonwhitespace position on the
current line.

(Move backward to the beginning of a sentence. A
sentence ends at a ., !, or ? followed by either the
end of a line or by two spaces. Any number of
closing),], ", and ' characters can appear between
the ., !, or ? and the spaces or end of line. If a
count is specified, the cursor moves back the
specified number of sentences.

If the lisp option is set, the cursor moves to the
beginning of a lisp s-expression. Sentences also
begin at paragraph and section boundaries (see { and
[[).

)   Move forward to the beginning of a sentence. If a count is specified, the cursor advances the specified number of sentences (see ().

{ Move back to the beginning of the preceding paragraph. A paragraph is defined by the value of the paragraphs option. A completely empty line and a section boundary (see [[above) are also interpreted as the beginning of a paragraph. If a count is specified, the cursor moves backward the specified number of paragraphs.

} Move forward to the beginning of the next paragraph. If a count is specified, the cursor advances the specified number of paragraphs (see {).

| Requires a preceding count; the cursor moves to the specified column of the current line (if possible).

+ Move to the first nonwhitespace character in the next line. If a count is specified, the cursor advances the specified number of lines (same as ^M).

, The comma (,) performs the reverse action of the last f, F, t, or T command issued, by searching in the opposite direction on the current line. If a count is specified, the cursor repeats the search the specified number of times.

- The hyphen character (-) moves the cursor to the first nonwhitespace character in the previous line. If a count is specified, the cursor moves back the specified number of times.

_ The underscore character (_) moves the cursor to the first nonwhitespace character in the current line. If a count is specified, the cursor advances the specified number of lines, with the current line being counted as the first line; no count or a count of 1 specifies the current line.

. Repeat the last command that changed the buffer. If a count is specified, the command is repeated the specified number of times.

/ Read a string from the last line on the screen, interpret it as a regular expression, and scan forward for the next occurrence of a matching string. The search begins when the user types a carriage return to terminate the pattern; the search can be terminated by sending SIGINT (or the user-designated interrupt character).

When used with an operator to specify an extent of text, the defined region begins with the current cursor position and ends at the beginning of the matched string. Entire lines can be specified by giving an offset from the matched line (by using a closing / followed by a +n or -n).

0 Move to the first character on the current line (the 0 is not interpreted as a command when preceded by a nonzero digit).

: The colon character (:) begins an ex command. The : and the entered command are echoed on the bottom

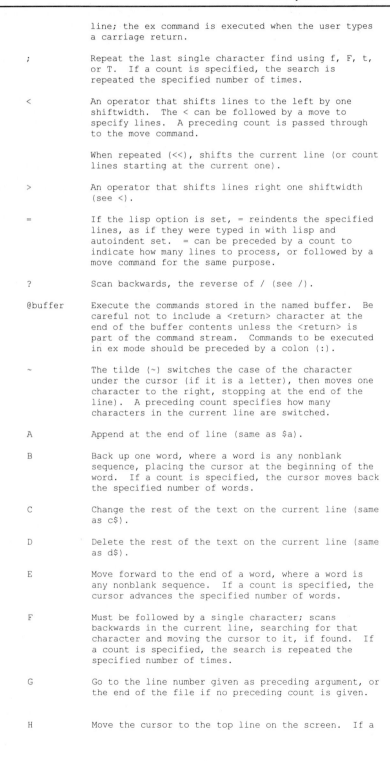

line; the ex command is executed when the user types
a carriage return.

;   Repeat the last single character find using f, F, t,
or T. If a count is specified, the search is
repeated the specified number of times.

<   An operator that shifts lines to the left by one
shiftwidth. The < can be followed by a move to
specify lines. A preceding count is passed through
to the move command.

         When repeated (<<), shifts the current line (or count
lines starting at the current one).

>   An operator that shifts lines right one shiftwidth
(see <).

=   If the lisp option is set, = reindents the specified
lines, as if they were typed in with lisp and
autoindent set. = can be preceded by a count to
indicate how many lines to process, or followed by a
move command for the same purpose.

?   Scan backwards, the reverse of / (see /).

@buffer   Execute the commands stored in the named buffer. Be
careful not to include a <return> character at the
end of the buffer contents unless the <return> is
part of the command stream. Commands to be executed
in ex mode should be preceded by a colon (:).

~   The tilde (~) switches the case of the character
under the cursor (if it is a letter), then moves one
character to the right, stopping at the end of the
line). A preceding count specifies how many
characters in the current line are switched.

A   Append at the end of line (same as $a).

B   Back up one word, where a word is any nonblank
sequence, placing the cursor at the beginning of the
word. If a count is specified, the cursor moves back
the specified number of words.

C   Change the rest of the text on the current line (same
as c$).

D   Delete the rest of the text on the current line (same
as d$).

E   Move forward to the end of a word, where a word is
any nonblank sequence. If a count is specified, the
cursor advances the specified number of words.

F   Must be followed by a single character; scans
backwards in the current line, searching for that
character and moving the cursor to it, if found. If
a count is specified, the search is repeated the
specified number of times.

G   Go to the line number given as preceding argument, or
the end of the file if no preceding count is given.

H   Move the cursor to the top line on the screen. If a

count is given, the cursor moves to count number of lines from the top of the screen. The cursor is placed on the first nonwhitespace character on the line. If used as the target of an operator, entire lines are affected.

I   Insert at the beginning of a line (same as ^ followed by i).

J   Join the current line with the next one, supplying appropriate whitespace: one space between words, two spaces after a period, and no spaces at all if the first character of the next line is a closing parenthesis ()). A preceding count causes the specified number of lines to be joined, instead of just two.

L   Move the cursor to the first nonwhitespace character of the last line on the screen. If a count is given, the cursor moves to count number of lines from the bottom of the screen. When used with an operator, entire lines are affected.

M   Move the cursor to the middle line on the screen, at the first nonwhitespace position on the line.

N   Scan for the next match of the last pattern given to / or ?, but in the opposite direction; this is the reverse of n.

O   Open a new line above the current line and enter input mode.

P   Put back (replace) the last deleted or yanked text before/above the cursor. Entire lines of text are returned above the cursor if entire lines were deleted or yanked. Otherwise, the text is inserted just before the cursor.

         (XPG4 only.) In this case, the cursor is moved to last column position of the inserted characters.

         If P is preceded by a named buffer specification (x), the contents of that buffer are retrieved instead.

Q   Exit vi and enter ex command mode.

R   Replace characters on the screen with characters entered, until the input is terminated with ESC.

S   Change entire lines (same as cc). A preceding count changes the specified number of lines.

T   Must be followed by a single character; scan backwards in the current line for that character, and, if found, place the cursor just after that character. A count is equivalent to repeating the search the specified number of times.

U   Restore the current line to its state before the cursor was last moved to it.

         (XPG4 only.) The cursor position is set to the column position 1 or to the position indicated by the previous line if the autoindent is set.

W	Move forward to the beginning of a word in the current line, where a word is a sequence of nonblank characters. If the current position is at the beginning of a word, the current position is within a bigword or the character at that position cannot be a part of a bigword, the current position shall move to the first character of the next bigword. If no subsequent bigword exists on the current line, the current position shall move to the first character of the first bigword on the first following line that contains the bigword. For this command, an empty or blank line is considered to contain exactly one bigword. The current line is set to the line containing the bigword selected and the current position is set to the first character of the bigword selected. A preceding count specifies the number of words to advance.
X	Delete the character before the cursor. A preceding count repeats the effect, but only characters on the current line are deleted.
Y	Place (yank) a copy of the current line into the unnamed buffer (same as yy). If a count is specified, count lines are copied to the buffer. If the Y is preceded by a buffer name, the lines are copied to the named buffer.
ZZ	Exit the editor, writing out the buffer if it was changed since the last write (same as the ex command x). Note that if the last write was to a different file and no changes have occurred since, the editor exits without writing out the buffer.
a	Enter input mode, appending the entered text after the current cursor position. A preceding count causes the inserted text to be replicated the specified number of times, but only if the inserted text is all on one line.
b	Back up to the previous beginning of a word in the current line. A word is a sequence of alphanumerics or a sequence of special characters. A preceding count repeats the effect.
c	Must be followed by a movement command. Delete the specified region of text, and enter input mode to replace deleted text with new text. If more than part of a single line is affected, the deleted text is saved in the numeric buffers. If only part of the current line is affected, the last character deleted is marked with a $. A preceding count passes that value through to the move command. If the command is cc, the entire current line is changed.
d	Must be followed by a movement command. Delete the specified region of text. If more than part of a line is affected, the text is saved in the numeric buffers. A preceding count passes that value through to the move command. If the command is dd, the entire current line is deleted.
e	Move forward to the end of the next word, defined as for b. A preceding count repeats the effect.
f	Must be followed by a single character; scan the rest

of the current line for that character, and moves the cursor to it if found. A preceding count repeats the action that many times.

h   Move the cursor one character to the left (same as ^H). A preceding count repeats the effect.

i   Enter input mode, inserting the entered text before the cursor (see a).

j   Move the cursor one line down in the same column (same as ^J and ^N).

k   Move the cursor one line up (same as ^P).

l   Move the cursor one character to the right (same as <space>).

mx   Mark the current position of the cursor. x is a lowercase letter, a-z, that is used with the ` and ' commands to refer to the marked line or line position.

n   Repeat the last / or ? scanning commands.

o   Open a line below the current line and enter input mode; otherwise like O.

p   Put text after/below the cursor; otherwise like P.

r   Must be followed by a single character; the character under the cursor is replaced by the specified one. (The new character can be a new-line.) If r is preceded by a count, count characters are replaced by the specified character.

s   Delete the single character under the cursor and enter input mode; the entered text replaces the deleted character. A preceding count specifies how many characters on the current line are changed. The last character being changed is marked with a $, as for c.

t   Must be followed by a single character; scan the remainder of the line for that character. The cursor moves to the column prior to the character if the character is found. A preceding count is equivalent to repeating the search count times.

u   Reverse the last change made to the current buffer. If repeated, u alternates between these two states; thus is its own inverse. When used after an insertion of text on more than one line, the lines are saved in the numerically named buffers.

w   Move forward to the beginning of the next word (where word is defined as in b). A preceding count specifies how many words the cursor advances.

x   Delete the single character under the cursor. When x is preceded by a count, x deletes the specified number of characters forward from the cursor position, but only on the current line.

y   Must be followed by a movement command; the specified text is copied (yanked) into the unnamed temporary

buffer. If preceded by a named buffer specification,
"x, the text is placed in that buffer also. If the
command is yy, the entire current line is yanked.

z   Redraw the screen with the current line placed as
specified by the following options: z<return>
specifies the top of the screen, z. the center of
the screen, and z- the bottom of the screen. The
commands z^ and z+ are similar to ^B and ^F,
respectively. However, z^ and z+ do not attempt to
maintain two lines of overlap. A count after the z
and before the following character to specifies the
number of lines displayed in the redrawn screen. A
count before the z gives the number of the line to
use as the reference line instead of the default
current line.

Keyboard Editing Keys
  At initialization, the editor automatically maps some terminal
  keyboard editing keys to equivalent visual mode commands. These
  mappings are only established for keys that are listed in the
  following table and defined in the terminfo(4) database as valid for
  the current terminal (as specified by the TERM environment variable).

  Both command and input mode mappings are created (see the map command
  in ex(1)). With the exception of the insertchar keys, which simply
  toggle input mode on and off, the input mode mappings exit input mode,
  perform the same action as the command mode mapping, and then reenter
  input mode.

  On certain terminals, the character sequence sent by a keyboard
  editing key, which is then mapped to a visual mode command, can be the
  same character sequence a user might enter to perform another command
  or set of commands. This is most likely to happen with the input mode
  mappings; therefore, on these terminals, the input mode mappings are
  disabled by default. Users can override the disabling and enabling of
  both the command and input mode keyboard editing key mappings by
  setting the keyboardedit and keyboardedit! editor options as
  appropriate (see ex(1)). The timeout, timeoutlen, and doubleescape
  editor options are alternative methods of addressing this problem.

terminfo entry	command mode map	input mode map	map name	description
key_ic	i	^[	inschar	insert char
key_eic	i	^[	inschar	end insert char
key_up	k	^[ka	up	arrow up
key_down	j	^[ja	down	arrow down
key_left	h	^[ha	left	arrow left
key_right	l	^[la	right	arrow right
key_home	H	^[Ha	home	arrow home
key_il	o^[	^[o^[a	insline	insert line
key_dl	dd	^[dda	delline	delete line
key_clear	^L	^[^La	clear	clear screen
key_eol	d$	^[d$a	clreol	clear line
key_sf	^E	^[^Ea	scrollf	scroll down
key_dc	x	^[xa	delchar	delete char
key_npage	^F	^[^Fa	npage	next page
key_ppage	^B	^[^Ba	ppage	previous page
key_sr	^Y	^[^Ya	sr	scroll up
key_eos	dG	^[dGa	clreos	clear to end of screen

EXTERNAL INFLUENCES
        Support for international codes and environment variables are as
        follows:

    Environment Variables
    UNIX95 specifies using the XPG4 behaviour for this command.

    COLUMNS overrides the system-selected horizontal screen size.

    LINES overrides the system-selected vertical screen size, used as the
    number of lines in a screenful and the vertical screen size in visual
    mode.

    SHELL is a variable that shall be interpreted as the preferred
    command-line interpreter for use in !, shell, read, and other commands
    with an operand of the form !string. For the shell command the
    program shall be invoked with the two arguments -c and string. If
    this variable is null or not set, the sh utility shall be used.

    TERM is a variable that shall be interpreted as the name of the
    terminal type. If this variable is unset or null, an unspecified
    default terminal type shall be used.

    PATH determines the search path for the shell command specified in the
    editor commands, shell, read, and write. EXINIT determines a list of
    ex commands that will be executed on editor startup, before reading
    the first file. The list can contain multiple commands by separating
    them using a vertical line (|) character.

    HOME determines a pathname of a directory that will be searched for an
    editor startup file named .exrc.

    LC_ALL This variable shall determine the locale to be used to override
    any values for locale categories specified by the setting of LANG or
    any environment variables beginning with LC_.

    LC_MESSAGES determines the locale that should be used to affect the
    format and contents of diagnostic messages written to standard error
    and informative messages written to standard output.

    LC_COLLATE determines the collating sequence used in evaluating
    regular expressions and in processing the tags file. LC_CTYPE
    determines the interpretation of text as single and/or multi-byte
    characters, the classification of characters as uppercase or lowercase
    letters, the shifting of letters between uppercase and lowercase, and
    the characters matched by character class expressions in regular
    expressions.

    LANG determines the language in which messages are displayed.

    LANGOPTS specifies options determining how text for right-to-left
    languages is stored in input and output files. See environ(5).

    If LC_COLLATE or LC_CTYPE is not specified in the environment or is
    set to the empty string, the value of LANG is used as a default for
    each unspecified or empty variable. If LANG is not specified or is
    set to the empty string, a default of "C" (see lang(5)) is used
    instead of LANG. If any internationalization variable contains an
    invalid setting, the editor behaves as if all internationalization
    variables are set to "C". See environ(5).

    International Code Set Support
    Single- and multi-byte character code sets are supported.

WARNINGS
        See also the WARNINGS section in ex(1).

Program Limits
vi places the following limits on files being edited:

Maximum Line Length
LINE_MAX characters (defined in <limits.h>), including 2-3 bytes
for overhead. Thus, if the value specified for LINE_MAX is 2048,
a line length up to 2044 characters should cause no problem.

If you load a file that contain lines longer than the specified
limit, the lines are truncated to the stated maximum length.
Saving the file will write the truncated version over the
original file, thus overwriting the original lines completely.

Attempting to create lines longer than the allowable maximum for
the editor produces a line too long error message.

Maximum File Size
The maximum file length of 234,239 lines is silently enforced.

Other limits:

- 256 characters per global command list.

- 128 characters in a file name in vi or ex open mode. On
  short-file-name HP-UX systems, the maximum file name length is
  14 characters.

- 128 characters in a previous insert/delete buffer.

- 100 characters in a shell-escape command.

- 63 characters in a string-valued option (:set command).

- 30 characters in a program tag name.

- 32 or fewer macros defined by map command.

- 512 or fewer characters total in combined map macros.

AUTHOR
vi was developed by the University of California, Berkeley. The 16-
bit extensions to vi are based in part on software of the Toshiba
Corporation.

SEE ALSO
ctags(1), ed(1), ex(1), stty(1), write(1), terminfo(4), environ(5),
lang(5), regexp(5).

The Ultimate Guide to the vi and ex Text Editors,
    Benjamin/Cummings Publishing Company, Inc., ISBN 0-8053-4460-8,
    HP part number 97005-90015.

STANDARDS CONFORMANCE
vi: SVID2, SVID3, XPG2, XPG3, XPG4

CHAPTER 11

Windows NT and UNIX Interoperability:

The X Window System

Interoperability Topics

I could spend another 1000 pages covering just Windows NT and UNIX interoperability. There are hundreds of technologies and products that enhance Windows NT and UNIX interoperability. Since covering even a small fraction of these technologies and products in this book would not be feasible, I decided to devote a few chapters to technologies that bridge the gap between some fundamental Windows NT and UNIX differences in operation. The following is a list of what I consider to be the top interoperability topics, which are covered in the interoperability chapters of this book:

- **UNIX Application Server That Displays on Windows NT Using the X Window System (covered in this chapter)** - X Windows is a networked windowing environment that is the standard on UNIX systems. If you install X Windows on your Windows NT system, you can run applications on your UNIX system and use X Windows on your Windows NT system to manage those applications. The UNIX system is acting as the application server, but the applications are controlled from X Windows running on the Windows NT system.

- **Network File System (NFS) Used to Share Data (covered in Chapter 12)** - The next chapter covers using NFS to share data between Windows NT and UNIX systems. NFS comes with UNIX, and by loading NFS on a Windows NT system, you can freely access the UNIX file systems on the Windows NT systems and vice versa. I focus only on accessing UNIX file systems on the Windows NT systems because, as I earlier mentioned, I think it is more likely the UNIX system will act as a data and application server and the Windows NT system will act as a client. There is, however, no reason that NFS could not be used to access Windows NT file systems while on a UNIX system.

- **Windows NT Functionality on UNIX (Covered in Chapter 13)** - Putting the X Window System and NFS on Windows NT brings important UNIX functionality to the Windows NT operating system. It is equally useful to bring Windows NT functionality to UNIX. Advanced Server 9000 is a software product that runs on HP-UX and brings important Windows NT functionality such as file and print services to HP-UX. Chapter 13 is devoted to Advanced Server 9000.

- **Common Set of Commands (Covered in Chapter 14)** - The Windows NT Resource Kit provides countless useful utilities, including a set of POSIX commands that are familiar to UNIX system administrators. Commands such as **chmod**, **ls**, and **mv** run on Windows NT. Chapter 14 is devoted to these utilities.

Although the system administration topics are pretty much the same going from operating system to operating system, the peculiarities of each operating system define how you perform a given function. For this reason, system administration is seldom covered as a general topic; rather, it is covered for a particular operating system. In this book, however, the assumption is that you have both Windows NT and UNIX in your environment. You need to manage both and manage them separately for the most part; however, advantages exist to implementing technology that can enhance interoperability between the two operating systems.

What I cover in the interoperability chapters of this book (Chapters 11-14) are some of the most basic, and at the same time some of the most useful, technologies you can put in place to help with interoperability between Windows NT and UNIX.

You could certainly go beyond the interoperability topics I cover to much more advanced functionality; however, what I cover in the interoperability chapters is a big interoperability gain for very little cost and effort.

This chapter and the next work together and build on one another. In this chapter, I cover Windows NT and UNIX interoperability by running an X server program on a Windows NT system, which provides graphical access to an UNIX system. Then in Chapter 12, I use a networking product on the Windows NT system that provides transparent access to the data on the UNIX system using Network File System (NFS). Using the X Window System (X Windows), you have a graphical means of connecting a Windows NT system to a UNIX system, and using NFS, you have a way of easily sharing data between these two systems. These two technologies, X Windows and NFS, provide the foundation for a variety of other useful interoperability between the two operating systems.

Why the X Window System?

The Windows NT user environment and the UNIX user environment, which is based on X Windows, are much different. There is no bundled support whatever for accessing Windows NT from UNIX and UNIX from Windows NT.

To go beyond logging into a Windows NT system to perform Windows NT system administration and logging into an UNIX system to perform UNIX system administration, you need some way of getting access to one of these systems from the other. The X Window System is an ideal way to get remote access to a UNIX system while sitting at your Windows NT system.

X Window System Background

X Windows is a *network*-based windowing environment, not a system-based windowing environment. For this reason, it is ideal for giving you a window into your UNIX system from your Windows NT system.

X Windows is an industry standard for supporting windowed user interfaces across a computer network. Because it is an industry standard, many companies offer X server products for operating systems, such as Windows NT (we'll get into the "server" and "client" terminology of X Windows shortly). X Windows is not just a windowing system on your computer but a windowing system across the network.

X Windows is independent of the hardware or operating system on which it runs. All it needs is a server and a client. The server and client may be two different systems or the same system; that detail doesn't matter. The server is a program that provides input/output devices such as your display, keyboard, and mouse. The client is the program that takes commands from the server such as an application.

The client and server roles are much different from those we normally associate with these terms. The X Windows server is on your local system (in this chapter, it is your Windows NT system) and the X Windows client is the application that communicates with the server; (in this chapter it will be the UNIX system running a program such as a System Administration Tool). We normally think of the small desktop system as the client and the larger, more powerful system as the server. With X Windows, however, it is the system that controls X Windows that is the server, and the system that responds to the commands is the client. I often refer to a powerful client as the "host" to minimize confusion over this distinction.

In X Windows, the software that manages a single screen, keyboard, and mouse is known as an X server. A client is an application that displays on the X server. The X client sends requests to the X server, such as a request for information. The X server accepts requests from multiple X clients and returns information and errors to the X client.

Sitting on one of the Windows NT systems on a network, you could open an X Window into several UNIX hosts. You could therefore have one window open to UNIX_System1 and another window open to UNIX_System2, and so on.

The X server performs the following functions:

• Displays drawing requests on the screen.

• Replies to information requests.

• Reports an error associated with a request.

• Manages the keyboard, mouse, and display.

• Creates, maps, and removes windows.

The X client performs the following functions:

• Sends requests to the server.

• Receives events and errors from the server.

X Server Software

There are many fine X Server products on the market. I loaded Exceed 6 from Hummingbird Communications Ltd. on my system for demonstrating how X Windows can be used in a Windows NT and UNIX environment. I will use Exceed 6 in the examples in this chapter. Figure 11-1 shows the full menu structure from having loaded Hummingbird's X Windows product Exceed.

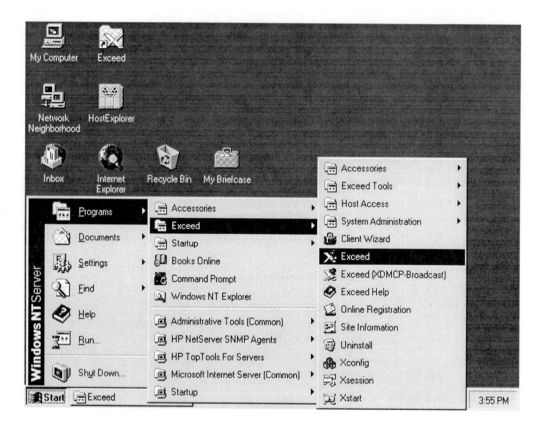

Figure 11-1 *Programs-Exceed* Menu

Selecting the Exceed icon from the very top of Figure 11-1 produces a group of Exceed icons that is an alternative to accessing items from the menu of Figure 11-1. Figure 11-2 shows the icon group.

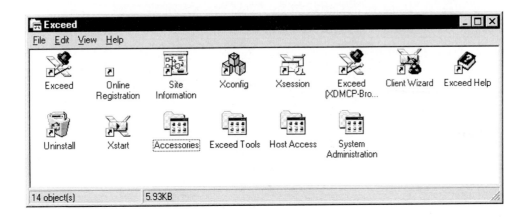

Figure 11-2 *Exceed* Group

The *Exceed* menu pick from Figure 11-1 allows you to establish an X Windows connection between your Windows NT system and UNIX system. You can specify the host to which you want to connect, the UNIX system in this case, the user you want to be connected as on the host, and the command to run on the UNIX system. Figure 11-3 shows the *Xstart* window.

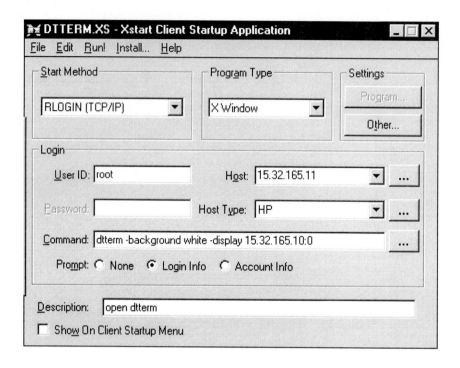

Figure 11-3 Establishing an X Windows Connection

The window in Figure 11-3 is labeled "DTTERM.XS." After you set up the *Xstart* window with the information you want, you can save the configuration. In this case, I am issuing the **dtterm** command, so I saved the window under this name. The system type can be most any system running X Windows. I used an HP-UX system in the upcoming examples, so the *Host Type* is *HP.* The complete **dtterm** command is:

dtterm -background white -display 15.32.165.10:0

Selecting *Run!* from the window in Figure 11-3 brings up the window in Figure 11-4, in which you can issue the *Password* and make other changes.

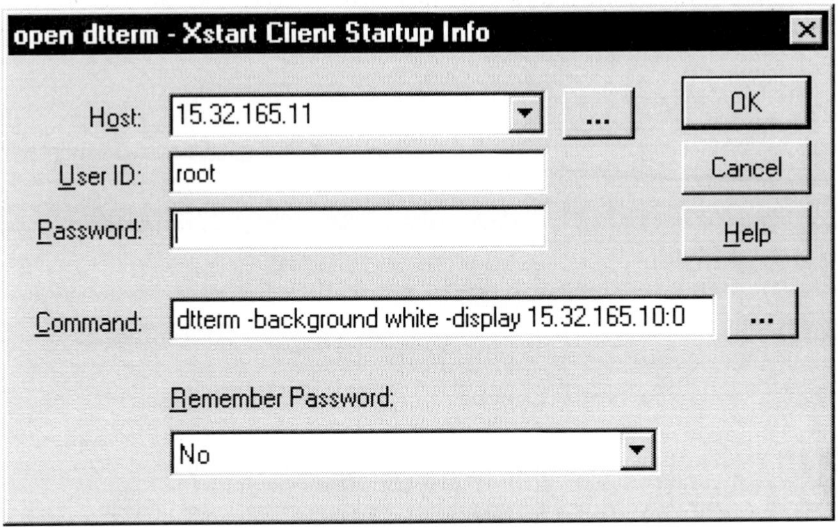

Figure 11-4 Establishing an X Windows Connection

This command starts a **dtterm** window, which is a standard window program on UNIX with a white background, and displays the window on the system at the IP address 15.32.165.11. The IP address in this case is the Windows NT system on which you are issuing the command, which is the X Windows server. The ":0" indicates that the first display on the Windows NT system will be used for **dtterm**, because in the X Windows world, you can have several displays on a system. The system on which the command runs is 15.32.165.10. This is the UNIX system that acts as the X Windows client.

Although you are typing this information on your Windows NT system, this command is being transferred to the UNIX system you specified in the *Xstart* box. This transfer will have the same result as typing the **dtterm** command shown on the UNIX system directly.

When you type your password and click *OK* a **dtterm** window appears on your Windows NT system that is a window into your UNIX system. Figure 11-5 shows the **dtterm** window open on the Windows NT system.

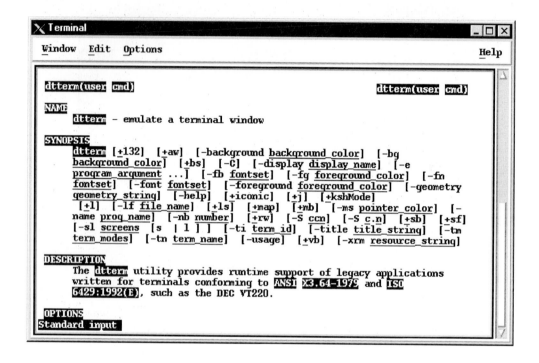

Figure 11-5 **dtterm** Running on UNIX and Displayed on Windows NT

Figure 11-5 is a **dtterm** window displayed on the Windows NT system but running on the UNIX system. The window currently has open the HP-UX manual page for **dtterm**. You can issue any commands in this **dtterm** window that you could issue if you were sitting on the UNIX system directly. Keep in mind, though, that your access to the UNIX system is based on the rights of the user you specified in the *Xstart* window.

You can use *Xstart* to run any program for which you have appropriate permissions on the UNIX system. Figure 11-6 shows an **xterm** window

that is displayed on the Windows NT system but is running on the UNIX
system.

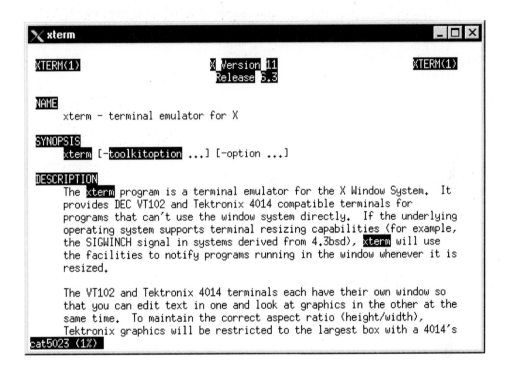

Figure 11-6   xterm Running on UNIX and Displayed on Windows NT

You are by no means limited to running only terminal windows such
as **dtterm** and **xterm** under X Windows in this environment. You can perform system management functions as well. Figure 11-7 shows the System
Administration Manager (SAM), which is the primary system administration tool on HP-UX, running on the UNIX system and displayed on the
Windows NT system with *Kernel Configuration* selected.

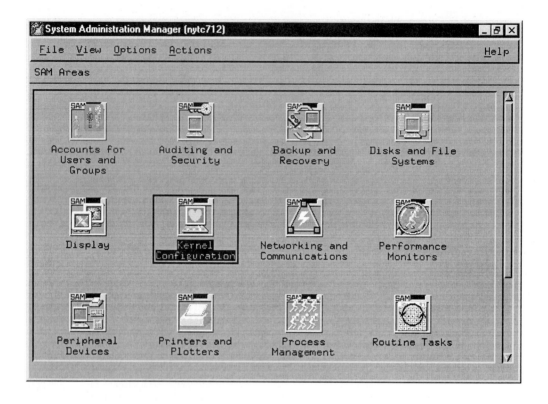

Figure 11-7   SAM Running on HP-UX and Displayed on Windows NT

There is no reason, however, to limit your use of Exceed to opening single windows or single applications. Exceed can also be used to run the Common Desktop Environment (CDE) used on most UNIX operating systems. CDE is a windowing environment that allows you to open several "desktops" which results in many windows.

By modifying a few parameters in Exceed, you can specify that the entire CDE environment run on your Windows NT system. CDE allows you to have multiple workspaces in with which you can organize the functional tasks you are performing. Figure 11-8 shows CDE running on our Windows NT system with the first of the workspaces selected called *program.*

Figure 11-8 CDE *program* Workspace

program is the first of the four workspaces shown on the bottom middle of Figure 11-8. There are three other workspaces for this user that we will view labeled *sam, files,* and *icon*.

Figure 11-9 shows the *sam* workspace in which we have invoked the System Administration Manager.

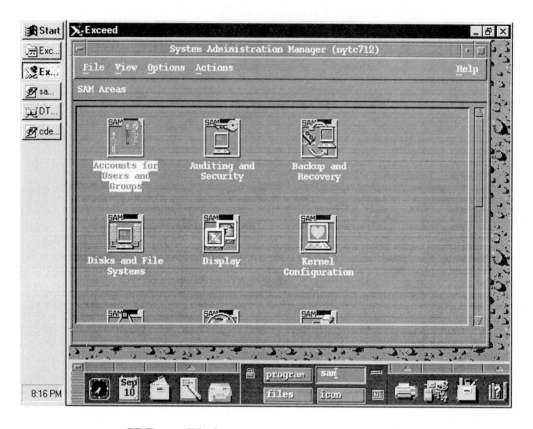

Figure 11-9   CDE *sam* Workspace

Figure 11-10 shows the *files* workspace in which we have invoked the
File Manager from CDE.

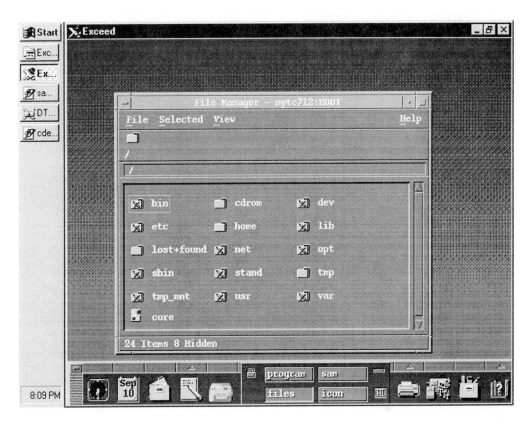

Figure 11-10 CDE *files* Workspace

Figure 11-11 shows the *icon* workspace in which we have invoked the icon editor.

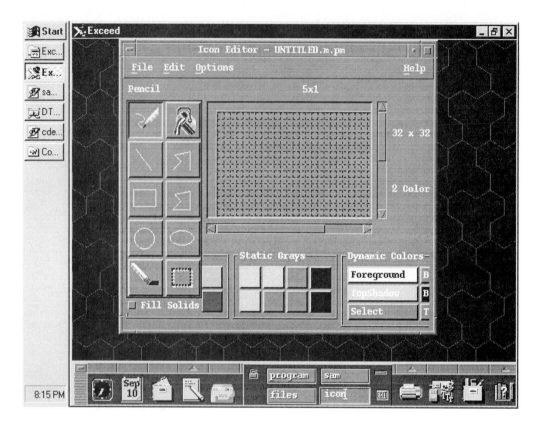

Figure 11-11 CDE *icon* Workspace

This technique, using X Windows on the Windows NT system to display applications running on the UNIX system, is powerful in this heterogenous environment. It is also inexpensive and simple to install. You have a choice using Exceed to either open individual UNIX windows while working on your Windows NT system or run the entire Common Desktop Environment from your Windows NT system. I find that users who spend a majority of their time working on the UNIX system, such as UNIX developers, like to run the entire Common Desktop Environment on their Windows NT system. Users who spend a majority of time on their Windows NT systems and need only occasional access to UNIX usually open a

dtterm or **xterm** window from the Windows NT system. Exceed gives you the flexibility to access UNIX from Windows NT using either technique.

We can also take this interoperability one step further by introducing data sharing into this mixed environment. Just as X Windows on UNIX and the Windows NT user interface are not compatible, the way in which data is shared in UNIX and Windows NT environments are different. Chapter 12 covers a way in which data sharing between UNIX and Windows NT takes place.

CHAPTER 12

Windows NT and UNIX Interoperability: Networking

Why Cover Interoperability?

Although system administration topics are pretty much the same going from operating system to operating system, the peculiarities of each operating system define how you perform a given function. For this reason, system administration is seldom covered as a general topic; rather, it is covered for a particular operating system. In this book, however, the assumption is that you have both Windows NT and UNIX in your environment. You need to manage both and manage them separately for the most part; however, advantages to implementing technology exist that can enhance interoperability between the two operating systems.

What I cover in the interoperability chapters of this book (Chapters 11 through 14) are some of the most basic, and at the same time some of the most useful, technologies you can put in place to help with interoperability between Windows NT and UNIX.

You could certainly go beyond the interoperability topics I cover to much more advanced functionality; however, what I cover in the interoperability chapters is a big interoperability gain for very little cost and effort.

This chapter and Chapter 11 combine to provide background of some useful interoperability. In this chapter, I use a networking product on the

Windows NT system that provides transparent access to the data on the UNIX system using Network File System (NFS). In Chapter 11, I covered Windows NT and UNIX interoperability by running an X server program on a Windows NT system, providing graphical access to a UNIX system. Using the X Window System (X Windows), you have a graphical means of connecting a Windows NT system to a UNIX system, and using NFS, you have a way of easily sharing data between these two systems. These two technologies, X Windows and NFS, provide the foundation for a variety of other useful interoperability between the two operating systems.

Although I provide TCP/IP background earlier in the book, I am going to include it again here so that you don't have to flip back and forth if you have to review TCP/IP.

TCP/IP Networking Background

You can see the seven layers of network functionality in the ISO/OSI model shown in Figure 12-1. I'll cover these layers at a cursory level, so that you have some background into this networking model. The top layers are the ones that you spend time working with, because they are closest to the functionality to which you can relate. The bottom layers are, however, also important to understand at some level, so you can perform any configuration necessary to improve the network performance of your system and have a major impact on the overall performance of your system.

Layer Number	Layer Name	Data Form	Comments
7	Application		User applications here.
6	Presentation		Applications prepared.
5	Session		Applications prepared.
4	Transport	Packet	Port-to-port transportation handled by TCP.

Layer Number	Layer Name	Data Form	Comments
3	Network	Datagram	Internet Protocol (IP) handles routing by going directly to the destination or default router.
2	Link	Frame	Data encapsulated in Ethernet or IEEE 802.3 with source and destination addresses.
1	Physical		Physical connection between systems. Usually thinnet or twisted pair.

Figure 12-1 ISO/OSI Network Layer Functions

I'll start reviewing Figure 12-1 at the bottom, with layer 1, and describe each of the four bottom layers. This model is the International Standards Organization Open Systems Interconnection (ISO/OSI) model. It is helpful to visualize the way in which networking layers interact.

Physical Layer

The beginning is the physical interconnect between the systems on your network. Without the **physical layer**, you can't communicate between systems, and all the great functionality you would like to implement will not be possible. The physical layer converts the data you would like to transmit to the analog signals that travel along the wire (I'll assume for now that whatever physical layer you have in place uses wires). The information traveling into a network interface is taken off the wire and prepared for use by the next layer.

Link Layer

In order to connect to other systems local to your system, you use the link layer that is able to establish a connection to all the other systems on your local segment. This is the layer where you have either IEEE 802.3 or Ethernet. These are "encapsulation" methods. This is named "encapsulation" because your data is put in one of these two forms (either IEEE 802.3 or Ethernet). Data is transferred at the link layer in frames (just another name for data), with the source and destination addresses and some other information attached. You might think that because there are two different encapsulation methods they must be much different. This conclusion, however, is not the case. IEEE 802.3 and Ethernet are nearly identical. So with the bottom two layers, you have a physical connection between your systems and data that is encapsulated into one of two formats with a source and destination address attached. Figure 12-2 lists the components of an *Ethernet* encapsulation and includes comments about IEEE802.3 encapsulation where appropriate.

destination address	6 bytes	address to which data is sent
source address	6 bytes	address from which data is sent
type	2 bytes	the "length count" in 802.3
data	46-1500 bytes	38-1492 bytes for 802.3
crc	4 bytes	checksum to detect errors

Figure 12-2 Ethernet Encapsulation

One interesting item to note is the difference in the maximum data size between IEEE 802.3 and Ethernet of 1492 and 1500 bytes, respectively. This is the Maximum Transfer Unit (MTU). The data in Ethernet is called a *frame* (the re-encapsulation of data at the next layer up is called a *datagram* in IP, and encapsulation at two levels up is called a *packet* for TCP).

Keep in mind that Ethernet and IEEE 802.3 can run on the same physical connection, but there are indeed differences between the two encapsulation methods.

Network Layer

Next we work up to the third layer, which is the network layer. This layer is synonymous with Internet Protocol (IP). Data at this layer is called a *datagram*. This is the layer that handles the routing of data around the network. Data that gets routed with IP sometimes encounters an error of some type, which is reported back to the source system with an Internet Control Message Protocol (ICMP) message.

Unfortunately, the information that IP uses does not conveniently fit inside an Ethernet frame, so you end up with fragmented data. This is really re-encapsulation of the data, so you end up with a lot of inefficiency as you work your way up the layers.

IP handles routing in a simple fashion. If data is sent to a destination connected directly to your system, then the data is sent directly to that system. If, on the other hand, the destination is not connected directly to your system, the data is sent to the default router. The default router, sometimes called a gateway, then has the responsibility to handle getting the data to its destination.

Transport Layer

This layer can be viewed as one level up from the network layer, because it communicates with *ports*. TCP is the most common protocol found at this level, and it forms packets that are sent from port to port. These ports are used by network programs such as **telnet**, **rlogin**, **ftp**, and so on. You can see that these programs, associated with ports, are the highest level I have covered while analyzing the layer diagram.

Internet Protocol (IP) Addressing

The Internet Protocol address (IP address) is either a class "A," "B," or "C" address (class "D" and "E" addresses exist that I will not cover). A class "A" network supports many more nodes per network than a class "B" or "C" network. IP addresses consist of four fields. The purpose of breaking down the IP address into four fields is to define a node (or host) address and a network address. Figure 12-3 summarizes the relationships between the classes and addresses.

Address Class	Networks	Nodes per Network	Bits Defining Network	Bits Defining Nodes per Network
A	a few	the most	8 bits	24 bits
B	many	many	16 bits	16 bits
C	the most	a few	24 bits	8 bits
Reserved	-	-	-	-

Figure 12-3 Comparison of Internet Protocol (IP) Addresses

These bit patterns are significant in that the number of bits defines the ranges of networks and nodes in each class. For instance, a class A address uses 8 bits to define networks, and a class C address uses 24 bits to define networks. A class A address therefore supports fewer networks than a class C address. A class A address, however, supports many more nodes per network than a class C address. Taking these relationships one step further, we can now view the specific parameters associated with these address classes in Figure 12-4.

Figure 12-4 Address Classes

Address Class	Networks Supported	Nodes per Network	Address Range		
A	127	16777215	0.0.0.1	-	127.255.255.254
B	16383	65535	128.0.0.1	-	191.255.255.254
C	2097157	255	192.0.0.1	-	223.255.254.254
Reserved	-	-	224.0.0.0	-	255.255.255.255

Looking at the 32-bit address in binary form, you can see how to determine the class of an address:

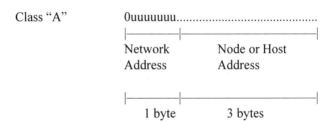

Class "A"   0uuuuuuu...

|————————|————————————————|

Network Address   Node or Host Address

|————————|————————————————|

1 byte   3 bytes

net.host.host.host

A class "A" address has the first bit set to 0. You can see how so many nodes per network can be supported with all the bits devoted to the node or host address. The first bit of a class A address is 0, and the remaining 7 bits of the network portion are used to define the network. There are then a total of 3 bytes devoted to defining the nodes within a network.

Figure 12-4 Address Classes (Continued)

Class "B"

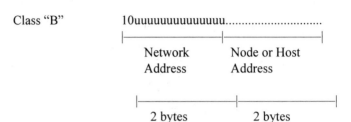

net.net.host.host

A class "B" address has the first bit set to a 1 and the second bit to a 0. There are more networks supported here than with a class A address, but fewer nodes per network. With a class B address, there are 2 bytes devoted to the network portion of the address and 2 bytes are devoted to the node portion of the address.

Class "C"

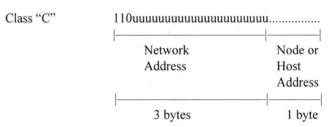

net.net.net.host

A class "C" address has the first bit and second bit set to 1, and the third bit is 0. The greatest number of networks and fewest number of nodes per network are associated with a class C address. With a class C address, there are 3 bytes devoted to the network and 1 byte is devoted to the nodes within a network.

Every interface on your network must have a unique IP address. Systems that have two network interfaces must have two unique IP addresses. I will cover some networking commands in Windows NT in an upcoming chapter.

NFS Background

I am not going to limit the discussion and examples in this chapter to NFS. There are other services used to share files that are also useful, such as File Transfer Protocol (FTP) which I'll show examples of as well. Because NFS is so widely used in the UNIX user community, it is one of my goals to expose you to how NFS can be used in a Windows NT and UNIX environment.

NFS allows you to mount disks on remote systems so that they appear as though they are local to your system. Similarly, NFS allows remote systems to mount your local disk so that it looks as though it is local to the remote system.

NFS, like X Windows, has a unique set of terminology. Here are definitions of some of the more important NFS terms:

Node	A computer system that is attached to or is part of a computer network.
Client	A node that requests data or services from other nodes (servers).
Server	A node that provides data or services to other nodes (clients) on the network.
File System	A disk partition or logical volume, or in the case of a workstation, this might be the entire disk.

Export   To make a file system available for mounting on remote nodes using NFS.

Mount   To access a remote file system using NFS.

Mount Point   The name of a directory on which the NFS file system is mounted.

Import   To mount a remote file system.

Before any data can be shared using NFS, the UNIX system must be set up with exported file systems. The **/etc/exports** file is often used on UNIX to define what file systems are exported.

This file has in it the directories exported and options such as "ro" for read only and "anon," which handles requests from anonymous users. If "anon" is equal to 65535, then anonymous users are denied access.

The following is an example **/etc/exports** file in which **/opt/app1** is exported to everyone but anonymous users, and **/opt/app1** is exported only to the system named system2:

```
/opt/app1    -anon=65534
/opt/app2    -access=system2
```

You may need to run a program such as **exportfs -a** on your UNIX system if you add a file system to export.

Although we are going to focus on exporting UNIX file systems to be mounted by Windows NT systems in this chapter, I can think of no reason we could not do the converse as well. Windows NT file systems can be mounted on a UNIX system just as UNIX file systems are mounted in Windows NT. Remote file systems to be mounted locally on a UNIX system are often put in **/etc/fstab**. Here is an example of an entry in **/etc/fstab** of a remote file system that is mounted locally. The remote directory **/opt/app3** on system2 is mounted locally under **/opt/opt3**:

system2:/opt/app3   /opt/app3   nfs   rw,suid   0   0

You can use the **showmount** command available on many UNIX systems to show all remote systems (clients) that have mounted a local file system. **showmount** is useful for determining the file systems that are most often mounted by clients with NFS. The output of **showmount** is particularly easy to read because it lists the host name and the directory that was mounted by the client. You have the three following options to the **showmount** command:

-a prints output in the format "name:directory," as shown above.

-d lists all the local directories that have been remotely mounted by clients.

-e prints a list of exported file systems.

Using Windows NT and UNIX Networking

I use the NFS Maestro product from Hummingbird Communications Ltd. on Windows NT to demonstrate the networking interoperability in this chapter.

You would typically run your NFS client, such as NFS Maestro, on your Windows NT system in order to mount file systems on a UNIX system. This setup means that all your Windows NT clients would run NFS Maestro. Depending on the number of Windows NT systems you have, you may find loading an NFS client on each and every system to be a daunting task. Hummingbird Communications has an alternative. Rather than loading the NFS client on each system, you can use a Windows NT system to act as a gateway between your Windows NT systems and your UNIX systems. NFS Maestro Gateway bridges your Windows NT network to your UNIX network. All Windows NT clients go through the NFS Maestro Gateway system in order to perform NFS access to the UNIX systems, thereby simplifying the installation and administration of NFS on Windows NT.

NFS Maestro Gateway bridges your Microsoft Server Message Block (SMB) network to your UNIX network by acting as a proxy. It forwards SMB requests from a Windows NT client to a UNIX NFS server and vice-versa.

The performance of using a dedicated NFS Maestro client is superior to that of using NFS Maestro Gateway. Like many system administration topics, there is a trade-off takes place between simplicity and performance. In this chapter I'll cover using a dedicated NFS Maestro client to access file systems on a UNIX server.

Figure 12-5 shows the menu for the Maestro product after I installed it.

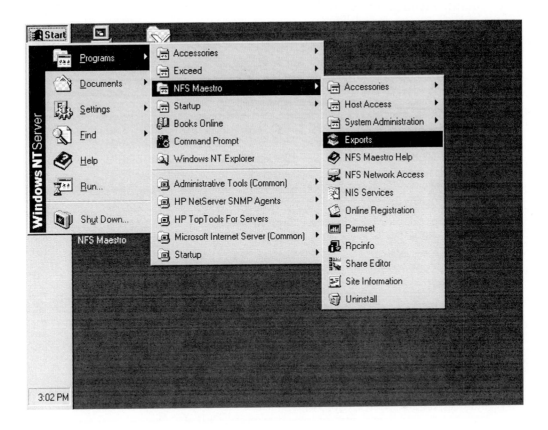

Figure 12-5 Hummingbird Maestro Menu in Windows NT

As you can see in Figure 12-5, there is much more than NFS function-ality is part of NFS Maestro. I will cover some additional functionality later in this chapter; however, my specific objectives are to cover the most important Windows NT and UNIX interoperability topics related to net-working.

The NFS icons can also be accessed as part of a group from the *NFS Maestro* icon as shown in Figure 12-6.

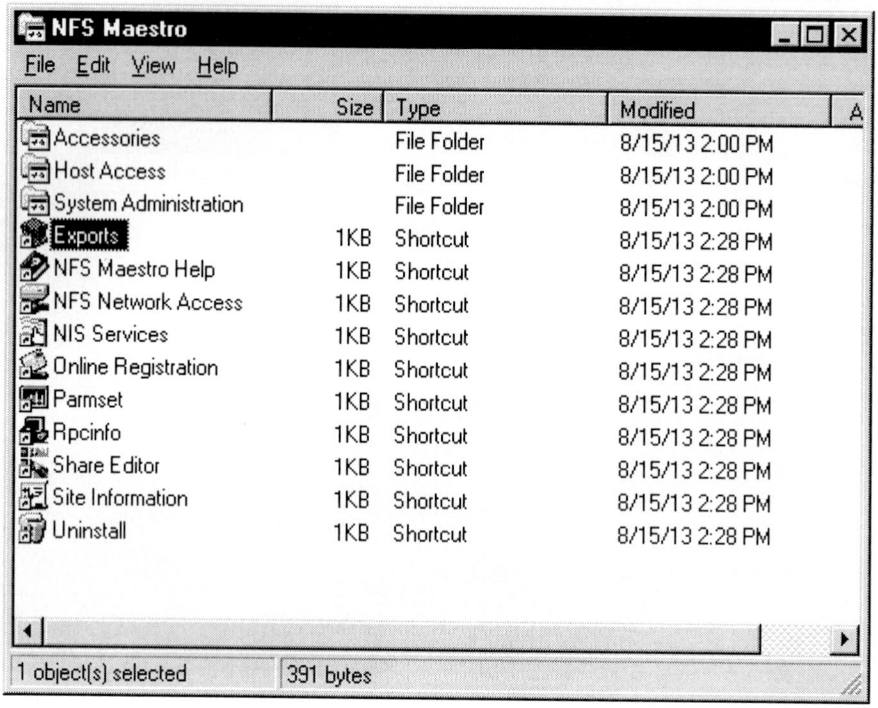

Name	Size	Type	Modified	A
Accessories		File Folder	8/15/13 2:00 PM	
Host Access		File Folder	8/15/13 2:00 PM	
System Administration		File Folder	8/15/13 2:00 PM	
Exports	1KB	Shortcut	8/15/13 2:28 PM	
NFS Maestro Help	1KB	Shortcut	8/15/13 2:28 PM	
NFS Network Access	1KB	Shortcut	8/15/13 2:28 PM	
NIS Services	1KB	Shortcut	8/15/13 2:28 PM	
Online Registration	1KB	Shortcut	8/15/13 2:28 PM	
Parmset	1KB	Shortcut	8/15/13 2:28 PM	
Rpcinfo	1KB	Shortcut	8/15/13 2:28 PM	
Share Editor	1KB	Shortcut	8/15/13 2:28 PM	
Site Information	1KB	Shortcut	8/15/13 2:28 PM	
Uninstall	1KB	Shortcut	8/15/13 2:28 PM	

Figure 12-6 *NFS* Group

Before we use NFS with our Windows NT and UNIX systems, let's first see what file systems we have available to us.

Using the Common Desktop Environment (CDE) on our Windows NT system from the Chapter 11, we can sit at the Windows NT system and work on the UNIX system. Figure 12-7 shows the Common Desktop Environment with a *Terminal* window open.

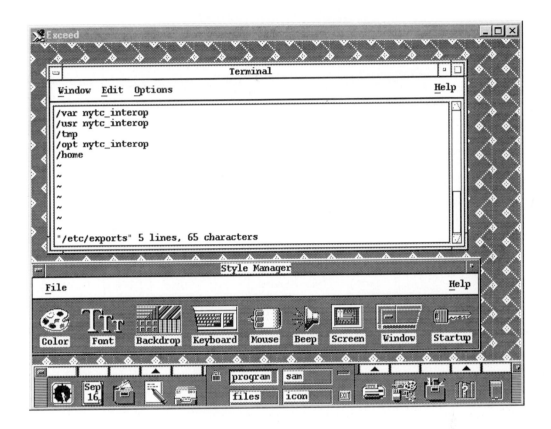

Figure 12-7 Common Desktop Environment on UNIX with **/etc/exports** Shown

There are several file systems exported on this UNIX system. Some, such as **/home** and **/tmp,** have no restrictions on them; others do have restrictions. We don't, however, have to open a *Terminal* in order to see this file. We can use the NFS Maestro menu pick *Exports* to bring up the window shown in Figure 12-8.

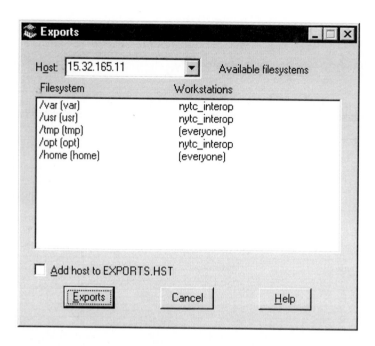

Figure 12-8 *Exports* Window Showing Exported File Systems

You can use the IP address, as shown in Figure 12-8, or the host name to specify the host on which you wish to view the exported file systems. You can see that this window takes the **/etc/exports** file and clarifies some of the entries. The entries that have no restrictions now have an "(every-one)" associated with them, and only system *nytc_interop* may mount the other file systems.

Now we can specify one or more of these exported file systems on the UNIX system that we wish to mount on the Windows NT system. Using the *NFS Network Access* from the NFS Maestro menu, we can specify one of these file systems to mount. Figure 12-9 shows mounting **/home/hp** on the UNIX system on the **F:** drive of the Windows NT system. Note that we are UNIX user *hp* when we mount this file system.

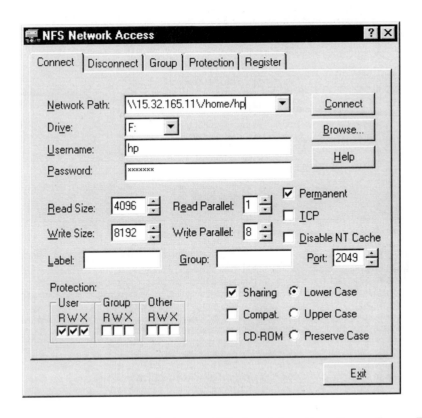

Figure 12-9 *NFS Network Access* Window Mounting **/home/hp** as **F:**

After you click the *Connect* button in the window, you have **/home/hp** mounted as **F:**. The means by which you specify the system and file system you wish to mount with NFS Maestro is two slashes preceding the IP address or system name, another slash following the IP address or system name, and then the name of the file system you wish to mount. Note that the forward slash is part of the file system name. I used the IP address of the system. To view all the mounted file systems on the Windows NT system, you can invoke Windows NT *Explorer*. Figure 12-10 shows several file systems mounted in an *Explorer* window, including **/home/hp** on **F:**.

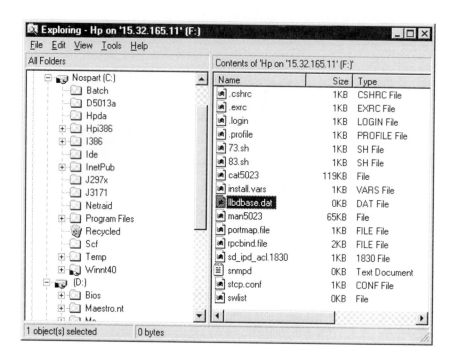

Figure 12-10 Windows NT *Explorer* Showing **/home/hp** as **F:**

This window shows **/home/hp** on drive **F:**. On the right side of the window is a listing of files in **/home/hp** on the UNIX system. These files are now fully accessible on the Windows NT system (provided that the appropriate access rights have been provided). You may need to adjust the *Explorer* to *Show all files* in order to see the hidden UNIX files. You can now manipulate these UNIX files in *Explorer* on the Windows NT system just as if they were local to the system. This is a powerful concept - to go beyond the barrier of only the Windows NT file system to freely manipulate UNIX files.

The permissions of these NFS mounted files are not shown in the *Explorer* window. We can select specific files and view their properties. Figure 12-11 shows viewing the **.cshrc** file.

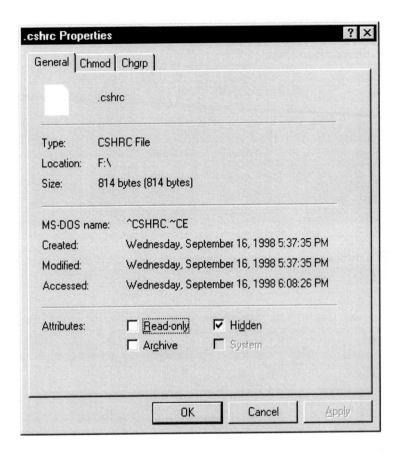

Figure 12-11 Viewing Properties of **.cshrc**

The **.cshrc** file is *Hidden* and is not *Read-only*, meaning that we can manipulate this file.

Next let's view the properties of **install.vars** as shown in Figure 12-12.

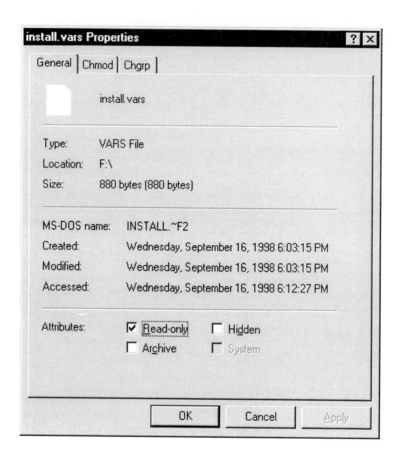

Figure 12-12   Viewing Properties of **install.vars**

install.vars is *Read-only* because this file is owned by *root* on the
UNIX system and not by user *hp*, which is the UNIX user under which we
mounted **/home/hp**.

We are unable to *Chmod*, or modify the permissions on this file,
because it is owned by root and we have mounted **/home/hp** as the user *hp*,
as shown in Figure 12-13.

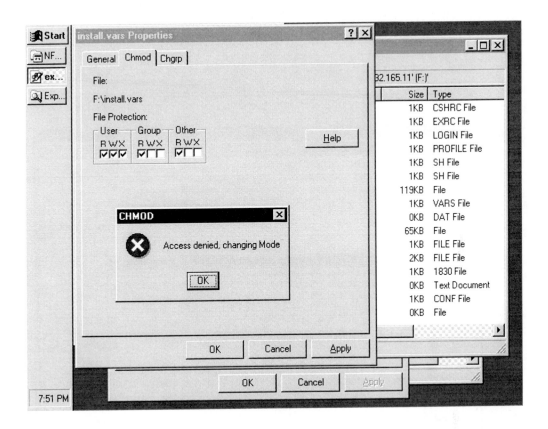

Failed Attempt to Change Permissions of **install.vars**

This error indicates that we are prevented from changing the permissions on **install.vars**.

An example of how you might go about using *Explorer* is to copy a Windows NT directory to UNIX. Figure 12-14 shows two *Explorer* windows. The top window has an **nfs** directory on the Windows NT system, which is being copied to a directory of the same name on the UNIX system in the bottom window. As the copy from the Windows NT system to the

UNIX system takes place, a status window appears, which shows the name of the file within the **nfs** directory (**exp2.bmp**) being copied.

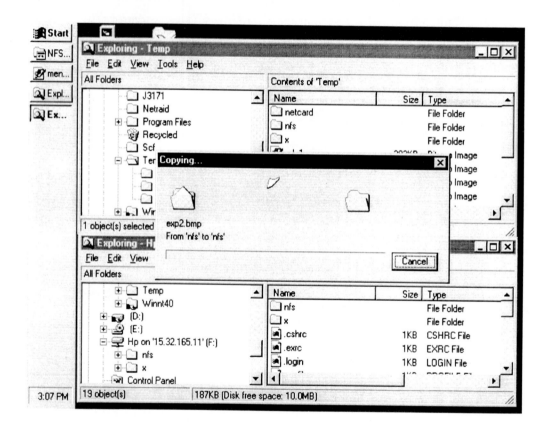

Figure 12-14   Copy a Windows NT Directory to UNIX Using *Explorer*

This copy from Windows NT to UNIX using *Explorer* demonstrates the ease with which files can be shared between these two operating systems.

File Transfer Protocol (FTP)

I started this chapter covering NFS on Windows NT and UNIX for interoperability, because NFS is the predominant means of sharing files in the UNIX world. NFS is used almost universally to share data among networked UNIX systems. NFS allows you to share data in real time, meaning that you can work on a UNIX file while sitting at your Windows NT system. This approach is file sharing. You can also copy data between your Windows NT and UNIX systems using FTP. This approach is not file sharing; however, the FTP functionality of NFS Maestro makes it easy to transfer files between Windows NT and UNIX.

Figure 12-15 shows the dialog box that you would use to establish a connection to a UNIX system from Windows NT.

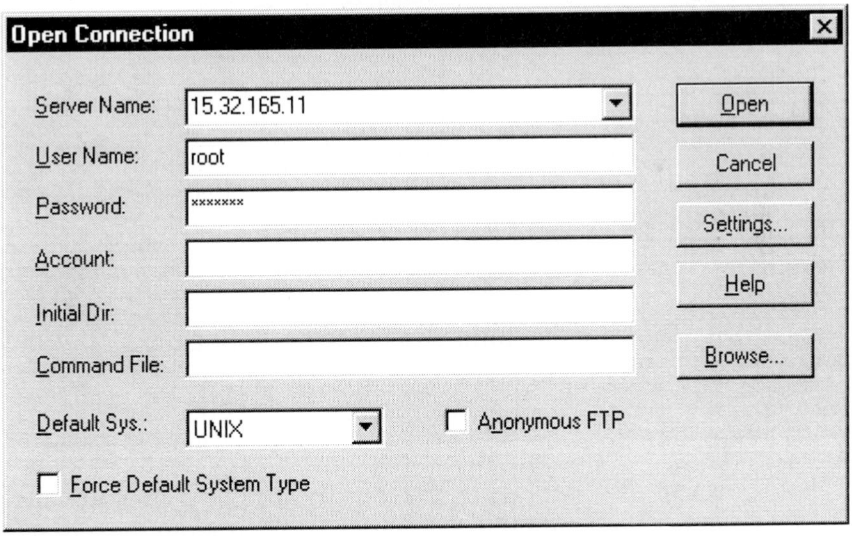

Figure 12-15 Establishing a Connection to UNIX from Windows NT

After having established the connection, a window appears in which you can traverse the UNIX file systems while working at your Windows NT system. Figure 12-16 shows viewing the **/home/hp** directory on a UNIX system through the *FTP* window.

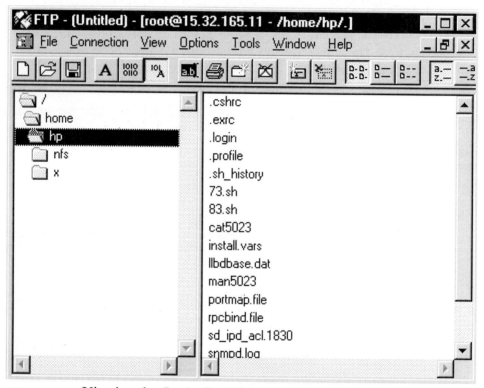

Figure 12-16 Viewing the **/home/hp** Directory Using the *FTP* Window

You can also copy files graphically using FTP. You can open two *FTP* windows and copy files and directories from one system to the other. Figure 12-17 shows copying the directory **c:\temp\x** on the Windows NT system to **/home/hp/x** on the UNIX system. This was performed using the icons in the two windows. The **x** directory did not exist on the UNIX system and was created as part of the copy. As the copy from the Windows NT system to the UNIX system takes place, a status window appears, which shows the name of the file within the **x** directory (**xmenu2.bmp**) being copied.

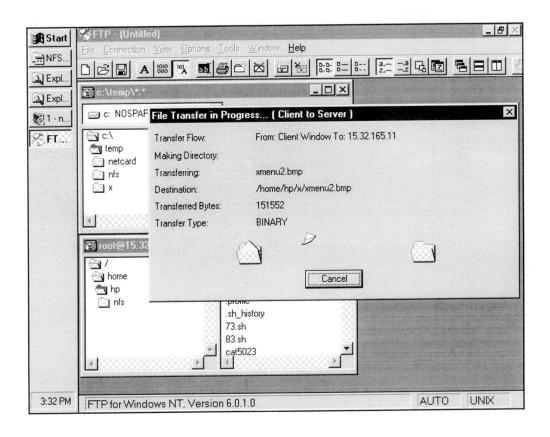

Figure 12-17 Using FTP to Copy a Directory from Windows NT to UNIX

There are a variety of options you can select when running FTP. Notice in Figure 12-17 that the "Transfer Type:" is binary. This is one of the options I selected prior to initiating the transfer.

Although this functionality is not as extensive as the file sharing of NFS, it is widely used to copy files from system to system and therefore can play a role in Windows NT and UNIX interoperability.

I used icons to specify the information to be copied in this example. You could also have used the FTP command. The following is an overview of FTP, including an example of running it from the command line and a command summary.

File Transfer Protocol (FTP) Transfer a file, or multiple files, from one system to another, such as Windows NT to UNIX. The following example shows copying the file **/tmp/krsort.c** from system2 (remote host) to the local directory on system1 (local host).

	comments
$ ftp system2	Issue ftp command
Connected to system2.	
system2 FTP server (Version 16.2) ready.	
Name (system2:root): root	Login to system2
Password required for root.	
Password:	Enter password
User root logged in.	
Remote system type is UNIX.	
Using binary mode to transfer files.	
ftp> **cd /tmp**	**cd** to **/tmp** on system2
CWD command successful	
ftp> **get krsort.c**	Get **krsort.c** file
PORT command successful	
Opening BINARY mode data connection for **krsort.c**	
Transfer complete.	
2896 bytes received in 0.08 seconds	

	comments
ftp> **bye**	Exit ftp
Goodbye.	
$	

In this example, both systems are running UNIX; however, the commands you issue through **FTP** are operating-system-independent. The **cd** for change directory and **get** commands used above work for any operating system on which **FTP** is running. If you become familiar with just a few **FTP** commands, you may find that transferring information in a heterogeneous networking environment is not difficult.

Since **FTP** is so widely used, I describe some of the more commonly used **FTP** commands.

ftp - File Transfer Protocol for copying files across a network.

The following list includes some commonly used **ftp** commands. This list is not complete.

ascii   Set the type of file transferred to ASCII. This means you will be transferring an ASCII file from one system to another. This is the default, so you don't have to set it.

Example: **ascii**

binary   Set the type of file transferred to binary. This means you'll be transferring a binary file from one system to another. If, for instance, you want to have a directory on your UNIX system that will hold applications that you will copy to non-UNIX systems, then you will want to use binary transfer.

Example: **binary**

cd　Change to the specified directory on the remote host.

Example: **cd /tmp**

dir　List the contents of a directory on the remote system to the screen or to a file on the local system if you specify a local file name.

get　Copy the specified remote file to the specified local file. If you don't specify a local file name, then the remote file name is used.

lcd　Change to the specified directory on the local host.

Example: **lcd /tmp**

ls　List the contents of a directory on the remote system to the screen or to a file on the local system if you specify a local file name.

mget　Copy multiple files from the remote host to the local host.

Example: **mget *.c**

put　Copy the specified local file to the specified remote file. If you don't specify a remote file name, then the local file name is used.

Example: **put test.c**

mput   Copy multiple files from the local host to the remote host.

Example: **mput *.c**

system   Show the type of operating system running on the remote host.

Example: **system**

bye/quit   Close the connection to the remote host.

Example: **bye**

FTP commands exist in addition to those I have covered here.

Other Connection Topics

There are other means by which you can connect to the UNIX system. Two popular techniques for connecting to other systems are FTP, which was just covered, and TELNET. NFS Maestro supplies the capability for both of these. I could sit at the Windows NT system using TELNET with a window open on the UNIX system and issue commands.

Figure 12-18 shows the *HostExplorer* window used to specify the characteristics of your TELNET session.

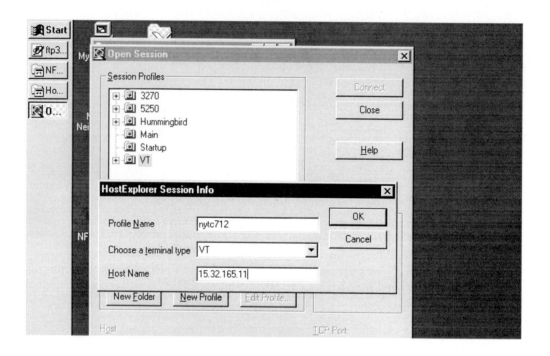

Figure 12-18   Specify Characteristics of *HostExplorer* Session

I selected *VT* in the *HostExplorer* window and was able to log in to the UNIX system, as shown in Figure 12-19.

```
1 - hp (15.32.165.11)

File  Edit  Transfer  Fonts  Options  Macro  View  Window  Help

$ ll -a
total 398
drwxr-xr-x   3 hp      users        1024 Sep 16 18:25 .
drwxr-xr-x   4 root    root           96 Sep 16 17:37 ..
-rw-r--r--   1 hp      users         814 Sep 16 17:37 .cshrc
-rw-r--r--   1 hp      users         347 Sep 16 17:37 .exrc
-rw-r--r--   1 hp      users         341 Sep 16 17:37 .login
-rw-r--r--   1 hp      users         446 Sep 16 17:37 .profile
-rw-------   1 hp      users          14 Sep 16 18:25 .sh_history
-rw-r--r--   1 root    sys            23 Sep 16 18:03 73.sh
-rw-r--r--   1 root    sys            23 Sep 16 18:03 83.sh
-rw-rw-rw-   1 root    sys        120922 Sep 16 18:03 cat5023
-rw-r--r--   1 root    sys           880 Sep 16 18:03 install.vars
-r--r--r--   1 root    sys             0 Sep 16 18:03 llbdbase.dat
-rw-rw-rw-   1 root    sys         66113 Sep 16 18:03 man5023
drwx------   2 hp      users        1024 Sep 16 18:17 nfs
-rw-------   1 root    sys           484 Sep 16 18:03 portmap.file
-rw-------   1 root    sys          1692 Sep 16 18:03 rpcbind.file
-rw-r--r--   1 root    sys            74 Sep 16 18:03 sd_ipd_acl.183
-rwxrwxrwx   1 root    sys             0 Sep 16 18:03 snmpd.log
-rw-r--r--   1 root    sys            60 Sep 16 18:03 stcp.conf
-rw-r--r--   1 root    sys             0 Sep 16 18:03 swlist
$
```

Figure 12-19 telnet Window

In this window, we can issue UNIX commands just as if we were sitting at a terminal connected directly to the UNIX system. This window shows **/home/hp**, including the **nfs** directory copied earlier and permissions, owner, and group of all files and directories.

telnet is widely used in heterogenous environments. With X Windows, you get graphical functionality that is not part of telnet.

The protocols running on the UNIX system are assigned to ports. We can view these ports, protocols, and associated information using the **rpcinfo** command on the UNIX system, as shown in Figure 12-20.

```
2 - nytc712 (15.32.165.11)
File  Edit  Transfer  Fonts  Options  Macro  View  Window  Help

         100021     4    tcp      0.0.0.0.3.111     nlockmgr    superuser
         100021     4    udp      0.0.0.0.3.112     nlockmgr    superuser
         100020     1    udp      0.0.0.0.15.205    llockmgr    superuser
         100020     1    tcp      0.0.0.0.15.205    llockmgr    superuser
         100021     2    tcp      0.0.0.0.3.113     nlockmgr    superuser
         100068     2    udp      0.0.0.0.192.11    cmsd        superuser
         100068     3    udp      0.0.0.0.192.11    cmsd        superuser
         100068     4    udp      0.0.0.0.192.11    cmsd        superuser
         100068     5    udp      0.0.0.0.192.11    cmsd        superuser
         100083     1    tcp      0.0.0.0.192.1     ttdbserver  superuser
         100005     1    udp      0.0.0.0.2.210     mountd      superuser
         100005     3    udp      0.0.0.0.2.210     mountd      superuser
         100005     1    tcp      0.0.0.0.2.211     mountd      superuser
         100005     3    tcp      0.0.0.0.2.211     mountd      superuser
         100003     2    udp      0.0.0.0.8.1       nfs         superuser
         100003     3    udp      0.0.0.0.8.1       nfs         superuser
         150001     1    udp      0.0.0.0.2.232     pcnfsd      superuser
         150001     2    udp      0.0.0.0.2.232     pcnfsd      superuser
         150001     1    tcp      0.0.0.0.2.233     pcnfsd      superuser
         150001     2    tcp      0.0.0.0.2.233     pcnfsd      superuser
      1342177279     3    tcp      0.0.0.0.192.20    -           superuser
      1342177279     1    tcp      0.0.0.0.192.20    -           superuser
      1342177279     2    tcp      0.0.0.0.192.20    -           superuser
      #

                    2 Sess-1     15.32.165.11                        1 24
```

Figure 12-20   **rpcinfo** Command on UNIX

There is a lot of information in this window in which we are interested related to NFS. We do not, however, have to establish a telnet sessionwith the UNIX system and issue **rpcinfo** to see this information. The *Rpcinfo* menu pick under Maestro will query the UNIX host and list the services it is running. Figure 12-21 shows this window.

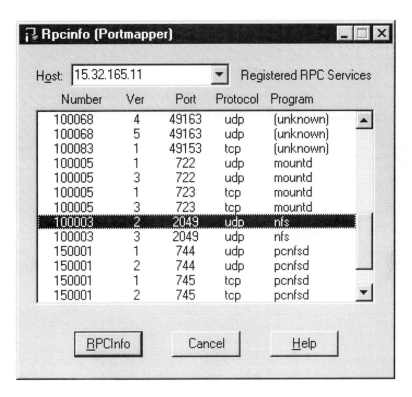

Figure 12-21 *Rpcinfo* Window on Windows NT

RPC stands for Remote Procedure Call. There are a variety of programs for which there is RPC-related information. Several programs are required to achieve the Windows NT and UNIX interoperability.

The first number shown is the program number. There are widely accepted RPC numbers for various programs. For NFS, the program number is 100003. The next number is the version of the protocol. In this case, NFS is version 2. The next number is the port. The port number is used by both the client, which is the Windows NT system in our case, and the server, which is the UNIX system in our case, to communicate using NFS.

The next field is the protocol used, which is usually UDP or TCP. The final field is the program name.

In the case of NFS, I had to ensure that NFS, portmapper, mountd, and pcnfsd were running on my UNIX system before I could use the NFS Maestro NFS product.

Rpcinfo is a useful tool for viewing all the information on the host to which your Windows NT system will connect.

CHAPTER 13

Windows NT and UNIX Interoperability: Advanced Server for UNIX

Windows NT Functionality on UNIX

To this point, we have been discussing moving UNIX functionality such as X Windows and NFS onto Windows NT in order to achieve interoperability. Why not do the converse? Having some Windows NT functionality on UNIX would certainly be helpful in some cases. UNIX resources such as printers and disks could then be shared with several Windows NT systems on the network.

Advanced Server for UNIX® is an AT&T product that serves as the basis for many products that bring Windows NT functionality to UNIX. Advanced Server for UNIX Systems is the result of a joint development agreement between AT&T and Microsoft Corporation. It provides Windows NT functionality that facilitates Windows NT and UNIX interoperability. With Advanced Server for UNIX, a UNIX system can act as a Primary or Backup Domain Controller, a file server, a print server, or other Windows NT functional component. Most major UNIX vendors have a product that is based on Advanced Server for UNIX. This chapter will use the HP-UX implementation of Advanced Server for UNIX called Advanced Server/9000. Other implementations of Advanced Server for

UNIX are similar, so you can use the examples in this chapter as a basis of understanding for other such implementations.

This chapter makes use of some of the **net** commands of Windows NT, especially the **net share** command. When I am working on the UNIX system (*dloaner*) in this chapter, I use the command line including some **net** commands. When I am working on the Windows NT system (*hpsystem1*) in this chapter, I will use graphical Windows NT functionality, which is preferable to issuing commands on the command line. I use both the command line and graphical methods so that you can see the difference in the two approaches. You may want to explore some of these **net** commands described in the "Command Line" chapter (Chapter 14) and using the on-line help of your Windows NT system as you progress through this chapter. Here is a list of some widely used **net** commands and a brief explanation of each:

net accounts	Used to maintain the user accounts database.
net computer	Used to add or delete computers from the domain database.
net config server	Displays or changes settings for a server service on which the command is executed.
net config workstation	Displays or changes settings for the workstation service on which the command is executed.
net continue	Reactivates a Windows NT service that has been suspended with the **net pause** command.

net file	Used for network file manipulation, such as listing ID numbers, closing a shared file, removing file locks, and so on.
net group	Used to add, display, or modify global groups on servers.
net help	Displays a listing of help options for any net commands.
net helpmsg	Displays explanations of Windows NT network messages such as errors, warnings, and alerts.
net localgroup	Used to modify local groups on computers.
net name	Used to add or delete a "messaging name" at a computer, which is the name to which messages are sent.
net print	Used to list print jobs and shared queues.
net send	Sends messages to other users, computers, and "messaging names" on the network.
net session	Used to list or disconnect sessions between the computer and other computers on the network.
net share	Shares a server's resources with other computers on the network.

net start   Used to start services such as *server*.

net statistics   Displays the statistics log for the local Workstation or Server service.

net stop   Used to stop services such as *server*.

net time   Synchronizes the computer's clock with another computer on the domain.

net use   Displays, connects, or disconnects a computer with shared resources.

net user   Creates or modifies user accounts.

net view   Lists resources being shared on a computer.

Installing Advanced Server/9000 on UNIX

You can easily install and configure Advanced Server/9000 on your UNIX system. Advanced Server/9000 is installed using Software Distributor on your HP-UX system, just as you would load any other software. After installing Advanced Server/9000, you run the configuration script called **asu_inst**. The following text shows running **asu_inst** to configure the UNIX system *dloaner* to be a Backup Domain Controller (BDC) for the Windows NT system *hpsystem1*:

```
# /opt/asu/lanman/bin/asu_inst
```

This request script will prompt you for information which is necessary
to install and configure your Advanced Server for UNIX Systems.

There are two installation modes:

Express Setup - the installation scripts use default settings so
installation is quick and easy. You may change these settings
after installation completes. The server is installed as a
primary domain controller in its own domain.

Custom Setup - this mode allows you to specify the settings at the
beginning of installation. If you select this mode, you must
specify the server's name, the domain it will participate in,
and the role in that domain.

NOTE: The installation requires a password for the administrative account.
A default password of 'password' will be used, although you may elect to
be prompted for a different password at the end of the installation.

If you are installing many servers it is strongly recommended that you use
the default password for all installations. Be sure to change these
passwords after determining that your network is operating correctly.

Do you want Express Setup [y/n]? y

Advanced Server for UNIX provides a NETLOGON service which simplifies the
administration of multiple servers. A single user accounts database can be
shared by multiple servers grouped together into an administrative
collection called a domain. Within a domain, each server has a designated
role. A single server, called the primary domain controller, manages all
changes to the user accounts database and automatically distributes those
changes to other servers, called backup domain controllers, within the same
domain. You may now supply a server name (the name which this server
will be known on the network), the role that this server will perform
in that domain (primary or backup), and a domain name.

Enter the name of the server
or press Enter to select 'dloaner':

Each server must be given a role in a domain. The possible roles are:

primary domain controller:
    Administration server. Distributes user accounts information
          to backup domain controllers. Validates network logon requests.
    There can be only one primary domain controller per domain.

backup domain controller:
          Receives user account information from the primary domain
          controller. Validates network logon requests and can be promoted
    to primary if the primary domain controller is not accessible.

Enter role (primary or backup): backup

This installation will configure the server as a backup domain controller.
You will be prompted to enter the name of the primary domain controller,
and an administrative account name on the primary along with its password.
In order for this installation to complete successfully, the primary domain

```
controller must be running and connected to the network.

Enter the name of the primary domain controller (eg, abc_asu): hpsystem1

Confirm choices for server dloaner:
                         role    : backup
                         primary: hpsystem1
Is this correct [y/n]? y
_&a0y0C_J
Enter the name of an administrative account on the primary
domain controller 'hpsystem1' or press Enter to select 'administrator':

This procedure requires the password for the administrative account on
'hpsystem1'.  If the password is the default ('password') created
during installation, you will not need to be prompted for a password.
If you have changed the password, you should allow this program  to prompt
for a password after the files have been installed.

Do you want to use the default password [y/n]? y

Advanced Server/9000
Copyright (c) 1988, 1991-1996 AT&T and Microsoft
Copyright (c) 1992-1996 Hewlett-Packard
All rights reserved

Adding Advanced Server for UNIX Systems administrative users and groups
Add
Comment <Advanced Server account>
Home Dir </opt/asu/lanman>
UID <100>
GID <99>
Shell </sbin/false>
Name <lanman>
pw_name: lanman
pw_passwd: *
pw_uid: 100
pw_gid: 99
pw_age: ?
pw_comment:
pw_gecos: Advanced Server account
pw_dir: /opt/asu/lanman
pw_shell: /sbin/false
enter addusr
pw_name = lanman
pw_passwd = *
pw_uid = 100
pw_gid = 99
pw_gecos = Advanced Server account
pw_dir = /opt/asu/lanman
pw_shell = /sbin/false
enter_quiet_zone()
exit_quiet_zone()
exiting addusr, error = 0
Add
Comment <Advanced Server Administrator>
Home Dir </var/opt/asu/lanman/lmxadmin>
GID <99>
Name <lmxadmin>
pw_name: lmxadmin
pw_passwd: *
pw_uid: 0
pw_gid: 99
pw_age: ?
pw_comment:
pw_gecos: Advanced Server Administrator
pw_dir: /var/opt/asu/lanman/lmxadmin
```

```
pw_shell:
enter addusr
pw_name = lmxadmin
pw_passwd = *
pw_uid = 0
pw_gid = 99
pw_gecos = Advanced Server Administrator
pw_dir = /var/opt/asu/lanman/lmxadmin
pw_shell =
enter_quiet_zone()
exit_quiet_zone()
exiting addusr, error = 0
Add
Comment <Advanced Server GUEST Login>
Shell </sbin/false>
GID <99>
Name <lmxguest>
pw_name: lmxguest
pw_passwd: *
pw_uid: 0
pw_gid: 99
pw_age: ?
pw_comment:
pw_gecos: Advanced Server GUEST Login
pw_dir:
pw_shell: /sbin/false
enter addusr
pw_name = lmxguest
pw_passwd = *
pw_uid = 0
pw_gid = 99
pw_gecos = Advanced Server GUEST Login
pw_dir = /usr/lmxguest
pw_shell = /sbin/false
enter_quiet_zone()
exit_quiet_zone()
exiting addusr, error = 0
Add
Comment <Advanced Server World Login>
Shell </sbin/false>
GID <99>
Name <lmworld>
pw_name: lmworld
pw_passwd: *
pw_uid: 0
pw_gid: 99
pw_age: ?
pw_comment:
pw_gecos: Advanced Server World Login
pw_dir:
pw_shell: /sbin/false
enter addusr
pw_name = lmworld
pw_passwd = *
pw_uid = 0
pw_gid = 99
pw_gecos = Advanced Server World Login
pw_dir = /usr/lmworld
pw_shell = /sbin/false
enter_quiet_zone()
exit_quiet_zone()
exiting addusr, error = 0

Creating Directory: /home/lanman
Setting owner, group, and permissions for installed files....
```

```
Enter the password for administrator on hpsystem1:
Re-enter password:

Contacting the server 'hpsystem1' ... Success

Creating Advanced Server for UNIX Systems accounts database.

Starting the Advanced Server for UNIX Systems...

The Advanced Server for UNIX Systems is now operational.
#
```

After the installation and configuration is complete, you have **netdemon** running, which is an essential component of Advanced Server/9000, as shown in the following **ps** command:

```
# ps -ef | grep netdemon
    root  1100     1  0 10:18:38 ?        0:00 /opt/lmu/netbios/bin/netdemon
#
```

In addition to netdemon, NetBIOS must also be running.

Advanced Server/9000 starts several processes on your UNIX system in addition to **netdemon**. You can also verify that the Advanced Server/9000 server is running by viewing its processes with the **ps** command.

```
# ps -ef | grep lm
    root  3285     1  0 10:37:19 ?     0:00 lmx.dmn
    root  3200     1  0 10:36:57 ?     0:00 lmx.ctrl
    root  3262  3200  0 10:37:07 ?     0:00 lmx.srv -s 1
    root  3295     1  0 10:37:20 ?     0:00 lmx.sched
    root  3289     1  0 10:37:19 ?     0:00 lmx.browser
    root  1100     1  0 10:18:38 ?     0:00 /opt/lmu/netbios/bin/netdemon
#
```

Many process are shown here, such as *lmx.dmn,* which is the daemon; *lmx.ctrl,* which is the control process; *lmx.sched,* which is the scheduler; *lmx.browser* which is the browser; and *lmx.srv,* which is a client session. If Advanced Server/9000 were not running, you would use the **net start server** command to start the server. Similarly, you stop the server with **net stop server**.

In addition, you have several users and groups that have been created on your UNIX system to facilitate using Advanced Server/9000 with your Windows NT systems. The new users are shown in the upcoming **/etc/**

passwd file, and the new groups are shown in the upcoming **/etc/group** file:

```
# cat /etc/passwd
root:jThTuY9OhNxGY:0:3::/:/sbin/sh
daemon:*:1:5::/:/sbin/sh
bin:*:2:2::/usr/bin:/sbin/sh
sys:*:3:3::/:
adm:*:4:4::/var/adm:/sbin/sh
uucp:*:5:3::/var/spool/uucppublic:/usr/lbin/uucp/uucico
lp:*:9:7::/var/spool/lp:/sbin/sh
nuucp:*:11:11::/var/spool/uucppublic:/usr/lbin/uucp/uucico
hpdb:*:27:1:ALLBASE:/:/sbin/sh
nobody:*:-2:-2147483648::/:
lanman:*:100:99:Advanced Server account:/opt/asu/lanman:/sbin/false
lmxadmin:*:202:99:Advanced Server Administrator:/var/opt/asu/lanman/lmxadmin:
lmxguest:*:203:99:Advanced Server GUEST Login:/usr/lmxguest:/sbin/false
lmworld:*:204:99:Advanced Server World Login:/usr/lmworld:/sbin/false
# cat /etc/group
root::0:root
other::1:root,hpdb
bin::2:root,bin
sys::3:root,uucp
adm::4:root,adm
daemon::5:root,daemon
mail::6:root
lp::7:root,lp
tty::10:
nuucp::11:nuucp
users::20:root
nogroup:*:-2:
DOS----::99:lanman
DOS-a--::98:lanman
DOS--s-::97:lanman
DOS---h::96:lanman
DOS-as-::95:lanman
DOS-a-h::94:lanman
DOS--sh::93:lanman
DOS-ash::92:lanman
#
```

In addition to the UNIX system modifications that have automatically taken place, the Windows NT Primary Domain Controller (PDC) now recognizes the UNIX system as the backup domain controller. Figure 13-1 shows a screen shot from the Windows NT system *hpsystem1*, which is the primary domain controller. The screen shot shows *dloaner* acting as the backup domain controller and the default shared directories on the UNIX system *dloaner*. The share properties for one of the shares, **C:\opt\asu\lanman** are also shown.

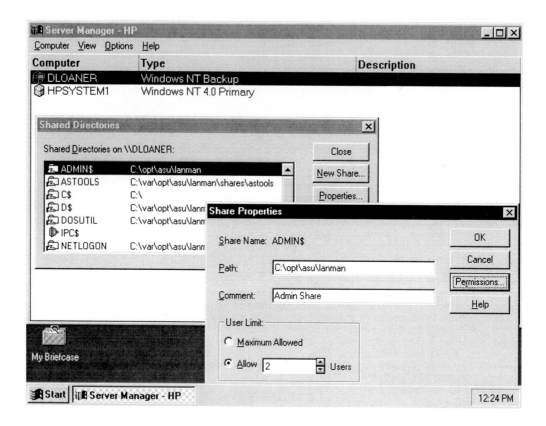

Figure 13-1 Default Shares after Loading and Configuring Advanced Server/ 9000

These shares can also be viewed on the command line of the UNIX system using the net command, as shown in the following output:

```
# /opt/asu/lanman/bin/net share

Sharename    Resource                      Remark
-------------------------------------------------------------------------
ADMIN$       C:\OPT\ASU\LANMAN             Admin Share
IPC$                                       IPC Share
C$           C:\                           Root Share
D$           C:\VAR\OPT\ASU\LANMAN\SHARES  SystemRoot Share
ASTOOLS      C:\VAR\OPT\ASU\LANMAN\SHARES... Advanced Server Tools
```

```
DOSUTIL      C:\VAR\OPT\ASU\LANMAN\SHARES... DOS Utilities
NETLOGON     C:\VAR\OPT\ASU\LANMAN\SHARES... Logon Scripts Directory
PATCHES      C:\VAR\OPT\ASU\LANMAN\SHARES... Client Patches
PRINTLOG     C:\VAR\OPT\ASU\LANMAN\SHARES... LP printer messages
USERS        C:\HOME\LANMAN                  Users Directory
The command completed successfully.
#
```

These are the default shares that have been set up by Advanced Server/9000. Those followed by a $ are hidden shares used only for administrative purposes. When you run *Windows NT Explorer,* you don't see these hidden directories.

You can set up additional shares, such as the printer and disk we will set up in the upcoming sections *Sharing a Printer* and *Sharing a File System* respectively.

Sharing a Printer

In addition to the default sharing that takes place with Advanced Server/9000, there may be additional resources you may want to share between Windows NT and UNIX systems.

For example, you may have a printer used in your UNIX environment, to which you want Windows NT systems to have access. The following commands show adding a shared printer and viewing it in UNIX.

The first command is **lpstat** on UNIX, which shows the status of the existing printer *laser*.

```
# lpstat -t
scheduler is running
system default destination: laser
device for laser: /dev/c2t0d0_lp
laser accepting requests since Feb 11 17:23
printer laser is idle.  enabled since Feb 11 17:23
fence priority : 0
no entries
#
```

Next we run the **net** command and specify the printer *laser* as a shared printer device.

```
# /opt/asu/lanman/bin/net net share laser=laser /print
laser was successfully shared
```

To see the configuration of the printer, we can issue the **net print** command as shown below:

```
# net print laser /options
Printing options for LASER

Status              Queue Active
Remark
Print Devices       laser
Driver              HP-UX LM/X Print Manager
Separator file
Priority            5
Print after         12:00 AM
Print until         12:00 AM
Print processor
Parameters          COPIES=1 EJECT=AUTO BANNER=YES
The command completed successfully.
#
```

After printing a text file from the Windows NT system onto the device *laser* connected to the UNIX system running Advanced Server/9000, I received a bunch of unintelligible information on the printed sheet. The Advanced Server/9000 printer was not configured raw. I issued the following command to make the printer raw:

```
# net print laser /parms:types=-oraw
The command completed successfully.
```

The new configuration, with the *TYPES=-oraw*, is shown in the following output. This device successfully printed from the Windows NT system to the UNIX system running Advanced Server/9000 to which *laser* is connected.

```
# net print laser /options
Printing options for LASER

Status              Queue Active
Remark
Print Devices       laser
Driver              HP-UX LM/X Print Manager
Separator file
Priority            5
Print after         12:00 AM
```

```
Print until          12:00 AM
Print processor
Parameters           COPIES=1 TYPES=-oraw EJECT=AUTO BANNER=YES
The command completed successfully.
#
```

We can now view all the shared devices with the **net** command.

```
# /opt/asu/lanman/bin/net share

Sharename   Resource                          Remark
------------------------------------------------------------------------
ADMIN$      C:\OPT\ASU\LANMAN                 Admin Share
IPC$                                          IPC Share
C$          C:\                               Root Share
D$          C:\VAR\OPT\ASU\LANMAN\SHARES      SystemRoot Share
ASTOOLS     C:\VAR\OPT\ASU\LANMAN\SHARES...   Advanced Server Tools
DOSUTIL     C:\VAR\OPT\ASU\LANMAN\SHARES...   DOS Utilities
NETLOGON    C:\VAR\OPT\ASU\LANMAN\SHARES...   Logon Scripts Directory
PATCHES     C:\VAR\OPT\ASU\LANMAN\SHARES...   Client Patches
PRINTLOG    C:\VAR\OPT\ASU\LANMAN\SHARES...   LP printer messages
USERS       C:\HOME\LANMAN                    Users Directory
LASER       laser                             Spooled
The command completed successfully.
#
```

The last item in this listing is the printer *laser* that was added with the **net** command. All the previous commands were issued on the UNIX system running Advanced Server/9000. We can now view the shared devices of *dloaner* on the Windows NT system using *Explorer* to confirm that the printer *laser* is a shared device, as shown in Figure 13-2.

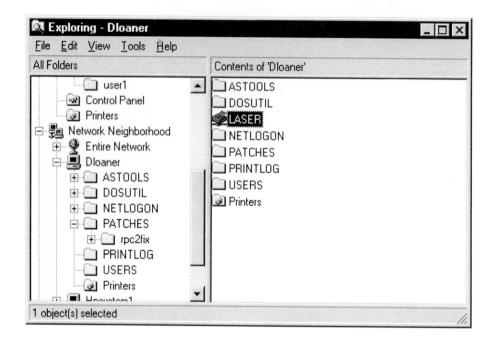

Figure 13-2 Windows NT Explorer Showing Printer *Laser*

The details of this shared printer can be viewed in *Printers* under *Control Panel*.

Sharing a File System

With the printer having been added, the shares that are now set up on the UNIX system running Advanced Server/9000 look like the following:

```
# /opt/asu/lanman/bin/net share

Sharename   Resource                                  Remark
-----------------------------------------------------------------------------
ADMIN$      C:\OPT\ASU\LANMAN                          Admin Share
IPC$                                                  IPC Share
C$          C:\                                       Root Share
D$          C:\VAR\OPT\ASU\LANMAN\SHARES              SystemRoot Share
ASTOOLS     C:\VAR\OPT\ASU\LANMAN\SHARES...           Advanced Server Tools
DOSUTIL     C:\VAR\OPT\ASU\LANMAN\SHARES...           DOS Utilities
NETLOGON    C:\VAR\OPT\ASU\LANMAN\SHARES...           Logon Scripts Directory
PATCHES     C:\VAR\OPT\ASU\LANMAN\SHARES...           Client Patches
PRINTLOG    C:\VAR\OPT\ASU\LANMAN\SHARES...           LP printer messages
USERS       C:\HOME\LANMAN                            Users Directory
LASER       laser                                     Spooled
The command completed successfully.
#
```

The shares shown include the printer that was added. We could now issue the **net share** command and add a UNIX file system to be shared. To share the **/home** directory on the UNIX system *dloaner,* we would issue the following command:

```
# /opt/asu/lanman/bin/net share home=c:/home
home was shared successfully
```

Note that the UNIX notation for the directory was issued with the slash (/) rather than the backslash (\), as you would on a Windows NT system. We can now view the shares on *dloaner*, including the new *HOME* share, with the **net** command.

```
# /opt/asu/lanman/bin/net share

Sharename   Resource                                  Remark
-----------------------------------------------------------------------------
ADMIN$      C:\OPT\ASU\LANMAN                          Admin Share
IPC$                                                  IPC Share
C$          C:\                                       Root Share
D$          C:\VAR\OPT\ASU\LANMAN\SHARES              SystemRoot Share
ASTOOLS     C:\VAR\OPT\ASU\LANMAN\SHARES...           Advanced Server Tools
DOSUTIL     C:\VAR\OPT\ASU\LANMAN\SHARES...           DOS Utilities
HOME        C:\HOME
NETLOGON    C:\VAR\OPT\ASU\LANMAN\SHARES...           Logon Scripts Directory
PATCHES     C:\VAR\OPT\ASU\LANMAN\SHARES...           Client Patches
PRINTLOG    C:\VAR\OPT\ASU\LANMAN\SHARES...           LP printer messages
USERS       C:\HOME\LANMAN                            Users Directory
LASER       laser                                     Spooled
The command completed successfully.
#
```

You could now view this share on the Windows NT system and map it to a drive, as shown in Figure 13-3.

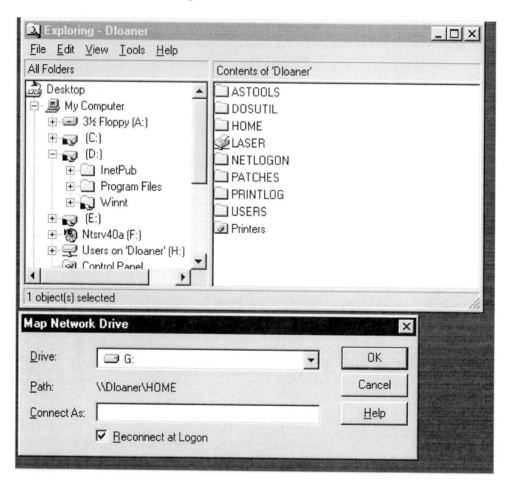

Figure 13-3   Windows NT *Explorer* Showing New Share *HOME*

I covered only a small subset of Advanced Server/9000 functionality in this chapter. I covered using a UNIX system running Advanced Server/

9000 as a backup domain controller, sharing a UNIX connected printer with a Windows NT network, and sharing a UNIX connected disk with a Windows NT network. These are some of the more common uses for Advanced Server/9000. Nearly everything you can do with a Windows NT system can be done with Advanced Server/9000, so don't limit yourself to only the functionality covered in this chapter.

CHAPTER 14

The Windows NT Command Line: NET Commands, POSIX Utilities, Others

Introduction for UNIX System Administrators

UNIX system administration is performed mostly from the command line. There are very good system administration interfaces through which many routine system administration tasks can be performed; however, the command line is still used before any graphical tool for most UNIX system administrators. The coverse is true for Windows NT. With Windows NT most system administration functions are performed with "point and click." There are, however, many functions you can perform from the command line in Windows. In this UNIX and Windows NT interoperability chapter I will cover the Windows NT command line in general, and a group of POSIX utilities that give you UNIX functionality in Windows NT in particular.

I'll begin with Windows NT "NET" commands, which are system administration commands for Windows NT. I'll then cover the POSIX commands you can run at the Windows NT command line that give you UNIX functionality in Windows NT such as **grep**, **ls**, and so on. I'll then cover some additional Windows NT commands you can issue to perform such tasks as backup and running a command at a specific time.

The POSIX commands are what really constitute the UNIX and Windows NT portion of this chapter. I think, however, that covering the other Windows NT commands gives UNIX system administrators an idea of the type of Windows NT system administration commands available.

The Windows NT Command Line

The whole Windows NT operating system is based on performing system administration tasks through the graphical user interface. Why, then, would I include a chapter on the command line? Well, many of us have used operating systems for which the lion's share of system administration work takes place at the command line - and old habits die hard.

The purpose of this chapter is to demonstrate some useful commands that are issued at the command line. You can then decide whether using such commands is helpful to the administration of your Windows NT server or whether you wish to use only the graphical user interface of Windows NT.

NET Commands

This section describes some of the **net** commands of Windows NT. Here is a list of some widely used **net** commands and a brief explanation of each:

net accounts   Used to maintain the user accounts database.

net computer   Used to add or delete computers from the domain database.

net config server

> Displays or changes settings for a server service on which the command is executed.

net config workstation

> Displays or changes settings for the workstation service on which the command is executed.

net continue   Reactivates a Windows NT service that has been suspended with the **net pause** command.

net file   Used for network file manipulation, such as listing ID numbers, closing a shared file, removing file locks, and so on.

net group   Used to add, display, or modify global groups on servers.

net help   Displays a listing of help options for any net commands.

net helpmsg   Displays explanations of Windows NT network messages, such as errors, warnings, and alerts.

net localgroup Used to modify local groups on computers.

net name   Used to add or delete a "messaging name" at a computer, which is the name to which messages are sent.

net print	Used to list print jobs and shared queues.
net send	Sends messages to other users, computers, and "messaging names" on the network.
net session	Used to list or disconnect sessions between the computer and other computers on the network.
net share	Shares a server's resources with other computers on the network.
net start	Used to start services such as *server*.
net statistics	Displays the statistics log for the local Workstation or Server service.
net stop	Used to stop services such as *server*.
net time	Synchronizes the computer's clock with another computer on the domain.
net use	Displays, connects, or disconnects a computer with shared resources.
net user	Creates or modifies user accounts.
net view	Lists resources being shared on a computer.

The following are brief descriptions of some of the NET commands and examples of using them.

Many of the descriptions include command summaries that were obtained by typing the command name followed by a **/?**. For instance, to get a command summary for the **NET ACCOUNTS** command, you would type the following:

```
C:\ NET ACCOUNTS /?
```

You can also get detailed help information by typing **HELP** and the command name, as shown in the following example:

```
C:\ HELP NET ACCOUNTS
```

NET ACCOUNTS

NET ACCOUNTS - Maintains user account database.

Here is a summary of the **NET ACCOUNTS** command.

```
C:\ NET ACCOUNTS /?
NET ACCOUNTS [/FORCELOGOFF:{minutes | NO}] [/MINPWLEN:length]
             [/MAXPWAGE:{days | UNLIMITED}] [/MINPWAGE:days]
             [/UNIQUEPW:number] [/DOMAIN]
NET ACCOUNTS [/SYNC]
```

Some commonly used options follow:

/DOMAIN	Perform the specified action on the domain controller rather than the current computer.
/FORCELOGOFF	Line numbers are displayed along with output lines.
/MINPWLEN:length	Specify the minimum number of characters for a password with *length*.
/MAXPWAGE:days	Specify the maximum number of *days* a password is valid, or use the *unlimited* option to specify no limit on password validity.
/MINPWAGE:days	Specify the minimum number of *days* that must pass before a user is permitted to change their password.

/UNIQUEPW:number   A user password must be unique for the number of changes specified by *number*.

/SYNCH   Synchronize the account database.

The following example shows **NET ACCOUNTS** with no options specified:

```
C:\ NET ACCOUNTS

Force user logoff how long after time expires?:     Never
Minimum password age (days):                        0
Maximum password age (days):                        42
Minimum password length:                            0
Length of password history maintained:              None
Lockout threshold:                                  Never
Lockout duration (minutes):                         30
Lockout observation window (minutes):               30
Computer role:                                      BACKUP
Primary Domain controller for workstation domain:   \\NISDEV
The command completed successfully.
```

We'll now issue **NET ACCOUNTS** with the *MINPWLEN* option to change the minimum password length to five characters:

```
C:\ NET ACCOUNTS /MINPWLEN:5

The request will be processed at the primary domain controller for domain
NSDNIS

The command completed successfully.
```

Reissuing **NET ACCOUNTS** with no options reflects the new minimum password length:

```
C:\ NET ACCOUNTS

Force user logoff how long after time expires?:     Never
Minimum password age (days):                        0
Maximum password age (days):                        42
Minimum password length:                            5
Length of password history maintained:              None
Lockout threshold:                                  Never
Lockout duration (minutes):                         30
Lockout observation window (minutes):               30
Computer role:                                      BACKUP
Primary Domain controller for workstation domain:   \\NISDEV
The command completed successfully.
```

NET COMPUTER

NET COMPUTER - Add or delete computers from the domain database.

Here is a summary of the **NET COMPUTER** command:

```
C:\ NET COMPUTER /?

NET COMPUTER  \\computername {/ADD | /DEL}
```

Some commonly used options follow:

\\computername	Name of the computer to be added or deleted.
/ADD	Add the computer.
/DEL	Delete the computer.

The following example shows adding a computer using the */ADD* option.

```
C:\ NET COMPUTER \\SYSTEM2 /ADD

The request will be processed at the primary domain controller for domain
NSDNIS.

The command completed successfully.
```

NET CONFIG SERVER

NET CONFIG SERVER - As a member of Administrator's group, you can change the settings for a service.

Here is a summary of the **NET CONFIG SERVER** command:

```
C:\ NET CONFIG SERVER /?

NET CONFIG SERVER  [/AUTODISCONNECT:time]
                   [/SRVCOMMENT:"text"]
                   [/HIDDEN:{YES | NO}]
```

Some commonly used options follow:

/AUTODISCONNECT:time   Use *time* to specify the number of min-
                                  utes that pass before an inactive
                                  account is disconnected.

/SRVCOMMENT:"text"

/HIDDEN:{YES|NO}

NET CONTINUE

NET CONTINUE - Reactivates a Windows NT service that had been suspended with **NET PAUSE**.

Here is a summary of the **NET CONTINUE** command.

```
C:\ NET CONTINUE /?
NET CONTINUE service
```

You can pause and continue many Windows NT services with the **NET PAUSE** and **NET CONTINUE** commands, respectively. The following example shows using the **NET PAUSE** command to pause the **NET LOGON** service and then restart it with the **NET CONTINUE** command.

Figure 14-1 is the *Services* dialog box from a system, showing some of the services running on a system.

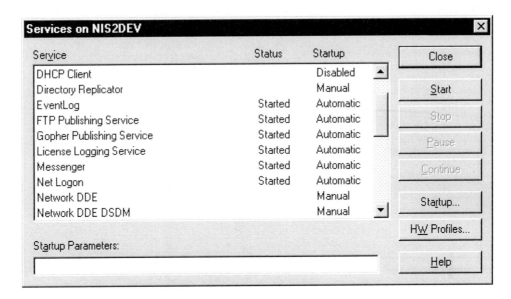

Figure 14-1 *Service* Dialog Box with Net Logon Started

We'll now use the **NET PAUSE** command to pause the *Net Logon* service:

```
C:\NET PAUSE NTLOGON
The Net Logon service was paused successfully.
```

Figure 14-2 shows the *Services* dialog box showing that the *Net Logon* service has indeed been paused.

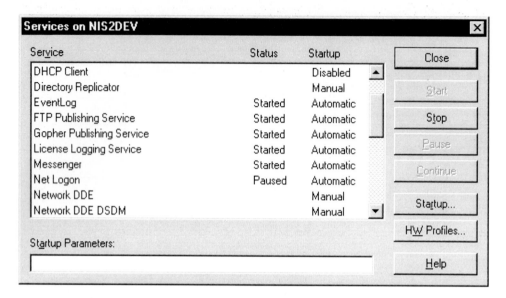

Figure 14-2 *Service* Dialog Box with Net Logon Paused

We can now resume the *Net Logon* service with the following **NET CONTINUE** command:

```
C:\NET CONTINUE NTLOGON
The Net Logon service was continued successfully.
```

NET FILE

NET FILE - This command lists and closes open files.

Here is a summary of the **NET FILE** command:

```
C:\ NET FILE /?

NET FILE  [id [/CLOSE]]
```

Some commonly used options follow:

id   Specify the identification number of
                                the file you wish to view.

id /CLOSE   Close the file specified by the *id* num-
                                ber.

The following example shows issuing the **NET FILE** command with no options:

```
C:\ NET FILE

ID        Path                              User name          # Locks
--------------------------------------------------------------------------
97         C:\tif_map_proj\sql              leung_k            0
147        \PIPE\samr                       administrator      0
148        \PIPE\lsarpc                     administrator      0
The command completed successfully.
```

This output shows the open files on the server. You can close one of these shared files or remove locks from the file.

NET GROUP

NET GROUP - This command displays and allows you to manipulate groups on a server. Without specifying any option, this command lists groups.

Here is a summary of the **NET GROUP** command:

```
C:\ NET GROUP /?
NET GROUP [groupname [/COMMENT:"text"]] [DOMAIN]
          groupname {/ADD [/COMMENT:"text"] | /DELETE} [/DOMAIN]
          groupname username [...] {/ADD | /DELETE} [/DOMAIN]
```

Some commonly used options follow:

/ADD	Add a group to a domain or a *username* to a group.
/DELETE	Delete a group from a domain or a *username* from a group.
groupname	Specify the *groupname* for the operation. With no options, the users who are part of the group are displayed. You can also use the *ADD* or *DELETE* options with the *groupname* to specify a *username* to add to the group.
/COMMENT:"text"	Add this comment to the *groupname*.
/DOMAIN	The operation will be performed on the primary domain controller. This option is the default for Windows NT server systems.

username
This user will be added or removed from the group. Any number of users can be specified.

The following example shows issuing the **NET GROUP** command to add the group *hp consultants*:

```
C:/ NET GROUP "hp consultants" /ADD
The request will be processed at the primary domain controller for domain
NSDNIS.
The command completed successfully.
```

Next we add the user *marty* to the group *hp consultants* on the local system:

```
C:\ NET GROUP "hp consultants" marty /ADD
The request will be processed at the primary domain controller for domain
NSDNIS.
The command completed successfully.
```

Next we add a comment to *hp consultants*:

```
C:\ NET GROUP "hp consultants" /COMMENT:"Group For HP Consultants"
The request will be processed at the primary domain controller for domain
NSDNIS.
The command completed successfully.
```

We can now view our handiwork by looking at the information we have added associated with the group *hp consultants*.

```
C:\ NET GROUP "hp consultants"

Group name     hp consultants
Comment        Group For HP Consultants
```

```
Members

-------------------------------------------------------------------------------
marty
The command completed successfully.
```

This output confirms that we have created the group *hp consultants*, that *marty* is a member of this group, and that our comment has indeed been associated with the group.

NET HELP

NET HELP - Use this command to get help on any of the NET commands.

A commonly used option follows:

NET HELP command | more   This provides information on the *command* you specify.

The following example shows issuing the **NET HELP** command to get a list of commands for which help is available:

```
C:\ NET HELP

The syntax of this command is:

NET HELP command
    -or-
NET command /HELP

    Commands available are:

    NET ACCOUNTS            NET HELP            NET SHARE
    NET COMPUTER           NET HELPMSG         NET START
    NET CONFIG             NET LOCALGROUP      NET STATISTICS
    NET CONFIG SERVER      NET NAME            NET STOP
    NET CONFIG WORKSTATION NET PAUSE           NET TIME
    NET CONTINUE           NET PRINT           NET USE
    NET FILE               NET SEND            NET USER
    NET GROUP              NET SESSION         NET VIEW

    NET HELP SERVICES lists the network services you can start.
    NET HELP SYNTAX explains how to read NET HELP syntax lines.
    NET HELP command | MORE displays Help one screen at a time.
```

The following example shows issuing the **NET HELP** command to get information on the **NET GROUP** command:

```
C:\ NET HELP NET GROUP

The syntax of this command is:

NET GROUP [groupname [/COMMENT:"text"]] [/DOMAIN]
        groupname {/ADD [/COMMENT:"text"] | /DELETE}  [/DOMAIN]
        groupname username [...] {/ADD | /DELETE} [/DOMAIN]

NET GROUP adds, displays, or modifies global groups on servers. Used
without parameters, it displays the groupnames on the server.
```

```
groupname          Is the name of the group to add, expand, or delete.
                   Supply only a groupname to view a list of users
                   in a group.
/COMMENT:"text"    Adds a comment for a new or existing group.
                   The comment can have as many as 48 characters. Enclose
                   the text in quotation marks.
/DOMAIN            Performs the operation on the primary domain controller
                   of the current domain. Otherwise, the operation is
                   performed on the local computer.
                   This parameter applies only to Windows NT
                   Workstation computers that are members of
                   a Windows NT Server domain. By default,
                   Windows NT Server computers perform
                   operations on the primary domain controller.
username[ ...]     Lists one or more usernames to add to or remove from
                   a group. Separate multiple username entries with a space.
/ADD               Adds a group, or adds a username to a group.
/DELETE            Removes a group, or removes a username from a group.

NET HELP command | MORE displays Help one screen at a time.
```

NET HELPMSG

NET HELPMSG - Gets information on four-digit network message codes. Use
only the four digits to get information on the code.

The following is the format of the **NET HELPMSG** command:

NET HELPMSG message#   Provides information on the four-digit
                                            messagenumber you specify.

The following command shows issuing the **NET GROUP** command
to add a group to a system. After issuing this command, an error number is
provided:

```
C:\ NET GROUP "hp consultants" /ADD

The group already exists.

More help is available by typing NET HELPMSG 2233.
```

We can now use the **NET HELPMSG** command to get information
on the specific four-digit code:

```
C:\ NET HELPMSG 2223

The group already exists.

EXPLANATION

You tried to create a group with a group name that already exists.

ACTION

Use a different group name for the new group. To display
a list of group names established on the server, type:

        NET GROUP
```

NET LOCALGROUP

NET LOCALGROUP - This command displays and allows you to manipulate groups on a computer. Without specifying any option, this command lists groups.

Here is a summary of the **NET LOCALGROUP** command:

```
C:\ NET LOCALGROUP /?
NET LOCALGROUP [groupname [/COMMENT:"text"]] [DOMAIN]
               groupname {/ADD [/COMMENT:"text"] | /DELETE} [/DOMAIN]
               groupname name [...] {/ADD | /DELETE} [/DOMAIN]
```

Some commonly used options follow:

/ADD	Add a group to a domain or a *username* to a group.
/DELETE	Delete a group from a domain or a *username* from a group.
groupname	Specify the *groupname* for the operation. With no options, the users who are part of the local group are displayed. You can also use the *ADD* or *DELETE* options with the *groupname* to specify a *username* to add to the group.
/COMMENT:"text"	Add this comment to the *groupname*.
/DOMAIN	The operation will be performed on the primary domain controller. If this option is not used, the operation will

take place on the local computer. This is the default for Windows NT server systems.

name

This is the user name(s) or group name(s) to be added or removed from the group. Any number can be specified.

NET NAME

NET NAME - This command adds or deletes a messaging name from a computer. This command is not to be confused with **NET USER,** which adds or deletes user accounts on a system.

Here is a summary of the **NET NAME** command:

```
C:\ NET NAME /?
NET NAME [name [/ADD | DELETE]]
```

Some commonly used options follow:

name	Name to add or delete.
/ADD	Adds a name to the computer.
/DELETE	Deletes a name from the computer.

NET PAUSE

NET PAUSE - Suspends a Windows NT service.

Here is a summary of the **NET PAUSE** command:

```
C:\ NET PAUSE /?
NET PAUSE service
```

You can pause and continue many Windows NT services with the **NET PAUSE** and **NET CONTINUE** commands, respectively. The following example shows using the **NET PAUSE** command to pause the **NET LOGON** service and then to restart it with the **NET CONTINUE** command.

Figure 14-3 shows the *Services* dialog box from a system, showing some of the services running on a system.

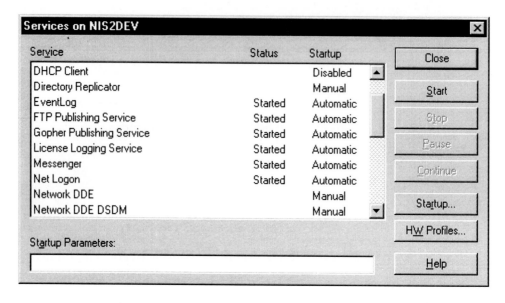

Figure 14-3 *Service* Dialog Box with Net Logon Started

We now use the **NET PAUSE** command to pause the *Net Logon* service:

```
C:\NET PAUSE NTLOGON
The Net Logon service was paused successfully.
```

Figure 14-4 shows the *Services* dialog box showing that the *Net Logon* service has indeed been paused.

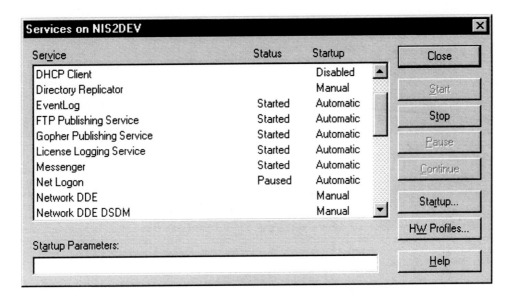

Figure 14-4 *Service* Dialog Box with Net Logon Paused

We can now continue the *Net Logon* service with the following **NET CONTINUE** command:

```
C:\NET CONTINUE NTLOGON
The Net Logon service was continued successfully.
```

NET PRINT

NET PRINT - This command lists print jobs and shared queues.

Here is a command summary of the **NET PRINT** command:

```
C:\ NET PRINT /?

NET PRINT \\computername\sharename
          [\\computername] job# [/HOLD | /RELEASE | /DELETE]
```

Some commonly used options follow:

\\computername	The *computername* sharing the print queues.
sharename	The print queue *sharename*.
job#	The unique number assigned to a print job.
/HOLD	The job is assigned a status of *HOLD*, which means it will not be printed until it is released or deleted.
/RELEASE	Releases a print job so that it can be printed.
/DELETE	Deletes a print job from the print queue.

NET SEND

NET SEND - Sends messages to other users, computers, or messaging names on the network.

Here is a summary of the **NET SEND** command:

```
C:\ NET SEND /?
NET SEND {name | * | /DOMAIN[:name] | /USERS} message
```

Some commonly used options follow:

name	The user name, computer name, or messaging name to which the message is to be sent. Use quotation marks if there are blank characters in the name.
*	Use * to send a message to all users within your group rather than an individual name.
/DOMAIN[:domainname]	Use /DOMAIN to send a message to all users in the /DOMAIN. You can also specify a *domainname* to which you want the message sent.
message	This is the text message you want sent.

The following example shows issuing the **NET SEND** command to send a message to a specific user.

```
NET SEND marty Our NetServer LXr has arrived for installation.
```

Figure 14-5 shows the alert box that appears on the screen of the computer on which *marty* is working.

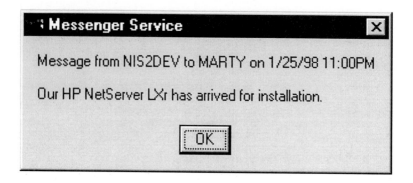

Figure 14-5   Alert Box Produced from the **NET SEND** Command

NET SESSION

NET SESSION - Views or disconnects sessions between computers.

Here is a summary of the **NET SESSION** command.

```
C:\ NET SESSION /?
NET SESSION [\\computername] [/DELETE]
```

Some commonly used options follow:

\\computername	Lists session-related information for *computername*.
/DELETE	Terminates a session between the local computer and *computername*, closing open files. Without a *computername*, all sessions are ended.

NET SHARE

NET SHARE - This command is used to list information about existing shares or to share a server's resources with other network users. The command lists information about existing shares if you don't specify any options.

Here is a summary of the **NET SHARE** command:

```
C:\ NET SHARE /?

NET SHARE sharename
            sharename=drive:path [USERS:number | /UNLIMITED]
                                 [REMARK:"text"]
            sharename [/USERS:number | /UNLIMITED]
                     [/REMARK:"text"]
            {sharename | devicename | drive:path} /DELETE
```

Some commonly used options follow:

sharename	Network name of the shared resource. Using the *sharename* only displays information about the share.
devicename	Used to specify printers to be shared with *sharename*. Use LP1-LPT9 as a *devicename*.
drive:path	Use this option to specify that a specific drive and path for a directory are to be shared.
/USERS:number	Use this option to specify the maximum number of users that can simultaneously access a shared resource.

/UNLIMITED	An unlimited number of users may simultaneously access a shared resource.
/REMARK:"text"	Associates a remark with the specified shared resource.
/DELETE	Sharing is deleted for the specified resource.

Let's now use **NET SHARE** to set up a new share on a system. To begin, let's look at the existing shares using the **NET SHARE** command with no options:

```
D:\ NET SHARE

Share name   Resource                        Remark
-------------------------------------------------------------------
ADMIN$       D:\WINNT                        Remote Admin
IPC$                                         Remote IPC
C$           C:\                             Default share
print$       D:\WINNT\system32\spool\drivers Printer Drivers
D$           D:\                             Default share
E$           E:\                             Default share
net_share    C:\net_share
NETLOGON     D:\WINNT\system32\Repl\Import\S Logon server share
HPLaserJ5    LPT1:                  Spooled  HP LaserJet 5MP
The command completed successfully.
```

Now we can set up a share of the **c:\measureware** directory with a sharename of *measure* and a maximum number of five users:

```
C:\ NET SHARE measure=c:\measureware /users:5

measure was shared successfully
```

Issuing the NET SHARE command shows that the share named "measureware" has been established.

```
C:\ NET SHARE


Share name    Resource                           Remark

------------------------------------------------------------------------------
D$            D:\                                Default share
ADMIN$        D:\WINNT                           Remote Admin
IPC$                                             Remote IPC
C$            C:\                                Default share
print$        D:\WINNT\system32\spool\drivers    Printer Drivers
E$            E:\                                Default share
measure       c:\measureware
net_share     C:\net_share
NETLOGON      D:\WINNT\system32\Repl\Import\S    Logon server share
HPLaserJ5     LPT1:                  Spooled     HP LaserJet 5MP
The command completed successfully.
```

NET START

NET START - This command starts services that have been stopped using the **NET STOP** command or that have not been started. Issue **NET START** without options to see a list of currently running services.

Here is a summary of the **NET START** command:

```
C:\ NET START /?

NET START [service]
```

The following example shows issuing the **NET START** command without any options to list currently running services:

```
C:/ NET START

These Windows NT services are started:

   Alerter
     Computer Browser
     EventLog
     FTP Publishing Service
     Gateway Service for NetWare
     Gopher Publishing Service
     License Logging Service
     MeasureWare Agent
     MeasureWare Transaction Manager
     Messenger
     Net Logon
     NT LM Security Support Provider
     OracleServiceTMI
     OracleStartTMI
     OracleTNSListener
     Plug and Play
     Remote Procedure Call (RPC) Locator
     Remote Procedure Call (RPC) Service
     Schedule
     Server
     Spooler
     STP/A - TCP/IP Page Server (TMI)
     TCP/IP NetBIOS Helper
     UPS
     Workstation
     World Wide Web Publishing Service

The command completed successfully.
```

There are many services listed in the example that are not native to Windows NT. For instance, MeasureWare (HP performance tools) and Oracle services. These can be started and stopped with the **NET START** and **NET STOP** commands, respectively.

NET STATISTICS

NET STATISTICS - Use this command to display the statistics log for a service. Issue **NET STATISTICS** without options to display statistics for all services.

Here is a summary of the **NET STATISTICS** command:

```
C:\ NET STATISTICS /?
NET STATISTICS [WORKSTATION | SERVER]
```

Some commonly used options follow:

SERVER   Displays server service statistics.

WORKSTATION   Displays workstation service statistics.

The following example shows issuing the **NET STATISTICS** command with no options:

```
C:\ NET STATISTICS
Server Statistics for \\NISDEV

Statistics since 1/21/98 8:49 AM

Sessions accepted                3
Sessions timed-out               32
Sessions errored-out             32

Kilobytes sent                   165941
Kilobytes received               33118

Mean response time (msec)        0

System errors                    0
Permission violations            2
Password violations              0

Files accessed                   12787
Communication devices accessed   0
Print jobs spooled               0

Times buffers exhausted
```

```
Big buffers                        0
  Request buffers                  0
```

The command completed successfully.

NET STOP

NET STOP - This command stops a service that was started using the **NET START** command.

Here is a summary of the **NET STOP** command:

```
C:\ NET STOP /?
NET STOP service
```

Option to the **NET STOP** command:

service   The name of a service that can be
                                           stopped.

NET TIME

NET TIME - This command is used to display the time for a computer or to synchronize the clock of a computer with the clock on another computer.

Here is a summary of the **NET TIME** command:

```
C:\ NET TIME /?

NET TIME [\\computername | /DOMAIN[:domainname]] [/SET]
```

Some commonly used options follow:

\\computername	The computer with which you want to synchronize the time or of which you want to display the time.
/DOMAIN[:domainname]	The domain name with which you want to synchronize the time.
/SET	Set's the computer's time with the time on the specified computer or domain.

NET USE

NET USE - Lists the connections of a computer, or establishes or removes shared resources. Without options, this command lists the connections of a computer.

Here is a summary of the **NET USE** command:

```
C:\ NET USE /?
NET USE [devicename | *] [//computername\sharename[/volume] [password | *]]
        [/USER:[domainname\]username]
        [[/DELETE] | [/PERSISTENT:{YES | NO}]]
NET USE [devicename | *] [password | *]] [/HOME]
NET USE [PERSISTENT:{YES | NO}]
```

Some commonly used options follow:

devicename	Specifies a name to be connected or disconnected. The possibilities include such names as drives and printers.
//computername	This is the name of the computer that controls the shared resource.
/sharename	The network name of the shared device.
password	The password that is required to get access to the shared resource.
*	Produces a password prompt for the user attempting to use the shared resource.

/USER	Specifies a different user name for the connection.
domainname	A different domain from the current domain is used.
username	Specifies a user logon name.
/HOME	Connects a user to their home directory.
/DELETE	Cancels a network connection and removes it from the list of persistent connections.
/PERSISTENT {yes | no}	Specifying *yes* means the connections are reestablished at the next logon. Specifying *no* does not save the connection for future logons.

The following example shows issuing the **NET USE** command with no options.

```
C:\ NET USE

New connections will be remembered.

Status      Local     Remote                  Network

--------------------------------------------------------------------------
OK          P:        \\DEVSYS\Disk_C         Microsoft Windows Network
The command completed successfully.
```

The directory *Disk_C* on remote system *DEVSYS* is viewed under **P:** on the local system.

NET USER

NET USER - This command creates and modifies accounts on computers. This can also be used without options to list accounts.

Here is a summary of the **NET USER** command:

```
C:\ NET USER /?

NET USER [username [password | *] [options]] [/DOMAIN]
         username {password | *} /ADD [options] [/DOMAIN]
         username [/DELETE] [/DOMAIN]
```

Some commonly used options follow:

/ADD	Adds a user account.
/DELETE	Removes a user account.
username	The name of the account to manipulate. You can add, delete, modify, or view the account.
password	Assigns or changes the password of a user account.
*	Displays the password prompt.
/DOMAIN	The action is to be performed on the primary domain controller.

additional options

You have many additional options such as expiration date of the account, path of the users logon profile, and many others.

The following example shows issuing the **NET USER** command with no options:

```
C:\ NET USER

User accounts for \\NIS2DEV

--------------------------------------------------------------------------
Administrator            arleo_j                 burgos_c
Guest                    IUSR_NIS2DEV            IUSR_NISDEV
johnt                    leung_k                 marty
mckenna_b
The command completed successfully.
```

Using the second form of the command shown earlier, we can add a new user to the system:

```
C:\ NET USER amyp * /ADD

Type a password for the user:

Retype the password to confirm:

The request will be processed at the primary domain controller for domain DEV.

The command completed successfully.
```

The asterisk in the **NET USER** commandmeans that we want to be prompted for the password for the new user *amyp*.

NET VIEW

NET VIEW - This command lists the resources being shared on a computer. You can use this command without options to display a list of computers on the domain.

Here is a summary of the **NET VIEW** command:

```
C:\ NET VIEW /?
NET VIEW [\\computername | /DOMAIN[:domainname]]
NET VIEW /NETWORK:NW [\\computername]
```

Some commonly used options follow:

//computername	Specifies the name of the computer for which you want to view shared resources.
/DOMAIN:domainname	Specifies the name of the domain for which you wish to view shared resources.
/NETWORK:NW	Displays NetWare servers on the network.

The following example shows issuing the **NET VIEW** command with no options, producing a list of computers in the current domain:

```
C:\ NET VIEW

Server Name          Remark

-------------------------------------------------------------------------
\\NIS2DEV
\\NISDEV
The command completed successfully.
```

The following example shows issuing the **NET VIEW** command while specifying the *DOMAIN* to be viewed:

```
C:\ NET VIEW /DOMAIN:nisdomain

Server Name              Remark

-------------------------------------------------------------------------------
\\HPSYSTEM1
\\KITTY
\\NIS
The command completed successfully.
```

The following example shows issuing the **NET VIEW** command while specifying a specific *computername* in the current domain to view:

```
C:\ NET VIEW \\nisdev

Shared resources at \\hpsystem1

Share name   Type        Used as   Comment

-------------------------------------------------------------------------------
HPLaserJ5    Print                 HP LaserJet 5MP
measure      Disk
net_share    Disk
NETLOGON     Disk                  Logon server share
The command completed successfully.
```

POSIX Utilities

The Microsoft Windows NT Server *Resource Kit* (referred to as *Resource Kit* throughout this chapter) has on it several POSIX utilities that UNIX system administrators find useful when using Windows NT. The *Resource Kit* in general is a fantastic system administration resource. Although I will focus on only POSIX utilities in this book, it has in it a wealth of information. The *Resource Kit* is available from Microsoft Press, Redmond, WA. The POSIX utilities include such useful commands as **cat, chmod, find, ls,**

mv, and others. The commands that are available on the *Resource Kit* vary somewhat from architecture to architecture. In this chapter I focus on only the "I386" utilities and not the utilities for other architectures in this chapter.

The *Resource Kit* has on it the file **POSIX.WRI**, which describes the POSIX utilities in detail. In this chapter, I'll just provide a brief overview of the utilities and examples of using some of the utilities. Most UNIX system administrators are familiar with these utilities in UNIX but may find differences in the options to these utilities when using the *Resource Kit* version.

I have made every effort to limit the number of "add-on" products, to Windows NT and UNIX covered in this book. The *Resource Kit*, however, is so useful to Windows NT system administrators that not covering at least some part of it, such as the POSIX utilities, would leave a void in the discussion of Windows NT system administration. You can find out more information about the *Resource Kit* on the Microsoft Web site. You can buy it at many computer, electronic, and book stores. Be sure to buy the *Resource Kit* for the version of Windows NT you are running. There is also a *Resource Kit* for both the Server and Workstation versions of Windows NT. I used the Server *Resource Kit* for the POSIX commands covered in this chapter.

Both the source code and executables for the POSIX utilities are on the *Resource Kit*. The following is a listing of the POSIX executables for I386 on the *Resource Kit* CD-ROM. I used the POSIX utility **ls -l** to produce this listing.

```
F:\I386\GNU\POSIX> ls -l

-rwxrwxrwx   1 Everyone Everyone   101748 Sep  6 12:39 CAT.EXE
-rwxrwxrwx   1 Everyone Everyone   116188 Sep  6 12:39 CHMOD.EXE
-rwxrwxrwx   1 Everyone Everyone   110920 Sep  6 12:39 CHOWN.EXE
-rwxrwxrwx   1 Everyone Everyone   111208 Sep  6 12:39 CP.EXE
-rwxrwxrwx   1 Everyone Everyone   173580 Sep  6 12:39 FIND.EXE
-rwxrwxrwx   1 Everyone Everyone   144256 Sep  6 12:39 GREP.EXE
-rwxrwxrwx   1 Everyone Everyone    90960 Sep  6 12:39 LN.EXE
-rwxrwxrwx   1 Everyone Everyone   128532 Sep  6 12:39 LS.EXE
-rwxrwxrwx   1 Everyone Everyone    88984 Sep  6 12:39 MKDIR.EXE
-rwxrwxrwx   1 Everyone Everyone    99096 Sep  6 12:39 MV.EXE
-rwxrwxrwx   1 Everyone Everyone   114564 Sep  6 12:39 RM.EXE
-rwxrwxrwx   1 Everyone Everyone    85004 Sep  6 12:39 RMDIR.EXE
-rwxrwxrwx   1 Everyone Everyone   362528 Sep  6 12:39 SH.EXE
-rwxrwxrwx   1 Everyone Everyone    91244 Sep  6 12:39 TOUCH.EXE
-rwxrwxrwx   1 Everyone Everyone   287628 Sep  6 12:39 VI.EXE
-rwxrwxrwx   1 Everyone Everyone    95392 Sep  6 12:39 WC.EXE
```

The directory in which these utilities are located is the **F:** drive, which is my CD-ROM, in **I386\GNU\POSIX**, which is the I386 version of these utilities. The following list is command summaries of the POSIX utilities. A brief description of some the utilities as well some of the more commonly used options to the utilities is included. In some cases, you also have an example of having run the utility. The **POSIX.WRI** file on the *Resource Kit* provides an exhaustive description of each utility.

cat

cat - Display, combine, append, copy, or create files.

Some commonly used options follow:

-n   Line numbers are displayed along with output lines.

-u   Output is unbuffered, which means it is handled character by character.

-v   Print's most nonprinting characters visibly.

The following example shows using the -n option with **cat**:

```
D:\WINNT\system> cat -n setup.inf

    1  [setup]
    2     help = setup.hlp
    3
    4  ;   Place any programs here that should be run at the end of setup.
    5  ;   These apps will be run in order of their appearance here.
    6  [run]
    7
    8  [dialog]
    9     caption  = "Windows Setup"
   10     exit     = "Exit Windows Setup"
   11     title    = "Installing Windows 3.1"
   12     options  = "In addition to installing Windows 3.1, you can:"
   13     printwait = "Please wait while Setup configures your printer(s)..."

                          .
                          .
                          .

   20  [data]
```

```
21  ; Disk space required
22  ; <type of setup>= <Full install space>, <Min install space>
23
24     upd2x386full = 10000000,6144000 ; 10.0 Mb, 6.144 Mb
25     upd2x286full = 9000000,6144000  ;  9.0 Mb, 6.144 Mb
26     upd3x386full = 5500000,5000000  ;  5.5 Mb, 5.0 Mb
27     upd3x286full = 5500000,5000000  ;  5.5 Mb, 5.0 Mb
28
29     new386full   = 10000000,6144000 ; 10.0 Mb, 6.144 Mb
30     new286full   = 9000000,6144000  ;  9.0 Mb, 6.144 Mb
31
32     netadmin     = 16000000          ; 16.0 Mb
33     netadminupd  = 16000000          ; 16.0 Mb
34     upd2x386net  = 300000            ;   .3 Mb
35     upd3x386net  = 300000            ;   .3 Mb
36     upd2x286net  = 300000            ;   .3 Mb
37     upd3x286net  = 300000            ;   .3 Mb
38     new386net    = 300000,300000     ;   .3 Mb,  .3 Mb
39     new286net    = 300000,300000     ;   .3 Mb,  .3 Mb
40
41
42
43  ; Defaults used in setting up and names of a few files
44     startup   = WIN.COM
```

chmod

chmod - Changes permissions of specified files using symbolic or absolute (sometimes called numeric) modes. Symbolic mode is described below.

Symbol of who is affected:

u	User is affected.
g	Group is affected.
o	Other is affected.
a	All users are affected.

Operation to perform:

+	Add permission.
-	Remove permission.
=	Replace permission.

Permission specified:

r	Read permission.
w	Write permission.
x	Execute permission.
u	Copy user permissions.
g	Copy group permissions.
o	Copy other permissions.

The following example uses both modes. Using absolute or numeric mode, the permissions on the file **cat1.exe** are changed from 666 to 777. Using symbolic mode, the execute permissions are then removed for all users.

```
D:\> ls -l cat1.exe

-rw-rw-rw-    1 Administ Administ    71323 Feb 20 11:34 cat1.exe

D:\> chmod 777 cat1.exe

D:\> ls -l cat1.exe


-rwxrwxrwx    1 Administ Administ    71323 Feb 20 11:34 cat1.exe

D:\> chmod a-x cat1.exe

D:\> ls -l cat1.exe

-rw-rw-rw-    1 Administ Administ    71323 Feb 20 11:34 cat1.exe
```

cp

cp - Copies files and directories.

Some commonly used options follow:

        -i   Interactive copy whereby you are prompted to confirm whether or not you wish to overwrite an existing file.

        -f   Forces existing files to be overwritten by files being copied if a conflict occurs in file names.

        -p   Preserves permissions when copying.

        -R   Copies recursively which includes subtrees.

The following example shows using the **cp** command to copy **cat1.exe** to **cat2.exe,** and then a listing of all files beginning with **cat** is produced:

```
D:\> cp cat1.exe cat2.exe

D:\> ls -l cat*

-rw-rw-rw-    1 Administ Administ     71323 Feb 20 11:34 cat1.exe
-rw-rw-rw-    1 Administ Administ     71323 Feb 20 11:47 cat2.exe
```

find

find - Recursively descends a directory structure looking for the file(s) listed.

Some commonly used options follow:

-f   Specifies a file hierarchy for **find** to traverse.

-s   When symbolic links are encountered, the file referenced by the link and not the link itself will be used.

-x   Doesn't descend into directories that have a device number different from that of the file from which the descent began.

-print Prints pathname to standard output.

-size n True if the file's size is n.

grep

grep - Searches for text and displays result.

The following example shows using grep to find the expression "shell" everywhere it appears inside the file **setup.inf**:

```
D:\> grep shell setup.inf

[shell]
00000000="shell versions below 3.01",,unsupported_net
00030100="shell versions below 3.21",,novell301
00032100="shell versions 3.21 and above",,novell321
00032600="shell versions 3.26 and above",,novell326
    #win.shell, 0:
    #win.shell, 0:
[win.shell]
    shell.dll
    system.ini, Boot,     "oldshell"        ,"shell"
```

ls

ls - Lists the contents of a directory.

Some commonly used options:

-a	List all entries.
-c	Use time file was last modified for producing order in which files are listed.
-d	List only the directory name, not its contents.
-g	Include the group in the output.
-i	Print the inode number in the first column of the report.
-q	Nonprinting characters are represented by a "?".
-r	Reverse the order in which files are printed.
-s	Show the size in blocks instead of bytes.
-t	List in order of time saved with most recent first.
-u	Use time of last access instead of last modification for determining order in which files are printed.
-A	Same as -a, except current and parent directories aren't listed.
-C	Multicolumn output produced.
-F	Directory followed by a "/", executable by an "*", symbolic link by an "@".
-L	List file or directory to which link points.
-R	Recursively list subdirectories.

I include several examples on the next few pages.

```
D:\> ls -a

Blue Monday 16.bmp
Blue Monday.bmp
Coffee Bean 16.bmp
Coffee Bean.bmp
Config
Cursors
FORMS
FeatherTexture.bmp
Fiddle Head.bmp
Fonts
Furry Dog 16.bmp
Furry Dog.bmp
Geometrix.bmp
Gone Fishing.bmp
Greenstone.bmp
Hazy Autumn 16.bmp
Help
Hiking Boot.bmp
Leaf Fossils 16.bmp
Leather 16.bmp
Maple Trails.bmp
Media
NETLOGON.CHG
NOTEPAD.EXE
Petroglyph 16.bmp
Prairie Wind.bmp
Profiles
REGEDIT.EXE
Rhododendron.bmp
River Sumida.bmp
Santa Fe Stucco.bmp
Seaside 16.bmp
Seaside.bmp
ShellNew
Snakeskin.bmp
Soap Bubbles.bmp
Solstice.bmp
Swimming Pool.bmp
TASKMAN.EXE
TEMP
Upstream 16.bmp
WIN.INI
WINFILE.INI
WINHELP.EXE
Zapotec 16.bmp
Zapotec.bmp
_DEFAULT.PIF
black16.scr
clock.avi
control.ini
explorer.exe
inetsrv.mif
inf
lanma256.bmp
lanmannt.bmp
network.wri
poledit.exe
printer.wri
repair
setup.old
setuplog.txt
system
system.ini
system32
vmmreg32.dll
welcome.exe
winhlp32.exe
```

```
D:\> ls -l

-rwxrwxrwx  1 Administ NETWORK    8310 Aug  9  1996 Blue Monday 16.bmp
-rwxrwxrwx  1 Administ NETWORK   37940 Aug  9  1996 Blue Monday.bmp
-rwxrwxrwx  1 Administ NETWORK    8312 Aug  9  1996 Coffee Bean 16.bmp
-rwxrwxrwx  1 Administ NETWORK   17062 Aug  9  1996 Coffee Bean.bmp
drwx---rwx  1 Administ Administ      0 Feb 10 10:39 Config
drwx---rwx  1 Administ Administ      0 Feb 10 16:22 Cursors
drwxrwxrwx  1 Administ NETWORK       0 Feb 10 16:23 FORMS
-rwxrwxrwx  1 Administ NETWORK   16730 Aug  9  1996 FeatherTexture.bmp
-rwxrwxrwx  1 Administ NETWORK   65922 Aug  9  1996 Fiddle Head.bmp
drwx---rwx  1 Administ Administ   8192 Feb 10 10:39 Fonts
-rwxrwxrwx  1 Administ NETWORK   18552 Aug  9  1996 Furry Dog 16.bmp
-rwxrwxrwx  1 Administ NETWORK   37940 Aug  9  1996 Furry Dog.bmp
-rwxrwxrwx  1 Administ NETWORK    4328 Aug  9  1996 Geometrix.bmp
-rwxrwxrwx  1 Administ NETWORK   17336 Aug  9  1996 Gone Fishing.bmp
-rwxrwxrwx  1 Administ NETWORK   26582 Aug  9  1996 Greenstone.bmp
-rwxrwxrwx  1 Administ NETWORK   32888 Aug  9  1996 Hazy Autumn 16.bmp
drwx---rwx  1 Administ Administ      0 Feb 19 15:10 Help
-rwxrwxrwx  1 Administ NETWORK   37854 Aug  9  1996 Hiking Boot.bmp
-rwxrwxrwx  1 Administ NETWORK   12920 Aug  9  1996 Leaf Fossils 16.bmp
-rwxrwxrwx  1 Administ NETWORK    6392 Aug  9  1996 Leather 16.bmp
-rwxrwxrwx  1 Administ NETWORK   26566 Aug  9  1996 Maple Trails.bmp
drwx---rwx  1 Administ Administ      0 Feb 10 16:23 Media
-rwxrwxrwx  1 Administ NETWORK   65536 Feb 11 10:35 NETLOGON.CHG
-rwxrwxrwx  1 Administ NETWORK   45328 Aug  8  1996 NOTEPAD.EXE
-rwxrwxrwx  1 Administ NETWORK   16504 Aug  9  1996 Petroglyph 16.bmp
-rwxrwxrwx  1 Administ NETWORK   65954 Aug  9  1996 Prairie Wind.bmp
drwxrwxrwx  1 Administ NETWORK    4096 Feb 10 16:32 Profiles
-rwxrwxr-x  1 Administ NETWORK   71952 Aug  8  1996 REGEDIT.EXE
-rwxrwxrwx  1 Administ NETWORK   17362 Aug  9  1996 Rhododendron.bmp
-rwxrwxrwx  1 Administ NETWORK   26208 Aug  9  1996 River Sumida.bmp
-rwxrwxrwx  1 Administ NETWORK   65832 Aug  9  1996 Santa Fe Stucco.bmp
-rwxrwxrwx  1 Administ NETWORK    8312 Aug  9  1996 Seaside 16.bmp
-rwxrwxr-x  1 Administ NETWORK   17334 Aug  9  1996 Seaside.bmp
drwxrwxrwx  1 Administ NETWORK       0 Feb 10 16:22 ShellNew
-rwxrwxrwx  1 Administ NETWORK   10292 Aug  9  1996 Snakeskin.bmp
-rwxrwxrwx  1 Administ NETWORK   65978 Aug  9  1996 Soap Bubbles.bmp
-rwxrwxr-x  1 Administ NETWORK   17334 Aug  9  1996 Solstice.bmp
-rwxrwxrwx  1 Administ NETWORK   26202 Aug  9  1996 Swimming Pool.bmp
-rwxrwxrwx  1 Administ NETWORK   32016 Aug  8  1996 TASKMAN.EXE
drwxrwxrwx  1 Administ NETWORK       0 Feb 20 09:59 TEMP
-rwxrwxrwx  1 Administ NETWORK   32888 Aug  9  1996 Upstream 16.bmp
-rwxrwxrwx  1 Administ NETWORK     239 Feb 10 16:23 WIN.INI
-rwxrwxr-x  1 Administ NETWORK       3 Aug  8  1996 WINFILE.INI
-rwxrwxr-x  1 Administ NETWORK  256192 Aug  8  1996 WINHELP.EXE
-rwxrwxrwx  1 Administ NETWORK    8312 Aug  9  1996 Zapotec 16.bmp
-rwxrwxr-x  1 Administ NETWORK    9522 Aug  9  1996 Zapotec.bmp
-rwxrwxr-x  1 Administ NETWORK     707 Aug  8  1996 _DEFAULT.PIF
-rwx---r-x  1 Administ Administ   5328 Aug  8  1996 black16.scr
-rwx---r-x  1 Administ Administ  82944 Aug  8  1996 clock.avi
-rwxrwxrwx  1 Administ NETWORK       0 Feb 10 11:18 control.ini
-rwx---r-x  1 Administ Administ 234256 Aug  8  1996 explorer.exe
-rwxrwxrwx  1 Administ NETWORK    1628 Feb 10 11:20 inetsrv.mif
drwx---rwx  1 Administ Administ  47104 Feb 10 10:56 inf
-rwx---r-x  1 Administ Administ 157044 Aug  8  1996 lanma256.bmp
-rwx---r-x  1 Administ Administ 157044 Aug  8  1996 lanmannt.bmp
-rwx---r-x  1 Administ Administ  67328 Aug  8  1996 network.wri
-rwx---r-x  1 Administ Administ 123152 Aug  8  1996 poledit.exe
-rwx---r-x  1 Administ Administ  34816 Aug  8  1996 printer.wri
drwx---rwx  1 Administ Administ      0 Feb 10 16:24 repair
-rwxrwxrwx  1 Administ NETWORK    2499 Feb 10 16:23 setup.old
-rwxrwxrwx  1 Administ NETWORK     138 Feb 10 16:22 setuplog.txt
drwx---rwx  1 Administ Administ   4096 Feb 20 10:07 system
-rwx---r-x  1 Administ Administ     219 Aug  8  1996 system.ini
drwx---rwx  1 Administ Administ 167936 Feb 20 09:50 system32
-rwx---r-x  1 Administ Administ  24336 Aug  8  1996 vmmreg32.dll
-rwx---r-x  1 Administ Administ  22288 Aug  8  1996 welcome.exe
-rwx---r-x  1 Administ Administ 310032 Aug  8  1996 winhlp32.exe
```

```
D:\> ls -C
```

```
Blue Monday 16.bmpGreenstone.bmpRhododendron.bmpWINFILE.INI     poledit.exe
Blue Monday.bmp Hazy Autumn 16.bmpRiver Sumida.bmpWINHELP.EXE   printer.wri
Coffee Bean 16.bmpHelp         Santa Fe Stucco.bmpZapotec 16.bmprepair
Coffee Bean.bmp Hiking Boot.bmp Seaside 16.bmp  Zapotec.bmp     setup.old
Config          Leaf Fossils 16.bmpSeaside.bmp  _DEFAULT.PIF    setuplog.txt
Cursors         Leather 16.bmp ShellNew          black16.scr    system
FORMS           Maple Trails.bmpSnakeskin.bmp   clock.avi       system.ini
FeatherTexture.bmpMedia        Soap Bubbles.bmpcontrol.ini      system32
Fiddle Head.bmp NETLOGON.CHG   Solstice.bmp      explorer.exe   vmmreg32.dll
Fonts           NOTEPAD.EXE    Swimming Pool.bmpinetsrv.mif     welcome.exe
Furry Dog 16.bmpPetroglyph 16.bmpTASKMAN.EXE     inf            winhlp32.exe
Furry Dog.bmp   Prairie Wind.bmpTEMP             lanma256.bmp
Geometrix.bmp   Profiles       Upstream 16.bmp lanmannt.bmp
Gone Fishing.bmpREGEDIT.EXE    WIN.INI          network.wri
```

mkdir

mkdir - Creates specified directories.

The following is a commonly used option:

-p   Creates intermediate directories to achieve the full path.
            If you want to create several layers of directories down,
            use **-p**.

mv

mv - Renames files and directories.

Some commonly used options follow:

-i   Interactive move whereby you are prompted to confirm whether or not you wish to overwrite an existing file.

-f   Forces existing files to be overwritten by files being moved if a conflict occurs in file names.

rm

rm - Removes files and directories.

Some commonly used options follow:

-d   Removes directories as well as other file types.

-i   Interactive remove whereby you are prompted to confirm whether or not you wish to remove an existing file.

-f   Forces files to be removed.

-r (-R) Recursively removes the contents of the directory and then the directory itself.

touch

touch - Changes the modification and/or last access times of a file, or creates a file.

Some commonly used options:

-c   Does not create a specified file if it does not exist.

-f   Forces a touch of a file regardless of permissions.

The following example creates **file1** with **touch**:

```
D:\> ls -l file1
ls:file1: No such file or directory

D:\> touch file1

D:\> ls -l file1

-rw-rw-rw-    1 Administ Administ       0 Feb 20 11:45 file1
```

WC

wc - Produces a count of words, lines, and characters.

Some commonly used options follow:

-l	Prints the number of lines in a file.
-w	Prints the number of words in a file.
-c	Prints the number of characters in a file.

The first example lists the contents of a directory and pipes the output to wc. The second example provides wc information about the file **system.ini**.

```
D:\> ls

CAT.EXE
CHMOD.EXE
CHOWN.EXE
CP.EXE
FIND.EXE
GREP.EXE
LN.EXE
LS.EXE
MKDIR.EXE
MV.EXE
RM.EXE
RMDIR.EXE
SH.EXE
TOUCH.EXE
VI.EXE
WC.EXE

D:\> ls | wc -wlc
      16      16      132

D:\> wc -wlc system.ini
      13      17      219 system.ini
```

Additional Commands

There are many additional commands in Windows NT that can be issued at the command line. I will present some of these commands in an informal manner.

Networking Commands

You have access to many useful networking commands on the command line in Windows NT. Some of the commands not covered here that you may want to look into include the following:

- **lpr**
- **route**
- **finger**
- **rexec**
- **ftp**
- **telnet** (opens a telnet window in the Windows NT environment)
- **hostname**
- **lpq**
- **tracert**
- **rcp**
- **rsh**
- **tftp**

You can find out more about these commands by typing the command name and /? at the command prompt, such as **telnet /?**. In the upcoming sections, I cover some additional commands that I often use.

arp

arp is used to display and edit the Address Resolution Protocol (arp) cache. This cache maps IP addresses to physical hardware addresses. The cache has in it one or more addresses of recently accessed systems. The following example shows issuing the **arp** command on a Windows NT system at address 113 and the address of the system most recently accessed at 111, with its physical hardware address shown.

```
d: arp -a

Interface: 159.260.112.113 on Interface 2
  Internet Address        Physical Address        Type
  159.260.112.111         08-00-09-f0-bc-40       dynamic
```

There are several options to the **arp** command that you can view by issuing the **arp /?** command.

ipconfig

ipconfig is used to display the current networking interface parameters. The following example shows issuing the **ipconfig** command on a Windows NT system at address 113 with the **/all** option set, which shows all information related to the networking interface.

```
d: ipconfig /all

Windows NT IP Configuration
```

```
                    Host Name . . . . . . . . . : hpsystem1
                    DNS Servers . . . . . . . . :
                    Node Type . . . . . . . . . : Broadcast
                    NetBIOS Scope ID. . . . . . :
                    IP Routing Enabled. . . . . : No
                    WINS Proxy Enabled. . . . . : No
                    NetBIOS Resolution Uses DNS : No

       Ethernet adapter Hpddnd31:

                    Description . . . . . . . . : HP DeskDirect
                                                  10/100 LAN Adapter
                    Physical Address. . . . . . : 08-00-09-D9-9A-8A
                    DHCP Enabled. . . . . . . . : No
                    IP Address. . . . . . . . . : 159.260.112.113
                    Subnet Mask . . . . . . . . : 255.255.255.0
                    Default Gateway . . . . . . : 159.260.112.250
```

There are several options to the **ipconfig** command that you can view by issuing the **ipconfig /?** command.

netstat

netstat provides network protocol statistics. The following **netstat** example uses the **-e** and **-s** options, which show Ethernet statistics and statistics for various protocols, respectively. The Ethernet statistics associated with the **-e** option are under "Interface Statistics" and end with "IP Statistics."

```
d: netstat -e -s
```

```
Interface Statistics
```

	Received	Sent
Bytes	3182007276	2446436
Unicast packets	11046	9604
Non-unicast packets	21827982	7932
Discards	0	0
Errors	0	1
Unknown protocols	4946670	

```
IP Statistics
```

```
      Packets Received                          = 20489869
      Received Header Errors                    = 133441
      Received Address Errors                   = 28222
      Datagrams Forwarded                       = 0
      Unknown Protocols Received                = 0
      Received Packets Discarded                = 0
      Received Packets Delivered                = 20328206
      Output Requests                           = 12004
      Routing Discards                          = 0
      Discarded Output Packets                  = 0
      Output Packet No Route                    = 0
      Reassembly Required                       = 0
      Reassembly Successful                     = 0
      Reassembly Failures                       = 0
      Datagrams Successfully Fragmented         = 0
      Datagrams Failing Fragmentation           = 0
      Fragments Created                         = 0

   ICMP Statistics

                                  Received       Sent
      Messages                    3702           23
      Errors                      0              0
      Destination Unreachable     4              5
      Time Exceeded               0              0
      Parameter Problems          0              0
      Source Quenchs              0              0
      Redirects                   3680           0
      Echos                       5              13
      Echo Replies                13             5
      Timestamps                  0              0
      Timestamp Replies           0              0
      Address Masks               0              0
      Address Mask Replies        0              0

   TCP Statistics

      Active Opens                              = 27
      Passive Opens                             = 8
      Failed Connection Attempts                = 1
      Reset Connections                         = 15
      Current Connections                       = 2
      Segments Received                         = 1888
      Segments Sent                             = 1854
      Segments Retransmitted                    = 3

   UDP Statistics

      Datagrams Received     = 607489
      No Ports               = 19718827
      Receive Errors         = 0
```

```
Datagrams Sent          = 10124
```

There are several options to the **netstat** command that you can view by issuing the **netstat /?** command. If you wish to see the changes in the value of statistics, you can specify an interval after which the statistics will again be displayed.

ping

ping is used to determine whether or not a host is reachable on the network. **ping** causes an echo request that sends packets that are returned by the destination host you specify. There are several options to the ping command you can specify. The following example uses the **-n** option to specify the number of times you want to send the packets, and **-l** specifies the length of packets for which the maximum of 8192 is used.

```
d: ping -n 9 -l 8192 system2

Pinging system2 [159.260.112.111] with 8192 bytes of data:

Reply from 159.260.112.111: bytes=8192 time=20ms TTL=255
Reply from 159.260.112.111: bytes=8192 time=20ms TTL=255
Reply from 159.260.112.111: bytes=8192 time=21ms TTL=255
Reply from 159.260.112.111: bytes=8192 time=20ms TTL=255
Reply from 159.260.112.111: bytes=8192 time=10ms TTL=255
Reply from 159.260.112.111: bytes=8192 time=30ms TTL=255
Reply from 159.260.112.111: bytes=8192 time=30ms TTL=255
Reply from 159.260.112.111: bytes=8192 time=20ms TTL=255
Reply from 159.260.112.111: bytes=8192 time=20ms TTL=255
```

There are several additional options to the **ping** command that you can view by issuing the **ping /?** command.

Permissions with cacls

You can view and change permissions of files from the command line with **cacls**. Figure 14-6 shows the help screen for the **cacls** command.

```
Command Prompt                                              _ □ ×
D:\>help cacls
Displays or modifies access control lists (ACLs) of files

CACLS filename [/T] [/E] [/C] [/G user:perm] [/R user [...]]
               [/P user:perm [...]] [/D user [...]]
    filename        Displays ACLs.
    /T              Changes ACLs of specified files in
                    the current directory and all subdirectories.
    /E              Edit ACL instead of replacing it.
    /C              Continue on access denied errors.
    /G user:perm    Grant specified user access rights.
                    Perm can be: R  Read
                                 C  Change (write)
                                 F  Full control
    /R user         Revoke specified user's access rights (only valid with /E).
    /P user:perm    Replace specified user's access rights.
                    Perm can be: N  None
                                 R  Read
                                 C  Change (write)
                                 F  Full control
    /D user         Deny specified user access.
Wildcards can be used to specify more that one file in a command.
You can specify more than one user in a command.

D:\>
◄                                                              ►
```

Figure 14-6   **cacls** Help Screen

cacls is used to display and modify the access control lists of files. You can see in Figure 14-6 that you have four different types of access rights for files that were described in detail earlier. The following list shows the abbreviations for access rights that are associated with the **cacls** command:

N   None

R   Read

C   Change

F   Full Control

Figure 14-7 shows using both **cacls** and the *File Permissions* window to view the existing permissions for **D:\WINNT\REGEDIT.EXE**. This is one of the most important files on the system that was used in an earlier chapter to view and modify registry information on the system. This is a file that you want to carefully manage access rights to in order to avoid any operating system mishaps.

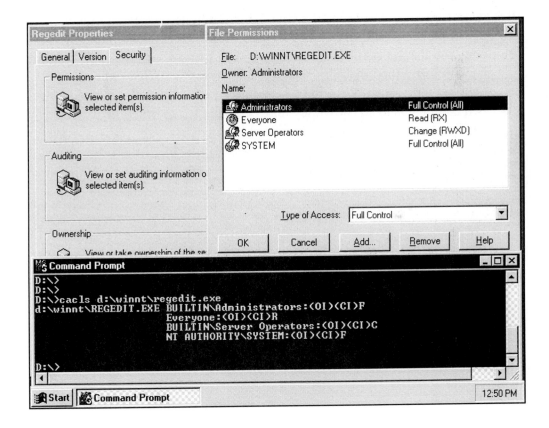

Figure 14-7   D:\WINNT\REGEDIT.EXE Permissions

Notice that *Server Operators* do indeed have *Change* rights to this file. You can, of course, modify the permissions on this or any file on the system. The *File Permissions* window and the output of the **cacls** command are in different formats; however, they contain the same information.

Command Line Backup

An alternative to using the graphical tools to initiate backups is to use the command line. Using the **NTBACKUP** command, you can initiate backups at the command line or build batch files using this command. You can combine the **NTBACKUP** command with the **AT** command to schedule backups. Provided that the *SCHEDULE* service is started, you can specify the time for which a job will be scheduled. Let's take a closer look at these two commands to see how they may be combined to schedule backups.

NTBACKUP

NTBACKUP - This command is used to initiate backups at the command line.

Here is a summary of the **NTBACKUP** command:

```
C:\ NTBACUKP /?
NTBACKUP operation path [/a][/v][/r][/d"text"][/b][/hc:{on | off}]
                        [/t{option}][/l"filename"][/e][/TAPE:{n}]
```

Some commonly used options follow:

operation	The *operation* to perform such as *backup*.
path	The directories you wish to back up.
/a	Append this backup to those on the tape rather than replace the contents of the tape with the current job.
/b	Include the local registry in the backup.
/d"text"	Description of the backup set is defined by the text in quotation marks.
/e	The backup log will contain only exceptions rather than the full backup log.

/hc:{on |off}	Specify whether or not to use hardware compression for the backup. You can use this option only if you don't use the /a option.
/L"filename"	The file name to be used for the backup log.
/r	Restricted access to the tape will be used. You can use this option only if you don't use the /A option.
/t option	Specify the type of backup such as normal, copy, incremental, differential, or daily.
/tape:{n}	Specify the tape drive to be used if indeed the server has more than one tape drive.
/v	Verify the operation.

To back up the **oracle** directory with a *normal* backup, recording exceptions only in the log file, performing tape verification, and including a description of "oracle backup," you would issue the following command.

```
C:\ NTBACKUP backup d:/oracle /e /v /t normal /d "oracle backup"
```

AT

AT - This command is used to schedule jobs.

Here is a summary of the **AT** command:

```
C:\ AT /?

AT [//computername] [id] [/DELETE] | /DELETE [/YES]]

AT [//computername] time [/INTERACTIVE][/EVERY:date[,...] | [/NEXT:date[,...]] "com-
mand"
```

Some commonly used options follow:

//computername	Computer on which the command will execute.
id	The identification number assigned to a scheduled command.
/DELETE	Cancel a scheduled command. You can use an id to cancel jobs associated with that *id* or cancel all scheduled commands.
/YES	Reply *YES* as confirmation of canceled jobs.
time	The *time* at which the job should be scheduled, in 24-hour format.
/INTERACTIVE	The job will run interactively rather than in the background.

/EVERY:date[,...]	Repeating jobs are scheduled with *dates* (Monday, Tuesday, and so on) or a day of the month (1-31).
/NEXT:date[,...]	Use this option to schedule a job the next time *date* occurs. Specify one or more dates (Monday, Tuesday, and so on) or a day of the month (1-31).
"command"	The *command* to be executed.

We can now combine the previous **NTBACKUP** command with **AT,** to perform a scheduled backup. By placing the previous **NTBACKUP** command in the file **backup,** we can issue the following command:

```
C:\ AT 03:00 /every:Monday,Tuesday,Wednesday,Thursday,Friday "backup"
```

CHAPTER 15

Windows NT and UNIX Interoperability: Services For UNIX (SFU)

Introduction to SFU

Microsoft Services For UNIX (SFU) provides interoperability between UNIX and Windows NT in many essential areas. Microsoft has packaged several widely used third-party interoperability products in SFU. Such important UNIX and Windows NT interoperability functions as NFS, Telnet, and UNIX utilities are part of SFU. Figure 15-1 shows these functions as menu picks that are produced when SFU is loaded on a Windows NT system. We'll go through the most important functional areas of SFU in the upcoming sections, starting with NFS.

Using Network File System (NFS) Functionality of SFU

With the NFS functionality of SFU, you would typically run your NFS client, such as the one included with SFU, on your Windows NT system in order to mount file systems on a UNIX system.

The NFS client of SFU bridges your Microsoft Server Message Block (SMB) network to your UNIX network by acting as a proxy. It forwards SMB requests from a Windows NT client to a UNIX NFS server and vice-versa. I always concentrate on the *client* aspect of NFS running on Windows NT. This is because the UNIX systems are usually bigger, more centralized systems to which Windows NT users want to get access. Therefore, Windows NT users usually mount UNIX directories on their Windows NT systems and not vice-versa.

This situation is not necessarily the case. With SFU, you can also set up your Windows NT system as an NFS Server. Figure 15-1 shows the menu structure of SFU after it has been installed. The *Server for NFS* menu pick is selected.

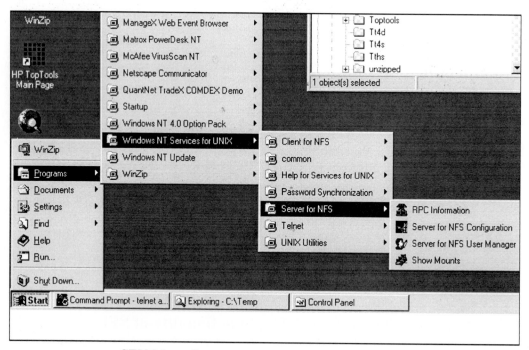

Figure 15-1 SFU Menu Structure

To begin, we'll focus on the *Client for NFS*, since this is very commonly used in mixed Windows NT and UNIX environments, and we'll then come back to the *Server for NFS* later in the chapter.

Under *Client for NFS Configuration* are the following six categories of information to enter related to NFS:

Authentication
Mount Options
File Access
Filenames
Configured NFS LANs
Symbolic Links

Let's walk through each of these, beginning with *Authentication,* shown in Figure 15-2.

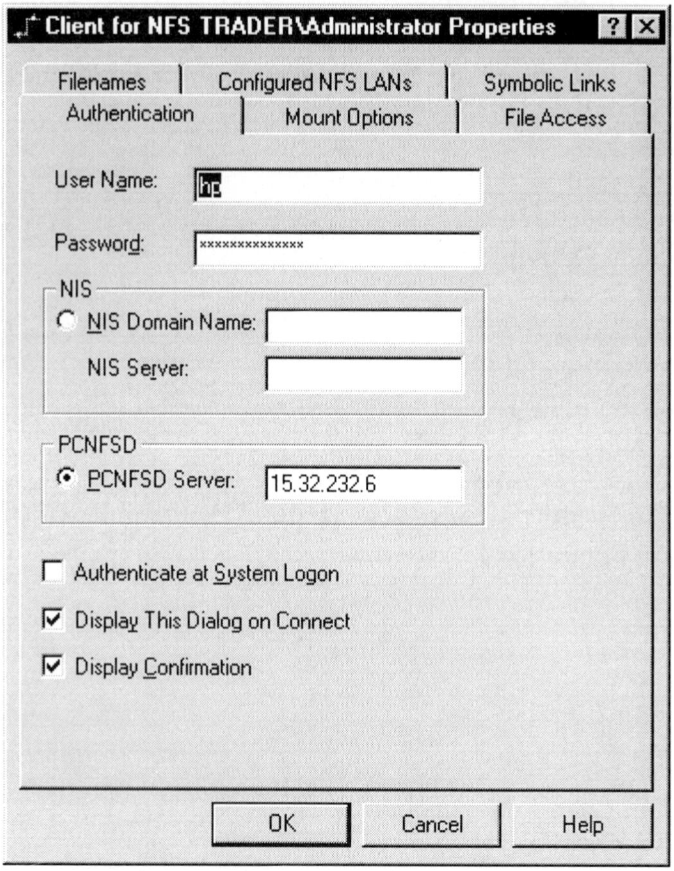

Figure 15-2 SFU *Authentication*

Authentication requires us to add some basic information about our connection to the NFS server. The *User Name* and *Password* are those we use to connect to the NFS Server. These should be set up on the server in advance of attempting to make a connection to the server. You also have the option to use NIS, which won't be part of this example. The server to which you are making an NFS connection must be running the PC NFS daemon. You can check to see whether your server is running this daemon. Figure 15-3 shows checking for PCNFSD on the NFS server:

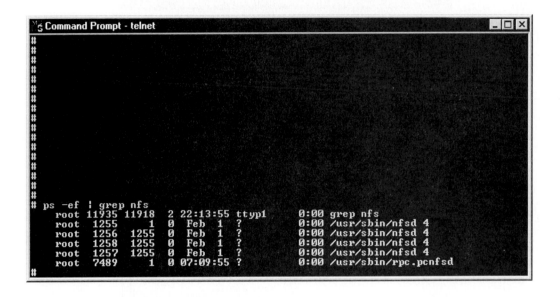

```
Command Prompt - telnet                                        _ □ ×
#
#
#
#
#
#
#
#
#
#
#
#
#
#
#
#
#
#
# ps -ef | grep nfs
  root 11935 11918  2 22:13:55 ttyp1      0:00 grep nfs
  root  1255     1  0  Feb 1  ?          0:00 /usr/sbin/nfsd 4
  root  1256  1255  0  Feb 1  ?          0:00 /usr/sbin/nfsd 4
  root  1258  1255  0  Feb 1  ?          0:00 /usr/sbin/nfsd 4
  root  1257  1255  0  Feb 1  ?          0:00 /usr/sbin/nfsd 4
  root  7489     1  0 07:09:55  ?        0:00 /usr/sbin/rpc.pcnfsd
#
```

Figure 15-3 Checking for **pcnfsd** on a UNIX System

The last entry shows that **pcnfsd** is indeed running on our NFS server.

With the *User Name, Password,* and *PCNFSD Server* specified, we can move on to *Configure NFS LANs.* Figure 15-4 shows that I have configured two LANs on which I want to use NFS.

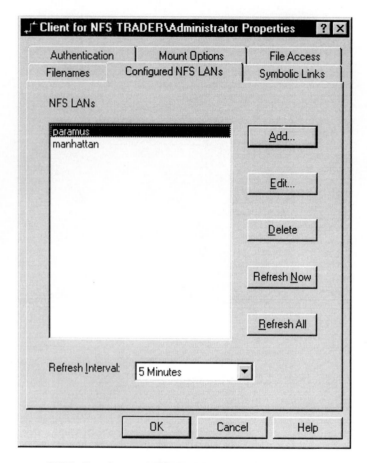

Figure 15-4   SFU *Configure NFS LANs*

You can *Edit...* these LANs to include such information as the *Broadcast Address,* as shown in Figure 15-5.

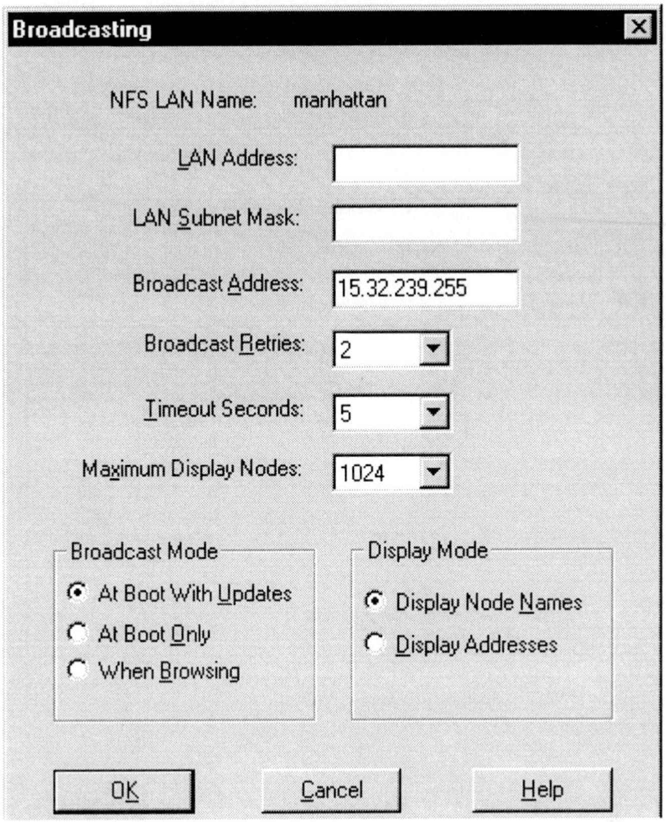

Figure 15-5 SFU *Configure NFS LANs*

Next you have options over the way symbolic links will be handled when you establish a client NFS connection. Symbolic links are a way of mapping a file or directory to an existing file or directory. If you select *Resolve Symbolic Links,* then you will be shown the actual path name to which the link is set. The options available for *Symbolic Links* are shown in Figure 15-6.

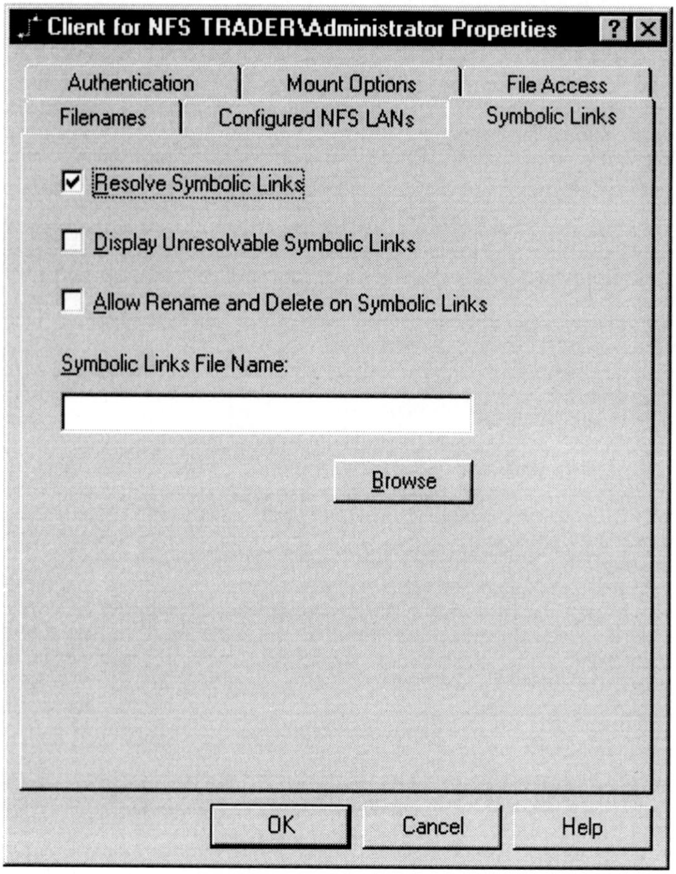

Figure 15-6 SFU *Client for NFS*

I typically like to resolve symbolic links but don't care to manipulate existing links or display those that cannot be resolved.

There are somewhat different conventions used in file naming on Windows NT and UNIX. SFU gives you several options related to *Filenames,* as shown in Figure 15-7.

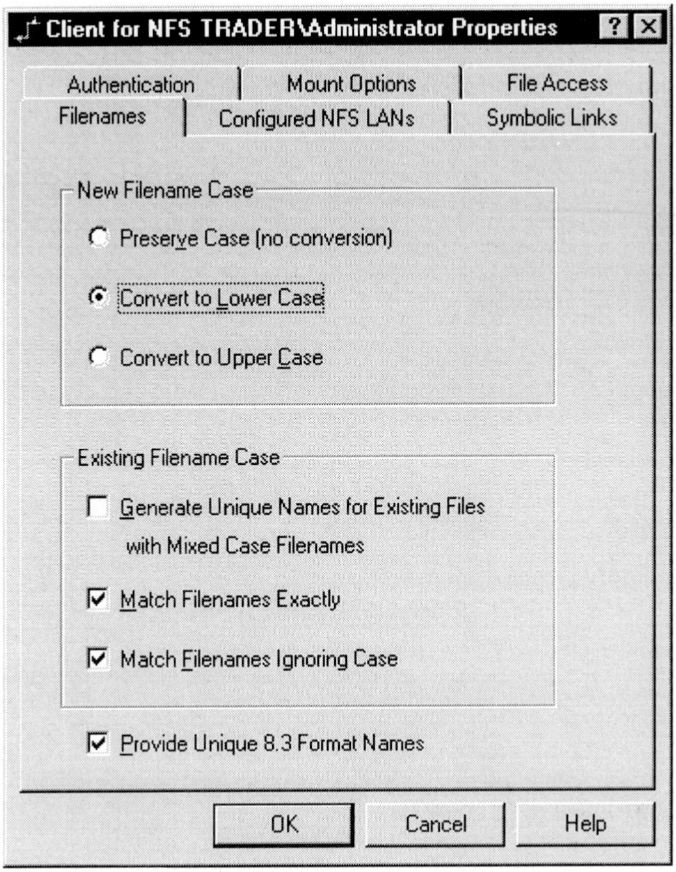

Figure 15-7 SFU *Client for NFS*

I like all new filenames to be lowercase. This seems to result in the minimum amount of confusion when working with multiple operating systems. I also like to work with existing filenames exactly as they exist, as indicated by the options I have chosen in Figure 15-7.

There are many mount options that you have when working with NFS. Figure 15-8 shows the *Mount Options* window.

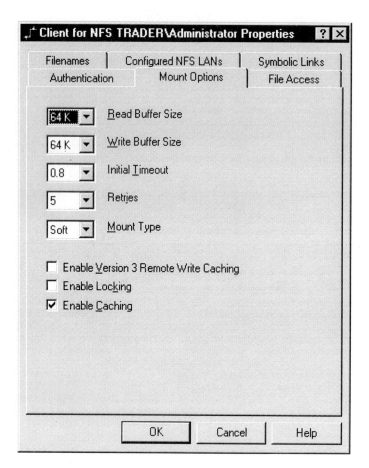

Figure 15-8 SFU *Mount Options*

We are using the default *Read Buffer Size* of 64,000 bytes. I like to keep this number large, since it is the data part of the packet used during NFS reads. In general, bigger is better. The same is true of the *Write Buffer Size*. The *Initial_Timeout* specifies the amount of time to wait for a response from the server before a retry. *Retries* specifies the number of times you'll attempt to access the server before dropping the operation altogether. I also use a *Mount Type* of *Soft,* as opposed to *Hard* and *Enable Caching.*

File Access allows you to specify privileges for users establishing NFS mounts. These are the privileges you're accustomed to seeing when working with files as shown in Figure 15-9.

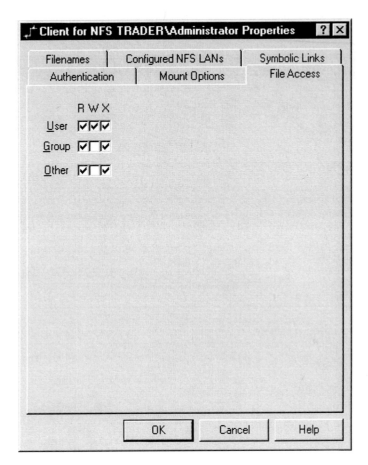

Figure 15-9 SFU *File Access*

By default, *User* will have unlimited access to files, and those in the *Group* and *Other* will have read (R) and execute (X) access only. These are common privilege assignments.

We can easily establish our NFS connection by selecting *OK* from the *Authentication* window shown earlier. A box appears asking you to confirm the user name and other information, such as that shown in Figure 15-10.

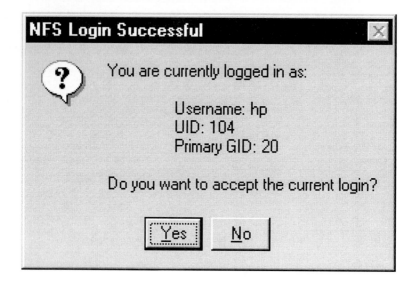

Figure 15-10 SFU *Login Successful*

The *Username, UID,* and *Primary GID* correspond to those on the UNIX NFS server. If we view the **passwd** file on the UNIX NFS server system and look for our user, *hp,* we'll see the following entry:

```
hp:EkyXw/N.EwFNw:104:20::/home/hp:/sbin/sh
```

The information in this **passwd** entry corresponds to that shown in our NFS Login window.

After login takes place, we can view the file systems exported on the UNIX NFS server using Explorer on our Windows NT system. Figure 15-11 shows the *Manhattan* LAN, with a specific system selected:

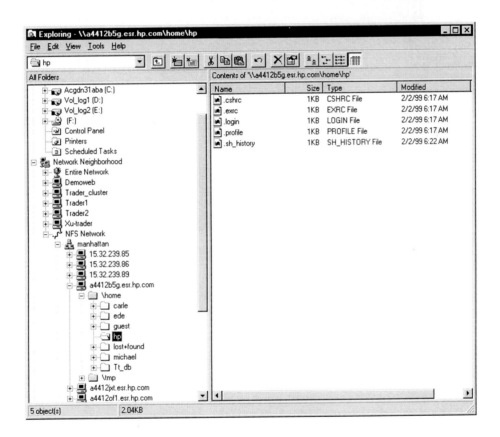

Figure 15-11   Viewing NFS Mounted File System

\home\hp is selected and the right Explorer window shows the files in the **\home\hp** directory. We have permission to manipulate the files in the

hp directory. We can check this by selecting a file, such as **.cshrc**, and viewing its properties. Figure 15-12 shows the *Properties* window.

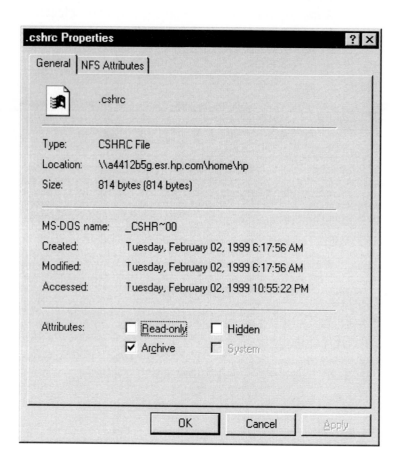

Figure 15-12 SFU *Properties*

The *Read-only* box in this window is not checked; therefore, we have full access to this file.

Telnet Client

There is also a Telnet client loaded as part of SFU. Selecting *Telnet - Telnet Client* from the SFU menu produces the Telnet window shown in Figure 15-13.

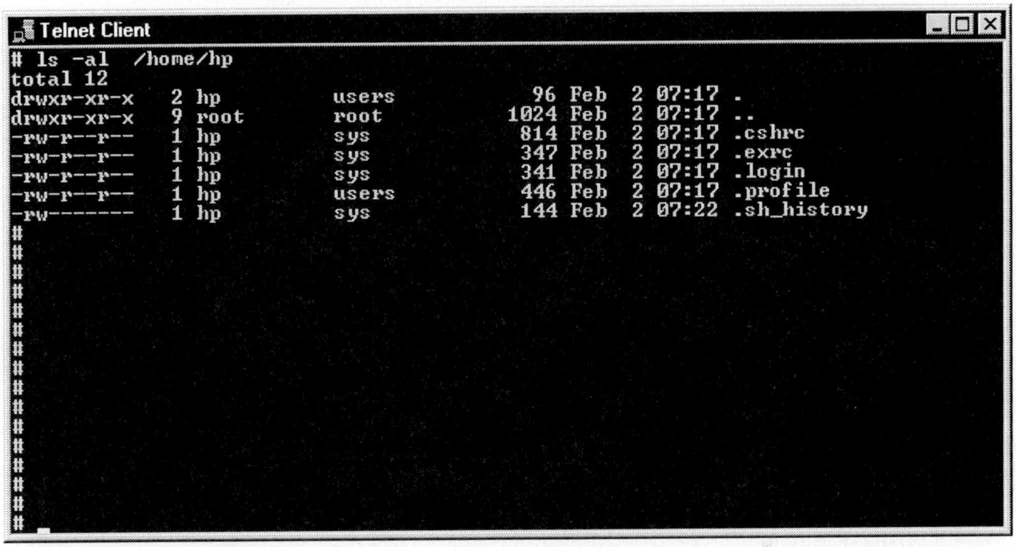

```
 Telnet Client                                                    _ □ ×
# ls -al  /home/hp
total 12
drwxr-xr-x   2 hp        users         96 Feb  2 07:17 .
drwxr-xr-x   9 root      root        1024 Feb  2 07:17 ..
-rw-r--r--   1 hp        sys          814 Feb  2 07:17 .cshrc
-rw-r--r--   1 hp        sys          347 Feb  2 07:17 .exrc
-rw-r--r--   1 hp        sys          341 Feb  2 07:17 .login
-rw-r--r--   1 hp        users        446 Feb  2 07:17 .profile
-rw-------   1 hp        sys          144 Feb  2 07:22 .sh_history
#
#
#
#
#
#
#
#
#
#
#
#
#
#
#
```

Figure 15-13 SFU *Telnet Client*

I have created a long listing of the contents of **/home/hp** in this Telnet window.

Telnet Server

There is also a Telnet server loaded as part of SFU. This means you can connect from a UNIX system, or any other system with a Telnet client, to a Widows NT system with the SFU Telnet server. Figure 15-14 shows accessing the Windows NT Telnet server from a UNIX system.

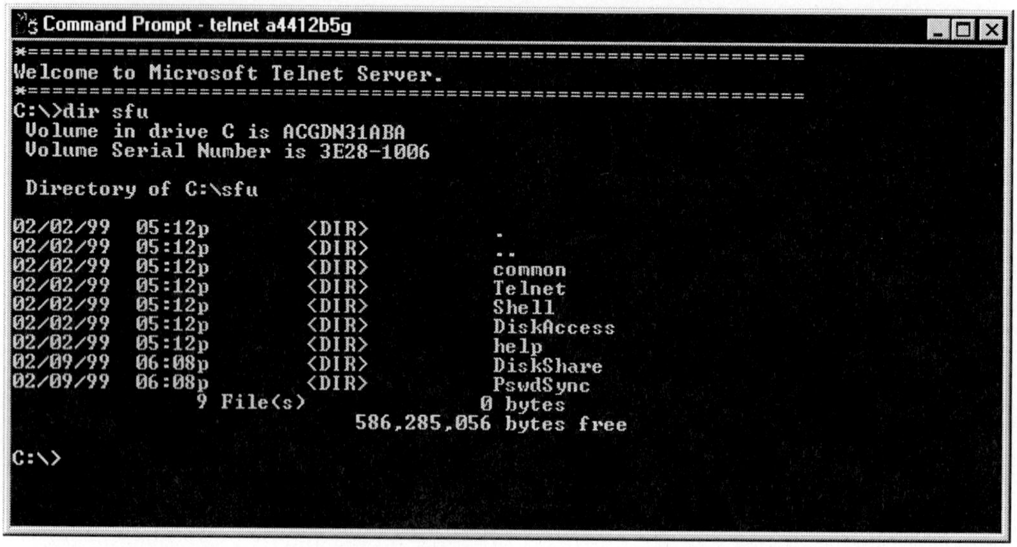

```
Command Prompt - telnet a4412b5g                                        _ □ X
*=============================================================
Welcome to Microsoft Telnet Server.
*=============================================================
C:\>dir sfu
 Volume in drive C is ACGDN31ABA
 Volume Serial Number is 3E28-1006

 Directory of C:\sfu

02/02/99  05:12p    <DIR>         .
02/02/99  05:12p    <DIR>         ..
02/02/99  05:12p    <DIR>         common
02/02/99  05:12p    <DIR>         Telnet
02/02/99  05:12p    <DIR>         Shell
02/02/99  05:12p    <DIR>         DiskAccess
02/02/99  05:12p    <DIR>         help
02/09/99  06:08p    <DIR>         DiskShare
02/09/99  06:08p    <DIR>         PswdSync
              9 File(s)               0 bytes
                        586,285,056 bytes free

C:\>
```

Figure 15-14 SFU *Telnet Server*

In Figure 15-14, I have initiated a Telnet session from my UNIX system to my Windows NT system. After receiving the welcome information from the Microsoft Telnet server, I can issue commands, such as the **dir** shown, exactly as I would from the prompt if I were working directly on the Windows NT system.

The Telnet server functionality of SFU gives some direct access from UNIX to Windows NT, which is a big help in mixed environments. This functionality is further enhanced by many UNIX utilities that you can run on the Windows NT system through this Telnet connection or on the Windows NT system directly. The next section "UNIX Utilities" covers these utilities.

UNIX Utilities

One highly desirable capability of SFU is a UNIX Command Shell invoked with *Unix Utilities - Unix Command Shell.* Figure 15-15 shows a window open with the UNIX utilities listed.

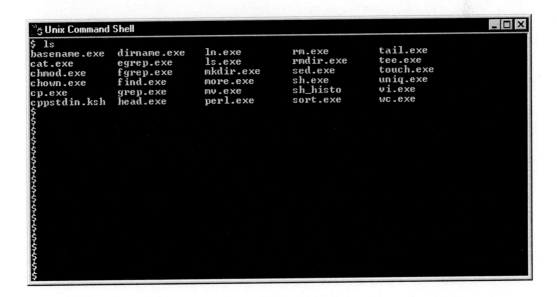

Figure 15-15   SFU UNIX Utilities Listed

The utilities listed in Figure 15-15 work in SFU just the way they work in UNIX. You also have access to these UNIX utilities through the Telnet session that you can establish from another system. To give you an idea how these utilities work, let's issue a few commands, as shown in Figure 15-16.

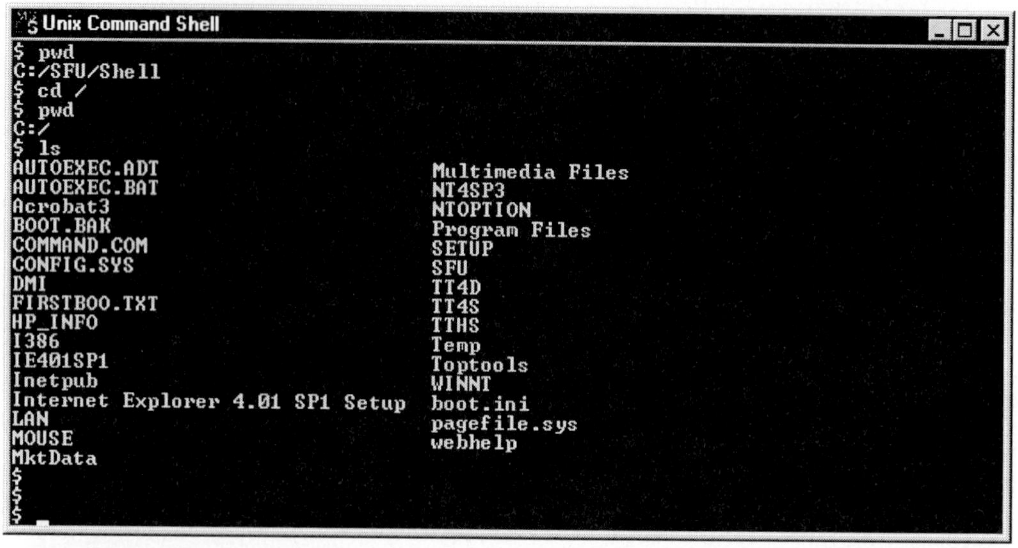

```
§ Unix Command Shell                                                    _ □ ×
$ pwd
C:/SFU/Shell
$ cd /
$ pwd
C:/
$ ls
AUTOEXEC.ADT                    Multimedia Files
AUTOEXEC.BAT                    NT4SP3
Acrobat3                        NTOPTION
BOOT.BAK                        Program Files
COMMAND.COM                     SETUP
CONFIG.SYS                      SFU
DMI                             TT4D
FIRSTBOO.TXT                    TT4S
HP_INFO                         TTHS
I386                            Temp
IE401SP1                        Toptools
Inetpub                        WINNT
Internet Explorer 4.01 SP1 Setup  boot.ini
LAN                            pagefile.sys
MOUSE                          webhelp
MktData
$
$
$
```

Figure 15-16   SFU Example of Using Some UNIX Utilities

This window shows that when we invoke *Unix Utilities,* we are in the **C:/SFU/Shell** directory on our Windows NT system. We change directory to **C:** by issuing **cd /** as we would on a UNIX system. **pwd** confirms we are at the **C:** level. We then issue an **ls** to see the files in **C:**.

Let's issue two more of the *Unix Utilities* to get a better feel for how these utilities perform in Windows NT, as shown in Figure 15-17.

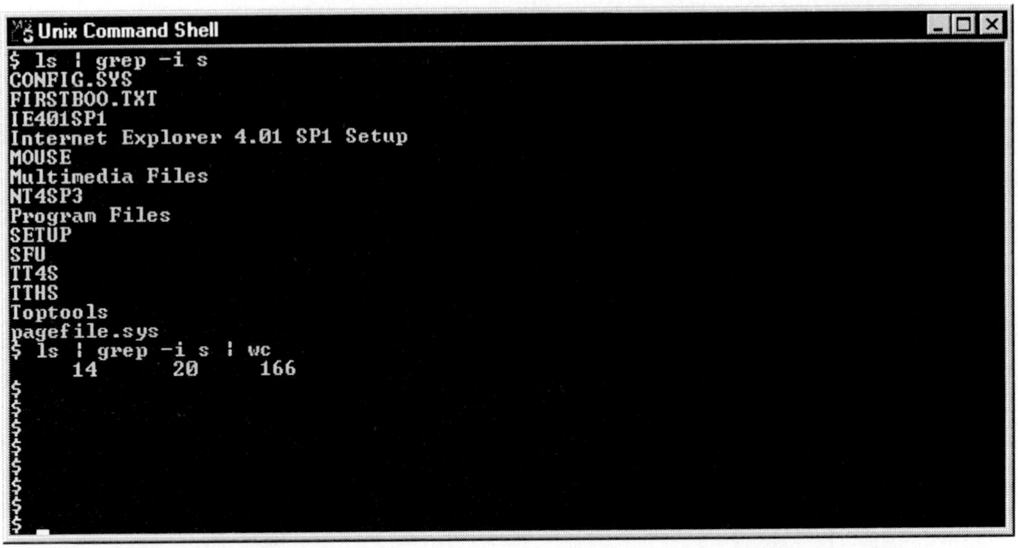

```
Unix Command Shell                                                    [_][□][X]
$ ls | grep -i s
CONFIG.SYS
FIRSTBOO.TXT
IE401SP1
Internet Explorer 4.01 SP1 Setup
MOUSE
Multimedia Files
NT4SP3
Program Files
SETUP
SFU
TT4S
TTHS
Toptools
pagefile.sys
$ ls | grep -i s | wc
     14      20     166
$
$
$
$
$
$
$
$
```

Figure 15-17   SFU Example of Using Some UNIX Utilities

In this window, we issued an **ls** and a **grep** command that ignored case (-i) and searched for *s*. Files that contained both upper- and lower-case *s* were listed. We then piped this same output to **wc** to get a word count.

NFS Server

Not only can the Windows NT system act as an NFS client but it can also act as an NFS server with SFU. A system running NFS can mount a file system exported on the Windows NT system.

Under *Server for NFS Configuration,* you can configure all aspects of your NFS server setup. The defaults for most categories of configuration are fine for initial testing, which we'll perform here. You may want to later perform additional configuration to tune your NFS server.

For our example, I've created one *Share Name,* as shown in Figure 15-18.

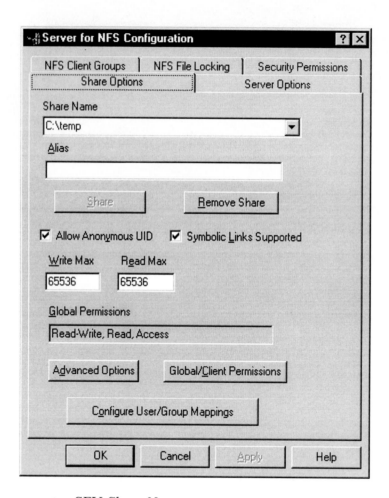

Figure 15-18   SFU *Share Name*

By selecting **Server for NFS Configuration** from the menu and then *Share Options,* I entered the *Share Name* **C:\tem**p shown in Figure 15-18.

We can view *Mount Information* to see what file systems we have exported, as shown in Figure 15-19.

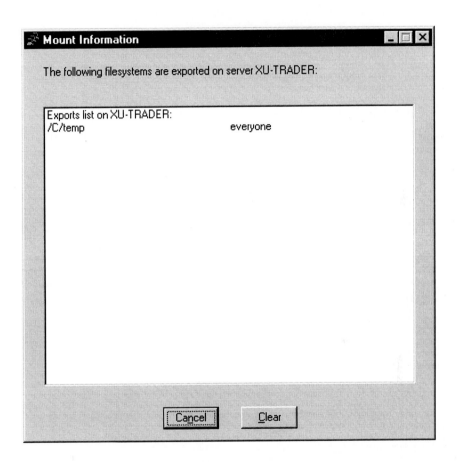

Figure 15-19 SFU *Mount Information*

Our file system of **C:\temp** is indeed in the exported list with no restrictions on who may access it.

With this *Share Name* having been established, we can use the defaults for all other categories of NFS server configuration and mount

C:\temp on a UNIX system. To mount **C:\temp**, you would issue the following command on your UNIX system:

```
# mount 19.32.23.112:C:\temp /ntmount
```

This command will work on most UNIX systems. We have first specified the mount command, which you would normally issue as root. Next is the name of the Windows NT system that has the file system we wish to mount on it; in this case, I have used the IP address rather than the system name. The system name, or IP address, is followed by a colon (:). Next is the name of the file system we wish to mount, as it appears on the Windows NT system, in this case **C:\temp**. Last is the name of the directory on the UNIX system under which we'll mount **C:\temp**, in this case **/ntmount**. You can also add a variety of different options with the **mount** command, but we'll use all defaults in our example.

Let's now check to see if indeed the NFS mount we specified has been established on the UNIX system. The following example shows issuing the **bdf** on the UNIX system to see if the mount has been established, then a **cd** to the **ntmount** directory, and finally an **ls** of the files in this directory.

```
# bdf
Filesystem             kbytes     used    avail %used Mounted on
/dev/vg00/lvol3        151552    53165    92162   37% /
/dev/vg00/lvol1         47829    14324    28722   33% /stand
/dev/vg00/lvol8        163840    87595    71039   55% /var
/dev/vg00/lvol7        339968   314984    23189   93% /usr
/dev/vg00/lvol6        102400    62284    37607   62% /tmp
/dev/vg00/lvol5       1048576   656649   367439   64% /opt
/dev/vg00/lvol4         69632    32448    34850   48% /home
/dev/vgCE/lvpatch     1024000     1357   958732    0% /ce/patches
/dev/vgCE/lvfw         512000     1294   478856    0% /ce/firmware
/dev/vgCE/cetmp        512000   419166    87028   83% /ce/ce-tmp
19.32.23.112:temp    2096160  1523360   572800   73% /ntmount
# cd /ntmount
# ls
_istmp0.dir       test.html       ~df8ec8.tmp      ~dfd65e.tmp
_istmp1.dir       tt2.exe         ~df8ee7.tmp      ~dfd65f.tmp
_istmp2.dir       tt3.exe         ~dfa393.tmp      ~dfd660.tmp
ie401sp1.exe      ttdemo.zip      ~dfa394.tmp      ~dfd66b.tmp
```

```
ie4setup.exe        ttwiz(1).exe       ~dfa3a3.tmp        ~dfd66c.tmp
jack.log            wbemcore.exe       ~dfa3a4.tmp        ~dfe649.tmp
jack1.log           winzip70.exe       ~dfb2a.tmp         ~dfe64a.tmp
jack2.log           ~df7e2f.tmp        ~dfb39.tmp         ~dfe64b.tmp
mmc14.tmp           ~df7e40.tmp        ~dfb3a.tmp         ~dfe64c.tmp
mmcaaa7.tmp         ~df7e41.tmp        ~dfd63c.tmp        ~dfe659.tmp
mmcaaad.tmp         ~df7e42.tmp        ~dfd63d.tmp        ~dfe65a.tmp
mmcaab1.tmp         ~df7e4f.tmp        ~dfd64c.tmp        ~dfe65b.tmp
nph-ntfinal.exe     ~df7e50.tmp        ~dfd64d.tmp        ~dfe65c.tmp
ntagt33e.exe        ~df7e51.tmp        ~dfd64e.tmp        ~dfe65d.tmp
ntoption.exe        ~df7e52.tmp        ~dfd64f.tmp        ~dfe669.tmp
sfu                 ~df7e53.tmp        ~dfd65b.tmp
sfu1                ~df8e99.tmp        ~dfd65c.tmp
temp.log            ~df8ea9.tmp        ~dfd65d.tmp
```

After issuing this command, we see **/ntmount** as one of the file systems mounted on the UNIX system. At this point, I changed to a user other than root, because it is inadvisable in general for root to be manipulating files on an NFS mounted file system. I changed to user *hp*. We can change directory to **/ntmount** and view its contents that correspond to those under **C:\temp** on the Windows NT system. Issuing a long listing, we see the files with ownership of *hp*.

```
$ ll
total 5710
drwxrwxrwx    2 hp        users          64 Feb  9 17:58 _istmp0.dir
drwxrwxrwx    3 hp        users          96 Feb  2 10:18 ~istmp1.dir
drwxrwxrwx    2 hp        users          64 Feb  2 10:19 ~istmp2.dir
-rwxrwxrwx    1 hp        users    24227193 Feb  1 19:50 ie401sp1.exe
-rwxrwxrwx    1 hp        users      443160 Jan 10 10:21 ie4setup.exe
-rwxrwxrwx    1 hp        users         218 Feb 10  1999 jack.log
-rwxrwxrwx    1 hp        users         218 Feb 10  1999 jack1.log
-rwxrwxrwx    1 hp        users         218 Feb 10  1999 jack2.log
-rwxrwxrwx    1 hp        users       60416 Feb  2 15:26 mmc14.tmp
-rwxrwxrwx    1 hp        users      102400 Feb  9 09:24 mmcaaa7.tmp
-rwxrwxrwx    1 hp        users      102400 Feb  9 12:40 mmcaaad.tmp
-rwxrwxrwx    1 hp        users      102400 Feb  9 12:40 mmcaab1.tmp
-rwxrwxrwx    1 hp        users      464200 Feb  1 19:33 nph-ntfinal.exe
-rwxrwxrwx    1 hp        users     5514240 Feb  1 17:43 ntagt33e.exe
-rwxrwxrwx    1 hp        users    38940572 Feb  1 20:07 ntoption.exe
drwxrwxrwx   20 hp        users         640 Feb  3 09:58 sfu
drwxrwxrwx    5 hp        users         160 Feb 10  1999 sfu1
-rwxrwxrwx    1 hp        users         218 Feb  2 11:34 temp.log
-rwxrwxrwx    1 hp        users          35 Feb  1 19:48 test.html
-rwxrwxrwx    1 hp        users     7046429 Feb  1 20:19 tt2.exe
-rwxrwxrwx    1 hp        users     5758110 Feb  1 20:21 tt3.exe
-rwxrwxrwx    1 hp        users     3232301 Feb  3 15:18 ttdemo.zip
-rwxrwxrwx    1 hp        users     1086772 Feb  1 16:53 ttwiz(1).exe
-rwxrwxrwx    1 hp        users     3456925 Feb  1 19:55 wbemcore.exe
-rwxrwxrwx    1 hp        users      943949 Feb  3 15:51 winzip70.exe
-rwxrwxrwx    1 hp        users        4096 Feb  2 15:26 ~df7e2f.tmp
-rwxrwxrwx    1 hp        users        3584 Feb  2 15:26 ~df7e40.tmp
-rwxrwxrwx    1 hp        users        3584 Feb  2 15:26 ~df7e41.tmp
-rwxrwxrwx    1 hp        users        3584 Feb  2 15:26 ~df7e42.tmp
-rwxrwxrwx    1 hp        users        3072 Feb  2 15:26 ~df7e4f.tmp
-rwxrwxrwx    1 hp        users        3072 Feb  2 15:26 ~df7e50.tmp
-rwxrwxrwx    1 hp        users        3584 Feb  2 15:26 ~df7e51.tmp
-rwxrwxrwx    1 hp        users        3584 Feb  2 15:26 ~df7e52.tmp
```

```
-rwxrwxrwx   1 hp          users        3584 Feb  2 15:26 ~df7e53.tmp
-rwxrwxrwx   1 hp          users        9728 Feb  9 09:24 ~df8e99.tmp
-rwxrwxrwx   1 hp          users        3072 Feb  9 09:24 ~df8ea9.tmp
-rwxrwxrwx   1 hp          users        5120 Feb  9 09:24 ~df8ec8.tmp
-rwxrwxrwx   1 hp          users        3584 Feb  9 09:24 ~df8ee7.tmp
-rwxrwxrwx   1 hp          users        6144 Feb  2 15:26 ~dfa393.tmp
-rwxrwxrwx   1 hp          users        9728 Feb  2 15:26 ~dfa394.tmp
-rwxrwxrwx   1 hp          users        3072 Feb  2 15:26 ~dfa3a3.tmp
-rwxrwxrwx   1 hp          users        5120 Feb  2 15:26 ~dfa3a4.tmp
-rwxrwxrwx   1 hp          users        3072 Feb  9 09:24 ~dfb2a.tmp
-rwxrwxrwx   1 hp          users        3072 Feb  9 09:24 ~dfb39.tmp
-rwxrwxrwx   1 hp          users        3072 Feb  9 09:24 ~dfb3a.tmp
-rwxrwxrwx   1 hp          users        4608 Feb  9 09:24 ~dfd63c.tmp
-rwxrwxrwx   1 hp          users       16384 Feb  9 09:24 ~dfd63d.tmp
-rwxrwxrwx   1 hp          users        4608 Feb  9 09:24 ~dfd64c.tmp
-rwxrwxrwx   1 hp          users        3072 Feb  9 09:24 ~dfd64d.tmp
-rwxrwxrwx   1 hp          users        3072 Feb  9 09:24 ~dfd64e.tmp
-rwxrwxrwx   1 hp          users        3072 Feb  9 09:24 ~dfd64f.tmp
-rwxrwxrwx   1 hp          users        3072 Feb  9 09:24 ~dfd65b.tmp
-rwxrwxrwx   1 hp          users        3072 Feb  9 09:24 ~dfd65c.tmp
-rwxrwxrwx   1 hp          users        3072 Feb  9 09:24 ~dfd65d.tmp
-rwxrwxrwx   1 hp          users        3072 Feb  9 09:24 ~dfd65e.tmp
-rwxrwxrwx   1 hp          users        3072 Feb  9 09:24 ~dfd65f.tmp
-rwxrwxrwx   1 hp          users        8192 Feb  9 09:24 ~dfd660.tmp
-rwxrwxrwx   1 hp          users        4608 Feb  9 09:24 ~dfd66b.tmp
-rwxrwxrwx   1 hp          users        3072 Feb  9 09:24 ~dfd66c.tmp
-rwxrwxrwx   1 hp          users        4096 Feb  9 09:24 ~dfe649.tmp
-rwxrwxrwx   1 hp          users        3584 Feb  9 09:24 ~dfe64a.tmp
-rwxrwxrwx   1 hp          users        3584 Feb  9 09:24 ~dfe64b.tmp
-rwxrwxrwx   1 hp          users        3584 Feb  9 09:24 ~dfe64c.tmp
-rwxrwxrwx   1 hp          users        3584 Feb  9 09:24 ~dfe659.tmp
-rwxrwxrwx   1 hp          users        3072 Feb  9 09:24 ~dfe65a.tmp
-rwxrwxrwx   1 hp          users        3072 Feb  9 09:24 ~dfe65b.tmp
-rwxrwxrwx   1 hp          users        3584 Feb  9 09:24 ~dfe65c.tmp
-rwxrwxrwx   1 hp          users        3584 Feb  9 09:24 ~dfe65d.tmp
-rwxrwxrwx   1 hp          users        3584 Feb  9 09:24 ~dfe669.tmp
$
```

We do indeed see that the user *hp* and the corresponding group of *users* are part of this long listing.

The NFS Server setup we have performed in this section can be combined with the NFS Client setup performed earlier to allow the Windows NT file system to be exported, as part of NFS Server, and imported, as part of NFS Client. The extent to which you use NFS as part of your file-sharing strategy depends on the makeup of your environment. Since NFS is available on most all UNIX variants, you may find that using NFS on Windows NT makes sense for your environment. If you expect heavy NFS use in a mixed Windows NT and UNIX environment, you may want to start small, with a few key directories shared using NFS, and test its performance to make sure it is adequate for your users. As you can see from the previous examples, NFS on Windows NT can greatly enhance the overall file sharing in your mixed Windows NT and UNIX environment.

Password Synchronization

SFU synchronizes Windows NT passwords to UNIX. I didn't include an example of this synchronization. There is an encrypted file sent from Windows NT to UNIX containing password information. The file should be set to read-only for root. There is also a daemon that is required to implement the password synchronization. After the setup is complete, user passwords on UNIX will be synchronized with those on Windows NT.

INDEX

X

Hewlett-Packard Computer Education and Training

Hewlett-Packard's world-class education and training offers hands on education solutions including:

- Linux
- HP-UX System and Network Administration
- Y2K HP-UX Transition
- Advanced HP-UX System Administration
- IT Service Management using advanced Internet technologies
- Microsoft Windows NT
- Internet/Intranet
- MPE/iX
- Database Administration
- Software Development

HP's new IT Professional Certification program provides rigorous technical qualification for specific IT job roles including HP-UX System Administration, Network Management, Unix/NT Servers and Applications Management, and IT Service Management.

In addition, HP's IT Resource Center is the perfect knowledge source for IT professionals. Through a vibrant and rich Web environment, IT professionals working in the areas of UNIX, Microsoft, networking, or MPE/iX gain access to continually updated knowledge pools.

http://education.hp.com

In the U.S. phone 1-800-HPCLASS (472-5277)